SCARRED BY DEATH

ANTOINETTE ZAM

First Edition

PAGE PUBLISHING, INC.
New York, NY

First originally published by Page Publishing, Inc. 2018

ISBN 978-1-64350-394-3 (Paperback)
ISBN 978-1-64350-395-0 (Digital)

Printed in the United States of America

PROLOGUE

Sarah Holland focuses on her hands, one crossed over the other resting on her lap, thinking she'd rather be anywhere else than the Presbyterian Church in her small town.

The reverend's jovial voice announces, "Today we celebrate …"

She stares at the ones standing before the reverend. The person sitting next to her is twitching one leg, a habit he has recently developed. Both have chosen to remain seated rather than on the altar with the others. Slowly she turns her head toward him, and his blank stare causes her eyes to well.

She faces forward to avoid a flood of tears. Suddenly she is aware of the large stained glass window above the altar. Jesus nailed to a wooden cross, his head slumped to the right, his face ridden with blood and scars. Smaller portraits in glass surround the cross. Mary holding her sweet child, Jesus, surrounded by children, and *The Wedding at Cana*, but the one that catches Sarah's eye is of Judas collecting his thirty silver coins from the high priest who wanted nothing more than to be rid of Jesus. Judas, who claimed to love Jesus above all, had betrayed him. Like Jesus, Sarah knows the pain of betrayal. Her betrayers are standing on the altar next to the reverend. They two have claimed to love one above all.

She moves her attention from Judas and stares at the faces of her betrayers, her brother and both sets of grandparents.

A voice proudly speaks a name. Sarah knows this voice and despises this person more than anyone. Her father's mother. Grandmother Catherine answers the questions asked of her by the reverend. She proudly answers yes. Sarah wishes she could wipe that smug look on her grandmother's face.

Sarah disconnects from what is taking place on the altar and thinks about her birthday. She'll be twelve in a few months. In six years, she'll be eighteen, old enough to make her own decisions, and her first will be to move from the town she calls home.

She made eye contact with her brother as the congregation applause. "She can't leave without him. Although he has betrayed her, she will forgive him, as she knows Jesus forgave Judas. Her brother is scared and confused, as she is. Two months ago, they were happy children looking forward to Christmas. Sarah is convinced George is a lost soul, and she, his only salvation. As Jesus died for our sins, she will find a way to save George.

Her religious revelation is interrupted when the person sitting next to her stirs in his seat. She turns to look at him. She knows he is uncomfortable. His chest moves quickly as if unable to breathe. A silent cry escapes from within. She places her hand over his and gently pats.

The people around them begin to stand. She takes the man's arm, and they do the same. The service has ended, and their new life now begins.

CHAPTER ONE

Greenwich, Connecticut, 2011
Allison

The phone rings, waking me from a deep sleep. I turn away from the sound. I'm too exhausted to talk with anyone. I just want to sleep. It stops after four rings, and I drift off again. With sleep comes the dream. The dream invades my sleep several times a year. Over the last twenty years, I never gave it much thought. *Till now.*

The dream is always the same, me walking slowly through a field of white daisies. The sun is shining. I lift my head and feel its warmth on my face. Suddenly I bend and gather a bunch of daisies. I pull five from the bunch and trim the stems with my fingernail. In no particular order, I place the trimmed flowers in my hair. The remaining flowers I hold tightly in my hand. Standing, I breathe in deeply, allowing the fresh air into my lungs. In the distance, I spy a white tent. My pace quickens, as I know this is where I should be. When I reach the tent, I step onto a red carpet covering the aisle, which separates two rows of chairs clad in white linen. At the end of this aisle is a man holding a book in his left hand. I know this man. It is Reverend Tom. He lifts his hand and motions for me to walk toward him. I look down, noticing my white dress and ballerina slippers. It occurs to me that this is my wedding day. I walk slowly down the aisle. With his back to me is a man in a white suit. The sight of this man makes my heart beat faster.

There are people sitting in the chairs, but they are of no interest to me. Someone steps in my path, and the happiness I'm feeling subsides.

I whisper, "Aunt Sarah."

She pleads, "No, Allison, you mustn't."

She keeps repeating the same words over and over. My face tightens as I ask her to step aside; when she doesn't, I walk around her. I look over my shoulder, making sure she isn't following me. I catch a glimpse of my mother sitting in the first row. Her presence only deepens the anger I am feeling. Someone touches my arm. It is the man in the white suit. My mood softens. Finally, I am beside him. I try desperately to see his face, but the sun's reflection obstructs my view. I place my hand in his, and the strength of his grip makes me feel safe. His grip loosens, and my hand slips from his. He drifts farther away from me. I reach for him, but he is gone.

My eyes fly open, and I am staring at the ceiling in my bedroom. I close them again, wishing the dream to return, but it doesn't. Frustrated, I get out of bed.

In the bathroom, I lean on the sink. Raising my head, I notice my reflection in the mirror. My eyes are swollen and smeared with black mascara. I blow a bit of breath from my mouth into my hand. I badly need to brush my teeth and shower, but before I do either, I look into the mirror once again. Staring back at me is a forty-year-old-woman.

My tangled hair is brown. There is a hint of natural blond streaks, inherited from my father. My eyes are blue, crystal blue in the sunlight, cobalt by night. I'm five feet, six inches tall, slender, but curvy in all the right places. My breasts are the perfect size for my stature, not too large, not too small. Everyone that knew my mother says I got my good looks from her. If this is true, looking alike is all we had in common.

I decide a shower may help, but I can't bring myself to step in. I begin to recite the Serenity Prayer. "God, grant me the serenity to accept the things I cannot change and to change the things."

All of a sudden, I can't remember the rest.

I wonder if there is a God. I have been taught there is. For years I believed in his existence, but now I'm not sure.

After five minutes of debating the existence of God, I open the door to the shower and step in. I turn on the water, making sure the temperature is set to hot, very hot. I'm tempted to step under the scalding water, but I adjust the temperature before making the move. I linger under the water for a very long time, finding it hard to breathe. I like the feeling. Again, I make an unconscious decision and step back to take a breath. I reach for the washcloth and start to scrub my body. I scrub so hard my skin turns red. I begin to cry, which turns to sobbing. I can't seem to control it. When my skin begins to tingle with pain, I stop scrubbing, but the crying continues.

I shut off the water and step out of the shower. The sobbing subsides. I reach for a towel, wrapping it around myself, and walk and sit at the vanity table, staring at myself in the mirror. I open the drawer and retrieve my makeup bag. Concealer is a must to cover my swollen eyes, little powder, mascara, finished with a clear lipstick. I run a brush through my wet hair.

As I walk into the bedroom, my first thought is to get into bed, but instead, I straighten the sheets and comforter. I walk to my closet and open the door. I pick out matching bra and panties, step into my favorite jeans, and scan the rack for a blouse. Unconsciously, I search for the shelf where I keep my sweaters. The red sweater is not hard to find. To preserve it, I wrapped it with white tissue paper. Gently I unfasten the pearl buttons and place my arms through the sleeves. I close my eyes as the soft cashmere touches my skin.

The memory of the day it was given to me comes flooding back. Grabbing a pair of shoes, I quickly close the closet doors and leave the bedroom. Making my way down the hall, I stop before descending the stairs, listening for sounds. I call out. No response. I make my way down.

I enter the kitchen, in need of coffee. As I prepare the pot, I stare out the window and notice my neighbor Marie and the postman in conversation. They're smiling, and I wonder what they're talking about. I look up at the sky. It is a beautiful day. I think of how nice it would be to just lie in the sun. I finish the coffee preparation and place the coffeepot on the stove.

I look back at Marie flipping through her mail. She's a stay at home mom, though she's rarely home. Marie loves to volunteer at the school, the hospital, and the library. She's always on the go. Right now, just watching her makes me tired. I long to go back to bed.

The smell of coffee is filling my nostrils. I need caffeine badly, but the coffee is not ready for consumption yet. I need something to do. The laundry comes to mind. More white clothes than dark. *White it is.* I retrieve the largest mug from the cabinet and wait. When the brewing stops, I pour the dark rich liquid. Coffee brings me clarity in the best and worst of situations. I close my eyes and breathe in the aroma, feeling warm, both inside and out. Satisfied, I sit at the kitchen counter. I focus on the clock, but not the time. From the corner of my eye I notice the blinking red light on the phone. There is a message. I try hard, but I cannot ignore the blinking red light. With each flash, my curiosity grows. I get up and push the button.

First call is from Pete. "Hi, I'm at the office. I felt so bad leaving this morning, but as you know, I had to clear my schedule for the … hey, before I forget, Julia insisted she couldn't leave this morning without giving you a kiss, so she tiptoed into our bedroom and gently placed a kiss on your cheek. So did I." Pause. "Allison, I don't want you to worry about a thing. I'll take care of everything, I'll be home as soon as I finish up here. Love you!"

I erase the message, but the red light continues to blink, so I press it one more time. The voice on the message makes me weak in the knees. I place my hands on the counter to steady myself. When the message ends, I press the Replay button. The contents of the message are of no interest to me. It's the voice.

"Hi, guys! It's me. I'm leaving Pittsburgh at 1:00 p.m. Allison, don't be upset with me. I decided to drive. Flying is such a chore these days, and it's only a ten-hour drive. I'm not driving the full ten hours. I plan on stopping at four, to get a good night's sleep. I should be back on the road no later than eleven and at your front door by six on Sunday. Can't wait to see you guys. It's been a while! I'm really looking forward to spending Thanksgiving with the family."

When the message stops, tears are flowing down my face. I ask out loud, "Why, Patrick? Why didn't you fly like you promised?" I grow angry, but not with Patrick; I'm angry with Pete. My good old reliable husband forgot to erase the damn message.

Patrick's voice repeats over and over in my head. *Can't wait to see you guys. It's been a while!* I feel empty, and my stomach begins to ache. I reach for the Delete button but cannot push it. I return to the seat at the counter and stare at the coffee mug in front of me, remembering the night Patrick and I last spoke.

"Patrick, would you please listen to me? Book a flight. You'll be here in no time. Pete or I will pick you up at the airport. It's such a long drive from Pittsburgh, and you will be driving by yourself. What if you get tired at the wheel?"

When Patrick and I had finished our conversation, I remember telling Pete, "He's not going to book a flight. He's determined to drive. Men are so stubborn."

Staring straight ahead, I notice the calendar on the back door to the garage. Tuesday, November 24. Where had the time gone since we first heard the news? I think back to Sunday, the twenty-second, the day Patrick was to arrive. I ask myself, "What did we do on Sunday?" I remember rushing the children so we would make Sunday services. We attended the breakfast that followed in the parish hall. Aunt Sarah was going on about the shopping she still needed to do in preparation for Thanksgiving. On the way home, we stopped at Patrick's favorite bakery and purchased dessert to share with him upon his arrival. We made a family decision to go bowling, got a bite to eat, and got home by four.

When six o'clock came and went, we assumed traffic was the cause of Patrick's late arrival. Julia, unable to wait any longer for dessert, convinced us that Pop wouldn't mind if we started without him. While we ate, Pete bored us with his high school football stories. The children and I, having heard these stories way too many times, ended the story mimicking Pete's exact words. Our laughter muffled the ringing of the phone. I stumbled to answer, thinking of Patrick. "That must be Pop." Instead, the voice on the other end asked my name and if I was Patrick Higgins's daughter. I corrected the woman by saying, "Stepdaughter."

The woman identified herself as Officer Hart of Station 106, right outside of Philadelphia. I listened to her for a second and then handed the phone to Pete. After he had taken the phone, I rested my body against his and repeated over and over, “This can’t be true! It’s not Patrick. They made a mistake.”

I held on to Pete, afraid if I released my hold, I would collapse to the floor. Pete hung up the phone, holding me tightly to him. He whispered, “Allison.” Over Pete’s shoulder, I spied my children, confused by our reaction to the call.

Andrew was the first to ask, “Dad, what’s wrong?”

I can’t remember what Pete said at that moment, but within seconds, our children were wrapped in our arms and crying. The last thing I remember is getting into bed that night. And now it’s Tuesday. Monday a total blur.

Placing my head in my hands, I cry out, “Patrick, you have no idea what—”

The doorbell rings, once, twice, several times. Frustrated, I get up to answer it. Ready to blast the person on the other side, I open the door to find the last person in the world I want to see, my aunt Sarah.

“Allison, I was going to call. I hope you don’t mind.”

I answer, “You should have called.”

She knows immediately that I have turned on my bitch attitude. She has seen it so many times before. She replies, “I should have called.” I stare at her, hoping this mishap may cause her to turn and leave, but instead, she remains stoic. Finally she asks, “May I come in?”

I walk to the kitchen with Aunt Sarah following like a puppy dog. I pour myself another cup of coffee and sit at the counter. Aunt Sarah stands in the kitchen doorway, asking, “Is there enough for another cup?”

I point to the cabinet. “You know where I keep the cups.”

She walks behind me and retrieves a cup. Now sitting directly in front of me, she questions, “I guess the children are at school. Is Pete upstairs?”

“No, he’s at work. An important client.”

"Of course. Pete wouldn't have left you today if it weren't important." An awkward pause. "Did you and he get a chance to discuss the arrangements?"

"Nope." I don't mention Pete's phone message from this morning. "Is that the reason for your visit? You were hoping I have information about the funeral arrangements? A call would have sufficed."

Aunt Sarah doesn't respond. Looking past her, I notice the time. "Allison, I know this is hard, losing—"

"Aunt Sarah, if this conversation is heading where I think it is, don't waste your time."

Aunt Sarah lowers her eyes.

When the silence between us has gone on too long, Aunt Sarah asks, "Allison, didn't Patrick tell you he was going to book a flight?"

"Guess he changed his mind."

"That was so unlike Patrick not to let you know …"

"Well, he didn't. That was real fucking considerate of him, wasn't it?" I deliberately neglect to mention Patrick's phone message. Aunt Sarah looks crushed. "Sorry. I know you don't really like me using the f-word."

"Allison, my intentions are not to upset you, but did Patrick ever talk with you, or Pete, about his wishes if something like this ever happened?"

"Not with me. Maybe with Pete. You should ask him."

"I spoke with Pete this morning, and he didn't mention anything to me."

"Aunt Sarah, don't take this the wrong way, but why are you here?"

"Where else would I be, Allison, if not with you? We're family."

Her eyes are filled with pity for me, and I can feel the tears building in mine. I stand, turning my back to her. I carry my mug to the sink, saying, "Right, we're family. Of course, where else would you be?"

I don't need to see her face to know that my words have hurt her. When I turn back to face her, she is staring at the coffee cup in her hands. I need to get her out of my house. "Aunt Sarah, I hate to rush you, but I have a lot going on today," I lie. "I have a dentist appointment. I promise, once Pete and I have finalized everything, I'll call you."

"You certainly can cancel that dentist appointment. They will under—"

"I'm going," I say, seething, the sharpness even surprising me.

"All right. Would you like me to pick the children up from school? I can bring them back to my house. I'll make dinner."

I stare blankly at her, knowing the only way to get rid of her is to agree to dinner. "That sounds like a great idea. I'll text the kids, let them know you're picking them up from school. Okay, then, I will see you later. I really have to get going."

"Of course, Allison. I understand."

"I'm glad you understand, Aunt Sarah. That makes me feel so much better."

"I do understand, Allison, more than you know."

The phone rings, but I make no move to answer it. By the third ring, Aunt Sarah asks, "Should I get that?"

I reach for the phone. It's Pete. "Hi, I'm doing fine. Aunt Sarah's here."

Pete whispers, "I feel better knowing you're not alone. Thank her for me."

"She was just about to leave when you called."

"She's leaving?"

"Yes, she is. I have a dentist appointment."

"And you're going?"

"Yes, I am. I also wanted to stop by Bloomingdale's to buy something appropriate for a funeral. Oh, before I forget, we are having dinner at my aunt's. She's anxious to know about the funeral arrangements. You'll have the information by then, correct?" Before Pete can answer, I say, "Pete, I'm running late. Love you."

Hanging up the phone, I smile at my aunt. "Dinner, five thirty, your house."

"Five thirty is fine. By the way, I love your sweater. Is it new? I've never seen you in *red*. The color looks nice on you."

I'm amazed she has no memory of the *red* sweater. "I don't wear *red*. I think it clashes with my hair. Be careful driving."

As she walks down the path to her car, I want to slam the door behind her, but I feel guilty about the way I've treated her, so I slowly and gently close the door.

* * * * *

Back in the kitchen, I have an overwhelming desire to run up the stairs, get back into bed, and place the covers over my head; instead, I place a call to my assistant, Kathy. The call goes to voice mail. "Hi, it's me. I'm sure you already heard my stepfather … an accident. I'm sorry to have to dump everything in your lap, but get Jane to help out. Tell Jon I said it was all right. The Stanleys, Johnsons, and Prezi files should be worked on before the others. They're coming to trial next week. If you have any questions, call."

I walk into the den and flop on the couch. I reach for the remote and turn on CNN. I'm half-listening to an economic guru, a.k.a. Know-It-All. "Mr. Heck, do you feel that we, the American citizens, should be held liable for bailing out these Fortune 500 companies? How, as a country, could we allow this to happen?"

Frustrated, I yell at the TV, "Greed, big bad bank CEOs found a way to convince blue-collar Joe that he can afford that million-dollar home. Now Joe yells foul, and the rest of us pay the price!" I hit the Off button on the remote.

I'm startled by the ringing of the phone. I decide not to answer since I already spoke with Pete and my aunt, but thinking it might be one of my children, I panic and answer.

"Hello."

"Allison, I'm so sorry for your loss. Patrick was a sweet man. Pete called yesterday and spoke with Jon."

Bingo! Good old reliable Pete never leaves a stone unturned. "Kathy, you didn't have to return my call. I was just heading out."

"I just wanted to say, don't worry about a thing. I pulled the files you spoke about. Jon already spoke with Jane. She was happy to help. I'll let you go. See you at the service."

"You're attending the service? Is anyone else coming?"

"Jon and your staff."

"That's not necessary, Kathy."

"We want to be there, Allison. I'll let you go. I know you have a lot to do today. If I can be of any help, please call."

"I will."

Hanging up, I know I have to get out of the house. I grab my coat and bag from the hall closet and head for the garage. I back out of the garage and down the driveway at record speed. I race to the corner and stop. In the rearview mirror, I notice Mr. Harris, my neighbor, and the stunned look on his face. I know he's thinking, *Of all people, Allison is speeding down our block, the woman who yells at the local teenagers when they drive five miles over the speed limit.* Humiliated, I rest my head on the steering wheel. I don't move until I hear a beep behind me. I turn left and drive the posted speed limit to the mall.

Traffic is light. With Thanksgiving only two days away, I wonder, Where is everyone? When I arrive at the mall, the parking lot is jam-packed. Everyone is at the mall. It takes another thirty minutes just to find a parking space near Bloomingdale's.

Finally in the store, I head straight for the women's department. I want something simple but not boring. After scanning the sales rack, I look up and spot the perfect navy-blue suit. The jacket is trimmed in *red*. I know it is the trim that I'm drawn to. I find my size and head to the fitting room. The mirror confirms that this is the suit.

A saleswoman approaches and says, "That suit is stunning on you, and I have the perfect shoes and bag to go with it. Would you like to see them?"

Looking at the complete ensemble in the mirror, I ask for the saleswoman's approval without saying a word. She says, "You look great."

After making my purchases, I head back toward the parking lot. At the door, my stomach starts to growl. I realize the last time I ate a complete meal was Sunday. I decide to visit the food court. I select a tuna salad and a bottle of water and then locate a table. I eat slowly, not enjoying the salad. What I do enjoy is people-watching. At the table directly ahead of me, there are two women approximately my age. I watch them carefully, one woman laughing at her friend's story. I can't hear what they are saying over the noise in the food court, so I try to read their lips. With no luck, I imagine the conversation.

"You know he decided to drive instead of booking a flight?"

"He drove?"

"Can you believe it? Now he's completely destroyed Thanksgiving! Wasn't that selfish of him?"

"He always put his needs before anyone else's."

"True. Now we'll be spending Thanksgiving at the funeral home. Maybe I'll drape the coffin in white linen, atop the turkey and all its trimmings. Ha, ha, ha!"

The ringing of my cell phone pulls me from my daydream. Upset by my thoughts, I ignore the phone, quickly dump my barely touched salad in the garbage, and make my way to the car. The phone rings again.

"Allison, what's wrong? Why are you out of breath? Where are you, sweetheart?"

"I'm at the mall. I just ran to my car. Give me a minute to catch my breath."

"Take your time, sweetheart. I wanted to let you know I met with the funeral director and finalized the arrangements. We'll talk later at your aunt's house."

"Fine."

"Also, I just spoke with your aunt. She suggested the kids sleep at her house tonight. She thought it might be good for you."

I'm backing out of the parking space and slam on the brakes as I try to comprehend what Pete is saying. A woman wanting my parking space beeps her horn. For the first time in my life, I give someone the finger. She isn't happy with the gesture and beeps her horn several times to let me know. I move the car so she can take the space.

"Aunt Sarah doesn't get to make decisions where my children are concerned! I don't need time to digest what has happened. Patrick is dead! There, I said it. Don't you think having the children around would be better for the both of us?"

"You're right, I'm sorry. Having the children around might be the best thing for us."

I lean my head on the headrest and close my eyes. Pete is right. All I want to do is sleep. How much time will I really spend with the children?

"Pete, wait. You're right. Forget what I said. The children can stay at Aunt Sarah's house, but only tonight. Tomorrow they come home. It's the night before Thanksgiving, and we've always spent that night together as a family."

"Are you sure? Because if it would make you feel better to have the children at home, I will call Aunt Sarah to explain."

"No, it's fine, but only one night. Now I have to hang up and get out of this parking lot."

Pete quickly says, "I'll pack for the kids when I get home."

"You're coming home?"

"Of course. We'll drive to Aunt Sarah's together. I don't want you driving home by yourself.

I want to argue and say he doesn't have to drive out of his way to get me, that I'll meet him at my aunt's, but I know this is an argument I won't win. "I'm heading home now. I'll pack their clothes."

"Don't forget to pack Julia's soccer equipment. She has practice tomorrow. And of course, Andrew will need his science book. Tomorrow is Wednesday."

Andrew, I think. Then clearing my son from my thoughts, I say, "I'll see you at home."

As I hang up, I hear Pete say, "I love you, Allison."

I don't respond.

* * * * *

Opening the front door, I call out, "I'm home!"

A chill runs through my body because I imagine Patrick responding, "Did you have a nice time at the mall?" But the house is silent, as I know it will be.

I close the door behind me, leaving my hand on the doorknob for several minutes before I remove my coat. I place my bag and keys on the table near the staircase, throw my coat over the banister, and head up the stairs to pack the children's clothes.

Julia's room is a mess, but I manage to find some clean clothes and move on to Andrew's room, which is the total opposite of Julia's. Packing Andrew's overnight bag is much easier; everything is where it should be, except the science book. I walk over to Andrew's desk, trying to locate the book, but instead I spot a picture of Andrew, Pete, and Patrick taken at a Yankee game last year. I reach for the picture and sit at the desk and softly say Patrick's name.

Andrew's arms are draped around Patrick and Pete. I brush my thumb over Patrick's face and smile. Then, as if the picture were on fire, I drop it on the desk and leave the room.

After gathering Julia's soccer equipment, I head for the office, where I know I will find Andrew's science book. Bingo! Right where I thought it would be. I wonder why this science book never makes it into Andrew's book bag.

When Andrew was in third grade, it was his math book that was forgotten at home. Once during an important meeting, my cell phone vibrated. *School* flashed on the screen, so I excused myself. Missing the call, I retrieved the message.

> *Mrs. Cane, this is Mrs. Hamill. Nothing serious. Andrew once again forgot his math book. With my daughter, it was her lunch bag. I swear that girl forgot her lunch at least twice a week. Anyway, if you can remember, on Wednesdays Andrew needs his math book. Have a nice day!*

I knew Mrs. Hamill's reference to her own forgetful daughter was to make me feel I wasn't alone, but the message made me feel like a failure as a mother.

The call from Mrs. Hamill upset me the entire day, and arriving home that night, I scolded my son, raising my voice two octaves higher than normal. "Andrew, I don't think it's my job to remind you every Wednesday not to forget your math book. I'm tired of being interrupted at work with trivial issues!"

Andrew would beg my forgiveness, and as always, I would melt, marking all the Wednesdays on the calendar, "Math Book." Two days after my outburst, I baked Andrew my famous homemade chocolate chip cookies, his favorite. That night at dinner, Julia commented, "Chocolate chip cookies! Thanks, Andrew, for ticking Mom off the other day."

Pete agreed with Julia. That night in our bedroom, he jokingly said, "Allison, I think Andrew forgets his math book so you'll bake his favorite cookies." Pete ducked as I threw my pillow his way.

Andrew is the child every parent longs for. He is kind and considerate, with an infectious personality. When my children were first placed in my arms, I melted, but their personalities were very different. Andrew hardly ever cried, slept well, and was a joy to be around. Julia, on the other hand, would often cry and then scream if her needs were not immediately met.

The memory of my children as babies makes my eyes well. My children mean the world to me. I thank God every day for them.

I suddenly become emotional, so I quickly leave the office with the packed bags, dropping them off in the garage. I hear the front door open and know Pete is home. He calls my name.

"I'm in the kitchen!"

Pete walks up behind me, hugging my waist, leaning his cheek against mine. He asks, "How's my girl?"

I whisper, "I'm good."

Turning me so we are face-to-face, he asks, "Are you really okay?" I try not to cry, but in the end, I lose the fight. Pete holds me tightly against him and kisses the top of my head.

He relaxes his hold, so we are facing each other once again. If someone asked me to describe Pete, I would say he resembles Brad Pitt. His hair is sandy brown, more on the blond side. He has emerald eyes, is six foot two, has a toned body earned from working out at the gym four times a week. My friends think he's hot and speak enviously, praising him as the perfect husband and father. I can't help thinking no one is that perfect, but if I were to look up the definition of *perfect*, I'm sure Pete's name would appear. As I stare into those eyes, I want to slap him hard and wipe that boyish, sympathetic look from his face. I break his hold.

"The kids' overnight bags are in the garage. We really should get going. With rush hour and holiday traffic, it's going to take longer than usual."

"I'll put the bags in the car, give me five minutes to change."

With Pete gone, I cup my hands to my face, asking myself, *What am I going to do now?* My chest begins to constrict. I am reminded of a family that was assigned to me early in my career. A young mother in her late twenties, with two small daughters, suddenly faced with the accidental death of her husband. While I reviewed the case, it was noted that the mother was severely depressed and incapable of caring for her children. When I met with this fragile young woman, I questioned if she feared losing her girls. With a blank stare, she said, "Three weeks ago, I kissed my husband goodbye. Two hours later, life as I knew it took an awful turn."

Pete enters the room. Noticing my blank expression, he asks, "What's wrong?"

"Just thinking, that's all."

"Are you sure, sweetie?"

I reach for my coat and purse hung over Pete's arm. "We should get going." Noticing the clean dishes, I say, "I should put the dishes away."

Pete reaches for my hand. "I'll take care of the dishes when we get home."

As we walk out the door, I cringe, knowing I will be seeing my aunt. I tell myself, *I'll get through this. Just a few hours, and I'll return to the safety of my bed, asleep, wishing for the dream to return.*

* * * * *

On the drive to my aunt's, Pete doesn't mention the funeral arrangements, and I don't ask. We talk about the kids, the holiday, and the suit I purchased at Bloomingdale's. Half-listening, I watch the people on the street rushing from one store to the next, and I think how Thanksgiving is my favorite holiday. One day to prepare, a day of eating and relaxing, looking forward to a full day of shopping on Black Friday.

"Allison, did you hear me?"

"Yes, you said you ordered lunch for the office."

Accounting is a tough business, and no one is allowed to take vacation between January and May 15 and August through the end of October. With such little flexibility, you'd think employees would come and go. But that's not the case. Pete's employees adore him.

"You're a good boss. Your staff is lucky."

Pete laughs. "I think it's the other way around. I'm lucky to have a great staff."

I think of this perfect man, our casual conversation, and realize we are getting closer to our destination. My chest begins to constrict. When we arrive, I exit the car and breathe in the fresh air. Pete comes around to meet me but stops when the front door to the house opens.

"Dad, Mom, what took you so long?"

"Traffic, sweetie," says Pete. Julia wraps her arms around Pete's neck. "Hi, my sweet girl. How was your day?"

"It was all right." Turning her attention from Pete to me, she calls, "Mom." Rushing into my arms, she places a kiss on my cheek. "I've missed you."

I welcome the warmth of my daughter. "I've missed you! It feels good to hold you. How was your day?"

"Good. Mrs. Garrett brought in cake mix and frosting. We made cupcakes for the fourth-grade elementary class. They're visiting our school tomorrow. The seventh graders are responsible for the meet-and-greet."

I smile at my girl. In less than two years, she'll be entering high school.

Julia takes Pete's arm. "Aunt Sarah said you're right on time. Dinner is almost ready."

I watch, envious of the special bond Pete and Julia share. I think of my own father, who died months before my fifth birthday. I breathe in several more times before I step forward and walk toward the house. Andrew is waiting at the entrance.

Standing before me, he asks, "How are you, Mom?"

He's wearing his favorite Yankee hat. I take him into my arms and say, "I'm fine. How are you?" As I release him, our eyes meet. My son is a foot taller than me.

"All right, I guess."

I smile. Seeing the concern in his eyes, I ask about his day.

"It was good. Did you remember to bring my science book?"

"I did."

Andrew man-hugs his father.

"Hey, buddy, how was school?"

"Fine. The coach said the baseball sign-up sheets are due tomorrow."

Pete smiles. "Got it right here, signed and dated."

"Mom, I need to make an appointment for a physical."

The children look sad, but not overwrought with grief. I wonder if they are keeping their true feelings hidden for my sake.

Our children love their grandparents, but Andrew and Patrick had a special bond. Whatever Andrew's latest interest, Patrick would surf the internet to be able to converse with his grandson. Patrick might've had more in common with Andrew, but he never neglected Julia. Younger Julia loved American Girl dolls, and Patrick knew more about dolls than Pete or me. I can't help but wonder how his death will affect them.

Aunt Sarah and Uncle George enter the foyer to greet us. Pete immediately kisses Aunt Sarah's cheek and shakes Uncle George's hand. Pete showers my family with affection. Sorry I can't say I do as well. Reluctantly I place a kiss on Uncle George's cheek, staring into his eyes. He whispers, "I'm so sorry, Allison. I know how close you were with Patrick. We're going to miss him."

Aunt Sarah asks, "How was your visit with Dr. Sass?"

"Dr. Sass?"

"Your dentist appointment?"

"Oh, yes. Dr. Sass is fine. And so are my teeth." I can tell she knows I'm lying, so I turn away from her and hang my coat in the closet.

"Nothing like a clean bill of health," says Aunt Sarah.

Pete asks Aunt Sarah if we have time to talk before dinner.

"We have fifteen minutes. Will that be enough time, Pete?"

"Yes."

Aunt Sarah places her arm through Pete's, and we follow them into the living room. As always, I glance around the room. Aunt Sarah's living room furniture is dated. The plastic that had protected it from stains has long been removed, and the chairs were reupholstered in 1998. God knows she has enough money to replace every piece of furniture in the house, but she chooses to live with the old stuff. Whenever I suggest replacing the furniture, she replies, "You can't replace perfection. This furniture will outlast me." She's probably right.

Andrew, Julia, and I sit on the sofa, Aunt Sarah in the armchair and Uncle George in the La-Z-Boy, which he brought with him, when he came to live with his sister. Pete grabs the desk chair and sits directly in front of us. Although I make fun of the furniture, the room is quite comfortable. There is a fireplace burning and casting an orange glow around the room. The fireplace is surrounded by an old English mantel and bookshelves. One of the shelves houses a TV. The TV became a staple when Andrew turned two. There are four large windows with built-in window seats, and an antique desk sits between two of the windows. As I look around the room, for some unknown reason, I feel safe and warm.

My thoughts are interrupted when Pete begins to speak. He uses the name our children so lovingly called Patrick. "Pop was involved in an accident on I-95 right outside Philadelphia. A man driving a tractor-trailer had a heart attack and hit Pop's car. I spoke with the man's family. He's in intensive care, but his doctors believe he will make a full recovery. I ask that we keep this man and his family in our prayers. Another driver did see the accident and called 911 immediately."

Andrew asks, "Only Pop was …?"

I gesture to Pete to be aware of what he says in front of the children. He acknowledges me and says, "Yes, son." Then he goes on to say, "The service will be at All Saints Church on Tuesday at ten. Reverend Tom will preside. My parents will arrive tomorrow as planned and will remain with us until the following Saturday."

Before anyone could respond, Andrew says, "Mom was right, Pop should have booked a flight. If he had listened, he'd be here, with us."

I sit stoic, thinking exactly what Andrew has just said out loud.

"Maybe he should have, son, but he chose to drive, and accidents happen every day. We don't have a crystal ball to avoid our destiny," replies Pete.

I turn to Andrew. "Pop was stubborn." I shock the adults with my statement and confuse the children, but I'm immediately forgiven because I am a person who is grieving, and a person dealing with grief doesn't always mean what they say.

Aunt Sarah breaks the awkward silence. "Thank you, Pete, for making the arrangements."

Julia asks, "Where will Pop be buried?"

Andrew steps up and says, "Pop wanted to be cremated."

Julia lowers her head. "Lizzy's cat was cremated. Where will we spread his ashes?"

Andrew again steps up. "This year at the egg hunt. I was sitting with Pop by the lake. He said when his time came, he wanted his ashes spread right at that very spot."

I stand up, saying, "I think we've covered everything."

* * * * *

During dinner, my eyes well as I remember that day, Andrew and Patrick sitting side by side at the lake. I was making my way toward them and heard Patrick telling Andrew he wanted to spend eternity at this lake. Reaching them, I say, "Magnificent view, isn't it?"

Patrick looks up at me and smiles. "I like to think it's one of God's greatest creations. I intend to make this my final resting place, close to the people I love most in the world."

I'm reminded of his eyes, crystal blue in color.

I force the memory from my mind and concentrate on the conversation going on at the dinner table. Julia and Aunt Sarah are talking about Julia's day at school. Pete and Andrew are discussing sports, and Uncle George is agreeing with whatever is being said.

After dinner, Aunt Sarah and I clear the table, Julia and Uncle George head to the living room to watch *A Charlie Brown Thanksgiving Special*, while Pete and Andrew discuss if he will get the short-stop position this year on the baseball team. Before my aunt and I disappear to the kitchen, Pete compliments my aunt on another fine dinner.

Aunt Sarah giggles like a schoolgirl and then asks, "Pete, do you know what time your parents' flight is arriving?"

"Mom had no idea when I spoke with her. I told her I'd call tonight to speak with Dad."

I interject by saying, "I can call your parents, Pete."

"No, you visit with your aunt." Pete turns to Andrew. "Buddy, do you mind if I just make a quick call to Grandpa?"

"Sure. I'll finish my math homework."

Aunt Sarah and I enter the kitchen. "I spoke with Mary this morning. She and Hank are going to stay with us during their visit. God knows we have the room."

"Why are they staying here with you?"

"What?"

"Why would they be staying here when you know damn well Pete would expect his parents to stay with us?"

"Pete was the one who suggested I call."

"What? When?"

"Pete called this morning and said his sisters would be staying at your house and he thought his parents might feel more comfortable staying with us."

"I don't know, Aunt Sarah. This sounds more like one of your ideas, not Pete's."

"Allison, why would I lie? I was more than happy to help. I'm looking forward to spending time with people my own age."

I begin to load the dishwasher. "I'm sure they're going to love spending time with Uncle George. The man doesn't say more than three words a day!"

Aunt Sarah looks hurt. To avoid being scolded, I say, "I'll set the table for dessert."

As I set the table, I realize that Perfect Pete was right to ask my aunt to extend an invitation to Mary and Hank. I'd forgotten about Pete's sisters and their families. Of course they will be here to support their brother. From the corner of my eye, I watch Uncle George as he tentatively listens to Julia explain what Lucy has planned for Charlie Brown. I'm overcome with guilt for faulting him for his strange personality, not so different from his own father's, my grandfather. I think, *The apple doesn't fall far from the tree.*

I was thirteen when my uncle moved back home. He lived outside the United State a little shy of thirty years, returning home at the ripe old age of forty-five. He resided with his father, till his death, at their childhood home in Cleveland. When Andrew was born, Aunt Sarah decided to move east to be closer to me and my family. I tried to talk her out of the move by asking, "What will Uncle George do without you?" but there was no changing her mind. She insisted that my family needed her more than he did. After two years, Uncle George sold the house in Cleveland and moved east.

When I was a child, Uncle George was the man who sent cash gifts on my birthday and holidays. Every card was signed, "Uncle George." No additional message. Whenever I received a card, Aunt Sarah went on about how much my uncle loves me, and never neglected to remind me, to send an acknowledgment of thanks. It excited me to think I had an uncle who lived overseas and had the ability to travel throughout Europe. Once, after receiving a gift, I decided to write Uncle George a letter in hopes of starting an ongoing conversation through cards and thank-you notes. I gave up after an hour and wrote thus:

Uncle George,

Thank you for the gift. I will buy something special, but not too expensive.

Love,
Your niece,
Allison.

As I grew older, I waited patiently for Uncle George's gifts and wrote the same thank-you note. My aunt, knowing Uncle George was a generous man, convinced me to save half the money in a savings account. "I promise you, someday you'll be happy that you made the decision to save half the money." Again, my aunt was right. As I grew, so did my bank account. Having that account gave me a sense of responsibility and freedom.

Uncle George was a career military man, so he rarely visited. The first time he visited was when my father died, but I was too young to remember. There were phone conversations and letters between him, Aunt Sarah, and my mother, and every so often, I got to talk with him. Our conversations were short. "How are you?" "I'm fine. How are you?" "Good." "Talk to you soon."

One day as I arrived home from school, I heard my uncle's name mentioned, so I stopped at the kitchen door to listen. My aunt was telling my mother that a local boy was again caught stealing. She said he was being held in the juvenile detention center. She went on to say, she knew the family and they were good people. The boys arrest reminds her of George at that age. Do you remember the late-night phone calls from the police station? Dad would leave the house, and an hour later, he and George would return. Then the fighting would begin. The military was the answer for George. "Maybe it can be a life-saver for this boy, as it was for George?"

I remember clamping my hands over my mouth to stop myself from laughing out loud. Uncle George, a teenage nightmare and not the refined young man Aunt Sarah had me believe he was?

Julia jumps from the sofa, waking me from my reverie. "Are we having dessert, Mom? *Charlie Brown* is over." As I glance at the man who had been sitting with my daughter, I can't imagine him as a child, or as a troubled teenager, the town menace.

Pete steps behind Julia and lifts her in the air. "So dessert is what you want, my pretty. Then it's dessert you'll get!" He gives Julia a kiss. "That's from Grandma and Grandpa."

Julia notices my sweater. "Mom, is that a new sweater? It's red. I've never seen you in red."

As if on cue, Aunt Sarah enters the dining room with a tray of desserts and coffee. “I told your mother earlier she looks good in red.”

Pete joins in the conversation. “You do look good in red, Allison. Why don’t you wear it more often?”

“I don’t think it goes well with my hair color.”

“Babe, you look beautiful in any color.” Pete winks at me.

“Dad, stop flirting with Mom—it’s gross.”

“What’s gross about me loving your mom?”

Julia waves her hand. “Whatever.”

Pete smiles.

Andrew rushes in, asking, “What’s so funny?” Sitting, he reaches for a piece of cake.

“Dad is flirting with Mom. I think it’s gross.”

Andrew ignores Julia. “Dad, tomorrow’s a half-day. Can I skip school and go with Uncle George to the airport?”

I answer instead. “You’re going to miss a few days next week, Andrew, for the funeral. You shouldn’t miss tomorrow.”

“Mom, there’s not much going on. It’s the day before Thanksgiving.”

Pete agrees with me. “Your mother is right, Andrew.” Pete diverts the conversation by saying, “Hey, I have an idea. Tomorrow night is usually pizza-and-movie night at our house. Why don’t we spend the night here with Aunt Sarah, Uncle George, and your grandparents?”

Andrew looks defeated, Julia elated. “Great idea, Dad! I get to pick the movie!”

Andrew throws Julia a look.

Pete, sensing Andrew’s disappointment, says, “I think we should let Andrew pick?”

“Let Julia pick. I really don’t care.”

Pete, realizing he isn’t one of his son’s favorite people at the moment, says, “Why don’t you guys get ready for bed? It’s been a long day, and I’d like to get Mom home.”

Andrew is the first to leave the table. I watch as he leaves shoulders slumped. Julia comes and places her arms around my neck and kisses my cheek. “You do look tired, Mom. But don’t leave without saying goodbye.”

"I won't, I promise."

With the kids gone, and trying hard to avoid any adult conversation, I rise to clear the table. My aunt follows my lead, leaving Pete and Uncle George talking about a problem Pete's been having with his car. I place the dessert dishes in the dishwasher.

"Thank you, Allison, for helping with the dishes."

"You're welcome. Thanks for offering your home to Mary and Hank. I completely forgot about Pete's sisters."

Aunt Sarah comes over and places a hand on my shoulder. "Always happy to help."

Trying to ignore the gesture, I ask, "Do you have enough food for Thanksgiving? I'm still making the pies and the cranberry sauce."

"Of course. I wouldn't have it any other way. Don't forget, it is a holiday weekend. You might want to place the order for the luncheon?"

I look confused. "What luncheon?"

"The luncheon following the service on Tuesday. I'm assuming it will be at your house, but if you're not up for it, we can have it here."

"Do we have to have a luncheon?"

"You don't have to have one, but usually the family has something after the service."

"This is ridiculous! I don't understand why we have to have a funeral service in the first place. These people didn't even know Patrick!"

Aunt Sarah looks shocked. "I think Patrick would have wanted a Christian burial!"

"I don't want to deprive Patrick of a Christian burial, but why couldn't we have a private service for just the family?"

"The arrangements have been made. I think it's too late."

"Too late? Fine, Patrick will have his Christian burial, the strangers will be fed, and all will be right with the world. I'll call the deli tomorrow." I finish loading the dishwasher and slam the door shut. "I blame Patrick for breaking my children's hearts and for ruining Thanksgiving. He was a stubborn and selfish man!"

"Allison, Patrick's death was an accident. You're hurting right now, and so is your family, but this, too, will pass. In time you'll be happy knowing you did the right thing."

"Do you have a crystal ball? How do you know how my family or I will feel in time?"

"Allison, you're angry."

"Yes, I am angry. I have a right to be angry. I don't want a funeral service or a stupid luncheon. How crazy am I to want a private service with just family? Who cares what people will think of us if we don't follow protocol? Are you afraid your friends at church will mock you for not showing your niece the error of her ways?"

I head for the door. She is after me like a fly on a horse, but I'm faster than the old bitch. Pete's still sitting with Uncle George at the dining room table, but from the looks on their faces, I know they've heard every word."

"I'm tired. Let's get the hell out of here."

Pete wants to intervene but changes his mind. "I'll warm up the car."

"Fine, I'm going to say good-night to my children." I run up the stairs to share a kiss and a hug with the kids and to tuck them in with the words I've spoken since their birth. "I love you with all my heart and soul. Never forget that." As I make my way down the stairs, Aunt Sarah and Uncle George are waiting at the front door.

"Allison, your uncle and I—"

"Not now, Aunt Sarah, please. I have another long day ahead of me tomorrow. I have to order the food and bake. Good night." I walk out the door, leaving them to wonder what they did to upset me.

When I get to the car, Pete says, "I didn't get to say good-night."

Afraid if I allow Pete to go back inside, my aunt or uncle will come to the car, I assure him by saying, "I said good-night for you. I hope you don't mind, but I really need to get home and get some rest."

As Pete pulls away from the curb, I look in the side-view mirror. I can see the hurt on my aunt's face, and it makes me smile.

CHAPTER TWO

Sarah

I remain at the front door and watch as the car disappears from sight. I glance up at the sky. During October and November, on a clear night, you can almost reach up and touch the stars. The chill in the air makes me shiver. Turning, I enter the house.

The children make their way down the stairs, concerned about their parents.

"Is Mom going to be all right?" asks Andrew.

I walk toward Andrew and Julia. "Of course, Andrew, she'll be fine. Your mother and Patrick had a special bond. She needs time to accept that he's gone. We all do."

"I know Pop was Mom's stepfather, but she told us she didn't think of him as a stepfather. She thought of him as a knight in shining armor," says Julia.

"Your mom was a teenager when Pop entered her life. She'll never forget the kindness he showed her. Young adults need someone to listen without judging. Patrick was a good listener."

"I guess her mom—I mean Grandma wasn't as understanding as Pop?" says Andrew.

I frown. "Parenting is a difficult job. Your grandma did her best," I say. "Enough about the past. It's late. Off to bed, you two. I'll be up in a few minutes to say good-night."

As I pass through the living room to check the back door, George says, "I already locked the back door."

"Thanks! It's been a long and stressful day for all of us, especially Allison."

"Most of your days with Allison are stressful."

"We're family, George. Maybe Patrick's passing will bring us closer."

"You're an optimist, Sarah. I hope for your sake that's exactly what happens."

I stare at George. Many years have passed since our childhood, but I can still see the boy he was in his eyes. I walk over to kiss George good-night. "I'll be up soon."

George smiles. "I'll drive the children to school tomorrow, and then I'll head to the airport."

I linger a while and listen as George says good-night to the children. Hearing his door close, I walk to the bookshelves and reach high for the book. The book that holds a lifetime of memories.

When I reach the top of the stairs, I hear Andrew scolding. "Julia, I'm tired. I don't want to talk anymore." Smiling, I know Andrew has agreed to let Julia sleep in his room. It reminds me of George and myself as children.

I address Julia first. "So you're sleeping in here tonight?" I wink at Andrew.

"Yup. Andrew's afraid of the dark." Julia laughs.

"Give your old aunt a hug and kiss."

Julia wraps her arms around my neck. "You're not old, Aunt Sarah."

Hearing the compliment, I say, "You'll make a great politician someday."

"I'm going to be a teacher, maybe a lawyer, but not a politician."

"Whatever makes you happy." I place a kiss on Julia's forehead. "You know how much I love you."

Giving Andrew the high five, I repeat the loving words my mother spoke to me, and her mother to her. "Love you with all my heart and soul."

* * * * *

Once in bed, I reach for the book and lay it on my lap, covering it with my hands. I open the book to the middle and touch the photos that were hidden between pages 599 and 600. The first photo is precious to me, and I allow the tears to cloud my eyes. I hold the photo to my heart for several minutes while staring at another dear to my heart. I place them aside. The next photo is of my mother, father, George, and myself. I focus on my mother. Closing my eyes, I breathe in, willing her scent to mind. *Lavender.* After several moments, I open my eyes and look at my father. I'm standing next to him in the photo, while George is sitting on our mother's lap. I think, the perfect family. I turn the photo over. The date is written in my mother's handwriting: "November 1945, Sarah, eleven, George, nine, and a short note to the little one to be born after Christmas or early in the New Year." The date is a reminder that World War II is quickly coming to an end.

My mother had three miscarriages, one before George was conceived and two after. With each miscarriage, my mother's pain and sorrow wore heavily on my father. He was concerned about the mental and physical health of his dearly beloved Erin. When my mother had reached six months into this pregnancy, my parents began to relax.

During their courtship, my parents dreamed of a house filled with children—five, to be exact.

When I was a child, it was no secret that Erin and Will Holland loved each other deeply. One would question how two people so different could find happiness. The "opposite attracts" theory was prevalent.

William James Holland, of English descent, born to Catherine and Charles Holland, their only child, resided in an affluent section of the Bronx known as Riverdale, New York. Erin O'Brien, of Irish descent, born to Margaret Ann and Timothy O'Brien, also an only child, was raised in a middle-class neighborhood in Brooklyn, New York.

My grandma Maggie, as I affectionately called her, suffered several miscarriages before giving birth to my mother. Maggie and Tim accepted God's will, feeling blessed to have a beautiful daughter to love.

Catherine Holland, content that her firstborn was a boy to carry on the Holland name, felt her job was done. Grandmother didn't enjoy being pregnant and made her feelings known to her husband, Charles. Grandfather accepted Grandmother's decision, knowing once his wife made a decision, there was no changing her mind.

Grandfather held an executive position with Bankers Trust of New York, and a company chauffeur was available to the family at all times. The Holland home was run by two live-in servants, Kevin and his wife, Polly. Polly was nanny to William James, my father, until the age of thirteen. While grandmother enjoyed her social status, Charles enjoyed his life outside the home. It was rumored that in his younger days, he was quite the ladies' man.

Tim O'Brien, my grandpa, worked for the Department of Transportation. His job was to repair and maintain the bridges and tunnels in New York City. He enjoyed the work because he loved working outdoors. Grandma Maggie was a skilled seamstress who worked at the local factory until the birth of her daughter, my mother, Erin.

Staring at the date on the photo, I think about my father and the war. I felt lucky then that my father didn't have to serve in the war due to a condition known as flat feet. His inability to fight for his country tormented him each time he read of another solider losing his or her life. Though, Mom tried to ease his suffering by saying, "Will, you're doing your part here at home."

Mom and Dad volunteered at the USO and local churches, boxing care packages for the soldiers. Dad and a number of well-body men in our community donated time to the women with husbands fighting the war. No job was too small; the men gave their time without complaint. Mom babysat for the women who took jobs at the local factory to support their children. I couldn't help thinking of a younger George and how much he enjoyed working side by side with our dad.

My earliest recollection of George as a baby was when he turned one. My grandpa and grandma O'Brien came to celebrate his first birthday. "You know, Mom, I still can't believe I let Will talk me into naming this beautiful precious boy George."

"George is a strong name, Erin."

Dad adored his grandfather Skip. Skip's birth name was George, and the nickname Skip was derived from his love of sailing.

Mom never tired of the stories my dad shared with her about Skip and his sailing adventures. Due to a severe case of seasickness, Grandfather Holland did not share the same love of sailing as his father, but his grandson did. My father admired his grandfather so much that he made a promise: if he ever were blessed with a son, he would name him George, after Skip. How could my mother refuse such a request from the man she loved?

Not pleased with the name George, Mom took to calling her son Georgie. She thought of calling him Skip, but Grandmother Holland wouldn't hear of it. I smile, thinking how frustrated it made my father when my mom called George, Georgie. Dad often scolded Mom for not using the birth name George.

"Erin, my love, why do you insist on calling the boy Georgie?"

"I could call him Skip and leave you to deal with your mother."

Dad chose the lesser of two evils.

Every child asks the question of their parents, "How did you and Dad meet?" George and I were mesmerized when Mom began the love story of how she and Dad met. If I close my eyes and will back the past, I can hear my mother's enthusiastic voice say, "Well, you know, when I attended Hunter College back in the day, my best friend was Peggy. She organized the spring dance each year. I'm not really sure how Peggy met John, but John and your dad were college buddies at Fordham University. Peggy invited John and your dad to the spring social." Then on cue, she'd ask, "Do you believe in fate? Well, I do. It was God's will that your dad and I met. When Peggy introduced me to your dad, I was smitten by how dapper he looked in his blue suit. Dad asked me to dance, and by the end of the night, I was hoping he'd asked me on a date, and he was hoping when he did, I'd say yes. Love at first sight?"

I never tired of hearing the story and prayed that when I met the love of my life, my story would be identical to my parents'.

Three months after my dad graduated college, he was hired by an accounting firm in Manhattan, and two months later, he asked Mom to marry him. Mom had one more year until graduation, and one year after she graduated, they married.

Catherine Holland did all she could to get her son to change his mind about marrying this Irish Catholic from a middle-class family, but not even God himself would change Dad's mind.

My grandmother Holland was a devout Episcopalian. Grandma and Grandpa O'Brien were devout Catholics but were willing to look past religious denominations, seeing how in love William was with their daughter, and she him. Their daughter's happiness was all that mattered.

Catherine Holland even threatened not to attend the wedding, but my father stood his ground, saying, "If you can't accept Erin, then, today, you can forget you ever had a son."

Charles Holland, with no intention of losing his only son, expressed to Catherine, "If you choose not to attend the wedding, it's your choice, but I will be there standing beside our son and daughter-in-law on their happy day."

On March 28, 1931, William James Holland and Erin O'Brien were married at St. Joseph's RC Church in Brooklyn. In attendance were their parents, family, and friends, including a not-so-thrilled Catherine Holland.

My parents resided in an apartment not far from Erin's parents'. Will was doing well in his job, while Erin taught second grade at the local elementary school. Shortly after celebrating their third year of marriage, Erin was expecting.

On the day I was born, my mom said her father brought several bottles of champagne to the hospital, which wasn't allowed, and charmed the nurses into letting him open the bottles. "Congratulations to my beautiful daughter and her handsome husband, Will, for this beautiful and precious child! She's as beautiful as the night is long." The Hollands, just as happy with the birth of their first grandchild, showered me with expensive gifts.

Shortly after my birth, my grandmother Holland pressured my father to move his family to the Bronx. "Private schools in the Bronx are superior to the schools in Brooklyn. You have to think of the child." My grandmother insisted her son do the right thing, putting the needs of the child before his own, but he didn't trust that his mother would keep out of their private lives and feared Erin, a gentle and compassionate woman, would fall prey to his controlling mother.

Hearing of a position with a steel company in Cleveland, Will decided to forward a letter of his accomplishments. The company showed interest and asked if Will would set aside time to meet with a member of their parent company in New York. The meeting went well, and one week later, my father received a call that a letter of intent would be mailed to him shortly. The salary was more than he presently was earning, including a yearly bonus and an approved mortgage on a home of his choice if he accepted the position.

Feeling guilty that he had not discussed the job with Erin, he was faced with the task of telling her. The conversation began with an immediate apology from Will, but to his surprise, Erin listened tentatively and said, "Will, that's wonderful news! If this is what you want, then you should accept the offer. We'll give it a go. If it doesn't work, we can always return to New York. With your qualifications, I don't think you'll have a problem finding a job."

So began the couple's exodus from Brooklyn to the suburbs of Cleveland, Ohio.

* * * * *

Christmas 1945, soldiers were returning home. The Christmas spirit was overwhelming in our small community.

The war ending added to this joyous season. Parents were overjoyed that their sons and daughters had returned home safe and sound. Wives longed for the love of their husbands; fathers beamed with pride to see how their children had grown during their time of separation. The streets were filled with well-wishes: "Happy Holidays," "Merry Christmas," "God bless our country and our soldiers." Christians celebrated the birth of Christ, rabbis read from the

Torah, but whatever the faith, we were thanking God for returning home these brave men and women.

My fondest memory of the Christmas season is when Mom, George, and I baked Christmas cookies. Mom would set aside the broken cookies for George and me to enjoy with a cup of hot chocolate topped with fresh cream. Dad would pop in, grab a cup of hot chocolate, pick at the broken cookies, then move on to his task of decorating our home, both inside and out.

On this night two weeks before Christmas, I asked Mom to repeat the story of how she and Dad met.

"Sarah, it amazes me how you never tire of hearing this story." After, George would request hearing about the wedding reception that followed, and I would ask that she start with the ceremony at the church. Mom ended the story by saying, "Your father is romantic."

"What does romantic mean, Mom?" questioned George.?"

Mom smiled. "*Romantic* is when a person does special things to win another's heart. "Mom placed her hand on her stomach. "You're father showered me with flowers, notes of love, and much more. Simple gestures to win your mom's heart. Someday you'll find that special person, and if you're as romantic as your dad, in no time, you'll win her heart."

George says, "I hope I'm as lucky as dad. I want a wife just like you mom." "Oh Georgie, that's so sweet."

I ask, "Mom, describe the wedding dress and how the women in the church gasped at how beautiful you looked when you walked down the aisle!"

"All brides look beautiful on their wedding day. I can't tell you if the women gasped or not—your grandma believes they did. And who's going to argue with the mother of the bride?" My father, always defending my grandma's description of the sounds echoing in the church as my mother walked down the aisle, said, "Believe me, there were gasps, but none louder than mine. My heart skipped a beat as she walked toward me, just as it does every day I wake up beside her."

Mom acknowledged the compliment with her usual "Oh, Will" then went on to describe the wedding dress my grandma sewed for her only child, sparing no expense on the silk and lace. When I was a little girl, my mother would place the dress on me and say, "One day I hope you'll wear this dress. If not, we'll have Grandma make you a new one." Today the wedding dress is wrapped in white paper, secured in a chest in the attic.

Another precious memory of that night is of my father calling out to us, "Enough about the wedding. Come see what your father has created." George was the first to join Dad in the living room. When Mom and I entered the room, our eyes widened seeing the transformation before us, a magical winter wonderland.

"Dad, it's so beautiful!" Looking out the large bay window to the outside, I called to George. "Look, George, there's Santa and baby Jesus, Mary, and Joseph. Dad, you hung a spotlight on the stable!"

As we stared out the window, my father placed his arm around my mother and gently kissed her cheek. "Will, it looks beautiful, but something's missing."

My father repeated her words. "I know, love. Children, Mom thinks something is missing. Can you guess what?"

George yells out, "The Christmas tree!"

"That's right, son. Why don't we get up early tomorrow and head to the farm and cut ourselves the prettiest tree in the forest?"

I corrected my father. "Christmas is two weeks away, Dad. The tree won't survive."

"In Mom's condition, I think she'd feel comfortable knowing we'll have a decent-size tree for Christmas."

The decision was made. The following day, the Holland family would venture out in search of the perfect Christmas tree and ease Mom's concerns.

I close my eyes to envision the scene as it was that night, my parents standing side by side, their arms wrapped around each other, the lights from the outside illuminating their faces. As George and I claim the stairs, I call to them, "Mom, Dad, I love you with all my heart and soul." In unison, their response was a repeat of those same words.

I open my eyes and look down at the photo while wiping away the tears running down my face.

The photo was Mom's way of welcoming each child to the family. In a photo album, stored away, there is a similar photo of Erin and Will. The back of the photo reads, "Two more months until we meet our firstborn."

The day Mom placed this photo in the old photo album, I asked her the meaning of the photos. I can envision her smile as she explained, "This might sound silly, but I wanted each of you to know how much Dad and I loved you even before we met you. See how happy your dad and I are in every one of the photos? We have you children to thank for those smiles."

At that moment, I felt her arms wrap around me as they did that day so long ago, she asking the same question she always did. "How much do I love you, Sarah Holland?"

Laughing, I'd answer, "You love me with all your heart and soul."

CHAPTER THREE

Allison

On the ride home from my aunt's house, Pete asks what happened between Aunt Sarah and me.

"Aunt Sarah was just being Aunt Sarah," I say and end it.

When we arrive home, I excuse myself, saying how exhausted I'm feeling. Halfway up the stairs, I stop and ask, "Pete, should we have gone to Philadelphia to identify the body?"

Pete gently answers, "The funeral director assured me he'd take care of everything."

I take a moment before saying, "He's not family." I lower my head, turn away, and climb the remaining stairs.

Pete calls to me, "Allison, you know I'm here for you, sweetheart. We all are. Especially your aunt and uncle."

At the mention of my aunt and uncle, I lash out. "Are you blaming me for what happened tonight? I know you and Uncle George overheard our conversation."

"Not at all." Pete decides to end the conversation. "I'm going to straighten up the kitchen. I'll be up shortly."

I shout, "No, you brought up my aunt, so tell me, Pete, did my aunt suggest we have a luncheon after the service? Because I don't remember being asked if I wanted to feed half the congregation."

Pete looks like a mouse who has just been cornered. "The reverend asked if he should make an announcement that a luncheon would follow the service, and I thought, since a number of people were traveling long distances to be here, it was only right—"

"Well, answer this question, How did my aunt know there was going to be a luncheon and not me?"

"I called and said I decided to provide a lunch after the service and to ask how many from the parish she thought might attend."

"If you had called me and asked me about this ridiculous luncheon, I would have told you I didn't think we needed to feed the congregation when half of them didn't even know Patrick. So you only have yourself to blame, because I was completely thrown off guard when she mentioned the luncheon. It sounded like one of her do-the-right-thing ideas."

"You're right, I should have called you. I'll call your aunt in the morning to explain, then I'll call the reverend and have him cancel the announcement."

Pete turns away from me, and the word *cancel* makes my head ache. I scold, "I will apologize to my aunt in the morning, from the both of us. Don't cancel the luncheon. I'll look foolish."

I walk up the stairs and close the bedroom door behind me.

I toss and turn all night as the dream invades my sleep.

* * * * *

The following morning, when I walk into the kitchen, Pete is pouring himself a cup of coffee and raises the pot in my direction. I take a seat at the counter and agree to a cup. Running my hands through my hair, I can't believe how tired I'm feeling.

Pete places a cup in front of me, saying, "Doesn't look like you got much sleep."

"I didn't."

"Same here. I kept thinking about all the people that might show up for the free lunch." Pete smiles.

"If you're asking to be forgiven, you'll have to give me a few days. You had to know that asking my aunt instead of me, your wife, would make me feel inadequate."

"Sweetie, that wasn't my intention. This is a first for both you and me."

"What if my aunt weren't around to offer her opinion? If you think that lame excuse is going to let you off the hook, you're sadly mistaken."

Pete rises, taking his coffee cup to the sink. "I wasn't planning on going to the office today, but Jim called. He's concerned about the Carlton account. He asked if I could stop by the office to update him on the file, since I'll be out next week."

"I hope you said yes. You wouldn't want him to mess up your largest account, would you?"

Pete turns and stares at me. "I didn't want to leave you alone, but the way you feel about me right now, you probably need a few hours to remember how adorable I am."

Pete is waiting to be forgiven, but I'm not ready to forgive or forget. "I think I can handle being on my own for a few hours. Besides, I have a lot to do today. Did you forget Thanksgiving is tomorrow? I need to go to the supermarket and the liquor store. And of course, there's the luncheon on Tuesday, or would you rather my aunt stop at the deli and place the order?"

Pete smiles. "You've made your point."

* * * * *

With Pete upstairs dressing, I find myself staring out the kitchen window, wondering what a difference a day makes. Yesterday the skies were picture-perfect, today dark as night.

Pete walks into the kitchen and says, "Looks like rain."

"Sure does. I should get going myself, before the skies open up."

As I get up from my chair, Pete places his hand on my arm. "I promise to be home by three."

"Sounds good."

"Again, I'm sorry." I don't offer a response. Pete says, "I love you. Be careful driving. The roads can be slick when it rains."

His comment infuriates me. "I didn't get my licenses yesterday. I know how to drive in the rain."

* * * * *

I shower without crying. It amazes me. Toweling myself dry, I lean over and become light-headed. Using the wall as my guide, I lower myself to the floor. The bathroom is steamy and warm, but a chill runs through me when the realization strikes that life as I've known it will be no more.

In the distance, I hear my cell phone buzz. The person trying to reach me is persistent. Annoyed, I lift myself from the floor and walk into my bedroom. The phone goes silent. Staring at it, I'm startled when it buzzes again.

"Hello."

"Allison."

"JoAnne, is that you? Where are you, are you still in China?"

"No. Didn't get in until two in the morning. I would have called last night, but it was too late."

"You're home?"

"We're in Atlanta. Remember, we're spending Thanksgiving with Gary's parents?"

"Yes, yes, I remember."

"Allison, I'm so sorry—"

"Patrick's dead, but I'm sure you already knew. The service is on Tuesday, at ten. You'll be home by Tuesday, right?"

"We arrive Monday night. Sweetie, I wish I were there with you. I promise I'll be there on Tuesday."

"I know you would have been here if you could." I begin to cry. "Don't go to the church, come to the house. I want you to drive with me. Be here by eight. JoAnne, something terrible is going … I need to tell you something." Then I whisper, "Something I should have told you years ago."

"Allison, I can't hear you."

I repeat myself, leaving out the last two lines of my statement. "Don't go to the church, come to the house. Eight o'clock. JoAnne, I need to talk with you, it's important."

"Gary and the kids are out with his mother. We have time before they get back. What's wrong?"

"Not over the phone. We'll talk Tuesday."

"Allison, you're scaring me. I'd rather you tell me what's wrong before I start thinking the worse. Is everyone all right?"

"Everyone is fine, I swear. We'll talk on Tuesday. Dolores and Gale arrive on Friday. They're staying with us. Pete's parents are staying with Aunt Sarah and Uncle George. We don't have enough room for everyone."

"I wish I could be there. This couldn't have happened at a worse time."

"Do you remember the last time we spoke? I said if Patrick says he's driving, then he's driving. JoAnne, he promised he'd book a flight. He promised!" I can't stop crying. "Patrick was a selfish man. He only thought about himself. It's true, JoAnne. I hate him!"

"Allison, calm down. You don't really hate Patrick. In all the years I've known you, you never said an unkind word about the man."

I dry my eyes. "I just can't believe he's gone. You're the only person that understands."

"I do. How are Pete and the kids holding up?"

"Pete's all right. I can't say the same for Andrew, though. JoAnne, you know how close he was with Patrick."

"Kids are resilient. How is Julia? She thought the sun rose and set in Patrick's eyes."

"She's good. She's strong, much stronger than Andrew."

"I'd keep an eye on them, especially Julia. The stronger they are, the harder they fall."

I lie when I tell JoAnne I will watch over my children. I should put my children's needs before my own, but it isn't registering. I'm more concerned about the future. Noticing the time, I shout, "Shit! JoAnne, I have to go, I have so many things to do. Pete wants to have a luncheon after the service, so I have to place a deli order. I have to bake three pies for tomorrow. I need to stop at the supermarket before there's nothing left, and would you believe it's raining? No, it's pouring!"

"All right, I'll let you go. Pete's probably waiting. Give the kids a kiss from Aunt JoAnne."

"Pete's not here. He had to go to work. Problem with a client."

"Pete isn't there? Is Aunt Sarah with you?"

"Hell no! Why?"

"I just thought …"

"She's the last person I want hanging around me. The woman irritates me, always interfering in my business."

"Allison, she's family, and I'm sure she'd be happy to help. I know it would make me feel better knowing you weren't alone."

"JoAnne, you're joking, right? The woman's a witch. She's bewitched you all into thinking how wonderful she is, but I know her true colors. She's a controlling bitch."

"I'd feel better knowing you were running errands with the controlling bitch instead of by yourself."

I smile for the first time since Sunday. "It's just like you to worry about me."

"You never stop worrying about the people you love."

As I've never had a sibling of my own, JoAnne has filled that void in my life. "I love you too."

"Then call Aunt Sarah and ask her to tag along."

"You know I can't do that. I have to go. Remember, Tuesday, our house at eight, and then we'll talk."

Ending my conversation with JoAnne, I question if confiding in her is the right thing to do. Will my best friend be understanding or judgmental?

* * * * *

Entering Ben's deli, I take a number and wait my turn. Lifting a menu from the counter, I glance over the different platter selections.

"Mrs. Cane, how can I help you?"

I lift my head. "How do you know my name?"

"You've been in several times with Mr. Cane."

Pete frequented Ben's deli quite often. I'm not fond of deli meat, but my family, on the other hand, can't live without it.

"Yes, of course. Ben, I need to order lunch for Tuesday."

"Ben is my father. I'm Sal."

"Sorry Sal."

"What's the occasion?"

"A funeral. My stepfather was in a fatal car accident on Sunday. The funeral service is Tuesday at ten. The luncheon will be at our house, following the service." I wondered why I have divulged so much information to a complete stranger.

"Was it Patrick?"

"Yes. Did you know him?"

"He lunched here several times with Mr. Cane. Nice guy. I'm so sorry."

Feeling uncomfortable, Sal reaches for an order form. "I see you had a chance to look over the menu. Would you prefer hot and cold or just cold? Dessert and drinks are included with several platter orders."

"I was leaning toward option A, both hot and cold."

"How many people?"

"I don't know. It's my first time."

"Thirty-five's a safe number."

Anxious and afraid I won't have enough food, which will cause my aunt to have a stroke, I increase the number. "Fifty sounds safer." Sal crosses out *thirty-five* and rewrites *fifty*. He also makes suggestions on the choices of meats and cheeses. I agree with his selections.

"I think we covered everything. All I need is an address, phone number, and access to your home."

"I'll leave a key with my neighbor Marie. Her address is 9 Penn Post Road. As I stated, the service is at ten. We should be home by eleven thirty."

"We should arrive by ten fifteen. Gina helps me set up. If you're interested, she is also available to serve and clean up. Her fee is reasonable."

"Yes, of course."

Sal promises I won't be disappointed. Forty-five minutes later, I'm heading for my final stop, the supermarket.

* * * * *

Before I enter the supermarket, my phone rings. It's my aunt. I want to forward the call to voice mail, but I decide to take the call. "Hello."

"Allison, how are you, dear?"

"Fine, Aunt Sarah."

"I'm happy to hear you're feeling better."

Upset with myself for answering the call, I calm myself and say, "I'm heading into the supermarket. I only have a few minutes to talk."

"Uncle George just called. I thought you'd like to know Mary and Hank arrived safely."

I breathe in slowly. "Thanks for letting me know. I'll call Pete."

"Uncle George said Mary already spoke with Pete. When no one answered at the house, Mary called his cell phone. Pete said he was at the office."

"The supermarket looks crowded. Can we talk later?"

"Of course. Allison—"

I know my aunt wants to end our conversation by saying she loves me, so I throw her a bone. "Oh, by the way, I placed the food order for Tuesday. I wasn't sure about the number of people, so I ordered for fifty. Sal at the deli recommended thirty-five, but I'd rather have more than less."

"I think you made the right choice. All right, then, I'll see you later."

From the tone of her voice when we say goodbye, I picture a big old smile on my aunt's face. I have shared the deli order with her, and by doing so, I have brightened her day.

* * * * *

When I arrive home, my cell phone rings. I curse, saying I'm going to drown this phone. I drop the packages on the counter, and Pete's picture is displayed on the face of my phone. I decide not to answer and send the call to voice mail. A few minutes later, I retrieve the message. He's running late. Should be home by three thirty. Also his parents arrived safely.

* * * * *

Rolling the piecrust, I think about JoAnne and how lucky I am to have her in my life. JoAnne has four siblings, whom she loves and adores, but she and I share a special bond. What has made our relationship more solid is that our husbands are best friends as well. Gary and Pete met in college, both earning scholarships to play college football. They didn't much like each other at first. Gary, believing he was the superior player, quickly realized that Pete was an excellent quarterback, and for Gary to shine as a player, he had to accept there might be others as good, if not better, than he was. He pleaded with the coach and got Pete as a roommate. Today, one would take a bullet for the other.

Preparing the fillings for the pies, I wonder how I would have made it through my teen years without JoAnne. We shared everything. Well, maybe not everything. There is one secret I haven't shared.

Placing the pies in the oven, I set the timer for an hour. I move to the den and flop on the couch, placing a blanket over my body. I lay my head back on the cushion, forcing all thoughts from my mind: funerals, luncheons, family, and most of all, death.

The aroma of apple, pumpkin, and sweet potato pie is helping me relax, and I drift off to sleep.

* * * * *

The dream is vivid. I'm standing next to the man in the white suit. The sun is blinding my vision, as it always does. I lift my hand and try to touch his face. As my hand draws closer, the figure begins to fade, and I'm left there alone.

I feel a hand pressing on my shoulder. "Allison." I open my eyes and see Pete standing over me.

"I must have fallen asleep."

He smiles. "The oven was buzzing. I turned it off."

I panic. Running to the kitchen, I say, "I hope the pies aren't burned."

"I checked. They look and smell great."

Moving the pies from the oven to the counter to cool, I comment, "Thank God you walked in when you did. If I had burned them ... Pumpkin was Patrick's favorite."

"Mine too."

How inconsiderate of me not to remember pumpkin is also my husband's favorite. My guilt makes me want to flee the kitchen. "Do you think I have time to take a shower and change? I'll be quick."

"We have time. I'll be up in a few minutes."

In the safety of my bathroom, I strip off my clothes and start the shower. Once inside, I lean against the wall, trying to fight back the tears. Last Thanksgiving, I prepared three pumpkin pies, knowing it was Patrick's favorite. Today I've only made one.

The bathroom door opens, and Pete calls, "Allison, are you all right?"

Pushing back the shower curtain, I apologize to Pete. "I'm sorry, I forgot how much you love pumpkin pie."

Pete moves toward me and takes me in his arms. "Sweetheart, I'm not upset. You also made apple. I like apple more than pumpkin, and you made two of those."

Pete kisses me. I welcome the kiss and the gentle touch of his lips on mine. Several kisses later, Pete lifts me out of the shower, and moving to our bed, we make love.

After, I lie beside my husband, resting my head on his chest. Pete gently touches my hair. I feel sick to my stomach for what I have just done. I lift myself up, saying, "I should dress."

"Just lie here for a little while longer," he asks.

"Your parents are waiting to see us. We have to go."

When I move to get up, Pete places his hand on mine. "Do you know how much I love you?"

I can't face him when I say, "I do."

He lifts himself and turns my face to his. “I need to tell you what happened to me today. I had a terrible thought. If something ever happened to you … I don’t think I could go on without you.”

I smirk. “My aunt says, as time passes, it gets easier and you learn to move on.”

Pete lowers his head. “I know it’s enviable that one of us will pass before the other. I just hope it’s me.”

“Death has a way of making us face our own mortality. As you and I know, there are no guarantees in life. If I went first, you’d learn to live without me.”

As Pete’s wife and soul mate, I know I should speak the words to ease his fears, but how do you explain to the one who loves you more than life that the end of us is near?

* * * * *

On the ride to my aunt’s house, the conversation that Pete and I have just shared is upsetting me. I need to calm down before we reach the house.

I ignore the holiday shoppers, deep in my own thoughts. What was I thinking making love to my husband while Patrick’s body lay cold as ice in some funeral home?

“There’s a lot of traffic. Looks like we’ll be eating cold pizza.”

I turn toward Pete. He smiles. It’s amazing how my husband and my family don’t seem as upset as I am regarding Patrick’s passing.

Pete continues, “I’m taking the entire week off next week. If you’re up to it, Thursday or Friday, we can get an early start on Christmas shopping for the kids. Maybe a leisurely lunch, just the two of us.”

Pete’s suggestion infuriates me. I scold him, “Christmas? Patrick’s funeral is Tuesday, and you want to go Christmas shopping on Thursday or Friday? Oh, and let’s not forget a leisurely lunch! I have an idea. If we have time, we can get the Christmas decorations from the attic and decorate the fucking house!”

Pete whispers, “I didn’t mean to upset you, Allison. I just thought—”

"No, you weren't thinking. How do I know how I'm going to feel next week, or the week after? No wonder you and Aunt Sarah get on so well. You think alike. Cremate your stepfather on Tuesday, shop on Thursday, life goes on."

"Allison, stop. I'm just as upset as you are about Patrick. I just thought keeping ourselves busy might help."

"Could have fooled me."

If looks could kill, Pete would keel over dead. Whoever said "Silence is Golden" hit the nail straight on.

* * * * *

Pete's mother, Mary, opens the door to greet us. As she opens her arms to me, my first thought is to run, but I graciously accept her embrace. "Sweetheart, I am so sorry for your loss."

"I know you are, Mary, I know you are."

Hank and Pete shake hands and hug. Hank steps forward and places a kiss on my forehead, saying, "Patrick was a good man."

"He was, Hank. Thank you."

I notice my aunt and uncle watching my reaction. I smile at them. Aunt Sarah raises her hand to her mouth, touched by my smile, assuming all is forgiven from the night before.

Andrew and Julia wait their turn to greet their parents. While Pete greets our children, I hand my coat and purse to my aunt and head for the kitchen, ignoring my children.

In the kitchen, I pour myself a glass of water. The kitchen door opens, and I know that my aunt has entered the room. I confess, "I don't know what's wrong. I'm so thirsty."

"I have your favorite wine. Would you like a glass?"

"A glass of wine might help."

While Aunt Sarah pours the wine, Mary walks in to see if she could be of any help.

"I was just pouring wine. Would you like a glass, Mary? It's Allison's favorite."

"I would love a glass."

I glance at my mother-in-law. I repeat the excuse I gave Aunt Sarah regarding my sudden departure and ask, "How was the flight?"

"Started out fine. Got a little bumpy around Washington. Flying wouldn't be so bad if I could handle the turbulence."

The doorbell chimes. "That would be the pizza. Allison, can you and Mary set the table? Nothing fancy. It's only pizza."

Feeling uncomfortable alone with Mary, I hand Mary the dishes, saying, "China and stemware—I'd say that's pretty fancy. But my aunt would disagree."

"We are women of the fifties. We can't live without our expensive china."

I smile. Mary has never made me feel any less than a daughter than her own two daughters. I have admired and felt a special connection to Pete's parents from the first day I was introduced to them. During our lives together, I have never heard Pete say one unkind word about his parents.

As I hand Mary the plates and glasses, I say, "Pete said Dolores and Gale arrive early on Friday."

"Their plane is scheduled to arrive at eleven. Hank and George will meet them at the airport. They were lucky to get two seats on the same flight one day after Thanksgiving. Vince, Mike, and the boys wanted to be here for you ..."

"I understand, Mary. Patrick's death was sudden, and during a holiday, no less."

"I know seeing Dolores and Gale will be good for my family. We'll see everyone over the Christmas holiday."

Mary gives an understanding nod. "I'll take these out and set the table."

* * * * *

After the Thanksgiving service, the reverend makes the weekly announcements, which includes a Christian burial for Patrick Higgins Tuesday at 10:00 a.m. "The family has requested that, in lieu of flowers, donations to Saint Jude Children's Hospital would be greatly appreciated. The family will be available to all after the service. A luncheon will follow at the Cane home."

The only difference this Thanksgiving is, Patrick is no longer with us, and I'm not hosting the holiday. I look over at the place where Patrick sat, between Uncle George, and Andrew. Pete to Andrew's left. Seated there today is Hank. Hank notices my stare. I sense his discomfort, and he asks, "Allison, are things getting any easier at work?"

"Work is the same. Defending mothers with drug addiction and criminal offenses from not losing their children to the foster care system is a difficult job."

Pete interjects, "If anyone can save these kids, it's Allison. She does all she can to keep these families together."

Again, I am remised by the casual conversation. "Every time I manage to keep a family together, I pray that no harm comes to the children. When the courts decide that it will be in the best interest of the children to be placed in foster care, I pray no harm comes to the children. It's a no-win situation."

"I've read several articles on the subject. The children always want to remain with their parents, even if it does more harm than good," says Mary.

"We are so proud of Allison."

"Are you, Aunt Sarah? So often you've stated I should leave that job and get a job with a high-paying law firm."

By the look on my aunt's face, I can tell she knows the conversation can get ugly. "You've misunderstood my meaning, Allison. I'm afraid for you. A disgruntled parent can do you harm. I pray every day that God keeps you safe."

"Is that so? I've always thought you felt it was all about the money. Why work your ass off as a social services attorney making peanuts when you could be making the big buckets at a large law firm?"

Pete, sensing the conversation is heating up, says, "That was a great dinner, thanks to the ladies. Andrew, Julia, help your old dad clear the table."

Depositing the Thanksgiving dishes to the dishwasher and the extra food in their containers, I continue to make myself busy, half-listening to Julia, my aunt, and Mary.

Julia is saying she can't wait for her aunts to arrive. Mary answers by saying the feeling is mutual. Julia questions how long the flight is. "Two hours," answers my aunt. Then trying hard to include me in their conversation, my aunt asks, "Am I right, Allison? The flight from North Carolina to JFK's about two hours?"

I ignore the question, having one of my own to ask. "Did you see the look on Andrew's face when the reverend mentioned the funeral service for Patrick?"

The room grows silent.

I continue, "He was crying. I'm worried about him."

"He misses Pop. We all do. It felt awkward not having Pop sitting between me and Andrew today at church," says Julia.

I turn to my daughter. "It did, didn't it, sweetie? Thanksgiving wasn't the same without him either."

"I believe he was here in spirit," adds my aunt.

Condescendingly, I ask, "So you believe that when we die, we float around, up there, keeping an eye on our family and friends?"

Julia ignores my comment and questions my aunt, "Aunt Sarah, do you really believe that our spirits remain here on earth?"

Aunt Sarah replies, "It makes me happy to think the ones I have loved and who have loved me are watching over me."

Julia smiles. My aunt takes Julia's hands in hers and speaks directly to her.

"Memories are a gift from God." My aunt points to Julia's heart and head. "He places those memories here and here. When that person wants to talk with you, they flood your mind with a memory of themselves. When this happens, a warm feeling will wash over you, and a smile will adorn your face. I believe it's our loved ones' way of saying, 'I'm always with you.'"

Mary agrees.

* * * * *

Waking to the smell of coffee, I check the time: ten o'clock. Stressing, I rise, knowing that Pete's sisters' flight is due to arrive at eleven, not giving much time to prepare for their arrival.

"Morning, Mom."

"Morning, Andrew."

My eyes scan the kitchen. It's a mess. As I make eye contact with Pete, my expression asks, "What happened?"

"Julia wanted to make breakfast for us—coffee!" With a pot of coffee in his hand, Pete winks.

Julia, giving her best impression of a waitress at a diner, shouts, "Two pancakes coming up for Mom. Andrew, are you ready for a third?"

"No, thanks." Andrew leans over and whispers, "Mom, her pancakes are the worst! Don't say I didn't warn you."

I glance at my family, one face at a time. There are no expressions of grief. I fix my eyes on Pete. He smiles.

I accept the plate of pancakes from Julia. Andrew is right; they are thick and heavy, and I find them hard to chew.

Julia watches as I swallow my first bite. Waiting for my approval, she says, "I think I make a mean pancake. Aren't they the best you ever had, Mom?"

I sip my coffee before answering. "Yes" is all I can muster.

"Can I get you another, Mom?"

"No, thank you."

"All right, since there are no more orders, I'm closing shop. Andrew, will you help me clean up?'

Andrew whines, "She makes the mess, and I get to help clean up. What's wrong with this picture?"

Pete laughs. "She meant well."

I wonder if I am awake or dreaming. The people in the room other than me show no remorse for the loss of a beloved family member.

Pete touches my hand and smiles. "Pass your plate. I'm good at getting rid of the evidence."

The phone rings. I reach to answer, wanting nothing more than to distance myself from my family. Seeing JoAnne's number on the display screen, I motion to Pete that I'm moving to the den. We talk for ten minutes before I hear a car pull into the driveway.

"JoAnne, I have to go. Pete's sisters just arrived. You promise you'll be here at eight on Tuesday?"

"I promise."

"I wish it were you outside my door."

"I wish it were me as well. I'll call again tomorrow. Love you!"

"I love you."

I sit for a moment and think, *I can do this.*

* * * * *

My sisters-in-law repeat the words I've heard many times in the last several days.

"Allison, sorry for your loss. Patrick was a sweet man." Uncle George and Hank look on, and I notice Uncle George's watchful eye.

"Thank you for coming."

Every condolence starts with "I'm sorry," ending with "Patrick was a good man," "Patrick was a sweet man," "Patrick was a wonderful man." But no one knows him as well as I do. He was a selfish dick.

We move to the den, and I excuse myself, fleeing to the kitchen. While brewing the coffee, I sigh, noticing the counters are still greasy from Julia's surprise breakfast. I retrieve a wet, soapy cloth and begin to wipe down the counters. My uncle enters the kitchen.

"Uncle George, can I get you something?"

"No, I'm fine. I thought you could use some help."

"I'm just waiting for the coffee to brew, but you can carry in the tray of cookies."

"I will, but before I do, how are you?"

"I'm fine."

"You didn't seem fine when you stormed out the other night."

"Uncle George, I know you mean well, but it's no secret that Aunt Sarah pushes my buttons."

"I'm not here to defend your aunt. She's pushed a few of my buttons over the years, but I knew she meant well, so I never gave her a hard time about it."

I can't believe, after all these years, and at this very moment, my uncle has decided to have a serious conversation with me. "Do you really think we should be having this conversation now, with Pete's family in the next room?"

"I'm a man of few words, and I guess when the moment hits, it hits. I'm only asking that you ease up on your aunt. She's not getting any younger, and I know how much she worries about you."

"I'd rather she didn't, but there's no stopping her."

"I think you're confusing love and concern as interference in your life. That woman loves you."

I can't deal with Uncle George right now, so I give the same answer to all that are convinced my aunt has my best interest at heart. "I will try harder, I promise."

Uncle George picks up the tray. "That's all I'm asking."

* * * * *

"Give us a few hours to freshen up," I hear Gale say to her father as he and my uncle leave the house.

Gale joins Dolores and me in the kitchen. "Pete took the kids to the mall, and Dad said he'd tell Mom we needed a little time to unwind."

"This has to be so overwhelming for you, Allison," says Gale.

"It is. If he were older, I think it would be easier to accept."

Dolores reflects, "I don't know. Vince's mom was so sick, and there were days he prayed she would pass, but when she did, he locked himself in our bedroom and cried. It took him close to a year to accept she was gone."

"Michael had a friend that died at the age of twenty-four. Michael told me his family never got over the fact that he died so young," says Gale.

"I guess it doesn't matter what the age. It's the living who suffer the loss." Dolores, changing the subject, asks, "Speaking of Michael, has he asked you to tie the knot? If not, my advice, little sister, is to move on."

I turn my attention to Gale, anxious to hear her response. "I have a mother, Dolores. I don't need another."

"It's our mother who is bugging me to find out if his intentions are good."

"Tell her to ask me herself, and you'll be off the hook."

"I've tried that. She doesn't want you to think she's interfering in your life."

"So it's all right if you interfere?"

"Let's stop this merry-go-round. Does the man want to marry you or not?"

Gale smiles. "You'll just have to wait and see."

"So that's a yes. Were you going to surprise us at Christmas?"

Gale frowns at her sister. "I've never liked you, Dolores."

"You love me, and you know it. By your reaction, I'd guess a Christmas engagement?"

Gale smiles.

Dolores jumps up and hugs her sister. "I'm so happy for you, Gale! Michael's a great guy, and you're lucky to have him."

"You were just telling me to dump him, now I'm lucky to have him in my life?"

I hug Gale. "You're going to make a beautiful bride, Gale." Stepping back, I think JoAnne is right; seeing Dolores and Gale has lifted my spirits.

* * * * *

That night, Aunt Sarah prepares a delicious dinner, and for the first time since Patrick's death, I'm able to eat half of my meal.

"Aunt Dolores, Dad said you and Aunt Gale are going to join us at the skating rink tomorrow?"

"The ice skating rink, I haven't been on the ice in ages," says Dolores.

"Oh, please," says Julia, sighing. "The Saturday after Thanksgiving, we always go to the ice staking rink, and it would be fun if you both came along. Pretty please?"

I had forgotten about our family outing to the ice skating rink the Saturday after Thanksgiving. Patrick always looked forward to skating with the children. So do Pete and I. I don't think it's something I can do so soon after his death. I sit stoic, wondering how I could get out of going.

"Mom, you have to convince Aunt Dolores and Aunt Gale to come along," begs Julia.

"I don't think—"

"You're going." Startled, I look at Pete, thinking he's speaking to me, but he's talking to his sisters. "Allison and I will need a break. These two can skate for hours. You're coming. It's been years since the three of us have been on the ice together. It'll be fun."

"All right, you shamed us into it. We'd love to go ice skating," says Gale.

That night, I plan to plead my case to Pete saying; *I don't think I'm emotionally ready for a family outing*. But on the way home, my daughter expresses how she so enjoys the day we spend at the rink, and I think about what JoAnne has said earlier that day. "It's always the strong ones you have to keep an eye on." So I don't have the heart to disappoint my child.

* * * * *

That night, I can't sleep. As I lie awake, an image of Patrick skating around the rink with Julia while Andrew flies by, hoping to throw Julia off balance, won't leave my thoughts.

I toss and turn, waking Pete.

"Can't sleep?"

"No. I can't seem to get comfortable."

"Come here."

Reluctantly I slide over to Pete's side of the bed. He holds me tight and turns on the TV. We watch a rerun of *I Love Lucy*, but tonight, even Lucy cannot calm me.

Saturday morning, I rise early, exhausted. The dream haunted my sleep. The man in the white suit holding my hand, then his image fading away while I struggle to see his face. Frustrated, I wake and lie still, listening to Pete's labored breathing.

I slowly move from the bed and tiptoe down to the kitchen. I prepare a full breakfast consisting of homemade muffins, batter for waffles, bacon, and scrambled eggs.

Dolores joins me in the kitchen. "Gale's in the shower. She should be down shortly. I heard the kids moving around in their rooms, but no sign of my lazy brother."

"He was sound asleep when I got up. I didn't have the heart to wake him. It's been a rough week with Patrick dying and work."

"He's still being pulled in a hundred directions by Hal?"

"Yes. It's been rough. Since the heart attack, Hal's doctors said the office is off limits. So the new office falls on Pete's shoulders. Patrick dying couldn't have happened at a worse time."

Gale enters the kitchen. "Good morning! Allison, what time did you get up to prepare this feast?"

"We always have a big breakfast on Saturday."

Gale smiles. "No fussing tomorrow. Dolores and I are heading out early. We're spending the day with Sammy."

Sammy was Dolores's roommate in college, and they've remained close. She lives in the next town over from Pete and me. "I've been meaning to call her ever since Mom told me about the divorce."

"I called her yesterday. Told her Gale and I were in town. Didn't tell her why. And I asked if she had some time this weekend. She was happy to hear from us and said she was free on Sunday."

"Does she still see Rich?"

"We only talked for a little while. She did say he was living in Manhattan and they haven't talked in three months."

"They were such a happy and devoted couple."

Dolores explains, "Sammy wanted children, Rich didn't. I knew it wasn't going to work out. She always thought once they were married, he'd change his mind. The more she pleaded, the farther apart they drifted."

"I don't blame Rich. Leaving her was the decent thing to do. In time, she'll find someone, she'll have a couple of kids, and Rich will be forgotten," says Gale.

"I don't know, Gale. Sammy was madly in love with Rich. They say you never forget your one true love."

I scramble the eggs and contemplate Dolores's last remark.

* * * * *

Andrew invites his best friend, Brian, to join us at the skating rink. Brian and Andrew crawl into the two back seats of the SUV.

"That means my precious niece will be sandwiched between her favorite two aunts," says Dolores.

Julia laughs. "Let's get going before there aren't any skates left."

As we pile in the SUV, I consider telling my family I'm not well enough to go and asking if they mind if I remain at home. Julia's excitement about the outing causes me to take my place in the passenger's seat, praying that I find the strength to get through this day.

Everyone is talking at once during the drive, but all I can hear is my son's voice as he talks with his friend Brian.

"I texted her yesterday, and she said she was going to be there today."

"She did?"

"Why didn't you text her yourself, Andrew?"

"I didn't have the time. Anyway, she talks with you more than me."

"You're kidding, right? You know you're the one she likes, not me."

I lower my head, wondering why my son has not confided in me about this girl. Who is she? I have to face the fact that my son doesn't want or need my opinion any longer. I begin to tear up. This week can't get any worse.

Dolores, sensing my pain, reaches over and says, "They grow up so fast, don't they?"

Dolores has two boys of her own. Dolores's husband, Vince, on occasion, reminds his wife that their boys aren't going to confide in her like girls do.

I always thought my relationship with Andrew will be different. How wrong I was!

* * * * *

Entering the skating rink, Pete asks everyone's shoe size, and Andrew and Brian go along with Pete to help.

Julia runs off to greet a friend. Dolores, Gale, and I are left to find a bench. I decide at that moment to play the sympathy card. "Dolores, I don't think I'm up to skating. I feel light-headed."

"I understand, Allison. Why don't you find a cozy spot? Gale and I will get you a hot chocolate."

I find a booth next to the glass wall overlooking the rink. I spot Dolores talking with Pete. She points in my direction, Pete smiles, and his expression says he approves of my decision to relax.

Gale places the hot chocolate in front of me. "It smells good. I almost got one for myself, but if I take the time to enjoy a hot chocolate, my sister will have my head."

I smile. "Thanks, Gale. Seeing you and Dolores has been good for me."

"Hey, that's what sisters do for one another. Enjoy the hot chocolate!"

I watch the family but notice Andrew is not with them. I scan the rink and notice Brian talking with a very pretty girl. Brian points in the other direction, and my eyes do the same. Andrew begins to skate toward Brian. My son and the pretty girl talk for a few moments and then begin to skate side by side. They skate in my direction. I wave to my son, but he doesn't notice me.

My cell phone rings. It's JoAnne.

"Hi."

"Where are you? I can barely hear you!"

"We're at the ice skating rink."

"Right, the Saturday after Thanksgiving is ice skating day."

"You remembered. Do you remember how much Patrick enjoyed this day?"

"I do. Are Dolores and Gale with you?"

"Yes." I look over and see Julia trying to lure her father away from her aunts. Pete wants so badly to throw his sisters off balance, but the sisters hold on to each tightly and ultimately they win the battle. Scanning the rink, I notice Andrew; he's holding hands with the pretty girl.

"It's good you got them out of the house. I'm sure their having a good time. How are you?"

"I'm feeling a little light-headed. I wish I had stayed at home, but Julia would have been disappointed, so I'm hanging in there."

"Good girl. I called to say tomorrow we are spending the day with Gary's aunt and I might not get a chance to call, but I'll text. We're traveling on Monday. I'll try to call. I can't wait to see you on Tuesday. Just two more days."

"Eight o'clock at the house, remember?"

"We'll be there as I promised. Try to enjoy the day."

"I'm trying."

JoAnne disconnects. I feel lost without her.

I stare at the hot chocolate. I can feel my eyes growing heavy when I am startled hearing my name.

"Mrs. Cane, I'd like to introduce myself."

I look up. A rather tall man, very distinguished-looking, salt-and-pepper hair, age late forties. He reminds me of an actor from the sixties, Gregory Peck in *To Kill a Mockingbird.*

"I'm Dr. Greenberg, Ellen's father."

"I'm sorry, Dr. Greenberg, I don't know Ellen."

Dr. Greenberg points to the girl skating with Andrew.

Looking at them, I say, "Oh, so the pretty girl's name is Ellen."

"Yes, Haven't you been introduced?"

"Not yet. My son is keeping her all to himself."

Dr. Greenberg waves Ellen and Andrew over. "Ellen, this is Mrs. Cane, Andrew's mom."

"It's a pleasure to meet you, Mrs. Cane," says the pretty girl with a beautiful smile.

Andrew looks embarrassed. "Mom, didn't you meet Ellen once before at school?"

Smiling, I say, "I don't think we've actually met, but I remember you pointing her out to me."

"That's right. I remember telling my mom you were the new kid at school."

Ellen smiles. "I was a little nervous when my parents told me we were moving to Connecticut and a new school, but everyone's been so nice to me, especially Andrew."

Ellen smiles. Andrew's cheeks turn a bright red. I think of the red sweater.

Andrews says, "There's Brian. See you guys later." The children skate off.

Smiling, I motion for Dr. Greenberg to sit.

"I'm guessing this is the first time you've met my daughter?"

"And you would be correct."

"I think our children are smitten with each other."

"I believe they are, Dr. Greenberg."

"Please call me David."

I shake David's hand. "Allison."

As we watch our children, David whispers, "Puppy love, the love you never forget."

I quickly respond, "Never." I pause, then ask, "What brings you to Connecticut, Dr. Greenberg?"

"My son attends Boston University."

"You're a long way from Boston."

"My wife works for Hartford Insurance. Right after my son was accepted to BU, coincidently, my wife was offered the CEO position here in Hartford." David smiles. "My buddy is a doctor, internal medicine. He owns a medical building not far from here. I rent space from him."

"Also internal medicine?"

"No, I'm a psychiatrist."

"Psychiatrist. Impressive."

"What impresses you about my profession?"

"It takes a special person to listen to someone else's problems all day long. I should know, I'm an attorney for social services."

"Impressive."

We laugh. Dr. Greenberg asks, “So what are we going to do about those two?”

“You’re the psychiatrist.”

“I’m thinking we let this infatuation run the course, and if it’s meant to be, then I guess one day we’ll be sitting here watching our grandchildren.”

“Grandchildren—I hope not for a very long time.”

Pete skates over, and I introduce him to Dr. David Greenberg. Pete and the good doctor talk for a while, and then David is introduced to Pete’s family and Julia.

While the others are conversing, I scan the rink, looking for Ellen and Andrew, and seeing them brings back memories of my days with JoAnn at the ice skating rink back home in Cleveland. The most handsome boy would always ask JoAnne to skate.

JoAnne and I met in seventh grade. Like Ellen’s, JoAnne’s parents had moved to our small town in August. She was in the lunchroom when she spotted me sitting alone and sulking. I wasn’t sulking; I was pissed. The prior evening, while ironing my favorite skirt, my aunt, who was a fixture at our home, asked how old the skirt was. When I answered about two years, my aunt insisted my mother take me shopping to update my wardrobe. My mother sulked and said my aunt was better suited for the task, saying she knew more about the latest fashions then her. After several moments, my aunt agreed and asked me to set aside some time on Saturday. I wasn’t sure whom I hated most, my aunt for agreeing to take me shopping or my mother for not wanting to spend the day with her only child.

JoAnne, taking the seat across from me, questioned, “A penny for your thoughts?”

JoAnne was pretty, probably one of the prettiest girls I have ever met. “If you want to know what I’m thinking, you’re going to have to pay more than a penny.”

“I’m JoAnne Daniels. And you are …?”

Crossing my arms in front of me, I turned my head to the side and didn’t offer my name.

My ignoring JoAnne didn't stop her from saying, "I just moved here in August. Haven't met a whole lot of girls my age. You're the first."

"I didn't ask you to sit down, and I sure don't need more friends."

JoAnne looked around. "Did all your so-called friends skip school today?"

I smiled at her remark. She noticed. "I'm pulling your chain. I'm sure you have a lot of friends. I, on the other hand, am in need of a friend."

Making eye contact, I said, "I'm Allison Marks, and I'm one of the more popular girls in this school."

"I'm sure you are. How long have you lived here?"

"Since I was born, but after I graduate high school, I'm out of here, heading to New York. And I'm never looking back."

"Well, Allison Marks, we have something in common. After high school, I'm also moving away, and New York sounds like a great choice."

* * * * *

"A penny for your thoughts?" asks Pete.

"I was thinking about JoAnne."

"Did you speak with her today?"

"I did."

Pete places his hand on mine in lieu of a response.

"I can't wait to see her on Tuesday. I told her to come to the house so she and Gary could drive with us to the church."

"The limo seats eight. I'm sure Gary won't mind sitting up front with the driver."

"Eight. We are only six."

"Aunt Sarah and Uncle George are in our car, their family. My family is in the second limo. I thought JoAnne and Gary could ride with them."

"Aunt Sarah and Uncle George can ride with your family."

"It's only right that they drive with us."

"I don't give a shit what's right. I don't want them in my car. I insist they ride with your parents, or I'm not going."

Dolores is nearby. She hears my outburst, and feeling uncomfortable, she says, "Pete, I think we should be heading back."

Frustrated, I say, "I've been ready to go since we got here. I'll be outside."

* * * * *

Arriving home, I excuse myself, saying I need to rest. "What are the plans for dinner?"

Pete softly says, "I made a reservation at Ping's. I thought Chinese for a change."

"What time is the reservation?"

"Six thirty."

"It's three now. Takes about thirty minutes to get to Ping's. I'll be down at five thirty. Dolores, Gale, if you're hungry, there's food in the fridge. Please help yourself."

"Allison, don't worry about us. We'll be fine."

* * * * *

Staring at the ceiling, I cry myself to sleep. The dream is vivid, as it has been for the past six days. It changes with each sleep. This time, I am lying in the field of daisies with my hands behind my head. I close my eyes and enjoy the warmth of the sun on my face. A moment later, I rise and begin to pick the daisies around me. I trim five and gently place them in my hair; the remaining I gather together, creating a small bouquet. I glance over and notice the white tent. Glancing up at the sky above the tent, I notice it has grown dark and black. I run toward the tent, hoping I arrive before the rains begin. Reaching the entrance, I anxiously look for the man in the white suit. His back is to me. I begin to walk down the aisle, but the aisle has grown longer, making it harder for me to reach him. I begin to run. The aisle grows even longer. My aunt appears before me. I stop. She is pleading for me to turn around.

"Go back, Allison."

I ask her to step aside, but she remains in place. I try to go around her, but she will not allow me to pass. I look past my aunt to the man in the white suit. His image is slowly fading, and then he is gone. I place my hands on my aunt's shoulders and shake her, screaming, "This is your doing! I wish you were dead, not Patrick! I hate you! Die, die, die!"

My eyes fly open. My body is drenched in sweat. I get up and head for the bathroom, where I can be alone.

Locking the door behind me, I step into the shower and slide to the floor. Covering my mouth with my hand, I begin to sob.

Later, dressed and sitting on the bed, I notice the time: five fifteen. I can hear voices downstairs, and if I don't make my way down, someone will be knocking on the door very soon.

With my stomach in knots, knowing I don't have a choice, I reluctantly leave the safe haven of my bedroom.

Aunt Sarah is the first to greet me. "Hello, sweetheart. You look lovely."

I accept the compliment with a "Thank you" and greet Mary and Hank with a kiss. "I'm sorry I wasn't here when you arrived. Please forgive me."

Graciously Mary says, "There is nothing to forgive. I'm happy you got a chance to rest."

I smile, adding, "We should be leaving. The reservation is at six thirty, correct?"

Everyone agrees, and we head out. I'm happy that Pete, the children, and I are alone in our car.

"I spoke with your aunt and uncle. They don't have a problem driving with my family to the funeral."

"Was Aunt Sarah upset?"

"No. Actually, she agreed it might be good for you to spend time with JoAnne."

* * * * *

At the restaurant, I sit silently, agreeing ever so often with the conversation taking place at our table. More often, I am glancing at the wall clock directly in front of me. I count down. Seven, the food order will be placed. By seven thirty, it will be served. By eight fifteen, the plates will be cleared. Dessert will be served by eight forty-five. Home by nine thirty.

Aunt Sarah interrupts my thoughts by asking, "Allison, did you enjoy your day at the rink?"

"Mom didn't skate with us," replies Andrew.

My response to my son is sarcastic and unwarranted. "I'm surprised you took time to notice, Andrew. You seemed bewitched by your new friend Ellen. Or should I say girlfriend?"

"Allison," gently whispers Pete so only I can hear, "you're embarrassing him."

My son's skin turns pink. Julia, coming to her brother's defense, corrects me by saying, "Mom, you sound so old. *Girlfriend, boyfriend.* Andrew and Ellen are just good friends."

Andrew builds strength from his sister and sarcastically says, "Mom, you're always preaching that we should be nice to the new kids. How many times have we heard, 'Put yourselves in their shoes, how would you feel if everyone treated you as an outcast?' I'm just doing my part making Ellen feel welcome."

The condescending remark makes me realize I owe my son an apology. "I'm sorry, Andrew. Yes, you're right. I'm proud of you for making Ellen's transition easier. So is her father, Dr. Greenberg." I excuse myself and head to the ladies' room.

In the bathroom, I lock the door and beat myself up for being so insensitive of Andrew's feelings. I'm startled by a knock on the door. "Allison, are you all right?"

"I'm fine, Pete. I'll be right out."

I know Pete is waiting, so I open the door and begin to walk. Pete grabs my arm. "Wait a minute. I think we should talk."

"About what?"

"About what just happened at the table."

Feeling guilty, I lean against the wall. "I feel terrible. I will apologize to Andrew when we get home."

"I think you should. It sounded like you were jealous of Ellen."

I confess, "I am. He never told me about this girl."

"Are you listening to yourself? He's fifteen, he's not a baby anymore. He has a right to his privacy. When he wants us to know, he'll tell us. If you want my opinion, I think he's confused. I don't think he's ever felt this way about a girl."

"How could he think about this girl when his … grandfather only died six days ago?"

"I'm happy he has Ellen to take his mind off Patrick. Aren't you?"

"No. I'm not happy that he's sharing his feelings with someone other than you and me." I walk away and take my seat at the table, under the watchful eye of my aunt. I smile at everyone. "I feel much better. Did you order desert?"

* * * * *

The outburst at the restaurant has worked in my favor. Dolores and Gale leave early on Sunday for the sleepover at their friend Sammy's house. They will arrive home late Monday night, long after I've gone to bed.

Pete, the kids, and Pete's parents spend the day at the aquarium, followed by a movie, then burgers and shakes afterward. I tell Pete I'm not up to another family outing. He understands and leaves me to rest.

Lounging on the couch, I try to read, and when that doesn't work, I watch a silly movie that doesn't make me laugh. I try to fight off sleep, but several minutes later, the dream is alive and embedded in my thoughts. The dream is a repeat of Aunt Sarah in the middle of the aisle, standing between the man in the white suit and me.

The more I dream, the more I hate my aunt. Waking from the dream, I'm reminded of the words JoAnne expressed quite often during our lives together. She said I resented my aunt because of the control I believed she had over my mother. Now I was convinced she was trying to control my life.

With everything that was going on in my life, I didn't have time to waste on my aunt. I had bigger fish to fry, like my feelings toward my husband. I kept dwelling on the day before Thanksgiving. We made love. As always, it was good, but I had to face the truth. I wasn't in love with Pete. Patrick's death has opened the wounds of my past. When will I approach the subject with my husband? The day after the funeral? Or should I wait three months, six months? My mind is filled with questions, and they're slowly driving me insane I can't stop thinking of my children. Their lives were about to change. Suffering the loss of the man they called, Pop, was upsetting enough, now I am head-fast in separating them from their dad.

I try to convince myself that we are the adults and together we will find a way to make things right for the children's sake. I will wait, until after Christmas. No, after our return from Florida, where we always spend the Christmas break with Pete's family.

* * * * *

Tuesday I wake at six. I lay out the outfit I purchased for this day. Sitting on the bed after my shower, I place the red sweater on my lap and run my hands over the softness of the wool. My eyes begin to well. I place the sweater to my face and weep.

Eight o'clock comes, and no sign of JoAnne and Gary. Gary calls, saying there is a terrible accident on I-95, causing a major traffic jam. He says he doesn't think they'll make it to the house and think it safer that they go directly to the church.

The distress I feel that my very best friend has deserted me has only heightened the tension I'm feeling.

Pete takes my hand, saying, "It's time to go, Allison."

Standing at my front door, I notice my aunt and uncle standing next to the limo Pete hired for his family. Before getting into the car, my aunt glances in my direction. For a slip second, I want to call to her and tell her to ride with me, but I can't find the strength. She steps into the car and sits beside Mary.

In the limo, I place my head on the car window. I watch the white lines painted on the road appear and disappear by the movement of the car. Pete places his hand on my lap. "Hal and Eve called this morning. Eve wanted me to tell you how sorry she and Hal were that they couldn't be with us today, but they are here in spirit."

"They're not dead. How could their spirits be with us?"

Pete reaches for my hand. I pull away. My children notice. I continue to stare out the window.

Arriving at the church, I walk alone in front of my family. The second limo pulls up, and everyone exits the car. I whisper to Pete, "I want to use the restroom before the service begins."

In the restroom, I pray that JoAnne knocks on the door, looking for me. After ten minutes, I meet up with my family in the vestibule. I question Pete, "Are JoAnne and Gary here?"

"No. Someone just said three people were pronounced dead from the I-95 accident. I'm not sure they are going to make the service."

Dejected, I lean on Pete. I always think of JoAnne as the sister I never had. A sister will be there, come hell or high water. As the saying goes, blood is thicker than water, and JoAnne and I were not blood related.

With everyone seated, the family procession begins. With Pete beside me and my family in front of us, I walk with my eyes cast to the floor. I stop dead in my tracks when I notice the open casket on the altar. The casket is directly in front of where my family will be seated. Willing myself to move, I step up to the casket and place my hand on Patrick's chest. I want to shake him awake from this sleep. I whisper his name.

Pete places his arm around my waist. My children stand beside me, Julia resting her head on my shoulder. She is whimpering. We move toward our seats. I sit and stare at the casket that holds the body of my stepfather.

I place my mouth close to Pete's ear and ask, "Why is there an open casket?"

Pete's and my eyes meet; he doesn't respond.

The service begins. *No sign of JoAnne.* Pete gives the eulogy. The congregation laughs on cue when something humorous is said and sighs when Pete says our family will forever miss this wonderful and caring man.

When the service ends, the family is asked to say their final goodbyes to the deceased. My aunt and uncle go first. Pete, standing between our tearful children, consoles them as they say goodbye to the man they lovingly call Pop. When it's my turn, I ask for a few moments alone.

I gaze at Patrick, thinking how handsome he looks even in death. "I can't believe that you're not going to be a part of my life anymore. Do you know how your dying has changed my life? I don't know how I'm going to handle." I start to cry. I place my hand on his dark hair. I continue, "If spirits do roam the earth, then you know the truth. I should have—"

"Allison, there are a number of people waiting for you. It's time to say goodbye." My aunt is standing next to me.

"And I shouldn't keep them waiting because that wouldn't be right?"

"You know he wouldn't want you to linger here. He'd want you to be with Pete and the children."

I place a hand on Patrick's chest, "Goodbye Patrick." Kissing my fingertips, I place them on his cold forehead."

I start my walk down the aisle. I walk faster and faster until my walk is a run. I run from the church, down the steps, and continue to run down the street. I hear JoAnne calling me, but I don't stop. There is confusion at the church, and I sense Pete, Gary, and JoAnne are after me. At the corner, I cross the street. The traffic is heavy, as luck would have it. I notice an empty cab and wave. In the cab, I instruct the cabdriver to quickly pull away from the curb. I notice Pete running toward the cab. He slows when he realizes he could never catch up.

At home, I notice Sal and the helper setting up the luncheon. They greet me. I smile and head for my bedroom. Locking the door, I remove my clothes, leaving them in a pile on the floor. I pull from a drawer a sweatshirt and pants. I head for the bathroom. In the medicine cabinet, I find the sleeping pills the doctor prescribed for Pete when he suffered a bad backache. I take two.

I get in bed and place the bottle of pills under my pillow. Lying still, I wait for them to work. I hear voices downstairs. Seconds later, Pete walks in the room. I pretend to be asleep. He closes the blinds and draws the drapes.

* * * * *

It's night when I wake. Pete is lying next to me, sound asleep. I ease my way out of bed to use the bathroom. I retrieve two more sleeping pills from the bottle under my pillow. I repeat the pattern until there are no sleeping pills left in the bottle.

I open my eyes and notice the sunlight peeping through the blinds. I don't know what day it is, but I know it's morning because I can smell the coffee brewing.

Lying in bed, I remember the dream. The sleeping pills have helped my mind relax. In the ever-changing dream, the man in the white suit and I are happy. In the field of daisies we run playfully, the man trying hard to catch me. When he does, we lie together, staring at the blue sky. When I turn to him, the sun's blinding light casts a shadow over his face, but that doesn't stop the happiness and pleasure I feel lying next to him.

"Allison, are you awake?"

"I am. What time is it, or should I ask what day it is?"

"Nine thirty Friday morning."

"Friday morning. I've been sleeping for three days."

"I think the pills might have helped."

"You knew about the pills?"

Pete sits on the bed and places a tray beside me. "I noticed they were missing from the medicine cabinet. I brought you coffee and toast. You've got to be hungry. You haven't eaten in days."

I push myself up and place the tray on my lap. Sipping the coffee, I ask, "Where are the kids?"

"They're out with my parents and your aunt. Tomorrow my parents have an eight o'clock flight for home."

"Dolores and Gale?"

"They left on Wednesday."

I place my hand over my eyes. "I'm sorry, I should have been there to say goodbye. Tonight I'll make dinner for your parents. It's the least I can do."

"I've got it covered. I placed an order with Dinner's on the Go. They come highly recommended. I ordered pork tenderloins with all the trimmings."

"Thanks." My stomach begins to growl, so I reach for a piece of toast. "What time will they be back?"

"Around four. You have plenty of time. You're probably going to nap on and off until the pills are out of your system. I'd recommend putting your head back on the pillow, reading, watching a little TV. No one is expecting you to come down before dinner. I'm going to be in the office, working on some files. I'll bring your lunch around twelve."

Pete gets up to leave.

"Pete, aren't you going to ask why I ran from the church?"

His mood changes. He looks sad. "I think I know. During the service, you asked why there was an open casket. You weren't expecting that."

"You're right, I wasn't. Why an open casket?"

"When I was asked opened or closed, I said I didn't know. I was told 50 percent prefer closed, 50 percent feel seeing the body gives them closure. I chose closure. Can you find it in your heart, once again, to forgive me for not thinking to ask what you preferred?"

I don't have the heart to scold him. "This is the first time you had … What's done is done. In time, I'll probably feel better knowing I was able to say goodbye. So will the children."

Pete smiles.

* * * * *

I nap on and off the entire day. Come dinner, it's pleasant enough. Aunt Sarah and Uncle George are happy to see that I look well.

When we get a few minutes alone, she comments, "You look rested. I'm happy to see you looking so well."

"How was the luncheon, Aunt Sarah?"

"Everything was wonderful. Just enough food."

* * * * *

Pete and the children drive Hank and Mary to the airport the following morning, after I apologize more than a number of times for my absence since the funeral. Mary consoles me by saying that when her mother and then her dad passed, her reaction was the same. My in-laws say they can't wait for us to visit during Christmas.

I head to the bedroom after their departure. I play the staring game with the bed but give up the thought of going back to sleep when the phone rings.

"Allison, I'm so happy you answered."

"JoAnne." My mood worsens at the sound of her voice.

"I checked in on you the day of the funeral, but you were out cold. I've called every day since and talked with Pete. What's going on, Allison? Pete said you've been taking sleeping pills."

"I'm in mourning, JoAnne."

JoAnne sighs. "I can tell by your reaction that you're not happy with me, and I'm truly sorry."

"I know there was an accident on I-95, whatever."

"Allison, I didn't cause the accident. Did you know three people were killed that day? I was shocked that we made it at all, but I was there when you took off. What was that all about?"

"You should have been with me. I would have been there for you."

"I asked Pete if I could stay, but Mary said she and Hank weren't leaving until today. I tried, I really did, but she insisted. Gary thought I should back off."

"You're my family, JoAnne. You should have been here. I needed you."

"With all the sleeping pills you were taking, I don't think you and I would have spent too much time talking. Allison, I'm sorry. I know you're upset with me. I wish things—"

"If you were dead to the world, I would have remained at your bedside. Nothing would have kept me away."

"You're right, and I'm truly sorry. I wish I could be there now, but I can't spare any time from work. I was thinking Gary and I could come and spend next weekend with you guys?"

"We're busy next weekend. We're going to spread Patrick's ashes at the lake. Andrew wanted to do it before the lake freezes over."

"We can come along. I'm sure it's going to be an emotional day. I'd like to be there to hold your hand."

"You're not family. I think it's best we do this as a family."

JoAnne sighs. "I understand. Maybe the following weekend."

"I'll have to get back to you, JoAnne. I'm not sure what's going on that weekend."

"All right, I'll wait for your call."

"Bye." Hanging up, I begin to cry. I hate being mad with JoAnne, but she deserves it. I needed her, and she was not there.

Through my sobs I hear the doorbell ringing. I let it ring. My cell phone begins to ring. Assuming it's JoAnne, I pick up.

"Allison, your car is in the driveway, but I wasn't sure if you were home or at the airport. I've been ringing the bell. I'm at the front door."

Son of a bitch. It's my aunt. *Perfect timing.* "I'll be right there."

I open the door and walk toward the den. Aunt Sarah follows.

"What can I do for you, Aunt Sarah?"

"I just wanted to stop by to see how you're feeling."

"Is this going to be an everyday occurrence, you stopping by?"

"Of course not. I was just concerned about you."

"Actually, Aunt Sarah, I'm glad you stopped by. We have to talk."

"About?"

"About my needing some space."

"Space?"

"Yes, space. Please don't take this the wrong way, and I'm not trying to hurt you, but you're smothering me. I need some time away from you and Uncle George. What I'm trying to say is, I'd like it if we spent less time together."

Aunt Sarah bows her head. "I see. What about Julia and Andrew? Would I be allowed to visit with them?"

"You realize, Aunt Sarah, that Andrew and Julia aren't babies anymore. Heck, Andrew has a girlfriend. I don't think he really wants to spend time with anyone but Ellen. The children still have their practices and games, and I can't stop you from going. You can check with Pete regarding their schedule."

"So you're saying you don't want to spend time with me or your uncle?"

I look at her not knowing how exactly to answer that question. I know the truth will hurt, so I go for it. "You're a smart lady, Aunt Sarah. That's exactly what I'm saying."

Aunt Sarah nods. "I see."

"I don't think you do. I don't think you see how I find you intimidating. I feel like a child when I'm in your company. Can you understand what I'm saying?"

"No, not really."

"Well, it would take too long to explain. I'm not saying I'm going to cut you and Uncle George from my life entirely. I'll still call once a week, or once a month, to see how you guys are doing. Every so often, we can have lunch or dinner to catch up. In time, I think you'll see that all we needed was time apart to make our relationship work."

Aunt Sarah plays with the gloves in her hands. Looking up, she smiles and says, "If it will help you to distance yourself from Uncle George and me, then we will abide by your wishes. We only want what's best for you, Allison. We want you to be happy. That's all we've ever wanted."

She turns to leave. I remain still. Something inside me is wishing I could take back what I have said, but it's been a long time coming.

"Goodbye, Allison. If you need us … Be well."

The door closes. I wait several minutes before the sobbing begins. I'm mourning my losses, the past, present, and the ones yet to occur.

* * * * *

I get through the week anticipating the spreading of Patrick's ashes. I tell Pete about my talk with Aunt Sarah, and by his expression, I know he isn't happy of my treatment of my family.

"I know you don't agree with me, but I had to do this for myself. I'm not stopping you or the children from seeing my family. I would never be that cruel. But I need to do this for my sanity, Pete."

"I'm glad I didn't call Aunt Sarah today. I was going to invite her on Saturday."

"I already told the kids, the church service was for anyone who wanted to attend, but this service was private, just our family, and I won't feel guilty about my decision."

* * * * *

Saturday arrives, and so do the knots in my stomach.

As we drive to the lake, Andrew holds the Japanese jar filled with Patrick's ashes tightly.

Pete, Julia, and Andrew hold hands walking toward the lake. I walk behind them alone. I sit on a very large rock as my family stands at the lake's edge. Julia looks up at Pete for guidance. Andrew gestures for me to come stand beside him.

I do as he asks.

"Julia, would you like to say something?" asks Pete.

"Yes, Dad. Pop, I know you're out there somewhere, watching over us."

I look straight ahead, hoping I might see a vision of Patrick. *Nothing.* So I lower my head.

"Pop, we will miss you. You were the best—no, better than the best. I know you're with God in heaven, and I know you're happy. Andrew said you wanted to spend eternity here at the lake, so I know you're happy with our decision. We love you, Pop, and we miss you so much. We'll never forget you. We promise."

My daughter's words bring tears to my eyes. Pete asks, "Andrew, would you like to say something?"

Andrew shakes his head no. Without looking at his sister, Andrew softly says, "Julia, that was nice."

Pete looks in my direction, wondering if I like to say something. I motion that I'd rather not.

Pete taps Andrew on the shoulder. "Whenever you're ready, son."

Andrew lifts the lid from the jar, and we watch as the ashes take flight. I can't help but wonder if Patrick's spirit is watching over us. If so, then he now knows what I never had the courage to tell him.

CHAPTER FOUR

Sarah

Back home, I decide not to tell George about the conversation I had with Allison. Stepping into the living room, I find George in his favorite chair, reading.

"Mrs. Blake stopped by to pick up the fabric you ordered for her. She said you told her to stop by at eleven."

"I would have been home sooner, but I went to check on Allison."

"How is she?"

"She looks rested."

After storing the food items I purchased in the panty, I join George in the living room. I have to find a way to tell George what Allison has requested without hurting his feelings. I retrieve the book I've been reading and sit directly across from him. After several minutes, I start a casual conversation.

"Are you going to help out at the church today?"

"No. Harry took the boys' choir on a hiking trip."

"He didn't ask you to tag along? That's strange."

"My knees have been giving me some trouble. Harry understood." Several minutes later, George says, "How was your visit with Allison?"

I smile. "Funny you should ask. I wanted to ask her why she ran from the church, but her mood was off. I guess I'll have to take Pete's word. She was shocked by the open casket."

"Not a fan of open caskets, so I can understand she might have been spooked."

"I know you are going to call me a worrier, but I think there's more to her behavior." I sigh. "But I'll never know, because I'm the last person she'll confide in."

"You're not going to ask me to find out what's going on, are you?"

"I think the best way to handle this is for us to keep our distance."

I know I'm not fooling George. He knows by the look on my face that my visit with Allison didn't go well. "She sure isn't going to take advice from a woman with one foot in the grave, that's for sure."

"I don't agree you have one foot in the grave, but I do agree that you might be a little overprotective of the girl. She might take your advice as controlling. I think keeping our distance from her can't hurt." Sensing the despair I'm feeling, George sympathizes. "You worry too much, Sarah. I know you mean well, but take it from one of the links in your chain of worry. Sometimes it's a little overwhelming."

I smile. Not wanting to discuss the subject further, I excuse myself. "I'm going up to clean out my closets. Goodwill is stopping by in two weeks, and I should get started."

* * * * *

After an hour of weeding through my closet, I decide to take a break. Lying on the bed, I try to relax, but all I can think about is my conversation with Allison. I reach for the book that contains the photos of my past. I glance through several photos and stop at the one dearest to my heart. Kissing the photo, I whisper, "I love you with all my heart and soul, and someday soon I know we'll be together." Moving on to the photo of my family, I question my mother, "How do you stop worrying about those so dear to you?" I close my eyes, transporting myself to another place and time, my childhood.

December 1945

I can faintly hear the knock on my bedroom door. "Sarah, you up?"

"Go away, George."

He pleads to come in. I place the pillow over my head to shut him out, but George is persistent. Having a soft spot in my heart for my younger brother, I allow him in.

"You're not dressed, Sarah. It's six o'clock. I hear Dad in the kitchen. You'd better hurry. All the good trees will be gone."

Before I can respond, George closes the door behind him. I stretch and force myself from the warmth of my bed. Finding my father and George in the kitchen, I ask, "Where's Mom?"

"Still asleep. I made your favorite, waffles."

I can't resist my father's waffles, so I quickly take a seat next to George and dig in. Mom shuffles into the kitchen. I notice her hands placed on the curve of her back. I can see she is uncomfortable. She sits. Dad rushes to her side and places a kiss on her cheek. "Feeling any better, sweetheart?"

"I feel like a balloon that's ready to pop."

George and I laugh. Mom asks, "What's so funny?" Sizing up our bellies, she says, "Looks like you've eaten your fair share of waffles. Did you leave any for the baby and me?"

Dad places a plate of waffles and a glass of milk in front of her. "You think I'd forget my one and only love?"

"Thank you, sweetheart. Did you eat?"

"I was waiting for you."

Mom asks Dad to sit. She places two of her waffles on his plate. She drinks the milk and picks at the remaining waffle, managing to eat half.

"Mom, you're not dressed! Did you forget what Dad said? We have to get to the farm early before all the good trees are taken!"

"It won't take me long to dress, Georgie, and don't mind your dad. There will be plenty of trees to pick from. Will, I have to stop at the library to see Claire. I also promised the children they could borrow books to read during the Christmas break."

I interject, "Mom, between the school library and the town library, I don't think there's a book in the children's section that I haven't read."

Mom laughs. "What about a love story? Maybe you'd like *Gone with the Wind*. It's one of my favorites. It is nearly a thousand pages. Do you think you can handle that?"

"Mom, did you forget I'm the best reader in my class?"

Mom reaches over and covers my hand with hers. "All right."

"What book can I read, Mom?" asks George.

"*Treasure Island* is a great book, George. I read it when I was your age," says Dad.

George replies, "If Dad says it's a great book, then that's the one for me."

Mom whispers to Dad, "You're a lucky man, Will Holland, to be loved by your children. There is no greater gift."

While Mom is dressing, Dad and George go out to sweep the light snow that has fallen during the night off the front steps. I'm just about to wash the breakfast dishes when Mom appears in the doorway. "Sarah, I don't think your brother can wait another minute, but those dishes can."

I notice the dark circles under my mother's eyes. "You're right, Mom. I'll just fill the tub with hot water, but when we get back, I'll do the dishes, and you have to promise you'll rest."

"You sure are your father's daughter." Then in a serious tone, Mom says, "God sure did pick the sweetest angel of all when he sent you to me. I'm so proud of you, Sarah. Never forget, I love you with all my heart and soul."

I run to my mother and place my head on her extended stomach, and wrapping my arms around her, I repeat, "I love you, Mom, with all my heart and soul."

* * * * *

I watch as my father walks my mother to the car, pleading with her to remain at home to rest. As he helps her into the passenger's seat, he continues, "The kids and I can manage the library and the tree. We won't be gone more than two hours."

I know he is going to lose this argument by my mother's response. "I want to visit with Claire, and you know I always have the final say on the tree we choose." Mrs. Peterson is Mom's good friend and the town librarian.

Dad closes the car door. Mom turns to George and me and says, "Your father's going to worry himself into an early grave."

Getting behind the wheel of the car, Dad asks Mom, "Are you comfortable?"

She smiles and says, "I'm as comfortable as I am going to be."

Dad returns the smile. "All right, then. Off we go!" My dad has a habit of making up songs for each of our family adventures, so he begins to sing. "We're off to get ourselves the prettiest tree in the forest." After repeating the verse a few times, George and I join in.

Abruptly stopping, Dad tells us that it's time to pray. Betsy was the name we had given the family car. Burt at the auto shop told Dad it was time to replace her, so a decision was made to purchase a new car after the baby was born. Until then, Dad would request God's help to get Betsy started. We begin to pray. "Dear God, please give Betsy the strength to get us to our destination and back home safe." Dad turns the key, and Betsy comes alive. We cheer and begin to sing Dad's song again.

Our first stop is the library. George pouts, but Mom promises we'll be back on the road in twenty minutes. The library was built in 1845. It was the second building constructed after the town hall, which had been built in 1840. The architrave at the top of the columns were magnificent. In the 1800s, buildings of importance usually had two or three levels of steps. The library had two levels, each level having twenty-five steps. The front doors of the library were constructed from cherrywood. They were tall, heavy, and hard to open.

Dad found a parking spot right in front of the library. George was the first to exit the car. He ran to the foot of the steps and challenged me to a race. "I bet I can reach the top before you, Sarah."

I stand beside him. "I'll race you, George Holland, but only if I can start the count." He agrees. "One … two …" Then I whisper, "Three!" Taking off before George, I reach the top first.

"You cheated. You never said three!"

I argue, "Maybe I did, maybe I didn't. Maybe you need to have your hearing checked!"

Laughing, I turn to look for Mom and Dad. My father is holding my mother tightly as they finally reach the top of the first set of steps. I want to run down to help, but my mother calls out, "Go in, tell Mrs. Peterson we're right behind you."

I do as I'm told. Opening the large door, I guide George in. Mrs. Peterson greets us. I tell her that my parents are behind us. She is livid. "Your mother is climbing those steps in her condition? Let me get a chair for her." Mrs. Peterson retrieves a chair from behind the counter and places it close to the front door, ready for Mom when she enters. Mrs. Peterson gives my father an accusing eye when he and Mom enter the library.

Sheepishly, my father says, "She insisted, Claire."

Patting Dad's hand, Mom says, "Exercise is good for the baby. Now stop fussing over me and help the children find their books while I visit with Claire."

When we return with our books, Mom is scolding Mrs. Peterson for forgetting to bring her grandmother's Christmas cookie recipe to church with her last Sunday. "No excuses, Claire. I'm not leaving until I get the recipe."

"I have it right here in my purse. I was going to stop by your house on my way home."

Mom looks suspiciously at Mrs. Peterson. "Were you now?"

"Are you calling me a liar, Erin Holland?" Spotting George and me, Mrs. Peterson says, "Children, your mother is impossible. She has badgered me into giving her my grandmother's secret cookie recipe. If my sisters only knew I was giving you this recipe, Erin, they would have me burned at the stake!"

"You're so dramatic, Claire. It was your sisters who told me to ask you for the recipe when they visited last Christmas!" Mom and

Mrs. Peterson share a chuckle. "I promise to only share the recipe with Sarah, and this new little one, if it's a girl."

Mrs. Peterson turns her attention to me. "Do you swear never to share this recipe with anyone for as long as you live?"

Crossing my heart, I say, "I won't share it with anyone. I promise!"

In unison, Mrs. Peterson and Mom laugh.

My knees are buckling from the weight of the book in my arms as we descend the steps of the library. A thousand pages! Was Mom right? Is it too much for a girl my age? No, I think. I can do it! In the car, I read about the author, Margaret Mitchell. Fascinated by her determination, I begin chapter 1. When I'm ten pages into the book, Dad begins to sing "Silent Night."

"You have a beautiful voice, Will," says Mom proudly.

"Thanks, sweetheart! You're my biggest fan."

I watch my parents, Mom looking adoringly at her husband, Dad blowing air kisses to his wife. I dream that one day my life will include a wonderful husband and children to love as much as my parents love each other and us.

* * * * *

At the tree farm, Mom walks without any help. Waiting at the entrance is Mr. Griggs.

"Good morning, Mr. Griggs."

"Good morning, Erin." Mr. Griggs shakes my father's hand. "How's work? Heard the plant is hiring again. Great news for the boys returning home."

My father agrees. "War destroys, and steel rebuilds. Prosperous times are ahead."

Mr. Griggs turns his attention to George. "Make a muscle for me." George flexes his right arm, and Mr. Griggs measures the muscle. "Wow, the boy is as strong as an ox! He'll be a great help with the saw."

Dad places a hand on George's head. "We're looking for an eight-footer, Bill. Where do you suggest we start?"

"Take the path on the right and walk a quarter of a mile. There are some beauties out that way. I'll send my son Joe to help haul the tree back to your car."

Dad lifts a sack containing two axes and a saw over his shoulder. George walks with Dad and Mom, and I follow, holding hands. Once we reach our destination, we stop to gaze at the beauty before us. George runs and points out several trees. My mother sits on a cut tree trunk and watches as George makes his final pick. Mother approves of his choice. She motions for me to come and sit beside her. I watch as Dad and George consider where to place the ax. I turn to look at my mother, and the sight of her takes my breath away. She is looking up at the sun peeking through the trees. She looks angelic. I whisper, "Do you think I'll be as beautiful as you when I grow up?"

Breaking the precious moment, my mother looks at me and smiles. "You are already beautiful, Sarah, very beautiful. It won't be long before the boys will notice and come calling. I can't wait to see how your father will handle his little girl going out on her first date."

I respond, "Oh, Mom, you have to say I'm pretty because I'm your daughter."

"Do you know that on the day you were born, the nurses fussed over you because you were the most beautiful baby in the nursery?" Mom looks out over the forest as if she were seeing it for the first time. "To me, Sarah, you are more beautiful than this landscape, but it is magnificent, isn't it?"

"It is pretty, Mom."

"God does good work."

* * * * *

Joe, Dad, and George haul the tree back to the car. Dad settles up with Mr. Griggs, and we wish Joe and Mr. Griggs a merry Christmas. Sitting in our car, we begin to pray. Betsy starts on the first try.

Back at home, I walk Mom to the sofa and demand that she sit and rest. Placing a blanket over her legs, Dad starts a fire then heads outside, where George is waiting. Mom closes her eyes, and I'm content knowing she will be asleep shortly.

While washing the dishes, I watch George and Dad secure the tree to the back of the garage. When my work is finished, I prepare lunch. Dad, George, and I eat, quietly chatting, while Mom sleeps. After lunch, Dad asks George to help him locate the tree decorations, and I prepare a plate of food for my mother to eat when she wakes. I curl up on the sofa next to Mom and open my book. An hour later, Mom wakes. I demand she stay put. Returning with her lunch tray, I place it on her lap. "I picked out some of your favorite cookies for dessert."

Mom eats her lunch, and together from the front window of our living room, we watch Dad and George toss a baseball. A light snow begins to fall, but Dad and George don't seem to notice.

"I see you started the book. How many pages have you read?"

"Eighty."

"Eighty? You'd better slow down, or you won't have anything to read over the Christmas break. Do you like it?"

"I do, Mom, but Scarlett is so spoiled. I don't think I'm going to like her very much."

"She's not easy to like, but I think when you finish the book, you'll respect her strength." Mom turns her attention back to Dad and George. "Sarah, how much do you want to bet that your dad is going to make a snowball and …" Before she could finish her thought, my father starts to make a snowball, but to our surprise, George is able to make two snowballs before my father could throw his first. It's obvious George has the upper hand. "That's my boy!" Mom and I begin to giggle.

Watching her, I ask, "Mom, what do you think, boy or girl?"

She pats her stomach then reaches over and pulls me closer to her. "I just want a healthy baby." Then she leans in and tickles me.

"You already have a girl and a boy. I guess it doesn't matter."

"If I had a choice, I say a sister for you. Wouldn't it be nice to have someone to tell your secrets to? I always wanted a sister when I was young, but I would have been just as happy with a brother."

"You have Grandma to tell your secrets to."

"I do, but if I had a sister or a brother, I would have had someone to complain to about Grandma and Grandpa!" She laughs and hugs me tighter.

"I guess a sister would be nice. Do you have a name picked out?"

"If it's a boy, we like the name Jacob. If it's a girl, I want to call her Rose. I'm not sure your father is crazy about the name, but since I agreed to name your brother George, he owes me this one."

"Rose, like the flower?"

"Exactly."

Mom looks out the window. I think she's checking on Dad and George, but instead, she points to the dormant rosebush in front of our window. "See the rosebush in the front yard?" I nod. "The first spring after your dad and I moved in to this house, the rosebush didn't bloom. Dad wanted to remove it and replace it with another, but I told him to leave it alone. One Sunday at church, I filled a small bottle with holy water and spread it around the roots. The following March, it sprouted leaves, and by spring it was filled with roses."

Staring at the rosebush, I say, "It was a miracle."

"I want to believe God had a hand in it. It always amazes me how something so barren in the winter produces the most beautiful and fragrant flowers in the spring. That gave me an idea, if the holy water worked for the rosebush, why not me? So I filled the same small bottle with holy water, and every night I rub a little ..." Mom touches her stomach and smiles.

"Then it has to be a girl! God wants you to name her Rose."

"God's already answered my prayer, so whatever the outcome, it's his will."

"Mom, I know it's a girl. It just has to be! I can't wait to meet Rose."

Mom kisses the top of my head. "Jacob or Rose, it won't be long now, Sarah."

* * * * *

The next day, Mom, George, and I make Mrs. Peterson's grandmother's Christmas cookies. They are as good as Mom says. The following day after school, we clean the china we would use for Christmas. Grandma and Grandpa O'Brien will be arriving in seven days, and Grandmother and Grandfather Holland will arrive on Christmas Eve.

While we wash the dishes, Mom asks about the books George and I are reading. George says he has only read twenty-five pages. I'm proud to announce that I have read one hundred fifty pages so far, adding that I still dislike Scarlett. Mom smiles and says, "After reading the book, I remember wanting to be just like Scarlett. She was strong yet soft. She was a woman with a head for business. She didn't let life get her down, and when she loved, she loved unconditionally. Once you come to understand her, Sarah, you might have a change of heart."

* * * * *

That night, I'm awaken by the shrieking cry. At first, I think it's two stray cats fighting, so I lay my head back down on my pillow. Hearing my father shouting, I jump out of bed. I run into the hall, bumping into George. I turn to see my father frantically pleading for us to hurry and dress. We hurry to dress, meeting outside our parents' bedroom door. The door opens, and we cannot look away from the scene before us. My father is holding my mother tightly to him as he helps her down the stairs. Both George and I notice the bloodstains on the sheets. The back of Mom's nightgown is soaked with blood, causing George and me to gasp. My father shouts to us, and we rush down and meet them in the foyer.

"Take hold of your mother. I'll get her coat." We do as we are told. Placing the coat over my mother's shoulders, my father yells, "Get your coats, we have to go!"

"Will, you're scaring them. Children, we have to get to the hospital. The baby has decided to join us for Christmas."

We get into the car, and Dad turns the key. "You better start!" But Betsy chokes, and for the first time in my life, I hear my father curse. "Start, you fucker!" He turns the key again, and the car comes to life.

When we arrive at the hospital, my father jumps from the car and runs through the emergency doors. My mother turns toward us. "I know you're frightened, but I'm going to be fine. Don't let the amount of blood scare you. It looks worse than it is. Tomorrow I'll have a talk with your father about his cursing." Then she blows us kisses. Reaching for my hand, she says, "I love you both with all my heart and soul."

Two nurses open the car door and help my mother into a wheelchair. With my father at her side, they walk into the hospital and disappear. The doors close behind them. I reach for George's hand. A few minutes pass, and the hospital doors open once again. A girl wearing a candy striper uniform opens the back door and looks in. "My name is Karen. I'm here to take you to the waiting area."

We follow her into the hospital. Once seated in the waiting room, I ask, "Will we be able to see my mom?"

"Children aren't allowed in the delivery room, but don't you worry, your mother is very close to having that baby. I'll take you to see her once she's settled in her room. Can I get you something to eat?"

"I'm not hungry, but I'd like my brother to eat something."

"I'll see what I can find."

After Karen leaves, George asks me, "Do you think Mom was lying to us when she said not to worry about all the blood?"

"Mom's been through this before. If she says the blood is normal, then I believe her."

George shrugs. "Karen said the baby should be here soon. I hope she's right."

"Me too."

Karen returns with milk and cookies. She sits and talks with us for a little while, then another nurse looks in and asks for her help. With Karen gone, George and I finish the milk and cookies. He looks tired, so I tell him to lay his head on my lap. I watch him sleep, and then I close my eyes and drift off.

Karen gently shakes me awake. "Sarah."

I wake, asking, "What time is it?"

"Eight o'clock. I thought you'd like to know that your mom is doing well. She asked me to tell you that your sister is beautiful and anxious to meet you."

"It's a girl!"

George moves and slowly wakes.

"George, it's a girl. We have a sister. Her name is Rose!"

"A sister? I wanted a brother."

"When can we see them?"

"Well, your sister was born at seven fifteen, so your mother should be in her room by eight thirty. I'll come get you when it's time."

Patiently we wait for Karen to come get us. A short time after, we follow her to the third floor of the hospital. As we walk toward the waiting room, Karen points to a room on the floor. "That's your mother's room. Nurse Jane and your father are with her. You know you have to be sixteen to visit someone in the hospital, but your mother asked Dr. Harris to bend the rules so you can see that she and your sister are doing well." Karen chuckles. "Dr. Harris is a softy. He agreed to make an exception."

Karen has just finished the story when the door to my mother's room flies open and Nurse Jane motions to Karen. She runs the length of the hall, is given orders by Nurse Jane, and then runs back past us and disappears around the corner. Nurse Jane also disappears.

Instinct tells me something is wrong. "George, wait here."

I start to walk toward Mom's room when I hear my father screaming, "Erin! Erin! No, no, sweetheart, don't! Please don't!"

Two men in white uniforms and one young man in a white coat pass me and enter the room. I am frozen in place, and George runs to my side. The two male nurses exit the room holding my father as he kicks and screams, calling my mother's name. I scream for them to let my father go. They continue to struggle with my father as he struggles to break away, wanting to get back into my mother's room.

I hear myself asking, "Dad, what's wrong?"

I run to him, pushing the two men. Karen is behind me, placing her arms around me, holding as tight as she can. The two male nurses carry my father off as he continues to scream my mother's name. Karen asks me to calm down. I question her, "Where are you taking my father?"

"If you promise not to run, I'll let you go. You're scaring your brother."

I can hear George sobbing.

The door to my mother's room opens. Nurse Jane steps out. I look past her. There is a young doctor making notes as my mother rests peacefully. Breaking Karen's hold, I run to my mother's bedside. "Mom, wake up! You have to help Dad. Two men just took him away! Wake up, Mom!"

The young doctor stares while I beg and plead with my mother to wake up. She looks as angelic as she did two days ago in the forest, and it is then that I realize that something terrible has happened.

George is behind me, crying. I turn my attention to the young doctor. "What's wrong with my mother?"

George whispers, "She's asleep, Sarah."

"Is my brother, right? Did you give my mother something to make her sleep?"

Dr. Harris enters the room with Nurse Jane and Karen. I notice that Karen is crying. "Dr. Harris, something is wrong with Mom, and these two men took Dad away!"

Dr. Harris ignores my pleas and asks Nurse Jane to take us from the room.

"I'm not leaving until you tell me what's wrong with my mother! Where is my father?"

Nurse Jane places her hands on my shoulders and tries to get me to move. I push her hands away.

The young doctor steps aside to allow Dr. Harris to examine my mother. Checking my mother's vitals, Dr. Harris takes the chart from the young doctor. "What the hell happened?"

The young doctor looks at us nervously. "An aneurysm would be my guess."

To their surprise, I yell, "Aneurysm? Does that mean that my mom is …?" I stop myself from finishing my sentence, not wanting George to hear.

Dr. Harris hands the chart back to the young doctor and approaches me. Kneeling before me, he says, "Your mother told me you were a smart girl, Sarah, so you know an aneurysm is a blood clot. If a blood clot goes undetected, it can cause—"

Knowing an aneurysm can cause death, I say, "Please don't say any more. I don't want my brother ..." I pause. "Where is my father, Dr. Harris?"

"Your father will be fine. We gave him a shot to help him rest."

"Can we see him?"

"I'd really like him to rest, Sarah. Maybe tomorrow. Do you want to meet your sister?"

"Right now, I'd like to spend some time with my mother. Will you ask everyone to leave, Dr. Harris?"

"All right, Sarah. Nurse Jane will be right outside that door. When you are ready, she will take you to see the baby."

With everyone gone from the room, George sits on the bed and begins to talk with our mother. I don't know how to explain to him that she isn't sleeping. Not being able to take my eyes off her angelic face, I wonder how we will survive without her. I reach for George's hand. "We need to check on the baby."

George kisses our mother and says, "See you tomorrow, Mom." Once he climbs down from the bed, I place a kiss on my mother's cheek, and my tears fall onto her face. George takes my hand and says, "Let's go, Sarah. Mom's asleep."

I turn to leave, and George pulls me back. "Sarah, we almost forgot." George climbs on the bed and whispers, "Mom, we love you with all our heart and soul."

* * * * *

After checking on my sister, I ask Nurse Jane if there is a chance we could see my father. "I'm sorry, Sarah, Dr. Harris gave strict orders. No visitors. Maybe tomorrow. Mrs. Peterson is downstairs, waiting to take you and George home."

I run into Mrs. Peterson's arms and sob. George is bewildered by my reaction. "I know, I know, my sweet child. Mr. Peterson is outside. Let's get you home."

That night, I explain to my brother that our mother has died. At first, George doesn't believe me, then I remind him of the scene at the hospital, of our father being dragged away screaming our mother's name. This confirms that I am telling the truth. George rests his head on my chest. Weeping, he asks over and over why God has taken our mother from us.

* * * * *

I wake to the sound of a garbage truck outside my window. George is sitting at the edge of my bed, staring at me. "I sneaked downstairs while you were sleeping. I overheard Mrs. Peterson telling Mr. Peterson that Grandma will be here later today. Mr. Peterson spoke with Dr. Harris. He wants Dad to stay in the hospital a few more days."

As we make our way downstairs, I notice that the steps are wet. Mrs. Peterson has done a good job of cleaning away the bloodstains. When we enter the kitchen, Mrs. Peterson is pouring the red water into the sink. Startled by our appearance, she runs the water to wash away our mother's blood.

"There's oatmeal and homemade corn muffins. The muffins are still warm."

George moves to his place at the table. I wait until he's seated then ask, "Has the hospital called to say when Dad will be coming home?"

Mrs. Peterson looks away as she answers, "He might not be home for a few days, but your grandmother is on her way. She should arrive by nightfall."

"What about Grandpa O'Brien?"

"The O'Briens arrive tomorrow."

"You just said my grandmother was arriving tonight."

"Your Grandmother Holland is arriving today."

"Grandmother Holland? Why?"

"Sarah, I'm only telling you what I know. You must be hungry. Eat your breakfast."

Mrs. Peterson fills the basin with clean water, and I know she's going to rinse the steps again to avoid answering any more questions. Mr. Peterson emerges from my parents' room carrying the blood-stained mattress. He pushes it out the front door, obviously trying to catch up with the garbage truck coming down the street.

Coming back into the kitchen, Mrs. Peterson tries to keep busy. Her back is to us, but I know she is crying by her actions. Every so often she lifts her apron and dries her eyes.

"Is it all right if we go to the park for a few hours?" I ask.

Without turning, she answers, "That's fine, Sarah."

I take a few dollars from Mom's secret hiding place without Mrs. Peterson seeing. When we leave the house, I tell George we're not going to the park. Instead, we take the bus to the hospital to visit Rose and find out what's going on with Dad.

Holding hands, George and I enter the hospital and approach the welcome desk. "Hello, I am Sarah Holland. My brother and I would like to visit my father and sister."

The nurse sitting at the desk was not on duty last night, but she has obviously heard about the tragic death of the young mother. Her face becomes solemn. "Have a seat in the waiting room while I page Dr. Harris."

Dr. Harris rushes down the hall and glances at the nurse behind the desk. She points to George and me in the waiting room. "Sarah, is Mrs. Peterson with you?"

"No, Dr. Harris. She doesn't even know we are here. I want to visit with my father and sister, please."

"You know the rules. You have to be sixteen to visit with someone at the hospital. Last night I made an exception."

"Dr. Harris, I know we're too young, but we're worried about our father, and Rose is all alone."

Dr. Harris looks at George. I realize that he's not sure how much he knows. "George knows that our mother isn't coming home. That's why it's so important for him to see our father."

Dr. Harris reconsiders his decision. "If I were in your situation, I would want know that my father and sister are doing well. I'm going to have a nurse take you to see your sister. I'd like to check on your father before you see him."

"Thank you, Dr. Harris." Taking George's hand, I follow the nurse to the nursery.

Staring at the tiny girl bundled in pink, George says, "She's pretty, isn't she, Sarah?"

Looking at my sister, I'm happy to know that our mother got to hold her daughter, if only for a brief time. I know my mother was relieved when they placed this beautiful and healthy baby in her arms. My mother got to kiss her small head, professing, "I love you with all my heart and soul." At that moment, I resent this tiny person for being the last to hear the words I treasure. Those precious last moments of my mother's life were wasted on this tiny human being. She will never gaze upon our mother's angelic face or see the proud smile of a loving mother when she is in the presence of her children or come to know the wife who loved our father unconditionally, and he her. My mother will never stand before the rosebush outside our home and tell this child the story of how she earned her name.

Dr. Harris approaches, saying we can see our father. I take one last look at the pink bundle and think what today will be like if the outcome were different.

* * * * *

Entering the hospital room with George beside me, I freeze. My father looks as peaceful as my mother did in death. When I notice the rise and fall of his chest, I step forward. I take his hand into mine and call to him, "Dad, George and I just saw Rose." Knowing Dr. Harris is behind me, I whisper, "Dad, wake up. I need to talk with you." He remains still. With my eyes fixed on my father, I ask, "Dr. Harris, why do you need to sedate my father?"

Dr. Harris steps forward. "Your father is in shock, Sarah. Your mother's death—"

"George and I are just as upset."

"I don't have all the answers, Sarah, but it is not uncommon for the brain to shut down when one is confronted by the sudden death of a loved one."

"How long until he's better?"

"It's hard to say. It's different with each patient."

"You might think I am too young to understand, Dr. Harris, how much my father loved our mother." I place my hand on my fathers and whisper, "Dad, George and I are going to go now. You rest." I'm startled when my father's hand closes tight around mine. His lips move, but there are no words. "Did you say something, Dad?"

Dr. Harris steps forward. "Will, it's Dr. Harris."

My father's eyes fly open, and with all his strength, he manages to say my mother's name. George places his head on my arm, hiding his face. I release my father's hand and hug George. My father starts to tremble, and Dr. Harris motions for George and me to step aside. Wanting to protect George, I do as he asks. My father begins to scream. Dr. Harris pushes a button, and within minutes, a nurse enters with a syringe. Pulling George along with me, I leave the room. We wait in the hall for Dr. Harris. George covers his ears when he can no longer listen to our father screaming my mother's name. A few minutes pass, and then silence.

Dr. Harris exits the room, noticing George and me.

I can see how uncomfortable Dr. Harris is feeling seeing us. "It's time for us to go. I don't want to worry Mrs. Peterson."

"I think that would be best, Sarah. Your father needs to rest."

I take George's hand. Before I make a move to leave, I ask, "Dr. Harris, did my mother get to hold our sister?"

"Yes, she did."

"Was she happy?"

"Extremely happy."

"Thank you, Dr. Harris."

* * * * *

It is nighttime when the car carrying our grandmother arrives. George and I run to the window just in time to see Grandmother Holland exiting the car. Looking up, she spies us at the window. She doesn't acknowledge us. I move away from the window. We listen at the bedroom door as Grandmother Holland cautions Mr. Peterson to be careful with her luggage, telling him one contains her favorite bottles of lavender water.

Mrs. Peterson offers a cup of hot tea, and the adults move into the living room, making it impossible for us to hear their conversation. Twenty minutes pass before Mrs. Peterson knocks on the door to inform us that our grandmother would like to see us.

Hand in hand we walk into the living room. Our grandmother is sitting on the edge of the sofa, sipping tea. She examines us from head to toe. "Children, you've grown since I last saw you. Don't just stand there. Come give your grandmother a hug."

George hesitates, but when I release his hand, he greets our grandmother. Looking past George, she speaks to me. "Sarah." I move closer. "I am very upset with you, young lady. I spoke with Dr. Harris. He said you visited your father at the hospital." Then she addresses Mrs. Peterson. "Were you aware that the children went to the hospital today?"

Before she can answer, I respond, "I didn't think I needed permission to go visit my father and sister at the hospital."

Grandmother and I lock eyes. She doesn't speak immediately, just stares. "You are eleven, young lady, and your brother is nine. You must always ask permission. Is that understood?"

I notice Mrs. Peterson's reaction to my grandmother's unsympathetic attitude toward her grandchildren.

"That goes for you too, young man. If you're going to leave the house, the polite thing to do is tell me or Mrs. Peterson where you are going."

Out of fear, George nods in agreement.

Mrs. Peterson, noticing that I'm about to lash out at my grandmother, says, "I think you'll find our town safe, Mrs. Holland. It's not uncommon for the children to come and go without too much worry to their parents. I think Sarah needed assurance that her father and sister are well."

I sense that Grandmother Holland doesn't take kindly to Mrs. Peterson defending George and me. I'm guessing she's assessing the situation and realizes it's not the right time to upset these good people who have graciously stepped in to help with the care of her grandchildren.

Grandmother smiles. "I'm from a large city, Mrs. Peterson. A child without adult supervision can come to great harm. I might be a little overprotective of these children." Turning her attention to George and me, she continues, "If you children would appease your grandmother by letting an adult know where you're off to, it will help ease my mind."

I think of my mother and wonder how she's tolerated this woman. I console myself by knowing her stay will be short, so I make a mental note to avoid her as much as possible.

"Are you hungry, Mrs. Holland? I made a roast for dinner. I can easily prepare you a plate."

"Thank you, Mrs. Peterson, but I had something on the train. I was hoping to visit with my son tonight. Is there a number I can call for a cab?"

"I'm more than happy to drive you to and from the hospital, Mrs. Holland," says Mr. Peterson.

"Thank you. I'm sure once my son is home, you'll be able to go back to your normal lives. I'm sorry for this sudden inconvenience."

My blood boils. This woman has the gall to come into my home and refer to my mother's death as an inconvenience! I look at Mrs. Peterson, who is equally shocked.

My grandmother rises to leave. "Good night, children. I don't want to hear you giving Mrs. Peterson any trouble."

* * * * *

In the morning, I find Grandmother Holland sitting at the kitchen table. "Where's Mrs. Peterson?"

"She hasn't come yet. I'll talk with her about arriving earlier. I'm usually up by six."

"Mrs. Peterson was my mother's best friend, not the housekeeper."

Grandmother doesn't respond but begins searching through the cabinets.

"What are you looking for?"

"A coffeepot."

"I'll make the coffee."

Grandmother Holland watches as I easily make my way around the kitchen. "I'm impressed that your mother taught you how to be domestic."

This is the first time since her arrival that this woman has acknowledged my mother. The tears begin to build in my eyes, but I hide my weakness from her. "I loved helping my mother in the kitchen. So did George."

"Then I'm sure you know how to start a wash. The sheets need to be removed from the beds. We need a schedule of chores for you and George. I don't want to consume Mrs. Peterson's time with household chores."

Turning, I notice the smile on my grandmother's face. I have an overwhelming desire to slap her, but instead I ask, "When you visited with my father, was he awake?"

"He was awake, but we really didn't talk. Your mother meant the world to him."

I soften at the mention of the love my parents shared.

"You'll soon find out what I have known since your father was a boy. He's not a strong man, Sarah."

This woman possesses the ability to run hot and cold. Before I can respond, she continues, "I remember when Skip, your father's grandfather, died. I'm sure he told you about him. He adored that man. A few days after the funeral, I had to order him back to school. Every day your father's nanny would have her hands full getting him to dress and leave the house. When he'd return, he'd lock himself in his room."

"How long did it take him to get over his grandfather's death?"

"About a year. I grew tired of his foolish behavior, so I had all the locks removed from the bedrooms and bathrooms in our house and threatened that if he continued in this way, I'd send him off to military school, where he'd have no contact with his friends."

"He was just a boy then. Things are different now."

Grandmother smirks. "Why is that?"

"Because he has us to help him."

* * * * *

I wait patiently for Mr. Peterson. When he pulls up to our house, my heart leaps.

My grandfather Holland is the first to exit the car, then my grandpa O'Brien, and finally my grandma Maggie.

"Grandma!" I yell through the closed window of my room. She lifts her head slowly and waves. George comes to stand beside me, waving and calling her name. It's then I realize she's feeling the same pain that George and I are feeling. The smile disappears from my face. I race down the steps with George behind me, rushing into my grandma's arms. I sob. Only she and Grandpa can understand the senseless loss I'm feeling. George clings to us and cries with me.

Grandpa O'Brien lifts George into his arms and tries to console him. "That's all right, George, you have yourself a good cry."

* * * * *

Sitting in the living room, George and I cling to Grandma Maggie. I sit very close to her, while George scoots over toward Grandpa. "Grandma, I'll make you and Grandpa a sandwich. You must be hungry."

My grandma tightens her hold. "I'm not very hungry, Sarah. Tim, would you like Sarah to make you a sandwich?"

"I'm fine, love. We ate on the train. But thanks for thinking of us, Sarah."

"How was your trip, Margaret?" asks Grandmother Holland.

"It was good, Catherine. And yours?"

"Exhausting!"

"How is Will?"

"The same, though I didn't visit today. I thought we would go together. Dr. Harris and Mr. Dickenson agreed to meet us at the hospital."

I lower my head when Mr. Dickenson's name is mentioned. He owns the only funeral home in our town.

"Charles has hired a driver. Mr. Peterson will take you and Tim to the boardinghouse to get settled. The driver will take me and Charles to the hospital after you've freshened up. You can meet us at the hospital."

I jump from my seat. "Boardinghouse? Grandma, why are you going to the boardinghouse? You're staying with us, aren't you?"

"There isn't enough room for all of us, Sarah. We are staying in town. It's only a ten-minute drive. We won't be far."

"No, you're staying with George and me. That's what Mom would want!"

"Young lady, where are your manners? You shouldn't raise your voice, especially to your grandparents," says Grandmother Holland.

Grandfather Holland places a hand on Grandmother's shoulder. "Catherine."

"Sarah, in a few days, your father and the baby will be home. Your grandmother needs to be here for them. I promise we'll be here when you wake up and kiss you good-night before you go to sleep," says Grandma Maggie.

Changing the subject, she turns to Mrs. Peterson. "Claire, thank you for helping with the children. You were a good friend to our Erin."

Mrs. Peterson pulls a handkerchief from her pocket. "Your daughter was my best friend. I loved her as much as one of my own sisters. She was such a beautiful person, inside and out."

"With her having no sisters of her own, I know Erin appreciated that you treated her like one of your own. I'm anxious to get to the hospital. Would you mind taking us to the boardinghouse now, Mr. Peterson?"

* * * * *

The following morning, my grandma Maggie greets George and me when we enter the kitchen for breakfast, just as she has promised. Grandpa O'Brien has been sent to the market with a list of items prepared by Grandmother Holland. Grandpa Holland is in the living room, reading the morning paper. Mrs. Peterson and Grandmother Holland are upstairs, reassigning bedrooms.

My mother's sewing room is now George's room. George's room is now the nursery, with a bed for Grandmother Holland.

On the third day after my mother's death, my father and sister return home. Rose is wrapped in a heavy pink-and-white blanket with a matching pink hat covering her tiny head. My mother had finished knitting two, one pink, one blue. One of the colors would be donated to the church once the sex of the baby was known.

George and I watch as our father shuffles into the house with a blanket over his shoulders. He looks so fragile. We can tell that he is heavily medicated. My grandfather holds on to his son, guiding him up the stairs, followed by two male nurses. As soon as they reach the landing, my father cries out, "No, please don't. Please, I can't go in there without Erin. No. No!" Everyone ignores his pleas. The screams grow louder as he is placed in bed, but after fifteen terrifying minutes, his pleas for my mother are silenced.

Grandfather Holland listens attentively to the male nurse. "The sedative should last until nightfall." He hands my grandfather a prescription bottle. "He'll need another at bedtime. Dr. Harris will be by tomorrow to check on him and answer any questions about his recovery."

* * * * *

On and off during the night, my father wakes and calls my mother's name. In the daytime, my father sits stoic in a chair, staring out the bedroom window. When night falls, the cries for my mother's return begins. After several nights, I can't stand it any longer. I gently knock on the door to my grandmother's room. When I'm told to enter, I inform Grandmother that she needs to call Dr. Harris to see if he can prescribe something stronger.

"It was my decision not to give your father any more pills. He has to come to terms with the loss. Now go back to sleep."

"Dr. Harris told Grandfather the pill at night would help my father sleep. His crying is keeping me awake!"

"Put a pillow over your head and don't raise your voice, young lady. You'll wake the baby."

My grandmother ignores my request, and closing the door behind me, I walk down the hall to my father's bedroom. I knock, but there is no response, so I enter the room. My father is still sitting in the chair, with the same blanket draped over his shoulders. I go stand beside him and look out as he does at the night sky. I ask, "Are you hoping you'll see Mom in heaven?"

I get no answer, so I continue. "I've stared out my bedroom window ever since that night. I haven't seen her either." I realize my few words have stopped my father's crying, so I kneel next to his chair and place my hand on his. "Dad, I need you. George and Rose need you. We miss Mom as much as you do, but she's not coming back, no matter how much we scream and cry. She's not coming back."

* * * * *

Grandma Maggie and George enjoy their time with Rose, but I manage to keep my distance. Something inside me doesn't want to accept that she exists. Dr. Harris says we should try to get my father to walk around, spend an hour in the living room, but he refuses to leave the room he shared with my mother. George and I take turns silently keeping vigil over him. Every so often, he whispers my mother's name. Yesterday he whispered my name, but when I tried to start a conversation, he remained silent. Dr. Harris says he needs time to heal. Grandma Maggie says something in my father died with my mother, and Grandmother Holland speaks of my father's weaknesses as a child.

* * * * *

After Sunday dinner, I'm sitting with my father in his room when Grandmother Holland enters with a tray of food. "You're losing weight, William. You should eat. Margaret made a roast with potatoes and vegetables. You wouldn't want to insult her by not trying a bite." When my father doesn't respond, she continues, "Tomorrow is the funeral service. Your father doesn't think you should be forced to attend, but if you truly loved the woman … Anyway, it's your decision. I know you've never asked for my opinion, but as your mother, I think it might help you to accept that Erin is gone. I had your shoes shined and your suit pressed. Your father picked out a tie. It's all right there in your closet." Without another word, she steps into the hallway and says, "Sarah, talk to your father. He might listen to you."

* * * * *

Monday morning seven o'clock, I wake to the sound of my father shuffling around in his room. Inside I hope my talk with him has convinced him to attend the funeral. I get myself out of bed and go look out my window. The sun is shining. The weather is uncommonly warm for this time of year.

At eight, my father descends the stairs and rides with us to the church. He makes it through the service holding my hand but loses control at the burial site and sobs. Grandpa O'Brien embraces him, but it's clear to all that my father can't go on, so my grandfather Holland helps him back to the car.

Grandma Maggie holds my hand and cries as the preacher reflects on my mother's short life. Grandmother Holland stands stoic, every so often raising her hand to dry away a tear. When the service ends, my grandparents ask for a few minutes alone with their daughter. I step back to give them privacy. George does the same. The wind is gently blowing through the trees as I watch my grandparents embrace and whisper loving words to their precious child. My grandma Maggie places three white roses on the coffin to signify the three children her daughter left in her care. Their last words are clear and familiar: "We love you, our sweet, beautiful child, with all our heart and soul."

My father goes back to his room, but every morning at seven, I can hear him dress and leave the house for three hours. Upon his return, he goes straight back to his room. No one questions where he goes. We all know.

On Christmas Day, my father sits and watches us open the presents my mother had hidden from us. There are several books and toys for my sister. One week before Christmas, my grandmother Holland has hired a woman of color named Pearl to care for the baby and the house. Pearl has prepared a Christmas dinner earlier in the day and then left to join her family. We eat in silence. The day after Christmas, George and I watch as my grandfather hauls the dead Christmas tree to the curb.

George and I return to school after the Christmas break. Arriving home from school, we usually find our grandparents keeping up with the household chores since most of Pearl's time is spent caring for the baby. After tucking us into bed, Grandma Maggie and Grandpa O'Brien will return to the boardinghouse, while Grandmother and Grandfather Holland sit before the fire to catch up on their reading.

Grandmother Holland has given orders that if my father wants to eat, he'll have to join the family at the table. No longer is he to have meals alone in his room. After two days of fasting, he joins us for dinner, and only dinner. George and I try to make conversation with him, but his answers are limited to a single word.

The last Sunday in January, after our Sunday meal, Grandmother Holland announces, "I spoke with Reverend Thomas at the Episcopal Church. Next Sunday after the ten o'clock service, Audrey will be christened."

I jump from my seat. "We are naming the baby Rose! Those were my mother's wishes."

"Rose is not a name for a child, it's a flower. My mother's name was Audrey, and your father has agreed with my choice."

I kneel in front of my father. "Dad, Mom told me if the baby was a girl, she wanted to call her Rose. It was Mom's wish."

My father stares at me and doesn't speak.

"William, tell the child of our decision. I've already presented the name to the congregation. Reverend Thomas listed it in the naming book this morning."

I yell, "We're Catholic! Rose should be baptized by Father Francis, not Reverend Thomas!"

"Since I will be overseeing the household, it makes sense that we worship together at the same church."

"Overseeing the household? Dad, what's going on?"

Grandma Maggie tries to console me by saying, "Sarah, your father will be going back to work in a few weeks, and someone needs to be here to care for you children. Your grandmother graciously offered to give up her life in New York to remain here until you are able to care for yourselves."

I want to lash out at Grandma Maggie for not taking my side. At that moment, I hate her more than anyone in the room. Ignoring her, I look at my father for help. "Dad, tell them we don't need help. Pearl can take care of the baby during the day. George and I will come straight home from school to take care of the house, and when you get home from work, the three of us can care for the baby. Please, Dad, tell them!"

For the first time since my mother's death, my father speaks in full sentences. "I can't take care of three children and work. We need help." He rises to leave the room.

"And what about the baby's name? You know damn well Mom wanted to name her Rose!" I yell as he walks away.

Grandmother Holland gasps. "Young lady, how dare you raise your voice to your father! And your mouth should be washed out with soap!"

My father turns and speaks directly to me. "I never agreed to name the baby Rose. She'll be Christened as Audrey."

As my father makes his way up to his room, I call to him. "I wish Mom were here and you were dead!" I run past him on the steps and lock myself in my room.

* * * * *

That week, my life takes on the same pattern as my father's. I go to school, do my chores, complete my homework, and only join the family for dinner, speaking few words to the family.

On the Sunday that my sister is Christened, the congregation claps when the reverend introduces its newest member, Audrey Holland.

The last week in February, my father returns to work. He leaves the house at seven and returns home at six. He eats dinner with the family then takes to his room.

Pearl praises my sister Audrey, who only cries when she is hungry or dirty, but the rest of the time, she is as quiet as a mouse. Pearl sings to the baby when she feeds her. I don't know anything about caring for babies, and I prefer to keep it that way, so I avoid Audrey as often as I can.

Pearl works until dinner is cleared and leaves after Audrey is down for the night. Grandma Maggie and Pearl work together well, so clothes are washed and ironed, the house is spotless, and dinners are cooked and ready to be eaten when my father returns home from work. Pearl and my grandma Maggie will walk Audrey every day if the weather permits, while Grandmother Holland acquaints herself with the women at the church. Grandmother Holland's only household task is to care for Audrey on Sundays before Grandma Maggie arrives.

Just as George and I are getting used to our new lives, my loving grandparents, with whom George and I spend most of our time, announce they will be leaving the week after Easter.

"Leaving? Where are you going?" I ask.

"We need to return home, Sarah. Grandpa is due back at work. We were lucky to stay as long as we have, but now we must get back."

I sneer. "Of course, you have to get back. Your dead daughter's children will get along just fine without you!" I scream and storm from the room. I shun my grandma and grandpa for the entire week.

Finally, they are scheduled to depart on the five o'clock train. That Sunday, I miss church services, convincing my grandmother that I feel feverish and have an upset stomach. It also gets me out of Sunday dinner with the family.

I am lying in bed when there is a knock on my door. "Who is it?"

"It's Grandma. Can I come in?"

I think if I don't let her in, I will hate myself for not saying goodbye. I get up and open the door. I rush back to my bed and lie with my back to her. She sits on the bed and places a hand on my hip. I begin to cry.

"Sarah, I know you're upset with me, but do you really want us to leave without saying goodbye?"

I don't respond. On my nightstand is the book. Grandma lifts it. "You're reading *Gone with the Wind*? It was your mother's favorite."

"I only read one hundred and fifty pages. I don't like it. I'm returning it to the library tomorrow."

Grandma puts the book down. "Sarah, I just had a nice talk with George, and I was hoping you and I could do the same."

"You're leaving. There's nothing to say but goodbye."

"We aren't leaving you forever, Sarah. Grandpa and I are coming back in July. We're going to spend our two-week vacation with you and your family. I'm planning on four trips during the year. It will give your grandmother time to go home and visit with your grandfather. We will spend every Christmas and Easter with you. Sarah, we're going to make this work. I promise you."

"Four times a year? That's all you're going to see us? Four times a year?"

"Sarah, I know you're too young to understand, but as you get older, you'll see that the efforts and decisions we made were for the benefit of you children. We love you with all our hearts and souls, and there is nothing greater than love."

The words hit me hard. “You don’t love us. You only loved your precious daughter.”

“You’re right, I did love my daughter and you’re a part of her, so how could I love you, George, and Audrey any less?”

I have no response.

“I don’t want to go away knowing you’re angry with me or your grandpa. Can you find it in your heart to forgive us?”

“I don’t think I can ever forgive you for leaving us here with Grandmother Holland. She’s not you. She’s not Mom. She’s mean!”

“Sarah, she’s your grandmother, your father’s mother! She has a right to be here. She needs your help. You have to promise me you’ll try to get along while I’m away.”

“I don’t have to promise you anything. Can’t you see that she and I don’t get along? How can you leave me here with her?”

Grandma sighs. “I have to leave, Sarah. You have to make an effort to make this work.”

I remain in place. Grandma rises, waits a few moments, and then leaves the room. When the door closes behind her, I bury my face in my pillow and cry.

George enters the room. “Sarah, Grandma and Grandpa are leaving! Won’t you come down and say goodbye?”

“Get out of my room, George! I already said goodbye.”

George leaves, and I move to the window, waiting for my grandparents to leave our house. A cab pulls up. I listen as everyone is gathered in the foyer, saying goodbye.

George is the first to step outside, then my four grandparents, and Pearl with Audrey in her arms. After a tearful goodbye with extra hugs and kisses for George and Audrey, my grandma and grandpa make their way toward the car. I bang on the window and yell, “Grandma! Grandpa!” They look up, and I run down the stairs and outside into my grandma Maggie’s arms.

“Oh, Sarah!” she cries.

“I love you, Grandma, with all my heart and soul. And it won’t be long until July!” I hug my grandpa Tim. “I love you, Grandpa, with all my heart and soul.”

When the cab pulls away, I reach for George's hand. "They'll be back. Grandma promised."

* * * * *

The following day, I return *Gone with the Wind* and *Treasure Island* to the library and spend a little time with Mrs. Peterson. She never asks if I enjoyed the book.

Grandfather Holland returns home two weeks after my grandparents left.

Soon after my grandfather's departure, Grandmother begins her new life. She turns on her charms with the ladies at the church. Soon she is on the social events committee. She begins a bridge, book, and ladies' tea club. They meet various times during the month. The fourth Tuesday of each month, promptly at 11 am, Grandmother has a set appointment for a cut, manicure, and pedicure, at the local salon. She becomes a member at the Country Club. Tennis was her favorite pastime back in New York. She joins a doubles team. Spending one hour, twice a week at the club, followed by lunch. Golf is new to Grandmother, in the fall she signs-up for lessons at the club. The following spring she joins the women's golf league. The women play every Thursday at 3 PM, weather permitting, followed by dinner. On Saturdays, Grandmother is often invited to someone's home for dinner. She has become popular with the elite of our town, having organized several fund-raising events for the hospitals and returning veterans. If there is a cause, Grandmother makes sure she's involved.

I myself am happy with Grandmother's new life, as it keeps her less involved with mine. When she is home, she passes out orders to George and me. "George, you're old enough to take care of the grounds. If you neglect your chores, you won't be allowed to go off and play ball on Saturdays. Sarah, Pearl said you've been a great help to her with the laundry, ironing, and dishes, but I've noticed you spend no time with your sister. I think you should take Audrey to the park on Saturdays. Spend a little time with the child. Your good deeds have not gone unnoticed. I spoke with your father, and he has agreed to an allowance of a dollar every week to spend as you wish."

It surprises me that my father has actually made a decision about something. The man we knew before my mother's death is gone, and in his place is a man who barely exists. He leaves the house each day at seven, even though he doesn't have to be at work until eight thirty. He arrives home at six. He eats dinner, and when dinner is done, he'll go directly to his room. Every so often, he'll inquire about what is going on in our lives. George is always eager to tell our father about his day. "Dad, the coach said I really have a strong arm. I'm probably going to pitch most of our home games. He said I'm also good at second base, so when Joe pitches, I'll play second. The team is really good, Dad. I can't wait for the season to begin! I signed up for football in the fall. I know it's not your favorite sport, but I borrowed a book from the library. I thought we could take a look at it together. Joe said with my arm, I'm sure to get the quarterback position. I read it's the most important position on the team."

George soon realizes it's always a one-way conversation and stops giving any details.

I begin to resent my father's treatment of George. "Dad, did you hear what George said? He's going to try out for the football team in the fall."

My father will look my way and stare. I'll narrow my eyes, hoping he'll notice how angry I am with him. One night, when he asks the question, I respond that I had disobeyed my teacher, was sent to the principal's office, and they were considering suspending me from school. He just looks at me and lowers his head. My grandmother interjects, saying, "I hope you haven't taken to lying to get your father's attention."

When my father has stopped going to his room several months later, it surprises everyone, but we all act as if we don't seem to notice. Pearl will place Audrey in her playpen next to my father, wherever he sits and reads the paper. There are times he'll just stare at his baby. When watching her becomes more than he can handle, my father, without a word, will take to his room. This action infuriates me, so one night, I stop him by saying, "She's a pretty baby, isn't she, Dad? Just like Mom said she would be." The mention of my mother's name causes my father to walk faster away from his children. It's then I lose respect for the man I've called Father. I no longer pray that God will return to us the father we once knew.

When it becomes clear to me that my father shows no interest in his children, I plan an escape for George and me. I go to my father and ask if our allowance can be raised to $5 a month. Since I'm too young to open a savings account, I ask my father if he can speak with Mr. Thomson at the bank. My father does as I ask. I then tell George that he has $2 a month to do with as he wishes and I will deposit the remaining half in an account that Dad has set up in his name. I choose to live on $1.50 a month and deposit $3.50 into my account.

Our grandparents have kept their promise. In July, they spend their two-week vacation with us. For Thanksgiving, Grandpa takes a week off without pay and returns Christmas Eve and remains with us till after the New Year. On Easter, he is with us for the Holy Days, leaving Easter Monday. Grandma Maggie has retired from her position as seamstress at the mill. She spends the entire month of July with us. Thanksgiving through New Year's and the week of our Easter break.

To our surprise, Grandmother Holland never returns to New York to visit Grandfather Holland. He visits us three times a year. At first, I'm saddened by the news that my grandmother will not be returning to New York, but my sadness soon turns to joy because we children are able to reside with my grandparents at the boardinghouse during their visits. I welcome the departure from the gloom that has invaded my home.

George and I are close, but the only time I spend with Audrey is on Saturdays, when I walk her to the park to meet up with my friends. George is more attentive to Audrey than me. I do treasure the times we spend with my grandparents. It's during their visits that I acknowledge Audrey's existence. Grandma Maggie will take charge of her grandchildren, and Pearl the household. Knowing that Pearl and Grandma Maggie enjoy each other's company, I begin to take on two more chores at home, freeing up Pearl's day. This is not a generous act. I notice when Pearl is around, she tends to Audrey and Grandma spends more time fuzzing over George and me.

It doesn't take long to notice that Pearl also enjoys the time she spends with my grandparents. We all seem happier away from the solitude of our home. One day at the park, George goes off with a friend and Pearl steps away to rock Audrey to sleep. I take the opportunity to share with Grandma the plans I have for George and me. "Dad gives us an allowance of five dollars each month, so I had Dad open savings accounts for us. George saves half of his allowance, and I all but $1.50."

"I'm very proud of you, Sarah. What are you and George going to do with all your savings?"

"We're going to move to New York to live with you and Grandpa. I've been reading about colleges in New York. I like New York University. I want to be a lawyer. The university has a great law program. I think George will make a great teacher or baseball player."

"He wants to be a teacher like your mother?"

"He hasn't said he wants to be a teacher, but I know he'd be happy living with you and Grandpa in New York."

"When the time comes, you might not want to live so far from your father and sister."

"I wish Dad would allow us to come live with you today. I don't think he'd care if we left."

"Sarah, your father loves his children! It would hurt him if you children were taken from him."

"That's not true, Grandma. He never talks to us. He doesn't even know Audrey exists."

My grandmother sighs and says in time I will understand.

* * * * *

I slowly adjust to my new homelife. I avoid Grandmother Holland as often as I can and ignore my absentee father. George, on the other hand, becomes defiant due to the lack of attention. That spring, my father is called to school to discuss George's bad behavior. Of course, my grandmother takes control of the situation. She meets with Mr. Klaus, our principal. George is getting into trouble at least once every two weeks. At first, Mr. Klaus has tried taking the fatherly approach with George, hoping to win the boy over. The town has taken on the role of both mother and father to us since the death of our mother and the living, breathing death of our father.

Mr. Klaus wouldn't have known about the fight between Charlie and George if Charlie's mom had not been more concerned with George's behavior than Charlie's swollen lip and lost tooth, which was on the verge of falling out anyway. She confided in Mr. Klaus that she felt George was looking for attention. It was time to talk with Mr. Holland, making him aware of George's problem. This might just help the man wake up and smell the coffee.

I'm called to Mr. Klaus's office because my father has not returned his calls. "Sarah, I didn't want to involve you, but I need your help in getting a message to your father. I need for him to set time aside to meet with me. It doesn't have to be during school hours. I will meet with him at night."

"Is George in trouble again, Mr. Klaus?"

"As I said, Sarah, I'd rather discuss George's situation with your father."

"I'll give him the message, Mr. Klaus. Would you mind if I attend the meeting with my father?"

"If your father agrees, I would respect his decision."

* * * * *

I wait for the right moment to speak with my father. "Dad, Mr. Klaus wants to meet with you about George."

My father doesn't respond. "He's been getting in trouble at school. I think—"

"I'll talk with your grandmother. Tell Mr. Klaus she'll call to set up a meeting with him."

"I want to be there when you and grandmother meet with him."

"I'll tell your grandmother you'll be at the meeting."

"You're not going?"

"I'm very busy at work, Sarah. I can't afford to be away from my job. I'm sure Mr. Klaus realizes I have three children to support. That's why your grandmother is here, to handle situations like this."

* * * * *

Sitting next to my grandmother, I watch her expression as Mr. Klaus expresses his concerns about George's behavior. She allows him to finish and then takes control of the conversation. "First, my son wanted me to apologize that he was unable to attend this meeting. He is not being neglectful of his duties as a father, but as you are well aware, I agreed to remain here to help my son with situations such as this. If I'm not mistaken, Charlie and my grandson are good friends."

"Yes, Mrs. Holland."

"And remain good friends even after this minor disagreement, correct?"

"Yes, Mrs. Holland."

"All right, then. I was told by my granddaughter that Charlie lost a tooth during the scuffle, and I want Charlie's parents to know that my son will cover any cost associated with the loss of the tooth."

"Charlie's parents aren't looking to be reimbursed. Mrs. Hansen wanted to express her concern for George's behavior. He was always a gentle and kind soul, but lately he seems troubled …"

"The boy just suffered a terrible loss. I'm sure this contributes to his poor behavior. When my son was a little older than George, his grandfather was taken from us. He and his grandfather were close. It was over a year before he began to bounce back. Mr. Klaus, I respect your professional opinion, and I hope in the future you will be available to me and my son if we need advice. Let's hope that George's behavior will cease once we have spoken with him."

Grandmother has a talent for gracefully letting you know that she doesn't appreciate any outside interference.

"Mrs. Holland, I would not have requested a meeting if I didn't think the problem with George is out of control. He holds the longest record for time served in detention. I was hoping Mr. Holland and I could get to the bottom of this."

"I promise you, Mr. Klaus, the woman sitting before you will make sure that George is aware that if this behavior continues, he will be shipped off to military school. Military men are accustomed to dealing with strong-willed boys."

Grandmother ends the meeting by standing. "I've taken up enough of your time. You do have a school to run. I can promise you George will not be giving you any more problems."

* * * * *

Once home from school, Grandmother Holland confronts George. "Please sit down. We need to talk. Sarah, you may as well hear what I have to say. George, it has come to my attention that you hold the longest record for serving detention at your school." George lowers his head. "I recently learned that you fought with you best friend, Charlie, and he lost a tooth."

"The tooth was ready to fall out, Grandmother. I swear."

"It's a sin to swear, George. Charlie's one of your good friends?"

"He is, Grandmother. And still is."

"Then what caused the fight?"

"He was upset with me when I said he threw like a girl. He threw the first punch, I swear. I mean, I'm telling the truth."

"So you were defending yourself?"

"Yes."

Grandmother smiles. "You do hold the longest record for detention, so this is not the first time you have been in trouble, but it will be the last. If this behavior continues, I will demand that your father send you off to military school. Do you know what that means? You will be sent away from your home, away from your family and friends."

I watch as the blood drains from George's face. "I won't get into any more trouble, Grandmother."

"Well, that's settled. Off with you. You have homework to do."

It's no secret that my grandmother favors George. His having the longest record for serving detention has impressed her. A few days after their confrontation, Grandmother asks, “How are things at school, George?”

“Fine, Grandmother.”

“Good. I’m not condoning using your fist to get your point across, but I can understand it’s hard to control yourself when you’re being provoked. I understand why you had reacted as you did, George. Wasn’t it Charlie who landed the first punch?”

“Hit me square in the jaw. But there won’t be a next time. Charlie cried after my first punch. He took one in the face and two in his stomach. I felt bad afterward. He is my best friend.”

I interject, “Mom would have had your ear for punching Charlie. What were you thinking, George?”

“What would your mother have said?” asks Grandmother.

“She would have told him to turn the other cheek and love thy neighbor.”

Grandmother smiles and rustles George’s hair. He beams from the attention. “I see a lot of myself in you, George. Just like you, I don’t take kindly to anyone having the upper hand over me.”

CHAPTER FIVE

Allison

Waking to an empty house, I think about all the things I have to do but don't have the strength to begin. I inform Jon, my boss, that I'm taking the entire month off and won't be returning to work until after the Christmas break.

Christmas is two weeks away. In Christmases past, shopping online for Pete's family is a given. All the presents are wrapped and shipped free of charge. Hank and Mary accept the deliveries and place the presents under the tree. Online shopping for my family is a capital *no*. The large Christmas tree placed in the center of the mall, the Christmas lights, the store decorations, and the hustle and bustle getting from one store to another for me is like a shot of heroin to a drug addict.

But this year is different. I surf online until every gift is ordered, wrapped, and shipped.

At the last minute, Andrew hints he wants the latest Madden video game, which I find online, but delivery won't be until December 28. Panicked, I call Game Stop and pay ten dollars to place the video on hold. If the item isn't picked up by four that day, the video will be placed back on the shelf for sale.

Lying in bed, I think about the dream that haunts my sleep. The face of the man is always blocked by the sun. Trying to push the dream from my mind, I think in two weeks I will be sunbathing on a lounge chair in Florida, surrounded by Pete's family. The thought makes my head ache.

The upcoming weekend, Pete and the kids want to decorate our beautiful fake tree and work on decorating the outside of the house. With Christmas two weeks away, I'm reminded of the phone call I have been avoiding.

I haven't heard from my aunt since the day I cut her from my life. Christmas Eve will be spent at my aunt's house, followed by Christmas Eve service, and Christmas Day is always at our house. In the past, Patrick would remain in Connecticut from Thanksgiving to the day after Christmas. He calls it his hobo holiday. One week, he'll spend with my aunt and uncle. Together they will travel to and from Manhattan, catching up on the most popular plays and restaurants. The week leading up to Christmas, he'll remain with us, helping out, making Christmas one the children won't forget.

The day after Christmas, we'll say goodbye to Patrick, who is off to spend New Year's with his work buddies in Maine. From there he'll make his way back to Pittsburgh until July. My family will head to the airport to catch the ten o'clock flight to Florida.

Thanksgiving is my family's first test of a holiday without Patrick. Christmas is going to be harder, with only five of us for dinner. No longer would I hear Patrick say as he did every year, "I don't know how you do it, Allison—the children, the house, work, and Christmas Day with a house filled with family and friends, and you still manage to be the most beautiful woman in the room."

"My secret? I let my fingers do the walking, call the caterer, stock the wine cellar, and moisturize, moisturize, moisturize."

He'd smile, and I'd blush from his compliment, that he thought I was beautiful.

My cell phone rings, reminding me that I have a hair and nail appointment at twelve.

The temperature has dropped thirty degrees overnight. Exiting the car, I lift the fur collar on my coat around my face. The gray sky warns that a snowstorm will be arriving later that day. As I walk closer to the lake, the wind picks up speed. I lift my collar closer to cover my ears.

I don't know why I feel a need to visit so often, with no grave or headstone to stare at, and the ashes long since washed away. I spend twenty minutes in limbo. I wonder if I should say a prayer, cry, or scream to the spirit who left a deep hole in my heart

My phone vibrates in my coat pocket. It's Pete. I forward the call to voice mail. I notice the number of calls waiting to be returned. I've listened to those messages several times—JoAnne's plea for me to call her. I still can't bring myself to speak with her. What's surprised me most is, there isn't one message from my aunt.

As I place the phone back into my coat pocket, my fingers touch the envelope. I hold the envelope in my hand, and my eyes scan the lake, searching for a sign that spirits do exist. What I wouldn't give for one last face-to-face talk with Patrick! As I open the letter, my throat constricts. I glance at the familiar handwriting. Gently I run my fingers over the words. I read the letter several times. Staring up at the gray sky, which has cast a black shadow over the lake, I speak into the wind. "Patrick, if there's a chance that the dead know all after death, you know that my world is falling apart." I fold the letter and place the letter back in my coat pocket then continue, "Pete's a good man, a loving husband, a wonderful father. He doesn't deserve what I'm about to do to him. I don't even know why I'm doing what I'm about to do. So many years have passed since …"

One snowflake falls on my face, mixing with my tears. Is this Patrick's gentle way of saying, "I'm here"?

Slowly I walk back to the car and beg for guidance from above.

* * * * *

I return Pete's phone call. He picks up on the third ring. "Hi, sweetie! I'm just going into a meeting, so I don't have long to talk. What's your day like?"

"I'm heading to the mall to pick up a video game for Andrew. Then I'm heading to the salon."

"Great! This might work out better than I thought. I made a reservation at Pierre's. With the holidays bearing down, the only reservation I could get was two thirty. I know how much you've been dying to try Pierre's, and I thought this would be a great time for you and me to spend some time alone."

My stomach knots up. "Pete, I'm dressed in jeans and a sweat-shirt. I don't have time to head back home, change, and make a two thirty reservation at Pierre's. Anyway, I've promised Andrew and Julia I'd pick them up from practice today."

"You're heading to the mall. Stop at Neiman Marcus—early Christmas present from me, whatever you need. You'll already have your hair and nails done. How hard could it be to pick out a slinky dress and a sexy pair of heels?"

I immediately take note of the beautiful diamond bracelet on my arm, a fortieth birthday present from Pete. It will work perfectly with a black dress. "Pete, it's impossible. I have too much to do today. Another time, maybe after Christmas. And the kids—"

Pete cuts me off. "I've already arranged for your aunt to pick up the kids after school. I told her we'll pick them up from her house."

"You've spoken with my aunt?"

"Yes. She was elated that I called her. Remember, the kids and I have nothing to do with this little spat you have going with your aunt—your words exactly. Anyway, you mentioned that you were going to call her to confirm the Christmas plans. You won't have to make that awkward call."

"You think my seeing her is going to make it easier?"

"Maybe not. What time is your hair and nail appointment?

"Twelve."

"It's ten now. Ten minutes to pick up the video, and with that body of yours, finding something to wear will be a walk in the park.

"Pete, I won't be done at the salon until two. It won't work. I'm sorry. Another time, I promise."

"Okay, you force me into it. It's time to play fantasy phone."

"Hi, Allison, this is Derek."

I'm very familiar with the game we're about to play.

Pete goes on, "Derek, the CEO of one of the largest Fortune 500 companies in the world. You're a famous art dealer, one of the best. Five months ago, I set up an appointment to meet with you at my penthouse so you can get the lay of the land, or should I say, laid. When I walked into the room, your back was to me, and I prayed the front was just as delicious. When you turned, our eyes met. For you, an instant orgasm, for me an uncontrollable desire to possess you. Today, I ring your cell phone. You excuse yourself to take my call. I tell you I have three hours before flying off to Paris. I don't ask if you can meet me at the penthouse. I insist you be there in fifteen minutes. You become flushed with the thought of what I'm going to do to you once you're in my arms. You return to your rich clients. Lying, you tell them that your eighty-nine-year-old grandmother was taken to the hospital—nothing serious, but you have to run to speak with the doctors. You say you'll meet them at eight for drinks and dinner. You rush away and hail a cab. Two thirty sharp."

The phone goes dead, and I begin to cry.

* * * * *

With the video safely placed in my purse, I head to Neiman Marcus. First stop: sheer black stockings. Moving on to the dress department, it doesn't take long to find a low-cut midnight-black dress with thick sequin straps that cross over my back midway to my waist. The prefect New Year's Eve dress, a no-bra dress. The stockings will replace the black thong panties I'm wearing. In the past, this rendezvous with Pete would excite me; today, holding the dress in my hand, I feel nothing but guilt, and I place the dress on the rack. Finding a high-neckline, straight, long-sleeve black number, I head for the dressing room. Along the way, I find a pair of black pumps.

Five hundred and eight dollars later, which isn't too bad for Neiman, I head for the parking lot, leaving me ten minutes to make the salon appointment. I call the salon to say I'm on my way. I look through my purse, hoping I hadn't left my makeup case at home. But I did. Then I realize the salon has a professional cosmetic consultant. I'm sure she won't have a problem fitting me in, if the price is right.

Rushing into the salon, I bump into Lori Grainger. Lori is a beautiful woman, early sixties. Her husband shits money, and he's one of Pete's richest clients.

"Allison."

"Lori."

"I can't believe I've bumped into you! I've been coming to this salon for five years. I'm surprised we haven't bumped into each other sooner."

"I usually come at night, or early Saturdays. You know, with work and the children, nights are more convenient."

"Of course. I was going to call you. Hunter told me about your stepfather. What a shock! Car accident? So sad."

Kristin, my hairdresser, looks over when Lori loudly continues, "His name was Patrick, correct? I think I might have met him once. Good-looking man."

"I believe it was a few times. He always attends the company Christmas party."

"That's right! Well, I'm sorry for your loss. Will you be attending the party this year?"

"If I'm up to it. But Pete will definitely be there." I have no intention of attending the company Christmas party. I already got an out-of-jail card from Pete.

Lori whispers, "It will make you feel better, and we always have such a nice time, don't we?"

"Yes, we do." In all the time I've been attending the company Christmas party, if Lori Grainger said one full sentence to me, it was one too many words.

"Well, if I don't see you at the party, have a wonderful Christmas."

Nothing is more relaxing than a pedicure and manicure after a long day at the office. I look forward to being pampered two times a month, but today all I can think about is the letter sitting in my coat pocket. It isn't the last piece of correspondence I've received from Patrick, but it is instrumental in setting the course my life has taken.

"You're done, Mrs. Cane. You can have a seat at Kristin's station."

"Thank you." Looking at my nails, I compliment Carmen for doing such a good job.

As I sit at Kristin's station, it doesn't take long for her to express her condolences. "Sorry to hear about your loss."

"Thank you, Kristin. It was an accident."

Kristin lowers her head. "I'm sorry."

"I'm meeting my husband for lunch at Pierre's. Would it be all right if I could change in one of the massage rooms? And if Janet has time, I like to have my makeup reapplied."

Kristin returns, saying, "You lucked out. Janet's next appointment isn't until two."

Usually, Kristin and I chat about the holidays, her children, my children, but today, I'm not up for idle chatting.

With my hair done, I move to Janet's station. At one forty-five, Kristin points me to a massage room where I can change. Once dressed, I move to the full-length mirror in the room. I gasp at the reflection in the mirror. Turning, I notice that the *V* on the back of the dress drops to the middle of my back, exposing my bra. I have no choice but to remove the bra. Staring at myself in the mirror, I realize the dress I thought safe is screaming to be noticed.

* * * * *

Being my first time at Pierre's, I'm impressed by the design of the restaurant. As I enter, there is a circular bar with a backdrop of mirrors. The reflection in the mirrors is of a circular dining area with floor-to-ceiling glass windows. Beyond the windows is a courtyard with a winter theme of white-light Christmas trees covered with white crystal snow, which can be viewed through the mirrors behind the bar. Each table is covered in white linen, with a centerpiece of red roses.

In the mirror behind the bar, I spot Pete sitting at the far end of the room, his face aglow from white Christmas lights reflected on the glass. I begin to walk toward him. Rising from his seat, he reaches out his hand to me and kisses me gently on the lips. Whispering in my ear, he says, "You look absolutely beautiful." He moves my chair, allowing me to sit. Leaning over me, he says, "You've caught the attention of every man in the room, but I'm the lucky guy leaving with you."

I don't offer a thankful response.

When Pete returns to his seat, he says, "My reaction was the same as yours the first time Hal brought me to the restaurant. I knew the transformation during the holidays was spectacular."

"The only word I have to describe the view is *magical*."

"Mrs. Cane, welcome to Pierre's."

"Craig, this is Allison, my wife." Pete announces *my wife* with pride.

"Mrs. Cane, it is a pleasure to meet you."

"It's a pleasure to meet you, Craig. I've been wanting to visit Pierre's for some time."

"We were happy to accommodate Mr. Cane when he called for a reservation. Can I start you off with a bottle of water?"

"Sparkling water, please."

"Of course, Mr. Cane."

When Craig returns, he pours the water and asks if we would prefer wine or a cocktail.

"Martini for me, three olives." Pete orders the same, and wine with dinner.

Pete and I are mesmerized by the winter scene beyond the windows. "It's beautiful, isn't it? So peaceful." Pete adds, "It's been a while since we spent a long weekend in Vermont."

I fumble with the napkin on my lap, knowing there won't be long weekends in Vermont for us. "Work is taking over our lives."

"Speaking of work, I got a call from Eve today. Hal's worried about the Florida office. So am I. You know how happy I was for Hal when he mentioned he was going to retire. Didn't picture him playing golf five times a week, so when he approached me with the idea of opening an office in Florida, it sounded like a great idea at that time, then the heart attack. Now it all falls on my shoulders." When I don't respond, Pete smiles. "No more shop talk. Have I told you how beautiful you look?"

"More than once, thank you."

"Did I tell you how much I love the dress? You took my breath away when you walked in, but then you've always had that effect on me."

Craig walks over to the table with a starter recommended by the chef and presents the specials for the day. Pete recommends the filet mignon.

Trying to keep the conversation light during lunch, we talk about the children, the excitement of the upcoming holiday, and our Christmas break trip to Florida.

Continuing to talk about our present lives, I dwell on how our perfect lives are about to change.

Craig arrives to ask how we enjoyed our lunch. We compliment the chef, and Craig announces the best is yet to come. Pete orders a port wine for himself and a chocolate cordial for me.

A bottle of champagne arrives. I say to Pete, "I don't think I can drink any more wine." Craig pours the bubbly and disappears. Pete raises his champagne glass in one hand and offers a little black box with the other. "Merry Christmas, sweetheart."

"What is this?"

"Open it and find out."

Untying the bow, I have a sudden urge to run. Staring back at me is a two-and-half carat solitaire diamond and a wedding band surrounded in diamonds.

Pete takes my hand. "May I?" he removes the rings from the box and places them on the ring finger of my left hand. "They look beautiful, but not as beautiful as the woman who will wear them."

"Pete, I don't know what to say."

"Say you love them, as much as you love me, and as much as I love you."

Staring into his eyes, I excuse myself and ask Craig where the restrooms are located.

Leaning on the sink, I lower my head and contemplate confessing everything, right here, right now. "O God," I call. And ask, "Why?" I splash water on my face, making sure I don't smudge my makeup, take eight deep breaths, and make my way back to the table.

Pete has a confused look on his face. "Allison, are you all right? That wasn't the reaction I was hoping for."

I try to make light of the situation. "I'm sorry, I wasn't expecting this. Of course, they are beautiful! But why such an extravagant gift?"

"I've always said that one day I'd replace your gold wedding band."

"Pete, these last few weeks, I know I haven't been myself, but you shouldn't have—"

"Sweetheart, I purchased the rings months ago. I was going to surprise you on Christmas Day. I guess … well, I thought the rings might cheer you up."

Tears fill my eyes when I think back at how many times over the years Pete would ask this question: "If you had to buy something special for yourself, what would it be?" My answer has always been "I have everything a girl could want, a handsome husband, two beautiful kids. What more can a girl ask for?"

"Humor me" would be Pete's response.

I'd respond by saying, "Marilyn had it right when she sang 'Diamonds Are a Girl's Best Friend.'"

Pete would laugh and say, "Someday, baby, someday."

"Pete, this gift must have cost a fortune! Can we afford—"

"Money's no object when you love someone as much as I love you."

* * * * *

Since we came in separate cars, I'm able to drive alone and wonder what just happened. The rings on my finger glisten from the sun. I can't deny that they are beautiful, but I don't deserve them.

I convince Pete to pick the kids up at Aunt Sarah's. He tries to convince me to follow him, saying, "Everyone is anxious to see the rings."

"Please, Pete, I'm not up to seeing my aunt and uncle. I promise I'll call tomorrow and confirm the plans for Christmas."

Arriving home, I enter the garage and place my head on the wheel, frozen in that position for several minutes. I exit the car and head for my bedroom, my place of solace. I leave the rings on my dresser before getting into bed. I fake sleeping when Pete enters the room. I can sense he's staring at the rings and wondering where he went wrong.

The gift of the rings has changed my demeanor toward my family. Faced with the dilemma of explaining my reaction to such a generous gift, I wear the rings the following day and let my children admire and compliment Pete's good taste.

"Mom, you are so lucky! Dad did a great job," says Julia.

Andrew, admiring the rings, says, "Congratulations, Mom! Aunt Sarah was disappointed you didn't stop by last night. She was anxious to get a look."

I promise my family that I will call Aunt Sarah to discuss Christmas and maybe stop by the house, which I have no intentions of doing.

* * * * *

"Hello, Aunt Sarah."

"Allison, how are you?"

"I'm fine. Sorry I didn't stop by last night. I guess I was overwhelmed by Pete's gift."

"I can't wait to see them! Were you surprised?"

"Surprised and shocked. The rings are not me. You know I like simple things, and I hope I never find out the cost. I'm a little annoyed that Pete would spend so much money without asking me first."

"You didn't share your feelings with him, did you?"

"Of course not. I couldn't do that to him. Enough about the rings. I'm calling about Christmas. Christmas Eve your house, and Christmas Day, I was hoping you'd understand that I'd rather not make a big deal out of the day. Just an early dinner, the five of us. I'd like to get the house in order before we leave for Florida."

I scheduled my cleaning service to clean the Thursday before New Year's Eve. I paid extra to have them remove the decorations, inside and out. Upon our return, the house and decorations will be cleaned and placed safely away until the following December.

"The first holiday is always the hardest."

"I'm sorry if it seems I'm being selfish, but I'm not up to it this year."

* * * * *

Christmas Eve, I stare at my finger, my aunt and uncle admire the rings, and again Pete is complimented on his good taste. Prior to Christmas Eve services, there is a gathering in the parish hall. Santa Claus arrives and showers the younger children with gifts. Watching Julia trying to comfort one little boy who is stressing out, saying Santa is wasting too much time at the parish hall instead of sailing across the sky to make his deliveries, is the only joy I feel that day.

Christmas Day, while I'm preparing dinner, the phone rings. Pete answers, and after a few words are exchanged, Pete hands me the phone. "JoAnne."

"Hello."

"Merry Christmas, Allison."

"Merry Christmas."

"I waited long enough for an invite to Christmas dinner, so I'm calling to tell you Gary and I are inviting ourselves. Don't you think you've punished me long enough for something I had no control over? It's Christmas, and I like to spend the day with you."

"I'm not punishing you, JoAnne. I just want to get through the day without too much drama."

"I promise no drama. Pete said dinner is at one?"

JoAnne had told me in September that her Mom and Dad were going to California for Christmas to spend time with JoAnne's brother and his family. Hearing the news, I said, "We get to spend Christmas together this year! This is going to be the best Christmas ever!" Remembering our conversation, I said, "Dinner's at one."

Pete sets the Christmas table for ten. Christmas music plays softly through the house while the kids read through the manuals of their latest technology gifts. I keep to myself in the kitchen, preparing the Christmas feast and pondering this day without Patrick.

*****

Earlier that morning, Pete was acting as Santa Claus and welcoming us to a den filled with gifts and his famous hot chocolate and my homemade Christmas cookies.

"Merry Christmas! I hope you're happy with Santa's choices this year."

"Santa, Dad? Really?" says Andrew.

"I'm sure Santa did a great job", says Julia."

Pete laughs, "That's my girl."

I sit on the sofa and watch my children open one gift at a time, big difference from when they were younger and clawed at the gifts, casting each gift aside until they had opened them all.

Julia looks at my hand. "Mom, you're not wearing your gift."

Startled, I said quickly, "I don't sleep with my rings on, sweetie."

"I would."

I glance at Pete. He looks sad. I feel like shit.

Andrew hands me several boxes. "Merry Christmas, Mom. These are from Julia and me."

One box contains a beautiful scarf with blue and green tones, blue leather gloves I've had my eye on, and two gift certificates for a massage at my favorite spa.

"Andrew, Julia, I love everything! You were reading my mind." I reach over and hug and kiss my children. "Thank you! I'm so lucky to have children as generous as you."

Again, glancing at Pete, I wonder if he is thinking why his gift didn't warrant the same reaction.

"The best part is yet to come," says Andrew. "We spent our own money. Didn't ask Dad to help out this year."

"You spent your own money? How sweet."

Beneath the tree there are four gifts remaining. Pete retrieves one and passes it to me. "Just a little something. Merry Christmas, Allison."

I reach under the tree and retrieve the last three boxes and hand them to Pete. Opening the gift, which contains my favorite Chanel perfume, I say, "Thank you, Pete." I reach over, kiss Pete on the lips, move to his cheek, and whisper in his ear, "I love the rings and the perfume."

Pete, moving me slightly in front of him, smiles and says, "Merry Christmas! You don't know how happy it makes me to know you love your gifts."

My aunt enters the kitchen, "Merry Christmas!"

"Merry Christmas, Aunt Sarah. Where's Uncle George?"

"The kids hauled him away. He's getting a lesson on how to play the Madden video game."

"Hey, girlfriend, Merry Christmas!"

I turn to see JoAnne turning around and around so I can admire her new sheer black mink. "Isn't it beautiful? And from the look on your face, I say I look like a million bucks in it. Let me see your hand!"

JoAnne, making sure that the tension between us is over, says, "First, do I look fabulously rich?"

Aunt Sarah laughs. "Fabulously rich."

JoAnne kisses my aunt. "Merry Christmas, Aunt Sarah."

"Merry Christmas, JoAnne."

Coming toward me, JoAnne asks, "Well, let me see them!"

I extend my hand.

"Allison, they look beautiful on your hand, just like I knew they would!" JoAnne leans in and takes me in her arms. "Merry Christmas! Friends forever—never forget."

I hug JoAnne and begin to cry, asking, "You knew about the rings?"

"I helped pick them out, and a little birdie told me you had a hand in my gift."

"When Gary asked, the answer was right on the tip of my tongue, since you reminded me over and over about the coat."

Laughing, JoAnne says, "A girl's got to do what a girl has to do."

I smile and wipe the tears building in my eyes, thankful JoAnne has invited herself. It's good to have her here today and always. Nothing is stronger than the friendship JoAnne and I share.

Aunt Sarah and Uncle George leave around six that evening. Gary wants to stick around a little longer, allowing the traffic to subside. JoAnne and I leave the boys and children playing video games.

We go into the kitchen for some quiet time. Sipping coffee and picking on the Christmas desserts, JoAnne begins the conversation. "You forgive me, don't you? I know you were hurt that I wasn't on time for the funeral, but believe me, it wasn't intentional. I should have been there, just like I was there when your mother died."

"Not the same. This was Patrick."

JoAnne has a strange look on her face after my last comment.

"Patrick understood me. He took an interest in me. Sorry to say I can't remember one precious memory that my mother and I shared, but there were many with Patrick." I pause. "I'm not being fair. There is one memory. The night before we left for college, she said she was proud of me."

"I know life wasn't easy for you. When we were younger, I envied you for not having to answer to anyone. Your mother wasn't June Cleaver, but she never did one thing that led me to believe she wasn't a compassionate woman."

"I know where you're going with this, JoAnne, but let me ask you, Didn't you find it strange that the woman couldn't show love to her one and only child?"

"All right, that was strange, and Patrick was the total opposite of your mother. That's why if he were able to be with you today, he'd shake you and tell you to snap out of it. Patrick wouldn't want you to waste precious time mourning his death. He'd want you to be strong for the people that meant everything to him, your family." JoAnne pauses before saying, "Pete told me you weren't overjoyed with his gift. That's not the Allison I know and love."

"Those rings must have cost a fortune. I'm horrified to think how much he spent."

JoAnne lifts her arms and gazes around the room. "Allison, by the looks of this place, you couldn't be hurting for money, unless you guys are drowning in debt that I'm not aware of?"

"Just because we're not hurting in the financial department doesn't mean he can go out and spend close to sixty thousand on diamond rings without my knowledge."

"Sixty thousand! The rings were not anywhere near that price, and I know because Pete used my jeweler and he gave Pete a great price on those rings."

"Whatever, forty-thousand, thirty-thousand, it's still a lot of money."

JoAnne shakes her head. "I know you're not a material girl, so I can understand why you might be a little upset, but still it's not like you to hurt anyone's feelings, especially Pete's."

"You'll be happy to know I told him this morning they were beautiful and I loved them, but I lied."

JoAnne sips her coffee. "And keep on lying, because that man thinks the sun rises and sets in you." JoAnne lowers her cup to the saucer. "Oh, before I forget, before the funeral, when we spoke on the phone, you said you had something to tell me, something we couldn't talk about over the phone. I've been going insane wondering what was so important that we had to speak face-to-face."

JoAnne's question sends chills down my spine. "It was nothing. I can't even remember what I wanted to say."

"Are you sure?"

"I'm sure."

It was only one month ago that I was willing to confess all to JoAnne, but now things are different. I don't want to share with the one person I will take a bullet for how my life is about to change.

CHAPTER SIX

Sarah

I glance at the clock: ten minutes to five. I wake at five, wanting to be on the road by six thirty. I pack snacks, water, and a thermos of coffee for our trip. Cleaning my coffee cup, I hear George's alarm go off. Twenty minutes later, he joins me in the kitchen.

"Do you want a cup of coffee and a buttered roll to go?"

"That would be nice."

I hand George a travel cup of coffee, and he asks, "Only the one bag in the foyer?"

"Yes, and the snack bag." I hand George the bag.

"This is heavy. You know there are rest stops along the way?"

"The bag is filled with bottled water. I'm not paying those ridiculous prices for water. Be out in a few. Just want to double-check before I set the alarm."

* * * * *

With George at the wheel, I say, "Not much traffic for the day after Christmas."

"I bet the airport is busy. Speaking of the airport, did you speak with Allison this morning?"

"No. They had an early flight. Should be boarding within the hour."

"This is a first for you. You usually call to wish them a safe flight and to remind them to call when they arrive."

Changing the subject, I continue, "The Christmas holidays went well. I think my plan of not interfering, or as you put it, worrying, might be working. Allison was cordial to us. Everyone got along beautifully. What made it even more enjoyable was JoAnne and her family joining us for dinner. That girl is such a hoot."

"I overheard Gary tell Pete JoAnne was coming even if Allison said not to come. I don't think you were the only one Allison cut out of her life."

"Allison was upset with JoAnne for not showing up on time for the funeral. All is forgiven, because they were getting along quite well yesterday. Speaking of JoAnne, I spoke with Rita. She was overjoyed we were coming for a visit."

"I'm sure she was. One more question, so how are you going to make it through the day not knowing if the family arrived safe and sound?"

"I spoke with Mary yesterday to wish the family a merry Christmas. I told her I wanted Allison to relax and enjoy the trip so I wasn't going to bother her with a phone call. Mary understood and said she would text me to let me know they arrived safely."

George approves. "Good thinking."

At ten, we make our first stop. It is my turn to drive until we stop for lunch. Back on the road, George begins to read the newspaper, and thirty minutes later, he puts his head back and drifts off to sleep.

Smiling, I'm amazed at how fast a motionless man can get his body to relax. Looking at George reminds me of the past. With the current situation with Allison, I feel a need to return home for a visit. It has been a while since I visited the grave and some old friends who still reside in the area, including Rita and Burt, JoAnne's parents.

I think about how fond Rita was of Audrey. She was one of many who never left Audrey's side in those final two years of her life. I think of Audrey often since hearing of Patrick's passing. Remembering the times I was forced to spend my Saturdays with my sister. As she grew older, before our walks to the park, we would stop and visit our mother's grave. When I tried to explain it was our mother's final resting place, she became frightened and confused. Showing her pictures of our mother only confused her more and frustrated me.

I took to visiting the grave site alone. Digging a small hole next to the tombstone, I'd leave mementos of items belonging to George, Audrey, and myself. Once I placed a lock of Audrey's hair and an old baseball of George's, one he'd never miss. I stopped buying wildflowers to place on the grave, because there would always be a dozen red roses lying on the grave, placed there by my father.

Even though our lives had changed for the worse, my grandmother Holland was enjoying the new life she created in our small town. George managed to keep his getting into trouble from Grandmother. I became a constant visitor at my friend Peggy's house. Dad existed, he worked and cared for his family, and the community respected and pitied him. Audrey created a world of her own through books.

George is fast asleep. The young boy and man who was so rebellious of our father's simple house rules is gone forever.

Many changes had taken place during those first three years. Two years had passed, and then another change. Grandma Maggie and Grandpa no longer could keep their promise to visit after Grandpa suffered a severe stroke that left him crippled on his right side. He died two years later, calling my mother's name as he passed away. We attended his funeral, and I remember how completely destroyed my grandma Maggie looked. The only good thing that came out of my grandpa's passing was my father's compassion for our grandma; he agreed that George and I were old enough to spend one month out the summer with Grandma in New York.

It was no secret that George and I resented Grandmother Holland's living with us. My father gave her carte blanche to rule the nest. During George's first year of high school, it was becoming clear that grandmother hadn't the time or strength to deal with George the delinquent. Audrey was turning five and, in the fall, would enter kindergarten. In July of that same year, my father received a call from Grandfather Holland's doctor saying he was experiencing back pain and an x-ray revealed it was lung cancer.

The night after hearing the news, during dinner, my grandmother was present, which was rare, since she was invited to a different home for dinner at least three nights a week. On the days she did join us for dinner, she brought us up-to-date on the latest news in our community. It was Grandmother that informed us Mrs. Peterson was moving back to Illinois; Mr. Peterson, who had become afflicted with severe arthritis, felt his dear, sweet wife needed the support of her family. This night, my grandmother sat stoic. Fork in hand, she pushed her food around her plate, never taking one bite. Sensing something was wrong, I caught a look from George mouthing, "What's going on?" I shrugged my shoulders.

Trying to break the tension, I asked, "Grandmother, are the ladies planning a going-away party for Mr. and Mrs. Peterson?"

"I'm not sure." This confirmed something was wrong.

Several minutes later, my father would reveal, "Children, your grandmother will be leaving us on Saturday. She's returning to New York."

I dropped my fork onto my plate, and the noise made my grandmother jump. George placed the fork filled with food back on his plate, and Audrey just stared, waiting for my father to continue.

Grandmother shouted, "I can't believe after all I did for you, George Holland, you're pushing me to the street like trash!"

"Mother, your place is with Dad. He needs you."

"These children need me more than your father. I will see to it. He'll have the best nurses money can buy. I'll visit more often, until—"

"I've already spoken to Dad. He'd prefer you come home. It's the least you can do."

"I have a life here, a life I'm not ready to give up, nor am I able to care for a sick husband."

"I've arrangement for day and night help. I don't expect you to care for him. He'll need moral support that only you can provide as his wife."

"Your children's needs take precedence over your father's. As you said, he will have around-the-clock help. How will you be able to cope without my help?"

“Mother, enough! Sarah will be sixteen soon, Audrey is entering kindergarten in the fall, and we have Pearl.”

“What about the boy? He’s this close to becoming a juvenile delinquent. He needs a firm hand to keep him in control.”

George smiled and waited for my father to respond. My father overlooked Grandmother’s last comment. “Your train leaves at ten on Saturday. That will give you enough time to pack. The children and I will drive you to the train station.”

“No, thank you. I’ll take a cab.”

I waited a few minutes before asking to be excused from the table. In my room, I began to dance and sing, “Ding dong, the witch is going.” Finally, we were getting back our home.

Later that night, I placed the pillow around my head, trying to drown out my grandmother’s weeping. I began to cry and hated myself for the way I had treated her. The following day, a Wednesday, I arrived home from school hoping to talk with her, but she was out. Pearl informed me she wasn’t due home until later that evening.

Thursday, I came home to find her packing two large suitcases. I asked, “Do you need any help?”

Grandmother turned. She was a broken woman, but it wasn’t long before the broken woman regained her strength. “You’re offering to help me?” Turning away from me, she said, “I bet you’re the one that fills your father’s head with all this nonsense. It’s no secret you hate me. You probably can’t wait till you’re head of the house. It’s what you’ve always wanted.”

I wondered if lying to her would ease her pain, but I knew she’d see right through me. “I’m not going to lie, I found your stay an intrusion of my father making a full recovery.”

“Don’t blame me for your father’s inability to face reality. I warned you he was weak. But I do respect your honesty. And if we’re being honest, tell me, did your mother think I was an uncaring, miserable witch?”

“My mother never spoke ill of anyone, not even you, but I bet you can’t say the same.”

Grandmother Holland smiled. "I thought your brother was just like me, but I might have underestimated you, Sarah Holland. You're more like me than George." She returned to her packing.

In the years to follow, Grandmother and I would be in a much better place.

* * * * *

Once Grandmother returned to New York, my brother was out of control. George became my main concern for living. I followed him whenever I could, questioned him about his choice in friends, and talked till I was blue in the face about how we were going to get away from all this, and the only way out was for him to get his grades back to where I knew they could be.

"George, I know you're smart. Hell, Mom even knew you were the brightest! George, I have a plan for us. In two years I graduate high school. I want to move to New York and attend NYU. I'll rent an apartment not far from Grandma Maggie's place. I want you to come live with me. You can finish high school in New York."

"You got it all figured out, this dream of yours, NYU, New York … You saving me from the inevitable—jail?"

"George, I'm not going to lie, I do worry about you. You and Dad are like night and day. Us moving away is the best thing."

"Your own apartment. And how are you paying for this dream of yours?"

"I've been saving, so have you, and I'm going to get our father to help. He owes us that much. He's not hurting for money. I heard him talking with Grandfather's attorney the other day. Grandfather appointed Dad executor to his estate."

"What does Grandfather's estate have to do with us?"

"It has nothing to do with us, but I know Dad would welcome the idea if it means keeping you out of trouble."

"What makes you think I want to live in New York? This is my home."

"You like living in this house with Dad, fighting all the time. Our mother is probably turning in her grave to see how you and Dad act toward each other. Even I don't get why you torment Dad. Just once, can you do what he asks of you?"

"I keep up with the chores, Dad has no complaints. Heck, I even help Pearl with Audrey!"

"I'm not talking about chores, George. He wants you to study, make something of yourself. He loves you, George."

"You're dreaming, Sarah. Dad only loved one person in his life, and that was Mom."

"He may not show us love like he did when Mom was alive, but I know he loves his children."

"That's what you want to believe. Dad pays no attention to Audrey. He pats her head, buys her books. If he noticed us at all, he'd notice that Audrey's not a normal little girl. She spends her spare time reading. She doesn't interact well with kids her age. Her teacher says she's gifted, I think she's weird."

"Are you blaming me for not taking an interest in Audrey?"

"I'm not blaming you, Sarah, but if we are being honest, I think we all blame Audrey for our mother's dying, especially Dad."

"George Holland, you take that back! No one blames Audrey for Mom's death, especially Dad."

Remembering that conversation still cuts through me like a knife. George was right; I did blame Audrey for my mother's death, and I blamed my father for not honoring my mother's wishes and naming her Rose. I've often asked myself over the years, Could a name have changed my feelings toward my sister?

George wakes. I ask, "Ready for lunch? There's a rest stop four miles ahead."

* * * * *

After using the restroom, George and I find a table.

"This salad is delicious. How's the BLT?"

"Good." My cell phone buzzes. Looking at the message, I inform George, "It's from Mary. Allison, Pete, and the kids arrived safely. She will text me during the week."

George acknowledges the news with a nod. "When are Rita and Burt due back from California?"

"Tomorrow. Rita's in charge of the retirement party for the reverend. It will be good to see him and some of our old friends."

"I'm sure Rita told everyone we're staying at the boardinghouse."

"It hasn't been called *the boardinghouse* for years. Today it's known as a *bed-and-breakfast.*" I smile. "We have five more hours before we reach Cleveland. You want to drive another three hours then stop for dinner before we check in? We can stop at that nice restaurant right outside of Cleveland. You know the one, George. Great steaks and even better martinis? With no traffic, we should arrive at the restaurant by six."

"Steak sounds good to me."

"Your turn to drive. I'll take the last two hours."

* * * * *

With the gas tank full, George makes his way back onto the highway.

"While you were asleep, George, my mind began to wander. I guess it's the trip back home that's stirring up memories."

"What memories?"

"I was thinking about our last summer trip to visit Grandma Maggie."

George turns to look out the side window.

"I'm sorry, does talking about Grandma Maggie upset you?"

"Funny you should mention Grandma. I thought about her yesterday when I unplugged the Christmas tree. Christmas always gets me thinking of Grandpa and Grandma. Christmas was their favorite holiday."

"Just like Mom and Dad."

"Well, Dad did until Mom … I guess you'll want to visit the grave first thing tomorrow?"

"Right after breakfast. I can go alone if you'd rather visit another day."

"I'll see how I feel tomorrow."

I rest my head back, remembering our last summer visit with Grandma Maggie.

Grandma's apartment had a clear view of the ocean. If I close my eyes, I can hear my father's voice as we boarded the train. "Sarah, Danny will meet you and your brother at Grand Central. If he's late, just stay put and he will find you." Danny was Grandpa's nephew from his younger brother. "Call me as soon as you arrive at Grandma's."

"I know the drill, Dad." I looked at my sister, who was standing next to our father, clutching a book to her chest, I bent down. "Audrey, can George and I get a kiss? We're going to be gone for six weeks this time. Will you miss us?" Audrey nodded. I pulled her close to me. She kissed my cheek, and I whispered in her ear, "When you get a little older, I'll take you to visit Grandma Maggie in New York. While I'm away, never forget, I love you with all my heart and soul."

My sister didn't respond, which was her usual reaction. George picked up Audrey, turned her around, and gave her a hug and kiss. "I'll miss you, little sis. I love you …" George stopped himself, knowing my father was close. He extended his hand to our father. "Goodbye." As usual, not an ounce of affection was passed between a father and his son. George boarded the train.

When George disappeared, I leaned in and hugged my father. "It's time to go."

My father wished me a safe trip. I smiled. "Maybe one year you and Audrey can come along?"

My father surprised me by saying, "We might come for a week at the end of the summer. I'll call to let you know."

Without another word, I boarded the train.

Waving goodbye to Audrey and my father from the window of the train, I whispered to George what my father said.

* * * * *

Danny met us at the train station, holding a sign that read, "Sarah and George Holland, Welcome."

On the drive, Danny told us how much our grandma was looking forward to our visit. I smiled, knowing that George and I were just as excited.

After Grandpa died, Grandma rented an apartment near to Grandpa's family. The area was called Sea Gate. The apartment was in walking distance to Coney Island beach and the amusement park. In the past two years, George and I had made friends with a few of the kids in the area, becoming good friends with a brother and sister, Camille and Jeff. Camille and I were the same age, George and Jeff one year apart, George being the older. Jeff was different from the boys George usually hung around with, but Jeff thought George was cool, and George liked the attention.

There was an elevator at the apartment house, and it took George a while to get used to the thing. Grandma Maggie was waiting in the hall when the elevator doors opened. George ran into her arms, and she showered him with kisses. George stepped aside, and I stopped dead in my tracks. Grandma had lost weight since Easter.

"Sarah," she whispered. I moved slowly into her arms, and she placed several kisses on my check.

George took Grandma's hand, and together they walked into the apartment. Danny and I followed. "Grandma, I've missed you so much!"

"Well, we have most of the summer to catch up. Come, I've made lunch." Turning to Danny, Grandma asked, "Danny, can you stay for lunch?"

"I have to get back to the shop, Aunt Maggie, but I'm all yours on Wednesday. Does eleven work for you?"

"Eleven is good. Thanks, Danny, and thank your father."

Danny worked for his father, and his father made sure he was available to chauffeur us around on Wednesdays, if we needed him.

The terrace door was opened, so George and I went outside to look at the ocean.

"It's still there," said Grandma.

I shouted back, "It's so beautiful, Grandma!"

"How was your train ride? Were you able to sleep?"

"Like a baby," said George.

I watched my grandma moving slowly around the kitchen. "Put your luggage in your room and come eat. You can unpack tonight."

I kept an eye on Grandma as we ate our lunch. "How are Audrey and your father?"

"Good," said George.

"I think they might come visit at the end of the summer if Dad can get the time off," I added.

Grandma was not surprised by the news, so I guessed my father had already mentioned the visit.

"Camille and Jeff are coming by at two. Thought you'd like to go to the beach for a swim. You're not going to believe how tall Jeff has grown since you last saw him."

George did most of the talking during lunch. I was amazed how George's personality changed when he was in the presence of my grandma. I knew my plan was what George needed to turn his life around.

A knock on the door interrupted George's story. "That must be Jeff. I'll get it."

"Jeff, Grandma was right. You must be six feet or more," said George.

"Hi, George! Five nine to be exact. Hi, Sarah! Camille said she'll meet us at the beach. She's with two of her friends. She can't wait to introduce you to them."

"I want to spend time with Grandma." I needed to plant my plan in Grandma's head. Turning to her, I said, "Maybe you and I can take a walk along the boardwalk?"

"I won't hear of it. There's plenty of time for walks. Go put on your swimsuits and make sure you don't swim too far from the lifeguard stand."

I open my eyes and stare at the sky. A vision of my grandma's face appears in my thoughts. Closing my eyes again, I remember the places Danny had taken us.

When Danny arrived on Wednesday, Grandma had a full day planned. The Museum of Natural History was on this week's schedule.

On the drive, Danny asked, "Sarah, your grandma said you're applying to NYU?"

"I am. This year I'm entering my junior year. My school counselor is going to help me with the application."

"What other colleges are you applying to?"

"None. Only NYU. I'm moving to New York to be with Grandma." I turned to smile at Grandma, but she turned her face away from me. I noticed Danny glancing at Grandma in the rearview mirror.

"Sarah's been dreaming of attending NYU ever since our mother died," said George.

Grandma looked at George at the mention of our mother. My grandma asked me, "Did you and your mother talk about you attending NYU, Sarah?"

I lied, "Yes, Grandma. I told her I wanted to be a lawyer. She said NYU was a good choice."

Grandma nodded in agreement then turned to look out the window.

First week of August, and I still had not talked with grandma about my plans of having George come live with me when I graduated high school. I would need her help convincing my father my plan could work.

July went by so fast, and Camille kept me busy. She introduced me to several of her boyfriends. One boy named Charlie had a crush on me. I wasn't interested in the boys back home, but Charlie was different. He was a little taller than me, handsome, and he knew the right things to say to a girl.

"So you have never kissed a boy. Do you think I could be your first, Sarah?"

"I'm waiting. I don't think a girl should be kissed before her sixteenth birthday."

"You'll be back home on your sixteenth birthday. I'll just have to come visit you in Cleveland."

"You'd travel that far just to kiss me on my sixteenth birthday?"

"I like you more than any other girl I've known."

Smiling at Charlie, I said, "If you're being honest about liking me, maybe, just maybe, I'll let you kiss me before I leave for home."

"I hope so. I really hope so."

Charlie did get his wish. He was the first boy I had ever kissed. In fact, I allowed him to kiss me more than once that August.

Time was running out, and I still hadn't gotten up the nerve to speak with Grandma. One night, I couldn't sleep. Overheated and thirsty, I woke and headed for the kitchen for a cool drink.

Walking into the kitchen, I felt a cool breeze from the terrace. Thinking Grandma had left the door open to air the apartment, I walked toward the breeze, hoping to step outside to cool myself off. But I stopped when I noticed my grandma sitting on the chair, wrapped in a blanket.

I stepped onto the terrace and asked, "Guess I'm not the only one bothered by the heat?"

As she turned toward me, I was mesmerized by the glow on her face. I was reminded of my mother and that day in the forest, how the sun shining on her face made her look angelic. The reflection of the moon off the ocean gave my grandma that same angelic look. I sat beside her then asked, "Grandma, is there something you're not telling me? Are you feeling well?"

My grandma smiled. "Sarah, this is your summer vacation. Don't tell me you've been spending this precious time worrying about me."

"Yes, I am worried about you. Tell me, Grandma, please. I have to know. I'd hate myself if anything were to happen to you and I wouldn't get the chance—"

"You don't want to miss the chance to say goodbye?"

"If I had known when Mom got out of the car that night, I wouldn't have let her go."

"I got to say goodbye to your grandpa. It doesn't make losing someone any easier. The goodbye I did get to share with your mother got me through the bad times. She was happy, sharing with me how excited you children were about the Christmas tree. Said she couldn't wait to see her dad and me. What I'm most grateful for is that I got to tell her how much I loved her before we said goodbye." Grandma sighed. "I'm not going to lie to you, Sarah, I have lost weight. My doctor is concerned. That's why he's scheduled a few test at the end of the summer."

"Why are you waiting so long?"

"A few weeks isn't going to change anything, sweetheart. I wanted to spend this time with my grandchildren."

"Is that why Dad and Audrey are coming to New York?"

"It will only be your father, Sarah. Audrey is going to stay home with Pearl. Your grandfather is not doing well. Your dad is going to spend some time at your grandparents' house. You'll go back together."

"I feel bad for Grandfather." Pausing, I searched for the words to ask. "Grandma, there's something I've been meaning to ask you."

"What is it, sweetheart?"

"In two years, I'm moving to New York. I hope I'll be accepted to NYU. If not, I'll attend whatever college will have me. I'll rent an apartment between the university and your place. I was wondering if you would help me convince Dad to let George come live with me. He can finish his two years of high school here in New York."

"Sarah, I don't think your father would even consider such a request."

"Grandma, you have to help me. George and Dad don't get along. They're always fighting. George is always getting into trouble. I can't leave him behind! Please, Grandma, help me convince Dad that you will keep a watchful eye over George. I promise I'll make sure George does his homework and graduates. Can't you see how much happier George is here with you?"

My grandma reached out and took me in her arms. "Oh, Sarah, it breaks my heart hearing that George and your father aren't getting along, but do you know what you're asking?"

"I'm asking you to help me save George."

At that moment, George stepped out onto the terrace. "Grandma, don't listen to Sarah. She's a worrier. Dad is being a dad, and I'm just a son who hates being told what to do."

I was embarrassed that George overheard what I told Grandma and appalled that he lied about his relationship with our father.

"George, I don't think Sarah would be this concerned if she didn't think the problem between you and your father is seriously endangering your future."

George lowered himself to my level and spoke softly to our grandma. "Grandma, I heard you tell Sarah you haven't been feeling well. Sarah had no right to worry you. She has this dream of moving to New York, but it is her dream. I have plans of my own. Maybe New York, maybe not."

"George, everyone is entitled to their own dreams, but you're not going to reach your dreams if you defy your father and not do well in school. I won't tolerate bad behavior."

George laughed. "Grandma, you sound like Grandmother Holland. I promise to do better in school and give Dad some slack, cross my heart. I'll keep my curfew, but I can't take on more chores than I've already been assigned. That's impossible!"

Grandma smiled and took George in her arms, "Thank you, George."

Grandma sent us off to bed, and as we walked toward our rooms, I confronted George. "You lied, George, about your relationship with Dad."

George whispered, "That's right, I lied, but you forced me to lie. You think you're all high and mighty, making decisions for me. Stay out of my life, Sarah."

That was the straw that broke the camel's back. "You're on your own. Screw up your life! I don't give a shit."

My mood for the remainder of our vacation didn't go unnoticed by Grandma.

"Sarah, why the sad face?"

"I'm worried about you. I wish I could move to New York and finish high school to be here with you."

"Two years will go by quickly."

"Anything can happen in two years. Grandma, you have to promise me that you'll tell me the truth if the doctors—"

"Sarah, you are a worrier. Let's hope it's nothing."

* * * * *

The second week of August, my grandfather Holland passed away. It was the first time I had seen my grandmother Holland since she left our house. The year hadn't been kind to her. She was officially an old woman, but she hadn't lost that mean streak she played so well. Sitting in her well-manicured living room, she chatted with Grandma. "How are you feeling, Margaret?"

"Not too bad."

"I heard you're moving into one of those facilities. I'm sure it won't be long before this one has me placed in one." This was the first I was hearing about a facility and a move.

"Catherine, I don't think Will has any intentions of removing you from your home."

"This house is worth a lot of money, but I have news for sonny. The only way I'm leaving this house is in a body bag."

"Mother, please," said my father.

Grandmother Holland looked over at the sofa where George and I were sitting.

"Do you know how lucky you are? Your grandfather remembered you in his will. If it were up to me, I'd have spent every dime or left it to charity, after how I was treated in your home."

I never disliked anyone as much as I disliked Grandmother Holland. "Then I guess we're lucky that Grandfather didn't ask your advice"

"Sarah," said Grandma Maggie.

Speaking to my father, Grandmother Holland asked, "Are you going to allow this little twit to speak to me in that tone?"

"Sarah, enough," said my father to me. Then gently speaking to Grandma, he said, "Maggie, it's been a long day. I'll have the driver take you and the children back to your apartment. I have to meet with the lawyers during the next several days. I'll see you on Tuesday."

"Take all the time you need." Grandma stood, and so did George and I. "I'll keep in touch, Catherine. Again, I'm so sorry for your loss."

George kissed our grandmother goodbye. Standing in front of her, I said, "Goodbye."

* * * * *

Later that day, I confronted Grandma about her move and why she neglected to tell me.

"Sarah, I'm moving into a building with people my own age. I'll still have a view of the ocean, but no terrace. I'll miss the terrace, but the building has a beautiful courtyard, where I can read and visit with my friends."

"Why the move? I know you're not telling me the truth. You're sick, that's why you're moving. This building is a care facility. We have them back home. They're called *nursing homes*."

"There is a doctor affiliated with the building in case of an emergency. I have my own apartment, two bedrooms, living room, small dining area, and an adequate kitchen. The rent is less, and as I said, I have a number of friends already living there."

"It doesn't sound like there is enough room for George and me to visit."

"We will make do."

* * * * *

Tuesday, George and I went to the beach with our friends to avoid our father's visit. Upon our return, our father greeted us at the elevator. "Did you have fun at the beach?"

I responded for George and me. "Yes."

"Your grandma has plans for tonight. She said it's a special dinner, with the family."

George and I entered the apartment with Dad. "Good. Right on time. Children, go clean up. We're having dinner at a restaurant tonight," said Grandma.

Danny arrived to drive us. When we entered the restaurant, we were greeted by people George and I had never met. Dad seemed to know some of the guests. They showered him with condolences on his father's passing, and then the party began.

The guests were singing, dancing, and drinking beer, lots of beer. I asked, "Grandma, what are we celebrating?"

"We're celebrating your family's visit. I wanted my family and friends to meet my grandchildren. I wish Audrey could be here, but we can't have everything we wish for now, can we? Come, let me introduce you to my friends. It will make you feel better about my move. Many of them already live at the building, and some attended your mother and father's wedding."

Grandma called to a friend. "Alice, meet Sarah. What did I tell you? Erin at this age! Do you see the resemblance?"

"You never lie, Maggie. She's Erin, all right, but I've seen a picture of that little one, Audrey. Erin through and through."

I notice the look on my father's face when my mother's name was mentioned. Amazing to me, George, didn't leave my father's side the entire evening. George and dad were gracious when spoken to, but for the most part, they just sat and watched the festivities.

The following morning at breakfast, grandma described the place she would soon call home. "It's really nice, Will. My room faces the ocean. Danny will handle my care. I'll have help four hours a day at first, then longer as needed."

I felt sick to my stomach listening to grandma describe what sounded like her final days. Her voice was filled with hope, but all I heard was despair.

"It sounds nice, Maggie. I'm sure you've made the right decision."

"It's the best decision for me, Will. I've depended on the family long enough."

I interrupted and said. "We're your family. You should be coming home with us."

"Sarah, I can't leave New York. It's my home. And in two years, New York will be your home."

My father didn't flinch hearing of my plans to move to New York.

* * * * *

Summer vacation was over. With Grandma standing by our sides, George and I took one last look at the ocean from Grandma's terrace. George's eyes were glassy when he said goodbye to Grandma. "Grandma, Christmas isn't that far off." Then he whispered, "I love you with all my heart and soul."

When it was my turn to say goodbye, I held back the tears. "Dad said we'll be coming for Christmas. Grandmother Holland can't make the trip, so I'll see you in four months. Remember, you promised to let me know the results of your tests."

"Cross my heart. I'll call as soon as I know."

"I love you, Grandma, with all my heart and soul."

My grandma smiled. "I love you with all my heart and soul. You promise to give Audrey a big hug and kiss from her grandma."

Back home in Cleveland, not a day went by that I didn't pray that Grandma's test showed no abnormalities.

One month later, we would hear that there was a small spot on Grandma's lung. The doctor prescribed medication and, in six months, another x-ray to check for any changes, good or bad.

My family couldn't wait for Christmas and our trip to New York. I would spend Christmas vacation at Grandma's, and George, Audrey, and Dad with Grandmother Holland. The guilt I was feeling about Grandma subsided when I greeted her that Christmas. She had gained a little weight, her apartment was cozy, and I felt comfortable in her new surroundings. There was a view of the ocean, though not as impressive as the view from the terrace. Female and male friends stopped by for tea and small talk. The courtyard faced east, and several blocks from the building was the beach, the ocean's scent filling the air.

We spent Christmas Eve and Christmas Day at Grandmother Holland's. She, too, seemed to have improved since the summer. She yelled out orders to her servants and her male caretaker. She still had the luxury of a driver, so we were escorted to Christmas Eve services, too, and from Grandma Maggie's house and a beautiful New Year's Eve dinner at the Hilton.

I was convinced my grandfather Holland provided well for his wife and son.

* * * * *

We arrive at the restaurant at four.

"Doesn't feel like we've been driving for three hours, does it?"

"Three hours exactly. You were asleep for two of those hours."

"I can't believe I slept that long."

A young lady informs us a table for two will be available in twenty minutes. George and I agree to wait at the bar.

George orders a beer, while I order a dry martini with three olives. Highlights of the prior week's football games are airing on ESPN. George listens attentively as the narrator comments on the strengths and weaknesses of each team.

"I think the Giants will make the playoffs."

"Your guess is as good as theirs."

"I think they have a chance."

"How can a girl from Cleveland be a Giants fan?"

"When I moved to New York, I became a fan."

I enjoy spending time with George, although I do most of the talking, which is normal, since George is a man of few words. I know we aren't getting any younger and our time together is precious.

"I can't wait to see Rita and Burt! It's been a while."

George agrees.

"Do you miss small-town living, George?"

"Can't say that I do or I don't."

"Sometimes I miss that neighborly setting. Good times, bad times, you can always count on your neighbors. But Grandma Maggie lived in the city, and she had a lot of friends, especially when she moved to home care. Remember, George?"

George stares into space. I have gone too far by bringing up our past.

"Does it bother you, all this talk about the past?"

George smiles. "You have been obsessed about the past ever since Patrick died."

"Patrick's death seems to have opened up old wounds for me."

"You don't practice what you preach, Sarah. You tell Allison she has to move on, but over the past few months, all you've done is reflect on the past. In May, when you received the invite to the reverend's retirement party, you declined, saying you didn't want to travel during this time of year. Then two weeks ago, you changed your mind. Why?"

The hostess interrupts George. "Your table is ready."

"Great. I'm starving!"

At the table, I decide George deserves an answer to his question. "In answer to your question, all I can say is, Patrick's death was a shock. Seems like my whole life has been nothing but one shock after another. Anyway, it's been a while since I visited the grave, so I reconsidered attending the reverend's retirement party. Thanks for agreeing to come along."

* * * * *

Back on the road, I start to analyze my actions since Patrick's sudden passing. George is right; I'm not practicing what I have preached to Allison about moving on, reflecting on the words Grandma Maggie instilled in me: "We don't have the power to turn back the clock, so as time marches on, so should we."

* * * * *

After I had set aside my obsession of George moving to New York with me, another obsession controlled my life, getting accepted to New York University. In my third year of high school, I was assigned Mr. Novak as my guidance counselor. I smile remembering how jealous Peggy was when she heard. Mr. Novak was in his early thirties and good-looking. He was young enough to understand my plight and quite willing to help me see my dream to fruition. We worked together creating an impressive application that I would submit in the fall to NYU. Mr. Novak expressed concern that I was storing all my eggs in one basket.

"Sarah, there are so many good universities. What about Michigan, Ohio State, Northwestern? You need to apply to more than one university."

"Mr. Novak, why would NYU reject me? I'm a straight A student."

"Sarah, universities look for more than just good grades."

"What more is there? If I don't have the grades, I won't be able to keep up."

"Universities look for well-rounded individuals, such as how involved you are with your school and community."

"I'm involved with the church."

"You attend services. That doesn't count."

"Tell me what I have to do, and I'll do it."

"I'm having a hard time writing a letter describing the woman Sarah Holland has become. I'm stymied after I finish writing about what an excellent student you are. If I had to write a letter of acceptance for George, I wouldn't have an issue writing about his accomplishments as an athlete."

"I'm sorry I don't possess my brother's attributes as an athlete, but I would think it harder to explain George's fluctuating grades. Anyway, what does George have that would be of interest to NYU?"

Mr. Novak defends George by saying, "I can sum George up in a paragraph. He's smart but unwilling to let the world see how smart he is. If he had given permission to have his science project entered in the science fair, he would have won state and probably came in second or third across the nation. He speaks fluent Spanish but maintains a C on tests instead of earning an A. He's not fooling anyone, he's quite intelligent. My letter would … most universities, they'd welcome the challenge to help George see the errors of his ways."

"Let me shed some light. George is rebelling against our father. Haven't any of you figured that out? My father preaches good grades, George defies him. I've tried to talk with George. If he's not going to listen to me, his own sister, what makes you think the professors at any university will get through to him? Just tell me what I have to do to make your writing that letter a lot easier."

"It's simple: get involved. You're not involved in one school organization. Your writing is exceptional. When the school paper posted a need for a reporter, I thought for sure you'd apply, but you didn't. Just like your brother, you're fluent in Spanish. Think outside the box. Approach the reverend and ask him if you can run a Saturday-morning class for the parents and children trying to make the transition from Spanish to English. This is what makes Sarah a well-rounded individual."

"Then I'll get involved. It's not too late, is it?"

"Better late than never. I can hold off writing the letter."

* * * * *

I began an English-speaking class at the parish. I was overwhelmed with how many parents and children showed up for the class. I spent Saturday mornings with Audrey, so I brought her along for the one-hour session, and within a year, Audrey was speaking full sentences in Spanish.

I needed to get involved at school, and so I begged for a job on the school paper, as Mr. Novak had suggested, and found I actually enjoyed the work. I sought the help of my friend Peggy. Peggy was elected class president in our sophomore year and held the position until graduation. She was good at organizing school dances, class trips, and any event of interest to our classmates. Peggy put herself out there to get the attention of the opposite sex. Since I had no interest in the opposite sex, she didn't see me as a threat and agreed to make me her assistant.

Then midyear, Michael Pratt moved in to our neighborhood. He was the middle child in his family. His eldest brother was in his first year of college at Pitt, the youngest seventh grade. Peggy fell madly in love with Michael, and Michael fell madly in love with me. After a few months, Peggy moved on, leaving the door wide open for Michael to become my first serious boyfriend.

I smile to myself remembering how George teased me when he heard through the grapevine at school that Michael Pratt was head over heels in love with me. "Sarah and Michael sitting in a tree.

What's Dad going to say when he finds out his precious little girl has a boyfriend?"

"I don't care what Dad thinks. And don't you dare tell him, George Holland! I've kept most of your secrets. You owe me."

"Maybe if I tell him you have a boyfriend, he'll get off my back and start focusing on his favorite child."

"Dad doesn't have a favorite child."

I never stopped worrying about George, as I had told him I would. I still held out hope that George would agree to move to New York when I graduated. I dropped the issue for now, but when, and if, I received an acceptance letter from NYU, I would start a dialogue on how we could both benefit by moving far away from this town.

There were times I underestimated George. In the summer before he started his freshman year, George tried out for the football team. The coaches were impressed by his performance in every position, but especially his ability to play quarterback. George had the talent the school board had been hoping for. The coaches would play the senior that year, but the junior that was hoping to play quarterback next year would soon find out there would be tryouts for the position. The school was dreaming of a state trophy, and George was their hope.

During his freshman year, George's bad behavior went unnoticed. The football standings that year: ten wins, four losses, with George playing defense. The school stats hadn't seen ten wins for quite some time. Baseball season, George proved to be the best pitcher on the team. The coaches played him often, and the baseball team won state for the first time in twenty years.

The thought crossed my mind that George might be planning his own escape through sports. The beginning of George's sophomore year, he earned the quarterback position.

George took a new approach at getting passable grades, because without good grades, he couldn't play sports.

Better grades did not stop the fighting at home, though. The fights escalated with my father threatening to pull George from the sports program and George threatening if he did, he would leave home in a heartbeat and never look back.

These fights occurred at night; the pillow covering my ears wasn't working. One night, I stormed from my room to the foyer of our home, where most of the fights occurred. The fight was over George not keeping the curfew my father had put in place.

I stormed down the stairs and yelled, "Stop it! There are other people living in this house besides you two!" Turning toward my dad, I asked, "Can't you see he's not going to keep a curfew, especially one given by you? His grades are improving! Can't you just be satisfied that he's trying? And you, your bad behavior … it's just so he'll notice you exist. Some attention is better than none, I get it."

George ran past me. I called to him. "George, stop running away! Tell him how you feel."

George slammed the door behind him, leaving me alone with our father. Turning toward him, I said, "Maybe now we can get some sleep. Good night, Dad." I climbed the stairs hoping that my father would stop me to talk, but he remained silent.

Changes seemed to be happening every day. I put my obsession with NYU aside and tried to enjoy my life. Thanks to Mr. Novak's advice, I found getting involved rewarding, and I was spending more time with Audrey. I knew I was smart—my grades proved it—but George and Audrey possessed a natural ability to learn.

Audrey's love of books was no secret, but her ability to read and comprehend went unnoticed until Mrs. Gould called my father to school to inform him his daughter was gifted. I blamed myself for not seeing what was so obvious; the lack of bonding as an infant had affected my sister emotionally and mentally. She found a way to bond with the characters in her books. Knowing this, I began conversing about the stories in those books. Once I asked what she wanted to be when she grew up, thinking her response would be a princess or a pirate, but her response was simple: she didn't know. Guilt in me was building by the knowledge that in a short time, I would be moving away from home, and I couldn't help but wonder what would happen to this little girl. I decided to confide in her that I would be leaving home soon to attend college. How did she feel about my leaving?

"Audrey, I'm going off to college soon, living away from home. My dream is to become a lawyer. Maybe someday you'll have the same dream or a dream of your own. How do you feel about me moving so far away?"

Audrey's response both impressed and disappointed me. Impressed that she spoke three full sentences, but disappointed she showed no remorse regarding my moving away. "I know. Where are you going to live, Sarah?"

"I'm hoping New York, not far from Grandma Maggie, and Grandmother. Maybe someday you might come live with me in New York."

"I don't want to live in New York. Too many people. I like where we live. I think I'll stay here with Dad and Pearl, but I'll visit you when I visit our grandmothers."

"You sound like our brother." Audrey looked confused by my comment. "Maybe you'll change your mind when you come visit and see how much fun I'm having living in New York."

"I don't think so."

I wanted to wring her neck. Was I really related to George and this little girl? She was nothing like me or our mother. I hated myself for the next unpleasant thought: she might be as beautiful as our mother, but she was dull and boring like our dad.

Mr. Novak put pen to paper. The letter that would accompany my applications—yes, *applications*—described a woman secure in herself, humble, passionate, and able to overcome adversity, such as the loss of her mother at an early age.

I received acceptance letters from three of the colleges I had applied to, but not NYU. Senior year began, and I still hadn't heard from them. With the new year soon approaching, I'd have to make a decision on one of the other three colleges.

"Michigan State is a great college," said Michael.

"It's cold there."

"It's cold in New York."

"It's freezing in Michigan. New York weather is bearable."

"I wish you had chosen a college closer to home. You know, with you in New York and me in Pittsburgh ... when will we see each other?"

"During the holidays."

"You spend the holidays in New York with your family."

"We'll see each other, I promise." That was a promise I had no intention of keeping. Wherever I went to college, my relationship with Michael would surely come to an end.

Early March, my dad informed us we'd be spending Easter in New York with my grandmothers. I wasn't looking forward to the trip, until the day I arrived home from school and Pearl handed me a letter. In the left-hand corner of the envelope, the school name appeared: New York University. My hands began to shake. This letter would change my life forever. At this late date, I was sure it was a letter informing me that my application was denied. I dropped into the chair nearest me and stared at the envelope.

Pearl, noticing that I wasn't in a haste to open the letter, asked, "For months you've waited for that letter to arrive, and now that it has, you aren't in a rush to open it. Why?"

"It's probably a rejection letter."

"I know you're a smart girl, Sarah, but I didn't know you had the powers."

"The powers?" I asked.

"Yes, the power to read a letter without opening it." Pearl smiled. She sat across from me. "Sarah, I've been with your family long enough to know what's in your heart. That letter doesn't change anything, it just changes how you'll reach your goal. How many times have you told me that your grandma Maggie said you can't change what's already happened? You have to move forward and make the best of it. My mother, would say, 'If the good Lord gave you two good hands and two good feet, then just keep doing and moving. You owe him that much.' I never did pay much mind to what Ma said, but I do know the letter is not going to open itself, but those hands will, and those feet will take the next step."

That night, I lay in bed. Pearl's words kept ringing in my head. Only my hands could decide what steps I needed to take to reach my dream. Flicking on the light, I sat with the letter in my hands and tore open the envelope. Reading the letter, I knew my hands had accomplished their task, and my feet were ready to take the next step.

That morning, I announced to my family, which included our beloved Pearl, that I had been accepted to NYU.

* * * * *

I was walking on air. Running into Mr. Novak's office, I threw my arms around him and said, "I'm in! Thank you, Mr. Novak, for all your help! I'll never forget you."

After school, I placed a call to Grandma. "I got in, Grandma! NYU! We're coming to visit at Easter time. I want to visit the campus again. God finally answered my prayers! I was starting to doubt he existed."

As I was sitting in my room, looking through magazines, there was a knock on the door.

"Come in, George."

The door cracked open. "Sorry to disappoint you, but it's only me. George isn't home."

Jumping from my bed, I walked to my desk and moved the chair for my father to sit.

When seated, he clasped his hands together and leaned on his knees. Lowering his head, he began, "I'm proud of you, Sarah. NYU … that's a great accomplishment. Your mother …"

Moving closer, I placed my hand on Dad's. "I know, Dad."

"Your grandma told me you'd like to visit the campus during Easter. Would you mind if I join you?"

My heart jumped in my chest. "I'd like that, Dad. Dad, I don't want to live on campus. I'd rather rent an apartment not far from Grandma. I'm going to get a job, part-time. Of course, my grades come first."

"I thought one of the great things about going away to college was living on campus."

"I want to rent an apartment near school but a train ride away from Grandma. I'm sure with the money I've saved and working, I'll be fine."

"Money isn't a problem, Sarah. That's why I wanted to talk with you. Your grandfather Holland created a trust for each of his grandchildren, stipulating that you receive a monthly allowance starting at the age of twenty-five, earlier if you continue your education beyond high school."

"Can I try it on my own at first? And if I run into a problem—"

"Sarah, you want to be independent, and I respect you for that, but I would like to provide for your college expense and rent. I'll leave the food and utility costs to you." My father smiled. "I don't have to lecture you on getting good grades. You're a model student, so I've been told many times over the years."

"Thanks, Dad."

Rising to leave, he said, "I just wanted to have this talk, ease your mind a little about the cost."

As he headed toward the door, I called to him, "Dad." I really didn't know what I wanted to say, but he stopped to listen. So I continued. "Dad, there's another reason why I choose an apartment over the campus. I was hoping you'd allow George to come and live with me and Grandma in New York." I had my father's attention, so I continued, "I'm afraid to leave George and you. He's a different person when he's around Grandma Maggie. I think she reminds him of Mom. You can oversee George's expenses, and I promise you and Grandma that I will keep a watchful eye on him. Please, Dad, say yes. I think it's best for the two of you."

My father lowered his head; he didn't answer immediately. Then in a voice so low, he said, "Has your brother asked to go with you to New York?"

"No, Dad. He doesn't even know I'm asking. I didn't want to mention it unless I had your approval."

My father paused to think before answering. "In two years, George will graduate high school, but two years is a long time, and I don't know if living in this town is good for the boy. But to allow a boy George's age to go off with his sister to live in another city …"

"Dad, I know it's hard, but you have to think of George. George would die rather than disappoint Grandma Maggie. This can be the best thing for George."

"Sarah, it's no secret your grandma is sick and getting on in age. I can't ask her to take on caring for your brother."

"Grandma comes alive when she's with us. I promise we will not depend on her to care for us. I want to give George this opportunity."

Dad contemplated my request. "If your brother wants to move to New York with you, I will agree to the move and make all the arrangements to make it happen, but if it doesn't work out, or he … then he has two choices: come home or make his own way in the world. His choice."

* * * * *

I couldn't wait to share the news with George, so I asked him to lunch.

"Lunch, you're asking me to lunch? Is Audrey coming?"

"No, just you and me."

"Lunch, you and me, no Audrey. Is Michael tagging along?"

"No, just you and me. Are you going deaf? I'm inviting you to lunch. Are you coming or not?"

"Only if we go to the diner. I like the diner."

"Not the one in town. Everyone goes there. We won't have any privacy."

"Why do we need privacy? What's going on?"

"Are you going to meet me or not? I'm meeting Peggy at Feldman's at ten, I have to pick up my and Audrey's Easter outfits. There's a diner not far from Feldman's on Hatfield. Meet me at twelve."

"I have practice till eleven thirty. Twelve thirty."

* * * * *

George arrived at twelve twenty-five. The bus was late, so I arrived twenty minutes later, and by the look on George's face, ten more minutes and he would have left.

"Sorry, the bus was late. Weren't you going to wait?"

"I've been sitting here for half an hour. I thought you weren't coming. That waitress has been giving me the evil eye ever since I sat down."

"She thinks you're cute. She's pretty cute herself. Not much older than you, maybe a year."

"Yeah, I don't need another girlfriend. My plate is full."

George had his share of girlfriends, what with his being the star athlete. It came with the territory, and several girls asked me to put in a good word on their behalf. But George's love life was of no interest to me.

We placed an order, two cheeseburgers, fries, onion rings, and two bottles of Coke.

"All right, why the lunch? Why the privacy?"

"I have great news. Dad gave his permission for you to move to New York with me."

"What?"

"I asked Dad if you can move to New York with me in September. He said it was your decision. That's great news, isn't it? You are free to go—no more fighting with Dad. I'm going to rent an apartment, two bedrooms. The deal is, you have to keep up your grades, no getting into trouble, because if you do, you'll be forced to come home or take care of yourself."

George wasn't as enthusiastic as I thought he'd be.

"What's wrong? Isn't that great news?"

"Dad gave his permission for me to move with you to New York. Isn't that sweet! He's found a way to get rid of me for good, no more fighting, no more problem child?"

"No, that isn't true. He left the decision up to you. You can't tell me living in New York isn't a step up from living here. I'd rest easier knowing you were with me than getting into all kinds of trouble and fighting with Dad just to get him to notice you."

"He'd agree if I said yes. He didn't right out say no. He didn't put his foot down and insist I finish high school first."

"He said it was your decision. He left it up to you."

The cute girl placed our lunch before us. "Can I get you anything else?"

I said, "No, we're fine. Thank you."

George stared at the food in front of him.

"George, think about the opportunity Dad's giving you. He's not trying to get rid of you, he's thinking of your well-being. There's nothing here for you."

"Sarah, don't you think you should have asked me before asking Dad? Do you know what it's going to be like for me living with Dad and knowing he was willing to ship me off rather than spend one more day living under the same roof as me?" George pushed his plate away. "I told you over and over, Sarah, New York is your dream, not mine."

"I was thinking of you and your future. I don't understand why you wouldn't jump at the chance to get away. When will you stop wanting his approval? Think of yourself and what's best for you. I'm offering you a way out. I wish I could make the same offer to Audrey, but I have no way of caring for a child. Be grateful for what I'm trying to do for you!"

George softened, and his silence gave me hope. "Thanks for the offer, sis, but no, thanks. Dad's stuck with me until I decide what I want to do with my life. Actually, I'm pretty happy with my life and this town. Thanks for the lunch, but I'm out of here."

I grabbed George by the arm as he passed to leave. "You're making a mistake. I'm not leaving tomorrow. Please promise you'll consider my offer. I love you, George, with all my heart and soul."

George squeezed my hand. "I know you do, Sarah, I know you do."

* * * * *

I knew that day George would never agree to the move to New York, so I told myself I did all I could and now it was time to concentrate on enjoying my last few months of high school.

Peggy took charge of the senior prom with me as her assistant. Together we would plan the prom our classmates would never forget.

I accepted Michael's invite to the prom and found the perfect dress.

I sat in the backyard with my hair in curlers, painting my nails. While Audrey read her latest book to me, George arrived home from baseball practice.

"Wow! I hope you're going for a better look than that!"

George was the only person that could awaken an emotion from Audrey—not a kiss or hug without asking, but she seemed to perk up when he was around.

George noticed the book in Audrey's hands. "Hi, kid! What's that you're reading?" Taking the book from Audrey's hands, he stated out loud, "*The Solar System*." George glanced in my direction. "Very interesting."

George took a seat on the step. "Are you excited about tonight? Heard Mike's pretty excited. He's hoping to get to first base before you run off to New York."

"George, not in front of Audrey!" I said. "He might be hoping, but it's not going to happen."

"I know that, but you can't blame the guy for trying."

Our dad pulled into the driveway. George watched as he exited the car. "Well, nice talking with you girls." George entered the house. Audrey and I had watched this scene play out so many times it didn't even faze us that George ran off before my father took one step toward us.

"Hi, Dad! You're home early."

Dad patted Audrey on the head and said, "It's a special night. I asked Pearl to make a special dinner for us. I'm going in to wash up."

* * * * *

As I sat at the dining room table in my robe, Pearl placed a fresh salad before everyone. Dad asked Pearl to join us, but as always, she refused, so we ate in silence.

When we finished the main course, Pearl placed a chocolate cake in front of me. "I made your favorite." Pearl was showing her age. I was partial to vanilla, and George chocolate. Rising, I placed a kiss on Pearl's cheek. "You're so good to me, Pearl. Thank you! It looks delicious. But why all the fuss? It's only a dance, not graduation."

Pearl glanced at Dad, and I followed her direction. In Dad's hand was a box. "I was going to give you this for your graduation, but Pearl convinced me it would look beautiful with your dress, so … happy early graduation."

Frozen in place by my father's show of affection, I slowly walked over to him. As I took the box from his hands, our eyes met. I reached down and hugged my dad. "Thanks, Dad."

Close to my ear, he whispered, "I love you, Sarah, with all my heart and soul."

I moved far enough away from him to notice a tear falling down his cheek. "I love you too, Dad, with all …" Choking up, I stopped. He smiled.

The box contained a delicate necklace, and from it hung a decent-size diamond surrounded by blue sapphires.

I had seen the necklace before; he had given my mother an identical one on their first wedding anniversary. I've worn the necklace often throughout my life. It hangs from my neck today. I place my left hand over the necklace, thinking about that day so long ago.

* * * * *

Seems like yesterday, the prom, graduation, and my move to New York.

I left for New York right after the July 4 picnic to room with Grandma Maggie and begin my search for an apartment. Grandma looked fragile, but she was overjoyed that I would be residing in New York.

"Here's one, Sarah, not far from college. Six train stops from my apartment. The rent is reasonable."

"It has two bedrooms, just in case George changes his mind."

With the help of the law firm originally hired by Grandfather Holland, whom my father continued to use, my father arranged for a letter-of-credit that allowed me to sign a two-year lease on the sweetest apartment ten blocks from the university and, as Grandma said, six train stops from her apartment.

The landlord, Mr. Parks, placed the key to my new apartment in my hand. "I was a little apprehensive to rent this apartment out to such a pretty young lady as yourself, but Mrs. Parks has the ability to know a good tenant versus a bad one. She said you have a good head on your shoulders. Told me not to worry about the rent. You know it's due the first of the month."

"Don't worry, Mr. Parks, I'll have the rent to you the day before the first. I promise it won't be late. I hope it's not a problem, but my sister and brother will visit over the holidays. I promise we'll be very quiet."

Mr. Parks smiled and said, "What you do in your apartment is your business. As long as you don't disturb the other tenants, we'll get along fine. I hope you don't mind Mrs. Parks checking in on you every so often. You might even come home to find a home-cooked meal outside your door."

"I don't have many friends in New York. I won't mind a little company now and then."

"NYU should keep you pretty busy. I'll make sure Mrs. Parks doesn't visit too often."

Walking around the apartment, I sized up which room I would take as my bedroom. I settled on the one with the largest closet space, with two windows that overlooked the main street, and the bathroom was right outside my bedroom door to the left. A fake window was centered high over the tub and shower, the hall light keeping the bathroom light day and night. The kitchen, dining area, and living area were one, and off this area was a second bedroom.

I sat on the floor and envisioned the furniture I would need to make my new home comfortable for me and for George and Audrey when they visited. A strange feeling of guilt came over me as I contemplated my leaving home. How could I abandon George and Audrey? Who would keep the peace while I was away?

I was startled by a loud sound outside my kitchen window. (It would take several months for me to recognize each sound—the backfiring of a bus, ambulance, and fire trucks, the horns and honks, the endless sounds of the city.)

With Danny's help, I furnished the apartment, took one last look, and was off to spend my last night with Grandma before leaving for Cleveland to begin packing up my belongings for my move in the middle of August.

Watching my grandma move around, filling our plates with dinner, I asked, "You're telling me the truth, the doctor was impressed with your latest blood work?"

"He said I was doing well. Thinks the move might have prolonged my life. I do like it here. Did I introduce you to Sam?"

I chuckled at the thought of my grandma having a male champion. "Yes, I did meet Sam. Think he has a crush on you."

"What would you know about crushes, Sarah Holland?"

"Grandma, I have a boyfriend back home. We went to the prom together. I sent you pictures."

"Yes. You looked beautiful, and Michael looked handsome in his tux. Long-distance relationships can be difficult, Michael heading west and you living on the East Coast. I think your romantic encounter might be nearing an end, just like Sam and me."

"Grandma, don't. I don't like when you talk that way. It was only a high school fling, but Sam and you will be around for some time."

Placing the plates down, Grandma sat across from me. "Sam's a nice guy. We take long walks by the ocean, reminisce about the early years, and I'm not going to deny, we've shared a kiss or two." Grandma laughed. "And I'll confess, he's a good kisser, not as good as your grandfather, but then no one can shine my Tim's shoes." She sighed. "I miss them every day, your mother and my Tim."

"I wish my father had … you know, maybe gone out, had some fun. I worry so much about them, Grandma."

My grandma reached for my hand. "You have to stop worrying. Your father is a grown man. He's chosen his path. I, too, wish he had chosen a different path, but it's the one he chose." Grandma leaned forward. "Do you know what I wish, Sarah?"

"What?"

"That someday you'll meet someone and have a family of your own to worry about."

The thought of knowing that my grandma would be a fixture in my life made my leaving home easier.

* * * * *

George interjects, and the memories are gone. "The bed-and-breakfast is right down the road. I need a hot shower and a good night's sleep."

After checking in, I say good night to George. "Breakfast is at nine. Should I wake you?"

"I'll be up at six. Probably take a long walk. I'll see you at breakfast."

"Don't get lost."

George laughs. "Always the worrier. Some things never change."

* * * * *

I could count on my hand the number of times George and I stood side by side at the grave.

I place a very large arrangement of fresh flowers into the water container. Pushing the can into the ground, I stare at the names on the large tombstone. I sigh softly as my eyes begin to tear.

"It's getting cold. I don't think the flowers will last through our visit."

"I'll come back and replace them before we leave," says George.

Silently I speak with my loved ones, saving the best stories for the two closest to my heart. Once I have shared my life and stories, I speak only to Audrey. *I'm worried about Allison. You need to watch over her.*

"Asking for guidance?" says George.

"No, help. Audrey's help. But you might want to ask our mom to intervene. You were her favorite." I smile.

"Sarah, I'm no fool. Allison would like nothing more than to push us totally out of her life. The only one stopping her is Pete."

I look toward George. "I know she'd like to disown me. That's why I'm trying to keep my distance, hoping we can salvage some sort of relationship."

"In your defense, I think she's acting like a child."

"Funny I felt the same way about you so many years ago, but then you were a child, so you had every right to act out."

George stares at the tombstone, and I'm sure the name he is eying is William James Holland.

"You know, George, I've often wondered, had Dad died instead of Mom, would our lives have been different? She was the stronger of the two."

"Maybe Dad's death would have had an adverse effect on you, then you could have been called the town delinquent." George and I smile at his comment. Going on, he says, "I don't know … I think I was doomed either way. If Mom had lived, I would have been a boy without a male figure to guide me. Actually, that was how it turned out."

I wonder why I have been spared the scars of our mother's passing. George wears the scars of rejection from our father, Audrey scarred by the lack of bonding with either parent.

"Every time I visit the grave since Dad died, I ask him why. I loved Dad, George. I know you did as well. As I grew older, I understood his pain, and I forgave him. How could I hate a man who loved our mother more than life itself?"

"I forgave him too."

I turn to George and ask, "Did you? When?"

"You know why I came back home to live?"

I shake my head. "No."

"When you wrote Dad's health was failing, I knew it was time to come home. I owed him that."

"Why did you feel you owed him, George?"

"I wanted the chance to ask why, but living under the same roof again didn't make my asking any easier. I often thought I should have accepted your offer and moved to New York, but I just couldn't give up the hope that someday, after winning a trophy, I'd look into the stands and he'd give me the thumbs-up, filled with pride for his only son."

"George …"

George is lost in his own world when he confesses standing with our father at this very grave. "I never shared this with you, I guess because I was embarrassed to repeat what happened."

Curious, I remain frozen and listen.

"You knew his routine, up at six, out the door by seven, a visit to her grave and home several hours later, but one day he woke at nine, found me, and asked if I wouldn't mind driving him to the cemetery. I dropped what I was doing and said, 'Of course.' We stood here just like we are standing now, but after several minutes, he dropped to his knees and began to sob. I was going to walk away, give him his privacy, but he called to me. 'Georgie,' he said, 'please kneel with me.' Hearing that name and the pitiful look on his face, I did as he asked. As I knelt next to him, he reached for my hand and begged for forgiveness. 'Can you ever forgive me, Georgie? I'm afraid to die. I'm afraid your mother will never forgive me if I don't make things right with you. I was wrong, Georgie. I should have been there for you and your sisters. How will your mother ever forgive me? I know you hate me, son, and you have every right to, but I couldn't be the father you needed me to be. When your mother died, she took my reason for living, but I should have lived for you and your sisters. I'm so sorry.'

"He collapsed in my arms, sobbing. I couldn't believe what I was hearing. Our father was asking to be forgiven by *me*. I didn't know whether to laugh or cry. I wanted to tell him it was too late, I'd never forgive him, but I knew there wasn't anything I wouldn't do to stop the pain he was feeling."

I have to know and ask, "What did you do?"

"I held him and told him there was nothing to forgive, that we never blamed him. It made us happy knowing how much he loved our mother. I lied."

I lower my head. "You did the right thing, George. He was in so much pain. He needed to be forgiven."

George smirks. "Looking back, I have to wonder, maybe our lives weren't that bad."

I smile. "See? I was right. It was time to come home and visit."

Taking George's arm, as I had done so many times during our lives, we walk away together. Grandma Maggie is right; we do not possess the power to turn back the hands of time and change the worst times in our lives, but what we do possess is the right to forgive and move on.

CHAPTER SEVEN

Allison

Five months have passed since Patrick's death and our Christmas trip to Florida.

Many different versions of the dream play in my head. Dancing together, laughing, lying together among the flowers, always ending with our standing before the preacher, waiting to hear, "I now pronounce you man and wife," and still unable to make out the face.

The dream is wearing on my nerves. When I do sleep, I feel happy. I dread facing the day, when I'm awake.

I return to work the second week in January. Kathy, my assistant, presents me with eight new cases. The children involved have already been placed in foster care. Their parents, coming down from their holiday high, realizing their children are gone, are sitting right outside my office.

My stress level is elevated not only by the dream, work, and Pete's traveling to Florida every three days, but I've also lost the ability to juggle work and home. I'm a woman on the edge.

Things that I've overlooked knowing life is too short to stress about have now become an obsession. I begin to nag and lecture my children about school and chores. Threatening to punish has never been a way I've chosen to get my point across, but now the threats are an everyday occurrence.

"If you don't help out, I'm not driving you to practice." Andrew's forgetfulness and Julia's whining about Andrew and her bitchy girlfriends are driving me insane.

The tension I feel is overwhelming, but Pete's ability to cope remains intact. During a phone conversation, which most times I half-listen to, I take pleasure when Pete confesses that the Florida office is wearing on his nerves. *Perfect Pete is losing it.*

Pete is running around like a chicken without a head to put out the fires created by Ray. Ray signed a three-year lease on office space. Ray's heart attack occurred several days before Ray was to meet with the lawyers to prepare the appropriate documents to file for a license to operate in the state of Florida. With all the confusion and Ray's hospitalization, the lawyers dropped a bomb—the documents were never signed or filed with the courts. The lawyers assured Pete they reached out to a higher authority to rush the licenses. Three months later, nothing. Pete had the office manager here in Connecticut working overtime to find extra cash to cover the rent on the Florida office.

January has also brought the news that Ray's health is not improving. Doctor's visits and bed rest have slowly become his new life. Pete has reached out to the landlord to see if he can sublet the space, but the lease specifies that the space cannot be sublet. Pete, with no other choice, has to bite the bullet and move forward. Traveling north to south and south to north is inevitable in trying to keep both offices operating, plus carving out time for his family.

When he is home, which isn't often, I half-listen to his work problems. If he's looking for a shoulder to cry on, I'm not available. Pushing the knife further through his heart, I say, "You should have held your ground and insisted Ray wait another year before opening an office in Florida. You're not Ray's office boy, you're an equal partner."

"If I only had a crystal ball."

"Life doesn't come with a crystal ball. You have to think outside the box. You allowed Ray to control you."

If Pete weren't discouraged enough, I had just dragged him through the mud.

"Gary thinks it's best to move forward. He said in a year or so, this will all be forgotten."

"Gary doesn't have to pay rent on an office that's not operating. Why are we talking about this? It doesn't change anything. Speaking of Gary, JoAnne wants to know when we'll have time to meet them for dinner. She thinks I've been avoiding them." JoAnne is right; I am avoiding seeing them. My excuse: Pete's never around, and when he is, we're busy with the children.

"Why don't we plan on seeing them next weekend?"

"Are you going to be here? Andrew has a game at two on Saturday. Of course, Julia's game is at nine. Maybe I can fit in a hair appointment between ten and one. Since you're not here most times during the week, it's become difficult to make time for myself."

"Why don't you ask your aunt to help out?"

"Is that your answer to every problem, ask my aunt for help? Anyway, the kids like to see a parent at their games. I'll work it out. Oh, shit, forget the hair appointment Saturday. I might have to work. I'm also backed up at work, being the only parent ..."

Pete is behind me. Placing his arms around my waist, he says, "I know my traveling has been hard on you and the kids. I promise I'll make it up to you."

Thinking what a bitch I've become and enjoying my new role, I turn on Pete. "You're lucky you get to put all this behind you and fly off to Florida. You might be stressed, but you have no idea what it's like for me."

"You have to know I hate being away from you and the kids."

"Then do something about it." I storm out of the kitchen and head for the bedroom.

Pete's answer to the problem, Gary recommends, is that Pete interview a CPA by the name of Emily Carter. Gary has worked with her on a construction project in Florida. She also comes with her own licenses and client base. She will manage the office, and in two years' time, if all goes well, there can be a partnership in it for her. Ray has also arranged for Emily to meet with his clients, and now there will be money to cover the rent. Of course, Emily can't handle all the clients on her own, so this doesn't cut down Pete's travels, and Pete still has to spend time with the attorneys to get the company licenses in place.

While Pete is trying hard to work out his problems, he works even harder at making our lives as normal as possible. But I, on the other hand, am working on a way to end my marriage.

I intended to speak with Pete as soon as we returned from Florida, but during our vacation, it became apparent to me that I was about to break my children's hearts. So I chickened out.

I devise a new plan: I will make myself unavailable to Pete, which, I hope, will result in a greater division and strain on our marriage. I know Pete is tiring of my complaining, so I escalate my bad behavior.

Pete has learned to keep his work problems to himself and become more attentive when he is home. This is not part of my plan, so I convince myself it is time for the talk, then I'll avoid the talk like the plague.

I also avoid dinner dates with friends. Date night with Pete is a thing of the past, and family dinners … well, I get through them. When Pete is home, I avoid going to the children's practices and games, using work as an excuse. I try to avoid any sexual encounters, but there are times when I welcome something other than the dream.

Pete is so understanding about my Saturdays at work. "I'd rather we spend time together, but if these few hours at work help make your week easier, I understand. The kids and I will be fine."

On the Saturdays I lie about working, I find myself at the lake, at Patrick's final resting place. I spend the time defending the decision I made all those years ago. "You left me no choice, Patrick. I had to consider …" This constant battle with Patrick is taking over my life. I have to make a decision. As the saying goes, "The truth will set you free."

Back home with my family, the strength I have at the lake diminishes as I watch Pete and the children interact. I fear becoming the outcast. My children will resent me for leaving their father.

Whenever I take notice of my reflection in a mirror, I see the woman I have become, uncaring, selfish, hard. I want back the woman I was.

If Pete notices the changes in me, he never brings it up or allows an open discussion. If he demanded to know what's wrong with me,

I know my unhappiness will flow like a river and I will ask to be free of our marriage.

The only people I am not fooling are JoAnne and Aunt Sarah. Aunt Sarah has kept her promise to me; she doesn't call. If I need her, she makes herself available, and if I need to vent, she listens. This should have changed my feelings toward her, but it hasn't, because I know once she hears I'm leaving Pete, I will have again been a failure in her eyes. Once a month after Sunday services, we share a dinner together as a family. Aunt Sarah makes sure the conversation is light and nonintrusive. "How is work?"

"Piling up. When I complete one file, three or four appear."

"Maybe it's time to hire someone."

"The State won't approve a new hire, not with the way the economy is headed. There are rumors of layoffs."

"Oh, sweetie, you're going to burn yourself out working so hard."

"I don't know how much longer I can go at this pace."

"Remember, I'm always here to help out. Just say the word."

Easter is fast approaching. It is my turn to host Easter dinner. I think about asking Dolores if she can host this year, but I want to keep up the appearance that all is well in Allison's world.

JoAnne isn't buying the overworked, no-time-for-anything stories. And I'm finding it hard to keep up a good front in front of JoAnne. She sees right through me.

"Why does it take you so long to return my calls?"

"I try, but there aren't any hours left in the day for talking. Work's become impossible, and with Pete being gone so often, I'm losing the ability to juggle."

"You can call me at night when the kids are asleep. You know I don't go to bed until midnight. It's a great time for you and me to catch up."

"I think about calling, but when my head hits the pillow, I'm out."

"Okay, I'm not hanging up until you give me a date. You can come to the city, or Gary and I will come to you guys. I won't take no for an answer."

"What about next Saturday? But I have to warn you, I can't promise Pete will be home, but I'll ask Aunt Sarah to sit with the kids, and I'll take the train to the city with or without him."

"I don't want you coming in by train, and I want to see the two of you. I'll make the reservation. If something comes up, let me know."

Pete already has said he may be spending the following Saturday in Florida, so I'm off the hook. I'm not expecting Gary to call Pete and Pete agreeing to take the red-eye home on Friday.

"I was so happy Pete was able to come this weekend. It's so good to see you guys! Last time we were together was St. Patrick's Day."

The name strikes a pang in my heart. "Yes, it was St. Patrick's Day."

"Pete said the kids are spending the night with Aunt Sarah. I guess you're seeing more of her, with Pete traveling so much?"

"I haven't seen her as much as you may think. I told you there aren't enough hours in the day. With Pete away, I try to be there for the kids."

"I'm so happy you guys will be staying the night. I think you both can use the rest. I ordered brunch for tomorrow. Should be here around eleven. Pete said he'd like to catch the four o'clock train back home. He has an early flight on Monday. I hate when Gary travels, but with the new hire, I'm assuming Pete would travel less?"

"By *new hire* you mean Emily Carter?"

"Have you met her?"

"No. All I know is she's smart and should be a great asset to the company."

"I met her. Did he tell you she's hot? I mean frying-pan hot!"

JoAnne's statement gets my attention. "He never mentioned she was hot."

"Charlize Theron hot, legs a mile long, blond hair, striking blue eyes, and a body to die for! If you want to check her out, she's on Facebook. I can't believe she's not married."

"She's single."

"Can you believe it? Maybe she prefers women? If it's women she prefers, I'm going to be pretty pissed. The night we met, I looked pretty hot, but I guess not hot enough for her to hit on me." JoAnne laughs.

I don't know why JoAnne's description of Emily Carter is bothering me, but it is.

On the train ride home the following day, I question Pete, "JoAnne says Emily Carter is a knockout. You only mentioned she was smart."

"She's smart, and I'm not going to lie, she's attractive, but the only thing about her that turns me on is her client base and her ability to get some cash rolling in."

"If she's so beautiful, how come some rich guy hasn't snatched her up?"

Pete smiles. "Maybe she prefers the muscular, blue-collar guys."

"You're not blue-collar, your kind of handsome, and the body ... well, it can use a little toning."

Pete laughs out loud. "Thanks for the compliment, I think."

"JoAnne suggested I check her out on Facebook."

Pete draws me to him. "It turns me on when you show your cat claws. Anyway, I prefer brunettes. Blondes don't do it for me."

"A normal man prefers blondes."

"This normal guy prefers you."

That night, I make love to Pete, not just the run-of-the-mill lovemaking, but one he won't soon forget. I'm ready to end my marriage, but I'm not ready to hand Pete over to Emily Carter. These feelings are conflicting. I can't get Pete and this Emily Carter out of my mind.

I lose sleep thinking about Emily Carter and spend my days wondering why.

Staring at the computer at work, I sign on to Facebook and search for Emily Carter. I find her as a friend under Gary's Facebook page. Two clicks later, I find Emily Carter.

JoAnne is right; she's beautiful. My next question: Why a Facebook page? She doesn't look like the type. Noticing her profile, I realize she hasn't updated her page since 2004. Just like me, she wants to be part of the new trend but has soon realized she has better things to do with her time.

For an entire week, I think about nothing but Emily Carter. The question I keep asking myself is, Once I end my marriage, can Emily Carter change Pete's mind about blondes? Emily Carter looks like the type of woman who can make a gay man question his sexuality. Is she the kind of woman who can offer a shoulder to cry on if there is a pot of gold at the end of her rainbow? Emily Carter definitely won't appreciate being called stepmom. I imagine her finding ways to exclude Andrew and Julia from Pete's life, sending my children off to boarding school. I have to snap myself back to reality. I'm not dead. Emily will have no say about my children's lives, or would she, once my separation from Pete becomes a reality?

Watching Andrew's baseball practice, Dr. Greenberg sits beside me.

"Mrs. Cane, it's been a while."

Looking up, I say, "Dr. Greenberg, so good to see you!"

He sits and says, "Last time we were together, we were on a first-name bases. Remember David."

"Hello, David. Remember Allison?" I search the field to find Ellen. "I didn't know Ellen was on the cheerleading team."

"She was a cheerleader at her prior school. She tried out in September but didn't make the team. She was devastated, then all the planets aligned, a girl dropped out, and here I sit cheering on my little girl. Pete was here when she cheered her first game. I believe you were at work?"

"With Pete traveling so often, I have no choice. I get so much accomplished working on Saturdays. No one to bother you."

Lying about working on Saturdays is becoming a reality for me.

David agrees; working on Saturdays is not a favorite of his, but what you can accomplish with no interruptions is amazing.

"Pete mentioned he's traveling, so you're experiencing firsthand what it's like to be a single parent?"

I take a moment to reflect on David's question, thinking this is what it will be like when I get around to asking Pete for a separation. "I guess I am. I thought life might get easier since Pete hired an office manager. Did he mention her to you, Emily Carter? I hear she's really good at her job."

"Ms. Carter, yes. He did mention he hired someone."

"He told you about Emily Carter?"

"Yes. He said hiring her took a huge weight off his shoulders."

I smile and think Pete has told Dr. Greenburg about Emily. I wonder, during their guy conversation, if Pete has mentioned she's hot.

"Did you say something, Allison?"

I cover up my expression by asking, "How is Mrs. Greenberg and your son?"

"Everyone's good, thanks for asking."

After the game, the kids beg and plead that we take them for cheeseburgers. Six boys, four girls, including Julia. The other parents go on to say the family is too busy for a cheeseburger break. I glance at David and ask, "You up for a cheeseburger?" After choosing the children according to the driving distance from our homes, we promise the parents their children will be home in three hours.

The kids are escorted to a table for ten, and David and I find a table for two directly across from them.

Watching the table of ten, David says, "Remember your high school days? Hamburgers, milkshakes, your favorite girl sitting next to you." He's referring to Andrew and Ellen.

"They sure do like each other, but in answer to your question, my favorite girl was my best friend, JoAnne."

"Are you trying to tell me something?"

"No. JoAnne wasn't a one-boyfriend kind of girl. We didn't hang around long enough in fear that certain demands might be asked of us. JoAnne and I were saving ourselves for college and the right guy."

"And how'd that work for you?"

"Dr. Greenberg—I mean, David, a girl never tells, but if you must know, there was someone else before Pete."

"Things were different back then. Sorry I can't say the same for my son. My wife and I tell him to be careful, and I hope he heard every word we said, but he's not Ellen. He likes to test the waters where Ellen thinks twice before jumping in."

"That's good to know. It's the opposite for me. Andrew is more like Ellen, Julia like your son. She'll test the waters. Pete and I will be gray before our time."

David is easy to talk with, and I truly enjoy my time with him, but more surprising, I haven't felt this relaxed in months.

*****

"Allison, let me help with Easter dinner. I'm willing to host it at our home."

"Thanks for offering, Aunt Sarah, but I like to have it at our home. I could use help with the shopping, though. Are you busy Saturday?"

My aunt is elated I've asked that she join me. "We could send the boys off with the children and make a day of it, a late lunch." Aunt Sarah offers to drive. "I'll pick you up at twelve. We can have lunch first."

*****

Aunt Sarah is in a joyful mood, excited to spend the day with me. I feel awful that my request to spend the day food-shopping brings on this kind of reaction. Why is it so hard for me to give this woman a few moments of my time?

"The quiche at this restaurant is to die for, so I'm opting for the quiche and a cup of onion soup. When I have a big lunch, I usually skip dinner. Uncle George can eat the leftover stew. Remind me to get a few rolls for home."

I place the order. "Today's quiche, two cups of onion soup, with a side salad, unsweetened ice tea, and one hot tea."

Aunt Sarah says, "Pete seems relaxed. I'm guessing things are moving along with the new office?"

"He's hired someone. Her name is Emily Carter. They made her an offer she couldn't refuse: 20 percent of her client base as a bonus and maybe partner in two years."

"Nice offer. Times have changed since I was a workingwoman. Good for Emily Carter."

"Makes me wonder if I should look for a job outside of social services. You did well as an attorney in the corporate world. Anyway, Gary recommended her, and you know how much Pete respects Gary's opinion. Pete was impressed with her client base, and she's easy to look at."

Aunt Sarah stares but doesn't ask if I'm bothered by this woman working so closely with my husband.

"I guess I should be grateful. Heck, once the operation is in full swing, it's not like Pete and Emily will be seeing each other every day." I'm talking like a woman who is in for the long haul with Pete, but in fact, I'm getting stronger about having the talk after Easter.

"And I'm sure Ray will be back at the helm soon?"

"I think Ray's working days are over. He's not doing well."

"I'm sorry to hear, but Pete said his doctors were optimistic. Has there been a change?"

"The doctors think Ray should take it easy, and so does Eve. I called several weeks ago, and Eve said she is demanding Ray and she enjoy their children and grandchildren. That was why she wanted to move to Florida in the first place. She was never on board with an office in Florida."

Lunch arrives. During lunch, Aunt Sarah makes idle chatter. I half-listen, as I've been doing since that God-awful day last November.

"I spoke with Hank and Mary. They're arriving on Holy Thursday. I offered our home, but she said she booked rooms at the Hilton since Pete's sisters were staying at the hotel."

"We offered our home as well. I can understand them wanting to stay at the hotel with the girls. Between my kids and their cousins, the house can get pretty loud. At the hotel, everyone can find a little refuge in their rooms." I know why I'm pleased Pete's family has decided to stay at the hotel; I'm having a hard time playing the role of good wife, daughter-in-law, and sister-in-law when I'm about to become an outsider.

"It will be nice to see everyone. Pete's family are good people."

"Speaking of family, I know this is going to sound strange, but did you ever keep in touch with my aunt Kerry? Do you know if she is still alive?"

"When your mother was alive, we'd exchange Christmas cards, but when your mother died, I did send a Christmas card that year and it was returned. When I was back in Cleveland this past January, Grace Perry told me she heard that your aunt and her husband had moved to Arizona. Three years after the move, your aunt passed away."

"She had one child?"

"Scott. He died in Vietnam. He was much older than you."

"I know."

"If your father's life hadn't been cut so short, I know he and your mother would have had more children. It's rough being an only child."

"I remember so little about my father, except his smile. I was close with him, wasn't I?"

"You worshipped him, as he did you. You were his little princess, his shining star."

"I remember how he used to swing me around, saying, 'You're as light as a feather, my little princess.'"

"He was a wonderful man, and you're right about his smile. I don't remember him without a smile on his face, and he knew how to make your mom laugh till it hurt."

"I can count on my hands the number of times I saw her smile."

* * * * *

The Saturday I spent with my aunt awakens sweet dreams of my father. The night he died, Aunt Sarah placed a picture of him in my room, which I left behind the day I went off to college. I make a mental note to look for the picture.

My father was a good-looking, well-built man with large hands and an even larger smile. As a little girl, I dreamed of him often and woke crying and calling for him. As I grew older, the dreams faded, but now I can see him so clearly when I close my eyes.

My grandfather and grandmother owned the lumber warehouse in our town, which, when my father became of age, he co-owned with his father. I remember waiting for him to return home from work, from the factory that would take his life and the life of a young boy.

When I was young, to keep my father alive in my heart, my aunt would tell me stories about him. I remember patiently waiting for the clock to strike five, and I would run to the door and watch for him as he made his way down our street. He would call my name as he got closer to our home, and I would run out and into his arms. He'd turn me around and around until I said stop, then he place me on the ground and we'd walk together into the house.

My father has been on my mind since Patrick's death. A few times he invades the dream, and I say, "Dad, I knew you'd come." He will smile that great smile of his, but no words will pass between us.

My father's silence also increases my stress level when I'm awake. I want him to speak as much as I want to see the face of the man in the white suit.

* * * * *

My mother and father were total opposites. He was warm and loving, she cold and uncaring. I can't remember my mother ever speaking of my father after his death. I would ask questions when I was young, and she would shy away from talking about him. Anything I wanted to know, I learned from my aunt. I asked my aunt why my mother refused to talk about my father. My aunt defended my mother's actions by saying it might be painful for her to remember how happy they once were.

Aunt Sarah was the one who comforted me the night he died, and many nights after, she told me when I wanted to talk with my father, I should look toward heaven, because he was now living with God.

My father was the younger of two children. Aunt Kerry, my father's sister, was seven years older than him. Aunt Kerry found working at the lumber factory boring; this was what my aunt said when I asked how Aunt Kerry and Uncle Billy met. Aunt Kerry took a job as a secretary at the steel mill, where she and Uncle Billy met. Uncle Billy was born and raised in California, and shortly after they married, they moved back to San Diego. Three years later, Scott was born. That was all I knew about Aunt Kerry.

The day my father died is one of my first memories. My fifth birthday was two months away. I remember sitting at the kitchen table, watching the clock as it struck four. Shortly after, my aunt Sarah and my grandpa Holland arrived at our home. Mom left with Grandpa, and my aunt tried to entertain me by coloring in the last coloring book my father bought me. When the clock struck five, I ran to the door and waited, with my aunt standing beside me.

As I grew older, I found out what happened the day my father didn't return home. My father was helping another man load lumber on his truck. The son of this man, a six-year-old boy, with a book of matches in his pants pocket, entered the lumber factory and struck a match. The boy didn't run from the building; it was assumed he hid behind a stack of wood, fearing he would be caught.

My father, first to see the flames, ran to sound the fire bell. The man, realizing his son was nowhere to be found, called out his name. The boy did not respond, and it soon became clear to my father that the boy was inside the building. My father ran into the building. My grandfather, hearing the commotion, ran out to see what was going on, and he noticed the flames and several men holding on to a man from entering the building. By the time my grandfather reached the men, the building was engulfed in flames. Shortly after, part of the roof collapsed onto my father and the boy he held in his arms.

The town honored my father for his heroic action. My grandmother and grandfather no longer wanted any part of the lumber business and decided not to rebuild. Grief-stricken, they decided to move to California to be near Aunt Kerry and her family.

My grandparents would call, I would inquire about my father, but my questions were unbearable for them. So the calls began to lessen. By the age of seven, I accepted my father was never coming home. At the age of ten, I was told my father's father had passed away, and my grandmother several years later.

On holidays, I did speak with Aunt Kerry. She would bring me up-to-date on life in California and hoped one day, when I was older, I would come for a visit. I spoke with Scott, my cousin, who I knew was forced into speaking with me. But he asked all the right questions and then passed the phone back to his mom. After Scott's death, my mom called Aunt Kerry several times a year, but I made myself unavailable, because talking with Aunt Kerry wasn't fun anymore since Scott's death.

It saddens me to hear my aunt say Aunt Kerry has passed away. I begin to question myself, *When I became an adult, married, had children of my own, why didn't I attempt to reconnect with Aunt Kerry?* The answer is simple: The apple didn't fall far from the tree. I was my mother's child.

* * * * *

Easter has come and gone without a hitch. Pete continues to travel, the State documents still haven't been approved, but hiring Emily has proved a smart move. The monthly office expenses are covered. Ray's former clients praise Pete for such a find, saying they will remain loyal to the firm as long as Emily is around.

Pete is losing sleep at night, feeling the lawyers aren't working hard enough to get the State licenses. With the new Florida laws regarding corporations and fraud, the State is dragging their feet. This problem has caused Pete to lose five pounds he can't afford to lose.

My depression has worsened. The change has been noticed by JoAnne, and definitely Pete. The desire to end my marriage is consuming me. Easter is long gone, and again I avoid the talk.

Summer is knocking at the back door, which causes my depression to heighten, because our two-week August vacation in Florida with Pete's family is right around the corner.

CHAPTER EIGHT

Sarah

Lunch with Allison was both rewarding and disappointing. I was elated my niece wanted to spend time with me, but after speaking with her, I wasn't sure about her state of mind. It appeared she had lost weight, and the dark circles under her eyes weren't because her plate was too full; it was from lack of sleep.

When you're a partner in an accounting firm, as Pete, there are months at a time you spend away from your family. Allison never complained in the past; she seemed to enjoy the full days she spent at work and with the children. Now there was something more going on, and I knew it had to do with Patrick's death, but my hands were tied. I promised to give her the space she needed, and it seemed to be working.

Her inviting me to lunch and asking me to help with Easter shopping was a triumph in my book. I had to confess, as she stated, the questions about her father and family were strange. Discussing death is not the Holland way, not even if it was a fond memory of the person who had passed.

My father loved his granddaughter, but after her father died, he saw Allison as a victim, like himself. Death had taken away another loved one, and nothing or no one could shield you from the pain.

After George returned home, I hoped he and Allison would bond and she might look to him as she would have her father, but it was Patrick who seemed to fill that need.

Easter was early this year, and the nights remained cold. Sitting by the fire, I thought of my own young life.

* * * * *

New York, college, and being close to Grandma Maggie was great, but there was a void. I missed my family. As dysfunctional as life was, there wasn't a day that went by that I didn't worry how they were getting along without me. I called twice a week, once in the day to speak with Pearl, and once during the evening to speak with Dad, George, and Audrey. If George wasn't at home, I told Dad to have him return my call. He always did.

The third week at school, while shopping at the bookstore, I met two interesting girls, Diane Steen and Eleanor Grant. They invited me to coffee, and a friendship evolved. Diane lived on campus, and Eleanor lived at home with her parents in Queens.

"Your own apartment? How did you convince you parents?" asked Eleanor.

"My mother died when I was young, and my father … well, since then, he pretty much says yes to everything. My grandmothers live in New York, so it's not like my father sent me off to live on my own. My apartment has two bedrooms, so you're welcome to use it when the weather is bad."

"Thanks, but I have a controlling father. Wants his little girl home every night. I'm not allowed to have a boyfriend, or live away from home until I graduate college and/or marry", say Eleanor.

"You're not allowed to have a steady boyfriend. How's that working out?" asked Diane.

"It's working. What my father says goes in one ear and out the other. I've had a steady boyfriend for a year. He's attending Florida State. With him away, it's working out just fine."

"Your boyfriend is in Florida, and you have no intentions of dating? Are you sure he's the one?"

"I'm not sure if he's the one, Diane, and yes, I do intend to test the waters. Isn't that what college is all about? While the cat's away, the mice will play."

Diane turned her attention toward me. "What about you, Sarah? Steady boyfriend back home?"

"I dated in high school. Nothing serious."

"Okay, then, this should be interesting, three single women out to find Mr. Right."

Looking for Mr. Right wasn't the way I spent my first year at college. I took a job at the corner diner, five hours, two nights a week, and Saturdays from six to four. Enjoyment was going out on Saturday night with Diane, Eleanor, and a few other friends. Sunday was spent with Grandma Maggie. The other nights, I locked myself in the apartment to study.

"How's school?" asked Grandma Maggie.

"School's good. Straight A's so far."

"Straight A's, part-time job, Sundays with me, all work and no play. When do you have time for just plain old fun?"

"Grandma, I'm enjoying my life. I get to meet a lot of interesting people at the diner. Mrs. Parks makes sure I'm fed. She even set me up on a date with her nephew. He was nice, but we had nothing in common."

"My only purpose in life is to see you, George, and Audrey happy. Are you happy, Sarah, living in New York far away from your family?"

"I can lie and say I don't miss my family, but I do. I'm still hoping George will call and say he's coming to live in New York, but I'm not banking on it."

"George will find his way. Boys develop slower than girls. I do have a question for you, young lady. Have you made time to visit your grandmother?"

"No, I haven't gotten around to calling her."

"Sarah Holland, you've been here two months, and you haven't called or visited?"

"The woman hates me, and I'm not crazy about her."

"Next Sunday, we're going to visit your grandmother. I'll call to say we're coming. Be here by ten. I'll arrange for a cab."

Several times I tried to place a call to Grandmother Holland, but then I thought I'd wait till Thanksgiving, when my family visited. I was relieved when Grandma Maggie insisted we visit with Grandmother the following Sunday. Grandma would be the go-between when it came to Grandmother and me.

I wasn't fooling myself; I knew my time with Grandma was limited. She wasn't getting any better. She asked that I didn't question her every time she visited with her doctor, and I made her promise if the news wasn't good, she would tell me. She said our time together shouldn't be overshadowed by the inevitable: we're born, we die, and it's what we do in between that matters. She was grateful to be spending her remaining days with me.

Sunday, I arrived at nine. Grandma was dressed and ready to go. "I'm so glad your early. It's such a beautiful day. I told your grandmother we'll be there by twelve. The cab is coming at eleven thirty, so there's enough time for a walk, coffee, and a cheese-Danish."

"A walk? How far?"

"To the boardwalk and back. If you're worried about me, don't be. This is one of my better days. A walk will do me good."

We walked arm in arm to the boardwalk. I found a bench for Grandma. After she was settled, I crossed the street and purchased breakfast at the deli.

We sipped our coffee, ate our Danish, and watched as the sun's reflection danced on the ocean. I could never get enough of the vision before us.

"Your dad told me about his plans for Christmas. We're spending it at Grandmother Holland's house. I can't wait to see George and Audrey! Pearl said she's growing like a weed."

"I was hoping to make Christmas dinner at my apartment. I think we can manage. I'll talk with Dad. We can spend Christmas Eve at Grandmother's."

Grandma slapped my knee in approval. "It's nice, you wanting us to spend Christmas Day at your place. I don't think that will be a problem."

I knew we were both thinking the same thought, that this might be my grandma's last Thanksgiving and Christmas.

"I told Dad I'm going to be spending Thanksgiving in New York with you and Uncle Charlie's family."

"I asked Charlie if I can invite your grandmother. He was fine with it. Are you sure you're not going to miss George and Audrey?"

"It's only one day, and I want to spend it with you. And I guess Grandmother Holland. I hope she behaves. You know Grandmother. She'll find a way to insult Uncle Charlie and his family. I convinced Dad to let George stay at my place over the Christmas holiday, even Audrey if she wants to."

"You're a good sister, Sarah. It's no secret how much you love George."

"I love Audrey as well."

"I'm sure you do, but you and George have a special bond."

"Not a day goes by that I don't think of that day. My mother was a special and good mom. She loved us, especially George. He was her little Georgie. Why was it so hard for our father to see that the loss was just as great for us as it was for him? I know they loved each other, but we were a product of that love. We were her children. A part of her was alive in us. Why couldn't he love us? Why can't he see how much George needs him? George and Dad were so close when Mom was alive."

"He does love the three of you, Sarah. I'm not denying it's as confusing to me as it is to you, but we'll never be able to understand what broke inside him the day my sweet daughter died. He blames himself just as I do. After each miscarriage, I tried to convince her not to try again. Your father did as well."

"And yet he got her pregnant."

"He couldn't say no to your mother, and now he's a shell of a man living with his guilt."

"Audrey would have been their last child. I overheard Mom tell him she was done. My father lived in fear the whole nine months. If only you had seen him that night … Mom covered with blood … he was sick with worry. We all were. Then the news that Mom and the baby were healthy, and in minutes our world was turned upside down."

"Sarah, I wish I could find the words to explain why, but I couldn't for your grandfather, and I can't for you and your family.

Promise me, when life gets tough—and it will—don't linger too long in the sorrow. It doesn't change a thing if you do."

* * * * *

When we arrived at Grandmother's house, we were greeted at the door by the butler, Gus.

"Hello, Gus, how are you doing?"

"Hello, Mrs. O'Brien. I'm fine. And yourself?"

"Happy for every day I wake up."

Gus escorted us to the living room. "Mrs. Holland will be down in a moment."

Didn't surprise me that grandmother wasn't there to greet us. Some things never change, like her having to make a grand entrance.

A small commotion began in the foyer.

"If you wouldn't struggle, it would be much easier to get you into the chair."

"I don't need that chair! I'm perfectly fine walking on my own."

My grandmother's entrance included a wheel chair and a male attendant around the age of fifty.

Grandmother looked older, but her complexion was pink, while Grandma Maggie's was gray.

"Margaret, so good to see you! How have you been feeling?"

"Still fighting the wheelchair, Catherine."

Grandma's comment regarding the wheelchair confirmed my grandmothers had seen each other often over the years.

"I keep telling this idiot I don't need that chair. I can walk perfectly fine on my own. I have to admit, my legs don't work as well as they used to, but I'm not a cripple."

Grandma Maggie laughed. "Catherine, everyone can use a little help every now and then."

Grandmother looked past Grandma to me. "Well, well, been living in New York two months and no time to visit your grandmother?"

"Hello, Grandmother. I've been busy settling in."

Grandmother sighed. "I bet you were. Well, come closer. Let me take a good look at you."

I moved closer. "You are a pretty little thing. I'll say that much for you. NYU, I'll admit you made a fool of me. Never thought you or that brother of yours would amount to much."

Before I could slap the old bitch, Grandma said, "Bet you can't wait to see George and Audrey at Christmas. By the way, Charlie asked me to extend an invite to you to spend Thanksgiving with his family. Sarah's also joining us."

"Thanksgiving, of course. Thank Charlie for me. I'd love to spend the holiday with you and my ungrateful granddaughter. And I'm looking forward to seeing the ungrateful grandchildren during the Christmas holidays."

I didn't respond to the comment.

* * * * *

I had to hand it to my grandmother, because as always, the food was delicious. I could get used to visiting more often if she promised to feed me. When we left, I promised I would visit once a month.

At Thanksgiving, George surprised me with a visit. Grandma Maggie already knew he was coming, so it was no surprise for her. Thanksgiving with George and my grandmothers turned out to be fun. Uncle Charlie made sure we had a good old Irish holiday, with music, lots of beer, and friends dropping by throughout the day. Grandmother Holland talked with everyone, drank beer, and sang along with Grandma Maggie.

Grandmother Holland ribbed George a little, but he cuddled up to her and she forgave him for being such a terrible grandson.

That night, when George and I were alone in my apartment, he commented, "Our grandmothers seem to enjoy being together. Grandmother Holland hasn't lost her feisty personality."

"No, she hasn't."

"Can't believe she's our father's mother. They're nothing alike."

"You mean pre-Mom's death? That father?"

George avoided an answer. "Nice place. Is it all what you dreamed it would be, living in New York?"

"Yes, and so much more. My offer still stands if you want to experience New York for yourself."

"I tossed and turned last night with all the noise going on outside my window."

"You get used to the sounds. I did a lot of tossing and turning when I first got here. Now I sleep like a baby."

"There sure are a lot of girly things thrown around my room."

"My friend Eleanor sleeps over every so often."

"Is she sleeping here tonight? I sure can use the company."

"Not under my roof. Anyway, Eleanor's all talk, no action. She's afraid of her father."

"I don't need the headache of a pissed-off father. I have one of those waiting for me at home. Speaking of boys, have you met anyone?"

"I've been on a few dates, but with work, school, and our grandmothers, there's not much time left for dating."

"Nothing but "A's" for Sarah Holland."

"You got that right, George Holland. In a few years, everyone in this city will know my name. Sarah Holland, the sharpest attorney this town has to offer."

George and I shared a good laugh. I enjoyed my time with George. Seeing him made my worries cease. He seemed happy, and in no time, he'd be off to college somewhere, anywhere but Cleveland.

* * * * *

I found it hard to concentrate at school, anticipating my family's visit at Christmastime. Convincing my father—or should I say, telling him—that I wanted to have Christmas dinner at my place was easy. I told him I had already spoken with my grandmothers and they were fine with it. As I looked around my place, I had to rearrange the furniture so we could fit.

School break began one week before Christmas, so my first thought was to shop, first for presents for the family, food, and lastly to purchase a Christmas tree.

Three blocks from my apartment, a local merchant occupied a small space and sold Christmas trees. Walking along the fence, browsing the Christmas trees for the perfect size and shape for the living room, someone called out to me.

"The trees at the end of the fence are all six feet. What size are you looking for?"

Turning, I was face-to-face with an extremely handsome man. I motioned with my hands the size that I needed.

"Guessing five feet might work. Follow me." We walked to the middle of the pile, and he proceeded to pull one out and untied it. "Five and half, has a great shape, round and full. What do you think?"

"It might be too wide. It's a small space. But she's pretty."

"I can see you don't know much about trees. This one here is a boy."

"A boy." I looked at the tree. "Forgive me, sir, I stand corrected. You're not pretty, you're handsome."

I turned to the handsome man, and together we shared a laugh. "I'm just joking with you. I know nothing about trees, but I do know a pretty girl when I see one."

I didn't respond to the compliment. "I'm not sure it will fit."

"There's only one way to find out. I get off in an hour. I can drop the tree off. If it doesn't work, you can pick another."

Staring at him, I said, "You want me to give you my address?"

"I'm harmless. Ask my boss."

I had to admit, I had no way of getting the tree to my place, so I had to take him up on his offer. I wrote down my address and apartment number. "My landlord is a little protective of the single girls living in his apartment building. I'll let him know I'm expecting a delivery."

"See you in an hour. I'll bring tools just in case the tree needs trimming."

"Wait, you haven't told me the cost."

"For this tree, I think my boss would agree on three dollars. Do we have a deal?"

We shook on it.

* * * * *

I felt a need to run a comb through my hair and apply a fresh coat of lipstick before my tree arrived. A little over an hour later, there was a knock on my door.

Checking myself one more time in the mirror, I called out, "One minute."

When I opened the door, the handsome man was leaning on the doorjamb, holding up the tree and breathing heavily. Behind him was Mr. Parks.

"Your landlord was nice enough to walk me to your door. I told him you were expecting me." The handsome man rolled his eyes and looked at the tree.

I smiled. "Mr. Parks."

"He said you ordered this tree. Did you?"

"I did." Feeling sorry for the young man, I said, "You can place the tree in the corner." With the tree and man in my apartment, I mouthed to Mr. Parks, "Thank you. I'll call if I need you."

Mr. Parks nodded in agreement.

Closing the door behind me, the man said, "Are you related to that guy? He's very protective of you."

"As I said, he and his wife are very protective of their tenants."

"You're right. Even a five-footer is too big for this space. But with a little trimming, we might get it to fit, or would you rather I take it back and pick out a four-footer?"

"You're willing to take the tree back and bring back a smaller one?"

"I will if you want me to, but I'm sure with a little trimming, this one will work."

Looking at the tool bag, I suggested, "I'm sure if you trim a little here and there, but not too much. I'm afraid it will ruin the shape."

I watch as the handsome man did a nice job trimming the tree. Finishing, he stepped back and admired his work while I admired the muscles in his arms.

I filled a teapot with water and placed it on the burner. "It looks perfect. Thank you so much."

"Are you going to decorate the tree? If you want, I can help with the lights. Do you have lights?"

"Of course, I have lights and Christmas ornaments as well. I will decorate the tree tomorrow."

"I don't mind helping."

"You just got off work. I'm sure you'd like to get home."

"Just have to pack some clothes. I leave for home tomorrow."

"And where's home?"

"Just outside of Niagara Falls, right across the border."

"You're Canadian?"

"I was born in the United States. My parents are Canadians. My mother lured my father to Canada three years after I was born. My mother wanted to be close to her family. Are the lights in this bag?"

"Yes, but only the lights. Can I at least offer you a cup of tea and some Christmas cookies for all your hard work?"

"Sounds great. I haven't eaten since breakfast."

"I waitress at the diner. I can offer you a day-old sandwich. It will only take a minute to warm it in the oven."

"A day-old sandwich sounds great."

I set the oven and then set the table, two cups, two dishes, two napkins, sugar, milk, and in the center of the table, a plate of homemade Christmas cookies. When the oven reached the required temperature, I placed the sandwich in the oven.

"Can you hand me the extension cord?"

I handed the handsome man the cord, and he connected the end of the lights to the extension cord and then ran the cord along the wall and placed it into the socket. The tree illuminated in red, green, blue, and yellow. I gasp. "Oh, how beautiful!"

Staring at me, the handsome man said, "Yes, she is."

"So I'm right, this tree is female." Smiling, I added, "Thank you."

"You can thank me with that sandwich and cookies."

He sat, and I poured the tea. "I have lemon, if you prefer it to milk and sugar …"

"Milk and sugar, Sarah."

Sitting across from him, I asked, "How do you know my name?"

Mimicking Mr. Parks, he said, "You're sure the tree is for Sarah in apartment 3?"

I laughed. "Does tree-man have a name?"

"My name is Lance Pickett."

"Pickett, not the Pickett who plays hockey at NYU?"

"Pickett hugs the net, he has a clear shot, shoots, scores! That's me."

"I also attend NYU. Been to two games this season. You're really good."

"I'm all right. These cookies homemade?"

"Yes."

Lance chose the secret recipe cookie. Taking a bite, he said, "This is really good." He took two more and three of the others.

I stood, and I removed the sandwich from the oven, placing one half of the sandwich on Lance's plate and the other half on mine.

We talked for hours. He spoke lovingly of his mother, father, and an older brother. I told him about my family in Cleveland, several times mentioning George. He never asked about a mother.

After finishing a light supper, together we finished decorating the tree, talking while we worked.

Lance was at NYU on a science scholarship. His first love was hockey, and he hoped to play professionally, and his second dream was finding a cure for cancer.

When it was time to say good-night, Lance asked if he could call when he got back from winter break. Of course, I said yes. He looked at the tree one last time, wished me a merry Christmas, then added, "See you next year. I have a feeling it's going to be a good year."

* * * * *

I woke early the following day. My family was arriving on the ten o'clock train Christmas Eve morning, so there was much to do with so little time.

Grandma needed help altering one of her favorite holiday dresses to fit her fragile body. I stopped at the deli and picked out Grandma's favorite dishes and dessert before boarding the train to Brooklyn. The train was filled to capacity with last-minute shoppers. A group of young teens heading home for Christmas break broke out singing "Jingle Bells," and a few of the riders chimed in. Their jolly mood made me think of Lance. I tried to put him out of my mind, but each time I remembered something he said or the way he laughed, I wanted to hear that voice and melt in that smile once again. He was taller than any boy I had dated—six one or two, maybe three. The full head of blackish-brown hair, hazel eyes, full lips, a square chin, and a muscular body, I assumed, formed from all those years on the ice. I had to remind myself, with my busy schedule, I was too busy to have a steady boyfriend, but I was no idiot; I knew damn well if he called, as he said he would, I would find the time to get to know him better.

When I entered the apartment, I shouted out, "I brought lunch!"

"I knew you would. My favorites, I hope."

"Absolutely."

"First, you'll help me pin the dress, then we'll eat. I have to sew by the light of day. My eyes don't work well at night."

Grandma set the oven to warm and placed the food inside. "It will keep while we pin the dress."

When my grandma removed her housecoat, I lowered my eyes, not wanting her to see how her fragile body upset me. "Pin the sides first, and let's see how it looks."

Looking in the mirror, I said, "I think that looks good. What do you think?"

"I made this dress for myself when I was thirty and had a shape. Did you know that in my younger days, your grandma was a good-looking woman?"

"You're just as beautiful today."

Grandma reached out and touched my cheek. "You're so sweet, princess."

I smiled. After the dress was pinned, my grandma placed her housecoat back on and laid the dress on her sewing table. "Sit down, Grandma, let me serve you today."

"You seem very happy. Is it because your family is coming to visit?"

"Yes. George agreed to stay at my apartment the entire week, and Audrey has agreed to spend Christmas Eve and two other nights during the week. I'm planning on spending a day just with Audrey. She wants to visit the New York library, and afterward, we'll catch up with George for lunch. Dad's planned a family dinner at the Hilton, but you already know about that. I think it's going to be a fun week."

"I'm excited to see Audrey. It's been a while. I'd like to come along when you visit the library."

"Grandma, that's a great idea!" I made a mental note to ask Grandmother Holland if I could borrow her driver for the day. Heck, I'd even extend an invitation for her to join us. "George says Audrey has gotten so tall and she's very pretty, just like Mom."

Grandma smiled. "You children get your good looks from your mother. Not saying your father isn't a handsome man, but your mother was a beauty." Changing the subject, she asked, "Were you able to find a tree to fit in your apartment?"

"Funny you should ask." I told my grandma about the tree and the tree-man who hauled it to my apartment. Grandma smiled as I told the story.

"Half-Italian, half-French. Nice combination. He must be handsome!"

"He was—I mean *is*." I looked over at my grandma, who had one eyebrow raised. "What? I have eyes. He's handsome and very tall for an Italian. His mother must be tall."

"If you and this boy remain friends, I might get the chance to judge for myself whether he is handsome or not." Grandma smiled.

* * * * *

The train came to a stop, and my heart leaped from my chest. Five minutes passed before the door opened. Patiently I watched as the passengers exited the train. I spotted George and called his name. He acknowledged me then reached to help Audrey down. My father waited at the top step and looked for me. I waved, calling, "Dad!"

My family walked toward me. I passed through the gate and hugged George. Reaching down, I lifted Audrey in my arms. Turning to my father, I said, "Dad, it's so good to see you!" We hugged. "I've missed you, Dad."

"I've missed you too, Sarah." When our eyes met, both were filled with tears.

"First, we have to stop at my apartment. George and Audrey can drop off their luggage and change if they want, but you have to see my tree. It's beautiful! Grandmother arranged for the car to pick up Grandma. I'm hoping she'll be able to attend midnight services with the family. If not, the driver will take her home."

I was babbling, but for a good reason. I was happy to see my family.

* * * * *

"William, you look a little peaked. You're working too hard. You should come home. Move the children back to New York. I think it would be good for them. Sarah is thriving in New York?"

Feeling sorry for my father, I said, "Not everyone enjoys living in the city."

"Are you forgetting your father was born here? He's a city boy through and through."

Grandma's arrival ended an uncomfortable situation.

"Margaret, you've arrived just in time. I need your help."

"Before I offer my help, Catherine, I just want to compliment you on how beautiful the Christmas decorations look, both inside and out. How did you find the time?"

"I had nothing to do with it. Gus arranged for the house to be decorated, and William arranged payment. Speaking of William, I think William and the children should move east. God knows he does not have to work. His father left him enough money. Why he chooses to live like a peasant, I will never understand. Maggie, help me convince him that the move would benefit him and the children."

"Catherine, you and I both know Will does not live like a peasant. He's done very well for himself. You also know we can't dictate where and how our children live their lives. Sorry I cannot back you on this one." Grandma looked over at George and me and winked. We smiled. After greeting everyone with a kiss, Grandma finally saw how tall Audrey had grown. "Hello, sweet girl, you've grown so tall!" Grandma took Audrey in her arms and whispered, "I love you with all my heart and soul." Audrey placed her arms around Grandma and held her close. It was the first sign of affection I had seen from the child.

"You have a way with children, Maggie. The child refused to hug me."

George and I laughed.

"What's so funny? I know what you think of me. You think I'm mean, a witch. You dislike me because I say what's on my mind. I'm honest. Can't fault me for being honest."

Grandma defended her friend. "You're the most honest person I have ever met, Catherine, and you're right, no one should fault you for being honest."

"Maggie understands me."

* * * * *

Christmas Eve, the family I knew and came to accept were together in the same room, enjoying family time together. George brought us up-to-date with what was going on back home. Grandmother inquired about the friends she had made during her stay with us. My father listened, unable to contribute a word to the conversation. This season only brought back the sad memories of the night so long ago when his precious Erin was taken from him.

Knowing my father was reliving that night, I sat next to him at the dinner table. Twice he reached out and took my hand. He asked about school and if the money he provided was sufficient.

"Dad, it's more than enough. I also have my job, which pays most of my expenses. I'm fine."

Watching my grandma Maggie with one arm around Audrey and holding my hand tightly, I thought what a gracious and unselfish woman she was to have joined us at the St. Vincent's Episcopal midnight services rather than the Catholic services at Our Lady of Mount Carmel.

When services had ended, I said, "Grandma, I'm really happy you're here with us. I noticed you brought your overnight bag. You accepted Grandmother's offer to spend the night?"

"Sweetheart, your grandmother and I enjoy our time together. I was happy she extended the invitation."

"I think you might be Grandmother's only friend."

Grandma Maggie smiled and waved her index finger at me. "Sarah Holland, respect your elders."

My grandmother was speaking with the minister, and I excused myself and asked if I could have a few words with her before George, Audrey, and I left.

"Of course, Sarah. Reverend Peters, have you met my granddaughter Sarah? She attends NYU."

"It's a pleasure to meet you. Merry Christmas."

"Merry Christmas, Reverend. Can I steal my grandmother away for just a few moments?"

"Of course."

I moved my grandmother's wheelchair somewhere private. "What's so important, Sarah, that you had to drag me away from the good reverend?"

"I just wanted to thank you for having Grandma stay at the house tonight. It was very considerate of you."

"I believe this is the first time you have thanked me in your life. You must be filled with the Christmas spirit!"

"You don't make it easy to be thankful." I smiled. She grunted just a little.

* * * * *

Christmas Day, George, Audrey, and I enjoyed a nice breakfast. After cleaning up, we began to prepare the Christmas feast.

My grandmothers and father arrived at eleven. I was elated when my grandmother and grandma Maggie expressed how beautiful my apartment looked. I gathered some pillows on the floor, and George, Audrey, and I sat and left the sofa and armchair for the adults. We opened our gifts before dinner.

Grandmother Catherine presented Audrey and me with pearl necklaces. "That was the first gift your grandfather gave to me. It was a double-strand. I had them separated as a gift for you girls. And, George, this is the first gift I gave your grandfather." It was a handsome ring, and George was elated that Grandmother wanted him to have it.

"Your grandmother gave me the idea, so I, too, have special gifts. These belonged to your mother." Grandma extended her hand to me. In her hand was an Irish ring with the tiniest of diamonds outlining the cross. I was told it was the gift my mother received on her first Holy Communion. Audrey received a delicate bracelet with a heart charm hanging at the clasp, and George the cross my mother wore on that special day.

Grandma told the story of the heart-charmed bracelet. "It was the gift every girl wanted." She smiled, remembering my mother at that age. "Your mother was determined to shame us into getting her the bracelet. 'Mom, Dad,' she'd beg, 'every girl in my Communion class is getting this bracelet. I'll just die if I'm the only one that doesn't have one.'" Grandma's story made us laugh, except Dad. He lowered his head. I knew where his thoughts were. He excused himself and headed for the bathroom.

* * * * *

"Audrey's asleep. Are you hungry?"

"Hungry! You made enough food to feed an army."

"I wasn't sure how much everyone would eat. The good thing is, we don't have to worry about cooking for the rest of the week." I made George laugh.

"I can't believe we all fit in this tiny apartment."

"We managed. Did Dad seem a little down to you?"

"Sarah, you haven't lived away from home that long. Dad is down 360 days a year, 5 of them he's downright depressed."

I sighed. "Audrey never left Grandma Maggie's side. Do you think … never mind."

"That she senses our mother in Grandma? Maybe. Grandma was overjoyed to see her. This might be—"

"She's lost more weight. I'm sure you noticed."

What does her doctor say?"

"She made me promise not to ask. She also promised, if something is wrong, she won't keep it from me. I'm just grateful for the time we have together, and I hope God will be generous."

"I'm jealous you're here and I'm not, but I'm happy she has family close by to check on her."

"The offer's still on the table."

George shook his head. "I know. Maybe someday I'll surprise you. Next year, I'll be a senior. I've been thinking about what I'm going to do after graduation. New York's one of the cities on my list, but don't go getting your hopes up. So is California and Arizona."

* * * * *

The week was all I'd hoped it would be. The time Audrey, George, and I spent at the apartment would surely be memories I would always have. George and I teased Audrey about her always having her head in a book. Grandma Maggie scolded us and then purchased ten books for Audrey. She and Audrey read every book twice. I took many pictures of my grandmothers and their grandchildren, even a few with our father. Audrey seemed to flourish when she was around Grandma Maggie. I knew that my father's biggest mistake in life was not allowing my grandma Maggie and grandpa Tim to care for us after my mother died.

Seeing my family off at the train station was difficult. "George, it's a long time until Easter. I'll miss you."

"Easter is right around the corner."

"Dad, take care of yourself. Maybe you have to cut back at work."

"You're sure you have enough money?"

"Yes, Dad." I turned to Audrey. "Audrey, will you tell Pearl I miss her?"

"Sarah, I promise to tell Pearl you miss her if you'll tell Grandma Maggie I love the books."

"I will."

* * * * *

It was three days since my family left. Standing before the tree, I had begun to remove the decorations when I was startled by a knock on my door.

"Lance, what are you doing here?"

"I would have called, but it's hard when I didn't get your number. I stopped at the diner, but Mr. Epstein said you had the night off. Mrs. Parks said she thought you were home. Mr. Parks just gave me the evil eye."

I leaned out the door and waved to Mr. Parks. As I stepped aside to let Lance in, he noticed the box of ornaments in my hands.

"Perfect timing! You'll need help getting the tree to the curb."

"I was wondering how I was going to manage. I tied a sheet around the bottom of the tree to catch the needles."

"All right, then, let's get started."

When the tree was safely to the curb, Lance looked at me and said, "Why so sad?"

"Once that tree happily lived in the forest, today it is trash."

Lance shook his head. "Now you've made me sad."

I smiled. Looking up at the sky, I said, "It's a nice night for a walk. You interested?"

"You read my mind."

I ran up to lock the door and grab my purse. Looking in the mirror, I fixed my hair, pinched my cheeks, and reapplied my lipstick. When did I become so concerned about my appearance? The answer: the night I met Lance.

"Did you have a nice Christmas?"

"Very nice. I mentioned my family was here? I got to spend time with my brother and sister. How was yours?"

"I got to spend more time than I wanted with my brother. My mother was happy when we left. Can you believe we still fight over anything and everything?"

"Sounds like fun."

"Not for my parents. We did get to play hockey. My brother is really good. His dream was to play professionally someday. It was also my father's. Unfortunately, my brother didn't make the cut. I'm my father's last hope."

"Is that your dream, to play professional hockey?"

"It's been my dream since I put on a pair of skates when I was three."

Walking, we talked about our time off and school. I spoke about Grandma Maggie and Grandmother.

"Your grandmother sounds like a piece of work."

"She is. She says we're exactly alike, but I refuse to see it. I like to think I'm more like my grandma Maggie."

"Grandma Maggie is your father's mother?"

"My mother's."

"I don't mean to pry, but you've never mentioned your mother, so I just assumed Grandma Maggie was your father's mother."

"My mother died when I was eleven."

"I'm sorry."

"It was a long time ago."

I was feeling chilled, so Lance offered to buy me a cup of coffee. He didn't ask what took my mother's life, and I didn't offer an explanation. Changing the subject, we talked about the professors and friends at school. He talked about the hockey team, how he earned a scholarship to play hockey at the university, and how, if his dream of becoming a professional failed, he'd be happy teaching science.

"So you're friends with Diane and Eleanor. Diane comes to all the games. I think she has a crush on Ted, our goalie."

"She does. I went to two games with her. Don't take this the wrong way, but the game is too violent for me."

"It looks worse than it is. I have a game tomorrow at four. Why don't you come?"

"I have to work tomorrow till six, then I have to catch up on schoolwork."

"What are you doing Sunday?"

"I spend Sundays with my grandma. I'm usually home by five. If you'd like to stop by, I'll tell Mr. and Mrs. Parks I'm expecting you."

* * * * *

Lance was becoming my newest obsession. When we weren't together, I wished the hours away until we were. When the hour drew near, I had butterflies in my stomach, waiting for his knock on my door.

My grandma saw the change in my demeanor and was anxious to meet my handsome friend.

It was March when I told Lance, "My grandma invited us to dinner on Sunday."

"I can't wait to meet her. What time should I pick you up?"

* * * * *

"Grandma, this is Lance Pickett. Lance, this is my grandma Maggie."

"It's a pleasure to meet you, Mrs. O'Brien."

"Hello, Lance. Welcome to my humble home. Dinner is almost ready."

I whispered to Lance, "My grandma is a fabulous cook. Her baking, not so good." Then I said, "I brought dessert, Grandma."

"Don't believe her, Lance. Dessert may not be my forte, but I'm not as bad as Sarah makes me out to be."

I cover my mouth, and Lance smiled at me. "Don't care much for desserts. I'm a meat-and-potato kind of guy."

"I wish I knew. Sarah mentioned you are French Canadian. Never cooked anything French. I hope Italian will do, pasta and meatballs."

"Pasta and meatballs—my favorite!"

My grandma and Lance talked the day away. When it was time to leave, while Lance waited at the door, my grandma and I said good-night. "I love you with all my heart and soul. Don't forget."

"I love you, Grandma, with all my heart and soul."

Then Grandma whispered, "Your friend is very handsome and sweet. I think he has a crush on you, and vice versa."

"Grandma, we're just friends."

On the train ride back, Lance leaned toward me and said, "I hope someday you'll think of me as more than just a friend."

Over the Easter holiday, I introduced Lance to the family. George took an instant liking to him. Grandmother Holland was smitten; she needled Lance about wanting to play professional hockey, saying there was no money in sports.

Lance charmed Grandmother by saying, "I'm really a scientist. I hope to find a cure for cancer. I should be able to eat at the best restaurants if I'm successful." Grandmother laughed a girlish laugh.

Grandma Maggie whispered, "Your grandmother approves of your choice in men."

During the visit, Dad never mentioned approving or disapproving of Lance, but upon his departure, when he kissed me goodbye, he said, "Lance is a very nice young man."

Audrey was drawn to Lance when he told her *Mary Poppins* was one of his favorite books.

* * * * *

That summer, Lance found employment in New York instead of going back home to Canada. I didn't have to wonder why. We spent the summer walking in the park, watching fireworks, and having picnics. Sundays, we spent with my grandmothers. That confirmed Lance and I were an item. The man was willing to give up his Sundays to spend time with my grandmothers. If that's not love, then what is?

"I'm sure you figured out that my grandmother Holland has a crush on you."

"She does, but I'm already taken. I hope you two won't get into a catfight over me." We laughed. "I'm impressed she's well versed in the sciences."

"She went to the best schools. So did my father."

Lance agreed by motioning his head. He talked openly about his family but never pushed me to do the same.

"Do your parents know about me?"

"Yes. My mother is anxious to meet you."

"You've never mentioned you told them about me."

"I didn't want you to think I was …" Lance stopped to think before speaking again. "I know how I feel about you, Sarah, but I'm not sure how you feel about me. I don't know if I'm the one or if you'd rather see other guys."

"What about you? Do you want to see other girls?"

Lance turned me toward him. "I don't want to see other girls, Sarah. I already know you are the one."

"What are you saying?"

Lance looked up at the night sky, looking for guidance. "I'm happy when I'm with you. I'm miserable when we're apart. What do you think I'm saying?"

I knew where this conversation was going, and it was exactly where I wanted it to go, but watching Lance trying to find the words that would seal our relationship … well, I just couldn't help myself. I enjoyed watching him sweat. "I like spending time with you, Lance."

"You like spending time with me. I was hoping for more."

"More? I'm confused. How much more were you hoping for?"

Lance stopped short and released my hand from his. "Sarah Holland, you sure know how to make a guy sweat. I'm trying to say I'm in love with you."

"Love? How silly! What do you know about love?"

Frustrated, Lance stepped toward me, taking me into his arms. He kissed me. I allowed the kiss. When our lips parted and our eyes met, he whispered, "This is the first time I've ever told a girl I love her, so I'm damn sure I love you, Sarah Holland."

"You've made a believer out of me, tree-man, and you'll be happy to know this is a first for me too. I love you, Lance Pickett, with all my heart and soul."

Lance knew the love I had confessed for him was true by the words I had just whispered to him.

* * * * *

It was hard to believe one year of school was behind me. I was again anticipating another visit from my family. They were coming for Thanksgiving and Christmas since Grandma Maggie's health was deteriorating with each passing day.

I took Grandmother Holland up on her offer to host both Thanksgiving and Christmas, knowing I needed to concentrate on my school assignments. I tried to make Sunday a day with both my grandmothers and Lance. Grandmother would send the car for Grandma Maggie; the driver would then pick Lance and me up at my apartment. Once a month, Sunday would be only for Grandma Maggie and me. Lance and Grandmother Holland understood that my time with Grandma was limited.

Everyone fussed over Grandma Maggie during the holidays. Lance decided to spend Thanksgiving with my family, telling his mother of my situation. I hadn't met Lance's parents, but I had conversed with his mother by phone. I knew she and I would get along if my relationship with Lance continued by the compassion she spoke when asking about my grandma's health.

"Grandma doesn't look well. Have you spoken with her doctor?" asked George.

"No. I decided it best not knowing. Anyway, did you forget about doctor-patient confidentiality?"

"You're her family."

"I have eyes. I don't need to hear a doctor tell me what I already know."

"It's not going to be easy letting go. She's all we have left of Mom."

*****

The day I feared more than any happened in the middle of March, when the phone rang and startled me from a sound sleep.

"Hello."

"Hello, Sarah, this is Sam."

"Sam, is it Grandma? Please don't tell me—"

"I found her lying on the floor. I called an ambulance. They took her to St. Joseph's in Brooklyn."

I hailed a cab, saying it was an emergency. I told the cabdriver I had to get to St. Joseph's in Brooklyn immediately.

Walking into my grandma's room and seeing her lying there so peacefully, I thought I was too late. Taking her hand in mine, I called to her, "Grandma, it's Sarah." Slowly she turned her head. I sighed with relief that she was still with me.

"Sarah, what are you doing here? It's late, and you have school in the morning."

I dropped into the chair near her bed and began to cry. "Grandma, I thought I wouldn't get a chance to say goodbye." I couldn't find the words to express how I was feeling.

"I'm still here, child. I'm not going anywhere. The doctor has been by to see me, and it's not my time."

Grandma had survived the crisis, and I had finally gotten to speak with her doctor. He informed me she wasn't able to live on her own, and as far as time, it was in God's hands. She was discharged from St. Joseph's hospital and placed in a nursing home adjacent to the hospital.

Working her magic with the other residents, she soon was surrounded with many friends. She cared for those who were worse than she was. She helped comfort people who were scared, not knowing where they were and why. She helped feed those who had lost their eyesight and found feeding themselves a challenge.

"Your grandma is a special woman. Since she's been here, we nurses have had less to do."

"She's amazing."

"She has a will to live. Something's keeping her going, and I think that someone is you."

Summer arrived earlier than expected. In late April, the temperature hit eighty-five four days in a row.

I found my grandma in the solarium with a blanket draped around her shoulders. Sitting beside her, I knew her time was near.

"Are you cold? Do you need another blanket?"

"I'm fine, sweetheart. I heard the nurses say it's another hot one out there. If that building weren't so high, I would be able to see the ocean."

"Do you want to go for a walk, Grandma?"

"I would like that, Sarah."

Gathering another blanket, I placed it on my grandma's legs. Pushing the wheelchair along the sidewalks, I began to sweat, but my grandma pulled the blanket around her. As we approached the boardwalk, I looked for an empty bench. I sat at the edge of the bench with my hand stretched out, holding my grandma's hand, but not able to look directly at her for fear I would cry. She spoke. "I never get tired of looking at the ocean. As you know, I met your grandfather on this boardwalk, about one mile that way."

Staring in the direction my grandma just pointed out, I said, "Love at first sight."

"Not exactly. Walking up to me, he said, 'Miss, don't think I'm rude, but I think your eyes are bluer than the ocean.' I soon found out he wasn't flirting. He truly couldn't get over the color of my eyes. Said they were the bluest he had ever seen, then he walked away. Two weeks later, while I was reading and looking out over the ocean, a voice from behind said, 'Blue Eyes, is that you? This must be my lucky day.'" She smiled while the tears flowed down my face.

"You're hoping it won't be long till you see him again?"

"I am, Sarah, but something is holding me back."

I knelt on the ground and placed my head on my grandma's lap, not caring if anyone was watching. "I know George and I are being selfish, but you're all we have left of our mother. We love you, Grandma."

"Sarah, listen to me. If I tell you I'm in pain, would you want me to suffer?"

"Of course not."

"I'm in pain, Sarah. Soon my body will give out, but before that happens, I have to know that my dying won't cause you to be bitter. We've been given a gift, Sarah. We've had two wonderful years to love and enjoy each other, and I feel blessed. I've got to see my girl reach her dream, NYU. I see happiness when you're with that young man of yours. I believe Lance is the one. He loves you, Sarah. You and he will begin a new life together, blessed with your own children. It's your time. Don't waste your time sulking about the past. I need to know you understand what I'm saying. I need to know you won't hate yet another person for leaving you sooner than you wanted."

"I could never hate you, Grandma. Remember, I love you with all my heart and soul."

That night, I sat at my grandma's bedside. Waking several times confused and disoriented, she asked over and over, "Sarah, where's George? Tell him that Audrey and I are going to the park. I love you with all my heart and soul."

The last names my grandma spoke were Tim and Erin. With a smile on her face, she went to them.

* * * * *

Lance helped me through the hard times. He never stopped me from sharing the memories of how much joy Grandma had brought to our lives.

"I'll never forget the first time we met. She made pasta and meatballs. I'm so happy I got to know her."

Grandma Maggie's death had affected Grandmother Holland more than I thought it would. I thought Grandmother's memory was failing when she asked, "Is Margaret home from the hospital? Should we stop by to check on her?" I grew tired of reminding her that Grandma was gone, so I played along.

When I shared this slight memory loss with her doctor, he said, and it was just an opinion, if Grandmother accepted that my grandma was dead, then she'd have to accept that her time was drawing near.

Grandma's passing caused maternal feelings to emerge from me for my grandmother. Sunday dinner was solely devoted to Grandmother. As time went on, she accepted my grandma's passing. No longer did I fear her mind was failing. Age had turned Grandmother into a caring woman. Often, I had to stop and check that the loving words came from Grandmother. "Thank God you got your mother's strength. She was a beautiful woman. I never told her how beautiful I thought she was when she was alive. I should have done a lot of things differently when I was younger. Your grandma made me want to be a better person. In my whole life, I never had a friend like your grandma. I'd say she was my best friend."

I came to understand and accept Grandmother. Lance was a big part of my seeing an old woman trying to make peace with her mistakes. One day, she started a conversation referring to my father when he was young. It was a happy memory, and she spoke of my father as being a good son.

I couldn't stop myself from saying, "Too bad you didn't share that with him when he was younger. Maybe you'd have a better relationship today."

"Sarah Holland, there's nothing wrong with my relationship with your father. We Hollands don't express our affection in public."

"My father did until my mother's passing."

"That's because your mother worked her magic on him. The same way your grandma did on me."

* * * * *

George was handling Grandma's death worse than I thought. When we spoke, he blamed himself for not taking me up on my offer to move to New York. I felt sorry for George. Those two years I spent with Grandma eased the pain of losing her. I had my memories, while George felt nothing but guilt.

"George, maybe this will make it easier. Grandma was suffering, it was her time. She loved us, George, and there are memories, lots of them. Try to remember the good times."

The start of my third year at college was also the beginning of George's senior year of high school. During our phone conversations, I asked George if he had intentions of applying to colleges. The answer was always the same: he'd been giving it some thought.

One day, while walking down the hall to my apartment, I hear my phone ringing. I rushed to unlock the door to my apartment in hopes I wouldn't miss the call. It was my father. George had been arrested. I packed a bag and headed to the train station.

My father met me at the train station, and seeing him, I asked, "Where is George?"

"Judge Garrison agreed to release him, but he refuse to leave."

"Why is he in jail? What happened? Did you get a chance to talk with him?"

My father bowed his head. "He doesn't want to see me."

"Why did he refuse to see you, Dad? I thought things were better between you and George?"

My father didn't answer.

"I'm guessing things are not as great as I thought they were. One more year, and he would be free of this place. I want to see him. Take me to where he's being held."

"Sarah, he doesn't want to see anyone."

"He'll see me."

We drove straight to the courthouse.

George refused legal counsel, but my father had already hired Mr. Stark, ESQ, and when he met with George, Mr. Stark informed George he was underage and had no choice in the matter since Dad was his legal guardian.

As we drove, I asked my father to tell me what happened.

George got into a fight outside the grocery store on Chestnut. George had landed a punch that put the boy in the hospital with a concussion. "The doctors assured me the boy would make a full recovery, but his parents are pressing charges."

I held my hand to my heart. "Thank God, the boy's alive."

My father and I drove in silence the rest of the way. When we arrived at the police station, I asked to see my brother.

The office in charge stated, "The inmate has requested no visitors."

"Officer, please tell my brother I only want a few minutes with him. I promise no more than a few minutes. I just have to see for myself that he's all right."

"Miss, I've tried. He refuses to see anyone from his family. Your brother's hearing is first thing tomorrow morning. You'll have to wait till then."

I lay in my bed looking around the room, blaming myself, then my father, and questioning why I didn't work harder to get George to see things my way. One more year, just one more year, and he'd be gone. All the bad memories this place had to offer would be behind him.

That morning, I found my father, Audrey, and Pearl in the kitchen. I went to Pearl, greeted her with a hug and kiss, and asked about her health and her family.

"I'm good, Sarah. Sorry to hear about your grandma. She was a special lady."

Audrey asked, "Where is George? He didn't come home last night."

I looked over at my father then added, "He slept at a friend's house. I'm sure he'll be home when you get back from school." I knelt down before my sister. "Audrey, can I ask you a question?" Audrey nodded. "Have Dad and George been fighting?"

Audrey looked over at our father. "George doesn't like Dad. There's the school bus. I have to go."

Pearl walked Audrey out to the bus.

With Pearl and Audrey gone, I stared at my father. "I'd like to get to the courthouse early to talk with Mr. Starks."

My father responded with a nod.

* * * * *

Mr. Stark arrived at nine forty-five. Speaking to my father, he said, "I have good news. The Gluck boy is up and speaking. He seems fine, just a bad knot on the back of his head. It took a lot of convincing, but the Glucks agreed not to press charges, but George will have to serve some community time. The court clerk just informed me Judge Garrison would like to meet with us before the trial. I'm pretty sure I can guess what he wants to talk about."

"What?" I asked.

My father introduced me to Mr. Stark.

"It's obvious your brother is troubled. George has been in and out of trouble on and off for some time now. This is the first time someone has gotten hurt, but the judge is not taking this last issue lightly. My guess is the judge will recommend George consider the military. He's a firm believer the military could knock some sense in the boy."

"The military? Do you know what's going on in the Pacific? We have to convince the judge that it would be in George's best interest if he left this town and moved with me to New York. I'll take full responsibility of my brother."

"I don't think the judge will agree with George moving to New York with his older sister. Mr. Holland, George is not eighteen, but if you agree to sign on George's behalf, he can enter the military."

"Dad, you can't agree to this! He could be killed!"

"Mr. Holland, you are good friends with Judge Garrison. Him being a war hero, I'm sure he has a lot of connections. Maybe he can pull some strings to keep George out of harm's way."

"Thank you, Mr. Stark. My father and I will meet with Judge Garrison. Once he knows my father is against sending his underage son off and placing him in danger of losing his life, he might reconsider and agree it would be in George's best interest to move to New York."

Mr. Stark looked at my father for his decision. My father said, "First, I'd like to meet with Judge Garrison to hear what he has to say."

My father's response assured me he was against signing his son into the military. The clerk walked us into Judge Garrison's chambers. We took the seats directly in front of the judge. "Sarah, it's so good to see you! Your father has told me you're doing well at NYU."

"Judge Garrison, I'm concerned about George's future."

"That is why I called for this meeting." The judge spoke directly to my father. "Will, I wanted to meet with you to discuss this latest issue involving George. As you are aware, I've given the boy several chances to turn his life around. Nothing has worked. I have two options, one-year prison time, out in nine months for good behavior—keep in mind, though, his record will be tarnished if he serves time—or two years in the military, which I hope will do the boy some good."

"You want my brother to serve time in jail? Did anyone speak with the Gluck boy? Maybe George didn't throw the first punch. Maybe he was defending himself. He has a right to defend himself."

"I know this is upsetting, Sarah, but you've been gone for two years. George is a troubled boy. Don't get me wrong, I like the boy. He won state for us. Thought he had a future in sports, but with that being said, I can't overlook the fact that the boy needs to know right from wrong."

"Please, Judge Garrison, I've asked several times to have George come and live in New York with me. I think he needs to get away from this town and my father. My father will agree to the move. Right, Dad? Please let me take responsibility for my brother."

"I'm sorry, young lady, I can't let Cleveland hand over our problems to New York. I took an oath to protect people. I have no other choice. As I said, George serves time or agrees to enter the military. Will, you'll have to sign for the boy."

I gasped. "You're sentencing my brother to death. He'll be shipped off to the Pacific, and he'll be killed. Dad, you can't agree to this."

While my father played with the hat in his hands, the judge and I anxiously awaited his answer. "Judge, I respect your opinion, but I think it should be George's decision whether he prefers to serve time or enter the military. If I'm forced to make a decision on his behalf, he'll only resent me more than he already does."

"All right, Will. I'll give George the choice, and let's pray he makes the right decision. The military will give him credibility. A jail sentence will remain with him for the rest of his life."

* * * * *

George was escorted into the courtroom. Seeing him, I reached out, hoping as he was seated at the table in front of me that he would take my hand. George sat and avoided eye contact. I drew my hand back.

Judge Garrison entered the courtroom and motioned for us to remain seated. He began, "George, as you know, this is not the first time you have faced me in this courtroom, but it is the first time that someone has been hurt by your actions. If you are wondering how Mr. Gluck is doing, I'm happy to say he is doing well. Probably will leave the hospital sometime today. His parents have agreed not to press charges and are leaving your punishment up to the court." Judge Garrison raised his voice. "Young man, please show me the respect I'm due in my courtroom. Look at me when I am speaking to you." George raised his head. The judge continued, "I have ruled with my heart in the past, and that has been of no benefit to you. This time, you'll have to pay for your bad decision. You can go to prison for a year, or your father can sign for you to enter the military." George lowered his head. "So I ask you, son, a stretch in prison or do the honorable thing and serve your country? It's up to you."

George's response was so low I moved forward in my seat to hear. The judge advised, "I don't think the court heard your response. Please speak louder so it can me noted."

"Military."

Judge Garrison smiled, relieved that George's arrogance didn't overshadow a chance at becoming a model citizen. "You've made the right decision."

When the judge finalized his decision, the officer tapped George's arm and he rose from his seat. I called out to him. "Please let me visit with you. I need to know you are all right."

The door closed behind George and the officer. I fell into the chair. My father reached for my hand, but I pulled away.

"Will," the judge called to my father, "please join me in my chambers to complete the paperwork. We can discuss what happens next."

I went to rise, and Mr. Stark placed a hand on my shoulder. "I think it might help if you remain here with me."

I wait in the hall with Mr. Stark. "Can you please try to get George to visit with me?"

"I can ask again, but he refuses to see the family." From the corner of my eye, I spotted my father coming toward us. "What did the judge say?"

"George will be sent to Parris Island in South Carolina tomorrow."

I asked, "Will he be traveling by train? What time?"

"No. The military will provide for his travel."

"Do we get to say goodbye?"

"Not unless he agrees to a visit."

Mr. Stark interjected, "I'm sure Judge Garrison will grant me another visit. I'll do my best to convince him to allow you and your daughter to see him."

"He won't want to see me. Just ask if he'll allow Sarah to visit. Say she's worried sick about him."

George denied any visitors.

My father drove me to the train station in silence the next morning. As he waited for me to board the train, I decided he needed to hear what I had to say. "Do you know why George didn't agree to move to New York with me? He was hoping that one day you'd wake up and love him the way you did before Mom died." Without saying goodbye, I boarded the train and left my father standing on the platform, crying.

* * * * *

Without George or Grandma Maggie, Thanksgiving was a solemn celebration.

Christmas was right around the corner, and I had not heard a word from George. I found comfort in Lance. He waited to walk me home after work, supplied the meals I half-ate, spent nights studying with me at my apartment, and brought a smile to my face when he brought home a Christmas tree for us to decorate.

"George will call. I know he will. He just needs time to think things over."

"You don't know him like I do. Ever since Grandma died, he hasn't been himself. This is all my father's fault."

* * * * *

The week before Christmas, Lance and I were lounging on the sofa when the phone rang. Feeling warm and cozy, I asked Lance to answer the phone, thinking it was my father checking up on me.

"Hello. Yes, this is Sarah Holland's residence. Oh, yes, she will accept the charges."

I leaped from my seat. "Is it George?"

Lance nodded and handed me the phone.

"George, is that you?"

The operator asked me to hold while she connected the call.

"George, where are you?"

"I'm in South Carolina."

"How are you doing? It's so good to hear your voice! Can I come see you?"

"I'm calling because I'm going to be in New York. I have a two-day furlough before I'm shipped off, and I thought maybe I could stay—"

"What day are you coming? I'll meet you at the train station."

"December 18. I'll take a cab to your apartment. I have to hang up. My buddy wants to call his girl. I'll see you in two days."

* * * * *

I sat patiently waiting for George to arrive. Four o'clock, and no George. The waiting was driving me insane. Then I heard footsteps outside my door. I ran to the door, opened it, and pulled George into my arms.

After greeting him with a *huge* kiss and hug, I explained the covered sandwiches at the table. "I thought you were going to be here for lunch. Are you hungry?"

George placed his duffel bag down, removed his coat and hat to reveal his uniform, and moving toward the kitchen table, sat. "I haven't had a good sandwich since I left Cleveland."

"I have cookies."

"The famous Christmas cookies?"

"Of course." I didn't want to ask too many questions. George seemed healthy; the only thing different was how short his hair was cut. "I can't get over how short your hair is."

George touched the top of his head. "I like it."

I smiled. "How are they treating you?"

"It's not that bad. They do wake you at five, sometimes four, maybe even three if the sergeant had a bad day. It's just as structured as sports training. So I don't mind it as much as some of the other guys."

"George, you mentioned you only had two days before you ship out. Where are they sending you?"

"Germany."

"Germany." I was relieved not hearing the Pacific. "Europe. Thank God it's not—"

"The Pacific? I think Judge Garrison had a hand in where I'd end up. He really likes Dad, or should I say felt sorry for him, having a delinquent like me for a son."

"Do you like the army?"

"I'm actually a Marine, and I don't hate it. I can finish high school and attend college all on Uncle Sam."

"Wow! I should have signed up for the Marines."

George looked tired, and soon after we finished eating, he asked if I'd mind if he went off to bed.

"No, of course not. We have two whole days to catch up."

"I have to report at ten on the third day. My flight is at eight that night."

"Flight? Your first flight, and it's to Europe. I'm jealous."

"Heading off to see the world. I'm living one of your dreams, sis."

* * * * *

We did some sightseeing, ate a lot of cookies, and lunched with Grandmother. Lance understood that I needed this time with George to be our time, so he called at night to ask about our day.

"Grandmother looks good. How's her health?"

"Strong as an ox. And her mind is as sharp as a tack. There was an episode after Grandma Maggie passed. She didn't want to accept that her friend, probably only friend, was gone, but then she did a 360-degree turnabout."

"It sounds like you've found a soft spot in your heart for her." He paused and said, "I wanted to apologize for not letting you visit me while—"

"It's all right. Water under the bridge."

"I owe you an explanation. I was embarrassed, plain and simple."

"As I said, water under the bridge."

George went on and explained what happened that night. As I had figured, he was provoked.

"Why didn't you allow Mr. Stark to defend you?"

"Guess I was tired of defending my actions to the town. After spending a few nights in jail, I liked Judge Garrison's suggestion. I can't lie, I was happy when I got my orders, Germany. My buddy Chip also got lucky."

"I guess it makes the trip a little easier having a friend to share it with."

"He's really a nice guy. Has a girl back home."

"And where's back home?"

"Atlanta."

"I like knowing you're not going to be alone in a foreign country."

* * * * *

We spent a lot of time talking those two days before George shipped out.

"Germany is so far away. Promise me you'll come home on leave."

"I can't promise every leave will be spent in the States. I was hoping to spend some time seeing that part of the world."

"It's what I've always wanted for you and for myself."

"I'm sure after you graduate and land that high-paying job, you'll be able to afford a trip or two."

"And my first will be to visit my baby brother in Germany." There was one question I hadn't asked George, but it was weighing heavy on my mind, so I asked before it was too late.

"Have you spoken to Dad and Audrey?"

"I'm going to call him now. Do you mind—"

"I'll be in my room."

* * * * *

Saying goodbye to George wasn't easy. I knew it would be a long time before I saw him again.

"Promise you'll call and write me at least once a week."

I hugged George as tightly as I could, and before he boarded the train that would take him to the airport, he held me and said, "Thanks, Sarah. Mom couldn't have left me in better hands than yours. I love you, sis."

CHAPTER NINE

Allison

Looking out my kitchen window, I watch my neighbor Marie share a kiss with her husband after she so effortlessly secures her three children in the car. For a split second, I wish I were Marie.

Pete enters the kitchen. "Another half-day at the office. I was hoping you'd pass up on work today to be with your family."

"Is that sarcasm I detect in your voice or your way of asking what I have planned for today?"

"Sarcasm"

Pete's attitude toward my working, or my presuming to be working on Saturdays, is taking a toll. "Coming from a man who spends more time in Florida than he does at home."

"What would you have me do, walk away?"

I decide to take a cheap shot. "Maybe it's Emily Carter you're having a problem staying away from."

"Is that why you're avoiding your family? Because you think I'm having an affair?"

"I'm not going to lie, the thought has crossed my mind."

"You know me better than that. The accusation is insulting, but truth be told, since Patrick's death, you've been avoiding your family I don't mind you using me as a scapegoat, but the kids don't deserve your mood swings. I think it's time you spoke with a professional or joined a group that deals with—"

"How dare you accuse me of avoiding the children! How do you think they get to school and practice? And what has suffered from all this? My work. So if I have to take a half-day on a Saturday so I can leave early during the week to chauffeur the children, then deal with it, like … like I deal with you being away from home, doing who knows what."

"You only have yourself to blame. By cutting yourself off from family and friends, you've added more pressure on yourself. And it's affecting the life we knew before. I can't remember the last time you and I … so yes, I think it's time you got professional help."

I drop a dish in the sink. It cracks, and I swear. Turning to Pete, I curse. "See what the fuck you made me do? That was one of my favorite dishes. Think whatever you want. I don't have time to fight. I have to shower." I walk past Pete, bumping into his shoulder.

In my room, I sit on the bed hating myself for prolonging the talk with Pete. He doesn't deserve the way I'm treating him. A knock on the door startles me.

"Mom, can I come in?"

It's Andrew. Julia is behind him, but she leans on the doorjamb, waiting for Andrew to ask his question. "Dad said you have to work, so you won't be coming to our games today?"

"I'm sorry, Andrew. You know I'd rather be with you guys, but it can't be helped."

"You've only been to one of my games all season, and two of Julia's. Can't we talk you into taking the day off?"

"With Dad away all the time, working on Saturdays helps me accomplish all we do during the week. I promise next year we'll be back on track. I'm doing the best I can."

"Are you and Dad getting a divorce?" asks Julia.

"What?"

"Casey's mom and dad are getting divorced. Casey told me her parents fight all the time and stopped doing things together."

Looking at Julia, I can see her eyes are glassy. "Your dad and I are not getting divorced. We are under a lot of pressure, but it won't last forever."

Andrew says, "Why don't you and Dad go to a movie tonight?"

Looking at my son, I say, "I can do better than that. Tonight, we'll see a movie together, and we'll go to that hamburger place you guys like so much."

Julia smiles. "That's great, Mom! I'll tell Dad." Julia runs down the hall, leaving Andrew and me alone. I hug my son. Smiling, I say, "Doesn't take much to make your sister happy."

Pete appears in the doorway. "It's time to go." Andrew passes Pete. "And make sure you take a jacket this time. It's not as warm as you think."

Pete watches to see that Andrew is far enough away before speaking. "Thanks."

"For what?"

"Hamburgers and a movie."

* * * * *

Grabbing my coat, I swing open the door, surprised to see Aunt Sarah.

"I was just about to ring the bell. I'm glad I caught you before you left."

"I'm off to work, but come in. I've got a few minutes."

"I just wanted to drop off Julia's soccer uniform."

I thank my aunt and invite her to go for coffee.

* * * * *

Aunt Sarah orders coffee and doughnuts. "There is steam rising from the doughnuts."

"Just came out of the oven."

I wave my hand over one, waiting for it to cool. "How did Uncle George's doctor's visit go last week?"

"It was two weeks ago. Doctor prescribed a CT scan. Should get the results in a few days."

"I'm sorry. I should have called."

"Don't apologize. I'm sure he'll be fine."

"What did the doctor think was wrong?"

"Acid reflux. He's taking medication, feels much better, but of course, I won't rest until I know the CT scan is clear."

Out of the blue, I say, "Pete thinks I should see someone, a professional. He thinks I've changed since Patrick's death."

"In what way? He realizes, I'm sure, this hasn't been an easy time for you? You're practically running the entire household without asking for help. Never knew Pete to be so insensitive."

"He's accused me of avoiding the family."

"Patrick's death was a shock. You haven't had a minute to grieve with Pete being gone most of the week."

"Do you think I should talk to a professional?"

Aunt Sarah reaches for my hand. "If you need to get something off your chest, it couldn't hurt to talk with someone."

* * * * *

Sitting at the lake, I think about what my aunt said.

I wonder what her feelings would be if she knew I wanted to end my marriage. Suddenly I am reminded of the promise I made earlier to my children. There will be no divorce. The hole I'm digging is growing with every lie I tell.

Speaking to the wind, I scold, "This is all your fault, Patrick! I wish I had never met you!" Then I think back to a day so long ago, and the thought warms my heart.

* * * * *

After Sunday services on a warm day in March, JoAnne and I, nearing the end of our sophomore year of high school, were sitting down to enjoy the drink and treats the parish women provided each Sunday when JoAnne spotted my aunt talking with an attractive man.

"Hey, your aunt is talking to a guy that could be Elvis Presley's twin. Elvis did have a twin brother, but I was pretty sure he died."

I turned to take a look. A man close to my mother's age was talking with my aunt Sarah. I watched as she motioned for my mother to join them.

"He's better-looking than Elvis. You think he might be the new pastor? I wouldn't mind him lecturing me for one hour every Sunday."

"I didn't think Reverend Scott was ready to retire."

"Maybe he's in training. I'm guessing late thirties, almost forty."

I couldn't stop staring. The man was handsome, very handsome. He didn't fit into our small town. "I'll bet you he's visiting. Probably related to one of the members."

"I wonder whom he's related to."

As JoAnne went on and on, the man, sandwiched between my aunt and mother, began to walk in our direction.

"Girls, I'd like to introduce you to Mr. Higgins," said my aunt.

"Patrick, please. It's a pleasure to meet you." I was at a loss for words. His eyes were the bluest I had ever seen, and his hair as dark as night.

"Hi, I'm JoAnne."

"Hello, JoAnne."

"Mr. Higgins will be moving to our town in June," said Aunt Sarah. "He is replacing Mr. Shuler as CEO at the Bank and Trust."

"Oh, how nice," said JoAnne.

I looked at my mother, who was listening intently as Mr. Higgins described the home he rented on Main Street.

"I haven't lived in a house since my childhood. That was why I decided to rent rather than purchase. I'm not sure I can adjust to so much living space. When you work in the city, you find it much easier to rent. I chose my apartment because it was walking distance from my work."

"And what city might that be, Mr. Higgins?" asked JoAnne.

"Pittsburg."

Aunt Sarah continued, "I must agree, renting is much more convenient when you reside in the city. I think you will enjoy living within our small community. If you need any help, just ask. I'm sure you will find that everyone is friendly and willing to help. Right, Audrey?"

My mother smiled but did not respond.

"Mr. Higgins, I would like to introduce you to my father and brother."

My aunt, mother, and Mr. Higgins made their way to my grandfather and uncle, leaving JoAnne and me behind.

"Oh my god, that man is gorgeous!"

Watching my family converse with Mr. Higgins, I said, "I can't believe he wants to live in this town."

"The women seem to be happy he chose our town, including my mother." JoAnne motioned in her mother's direction. "She can't take her eyes off him."

It was hard not to notice that my aunt slowly moved my grandfather and uncle away, leaving Mr. Higgins alone with Mom. Mr. Higgins was chatting while my mother smiled, not adding much to the conversation. What amazed me was Mom hadn't broken eye contact.

"Hey, Mr. Higgins seems to like your mom. I don't blame him. She's beautiful. The single women don't have a chance in hell."

My mom was beautiful. Everyone said I looked like her, but I didn't see it.

"You sure have good-looking people in your family."

I laughed.

"Didn't you say he was married?"

"Who?"

"Uncle George?"

"That's what I've heard. A German girl. It only lasted three years."

* * * * *

The next time I saw Patrick was at the Fourth of July church picnic. My mother and he had somehow developed a relationship that I knew nothing about. JoAnne noticed. "Your mother and Mr. Higgins seem pretty friendly. How did that happen?"

"I'm betting my aunt had a hand in it."

"Has she been going out lately without you knowing?"

"Same as usual. I don't ask, she doesn't say, but they do seem friendly for only knowing each other a little more than three months."

I watched my family interact with Patrick. Surely, something had been going on behind my back. I decided to have a talk with my aunt.

"Allison, are you having a good time?"

"Yes."

"Where's JoAnne?"

"She went to get the potato sack for the three-legged race."

"The Harvey boys have been practicing. They're going to be hard to beat."

"I didn't want to run the race this year, but you know JoAnne. She's so competitive."

"I know she is."

"Aunt Sarah, what's going on between Mom and Mr. Higgins?"

"Isn't it wonderful? I haven't seen her this interested in a man since your father."

"How did they become so friendly? Didn't he just move to town a month ago?"

"They both like to read. Your mother said one day he stopped by the library and was surprised to hear she was the librarian. He visits the library quite often. I don't think it is books he's interested in. Who can blame him? Your mother is a beauty. Oh, there's JoAnne. She's waving you over. I think the race is about to start." Aunt Sarah pointed in JoAnne's direction.

This was the fifth year we won. While we were awarded our sashes, JoAnne couldn't resist a little tongue-pointing at the Harvey boys. Patrick came by to congratulate us.

"Great job, girls. I was told you hold the record. Five straight wins?"

"Thanks, Mr. Higgins!"

JoAnne ran off when her mother called her name. "I'll be right back."

Being alone with Mr. Higgins made me feel uncomfortable. "Your mom tells me you and JoAnne are inseparable."

"She's my best friend. We're going to live in New York when we graduate."

"New York? Beautiful city."

"You've been to New York?"

"More times than I can count. Business trips."

"I guess you've traveled the world. Uncle George lived in Germany, so he's been everywhere in Europe."

"I've never been, but I hope to someday. Can I ask why New York?"

"JoAnne and I are applying to NYU."

"What if one gets accepted and the other doesn't? What then?"

"Aunt Sarah went to NYU. Maybe her being an alumna might help. I guess if one of us isn't accepted, we'll figure something out."

My mother walked over. "Allison, JoAnne needs help at the dessert table."

"Nice talking with you, Mr. Higgins. Mom, are you coming?"

"Patrick and I were going to take a walk. Save us a piece of berry pie."

* * * * *

"I think he's younger than your mom. My mom said he's thirty-seven."

"The age difference doesn't seem to be a problem. They have been out every Saturday, and they lunch several times during the week. Soon he'll be joining us for Sunday dinner."

"Your aunt seems to be thrilled. I heard her telling my mother she thinks Mr. Higgins is the one."

"My aunt doesn't know when to butt out. If Mr. Higgins even considers marrying my mother, it would be the biggest mistake of his life."

"Why?"

"She's so boring. I can't believe he's lasted this long. It's been five months."

"I think they look good together."

"You're getting ahead of yourself. My mother is not the marrying type."

* * * * *

One night, I arrived home to find Mr. Higgins sitting in my kitchen.

"Mr. Higgins."

"Hi, girls."

I asked, "What are you doing here?"

"Patrick stopped by to drop off the bank's donations to the Thanksgiving meal fund-raiser."

"Oh, how long are you staying?" Not waiting for an answer, I asked, "Mom, I need to talk with you. It's important."

"What's on your mind, Allison?"

I looked from my mother to Mr. Higgins. "Mom, it's important."

"Allison, stop being so secretive."

Angry with my mother, I blurted out, "I need a dress for the Christmas social. I was hoping you could drive us to Canton on Saturday?"

"I'm sure your aunt wouldn't mind driving you and JoAnne to Canton. I'll talk with your aunt."

My aunt kissed the top of my head, arriving just in time to hear her name mentioned. "Talk with me about what?"

It never failed. Whenever I tried to have a conversation with my mother, my aunt always managed to show up. I was convinced she hid in the closet and appeared on cue.

"This is between me and Mom, Aunt Sarah."

"Allison." My mother shook her head at me. I apologized.

"Sorry, I was just asking Mom to drive JoAnne and me to Canton to check out the dress shops. Feldman's doesn't have anything worth wearing."

"Maybe the Christmas shipment hasn't arrived. Why don't you give it another week?" said my mom.

"Allison has a point. The dresses at Feldman's are nice, but not as nice as the ones in the dress shops in Canton."

"Sarah, I don't want to drive to Canton. Can you take the girls?"

"I think Allison would prefer to go with you."

Patrick interjected. "I know it is not my place, but I'm driving to Pittsburg around five on Friday night. I have an appointment early Saturday morning. If you would like to come along, I'm sure you will find something in one of the dress shops along the avenue."

The only sound being heard was JoAnne's delight regarding Mr. Higgins's suggestion.

"Patrick, that is so kind of you, but I'm working at the library on Saturday. Maybe Sarah ..."

My aunt and I know my mother was not going to change her mind. My aunt moved her stare from my mother and smiled at Mr. Higgins. "The girls and I would be happy to join you. I'll speak with JoAnne's mom. What hotel are you staying at?"

"I'm staying at the Hilton. The bank has several rooms on hold. No need to make a reservation. I'll see to it that the girls and you have adjoining rooms. I might be able to get four tickets to the opera, *Romeo and Juliet*."

"Ms. Holland, you have to convince my mother. I've never been to the opera!" said JoAnne.

"I'll do my best, JoAnne."

"How exciting! The opera, shopping, two nights at the Hilton. Allison, I'm sure we died and went straight to heaven!"

* * * * *

I hated my mother for not coming along. If she was head over heels for Mr. Higgins, why hadn't she agreed to come on the trip? I was sure it was because spending time with me was not on her radar screen. While Aunt Sarah and Mr. Higgins talked, I stared out the car window.

JoAnne bought several style magazines. "Look at this dress! My mom gave me enough money to spend on a dress and accessories, but this might be more than I can afford. Are you listening to me?"

I looked over at the dress. "It's nice. Maybe you can find something similar and less expensive."

"That would be great. I'd look really good in this dress."

* * * * *

"Can you believe this room? The bathroom is larger than the kitchen at home."

"Way too large for the two of us."

"What is your problem?"

"I don't want to be here."

"Are you out of your mind? Did you have something better planned for this weekend?"

I didn't answer.

"I get it, you're pissed at your mom for not coming. Heck, I'm happy to be away from my mom."

"I hate that woman."

"I know you're not talking about my mom, so who is it? Your mom or your aunt?"

"Both. I really hit the jackpot when I got her for a mom. I bet if my father were alive, he'd be here."

"Your mom's not so bad. I just think she's not as outgoing as you'd like her to be."

"What mother doesn't want to spend any time with her only child? Why does she hate me?"

"She doesn't hate you. She never did one thing that makes me believe she hates you. She's just different from Aunt Sarah. Aunt Sarah has social skills, your mother not so much."

"My mother would be different if my aunt would just step aside and give her some breathing room. I hate that woman."

"Hey, remember, I was there that night. Your aunt did all she could to get your mother to come along on the trip with Mr. Higgins. Your aunt's here for you. She cares."

* * * * *

Waking early, I dressed. JoAnne was still asleep. I left her a note to meet me in the dining room.

When I reached the dining room, I spotted Mr. Higgins. As I was about to leave, I heard him call my name.

"Allison."

"Good Morning, Mr. Higgins." Patrick motioned for me to sit. "Where is JoAnne?"

"Still sleeping."

"And your aunt?"

"I don't know."

Mr. Higgins called the waiter over then asked, "Tea, coffee, juice?"

The waiter poured water. "I don't drink coffee, and it's too early for tea. Orange juice, please, thank you."

The waiter smiled. "You're welcome."

"Did you sleep well?"

"Yes. JoAnne decided around 11 last night to order dessert."

"I'm glad. The Hilton is well-known for their desserts."

"The desserts were really good." I began to relax with Mr. Higgins. "JoAnne is really excited about the opera."

Mr. Higgins smiled. His smile was mesmerizing. "First for JoAnne?"

"First for me as well."

"Your first opera—the experience is one you'll never forget. I have meetings until twelve, but your aunt agreed to meet back here for lunch. I hope lunch won't interfere with your plans?"

"No, of course not. Thank you, Mr. Higgins."

"Please call me Patrick."

"I don't think my aunt would think it appropriate for me to call you by your first name."

"Then we'll have to get your aunt's permission."

The waiter arrived with my drink and a basket of muffins. "Today's breakfast special is eggs Benedict."

"I'll have the eggs Benedict, please. Thank you."

The waiter smiled at Mr. Higgins. When the waiter left the table, Mr. Higgins said, "Preston likes you."

"You know the waiter's name?"

"I practically live at the hotel when I'm in town."

"How much time do you spend in Pittsburgh?"

Mr. Higgins lowered his head. I got the feeling I hit a nerve. "Several times a month. There's always a meeting about one thing or the other."

"Because the main branch of the bank is in Pittsburgh?"

"Yes. Seems like I spend my life in meetings."

I laughed. "Seems like I spend my life in school."

"I wish I were back in school." Mr. Higgins smiled.

If anyone could bring my mother to life, it was this man. That day, my hatred for my mother was replaced with jealousy of my mother's relationship with Patrick.

* * * * *

JoAnne and I shopped until we found the perfect outfit. My aunt followed along, never tiring of us. We met Patrick for lunch. JoAnne and I showed him our treasures. My dress had the slightest hint of red on a white fabric, and JoAnne's was solid blue. JoAnne found the perfect sweater for hers. After lunch, we would shop for a sweater for me.

Patrick decided to join us on the afternoon shopping spree. He said he knew the perfect shop to find a cover-up for my dress. Twenty minutes after we arrived, Patrick eyed the most beautiful cashmere sweater; it was red with tiny white pearls placed spaciously on the collar.

"It's beautiful."

"A gift from me to you."

"I couldn't accept this."

My aunt looked from me to Patrick. "A woman graciously thanks a man when he presents her with such a beautiful gift."

Amazed, I looked at my aunt. "I can keep the gift?"

My aunt smiled. "Yes."

"Thank you, Mr. Higgins. I've never owned something as beautiful as this."

"Your aunt has agreed you can call me Patrick. Mr. Higgins makes me feel old."

Saying his name made me feel older than my years. "Thank you, Patrick."

* * * * *

Patrick was now the newest addition to our small family. He joined us for Sunday dinners. My uncle George hung on his every word and even offered an opinion or two. Patrick was a nice addition to our family. There was only one problem: I was falling head over heels in love with him.

My junior year of high school, I was rethinking attending NYU. How could I leave now that Patrick had entered my life?"

I found ways to monopolize Patrick. When my mom invited him to dinner, I'd tell him I was having trouble with a math assignment or a science project. He so easily offered to help, and we laughed and talked while we worked. I knew he enjoyed my company to my mother's. Earning Patrick's affection became my quest. I set out to destroy the relationship he had with my mother and replace it with one with me. I'd look through magazines and read articles on how to keep a man interested. I began to open one too many buttons on the shirt I was wearing and always made sure I sat on the floor so Patrick would have to look down at me. A few times, he couldn't help himself, and I watched as he checked out my cleavage. The shorts and skirts I wore became tighter and shorter.

* * * * *

"I'm not sure I want to live in New York City. I think I'd rather stay closer to home."

"Why are you bailing on NYU? It's been our dream and your aunt's. She loved living in New York."

"I don't know if I should leave my mother."

"Is this about your mother's relationship with Patrick? My mother thinks he's going to ask your mom to marry him. Do you really want to live under the same roof if they do?"

JoAnne's suggestion that Patrick might ask my mother to marry him upset me. Aggressively I said, "He doesn't love her. Why would he ask her to marry him?"

"Hey, don't bite my head off. Listen, I know she's not your favorite person, but if she were my mother, I'd be happy knowing someone is taking care of her while I'm away at college."

"I think my mother is better off alone, and I don't think she'll make a good wife."

"I've noticed your mother's been reading less and smiling more. I don't want to bust your bubble, but I think she's happy."

* * * * *

I needed time alone with Patrick, and I got my chance after Sunday dinner. It was a beautiful day, and my mother convinced Patrick to sit on the front porch and relax. After a few minutes, I made my way outside.

"It's a beautiful day, isn't it?"

"It is."

I sat on the step, looking up at Patrick. "You were quiet during dinner. Are you feeling all right?"

He smiled, looking off in the distance. "I've been consumed with work. I feel like my life is slipping away. George was telling me all the places he visited in Europe. Made me want to rush home, pack a bag, and head to the airport."

My heart leaped in my chest. "You're not happy living here, are you?"

Patrick made eye contact but took a minute or two to answer. "No, I'm happy. A trip to Europe sounds good right about now. Someplace other than the good old USA."

He took a moment before continuing.

"Hearing George describe the places he saw makes me sorry I didn't travel when I was younger. I had a few dollars, could have purchased a cheap flight, backpack in hand, and the two good feet God gave me. I'd have some memories of my own to talk about."

"What's stopping you?"

I connected with those sad eyes, and that fabulous smile had faded. "If only I could …"

I melted.

He reached for my hand. "Has anyone ever told you how pretty you are? Is it wrong for me to tell you you're pretty?"

I answered, "No."

"Let me correct myself, *pretty* describes a child, but a woman should be told she's beautiful. You're beautiful." Patrick removed his hand from mine, and the disconnection made me shiver. He rested his face in his hands and sighed. "I've been questioning every decision I've ever made and the ones I'm about to make." Removing his hands from his face, he said, "If only we could follow our hearts, but sometimes our hands are tied, and we have to walk away, suppress the urges, the feelings, because it's wrong." He stared at me, lingering.

I could feel the blood rushing to my face. I began to sweat.

"Soon you'll be off to New York City. How great would it be if I could toss aside everything and join you in New York?"

The screen door opened, and my aunt announced she was serving dessert.

I often wondered if she listened at the door when Patrick confessed his love for me.

* * * * *

My original plan was back on track. I would be accepted to NYU, and Patrick, of course, would follow me to New York.

I was convinced our last conversation was Patrick confessing his love for me. He wanted to follow his heart, but our age difference was holding him back. In New York, we could be together without the accusing eyes. My family would, of course, disown me, but as far as I was concerned, it was no great loss.

Then my world came tumbling down when Patrick announced in November, during Sunday dinner, that he had asked my mother to marry him and she had accepted. They would be married in late June, after I completed my third year of high school. My mother flashed a nice-size diamond Patrick had given her the night before. I sat silently watching my aunt, uncle, and grandfather congratulating the happy couple. My mother smiled at me, hoping I was just as happy as the others.

I ran from the house and sat on the porch. My aunt was the first to come find me.

"Here you are." Sitting beside me, she put her arm around me and said, "I'm as shocked as you are."

"Are you? Isn't this what you were hoping for?"

"I want your mother to be happy. Don't you?"

"How do we know he really loves her? They haven't known each other very long. We know nothing about his family or where he is from."

"I know this is hard, but it won't be long before you're off to college. Aren't you happy she won't be living in that big house all by herself?"

"She has you, Uncle George, and Grandfather. She's not alone."

I could sense Patrick's presence, so I turned and asked, "Is your family coming to the wedding?"

"Sarah, can I have a few minutes with Allison?"

My aunt stood, and Patrick took her place next to me on the step.

"I want to apologize to you. Your mother and I just realized we should have told you before telling the rest of the family. I don't have children of my own. Like you, I'm an only child. My parents died three years apart. Five years an orphan."

"You have no aunts, uncles, or cousins?"

"Yes, I do. They live in Ireland. My father had a brother, and my mother two sisters. Haven't been in touch with anyone since my parents passed. My father wasn't fond of the old country and never had any desire to go back. But maybe one day I'll get the chance, have a few beers with my cousins."

I couldn't fault Patrick his misfortunes because he was describing my life—an only child, no siblings, no cousins. I wasn't an orphan with one parent still alive, but with my mother's inability to love her only child, I felt as alone in this world as the man sitting beside me.

Back in the house, I hugged and congratulated my mother. She returned the hug and said, "Don't worry, nothing's going to change. I promise."

* * * * *

I tried hard to stay focused on my own life, ignoring most of the planning regarding the wedding.

"Allison, do you have a few minutes to talk?"

My aunt, of course, was very much involved with the entire affair. After she had knocked several times, I reluctantly gave her permission to enter my domain.

Standing behind me, she announced, "Math homework. It was one of my favorite subjects when I was your age. I won't take up too much of your time."

"I need to turn this assignment in by Friday. JoAnne and I have been helping Diane with the school social, so I'm a little behind."

"The social is why I wanted to talk with you. I was wondering if you purchased a dress."

"It's hanging on the back of the closest door. Patrick and JoAnne helped me pick it out."

"Can I take a look?"

I pointed in the direction of my closet. "Sure." I was wondering why the sudden interest in the dress I was wearing to the school social.

"It's beautiful. I can't wait to see it on you. It's the perfect color! The reason I wanted to see the dress is, your mother asked that you and I stand in as her witnesses. I thought it would be nice if the colors of our dresses were of a similar shade."

"Fine with me, if you think this one works. I don't have time to shop for another dress."

"No one will pay much attention to what we're wearing after they get a glimpse of your mother. When your mother entered the church the day she married your father, the congregation fell silent, mesmerized by how beautiful she looked. I'm sure the reaction will be the same. Her dress is stunning!"

As my aunt continued talking, I realized why I had distanced myself from the planning of the wedding.

I was jealous.

* * * * *

The day had arrived, June 29. The perfect day for a wedding.

"This dress accentuates my figure in all the right places. I don't think I'll ever take it off. You know, the night of the dance, Scott asked if I was going to wear this dress to your mother's wedding. I said of course. I wasn't looking, but I did notice a bulge in his pants." JoAnne laughed.

"You know, if you continue on this path, you'll make a name for yourself. I'm thinking *class slut*."

"Hey, you know me better than that. I'm not giving it up to one of these high school boys. I'm saving myself for those college hunks."

My aunt called out to us, and JoAnne ran into the hall. I heard aunt Sarah ask if JoAnne would be kind enough to run down and get the veil, which was draped over the sofa in the living room.

JoAnne ran down to retrieve the veil.

With JoAnne gone, I glanced in the mirror. I spied the look on my face. It read, "This has to be the worst day of my life." My mother the bookworm was marrying the most eligible bachelor in our town, *my* bachelor.

JoAnne popped her head in the door. "Allison, you have to see this!"

Seeing the expression on JoAnne's face, has heightened my curiosity. Entering my mother's bedroom, I freeze. Seeing my mother in her wedding gown has cause me to exhale. My mother turns hearing me, "How do I look?" JoAnne responded, "Mrs. Marks, you look amazing! You're beautiful, your dress is beautiful, and I can only dream of looking as beautiful on my wedding day!"

My mother looked at me. "Mom" was all I could manage.

My mother laughed. "I'm guessing by your response that you approve."

The word *approve* hit me like a ton of bricks. No, I didn't approve of my mother marrying Patrick, but for the first time in my life, I understood why he would want to marry my mother. *She was beautiful.* I always knew my mother was an attractive woman, but the woman standing before me was beyond attractive. She was perfect.

"You look beautiful, Mom." I went to her, and as I stood before her, she took me in her arms. I placed a kiss on her cheek. "You look amazing, Mom. Patrick is a lucky man."

* * * * *

My aunt was right; my mother had again enchanted the congregation when she appeared at the doorway of our church. But it was Patrick's reaction that pulled at my heartstrings. He showered his bride with praises of adoration at the sight of her.

The day was drawing to an end and not soon enough for me. My grandfather surprised us all when he congratulated the happy couple by reading a poem of love, one of my grandmother Erin's favorites he proclaimed. My aunt cried as he read the poem. Uncle George bowed his head when my grandfather's voice cracked a few times during the reading.

The cake was cut, the happy couple danced a waltz, and I calculated an hour was left before this day would be over. While I was watching the clock, I heard a familiar voice. "Can I have this dance?" Looking into those eyes, I couldn't refuse his request. Entering his arms, I took notice of the song, "I Will Always Love You."

Patrick began to hum the song in my ear. I wanted to break free and run, but wasn't this what I'd been dreaming of since the day I knew he was the one? Being in his arms felt right.

"I like the story behind the song. She's strong enough to let go of the man she loves because she knows their differences will ruin the love and respect they already have for each other. She gives up what she wants most of all."

I moved my face far enough away to stare into his eyes.

"She's giving up a life with the person she loves. I don't agree she's doing the right thing. What's the saying, 'Love conquers all'?"

"You're a romantic."

"I believe if you love someone, you make sacrifices. Who cares—"

My aunt tapped Patrick's shoulder. "Patrick, your wife is calling. The sun is setting. The photographer would like several shots of the bride and groom with the sunset as a backdrop."

Patrick smiled and bowed to me. "Thank you for the dance. I hope it won't be our last."

Pushing my feelings of jealousy aside, I got a strong sense of concern. I was fearful my mother might have made the biggest mistake of her life.

* * * * *

My mother was right; life had not changed since she married Patrick. It seemed to me Patrick's business trips to Pittsburgh were more frequent. I began to wonder if he already knew marrying was a mistake.

"He travels a lot more since you've married," said Aunt Sarah.

My aunt wasn't the only one that was worried. I had no doubt this marriage was going to end and end badly for my mother. Seeing her hurt wasn't top on my list, but the marriage ending opened new possibilities for me. My aunt would be devastated, but maybe it was time for my mother to figure out that her sister's interference was her ruination.

I watched Patrick like a hawk on the nights he was home with us. I had to admit, he was attentive to my mother. They went out to dinner, held hands, laughed, and there was an occasional kiss, and with each kiss my jealousy grew stronger. In my heart I knew Patrick couldn't live this lie much longer. No man could. And I was going to help him see the errors of his ways.

I walked around the house in my bikini when the weather permitted. My robe would "accidentally" fall open, revealing a sexy bra and panties. My blouse … well, the button trick worked before, and so did the short shorts. It was exhausting dressing to be noticed, and with Patrick being away so often, I wasn't sure if it was working at all.

Early October, Indian summer came in like a lion. For one week straight, the temperature never dropped below ninety degrees. The temperature inside the school averaged between ninety-five degrees to a high of one hundred degrees. Arriving home from school, I ran to my room. Forgetting to close the door behind me, I stripped naked and headed for a shower. Emerging from the shower with a towel wrapped around my head and body, I sat at my dressing table. Looking into the mirror, I caught sight of a familiar figure discreetly positioned, giving me the perfect opportunity to execute my plan.

As I removed the towel from my head, my hair dropped to my shoulders. Taking my hands, I rustled my hair, moving my head slowly right then left. The movement released the towel around my body, exposing my breast. I carefully applied lotion to my upper body, not rushing the movements. Then the feast of resistance. I stood totally naked and began to apply the lotion to my legs. The thought hit me: *Why stop there?* I applied the lotion to my private parts. After ten minutes of rubbing, I exhaled with excitement. When I thought the intruder had seen enough, I slowly walked toward the door and gently closed it behind me. I leaned on the door and covered my mouth to control the laughter. I hoped the naughty me had aroused the intruder so much so that he'd rethink what woman he'd rather be with.

Patrick was gone the next day after the incident, but his travels lessened, and during the times we were in each other's presence, there was no sign of embarrassment on his part. His affection toward my mother was apparent, but I had to wonder if he thought of me when making love to her. The thought excited me.

* * * * *

JoAnne and I were accepted to NYU. Shortly we would be leaving for college. My mother, without coasting from my aunt, made the decision to shop with me for the things I'd need for college. How many times had I prayed for this day, my mother and I spending quality time together! But us together only depressed me. I told myself she was probably elated that soon she would be rid of me.

My graduation party was a dinner with the family. My grandfather, who spoke very few words to me, joined me on the porch. "This is a special day. Our little girl is off to college. We're so proud of you, and for all your hard work!" He handed me a box wrapped in gold paper. "This is for you. I hope you like it."

My family's gift for any occasion such as this was to shower me with money, which they so generously did. Opening the box, I discovered a heart necklace, and in the center of the heart was a diamond.

"This is the first present I gave your grandmother. I wanted to give it to your aunt when she graduated high school, but I didn't have the heart to part with it. So I had an identical one made for her and your mother. I'm sure you've seen them wear it from time to time."

"Why are you giving Grandmother's necklace to me?"

"Because a little birdie whispered, 'It's time, Will. Give the heart to our granddaughter so she will have something to remember me.'"

Gaping at the gift, I said, "Aunt Sarah says you loved Grandmother more than life itself."

My grandfather put his arm around me. "There isn't a day that goes by that I don't think of her. I go to bed each night with these words, her words, on my lips: 'I love you with all my heart and soul.'"

"I guess when you love someone that much, it's hard to let go. Aunt Sarah says my mother loved my father, but my mother found love again."

My grandfather sadly said, "And I'm happy for your mother, but for me, there was only one, your grandmother. No one could replace her in my heart."

* * * * *

Sitting here at the lake reminds me of my grandfather's words. I feel a powerful connection to him. I, too, have lost the love of my life.

CHAPTER TEN

Sarah

"You look happy," says George.

"You can say I'm both happy and a little concerned."

"Let me guess, Allison?"

"I stopped by to drop off Julia's soccer uniform. She invited me out for coffee."

"Keeping your distance seems to be working."

"Well, I have a confession. It wasn't my idea, distancing myself, but I think you already figured that out."

"I did, but why the invite for coffee? Change of heart?"

"I'm not sure. While I was in line at the coffee shop, I caught a glimpse of her from the corner of my eye. I knew something was wrong."

"Did you find out what was bothering her?"

"I did. She told me Pete wants her to speak to someone, a therapist."

"A therapist? I don't think she will agree to that."

"You hit the nail on the head. She doesn't think anything is wrong, but her behavior is affecting the children and Pete as well."

"Julia mentioned she's been working every Saturday."

"Every Saturday since—"

"Patrick's death. I'm no expert, but it seems history is repeating itself."

"You're referring to Dad. You think Allison is pushing everyone away because she can't deal with Patrick's death?"

"As I said, I'm no expert, but it might be in our DNA, the inability to deal with death."

"We've managed to survive."

George sighs and tilts his head. "What advice did you give her?"

"I didn't want to upset her. I didn't say Pete was right. I told her that I respected him for being a concerned husband, but no one could fault her for mourning the loss of a loved one. I said if in the future she truly feels she needs to speak with someone, a therapist is an option, or maybe a support group."

"And what was her response?"

"She smiled. I can tell she appreciated having someone on her side. I even got a hug and kiss when we parted."

George smiles, knowing that the hug and kiss have made my day.

"I'm happy for you, but sad for Allison. There's something going on, and she better wake up before it's too late."

* * * * *

George's comment weighs heavy on my mind. Both he and I know the effects of depression going untreated and how it can cause havoc not only to one's life but also to the lives of our loved ones.

I often wonder, had my father, who suffered a major form of depression after our mother's passing, lived during these times, with the right medication, would our childhood have been different?

As we grew older, we knew our father loved us. We saw that love in different ways. George and I stopped blaming him for what he had no control over. Audrey never knew the father George and I knew, so in Audrey's eyes, he was normal. She heard stories of our mother, my father's stories; he never blamed my mother's passing on her. Up until the day he died, I knew the only person he blamed was himself.

Sitting in the armchair, I wrap a blanket around me, with the book in my hands. I retrieve the first picture, lingering on the face. I place the photo to my lips and gently place a kiss on the person's cheek, whispering, "I love you with all my heart and soul." Looking upon the photo in my hands, I think back on a life so long ago.

* * * * *

Grandmother Holland adored Lance. Several times she said that if she had control over her estate, she'd leave all her money to him. Lance always laughed and said, "And I would spend every dime on Sarah."

"You foolish boy!" she would say. "Now, what do you two have planned after graduation? Are you applying to law school?"

I said, "That's the plan. I'm applying to Columbia University."

"And what are your plans, young man? Math teacher, science teacher? You'd make a fabulous lawyer. With your looks and charm, you'd be turning clients away."

"Thanks, Mrs. Holland, but my first love is hockey."

"Hockey? If I were the younger me, I'd belittle you until you changed your mind, telling you to grow up and get a real job. But age mellows a person. Makes you say things you never thought you'd hear yourself say, like follow your heart."

"Oh my god, did I hear those words coming from my grandmother's mouth?"

"Young lady, don't take the Lord thy God's name in vain."

"What if I told you I'm not sure there is a God?"

"Since you were a little girl, you've been trying to get rid of me. Do you want me to have a heart attack right here, right now? Of course there's a God! And we all have to answer to him."

"I want to be a fly on a cloud when you meet your Maker. How are you going to defend yourself for being a b—"

"Don't you dare say it, missy. I've told you many times, God can't fault me for being truthful."

We all laughed. Never in my wildest dreams would I have ever thought that in the end, I'd come to love and respect my grandmother. It wasn't the special love I shared with Grandma Maggie, but a different kind of love.

"Got a letter from your brother the other day. He's seeing a German girl. Did he tell you? How easily we put behind what they did during the war."

"Have you expressed your feelings to George?"

"Of course. Mailed a letter to him yesterday, telling him to keep one eye open if he's sharing a bed with her, which I'm sure he is. German women have been known to be very generous with what God gave them."

"And how did you come to that conclusion?"

"European women are not like American women. American women don't sleep around. We wait for the right man to come along. After he places a ring on our finger, then and only then do we share a bed with him."

Grandmother reached out and patted Lance on the hand. "Isn't that right, young man?"

"Yes, Mrs. Holland. Sarah has made that very clear."

I interjected, "I did not say we have to be married to have sex. I said I'd like to wait until after we graduate."

"Graduation doesn't give you the right to sleep around. I'm so happy you live far from your sister, so you can't corrupt her. She's a sweet girl. Keeps her head in her books, not at all interested in boys."

"You know how I found out about sex, Grandmother? I borrowed a book from the library. I'm sure the bookworm will find out the same way I did."

Lance covered his mouth and laughed.

* * * * *

"Did you really read books on sex? How did you get them out of the library?"

"Mrs. Peterson, the librarian. I told her I couldn't ask my father about female issues, and she was too embarrassed to have the talk with me, so she did the next best thing: books."

"I see."

"George and I became aware very soon that our town had a soft spot for the Holland children."

"So did Mrs. Peterson care for you after your mother died?"

"Not exactly. Grandmother Holland moved in for several years, but not the Grandmother Holland you've come to know. And there was Pearl. Pearl was hired by Grandmother to care for Audrey, George, and me. Pearl left a year ago. Pearl is and will always be family. She now lives with her son and his family. Audrey visits her often. Pearl is the only mother figure Audrey ever knew."

"I feel blessed to have had both my parents growing up. My mom took care of our home, and my father worked his tail off. On the weekends, my father, brother, and I would walk a mile to the frozen lake, where my father taught us to play hockey. I hope I'm as good a dad as my father was."

I lay on top of Lance, knowing it excited him. "You have to have sex to become a father."

"And one day I will have children with you, and when they're older, I'm going to tell them how you held out until we graduated NYU."

I unbuttoned Lance's belt, then his pants, and reached in. "Are you going to tell them how we satisfied each other before we did the dirty deed?"

* * * * *

George and I spoke once a week. He spoke about his girlfriend, Hilda, and how her grandfather hid several Jewish families under the barn floor where they lived for several years.

"You really like this girl?"

"She's a friend, nothing serious. Don't read anything into what Grandmother Holland's been telling you. How's the old girl doing?"

"As feisty as ever. Where did you meet Hilda?" "At school. We attend the same college."

"I'm happy for you, George, but I'm elated you're earning a degree!"

"Still seeing Lance?"

"Yes. I'm in love. I'm going to marry him."

"He has my permission to marry you."

I laughed. "Have you spoken to Dad? He's coming for the holidays."

"I've booked a flight. Dad deposited money for me to pay for the ticket. I keep telling him not to do that, but he doesn't listen."

"He wants to do it, and we both know he has the money."

"I can't wait to see everyone. Will Lance be there for Christmas?"

"No. He's going home. It will just be us, but he will be back for New Year's, so you'll get a chance to see him before you leave."

* * * * *

I treasured the time I shared with George, Audrey, and my father during the holidays. Dad and Grandmother seemed to be getting along much better. The old woman was right; she mellowed in her old age. She worried about my father as a mother would.

"How's work? You've cut back a little, haven't you?"

"I have. Have enough years in to retire, but I'll wait until Audrey is out of high school."

"You look tired."

"I always look tired in your eyes."

"You're my son. I worry about you." When my father didn't respond, Grandmother's next question was to George. "George, tell me about your German girlfriend. Is she as strong as a bull?"

"Her name is Hilda. She's no pushover, that's for sure."

"Are you serious about this girl?"

"No. As I wrote you, Grandmother, we're just friends."

"William, did you know George is seeing a German girl?"

"Yes, Mom."

"And you approve?"

"Yes, I do approve."

* * * * *

Shortly before Easter, my grandmother developed pneumonia. My father remained at her side until she took her last breath.

While Lance and I sat in the distance, giving my father time to say goodbye to his mother, I heard him whisper, "I love you with all my heart and soul."

* * * * *

I thought my grandmother would live long enough to see me graduate with honors from New York University. I was happy with the notion that somewhere above, my mother and my grandparents were watching and beaming with joy that my dream had come true.

My father, George, and Audrey clapped and cheered when my name was called and I accepted my degree.

It was the first time I had met Lance's family, and they were very warm and welcoming. My future mother-in-law, as I knew someday she would be, was everything I had hoped a mother-in-law to be, kind and caring.

"You do have the perfect parents. They are so sweet!"

"They've wanted to meet you for a very long time. My father's taken double shifts for the past six months to pay for plane tickets. He's never flown before. He's been over the top. Couldn't wait to see his son graduate from such a prestigious school."

I smiled. "I wish your family lived closer to us."

"Mothers-in-law and daughters-in-law, I've been told, are like water and oil—they don't mix."

I punched Lance in the arm. "Your mother is sweet, and we'd get along just fine."

Life with Lance was heading in the right direction. In July, I was accepted to the law program at Columbia, and Lance would land a job at NYU in the science department and earn his master's. That night, I planned our reward would be my virginity.

"Lance, with my acceptance to Columbia and your being offered a job in the science department and a chance to earn your master's, we are well on our way to saying I do in two years."

But Lance wasn't sharing in my happiness. "Lance, what's wrong?"

"We need to talk."

By the expression on his face, I immediately knew there was something wrong.

"I'm not taking the job at NYU, and I'm going to hold off on my master's. I've been offered a contract to play hockey for two years with a Canadian team. It pays eight thousand a year. I received the offer about a month ago."

Shocked, I scolded him. "So you've already made your decision without talking with me?"

"It's been my dream. Two years isn't that long. I can get my master's degree later . . . ?"

"What about us, our relationship? Am I just supposed to put my life on hold while you skate around Canada for two years?"

"I'm just asking for two years. I promise no more than two years, at the most three."

"Is it two years or three years?"

"I have a two-year contract. If I do well, they could extend my contract."

"No, no, this can't be happening. In two years, I'll have my law degree, hopefully a good position with a high-paying job. What about our plans?"

"In two years, you'll achieve your dream and I'll be happy for you. But this is my dream. All I'm asking is—"

"For me to wait for you two, maybe three years. You said you loved me, wanted to marry me. You never mentioned anything about a hockey contract."

"My agent—"

"You have an agent? You never mentioned having an agent, or a contract. How long have you been lying to me?"

"There was no guarantee I'd be offered a contract. I didn't want to upset you if nothing came out of it, but you're right, I should have told you."

I rubbed my hands through my hair. "I can't believe this is happening! You said you loved me!" I yelled. "I'm not putting my life on hold for you. If you go and someone else comes along, well, you get the picture."

Lance knelt in front of me. "Sarah, please, this can work. You're going to be busy with law school. I might be kicked out after the first year, but I'll still have eight thousand in my pocket. That money means the world to my family. I can't turn down eight thousand dollars."

When Lance mentioned his family, I inhaled. Money wasn't an issue for me. I had a sizable bank account from my father's estate, but Lance's family was depending on him. I had hoped that once we were married and had full employment, we could help his family financially.

"I won't come between you and your family, but you can help your family just as well by staying. I hoped your family would soon be my family. Together we can help them. I would never turn my back on our families."

"You always talk about dreams. This is my father's dream. I can't let him down. I love you, and there's no one else for me. I'm coming back, we're going to be married, I promise you. It hurts me to hear you say you won't put your life on hold. I can't stop you from seeing other men, but in your heart, you know I love you."

"Then stay. Your father will understand. If you love me, stay."

"You won't be happy if I stay. You'll blame yourself if I don't follow my heart. Two years is not that long."

Lance pleaded for me to understand, but I heard myself say, "Get out! I don't want to see you! Don't call me, don't tell me when you're leaving. Just go! Follow your dream, do what you have to do."

To avoid Lance, I left the apartment early and didn't return home until late at night. There was always a note attached to my door, a note I didn't read. Lance tried reaching me by phone, but I removed the phone from the cradle and listened to a dial tone for hours. The night before Lance left, he gently knocked on my door for fifteen minutes. I almost gave in and opened the door. As I leaned against the door, from the other side, he vowed we'd be married, that he'd come back. He begged me to wait, telling me he'd write, he'd call, as often as he could. I had never seen Lance cry, but I knew he was crying by the cracks in his voice as he spoke. I cried myself to sleep for two weeks, then I stopped convincing myself. It was time to move on.

Lance kept his promise. He called every night. I'd lift the phone, hear him call my name, then hang up. Letter after letter arrived. I placed them unopened in a box, which I hid in my closet. If Lance decided to come home, I'd welcome him with open arms, but until then, I would have no contact with him.

As a month turned into two months, my anger turned to hate. I began to tear the letters in two and throw them in the box. The phone calls had lessened, but the letters continued to arrive.

I dived into my studies. Lance and my mutual friends made sure my social life didn't suffer, with our girlfriends saying, "Men, you can't trust them as far as you can throw them," and our men friends adding, "It is only two years. What's the problem? Give the guy a break?"

At NYU, Lance and I had befriended Professor Powell and his wife, Sophie. Sophie had taken a liking to me. She was appalled with Lance's behavior. Professor Powell kept his opinions to himself, saying, "Relationships are either meant to be or not."

The older couple invited me to dinner at least once a month, and I made myself available, knowing they enjoyed the company of a younger person.

This night, Professor Powell started the conversation by asking, "Are you familiar with the law firm Clark and Hutch?"

"Yes, one of the top five law firms in New York."

"Doris Clark is a close friend. We had dinner with her last week. She informed me that the law firm is seeking highly qualified interns. Would you be interested?"

"Of course I'd be interested!"

"As you know, internships are only for experience. There are no wages involved."

"I know. I've placed my name on the list at Columbia for internships with several law firms. Should I hold off until I hear from you?"

"I will speak with Stephen Collins. He's a partner with the firm, or should I say, he *is* the firm. Go forward with your plans but speak with me before you make a decision."

* * * * *

In December, I began my internship at Clark and Hutch. My hours were set around my classes. Two days a week, I started at nine, left at twelve for classes that ran until four, then return to work and work until eight. The other three days, I had three morning classes, arrived at work at twelve, took lunch, and worked from one to eight each day.

This didn't leave me much time to think about Lance. The letters arrived, and I placed them in the box. The phone rang, I'd answer, and hearing Lance's voice, I'd hang up. Then I took to not answering at all.

Being away from home so much, consumed by school and work, helped me avoid Lance's calls. I still kept my job at the diner, working Saturdays and the Sunday-morning shifts, because I loved working for the Epsteins. The Epsteins, Parkses, and Powells became my family in New York City, each couple keeping a watchful eye on my comings and goings.

"I made stew. There's enough for two dinners. You can freeze one, eat the other tonight. You look skinny."

"Thank you, Mrs. Parks. I appreciate all that you do for me, but look at the size of my freezer. I can't fit any more of these delicious dishes."

"You should defrost some of it and take it for lunch. You'll save money if you don't eat out every day."

With all this food, you'd think I would gain weight, but Mrs. Parks was right. I had lost weight.

I often wondered if I would be able to keep up this pace, but truth be told, I was enjoying my hectic life. I was driven to be the best at both school and work. That was my goal.

With my busy schedule, I began to rethink what Lance had said. If he were here, would we be spending quality time together?

After work on Sunday, I would study, and around five each Sunday, the phone would ring. Already having spoken with Dad, Audrey, and George, I knew the caller. Many times, I wanted to reach for the phone and have a civil conversation with Lance, but my pride was stopping me. I wanted him to come crawling back, to beg me to forgive him, and maybe after a while, I would.

* * * * *

The first day on the job, I was escorted around by a sweet girl named Sally Hamill.

"Ellen said to show you around before I take you to the research department." Sally smiled. "I hope you fit in with the other interns. You seem really nice. Most of the interns ... well, you'll see their kind of stuck-up."

After my tour of the office, Sally took me to the research department. The room was an oversize library. Bookshelves surrounded the walls from floor to ceiling. There was a landing halfway up the wall and ladders with wheels placed twenty-five feet apart on the upper and lower level. There were desks everywhere, each having two typewriters on top.

"This is your desk. I placed you as close to the window as I could. It can get pretty depressing in here."

"Thanks, Sally." Sally was right; the room was depressing, and I soon noticed that not one intern looked up to introduce themselves.

"Are they always like this?"

"They're trying to make a good impression. Never know when Mr. Collins or Ms. Church will walk in. Mr. Collins doesn't look favorable on seeing people sitting around and chatting. Ms. Church doesn't mind as long as you don't abuse the socializing. I'm Ms. Church's assistant-slash-secretary. I think she's the nicest person in the office. Between you and me, this firm couldn't survive without her." She smiled. "She wants to meet with you at eleven. I'll call you." Sally pointed to the phone.

"She wants to meet with me. Why?"

"She meets with all the interns. Lunch is at twelve on the days you're here. Everyone eats in the cafeteria. It's frowned upon if you leave the office for lunch. You can eat lunch with me and Jimmy. Jimmy works in the mailroom. You'll like him."

"I'd like that."

Sally walked away, and I sat at my desk, staring at the typewriter.

"Hi."

I looked up. "My name is Frank. I've been working here for a year, but I'm leaving at the end of this week. Got myself a real job at a small law firm."

"Congratulations!"

"Thanks! No one in here will help you, and I would have let you figure it out for yourself if I weren't heading out the door. See that basket over there? It contains requests for research. Each brief describes a case. You do the research using these books as your guide. After you've typed the report, you place it in the Out basket." Frank pointed to the basket closest to the door. "Interns try and turn in at least two or three reports a week. Like I said, I have one foot out the door, so here is a little advice. It's not quantity, it's quality they look for. On the wall you'll find a reference guide to where to locate the books that reference the case you're working on. I'm sure this isn't new to a girl who graduated with honors from NYU."

"How do you know I went to NYU and graduated with honors?"

"I was in Ellen's office when she got the phone call from someone singing the praises of a certain female graduate from NYU now attending Columbia. From the questions Ellen asked, I could tell she was impressed. I guess since you're the newest intern, that might be you."

"Good guess."

"If you impress Ellen, you might be able to call this place home for the next twenty years."

"Maybe I don't want to hang around here for twenty years. My main goal is to be appointed to the Supreme Court."

Frank laughed. "Your association with this firm can get you there."

I laughed.

* * * * *

While I was reviewing my first case file, the phone on my desk rang.

"Ms. Holland, Ms. Church would like to meet with you."

I recognized the voice. "I'm on my way."

"Please have a seat. I'll let Ms. Church know you're here." Sally winked at me.

When I entered the office, the woman's back was to me. By the tone of her voice, I could tell she wasn't too happy with the person on the other end of the phone. Ellen turned toward me and pointed to the chair directly in front of her desk. I sat.

"Stephen, he's got to make a better offer or kiss the plant goodbye." Ellen listened to the person on the other end of the phone. "Do I have a choice? If you can't get him to agree on increasing the offer, then I'll step in. Let me know how you make out."

Ms. Church hung up the phone and took a few minutes before speaking. Extending her hand, she introduced herself. "I'm Ellen Church. If we are alone in this office, you can call me Ellen. Anywhere outside this office, I'm Ms. Church. Professor Powell is a loyal friend of the firm, and he speaks highly of you. Graduated with honors from New York University. *Impressive.* But you're not in Kansas any longer. You'll soon come to refer to this place as the jungle. The university gave you knowledge, and working for a law firm such as Clark and Hutch shows if you have what it takes to be a damn good lawyer or just a lawyer. Time will tell. Sally gave you the tour?"

"Yes."

"Did you figure out what's expected of you daily? Because I'm sure your fellow coworkers weren't very helpful."

"Actually, Frank was very helpful."

"That's because he's on his way out. Sorry to see him go. If you have any questions, you can run them by Sally. If she can't figure it out, she'll ask me. Your reports are due on Friday no later than six. I'm sure Frank told you it's not quantity we're looking for, it is quality."

* * * * *

When I exited Ms. Church's office and passed by Sally's desk, she whispered, "We'll talk at lunch, twelve. Don't forget."

* * * * *

Looking at my watch, I noticed I was ten minutes late for lunch. Sally was watching the door when I entered. She waved.

"Sorry I'm late. I lost track of time."

"Jimmy, this is Sarah."

Jimmy touched his forehead and saluted. "Nice to meet you. So how's your day going? And how are those stuck-up interns treating you?"

"I've met Frank. He seems nice, but he's leaving by the end of the week."

Jimmy said, "Just between us, I don't think he's fond of Mr. Collins."

"Sarah hasn't met Mr. Collins."

"You're lucky. The guy thinks his you-know-what doesn't stink like the rest of us."

"He's not so bad. He's always been nice to me," said Sally.

"That's because you work for Ellen."

"Where is his office?"

"His office is way down the hall. All the partners are far, far away from the working folks. You could go months without seeing any of them."

"Mr. Collins is very handsome," added Sally.

* * * * *

After three weeks, I had contributed five reports. I hoped I had achieved quality rather than quantity. Before turning in my first report, I had Professor Powell read it, knowing I'd receive an honest opinion. He made a few corrections, but overall, he thought I had succeeded in producing quality work.

I thought less and less about Lance and more and more about the letters that were overflowing in the box. I broke down and read two.

Dear Sarah,

I know you hate me, and you have every right, but three months have gone by out of the two years I've asked you to wait. I'm not going to bore you with what is going on in my life. I'm just going to ask you to wait. I will come back, and we will be together. Please don't give up on us. Twenty-one months will go by just as fast as the last three.

Remember I love you and only you. I love you with all my heart and soul.

Lance

The next letter was a reflection of the first. I didn't bother to read any of the others.

Every Friday night after work, Sally, Jimmy, and I would unwind at the pub. Saturday nights, I set aside for college friends. Once or twice, I accepted a date. I had no intentions of getting serious with anyone. My mood was starting to mellow. Two years wasn't all that long. Lance was right; three months had gone by in a flash.

I loved working at Clark and Hutch and had developed a relationship with Ms. Church, several times being called into her office to discuss a report I had submitted. Frank was right; quality outweighed quantity.

"I met Professor Powell at a dinner last week. I told him what a wonderful job you are doing. He said he never doubted you wouldn't give it your all."

"I've learned a lot from him."

"So did I. He was my most favorite professor when I attended NYU."

"I didn't know you graduated NYU, Ms. Church."

At that moment, the door burst open and in walked a man. He was handsome and well-dressed. I assumed this was Mr. Collins.

"He won't listen to reason. We've been over this for months. I can't get him to dig into that large bank account and seal the deal. The town council told the mayor they are not going to let some hotshot businessman come into their town and take control of the building without some compensation. You have to talk with him, Ellen. He'll only listen to you."

"I'll give him a call."

"I need you to call him now. The mayor is waiting for an answer. If he doesn't have one in two hours, they are walking."

Ellen lifted the phone and asked Sally to get Jack Kenny on the line. The name rang a bell—oil or steel—but I knew he was a Texan.

"Jack, how are you? It's Ellen. Yes, Steve is here. No need for name-calling." Mr. Collins raised him arm, made a fist, and placed his other hand over the muscle. I lowered my head. "Jack, this building is perfect as a pharmaceutical and research facility. It's cheap enough. You can't blame a small town in Atlanta for wanting to get a nice return in real estate taxes. The figure is not out of the ordinary. We've had this conversation. You're getting a bargain, and you know it. They are ready to walk, and I'll guarantee you, you won't find a sweeter deal. Jack, don't tell me your business is doing badly—not in this booming economy. Two hours, they want an answer in two hours. I'm not calling you again. In two hours, I tell Atlanta the deal is off." Ellen was silent for a few minutes. "The figure we discussed will make them happy, very happy. You're making the right decision, Jack. I'll bet my salary on it." Ellen looked at Mr. Collins and nodded. Mr. Collins threw her a kiss. "I'll tell him." Ellen hung up.

"He said to tell you he'll see you next month in Texas. Duck-hunting season. Said to wear a bulletproof vest."

"Duck-hunting season! Fuck him! He loves busting my balls."

"You know why he makes your life so miserable. He knows you don't value his business as you do your other clients."

"Screw him! He gets enough of my time. You know he's only with us because of Mrs. Clark. Her husband's clients are loyal to her and this firm. Jack's not interested in the pharmaceutical and research business bullshit. This is for that spoiled bitch of a daughter who, against Jack's wishes, went and married the medicine man. Jack is crying over every penny he's investing in his good-for-nothing son-in-law."

"I happen to like the good-for-nothing son-in-law, and I'm ashamed of you. The medicine man, as you call him, is trying to find a cure for cancer."

"Whatever! I've got bigger fish to fry. Speaking of Mrs. Clark, you heard?"

Ellen looked at me and then to Mr. Collins. "Stephen, this is Sarah Holland. She's our newest intern. She's friends with Professor Powell."

Mr. Collins extended a hand. Looking up, I realized I'd have to agree with Sally. He was handsome—brownish-blond hair, green eyes, square jaw, and high cheekbones. He wasn't Lance handsome, but a close second. Something about the way he handled himself was impressive.

"Hello, Ms. Holland. How long have you been with the firm?"

"Four months."

He shook his head. "Four months. Think you got what it takes to make it to five?" He didn't wait for a response. Speaking to Ellen, he said, "Call me when you have a few minutes. We have to talk. It's important."

* * * * *

Two weeks after that meeting, Ellen called and asked me to meet her for lunch.

Sally approached me. "I made a reservation for two at Pat's. It's on Perry Street, directly across from the building. You must have made quite an impression on Ellen. This is the first time I've made a reservation for her to dine with an intern. I'm so happy for you, Sarah!"

"I hope she's not going to tell me I'm fired."

"When she asked me to make the reservation, she didn't have the dreaded 'You're fired' look. I think you're safe."

I arrived ten minutes early to avoid being late. To my surprise, Ms. Church was already seated.

"Sorry I'm late."

Ellen looked at her watch. "You're ten minutes early."

"I left early not to be late."

Ellen smiled. "Early is always better than late, unless you're trying to make a grand entrance. Then twenty minutes' late works." Ellen looked down and continued to read the brief in her hands. When the waiter came by, she said, "Order something. I'll have the same."

I placed an order for two turkey sandwiches and coffee.

When the sandwiches arrived, Ellen put down the brief and studied the sandwich in front of her. "Turkey, not one of my favorites. At least it's the real thing."

Strike 1 for me.

"You were probably wondering why I wanted to meet."

With my mouth full of turkey, I nodded.

"That day you were in my office, the day I had to convince Jack Kenny to stop being an asshole, you might have overheard Stephen mention Mrs. Clark. Do you remember?"

I contemplated my answer. Was the correct answer yes or no? I went for honesty. "I did."

"Mrs. Clark, of course, is the wife of the late Mr. Clark, the founding partner of the firm. She's also a client. Mrs. Clark didn't just sit around and enjoy the comforts of the lifestyle Mr. Clark created for her. She took the fruits of his labor and invested the money well. She sits on the board for several of the firms she's invested in and more than several charitable organizations. She's rich, very rich, and she's the firm's top priority. Mrs. Clark has been faced with a situation. Without going into details"—Ellen reached inside her briefcase and handed me a file—"I'll need the report on my desk by the end of this week."

Placing the file on my purse, I continued to finish the sandwich on my plate and try to avoid eye contact with Ellen, who had finished her sandwich and was again working on the file. Finishing my sandwich, I called the waiter over and requested the bill. Ellen stopped the waiter in his tracks. "The firm has a running tab with the pub. You should be getting back to the office. As I said, the report is due by the end of the week."

* * * * *

International law. What did I know about international law? And to add salt to my wounds, it involved a child custody case. I couldn't talk about the case to anyone, but I needed help.

"Thanks for meeting me, Professor Powell. I hope you won't think this wrong, and I can be fired for even talking with you, but I need information on a personal level. If you're not comfortable, just say so. I'll understand. I've been given a brief involving Mrs. Clark. It's an international case. I know little about international law, and there's a child involved."

"Doris's grandson Christopher. Sophie told me Doris's daughter-in-law took the boy to live in Italy."

"She's being accused of kidnapping her own child."

"Ridiculous as it may seem, the child is a US citizen. In my opinion, the firm is desperate. Even if they win the case in the US, the Italian government will drag their feet returning the child to the States."

"Is it a story you're willing to share."

"Every story has a beginning. Let's begin with acquainting you with the people involved. Mr. and Mrs. Clark were blessed with three daughters and one son, Michael. Mr. Clark assumed Michael would follow in his footsteps, but Michael wanted to follow his own heart. He wanted to own and operate a vineyard on Long Island. Knowing nothing about running a vineyard, Michael, through a mutual friend, was introduced to Louis De Lorenzo. Louis and his wife were raised in Tuscany and worked the vineyards most of their lives until they left Tuscany in search of a better life in America. Louis was also a mason. Arriving in America, he found a job as a bricklayer, but his heart was in growing the grapes that produced the wine. After a short meeting, Louis invited Michael to his house for a home-cooked meal and a taste of his homemade wine. That night, wine wasn't the only thing that impressed Michael. Louis introduced Michael to his daughter Constance, and Michael fell hard for the girl."

"Mr. and Mrs. Clark didn't approve?"

"On the contrary, they loved the girl. Michael and Constance were married one year later. Mr. De Lorenzo found the perfect land for the vineyard, and Mr. Clark purchased the property. Two new homes were built on the land, a small mansion for the newlyweds and a modest home for Mr. and Mrs. De Lorenzo. *The New York Times* wrote a full-page article on the Clarks' newest adventure. If the Clarks invested in the vineyard, it would be a success."

"So what went wrong?"

"The Korean War. Actually, the war was nearing an end. Michael was a fine young man. He was smart, respectful, and caring. When he set his mind on something, no one could change it. Reminds you of anyone? He watched as his friends were drafted and sent off to fight for their country. It didn't take Michael long to figure out that his father might have pulled some strings to keep him out of harm's way, so he enlisted. After training camp, he spent two weeks with the family before being shipped to the Pacific. Soon after, Constance would announce she was expecting. For the first time in Michael's life, he asked his father to pull some strings so he could return home to witness the birth of his son. He returned to his post one month after Christopher was born. Two months before he was to be discharged of his duties—"

"He was killed?"

"Not by the enemy. He was killed in a freak accident. After the war had ended, Michael became the official driver at camp. On his way back to base, while joking with his passenger, he took his eyes off the road. An army truck carrying heavy equipment had just entered the bend in the road. It was a head-on collision. Michael was thrown from the jeep. He was killed instantly."

I sighed.

"Mr. Clark died one year later. Doris would say he died of a broken heart. She became obsessed with Christopher. She insisted Constance and the baby move to the city. Keep in mind, Constance was mourning the loss of her beloved. Living at the vineyard kept her connected to Michael. Doris's good intentions were wearing on the girl. Her parents were convinced that Doris was trying to replace Michael with their grandson. They wanted to protect their daughter and grandson from the wealthy, powerful Mrs. Clark. When the family arrived in America, they filed for dual citizenship, so her parents insisted she return to Italy with the boy. Smart move by Constance's parents. World War II was still fresh in the minds of every Italian. The government dragged their feet when the attorneys filed a petition to have the child, a US citizen, returned. If the mother chose to remain in Italy, so be it. When Doris's pleas went unheard, she was forced to seek legal counsel."

"Why do you think I was asked to work on a case that doesn't have a chance in hell of being resolved?"

"Now, that is a question I can't answer. My only guess is, they're not looking for an answer. They're curious to see how you would approach a case as complicated as this."

* * * * *

I was sure this was the end of my job at Clark and Hutch.

On Friday at three fifteen, I placed the report on Sally's desk. Sally said she would hand-deliver the report to Ellen and wished me luck.

I passed up on drinks with Sally and Jimmy that night and canceled on a blind date Saturday night. I had to play catch-up on my homework.

On Sunday, while speaking with George, I told him about the Clark family's dilemma.

"Mrs. Clark sounds very much like Grandmother Holland."

George's words convinced me that I had made the right decision ending the report with my own personal opinion.

* * * * *

I found it difficult to concentrate at work. Almost a week had gone by, and I still hadn't heard a word from Ellen. By Friday, I assumed that Professor Powell was right; I was being tested. Ellen knew my knowledge of international law was limited. She probably was critiquing the report. I questioned my ability. Had I referenced the correct law books? Were my findings precise?

Wednesday of the following week, I was called to Mr. Collins's office.

I was escorted into his office by an elegant woman of age. The few times our paths had crossed, I assumed she was a client of the firm.

With the phone gently hanging from his ear and him casually leaning back in the chair, Mr. Collins didn't acknowledge that we had entered his office. The woman motioned for me to sit then left the office. Mr. Collins looked up and made eye contact with me. Ignoring me, he continued his conversation.

"Phil, come on, admit it, you doubted we had a chance in hell of winning. Aren't you glad I convinced you to change firms? I'm happy everything worked out. When are you and that beautiful wife of yours going to be in New York?" He paused, listening. "Great! Dinner is on you. You owe me big-time." He laughed a phony but convincing laugh. "Have a great night."

Mr. Collins hung up the phone. Immediately I could tell his mood had changed. He began to look for something on his desk, still ignoring my presence.

The office door swung open and then slammed shut. Ellen took the seat next to me, also ignoring my presence.

Mr. Collins located the file, and without looking at Ellen, he stood and walked to the window. "We've been working together about seven or eight years." I knew this question was not directed at me.

"It will be eight in January," corrected Ellen.

"Eight years, and over that time, I've ignored your mistakes, but I don't want to waste time hashing them over one by one."

From the corner of my eye, I noticed Ellen rolling her eyes like a teenager who had heard it all before. "Stephen, stop wasting my time. Just get to the fucking point. You don't agree with me. Why?"

Mr. Collins turned to face us. "Why? You have the balls to ask me why? This is Mrs. Clark, not some small-cash client we can dick around. She deserves the best we have, not some intern who came highly recommended by your precious Professor Powell."

My heart skipped ten beats, and I felt the sweat beading on my forehead. Knowing I was the topic of their conversation, I felt the need to talk. "Excuse me, are you referring to me?"

Mr. Collins waved for me to stop talking. I did.

"You asked for my opinion. I gave you my fucking opinion. It makes a hell of a lot of sense to me. If you have a better idea, go ahead, I'm listening."

Mr. Collins was at a loss for words, leading me to believe he didn't have a better idea.

"Stephen, this is a no-win situation. I think we should let Mrs. Clark read the report. She might have hoped we'd find a loophole, but there isn't one."

Mr. Collins rubbed his forehead with his free hand. "This is bullshit! I worked hard to get to this position, and this little spoiled bitch is going to destroy my life."

My eyes widened, and I assumed he was referring to me.

Ellen said, "I don't think Constance was out to destroy you. She was protecting her child."

"Protecting him from what? A wealthy grandmother who could open every door? The girl is crazy!"

"Constance is not a spoiled child. She felt threatened. All I want to do is send Doris the report and have her read it for herself. What harm could it do?"

Mr. Collins threw the report on his desk. "I have a bad feeling about this." He spoke directly to Ellen. "I never saw this report, nor did I give you permission to send it to Doris. If you're wrong, it's your ass on the line, and I'll have no other choice but to fire your ass out of here."

"I'll take my chances."

Mr. Collins turned away from us. Ellen stood and walked from the room. I followed.

I walked behind her confused and wondering what just happened. Ellen stopped. "My office." After I had closed the door behind us, she leaned on her desk, motioning for me to sit. She began by saying, "Trust, can you be trusted?" She didn't wait for me to respond. "When Mr. Collins said he never saw that report, he never saw that report. Trust." Ellen looked toward the door, referring to the office beyond. "They're wondering what went on behind closed doors. A good attorney has to have the ability to give a great performance. Tell them we criticized your work. Cry if you have to. If they sympathize with you, you've accomplished what was asked of you."

Ellen turned and walked to her desk.

"Ms. Church, can you tell me if my report—"

Ellen turned to face me. "If you have what it takes to make it?"

"Yes."

"I think you already know the answer."

* * * * *

I took pleasure in the attention I received from my coworkers. If the law weren't my thing, I'd try acting.

The following week, Sally personally came to get me. "Ellen wants to see you." Then she whispered, "Mrs. Clark is in her office. I hope whatever happens, we can still be friends."

Sally and I walked in silence to Ellen's office. Sally knocked several times, and Ellen personally opened the door. "Come in."

Ellen introduced me to Mrs. Clark. "This is Sarah Holland."

The woman had soft blue eyes and chestnut-brown hair, but it was her complexion that I was drawn to. Similar to a china doll. "It's a pleasure to meet you."

"It's my pleasure, Mrs. Clark."

The woman smiled. "Ellen, can I have a few minutes with Ms. Holland?"

"Of course." Ellen squeezed my arm before releasing it.

"Please sit. I wanted to talk with you about this report."

"I haven't completed my master's, so my knowledge of international law is limited, especially involving a child of American citizenship. I was grateful to be given this opportunity. What I have learned should be advantageous to my career."

"I'm sure it will. To discount your abilities would be unjust. I was impressed, but what most impressed me was your personal opinion."

"Please accept my apologies if I overstepped my boundaries."

"No need to apologize. I'm assuming you might have connected the dots when I asked to meet with you privately, that the case in question is a family matter. Explain to me why you think it's wrong for me to seek legal help in solving this situation."

"The matter in question is of the heart, not a legal issue. It became obvious to me that your daughter-in-law felt threatened. She ran to protect herself from losing her son. Excuse me for being forward, but if anyone knows what it feels like to lose a child, it's you." Mrs. Clark lowered her head. "Lawyers and governments will only cause more harm than good to your relationship with your grandson and his mother."

"I've tried reasoning with Constance. She doesn't believe that I will not interfere with her raising Christopher. As you stated, Ms. Holland, I do know the pain of losing a child, and if my daughter-in-law truly knew and understood, she would know that I would never want her to suffer as I do today, and always. This was all a misunderstanding. I only suggested that she consider moving to the city, where Christopher could take advantage of the best schools and all the city has to offer. My husband and I were very supportive of Michael's marriage. It is a complete shock to me that Constance and her parents chose fleeing over a simple conversation. No, it was my wealth they feared. Fear controlled their actions. If I paid the Italian government the cost to return my grandson to the States, that could cause more harm than good. If I fought her in court, bought a win, to secure that Christopher receives all I can offer, I can lose the respect of the boy. For Constance, to fight me in court for the right to raise her son, as she wishes, could cost her the inheritance Michael left, including the vineyard." Mrs. Clark took a moment. "I myself, if having somewhere to run, would have done the same."

I could see the woman before me was sincere. "I'm sure if you've put your feelings in writing, your daughter-in-law might reconsider and return home."

"I've sent numerous letters and received only one that said she needed to protect her child. That was why after reading your opinion, I was convinced that if anyone can change Constance's mind, it would be you, Ms. Holland."

Confused, I questioned, "Me?"

"I want you to go to Italy and speak with Constance. You're the same age as Constance. I think if anyone can get through to her, it could be you."

"Why would she trust me, someone she's never met? Mrs. Clark, forgive me for being blunt, but why would I convince a complete stranger to return home with her child with no guarantee that she would be treated fairly? I don't want to be a part of a conspiracy. I couldn't live with myself if this was all a trick, and I the pawn."

"I will have a contract drawn, filed in the county, that if, at any time, I bring legal action against Constance in the raising of Christopher, at that time, Christopher will inherit my entire estate. Ms. Holland, Michael was not my only child. I have three daughters and five other grandchildren. Any legal actions against Constance would jeopardize their rightful inheritance."

"I would be remiss if I didn't legally advise you that to offer such a contract would not be wise."

Mrs. Clark smiled.

"Why not make the trip yourself, a face-to-face talk? I'm sure if you expressed your feelings as you did to me, leaving out the contract, I think she will see you are sincere."

Mrs. Clark sighed. "The answer is simple: She refers to the last sentence in the report. Do you remember what you wrote?"

Staring at Mrs. Clark, I said, "Only death can separate a mother from her child."

"Correct. Which leads me to believe you have a story of your own, and I hope someday you'll feel comfortable to share it with me." Mrs. Clark reached for my hand. "Please do this for me. Go to Italy and talk with Constance."

* * * * *

I had no idea why I had agreed to go to Italy, but I did.

"I don't know why I doubted you, Ellen," said Mr. Collins. Turning to me, he said, "Good job, Ms. Holland."

"Did you know she was going to ask me to go to Italy?"

Mr. Collins answered, "We had no idea. We leave in three days. That should give you enough time to pack."

"We?"

"You and I."

"I thought Mrs. Clark was discontinuing legal action?"

"She's not thinking clearly. You think Constance is just going to look into your baby-blue eyes, pack up Christopher, and return home? I'm not leaving Italy until every legal document the Italian government requires is signed, sealed, and dated."

"Does Mrs. Clark know you're pursuing legal action? She promised me she wouldn't. I'm sorry, but I can't be a part of this. Anyway, I completely forgot about school when I promised Mrs. Clark I'd go."

Mr. Collin's face turned beet red. "Mrs. Clark has no idea I'm proceeding filing all the legal documents the Italian government can dig up, and let's keep it that way. Have I made myself clear?" He waved his hands in the air. "Don't worry about school. I'm good friends with the dean at Columbia. I'll get him to agree that you will receive credit for the legal work, which you won't be involved in, in international law and all that other bullshit. So it would benefit you to rethink your going."

"Mr. Collins, you're not listening. I don't want to be a part of your deception."

Furious, Mr. Collins yelled, "If your intentions are to practice in this state, or, for that matter, any state in this country, you better be on that plane!"

Ellen interjected, "This is a great opportunity for you, Sarah. Have you ever traveled overseas?" I shake my head. "Don't you have a brother serving in Germany? Take two weeks, visit with your brother, all expenses paid by the firm."

"Ellen, you have to know, two weeks away from school? How could I make that time up?"

"Professor Powell has agreed to tutor you upon your return. Whether you succeed or not, the firm will pay two weeks' paid vacation and another two weeks' pay during your time with Professor Powell."

Mr. Collins walked toward the door, calling out, "Listen to your mentor, young lady. It takes balls to get by in this business. Don't be a fool." He slammed the door behind him.

"He's right, you know. My job was on the line. Stephen wasn't kidding. If this had backfired, I'd be packing up my office. If this pans out, well, I'll be looking at a pretty sizable bonus." Ellen smiled. "The research you did was spot-on, but what caught my eye was your personal opinion. My gut told me Mrs. Clark would want to meet the person behind the words. Heck, you knew we didn't have a chance in hell in court. Yes, Christopher is an American citizen, and yes, Mrs. Clark has enough cash to buy off the Italian government, but sometimes the heart speaks louder than the law."

"There's no guarantee I can convince this girl to return home. I don't think I'm the answer."

"What do you have to lose? You'll always have a spot here at Clark and Hutch. Mrs. Clark will see to that. I wouldn't have stuck my neck out if I didn't think you could pull this off."

* * * * *

That night, I spoke with my father. He was concerned about me traveling with a man I hardly knew. I felt that was the least of my problems. Deep down, I didn't know if I could trust these people.

I reached out to George and asked his opinion.

"Should I just quit? I can't allow Mr. Collins to make a liar out of me."

"Why quit? Sarah, just be yourself. Find a way to tell this girl she has to protect herself, without uttering one word that will harm the firm. Whatever the outcome, you earned yourself a trip to Italy."

George was right; I would find a way to protect Constance and her son. "The trip sounds intriguing. You have to come visit. Can you get some time off?"

"I'll see what I can do."

* * * * *

Arriving at the airport early, I waited to board the plane.

An hour later, the flight attendant called for me to board. "Excuse me, I'm traveling with someone. He hasn't arrived."

"Ms. Holland, correct?"

"Yes."

"Mr. Collins has already boarded."

I noticed Mr. Collins as soon as I boarded. He acknowledged me. "I saved you the window seat. Am I correct in saying this is your first time flying?"

I wanted to lie and say no, but lying wasn't one of my strong points. "It is."

"Then I was correct in saving the window seat. First flight, you'll want to watch as the plane takes flight."

Mr. Collins worked during the flight, and I studied. Professor Powell weighed me down with material we would review upon my return.

The silence between us was uncomfortable. When dinner was served, Mr. Collins put away his work and said, "I always fly this airline. The food is good. Did you order the steak or the chicken?"

"The steak."

"Good choice."

"The usual for you, Mr. Collins?" said the flight attendant.

"Yes, Carol."

"And you, Ms. Holland?"

"Water, please."

"Nothing stronger?" asked Mr. Collins.

"I only drink white wine."

"Water and a glass of white wine for Ms. Holland. Thank you, Carol."

"You must travel quite often."

"Not as much as I like. Just met Carol today. It's her job to be friendly."

"Then how did she know what you wanted to drink?"

"I boarded early, remember? I had a drink before you boarded the plane."

Embarrassed, I say, "I see."

"So have you decided how you're going to convince Constance to return home with the boy?"

"I'm not sure I can."

"What's your strategy?"

"I don't have one."

"Are you sure you want to be an attorney?"

"I'm sure."

"Then strategically, you should devise your plan of action."

"Why do you care about my strategic plan? You're already convinced my meeting with Constance Clark is doomed to fail."

My response got his attention. As I looked directly into his devilish green eyes, he said, "I do, but if you'd like to hear my suggestion, I'd be happy to share it with you. If not, then I wish you luck."

"Why wouldn't I be open to hearing your suggestions? We do work for the same firm."

"Good answer. I wouldn't have looked favorably on you for not taking the advice from someone as experienced as myself." Mr. Collins raised one brow before continuing. "Constance Clark is a girl who is suffering from the loss of a husband she adored and strapped with a baby to raise without a father. Approach her as you would a best friend."

I had a number of responses rolling around in my head, many of them condescending, but I didn't think this was the time or place to address them with Mr. Collins. I'd follow my heart, not his advice.

When our driver pulled up in front of the home we would occupy during our stay, a man of small statue greeted us. "Hello, Mr. Collins. How was your flight?"

"Good, Michel. This is Ms. Holland."

"So happy to have you as a guest in our home."

"Where's Antonia?"

"Tonia went to the market. She'll be home soon. Come, I'll show you to your rooms."

I was amazed by the number of flowers surrounding the house. "I've never seen so many flowers. The grounds are beautiful."

"Tonia plants some flowers, but mostly it's the birds doing what birds do." Michel smiled.

Michel escorted me to a small room. When entering the room, I gasped. A quaint room decorated tastefully in pastel colors awaits me.

Mr. Collins explained why I was standing frozen with my mouth wide open. "This is Ms. Holland's first trip overseas."

"You've come to the right place. I think my country is beautiful."

"Thank you for having me. I can't wait to meet your wife."

"You will meet her, but you will never talk with her. I'm the only one that speaks English, but I'll translate for you. Down the hall is a bath with a toilet. You have to share, of course."

Mr. Collins said, "The rule of the house: knock before entering. There are no locks on the doors."

"Tonia and I use the outhouse. The bath is for the guests. You can freshen up and take a nap. We will eat later."

Turning toward Mr. Collins, I asked, "When will I be meeting Constance?"

"Not until tomorrow. I'd take Michel's advice. A bath and sleep sound good to me."

"I will call you for dinner. While you bathe, I'll bring tea and cookies to your room. I know Americans like their tea."

First thing I do as I enter the room is step outside onto the balcony. To my left is a lounge chair surrounded with decorative pillows. I breathe the smell of flowers and the clean air of Italy. A knock at the door startled me. Michel enters with a tray of tea and cookies.

"You didn't want to use the bath? Tonia made it pretty for you."

"I'll let Mr. Collins go first."

"Mr. Collins went into town."

Oh. I'll bath later. Can you place the tray of tea and cookies on the balcony, please? The view is beautiful."

"Si. I'll let you know when dinner is ready. Tonia's been cooking all day."

I couldn't get enough of the magnificent view from the balcony—small green mountains, with vines filled with grapes and flowers scattered everywhere. I breathed in deeply, thinking, *How lucky are you, Sarah Holland! Your first trip to Italy, of all places!*

The bathroom was quaint and filled with flowers, and the bathwater warm. Spying beneath the tub, I noticed a metal tray filled with hot coal. While I was bathing, the door opened. I immediately covered my naked body. The smallest woman with a sweet round face appeared. Without making eye contact, she placed fresh towels on the ledge. "Excuse, excuse." It must be Tonia.

I fell asleep on the chair outside my bedroom, awakening to a knock on my door.

"Miss dinner."

I threw a dress over my head and stepped into my shoes. I walked down the stairs and through a small hallway that led to a large kitchen half-open to the outdoors. Looking ahead, I noticed there was a colorful garden. Beyond the garden were the mountains.

Michel said something in Italian to Tonia, and she came to stand next to me. She bowed and took my hand, shaking it gently, while Michel repeated my name. "Excuse me, Tonia can't say Ms. Holland. Do you have another name?"

"Sarah." I repeated my name to Tonia several times, and she came close to getting it right.

"Is Mr. Collins joining me?"

"No. He's not back from the town. You enjoy the view and dinner."

They placed a plate of pasta, meat, and bread on the table, and I noticed that Michel and Tonia sat at a very small table in the kitchen area. I turned and asked if I could come sit with them. They looked confused and spoke to each other in Italian. "This is a small table, Sarah. You won't be comfortable."

"Then please come sit with me."

"The guests sit at the large table."

"Michel, I'm all alone. Will you and Tonia please sit with me?"

"If it will make you happy."

"It will make me happy."

Soon the difference in language began to subside. Tonia and I were getting our points across in sign language. I couldn't count how many glasses of red wine I drank, but by dessert, I welcomed the black coffee Tonia served.

That night, I slept like a baby.

In the morning, I came to find Mr. Collins sitting at the large table in the kitchen. He was dressed in casual clothes, light slacks and a white shirt. With the sun behind him, he looked extremely handsome.

"Good morning."

"Good, you're up. You have a long day ahead of you. Your driver—his name is Rocco—will take you to where Constance lives. Her home is on a steep hill. Rocco will drop you off at the bottom of the hill. You'll have to climb to the house. He won't leave, so when you're finished, just walk down to where he is."

Mr. Collins pointed to the small table. Rocco waved.

I buttered two slices of thick bread and drank dark coffee while Mr. Collins studied the papers in front of him.

"Are those the legal Italian documents you need to complete?"

"They are. I can speak Italian, but reading is difficult. Michel is paid well for his help."

"Is it always about the money with you?"

Mr. Collins smiled. "Always."

Finishing my breakfast, I got up to leave. "Good luck," said Mr. Collins.

* * * * *

Rocco spoke broken English, but I was able to make out what he was saying during the ride. Rocco stopped the car and pointed up the hill. Mr. Collins wasn't joking; it was a steep hill. I began to climb, stopping twice to catch my breath. When I reached the top, there was a gate similar to the gate at Michel and Tonia's home. Of course, the front garden was filled with flowers. I opened the gate and walked toward the house. A playpen is outside the open front door. Inside, a small child sat playing. He stood when I approached him. I knelt down and said, "Hi! Is your name Christopher?"

From the front door stood a young woman. "And who are you?"

I stood, and before me, I assumed, was Constance. She was five foot six, with an olive complexion and dark curly hair that reached her shoulders. She was exotic.

"Hi! My name is Sarah Holland." I extended a hand. She didn't acknowledge it. She remained with her arms crossed over her ample breasts.

"And how can I help you?"

"Are you Constance Clark?"

"If he is Christopher, then yes, I am Constance Clark. Did she send you? I was wondering when someone would show up. I thought it'd be that slick attorney or his sidekick."

"Mr. Collins. And the sidekick, I'm guessing, is Ellen Church?"

"That's the one. Are you here to give me some documents from the government forcing me to bring my child back to America because America held him in her womb for nine months and gave him life?"

"No. All I have is a letter. Mrs. Clark asked that I deliver it to you personally." I pulled the letter from my bag and handed it to Constance. She stared at it long enough to make my extended arm start to hurt. When she took it from my hand, it was with force. I was sure she was going to tear it into pieces, but she placed it in her apron pocket.

"You delivered the letter, you can go."

"I'm a little thirsty after walking up that very steep hill. Can I bother you for a glass of water?"

Constance stared at me.

Assuming I wasn't getting a glass of water, I asked, "How old is he?"

"He's two."

"He's a good-looking boy."

Constance stared at her son then took him from the playpen. "He looks like his father. Come, I have some orange soda in the fridge."

"Thank you." I followed, watching the woman's dress sway from side to side. This woman was a woman men dream about. I took a seat and glanced around. "The homes in Italy are so quaint and beautiful, and the gardens are amazing."

"Where are you staying?"

"Can you believe I never asked Michel or Tonia their last name?"

"DeLuca."

"DeLuca."

"Nice house. Tonia's a good cook."

"She is."

"Everyone here knows everyone. My uncle owns all the land on this hill. His house and my cousins' houses are behind this one, but you'd have to walk past the trees to see them."

Constance placed two glasses of soda on the table. Christopher reached for the empty bottle, and Constance retrieved it and gave him a full bottle with a nipple. She smiled, making me smile.

"He's so sweet."

"He is sweet. You know, this sugar-and-spice approach is not going to work."

"Anyone who knows me would never refer to me as sugar and spice, believe me. I'm not married, no children of my own, so the only contact I've had with sweet babies has been with my sister Audrey. And that was many years ago."

Constance stared when, in one gulp, I drank the soda. "You weren't lying when you said you were thirsty. What's your name?"

"Sarah Holland. But you can call me Sarah."

"I don't have any more soda. Would you like some water?"

"No, thank you." I stood to leave.

"So that's it? You came all this way just to give me a letter?"

"That's it. I got a two-week paid vacation to Italy to deliver a letter. My job is done."

I said goodbye to Christopher and walked toward the door. "Aren't you a little bit curious why I won't read the letter?"

I turned. "Not at all."

"That leads me to believe you know what the letter says."

"No. Believe me or not, I only met Mrs. Clark one time, and I believe the woman is sincere."

"You are telling me you met Doris one time and she offered you a paid vacation if you delivered this letter?"

"Yes."

"Why you?"

"Why me? Good question. See, there was this report … long story. Read the letter. If you want to talk, you know where to find me."

* * * * *

Walking into the kitchen, I found Michel and Mr. Collins sitting at the table with a slew of papers spread between them. "Need help?"

"No. I think we're about done for today. So how did your day go?"

"Just as I thought."

"I hope you took my advice?"

"We're playing for the same team, aren't we? Teamwork—isn't that what it's all about? Oh, no, I forgot, it's all about the money."

* * * * *

Changing my clothes, I took a long walk through the mountains and gardens. Winded, I sat and took in the view. I hugged myself and wondered how I got so lucky.

The following morning, Michel told me I had company and she was waiting up there at the top of the mountain.

"All the way up there?"

Reaching the top of the mountain, I called, "Constance."

She turned. "Hello, Sarah."

"Where is Christopher?"

"He's with my aunt. Let's walk toward her house. She's expecting us for lunch. I'll show you where my father and mother grew up, unless you have to get back?"

"I'd love to meet your family." With her eyes she questioned the truth in my statement. "I really mean it. I'm so enjoying your country and the people."

As we walked through the hills, Constance pointed out vineyards and talked about the history. "A man whose family worked the vineyards would save his money, marry, and take his wife to purchase a small plot of land. On this land, they would plant twenty to thirty vines and ten olive trees. If the grapes didn't grow, maybe the olives would. If after a year the man was successful and the grapes were good to harvest the wine, he would find one or two men to help. Within five years, he would have developed a town of fifteen families. My great-grandfather created this town, but my grandfather, his only son, spent the profits on fast women, drinking, and gambling. He was forced to divide the land and sell it off, except for fifty acres, where my family now lives. Michael, my husband, had the same dream. His parents bought him the land, and he followed his dream with the help of my parents." She paused. "I read the letter. Doris swears that if Christopher and I return home, she won't interfere in our lives. Her only request is that she remain a part of Christopher's life." Constance paused as she glanced over the countryside. "When Michael died, I was heartbroken, but Doris was broken. Losing Michael took the life from her. If it weren't for Christopher, I don't think … My mother thought Doris was overbearing, and she convinced me to take a trip to visit with my family. I was hurt when Doris accused me of kidnaping my own son. You know who was behind this? That snake Mr. Collins. The man has no heart, but Michael said he was the best attorney, and to be the best, I guess you have to be heartless."

"Constance, I might agree with you about Mr. Collins. Maybe he did advise Mrs. Clark. As her attorney, it's his job. You could have talked with Mrs. Clark, told her you needed to get away. I think she might have understood. But when you didn't confide in her, how could she not think the worst?"

"Do you believe what Doris said in this letter?"

"I did believe her when she said she wanted what was best for you and Christopher. You're her family. Christopher sealed that relationship the day he was born."

Constance pondered what we spoke about then said, "It's getting late. My aunt will be wondering what happened to us."

Constance's family was as hospitable as Michel and Tonia were. Not once did they make me feel like I was the bad attorney from New York. Constance was happy. She laughed with her male cousins, who asked if I was in search of a husband. Constance said she didn't know me well enough to ask about my personal life.

With Christopher lying in a carriage, we walked back to Constance's house after dinner. Christopher pointed and said the word *trees* and then repeated over and over the word *dad*. "I taught him to say Dad. I wish Michael were here to hear his son."

When we arrived, Rocco was leaning on the gate. He removed his hat and bowed at the waist. "Your ride is here."

"Thank you for a wonderful day! If you'd like, Rocco can pick you and Christopher up tomorrow. We can go to town for lunch. I need to do some shopping for my family."

"That's a great idea!" Constance spoke to Rocco in Italian.

He repeated, "Eleven."

"I know a nice place to have lunch." Constance kissed me on the cheek. "See you tomorrow!"

* * * * *

Hearing the knock on the door, I opened it to find Mr. Collins.

"I got home late last night. What happened with Constance? It better be good. The town officials are nothing but a bunch of idiots. They find something wrong with every document."

"Today we are going shopping and having lunch."

“Sounds good. You’re building a friendship. I’m glad you took my advice.”

“I don’t think she sees me as a threat.”

“All right, then. Have a great day. The bath is yours. I’m hoping this nightmare will soon be over. I need to get back to New York.”

* * * * *

“I haven’t felt this relaxed in a long time. You’re so lucky to call this place home.”

“Far from the hustle and bustle of New York. You’ll need another suitcase for all the treasures you found.”

“I couldn’t resist. The books are for my sister, Audrey. The sweaters and hats are for my brother and dad. This bag is filled with gifts for my friends.”

“I can see you have a generous heart. Doris saw this as well.”

“She seems like a very nice person, but as I said, I only met her once.”

“I still don’t understand why Doris sent you. Why didn’t she come herself?”

Finishing my story, Constance asked if I would share with her what I said in my final statement.”

There was a lot of legal words, but my last and final paragraph was derived from my own personal experience. “My mother died when I was eleven. Her dying destroyed life as we knew it. Believe me, Doris is no fool. She knows bringing legal action against you will only sever your relationship. I don’t know why me. My only answer is, she knew she and I were on the same page.”

“How did your mother die?”

“A brain aneurysm after delivering my sister, Audrey. My father lost the will to live. They were very much in love.”

After speaking the words out loud, I watched as Constance’s facial expressions changed.

“I know exactly how your father felt. I guess it’s different when you’re a mother. I don’t think I could just stop living. If I did, what would happen to Christopher?”

"Funny you should say that. I always felt if my father had died, I believe my mother would have gone on for her children. It was hard losing our mom so young, but when we lost our father as well, it almost destroyed us."

"When your brother arrives in Italy, you must bring him by the house. I'll make dinner."

* * * * *

That night, Mr. Collins was happy when I reported that Constance and I had a wonderful day, but the subject of her returning to the United States never came up. To my surprise, his reaction was calm. I thought he was confident that my relationship with Constance would spark her to make a decision soon.

* * * * *

"I spent yesterday with Tonia. We went to the market. I wanted the kitchen fully stocked. I can't tell you how excited I am to see my brother."

"You love your brother. I have two brothers. I miss my family. That's why I've decided to return to the States."

"You're coming home?"

"I made the decision long before you arrived. After we had lunch, I called Doris. We had a long talk. I told her she made the right decision to send you in her place."

"But you had already made your decision. Doris should know I had nothing to do with you and Christopher returning to the States."

"When I first met you, when you spoke, you reminded me of someone. That night, while I lay awake, it came to me. Michael. I wanted to believe that Michael sent you to me. It was his way of saying it's time to go home. It wasn't easy for me to accept that Michael's mother accused me of kidnapping my own son, but I know it wasn't her choice to take legal action against me. It was the snake Mr. Collins." Constance paused to remember. "What Michael and I shared was special. I thank God for blessing us with Christopher. I couldn't imagine my life without Christopher, but Doris also lost a child. She's suffering. She needs Christopher in her life to lessen the pain."

"She also needs to know the truth. That it was your decision, not mine."

"It's too late. I told Doris it's because of you that I decided to come home. If it weren't for Doris, you and I would never have met." Constance smiled. "I made a reservation for Christopher and me to fly back with you. I'll need help with the baby."

* * * * *

A knock on the door left me to believe that Mr. Collins was announcing the bath was free. The knocking continued.

When I opened the door, he lifted me up and spun me around. "I don't know how you did it, but you did it! Constance booked a flight for her and the boy. She's returning home with you! You better make sure she boards that plane."

"I didn't do a thing. It was Constance's decision to return home."

"Listen to me, I never want to hear you say that you had nothing to do with her return. The girl is singing your praise. She's your ticket to success. Do you have a really nice dress? Get yourself all prettied up. I'm taking you to a nice restaurant to celebrate."

Mr. Collins lifted me again. When he placed me down, he kissed the top of my head. "We leave in thirty minutes."

* * * * *

"Every place I've been is more perfect then the last."

"This is the restaurant I frequent when I'm here."

"You've been here before?"

"Yes, many times. One of our clients is Olive's, the olive oil company. Robert Morgan's the owner. He loves this restaurant."

"Have you traveled much?"

"I've seen most of Europe, mostly on business. Sometimes I'll take a day or two to sightsee, but New York is my home. I love that city more than life itself."

"I also like New York, Mr. Collins."

"Stop with the Mr. Collins. You earned the right to call me Stephen."

"I like New York, Stephen."

Stephen smiled. "I said we were going to celebrate, so let's start with a nice bottle of red wine."

The owner of the restaurant began to sing. After three bottles of wine, Stephen and I swung our white napkins in the air, mimicking the owner.

When we left the restaurant, Rocco had to help me into the car. The wine made me feel dizzy. Stephen continued to sing on our way back to the house. Entering the house on our tippy toes, Stephen asked me to wait. He went into the kitchen, returning with a bottle of wine and two glasses. On the balcony in my room, we drank and star-gazed in silence.

After we finished the wine, Stephen said, "Well, I should be going. I have a long walk home."

Laughing out loud, I covered my mouth not to wake anyone. I lost my balance. Stephen reached for me. "Steady, girl. We can't have you going over the railing!"

In his arms, looking into those eyes, surprising myself, I kissed him. Pushing away from him, I apologized. "I'm sorry, I shouldn't have."

Stephen pulled me back to him. "Don't apologize. I liked it. Can we do it again?"

My first impulse was to stop, but I wanted to kiss him again. Thoughts of Lance crept in and my promise to save myself for him. But why should I honor such a commitment when he never thought our relationship was worth holding on to? "Yes, I would like you to kiss me again."

After several minutes of us kissing, I felt Stephen's hand slowly lower the zipper on my dress. I easily slipped from the dress, standing before him in my slip. He didn't reach for me, so I removed one strap of the slip at a time, revealing my breasts. Stephen seemed pleased, which caused me to blush. He said, "You're beautiful." He stepped forward and took me in his arms. Staring into my eyes, he smiled, then placed his lips on the side of my neck. I inhaled. Slowly he moved to my breast. I exhaled with delight. When he felt he had succeeded in pleasuring me, he lifted me in his arms and placed me on the bed. For a few seconds, he stared down at me and then lowered himself on top of me. The weight of his body and feel of his skin touching mine was exciting. I placed my hands on his lower back and pressed him closer to me, then he whispered, "I've pictured this moment many times."

My eyes widened with his confession. Our intimate moment was broken when I asked, "You imagined us together?"

"I could lie and say I haven't, but I'm sure every guy that meets you imagines himself lying with you."

My mind rushed off to another place and time. I thought of Lance. I had convinced him postponing intercourse was the right thing to do. It was at this moment I decided to reveal my own confession. "Stephen, this is the first time for me."

Stephen cocked his head and said, "Then I promise to be gentle."

After a gentle kiss, he moved down upon me, finding that special place. When his lips touched me there, I willingly opened up to him. Again, I thought of Lance, for this was the way that he and I found pleasure without intercourse. I wasn't sure if it was the wine or the cool breeze blowing in from the mountains or the view that I spied when I turned my head, but Stephen aroused me like no other. I wanted this man, who was experienced in the art of making love, and I was elated above all that he was my first. When I pleaded for him to enter me, the pain only lasted a few moments. When I opened my eyes to look into his, I saw him watching me. I blushed. For a brief moment, I was ashamed of my behavior. He moved to a sitting position and placed me on top. We were face-to-face. With every movement and the touch of his hands upon me, I climaxed not once, but twice.

We made love several times that night, until Stephen said, "It's almost morning. I need to sleep."

"I don't want to sleep. Let's do it again."

"Are you sure this was your first time?"

"Yes, and it was perfect! Better than perfect."

Stephen kissed me, "The sun is coming up." Stephen turned me toward the open window with his body perfectly positioned with mine and said, "It wasn't my first time, but a time I will never forget. Now close your eyes."

* * * * *

I woke to the sound of chickens outside my window. I reached for Stephen but soon realized I was alone. Pushing back the covers, revealing my naked body, I reached for my robe.

I walked into the kitchen to find Rocco drinking an espresso. "Where is everyone?" I asked.

"The boss is gone. He left an envelope for you. It's on the table. Tonia went to the market. You'll have to make yourself something to eat. You missed breakfast."

I rushed to the table to retrieve the envelope. Opening the letter under a tree in the backyard, I read.

Sarah,

I didn't want to spoil our perfect evening by telling you that I had to fly to England today to meet a client, then I'm heading back to New York.

I'm sorry I will not get to meet your brother. When duty calls, as you will soon find out, the client always comes first.

Please enjoy the remainder of your vacation. Have a safe flight home.

Stephen

The letter was short. I asked myself if I was hoping for more. Words of love? Not really. I hardly knew this man, but for the short time I knew him, I was willing to give of myself freely. I was swimming in unfamiliar waters. I told myself this was life in the fast lane, the big leagues. I was far from the secure relationship I had with Lance. Laughing, I asked myself how secure that relationship was. Lance easily walked away to follow his dream.

I hated Lance for leaving me. I hated myself for cheating on Lance. I couldn't find it in my heart to forgive him, but this stranger, this man, I understood, had his priorities. He took my virginity and flew off because the client's needs came first. I had to remind myself it was all about the money.

I spent the days before George's arrival lying in the grass, thinking of my night with Stephen. Stephen Collins had taken control of my mind. I couldn't stop thinking of that night without smiling. Sex did not disappoint. Having a man inside me, giving him pleasure, him pleasuring me—it was exciting. I was glad I had crossed over from a girl to a woman. If Stephen was a fling, when I returned home, the search to find that special someone would be my next quest.

"You seem different, Sarah. You're falling in love with Italy, yes?"

"I am, Constance. It's so beautiful here. I'm relaxed and at peace with the world."

"You're on vacation. If Italy were your home, you'd feel differently. What time is your brother's train?"

"He should be arriving now. Rocco went to pick him up at the train station."

"You didn't want to meet the train?"

"I overslept. Rocco left without me."

* * * * *

The car approaches, I ran to meet it, calling George's name.

George exited the car, and I jumped into his arms. "I can't believe you're here!" Pulling back, I couldn't believe that my brother had grown taller than me, much taller. "You're taller and leaner. You've aged!"

"I'll take that as a compliment. You look great. Nice tan. Italy agrees with you."

I smiled. "Come, you have to meet everyone!"

"George, this is Michel and Tonia. You've already met Rocco, and this is Constance and her son, Christopher."

"It's nice to meet you. Sarah goes on and on about you," said Constance.

George smiled. "Only good things, I hope."

Constance smiled. "Yes, only good things."

"And this little fellow must be Christopher?" George lifted the boy in the air. The child giggled with delight.

"See, George? Just as I told you, he's always happy, never cries."

I allowed these special people to fuss over my brother and knew this would be a wonderful vacation.

* * * * *

Our days were spent exploring, and our nights were filled with wine and laughter with our new friends. Michel, Tonia, and Rocco were comfortable to now sit with us at the big table, as Constance translated English to Italian and vice versa. On our last night together, Tonia prepared a special dish of trout and a special desert of sponge cake soaked with sweet wine set in a creamed pudding made from mascarpone cheese.

When everyone went off to bed, George and I went out back, lay on the grass, and marveled at the stars above us.

"So was I telling the truth? Constance is an exotic beauty, right?"

"She is beautiful and very sweet. Hard to think of her as a kidnapper."

"I knew you'd like her, and you two seem to have hit it off. And the boy … well, you just want to eat him up. I know he's taken a special liking to you. He just lights up when he sees you."

"Sarah, where are you going with this conversation? I have a girl, remember? Hilda. She'd be lying here with us now if she hadn't promised her sister she'd be there to help with the baby."

Changing my position to face George, I asked, "Are you going to marry this girl?"

"I've thought about it, but I haven't gotten up the nerve to ask."

"Did she agree to move to the States?"

"We've talked about it, but I'm not sure I want to move back to the States."

My heart sank. "You're never coming home?"

"Never say never. Maybe someday. Hilda's close with her family. Worries about everyone, just like you. I can't wait for you two to meet."

Furious with George, I said, "How can you live in a country with people responsible for the death of six million innocent people? She's German, George. Her family were Nazis!"

George faced me and said, "You sound like Grandmother Holland and just as stubborn. As I told you many times, Hilda's grandfather owned a farm way out in the country and he hid several Jewish families for years. Not all Germans fell under Hitler's spell."

"You're just doing this to get back at Dad. You know he wants nothing more than for you to return home. He's different, George. You should give him a chance."

"I speak to Dad every week, Sarah. He's happy for me, and he's never once mentioned my returning home."

"What about me? I want you to come home. Since you've been here, you never once asked about Lance and what his leaving did to me. I'm lonely. When our grandmothers were alive, it was different because I had them to care for. I was sure once you got your head on straight, you'd realize New York is where you can make a life for you and this Hilda."

I choke up, and George's face softened. "You're right, I never ask about Lance because you told me it was over and if he came crawling back, you might not be able to forgive him for leaving."

What I said and what I felt were different now with Stephen in the picture. What was confusing, I felt no guilt about making love to

Stephen, and the man I once loved and respected, whom I convinced to wait until I thought the time was right, I tossed aside like an old dishrag.

Glancing at George, I said, “Lance and I are over. I met someone else.”

“Good. I’m happy for you.”

“We’re not serious, not like Lance and I were. Anyway, it’s too soon to know if he is the one.” I ended the conversation. “We should go back. I haven’t finished packing. Rocco said we have to be on the road by seven so you’ll make the train back to Germany.”

“Is Constance driving with us?”

“No. Her entire family is driving her and Christopher to the airport. I’ll meet them after, when the family is all cried out and on their way back home.”

* * * * *

I kissed my brother goodbye. He whispered, “I love you with all my heart and soul. Don’t be mad at me.”

Hugging my brother, I whispered, “I could never be mad at you.”

After we had boarded the plane, Constance asked if I was feeling well. I told her I was fine, just sad to be leaving my brother and this beautiful country.

CHAPTER ELEVEN

Allison

School is nearing an end, and summer is right around the corner, which causes my anxiety to heighten. My children are looking forward to camp, and Pete is looking forward to our annual two-week vacation in Florida.

It is Andrew's last baseball game of the season. He's hit a home run, and I'm giving thanks that this Saturday Pete is stuck in Florida. There is no reason to make excuses about work. Deep in thought, I reconnect when a familiar voice says, "Hi, Allison!"

"Dr. Greenberg! It's been a while."

"Allison, remember first names only. I don't see Pete?".

"Is Pete around?"

"He's in Florida."

"Things aren't easing up?"

"No. If anything, I think it's gotten worse. The Florida State Department is dragging their feet on executing the license to get the office open and operating."

"I know. Pete's shared his frustrations with me."

"Professionally?"

"No, just guy talk, watching the game. I'm happy you're here. My wife's been wanting to meet you." David points. "That's Alice, the woman leaning over the gate. She wants as many pictures as possible of her little girl as head cheerleader."

I smile. "They grow up so fast."

"Since our son went off to college, Alice makes sure she spends as much time with Ellen as she can. The first child gets all the attention. She's trying to make up for lost time before the last bird leaves the nest."

David's words hit home, as I know shortly Andrew will be off to college. "I don't know about that. Julia demanded all our attention the first time she opened her mouth."

Alice makes her way toward us. She's five seven, slender, her shoulder-length naturally blond hair swinging into place with each move of her head. She has a classic look, the look women pay big bucks to achieve.

David kisses his wife's cheek. "Did you get enough pictures of our daughter?"

"Stop teasing me, David."

"Alice, I like to introduce you to Mrs. Cane."

I reach out my hand and correct David. "First names only, remember? Allison, it's so nice to finally meet you."

"Same here. Allison, I don't think it will come as a surprise that our daughter is very smitten with your son, Andrew, and David and I couldn't be happier. He's a fine young man."

"Ellen is a sweet girl. Andrew is the lucky one."

"All right, I'll have to put a stop to this before you two start planning a wedding," says David.

"I wouldn't be upset if Andrew is Ellen's choice ten years from now," says Alice.

Not to offend Alice, I agree our children seem right for each other, but deep down I know Andrew's wife is out there somewhere, as sure as I am that Ellen will someday meet her prince charming.

On the ride home, I want to question my son about his feelings for Ellen, but he surprises me when he asks, "Mom, how long were you and Dad dating before you knew he was the one?"

"At first, your father and I were just friends."

"Like Ellen and me?"

"Yes, but we were much older, college age, and there were a few boyfriends and girlfriends before we started seeing each other."

I look in the rearview mirror. By the look on Andrew's face, he's sure Ellen is the one. My heart begins to ache. I wonder if he is a chip off the old block. Has he fallen so hard for this girl that he can't see a life without her? How do I stop him from making the same mistake I did? My hands are tied. If I try to talk with him about seeing other girls, he will shut me out completely. I think about how important it is to stay close to Andrew. He will be most affected by my leaving Pete.

My relationship with Pete has been severed. Pete's being away so often is working. When he is home, he doesn't have the energy to work at fixing our marriage. He's hoping our two-week vacation will help repair our broken relationship. I, on the other hand, am not going to let that happen. I'll fight and whine that my passing on the trip will get me caught up at work and give me clear sailing to face the upcoming school year.

The following weekend with Pete home, the children fast asleep, and Pete and I resting comfortably in our bed, I start a conversation. "I met Alice Greenberg last weekend."

"You did? I was sure she thought you a figment of my imagination."

"She was sweet. I think we should start monitoring the time Andrew spends with the Greenbergs."

"I've allowed Andrew to join Ellen and her family for a hamburger a few times after the game. Has he been abusing the time he spends with Ellen during the week?"

"No. He knows schoolwork is top priority during the week. I think we should pull back on the time he spends with Ellen and her family."

Pete questions, "What's brought this on?"

"They're becoming too close. Andrew gives me the impression he can't live without her."

"Have you said anything to him about the way you feel?"

"No. The last time I expressed my opinion, you jumped down my throat. Told me to get off his back. So I thought you might address the issue. You know, man to man. When you're not so consumed by work."

I can feel Pete's stare, but I avoid looking at him. I'm trying to get Pete riled up so I can bring up the vacation issue.

"You want me to talk with him about his seeing too much of Ellen on the weekends, the only time he's allowed to see his friends? How well do you think this little talk will go when soon they will be seeing each other every day for five weeks?"

I sit up in bed, realizing Pete is talking about summer camp. "Ellen signed up at the same camp?"

"Most of the kids at his school are signed up for the same camp. It's been that way every year."

"I know you think I'm making a mountain out of a molehill, but recently, he asked about how I knew you were the one. Those are questions someone asks when they think they found the one."

"Allison, why don't we just let this little romance play itself out? Right now, I don't think I'd be able to preach to our son about relationships. I wouldn't know how to respond if he changed the subject and asked what was going on with us. 'Oh, I don't know, Andrew. Sometimes relationships …'" Pete pauses, not wanting to create a scene. "Let him be. Who knows? He might meet someone else at camp or when we vacation in Florida."

Bingo. Florida. *Go for it,* I tell myself. "Since you brought up Florida, I might need to pass up on the family vacation. I thought with the seven weeks the children will be away, I could clear a lot of work sitting on my desk."

"You're kidding me, right? You want to pass up on our vacation? Did you mention this to the kids?"

"No. I thought I'll talk with you first."

"You are not passing on this vacation. The kids and I were looking forward to all of us being together. I don't care if you have to work around-the-clock. You're not. I won't—"

"Won't what? Allow it? No, it wouldn't be right to put myself first. Once the kids are back at school, my day doesn't end till I put my head on the pillow. I'm sure you can understand missing one trip will make my life much easier. You're not blaming me for what's going on in our lives, are you?"

Pete runs his hands through his hair. Calming down, he says, "Allison, I'm so looking forward to us being together, you and me, and you, me, and the kids. We need to get back the life we once had. I'm not blaming you, I blame myself. I was against this new office. I should have stood up to Hal, but I didn't, and here I am with no other choice but to see it through. I'm not trying to make your life miserable, but these two weeks together as a family … it's what we need."

All I have put into making Pete's life as miserable as I can isn't working; he isn't giving up on us. "I can't make any promises. Let's see how July goes. But you have to promise, if I can't get away, you have to help me explain this to the children."

Lying in bed, Pete tosses and turns. I know he's not asleep. The pain he is feeling brings tears to my eyes. Over the months, I have accused him of having an affair, neglecting his family, and discounting my feelings regarding my job, and still his love for me has not wavered. He is still the same loving man I met those many years ago.

* * * * *

When JoAnne and I arrived at college, we roomed together. School policy was that students should room with people they didn't know. Luckily, our dorm supervisor, a junior from Pittsburgh, took pity on JoAnne and allowed us to room together.

"I didn't think she was going to bend, but she was a pushover. 'Oh, please don't separate my best friend and me. I'm so frightened to be without her. Maybe next year, please?'"

"I think the tears were the frosting on the cake. It is amazing how you can cry on command."

"I think about the worst thing that could happen to me, like hearing my mother was in a bad car accident and death was knocking at the door."

"That's terrible. Remember, my father died in a freak accident."

"I'm sorry, but it works. You should try it sometime. I think in all the years we've been friends, I've seen you cry twice, maybe three times."

JoAnne was right; I wasn't much of a crier. I did cry myself to sleep the night before we left for college.

Earlier in the night, I was sitting on the porch, staring at nothing in particular, when the door opened and my mother stepped outside and sat beside me. I had hoped it would be Patrick.

"It's a beautiful night."

"Sure is."

"I can't believe you're going off to college. Where does the time go?"

"Everyone has to grow up."

"Yes, we do. Are you nervous? I would be. City life isn't for me. Your aunt loved living in New York. You and her are so much alike. When we were younger, she was always trying to convince your uncle and me that moving to New York was the right thing to do, but I've never wanted to live anywhere else."

"I don't know why. There's not much going on here. You have to go to Pittsburgh to have any fun."

"I guess. If it weren't for the lumber business and your father's loyalty to his parents, we would be living in Pittsburgh."

My mother's mentioning my father made me lie and say, "I don't remember him."

"He loved you. The day you were born was the happiest day of his life."

I couldn't believe on the last day of my living in this home, my mother picked this night to mention my father. Staring at my mother, I said, "That's what Aunt Sarah says. I was his shining star. Were you jealous he loved me more than you?"

My mother looked into my eyes. "What a strange thing to say. Of course I wasn't jealous. You were our child." She smiled, remembering. "I loved the way he used to fuss over you. The love you and he shared was special."

My question caused me to feel guilty. My mother wasn't jealous of the love my father bestowed on me. For years I thought her jealousy caused a rift between us. I wanted to scream, "Why now? Why, after all these years, are you sharing how happy we might have been if my father had lived or how loving each other could have been our consolation for losing him?"

"I remember the night he died. Aunt Sarah came to tell me he was in heaven with God. For years I hated God. I don't think I believe in God, not the way you do."

"Many people lose their faith when tragedy strikes. I had my doubts after your father was taken from us."

"What made you change your mind?"

"I try to remember that God places us on this earth and when he says our time is up … well, who can argue with God?" She placed her arm around me, and the feeling of her arm around me warmed my heart. "Anyway, I know if your father were here with us today, he would tell you how proud we are of you. Moving to a big city can be a challenge, but you're strong, and if you don't take this opportunity, you'll be sorry later in life."

I didn't ask why she never wanted to take a chance and leave this town, since she had already told me that she loved living here and had no desire to leave. If my father insisted, would she have followed? I asked the only other question that had plagued me most of my life. "Mom, did you and Dad ever talk about having more children?"

"Yes. He wanted three children. He talked about all the summer vacations we would take with our children. If he had lived, we would have traveled, I'm sure."

I pictured what life would have been if he had lived, but mostly I wondered if my relationship with my mother would have flourished. My desire to lash out at her was subsiding the more she opened up about her life. She went on to tell me about the crush my father had on her in third grade. She said during their short marriage, he repeated over and over that she was the only woman he ever loved.

That night, as I was lying in bed, the tears I shed weren't because I was leaving Patrick; they were for the woman I called mother, who, for one night, allowed herself to love and open up to her only child the night before she sent her away.

* * * * *

I was reminded of that night, the night before I went off to college, whenever I was in my mother's company. As much as I wanted to treasure what my mother and I had shared, I found I hated her for waiting my entire life to show me any kindness. These mixed feelings only enhanced my love for Patrick. On holiday visits, I was convinced he grew more handsome than the time before.

On one visit home, I noticed my mother had lost weight. I was concerned, but not concerned enough to question.

While we were sharing breakfast together, my mother asked, "Are you dating anyone special?"

"Why do you ask?"

"A girl with your looks must be turning the boys away."

Her reference to how pretty I had become was another first in this new mother of mine. "I've had my share of boyfriends. If you're trying to find out if I'm still a virgin, I have to say that ship sailed long ago," I lied.

"I trust you. I'm sure you're protecting yourself."

"I am. I don't want children until I'm sure I can love them the way children deserve to be loved, like my father loved me." I went in for the kill.

My mother lowered her head. For some unknown reason, I was reminded of the time I exposed myself to Patrick. Patrick walked into the kitchen and placed a kiss on my mother's head.

"What are you girls talking about?"

"I asked Allison if she's met anyone special."

Patrick looked startled. I raised my eyebrow and smiled. He blushed. "I'm sure the boys are very impressed with Allison. She's beautiful and smart." With his eyes still upon me, I licked my spoon in a playful way.

Taking a seat at the table, placing his napkin on his lap, he said, "It's nice having you home. I've missed you, Allison." Then he added, "More than you can imagine."

Another confirmation that Patrick wasn't happy with his present life. I made sure I spent most of my time with Patrick on this visit and future visits.

* * * * *

As much as I missed Patrick after my visits home, I was always happy to be back in New York. It would take several weeks to stop daydreaming about Patrick. I hoped against all hope he would wake up and realize if he wanted any happiness in life, he could find it with me in New York.

JoAnne, as usual, took charge of our social lives. We were invited to the best parties on campus. JoAnne set her sights on a guy who played on the rugby team, Jason Grant. Jason hung around with a guy named Gary Graves. Gary didn't much care for JoAnne and tried his best to make his feelings known to Jason.

"I know why Jason is acting cold. His friend Gary doesn't like me. He's a prick."

"Did you come on to him and then give him the cold shoulder?"

"No. I met him through Jason, at the Valentine's party."

"I think the college guys have your number. You're a dick tease."

"You might be right. No great loss. I wasn't that crazy in love with Jason. What's with this Hank guy? He calls you every day."

"Hank's part of my study group. We're good friends. Don't go reading more into it."

"Oh, by the way, I pulled this job posting off the bulletin board today. Two families are looking for nannies to travel with them to London, leaving June 15 and returning August 18. I added our names to the list. We won't get an interview. There's an age requirement, twenty years or older."

"I was going to ask Patrick if there were any summer openings back home."

"What? You're going to go back home for the summer? I'm sure you can land a job here. There's a bank on every corner. It took me all of Christmas break to convince my parents that it would be easier for me to find a job here than back home."

"Maybe next year. I think this year I'd rather go home."

"I'll miss you! Have fun. There's nothing back there for me. Never a day goes by that you don't surprise me, Allison. When we were growing up, you couldn't wait to leave. Now you're packed several days before a holiday break. What's up?"

I was happy JoAnne decided to stay in New York. My intensions were to get a job at the bank, working side by side with Patrick. If JoAnne were home, she'd demand my time nights and weekends, and I had other plans. And those plans included spending most of my time with Patrick.

* * * * *

"I have great news. Remember the job I told you about traveling overseas as nannies? I got a call back. We both have interviews tomorrow. I know we can do this. Remember, whatever JoAnne wants, JoAnne gets."

"I told you I was going home for the summer."

"I spoke with your aunt last week. There are no jobs at the bank. What are you going to do all summer, work at the supermart, if there are openings, or travel to England? This is a no-brainer—travel to England!"

"You spoke with my aunt and told her I was planning on coming home for the summer to work?"

"No. I told your aunt I was planning on staying in New York for the summer and you were planning to go back home and find a job at the bank. She said Patrick recently mentioned the bank had placed a freeze on hiring."

I confirmed that the bank wasn't hiring and went on the interview with JoAnne, convinced we wouldn't get the job. To my surprise, the women took a liking to us and immediately offered us a position, overlooking our age.

Sitting in the lounge at school, JoAnne was out of control with excitement. "I can't believe in two weeks we'll be on our way to England, all expenses paid! I did some calculations. We set aside one day's pay, and on our day off, we sightsee during the day and hit the pubs at night. There are a million pubs in London. Who would have thought, you, me, London? I told you whatever JoAnne wants, JoAnne gets. Stick with me, kid. You'll go places."

A familiar voice asked, "You seem pretty happy for a girl that just got dumped."

JoAnne turned slowly in her chair. "Gary Graves, how nice of you to stop by to say hi. Goodbye."

Gary took the liberty to sit at our table. "Come on, JoAnne, you know Jason wasn't your type."

"And how would you know what my type is?"

Gary chose his words carefully. "Because your type is right here waiting for you to come to your senses and go out with him Saturday night."

JoAnne was thrown off guard. I choke on my sandwich. This guy exuded charm, and he was handsome.

JoAnne half-smiled. "Gary Graves, have I heard you correctly? You want me to go out with you on Saturday night? Do you take me for a fool? I don't like you, and if I'm not mistaken, the feeling is mutual."

"Oh, but you're wrong. Anyway, Jason is definitely not your type. You and me, now that's a story waiting to be told."

I waited and watched as JoAnne gathered her thoughts. In a minute or two, Gary wouldn't know what hit him. JoAnne smiled. I waited patiently. JoAnne the smart-ass was evolving. Then to my surprise, she said, "Eight o'clock Saturday. I'll meet you in front of my dorm. If you don't show, Allison and I will catch that chick flick we've been dying to see."

Gary smiled. "I'll be there at seven fifty-five, just in case you're early. I wouldn't want to keep you waiting."

Gary got up and walked away. JoAnne turned to me. "Now, what was I saying before we were so rudely interrupted?"

* * * * *

Gary was right; he was JoAnne's type, and from their first date till the day we left for Europe, they were joined at the hip.

"I'll call."

"I want you to write me love letters. If you don't, we're over. I mean it."

"I promise nothing but love letters. I'll call once a week." Gary pulled the number from his pocket. "And I promise to dream of you every night—wet dreams, of course."

JoAnne was like a lovesick schoolgirl. "You're so bad! Now kiss me before I miss my plane."

In a beautiful oversize English cottage, JoAnne and I spent every minute together. When the children napped, we sat under a tree and planned our day off. We retired early, exhausted from caring for four small children.

We rose early on our day off, fully energized to explore London and frequent as many pubs as possible, arriving home at ten.

The last week of our time in London dragged. JoAnne was anxious to get back to Gary, and I wanted to get back to a normal life that didn't include children. Gary kept his promise; he called once a week, and JoAnne accumulated a nice stack of love letters.

"I can't believe we're going home in three days. Although exhausting, it beats working at the supermart."

"I spoke with the ladies this morning. They were singing our praises. Said the children adore us. Offered us the job next year if we want it."

* * * * *

Back in New York, JoAnne kept herself busy with Gary, school, and a small part-time job.

"Gary has a game tomorrow at one. I don't want to go alone. Please come with me! Please?"

"I took the four-to-nine shift at the store. I was going to get up early tomorrow and study."

"You can study on Sunday. If you were a true friend, you'd say yes. Please, pretty please?"

"I was going shopping with Stacy on Sunday. I promised her."

"Stacy, I'll agree the girl needs to up her game in the clothing department. I have the answer: wake early on Sunday, you can study till twelve, then take the girl shopping, dump her by four, and study the night away."

"You always put your needs before mine."

JoAnne raised her hands, placed them together, and extended her lower lip.

"All right, but if you and Gary come back to this apartment to do whatever you two do before ten o'clock Sunday night, I swear I'll throw hot water on your naked bodies."

"Hey, what makes you think I've given it up? I told you I'm saving myself for the right guy."

I stared at JoAnne until she confessed, "All right, I confess. I'm sure he's the one, my one and only. Wait till it happens to you. There's nothing like having an orgasm with a guy inside you."

* * * * *

JoAnne waved to Gary. He didn't look directly at her, but he jerked his head in response to her wave.

"Doesn't he look hot in his football uniform? He hates when I wave to him. He says he can't wave back. The coach doesn't like it."

"So why do you do it?"

"I want these other bitches to see he belongs to me."

"But he doesn't wave back, so how are they going to know you're his girl?"

"Look, look, he's running out on the field. Go, Gary! Go, Gary, baby!"

"You're embarrassing me. Sit down."

Friday nights were spent at the high school field back home for the young and the old. JoAnne and I had a pretty good understanding of how the game was played. I was pretty impressed with the quarterback; he knew his stuff. Third quarter, the quarterback was sacked pretty hard, so hard that the crowd rose to their feet. I sat and watched as the medical team ran out on the field. "Do you know any other players on the team, like the quarterback?"

"I think that's Gary's roommate. His name is Pete. I haven't met him, so I can't tell you his last name."

Someone from behind said, "Pete Cane. He's a good quarterback. I hope he's all right."

Just then, the quarterback stood, removed his helmet, and lowered his head. He was assisted off the field. The crowd cheered, and I joined in.

* * * * *

"Allison, this is Pete Cane, Gary's roommate, the quarterback."

"Hi! How are you feeling?"

"I've been hit harder. I'm sure I'll feel it tomorrow. This beer should help." Pete called to Gary, "Keep them coming."

I smiled.

"It's noisy in here."

"You're right, it is noisy."

"Your drink is almost empty. Can I get you a refill?"

"Diet Coke. I'll be out in the hall."

Several minutes later, Pete handed me a fresh drink. "There weren't any diet Cokes left, so I got you a diet Sprite."

"You read my mind. I prefer Sprite."

"I've seen you a few times walking around campus. Gary says you and JoAnne are from Cleveland."

JoAnne and I met in grade school."

"No kidding? Grade school, and you wound up at the same college?"

"It was our dream to live in New York, attend NYU. Did you know Gary before college?"

"No. I met Gary during practice. We didn't like each other at first. I thought Gary was a snob. Turns out, he and I have a lot in common. I mean, I'm not a snob. Neither is Gary. He and JoAnne really like each other. They say opposites attract, but those two are exactly alike. It's all about them. Please don't repeat that."

"You aren't telling me something I don't already know."

Pete laughed. I thought him handsome, beautiful green eyes, thick blondish-brown hair. Later, I would refer to him as Brad Pitt's double.

Pete continued to tell me the story of how he and Gary ended up as roommates. "Gary and I connected on the football field. He's a great receiver. He convinced the coach that we should room together. At first, I wasn't sure it would work out, but now I'm convinced the guy would take a bullet for me, and I would do the same for him."

"That's pretty much how it is between JoAnne and me."

"Gary comes on strong, but there's a teddy bear locked deep inside him."

Smiling, I said. "JoAnne and Gary were cut from the same mold."

"They sure seem head over heels in love with each other. Heck, he got Jason to dump her so he could make his move. Again, please don't repeat that."

"Cross my heart. My lips are sealed."

I spent the entire night talking with Pete Cane, about music, books, school, professors we liked, professors we tried hard to avoid. I told him my uncle George won state three years for baseball, two for football. His picture and the trophies were encased in the school hall. I was told he was really good.

Pete laughed out loud. "I've been told I'm pretty damn good. Did your uncle go pro?"

"No. He joined the Marines."

"A Marine? Good choice. My father was a Marine, served in Vietnam."

"Did he play football?"

"He did, high school and college."

"Do you want to play professionally?"

"No. I'm majoring in accounting. I love football, but I wouldn't want to play professionally. Good money, but hard on the family."

"Your parents afraid you might get hurt?"

"No. I didn't mean my parents. I meant my wife and children. Traveling can destroy a marriage."

Now I reflect back on Pete's words during our first meeting. "Traveling can destroy a marriage." Does he ever think about that night and think how ironic that those very words will come back to haunt him?

* * * * *

Thanksgiving, I returned home to find my mother looking paler than she did during my Easter visit.

"Are you seeing anyone?" asked Aunt Sarah.

"I met a boy in the fall."

"Where is he from?"

"Connecticut."

"Northeastern boy."

"So if he were from California, he'd be a western boy?"

Aunt Sarah smiled.

"Enough about me and the boy. Aunt Sarah, I'm glad we're alone. Is Mom feeling well? She looks like she's lost more weight, if that's possible."

"She's been seeing the doctor about stomach issues. I think the medication she's taking is causing her to lose weight. Dr. Pratt said the medicine should help her appetite, but I think she's eating less. Patrick is going to call the doctor next week. Uncle George and I have been consumed with your grandfather's health. Now this stomach issue with your mother, I'm worried sick."

"Why doesn't the doctor schedule a CT scan?"

"Oh, Allison, you don't think—"

"It might be an intestinal bug, but a scan can rule out anything worse."

* * * * *

When I confronted Patrick, he told me my mother refused any tests, saying she wanted to see if the medication worked.

"Patrick, if she's not feeling better in two weeks, you have to promise me she gets a CT scan."

"Don't worry, Allison, if I see there is no improvement, she will have the scan. I think she was avoiding the test because of your grandfather's health."

"He's lucky to have such caring children. She should spend more time caring for herself and less time caring for my grandfather."

* * * * *

Shortly after Valentine's Day, I received a call that my grandfather William James Holland had died. JoAnne and I returned home for the funeral.

My mother looked healthier and was in complete control. She saw to all the arrangements and shed only a few tears at the burial site while Aunt Sarah and Uncle George held on to each other and cried easily.

That night after the service, I found my mother on the porch swing, sipping hot tea.

"Allison, would you like a cup of tea?"

"No, Mom, I'm fine. Did Patrick drive Aunt Sarah and Uncle George home?"

"He did. I wanted them to stay with us, but they insisted they would be fine."

Sitting on the swing next to my mom, I finally got the nerve to ask, "Mom, how is the new medication working?"

"Good. I'm feeling much better, but I can't seem to gain back the weight I lost. I was speaking with a friend at church. She said her cousin developed an intestinal infection. Took him over a year to gain back the ten pounds he lost."

"I think you should have the doctor perform a CT scan. I can't believe he hasn't scheduled one already."

"I pushed it off because your grandfather was so ill. Don't blame Dr. Pratt. If I don't gain back at least a pound in two weeks, he will personally take me by the hand to get the test."

"Good. That makes me happy. Mom, I'm sorry about your father."

She reached for my hand; her hand was warm from holding the teacup.

My mother smiled at me. "I know you might find what I'm about to say cruel, but I'm actually happy for him. He's where he's always wanted to be."

"With Grandma Erin."

"Yes, with Grandma Erin. I never knew my mother, but it was no secret how much your grandfather loved her."

"Did it bother you, never knowing your mother?"

"Yes and no. Yes, I wish I had known her. From what I've been told, she was a special person. And no, because I'm happy I was spared all the sorrow everyone felt when she was gone."

I considered my mother's response. The hurt you feel after losing someone you love is devastating, but I was happy I had, even though faded, memories of my short time with my father.

*****

"Patrick, Dr. Pratt told my mother, if she doesn't gain back some weight, he will schedule the scan."

"Your mother has agreed to have the scan. She told me last night. I have to be in Pittsburgh tomorrow. I won't be back before you leave, but I'll call you every week with an update."

"You're going away?"

"Yes. Lots of changes in the banking world."

"We've seen so little of each other."

"I'm sorry. I'm taking the six o'clock shuttle to Pittsburgh. That's why I'm going to say good-night. Will you be home for Easter?"

Furious knowing Patrick was leaving, I said, "I don't know. I've met someone. I might be spending Easter with his family."

"You're seeing someone? Why didn't you tell me?"

"I don't have to tell you everything that's going on in my life. I'm sure you have a few secrets of your own."

Patrick paused before answering, "You're right, if you wanted me to know, you would have told me. Will you be home in the summer?"

"No. JoAnne and I were offered the same positions as last summer."

"You're off to Europe again? I'm jealous."

"Maybe while I'm there, you can take a week or two off and join me. I can show you the sights."

Patrick looked around the room, making sure no one was near to hear. "Wouldn't that be wonderful! Europe, time away from death and sickness."

"Exactly. Mom might feel better by the summer. I'm sure she wouldn't mind you taking some time away from all this."

"Maybe." He moved toward me, and I was sure he was going to kiss me, but he placed a kiss on my forehead and said, "Good night."

* * * * *

Again, I set my sights high. I and my mother's husband traveling through Europe. I was overjoyed by the thought, then sickened, asking myself, *What is wrong with me?* Once I was a levelheaded, compassionate individual, but now what I wanted more than anything was to spend time alone with my mother's husband. How screwed up my life had become once Patrick came along. But I couldn't deny, if he agreed to a week's visit, I'd be anxious to find out his true feelings for me.

"I haven't seen you in a few weeks. I was sorry to hear about your grandfather," said Pete.

"Thanks, Pete. Sorry I haven't called. I've been busy. JoAnne and I are leaving in two weeks. I had to do a little shopping for the trip, and with finals, no time for fun."

"I understand."

I was avoiding Pete, dreaming of my upcoming trip with Patrick, which I'd convinced myself he wouldn't miss. But miss he would. The following Sunday, when I called my mother, she informed me she hadn't gained one pound of the weight she lost, so Dr. Pratt scheduled the scan. Later, when I spoke with Patrick, our trip to Europe never came up.

The night before the trip, I called home, and Patrick answered the phone.

"Patrick, can you talk?"

Patrick called to my mother, making it clear that he wasn't alone. "Audrey, Allison is on the phone," he said. "Your mother wants to know if you're excited about your trip."

"Did my mother have the scan?"

"Yes, she did. We haven't gotten the result yet. She's lying down. She seems extremely tired these days." Patrick lowered the phone. When he came back on the line, he said, "Your mother wants to know if the phone number where you are staying is the same as last year?"

"Yes, the same number. Let her rest and assure her I'll call when I land."

Patrick relayed the message. "Thanks, Allison. She would have been worried sick if you forgot to call. Have a safe trip." By the muffled sound, I knew Patrick had placed his hand over the mouthpiece so as not to be heard. "I promise we'll talk. You can tell me all about your trip. The only way I'm going to see the world is through your eyes."

The phone went dead. I whispered, "Patrick."

* * * * *

"Allison, I know you're worried about you mother. Did she say anything when you spoke with her yesterday?"

"She said she hadn't heard from Dr. Pratt. I don't know whether to believe her or not."

"I can understand why you're concerned. Your mother is a private person, but I'm sure if something's wrong, she would tell you."

"If your child was in Europe and your test results were positive, would you tell them or wait till they got back to the States?"

JoAnne pondered the question. "I'd wait."

"Of course. So would I."

"Allison, I know my timing isn't perfect, but there's something I've been meaning to tell you. I've got us a week off at the end of July."

"How did you manage that?"

"Early this morning, Stacy said the families were flying to Monaco to meet up with a friend. They planned a one-week cruise around the Mediterranean with the children on their friend's yacht. There is a full staff, which includes a nanny. She said we would be paid for the week and we should take the time to do something special. I told her we were dying to see Paris. Would you believe they have an apartment in Paris? She said it's hardly ever used. She insisted we stay there for the week."

"You're kidding me?"

"Scout's honor."

I smiled. "That is great news! Paris … I thought I'd have to work a few years before I ever crossed the Atlantic, and in just two years, London and Paris!" I leaned back my face to the sun and pondered my good fortune.

"I have more good news. Well, good news for me. I hope you're all right with it."

I stared at JoAnne, knowing I was not going to be happy with the news. "Okay, what's the downside to our visit to Paris?"

"It's going to be fun, I promise. Having Gary and Pete along will make it that much better."

I shouted, "Gary and Pete are coming here? Why?"

"Well, after I got the news, I called Gary to tell him we would be in Paris at the end of the month. He said I wasn't seeing Paris without him, and he's asking Pete to come along."

"What did you do with the JoAnne I grew up with? This guy has you all wound up. You're acting like a lovesick fool!"

"I love him, Allison. He is the one, and I know he loves me."

"What happened to career first, earn lots and lots of money, then and only then the husband and a family?"

"That's still the plan, but you know what they say, love comes along when you least expect it."

I had no response to JoAnne's statement. She was right; love has a funny way of capturing your heart. Prime example: Patrick. I snapped back to reality. "Pete will never agree to the trip, so the way I see it, I'm the third wheel. Did you invite Gary to stay at the apartment?"

"Not without Stacy's permission, and yours, of course."

I had no right to lecture JoAnne. I had planned on having Patrick come for a week in hopes that JoAnne would understand, leaving me time alone with Patrick. "I don't want to be a third wheel. Why don't you and Gary go to Paris alone? An early honeymoon. I'll be fine."

"Then Pete will be the third wheel."

That was JoAnne's way of saying Pete had agreed to the trip.

* * * * *

When Pete waved to me from the train, to my surprise, I jumped with joy.

JoAnne, taking notice, said, "Look at you, you're grinning from ear to ear. I thought you didn't like this guy."

"Allison." Pete lifted me in his arms and turned me around. Placing me down, he said, "I can't believe I'm in Paris with you! I've missed you. Did you miss me?"

"I have missed you. Wait till you see the apartment. It overlooks the Eiffel Tower."

As I placed my arm in Pete's, the four of us hailed a cab.

JoAnne planned the itinerary, of course. We were up and out by nine, coming back no earlier than two in the morning. The apartment had two large bedrooms. Gary and JoAnne occupied the master, me the other bedroom, and Pete got stuck on the couch, which he insisted was comfortable.

JoAnne was right; I had been in a slump over Patrick and my mother's health. During Pete's visit, he asked about my mother. I shared with him our conversations, which occurred twice a week. "She says she hasn't gotten the results. It doesn't take this long. I'm afraid she's keeping the truth from me."

Pete's arrival and concern about my mother's health overshadowed my fantasies regarding Patrick.

"I have to admit, I was surprised when I heard you agreed to the trip."

Pete placed his arm around me and said, "I knew what was waiting across the ocean."

I blushed. "I like you, Pete. That's why I want to be honest with you. I'm not ready for a serious relationship, not with all I have going on."

"I'm not going anywhere, but if we're being honest, I miss you when we are apart. I think about you all the time. I wonder if you're seeing other guys. A beautiful girl like you, they are probably lined up around the block, waiting their turn."

I laughed. "No such luck."

Pete asked, "Do I sound like a lovesick puppy?"

"You sound like a guy who likes a girl."

Pete looked into my eyes. "Would it be all right if I kiss you in the most romantic city in the world?"

I leaned into him, placing my lips on his, very much enjoying our first kiss and the ones that followed.

When I kissed Pete goodbye at the airport, I said, "I had fun with you, Pete Cane, in the most romantic city in the world. I get back on August 8. Call me."

Pete smiled. "I can't wait."

* * * * *

"What are the rules? You have to digest your food before you are allowed to swim." JoAnne grunted. "Is it my imagination, or were these kids better behaved last year? I don't think I can do this next year."

"I intend to intern next summer, so my nanny days are over."

"Sounds like a plan. Seems like yesterday we were on the train heading to New York. Now we're entering our third year of college. Talking about home, my mom said your mother's name was added to the prayer list at church. Doesn't mean anything. You can have an ingrown toenail, and your name will show up on the prayer list. Have you spoken with your aunt? She'd tell you the truth. I know she would."

"No, I haven't spoken with her, but I'm sure she was given strict orders not to say anything while I'm away."

"My mom said Dr. Pratt ordered more tests. I felt I had to say something. I know you'd never forgive me if I didn't."

I called my mom that night. "Mom, I want the truth. Did you get the test results back from Dr. Pratt?"

My mom whispered, "Allison, can't this wait until you're back home?"

"No. The results aren't going to change whether I'm here or there."

For a moment, I thought my mother hung up the phone.

"Mom, just tell me. I'm your daughter, for heaven's sakes!"

"Allison, don't swear. The blood work showed some abnormalities. Dr. Pratt ordered an MRI. I had the test yesterday. When you get back from Europe, I'm sure I will know exactly what's going on."

"It's going to take a week to get the results back? Why?"

"There's more than just the MRI. There's a series of blood tests. I'm sure by the time you're back, I'll have more information. Your aunt, uncle, and Patrick are just like you. They want answers now, but Dr. Pratt doesn't feel comfortable giving his opinion until all the results are back."

My mother's analogy made sense. "Mom, I'm worried."

"I know you are. Let's talk about something cheerful. I heard through the grapevine that some college friends came to visit?"

I felt guilty telling my mother about Pete and Gary's visit when she had so much going on in her life. I knew JoAnne probably told her mother, and it was surely conveyed to my mother. I wondered if my mother felt hurt that I didn't tell her myself. "I'm sorry I forgot to tell you. Every time we talk—"

"It's about my illness. I understand. Sounds like JoAnne really likes this guy. Is your relationship with Pete as serious, or are you just friends?"

"I was honest with him, Mom. I said I wasn't ready to have a serious relationship, but we had a great time together in Paris. I'm hoping we'll see more of each other when I get back to the States."

My mother agreed with my decision. "Honesty is always the best policy, Allison. You did the right thing. When you get back, if you continue to date the boy, then you'll make a decision about the future. I'd like to take credit for raising such a well-adjusted woman, but …"

In my mother's defense, I added, "Mom, you did the best you could as a single parent. I didn't turn out so bad."

That night, I cried. I couldn't shake the feeling that my mother's test results weren't going to be good. Our phone conversation played over and over in my mind. My mother asked about my relationship with Pete. She praised me, not only for my honesty, but also for growing into a well-adjusted woman. We were bonding as a mother and daughter. *Why, oh, why?* I cried. All these wasted years. Why was I cheated of having a best friend in my mom? A mother, the only person who has your back, right or wrong. Through the miracle of childbirth, she is your protector.

* * * * *

Patrick picked up on the first ring. "Hello, Allison. Your mother and aunt are out. I'm assuming you arrived home safe and sound."

A chill ran up my spine when I heard Patrick's voice. "How was your summer, Patrick?"

"I'd rather hear about your summer, Allison. Your mom said the boy you're dating visited you in Paris. How romantic."

"He's just a friend."

Patrick paused before speaking. "Last time we talked, I forgot to ask your friend's name."

"Peter Cane."

"Peter. And did you and this Peter have a good time?"

I detected sarcasm in Patrick's voice. It infuriated me. "Yes, we did. It was his first time overseas. He wanted to see Paris before he got too old to enjoy it." I let him digest my last statement before saying, "I didn't call to talk about my summer. I called to speak with my mother. I wanted to know if she heard from Dr. Pratt."

"She did."

"And ...?"

"It's not my place. I'll tell your mother you called."

"Fuck that, Patrick. You're her husband! Tell me what the doctor said."

"I'd rather—"

"Patrick, tell me what the doctor said, damn it!"

In a voice so low I could hardly hear him, he said, "Your mother has cancer, pancreatic cancer."

I wanted to drop the phone and scream, "That's the worse, isn't it? Pancreatic cancer—there's no cure? What level?"

Patrick whispered into the phone, "Stage III."

I breathed in deeply. The tears were building. I was speechless.

"I'm sorry, Allison, but I'd rather we kept this between ourselves. Your mother would prefer you didn't know."

I yelled into the phone, "She wasn't going to tell me? I'm her fucking daughter! If not me, then who?"

Patrick changed the subject. "Today is your mother's first chemo treatment. Your aunt is with her."

"She's already started chemo? She's known for some time, hasn't she?"

"Three weeks."

"Three weeks? I've talked with her at least six times over three weeks, and she never said a word, even though she promised I'd be the first to know. Why aren't you with her?"

"I've gone with her every day since she started the treatments, but I had a meeting this morning, so your aunt was kind enough to help me out." Patrick began to cry. "Her beautiful hair is falling out. She's having her head shaved tomorrow."

I yelled, "I'm taking the next train home!"

Patrick regained control. "What about school? Your mother wouldn't want you to miss school because of her."

"School doesn't start for a week. I'm coming home. She'll just have to deal with it."

* * * * *

When my aunt and I were alone, I asked, "What is wrong with you fucking people?"

"Allison, there's no need—"

I cursed Aunt Sarah. "Get over it. Not one of you had the decency to call me and let me know my mother had cancer."

"Sweetheart, it happened so fast. Monday, we get the results. Four days later chemo treatments."

I heard the cracking in her voice, but that didn't stop me from scolding her. "And while she and Patrick were at the hospital, you couldn't find the time to call me?"

Aunt Sarah pleaded, "Allison, your mother—"

"My mother what? Didn't want her daughter to know she had cancer? I can't believe this!"

"Allison, you know how your mother is. She doesn't like anyone fussing over her. She's—"

"She's different, I get it." I took a seat at the kitchen table and whispered, "I thought we were getting closer. What a fool I was! Why does this woman refuse to acknowledge my existence? Why does she constantly shut me out?"

My aunt moved closer to where I was sitting. "Allison, that's not true. She loves you! She's not trying to hurt you, she's trying to protect you. Can't you see that?"

"She wants to protect me? That's bullshit! She doesn't have a compassionate bone in her body. I begged her, as soon as she found out the results, I wanted to know, and she promised to tell me. But she lied. I curse the day I was born! She should have died instead of my father."

My words cut like a knife. My aunt lowered her head. "Don't speak that way, Allison. Someday you will regret those words. Accusations are not what your mother needs. She needs you to be there for her. You have to try your best to forget the past."

I laughed. "All my life I've been trying. I'm tired of trying. If she wants to die alone, then so be it. Oh, I forgot, she won't die alone. She has you, Uncle George, and her beloved Patrick."

Aunt Sarah continued her plea. "I couldn't go against your mother's wishes. She didn't want you to get the news while you were overseas. Put yourself in her shoes."

"I figured that out while I was in Europe, but I got home on Friday. I called Patrick on Monday. If I didn't squeeze the truth from him, I wouldn't have known. What's your excuse for waiting to tell me?"

"I swear, your mother promised me she would call you. If you want to hate me for not calling, so be it, but it won't do you any good to hold this against your mother. I know you're hurt, and I'm hurting for you, but your mother needs you to be strong. Please find a way to put aside your feelings. If God's will is to extend your mother's life, tell her how you feel, mend the fences between you, but for now, just be there for her. I know you won't believe what I'm about to say, but your mother is proud of you and all you've accomplished. And never, ever again let me hear you say you wish you were never born. You were loved before we even met you."

I did as my aunt suggested. I didn't scold my mother for breaking her promise. I wanted to believe she was trying to protect me, but I couldn't shake the knowledge that she didn't see me as her daughter and best friend.

I made the decision to be the better person. I would be there for her, right or wrong, good or bad. I would do whatever it took not to feel guilty that I had failed her as she had failed me.

* * * * *

Patrick drove me to the train station. "Your mother was happy to see you. Thank you for coming home."

"I wish she had asked me to stay, but she insisted I return to school. She said she'd be just fine without me."

"Your mother doesn't express her feelings very well, but I know she appreciated your wanting to stay. She wants you to get back to your life in New York. She hates being a burden to anyone."

"She's not a burden to me. I'm her daughter, but I'm sure this isn't easy on you. Are you happy, Patrick?"

Patrick was shocked by the question. "I'm not happy. My wife, your mother, is fighting for her life."

"I realize that, but before my mother became ill, were you happy with your life?"

Patrick took a moment to answer. "Life is complicated, Allison. It's not all peaches and cream. Some days are happier than others."

"I can't believe you like living in this town, and excuse me for being blunt, but your life is more like sour cream than peaches and cream. My mother's very sick. She might not be around much longer. Where do you see yourself in five years?"

Patrick pulled up to the train station. Leaving the engine running, he turned to me and said, "I hope still married to your mother." I smiled. This annoyed Patrick. "There's a 5 percent chance your mother will beat this, so keep your mother in your prayers and don't worry so much about my happiness."

"You're upset because I sound so cold, but truth be told, I never thought you and my mother were right for each other. You're younger than her by a few years, she was never one to travel, so I didn't see your dream of traveling becoming a reality. You also gave up the joy of having children of your own because, in case you haven't noticed, she's not the motherly type."

Patrick scolded me. "I get it. You're pissed at your mom for not calling and messing up your day by telling you she had the big 'C.' My father didn't tell me he had cancer until two weeks before he died. He had his reasons, and I got over it. You've asked if I'm happy with the decisions I've made in my life. When you find the person that has no regrets, let me know." Patrick looked at his watch. "Your train will be arriving in ten minutes. I wouldn't want you to miss it."

"Patrick, all I ever wanted is for you to be happy—"

"Your timing is all wrong, Allison." I waited a few moments, assuming there would be a goodbye kiss. Patrick remained in place. "Call your mother to let her know you arrived safe and sound."

* * * * *

On the train ride home, I was filled with guilt. I wanted Patrick to confess that he was miserable, but instead, he scolded me for thinking only of his and my happiness while my mother faced the worst fight of her life.

As time passed, I thought more of what my mother was going through and less of my hurt feelings.

I was sitting on a bench outside the campus cafeteria when Pete sat beside me. "Allison, why haven't you returned my calls? Are we still on Saturday night? We need to be there by eight. Should I pick you up around seven?"

"I'm sorry" was all I could manage.

Softly Pete asked, "How is your mother?"

"She looked much better when I saw her over the Christmas break. Dr. Pratt scheduled a scan at the end of this month, and I'm keeping my fingers crossed the chemo is helping."

Pete took my hand. "Are you going home for Easter?"

"Easter? I can't think that far ahead."

"Easter is less than six weeks away."

"Really? Only six weeks till Easter? I better get working on a summer job."

Pete questioned, "I thought you were going to intern over the summer? Did you check the employment bulletin board? There's a number of law firms looking for help."

"I did complete several applications, but I'm not sure if I should remain in the city or go home for the summer and spend some time with my mother."

"What did JoAnne have to say about your going home?"

"I didn't have to ask her. If the shoe was on the other foot, I know JoAnne would go back home to be with her mom."

Pete squeezed my hand. "I think you've already made your decision. You and your mother must be very close."

"Not in the traditional way. Daughter wants Mom to butt out of her life, then the shit hits the fan, and who does she call? Who else but her mother? Not this girl. I call JoAnne. It must be hard for you to understand, you being so close with your parents."

Pete agreed. "They've always been supportive of me and my sisters."

"I was little when my father died, but I can still remember how close he and I were. I want to believe life would have been different if he had lived."

Pete shrugged his shoulders. "When I spoke with my mom, I mentioned coming home for the summer and working with my dad. She said I'd be happier staying in New York. Can you guess why?"

I smiled. "Because of me?"

"I guess your name has come up once or twice during our conversations."

I was lucky to have a guy like Pete interested in me. Whenever we were together, I put all the bad things in life aside, envisioning how perfect my life would be if I gave Pete a chance. "You know what's upsetting? If I told my mother I was coming home to spend the summer with her, she'd try to talk me into the internship."

Pete placed an arm around my shoulder. "Then don't ask, just do what's in your heart."

"You have a way of lifting my spirits. I like that about you, Peter Cane. I like having you as a friend."

* * * * *

Before I left to spend the summer back home, JoAnne and I signed a lease on an apartment in Lower Manhattan. In one year, we would be graduating. It was time to move on.

As we were walking arm in arm, JoAnne said, "I promised my mother I would come back for a week's vacation before school starts. I thought the second week of August, so you'd have company on the trip back."

"Thanks, JoAnne."

JoAnne lowered her head. "Don't thank me. I wanted to come home and check up on your mom."

I stopped, and JoAnne asked, "What's wrong?"

"Nothing. I just wanted to thank you for being my best friend. You're not fooling me, you're coming back home to check on me. You're worried my mother might not be appreciative of my good intentions."

JoAnne confessed, "Allison, I'm wishing and praying that you fix what's broken between the two of you."

I hugged JoAnne. "We'll see, but now we have to hurry before I miss my flight, courtesy of Aunt Sarah."

* * * * *

My aunt waved as I entered the airport. Taking me in her arms, she said, "I'm so glad you're home!"

"I wasn't expecting you. I thought—"

"You were expecting Patrick?"

"I guess."

"Patrick is in Michigan."

"Michigan."

"We'll talk in the car. Have you eaten?"

"Yes. I had lunch on the plane."

"Then I'll get you home. I'm sure you're anxious to see your mom."

In the car, I asked, "So why is Patrick in Michigan?"

"Didn't he tell you the bank was acquired by BTC Bank and Trust? The main headquarters is located in Michigan. That is why I'm happy you're home for the summer. Patrick's been under an enormous amount of stress, burning the candle at both ends ... caring for your mom, work. I'm actually happy he'll be away for a few weeks."

"A few weeks? How many is a few weeks?"

"I'm not sure, but I assured him with you home, we'll be just fine."

I was not happy with the news that Patrick would be gone for an extended time, but I wasn't here for him; I was here to care for my mother.

"Aunt Sarah, tell me the truth, how is Mom doing with Patrick away?"

"I think she needed a break from Patrick. He watches over her like a hawk. I'm just as guilty as him. It's not easy not to. You'll see."

"I'll try not to hover."

"Oh, no, sweetheart, you have every right to care for her as you see fit."

I asked, "What's the next plan of attack?"

"No more chemo for a while. Dr. Pratt said your mother needs a break." My aunt looked in my direction, and by her expression, I knew something was wrong.

"You're not happy with Dr. Pratt's decision?"

My aunt turned away. "I'm not a doctor. If Dr. Pratt says she needs a break, then I'm on board."

I could see my aunt was holding back. "There's nothing more the doctors can do, is there?"

"There's no change in the size of the mass. This regiment of chemo didn't help, but in several weeks, Dr. Pratt has recommended we try this experimental drug. It has lots of side effects, but it has been known to be affective with this type of cancer cells."

I could read between the lines. "Mom hasn't agreed to the new drug, has she? Sounds like she wants to live out her remaining days in peace."

Aunt Sarah didn't respond. I could see she was upset with my mother. She thought she was giving up, and my aunt didn't want to lose her baby sister.

* * * * *

My mother was asleep. Not wanting to wake her, I remained before her, holding a tray. She stirred then opened her eyes. "Allison."

"Mom, you haven't eaten."

"Thank you, sweetheart. I'm not really hungry."

"Mom, it's just a little. Won't you at least try just a few spoons?"

Forcing herself to a sitting position, she woke from her semi-conscious state. It had been seven weeks since I arrived. The temperature had remained in the high eighties since July 4. Every day I prepared the same lunch, chicken broth with smashed carrots, and one slice of unbuttered toast. My mother ate less than half of what I prepared. The house was as hot as an oven, and my mother shivered.

I placed a spoon of soup to my mother's lips. "Aunt Sarah is stopping by. I'm going to the supermarket. Would you like something special for dinner?"

"No, thank you. Patrick said he was stopping by the bakery. He always buys one pound of my favorite cookies."

Another ritual. Patrick bought the cookies, my mother ate half of one each day, and after several days, we discarded the rest, tired of eating them ourselves. Patrick had been in and out over the course of my visit. If he was not out of town, he worked till eight every night.

"He knows how much you like them."

She nodded. "I think, when you get back from the supermarket, you and your aunt should sit out back and enjoy the sun."

"I will, Mom. I'll read one of those books Patrick bought for you. I'm sure Aunt Sarah can find one that interests her."

My mother stopped my hand. "I can't eat another bite. I'm sorry, Allison."

I placed the cup and spoon on the coffee table. "That's all right, Mom. You did fine."

"I'm sorry you weren't able to take an internship at one of those prestige law firms. Will it affect your classes in the fall? She asked the same question at least three times a week.

"No, Mom, I can work during the school year. I'll be fine."

My mother repeated, "You should have worked at Mr. Gordon's office while you were visiting. It's not a New York law firm, but it is a law firm."

Before I could answer, she drifted off to sleep. She had eaten less than the day before.

* * * * *

JoAnne called every day. At first, I asked about New York, Gary, and Pete, but then our conversations became strained. "Allison, I'll be there in less than a week to help out."

"I thought coming home was the right thing to do, but I hate seeing her waste away. And Patrick is away most of the time. I can't blame him. I don't know why anyone wants to live in this town."

I knew JoAnne sensed the exhaustion in my voice. "My parents couldn't fathom living anywhere else. Is there any improvement?"

"No. She sleeps most of the day. There are days that are better than others."

"Having Patrick away all the time can't help."

"It's worse when he's here. He spends most of his time asking Mom what he can do to make her comfortable. I want to scream. He told her you're coming to visit, and he's going to take the family to dinner before we return to New York. My aunt already arranged to have dinner brought in because Patrick isn't thinking straight."

"Allison, if there were words I could say to make this all go away, I would have said them. Are you still planning on meeting me at the train station?"

"Yes. Aunt Sarah and Uncle George will stay with my mom."

"If you can't meet me, I'll arrange to have my brother Jake pick me up."

"If something comes up, I'll call."

* * * * *

When I hung up the phone, my mother asked, "I bet you can't wait to see JoAnne?"

"Mom, I thought you were asleep."

"My back was bothering me. When it kicks-up I walk up and down the hall so I don't wake Patrick."

I ran to my mother's side. "Does this happen often?"

"Yes, but usually it's later in the night. I know exactly where to step so the floor doesn't creek. I wouldn't want to wake you."

"You can wake me. I wouldn't mind."

We walked into my room, and my mother sat in the chair by the window. "I've always liked this chair. Your father bought this before you were born. He sat in this chair a lot when we first brought you home from the hospital. He was afraid you'd stop breathing during the night."

I wanted to ask if she had the same fears, but I didn't want to interrupt her when she was willing to share memories with me. She looked out the window. "'The August moon lights the room. No need for a night-light.' Do you remember you father saying those words to you, or were you too young to remember? Every night when he tucked you in bed, you'd say, 'Don't forget to turn on the night-light.' His reply would be, 'Every month should be August. The August moon lights the room. No need for a night-light.'" She smiled, remembering.

My mother was amazed when I said, "I do remember."

She smiled. "I'm not surprised." Contemplating what she wanted to say, she said, "Oh, yes, I should apologize to you for taking you away from your work and friends in New York."

Her words sicken my stomach. "You don't have to apologize. I wanted to come home for the summer."

"You didn't have to."

I wanted to get up and shake her, wishing she had instead said, "Thank you, sweetheart, for wanting to come home and spend time with your dying mother."

"Time goes by so fast. Next May you'll graduate college. Are you planning on remaining in New York?"

"Yes. I'm applying to law school. I thought I'll follow in Aunt Sarah's footsteps, but unlike her, I'm thinking of heading to California to practice law."

With no remorse, she said, "Only been to New York, never California. I don't think I would like the West Coast. I love the change in seasons too much."

"It would have been nice if Aunt Kerry were still alive. Then I'd have family to visit."

"Yes. They did move to California after your father died," my mother said. "Your aunt Sarah will be disappointed when she hears you want to move to the West Coast. Ever since you were a little girl, she filled your head with grandeur about living in the big city. She'd make up stories about the princess finding her prince charming while crossing Fifth Avenue. She was always trying to get your uncle and me to come and live with her in the city, but you already knew that."

"I think Patrick would like living in a major city. If he wanted to move, would you go?"

"Patrick has the best of both worlds. He spends more than his share of time in Pittsburgh and then comes home to relax. I don't think that conversation would ever come up." She rose from the chair. "Talking has suddenly made me very tired. We'll talk more tomorrow."

As she slowly made her way to the door, I said, "Mom, I was hoping you and I could talk. I have so many questions—"

"There's plenty of time to talk. I want to know more about that boy Peter, who calls twice a week. I hope to meet him at your graduation in May."

"Mom, I'd like to talk more. I have so many questions, about my father, you, me ..."

My mother turned to me. Her eyes had lost that beautiful crystal blue color; they were black and cold in this dim light. "Allison, what I admire most is your tenacity, always wanting answers to questions that I have no answers for. You were such a difficult child. I only have myself to blame. I never stepped in and stopped your father from spoiling you as he did. You learned very early, if you didn't get your own way, pouting always helped. After your father died, I knew I had to approach raising you differently, so if you feel my treatment of you was unjust and you're hoping for an apology, I have none to offer." She paused for a moment. "Did you ever consider how hard it was for me, a young woman, to be left to raise a spoiled child? Nothing I did ever pleased you, Allison."

My mother closed the door behind her. I lay awake, dissecting my mother's confession. I never considered myself a difficult child, or was I as a small child? I didn't remember making her life miserable as I grew older. I worked hard at keeping my feelings to myself not to widen the riff between us. Was the trouble between us all my doing?

She felt she had nothing to apologize for. I wasn't searching for an apology. She did not see herself as the problem, and I only saw her lack of affection as our problem. She defended her actions. What question could I ask that would make her understand my side? At this point, I didn't want her explanation. I was done.

The anger I felt toward my mother was building. At one point, I wanted to storm down the hall, burst into her room, and call her a coldhearted asshole. I wanted her to admit that she blamed me for my father's death or blamed him for leaving her with a spoiled little girl.

Most of all, I wanted to hurt her. I wanted to tell her that the man lying next to her, her precious husband, was never in love with her, that his true love was me. I wanted her to suffer as I had all those years living with her. As the night went on, I controlled my anger, knowing death was knocking on her door.

The next day, I did my chores as a good daughter would and made little conversation with the woman I called Mom.

* * * * *

Back at school, I pushed my mother from my mind. I only focused on the people I knew loved me. Upon my return to New York, Pete and I became close. I knew it was wrong, considering that I was still bent on Patrick and me someday finding true love.

In September, I was offered an internship at the Brown and Schuler's law firm. I was lucky to land the job since most of the interns worked during the summer, but hearing of my mother's plight, they reconsidered when it was noted that my name appeared on the dean's list for three years. The job also gave me a way out of holiday visits back home.

I lied, telling my mother I had to work. "I'm happy you're feeling better, Mom, and I hope you're not upset that I won't be able to make it home for Christmas. I'm working Christmas Eve," I said. "No, I'm not going to be alone on Christmas Day. Pete's family invited me to dinner. I'm going to spend Christmas night at Pete's house, then I'll take the train back. I have to work on Tuesday." I paused. "I knew you'd understand."

My aunt wasn't as understanding. "Allison, you missed Thanksgiving, now Christmas. I really thought you'd be home for Christmas. You haven't seen your mom since August."

"My mother understood. Aunt Sarah, if I could clone myself, I would. I promise I'll be home for Easter."

"I find it strange that you haven't even asked about your mother's health."

"I spoke with Mom. She said she's doing fine. Patrick said Dr. Pratt told him she might be one of the lucky ones."

"Dr. Pratt is amazed she's doing so well. Even gained back a few pounds. Your mother was very helpful at the church Christmas party. Maybe God has taken pity on our family."

"A Christmas miracle."

"Miracle—wouldn't that be wonderful? But what if this is just a—"

"Aunt Sarah, don't be such a pessimist. Think positive. She might beat this. She told me she was looking forward to her only child graduating with honors."

"She's looking forward to that day. She's mentioned it to me more than once."

I tried not to sound too sarcastic. "I'm sure she is. Aunt Sarah, I've got to run. I'll call home on Christmas Day, I promise. Say hi to Uncle George for me."

* * * * *

I had been avoiding conversations with Patrick now that my mother was feeling better. My hopes of a future with Patrick were growing dim, and brighter with Pete.

"My family was happy to hear you'll be spending Christmas Day with us. My mother goes all out for Christmas."

I smiled. "I wish I could spend more time with your family."

"They understand, but you're off on New Year's Eve and New Year's Day. You can't miss the Canes' New Year's Eve blast."

"I couldn't intrude on the family's New Year's Eve blast."

"When I say *blast*, I mean everyone in a radius of two miles is invited. I'm sure one more person isn't going to make a difference. You have to promise you'll come."

"If you insist, I'd love to be included. I'll take the early train. Tell your mom she has to put me to work. I don't want her to think I'm a freeloader."

* * * * *

I had also disappointed JoAnne when I didn't take the train with her back home for the Christmas holiday. "I can't believe you got away with not going home for Thanksgiving and Christmas. How did you pull that one off?"

"It's different in your family. Siblings, aunts, uncles, cousins—they all show up for the holidays. My holiday consists of five people. Anyway, I had a blast with Pete's family. His mother is so sweet. I think one day I'd like the life Pete's mom has, a loving husband, three children who believe the sun rises and sets in her smile."

"She sounds like June Cleaver. June's life was boring. All she does is cook, clean, and worry about Beaver and Wally. Are you going home for Easter, or are you celebrating with June's family?"

"I really don't want to go home for Easter. Graduation is four weeks later. I think I can convince my mother it's impossible for me to come home for a long weekend."

"Speaking about your mother, I stopped by to visit with her. She looks good. Do you think the cancer is dormant?"

"I have no idea. You said she looks better. My aunt says the same. So maybe she beat the big *C*. I guess I'll come to my own conclusions at the graduation."

"Graduation. You've decided not to go home for Easter? Allison, cut the shit. What happened over the summer? I thought things would get better between you and your mom, but it's gotten worse!"

"JoAnne, drop it. I went home and cared for my ailing mother, just like a good daughter. Nothing more."

"I'm sorry. I know you're going to tell me to butt out, but did you get a chance to talk with your mom?"

"Why do care so much about my mother and my nonexistent relationship with her?"

"I bring it up because I love you. No matter what the outcome, I think you have to make your feelings known before—"

"Before she dies? That's why I went home this past summer, and I gave it my best shot. If you're bent on knowing the truth, I tried to talk with her. She told me I was always a difficult child. She doesn't blame herself, she blames my father. She doesn't owe me an apology. She did say her life wasn't easy. Raising a child on her own was an added burden. Now you know the truth. If you were hoping for 'Allison, sweetie, I love you, I've always loved you,' that didn't happen. That isn't going to happen. This day started off perfectly fine until you fucked it up butting in my business."

* * * * *

I didn't go home for Easter. With three weeks till graduation, I found myself wanting nothing more than to pass up on the graduation totally. My aunt booked a number of rooms at the Hilton for JoAnne's family and ours. Pete and Gary's family did the same.

"I thought you and JoAnne would like to room together. Your mother is so excited about the trip. We all are. We are proud of you, sweetheart! I can't wait to see you. It's been a while."

"It hasn't been that long, Aunt Sarah."

* * * * *

"I think my mother is more excited about my graduation than me. I'm a little nervous introducing Gary's family to mine. Gary's mother's a snob but sweet. I thank God every day that she took a liking to me. I already warned my mother. Told her to be on her best behavior. I bet your family is anxious to meet Pete!"

"I wish I could find a way to keep them apart, but that would be impossible. Pete and I are close, but not walk-down-the-aisle close."

"From the outside looking in, I'd say you look pretty close. I've been waiting for you to spill the beans, but if someone asked if you were still a virgin, my answer would be heck no!"

"We sleep in the same bed, right across from the room you share with Gary. I'm sure you didn't think all we were doing was sleeping?"

"No! You could have shared with your best friend how it felt having a man inside you. The apple doesn't fall far from the tree. You're a private person, just like your mom."

JoAnne hadn't mentioned my mother since I told her it was a dead subject.

"I'm nothing like my mother, and to answer your question, I like being with a man. If I had known it felt this good, I would have given it up long ago."

JoAnne smiled. "Pete's a nice guy. He might not exactly know how to light your fire."

"Oh, he knows only too well. No complaints from this gal."

JoAnne smiled then changed the subject. "It was nice of your aunt to arrange a dinner at the Plaza for our families. She's lucky only my parents are coming, because if my siblings were joining us, we'd be eating at McDonald's. My mom said my dad hasn't stopped complaining about the cost just to come see me receive a piece of pig's skin."

"You know, it's not mandatory that we attend the graduation ceremony."

"Not attend graduation! Why not? I worked my ass off for this degree. Both of us earning high honors, we deserve every bit of the praise our families are about to bestow on us. You're not fooling me. You just don't want to spend time with your family. Lighten up. You, me, our boys, a weekend at the Plaza. After the dinner, it's 'Good night, family,' 'Hello, drinking, dancing, and a little celebration.' Just us and our honeys."

* * * * *

I met my family at the Hilton. Aunt Sarah was front and center when JoAnne and I entered the hotel.

Taking me in her arms, she whispered, "It's so good to see you! I've missed you." Releasing me, she said, "You look beautiful. I can't tell you how proud we are of you graduating with honors."

"A Holland not graduating with honors. Do you think I'd want to be responsible for placing the first crack in the Almighty Holland Foundation?"

My aunt smiled, and I could read her mind. "*Can't you set aside the sarcastic attitude for just one day?* Come, your mother is anxious to see you." Taking my arm, Aunt Sarah escorted me to where my family was sitting and enjoying a cup of tea and biscuits. Patrick and my uncle rose when they saw me coming, each greeting me with a congratulatory kiss and hug. My mother remained seated.

"Hello, Mom. You look well," I lied. She looked exhausted, and I felt guilty. I hated myself for acting, as she said, like a spoiled and difficult child. Sitting beside her, I decided to set aside my feeling. I placed a kiss on her cheek and whispered, "Mom, truthfully, how are you feelings?"

"I'm fine. A little tired from the flight, but your uncle, against my wishes, asked for a wheelchair. Patrick made the ride fun."

Patrick spoke. "We did a few wheelies through the terminal."

I smiled at him and thought he grew more handsome each time I saw him. My feelings for him returned when my stomach flipped at the sound of his voice. "Wheelies? That sounds like fun."

* * * * *

My mother sat when everyone else jumped to their feet to applaud the graduating class. As the graduates tossed their caps in the air, I searched the grounds for my family. I spotted Uncle George. As I ran toward him, he opened his arms and I wrapped my arms around his neck. "Your speech was outstanding! Did you ever consider being a writer?"

"Thanks, Uncle George. Good point. If lawyer doesn't work out, I'll consider writing the next classic novel."

My mother was securely standing with Patrick's support. I went to her. Looking into my mother's beautiful crystal blue eyes, I felt nothing but regret for my bad behavior. Regretful tears filled my eyes when I said, "I did it, Mom! Did I make you proud?"

My mother smiled then took my hand in hers and said, "Very proud." And we hugged.

The feeling I had to skip graduation was gone. I searched the crowd until I eyed Pete and his family. "Mom, there's someone I'd like you to meet." I introduced my mother to Pete and his family. My uncle snapped picture after picture, making sure he got pictures of every family. One picture that hangs on my den wall is of Gary, JoAnne, Pete and myself, Gary trying to lift JoAnne in the air, Pete laughing as I hold on to JoAnne, making sure she didn't fall, diplomas held high in our hands, with the uncertainty of what the future would bring.

* * * * *

I dressed and left the hotel room, leaving Gary and JoAnne time to celebrate. Pete and I decided to postpone our special celebration for after our families had returned home.

Standing in the hotel lobby early for the dinner celebration, I heard my name called. "Allison, you're early. Your aunt is helping your mother dress. They should be down in twenty minutes." He took my arm, and we walked to the lounge.

Patrick sat in the chair opposite mine. The waitress approaches and asked if we would like to order a drink. "Yes, thank you. Allison, would you like a drink?"

"No, thank you. I'll have wine with dinner."

Patrick smiled at the waitress. "I'm interested in a glass of red wine, not too sweet, not too dry. What would you recommend?" The waitress melted and described a wine that fit Patrick's description. Looking at me, he said, "This is how I broaden my knowledge of wines. I allow the waiter or waitress to make the choice. Their selection is always perfect, but a little pricey."

When his drink arrived, Patrick made a toast. "Congratulations, Allison, an NYU degree. You did it! I'm sure you'll be the most successful attorney New York has to offer."

"I hope to be and much more."

Patrick placed his wineglass down. "As I said, perfection. You should taste it."

"I prefer white."

"White, the lady prefers white." I noted a little sarcasm in his tone. "Your mother wants to drop by your apartment before we leave. She wants to make sure her daughter isn't—"

"Living in the slums of New York. I can assure you our apartment is in the nicer side of Lower Manhattan."

"I'm sure once you and JoAnne have secured a high-paying job, you'll move uptown."

"We intend on remaining in this apartment while I'm in law school and she's earning her master's."

"Smart move."

I fought hard to suppress the feelings that resurfaced whenever I was in this man's company. I controlled my feelings, thinking of Pete and my sick mother when my thoughts were interrupted with a question. "Are you happy, Allison?"

Thinking back on the conversation Patrick and I had not so long ago regarding happiness, I said, "Is anyone ever 100 percent happy, Patrick?"

Patrick smiled, knowing I had just given him a taste of his own medicine.

Patrick smirked. "Let me put it another way. Does Pete make you happy?"

This perfect day had become sensational. Was Patrick jealous? Was he jealous of Pete, or what I had accomplished? "Very happy."

Patrick had no response. Without breaking eye contact, he said, "Dr. Pratt didn't want your mother to make the trip, but she was determined to see you graduate."

The moment was broken with Patrick's sharing Dr. Pratt's concerns. "I knew she wasn't doing well from the moment I laid eyes on her. What is she keeping from me?"

"She's scheduled for an MRI on Wednesday. I believe the cancer—"

"I'm surprised Aunt Sarah allowed her to make the trip."

"Your mother insisted, and she wanted to meet Pete. That was all she talked about, meeting Pete. I guess like all mothers, she wants you to be happy."

I didn't respond.

He continued, "I must admit, I was curious about this boy, but now that I've met Peter, well, I hope we get to see more of him."

Whatever possessed me to announce out loud for Patrick's sake astonished me. "Pete and I are friends, but for my mother's sake, I'd rather we keep that between us."

"Of course. Your secret is safe with me."

* * * * *

That night, lying in bed, wondering where JoAnne and Gary had wandered off to, I was startled by a knock on my door. I asked before opening the door, "Who is it?"

"It's me."

"Mom, it's late. What are you doing walking the halls at this hour?"

"I couldn't sleep. I have something for you."

In her hand was a bracelet box wrapped and adorned with ribbon. "Mom, you're short of breath. Why didn't you call? I would have come to you."

Walking my mother toward the bed, I helped her sit. She handed me the box. Unwrapping the box as quickly as I could, I found a delicate bracelet of blue sapphires and diamonds and a small envelope that contained a note. The writing on the envelope was unfamiliar to me. I looked at my mother. "Open it."

> *Dear sweet, precious little girl,*
>
> *I discovered this bracelet among your grandmother's treasures, and she promised whoever presented her with her first granddaughter would win this beautiful treasure.*

On the day you were born, your grandmother Marks presented this gem to your mother and me, saying, "A beautiful jewel for the most precious of all jewels, a daughter."

Your mother and I pondered when we would present this gift to you. Of course, we chose your wedding day.

To our most precious jewel, today, I am sure, is the happiest day of your life. Know how much your mother and I love you.

Love you with all our heart and soul,
Mommy and Daddy

I read the note several times before I said, "Mom, it's beautiful, but why now? I'm not ..." I knew the answer before I asked the question. "Mom." Gently I held my mother in my arm and whispered, "Why?"

"It's God's will. Allison, do you like the bracelet?"

"I love it, Mom! I love it even more because you held on to it all these years. Of course, you held it for my wedding day ... oh, Mom."

"I know the last time we spoke, I was ... well, let's just say I wasn't myself. I know you had a lot of questions, especially about your father. When it first happened, if anyone mentioned his name, you became moody, depressed, causing terrible nightmares. Were we wrong not to discuss what a wonderful human being he was? Maybe, but the less we spoke of him ... well, I hope you understand. It's no secret how much he loved you. I hope that brings you happiness and closure."

The question I truly wanted to ask hung over us like a cloud. I wanted to tell her, "I never doubted his love for me. It was your love I questioned." A strange feeling came over me at that precise moment. I didn't want to upset my mother. I wanted our time together to go on, with her sharing whatever she thought would bring happiness to my life. It was then I realized that it took a lot for her to share these precious memories with me. It was clear she loved my father, maybe the only person she could ever love, and since I was my father's daughter, maybe she found a bit of love for me as well.

We talked for over an hour that night, ending with her promising to be truthful with me about her health. "Good or bad, Mom, you have to tell me everything. You promise?"

As we walked arm in arm back to my mother's room, and before she closed the door behind her, I reached for her hand. "Mom, Daddy is so proud of you tonight. You did a great job raising his little girl."

* * * * *

JoAnne was rushing around our hotel room, gathering up her clothes from the floor.

"We've been here three days, and we spent maybe six hours dressing, the other six sleeping, and look at this mess, your mess!"

"Put a lid on it. We have three minutes to get to the lobby. My father said if I'm not in the lobby in three minutes, he'll see me at Thanksgiving. He's afraid he'll miss his flight. By the way, nice bracelet. Was it a gift from Mr. Perfect?"

For a second I thought JoAnne was referring to Patrick, whom I referred to as Mr. Perfect many times in my mind, but I soon realized she was referring to Pete.

"No. It was a gift from my mother. Actually, it was a gift from my grandmother Mark. She gave it to my father and mother to give to me when I married. My mother wanted me to have it just in case …"

JoAnne stopped what she was doing and cradled my wrist in her hand. "It's beautiful, Allison." JoAnne was at a loss for words. What more was there to say? My mother was fading away with each passing day.

* * * * *

When JoAnne and I arrived at the lobby, Pete and his family were talking with our families.

Pete called to me. "My parents didn't want to leave without wishing your family a safe trip."

I didn't know how to respond, so we joined our families. "Mr. and Mrs. Cane, are you having lunch with your daughters?"

"We are, sweetheart, but we wanted to drop by and say goodbye to your family. It was a pleasure to meet you, Mr. and Mrs. Higgins. Sarah, George, it was a pleasure to meet you."

Pete turned to me. "I'll call you later. They're leaving later this afternoon."

Standing beside my aunt while my mother was seated and my uncle and Patrick were checking out of the hotel, I motioned to my aunt to step back so we could talk in private. "Aunt Sarah, I want to know everything that is going on with my mother. I made her promise to tell me the truth, but we both know she's not going to keep her promise. That is why I'm depending on you."

"I promise, sweetheart."

My mother motioned for me. I sat next to her, and she passed a decorative bag to me. "Don't open it now. Wait till after we leave."

I smiled. "Thank you."

My aunt hugged me tightly when she said goodbye. "Allison, please try to make it home for the holidays this year."

"I will, I promise. And don't forget your promise to me."

"I won't. And don't forget, I love you, sweetheart, with all my heart and soul."

* * * * *

I slowly opened the bag and reached in to find a cardboard box with a tiny lock and key. I unlocked the box to find a mound of pictures, of my father, mother, and me from my birth till my fourth birthday. Looking them over several times, I retrieved a sealed envelope. I opened it to find my parents' wedding rings and a watch attached to a chain, which I remembered my father wearing. At the bottom of the box was a note and several documents.

Allison,

Attached is my will and the deed to our home. The will is simple. All my assets will go to you, including the house. All I ask is that you allow Patrick to remain in our home until he decides to leave.

My mother didn't need more than two sentences to express her wishes. There were no words of love or regret, just the simple fact that I would inherit her worldly goods.

* * * * *

I kept the promise I made to my aunt. I went home for Thanksgiving to find a shell of a woman waiting to greet me. Christmas, I spent five days with the family. My mother spent most of her time in bed, except Christmas Day. At night, I listened as Patrick prepared my mother for bed. During the night, I was awakened by the shuffling of her feet as Patrick helped her to the bathroom. My heart was breaking, for my mother, and also for Patrick.

Easter was the last holiday I got to spend with my mother. My mother was admitted into the hospital on May 30. My uncle called me on June 5. That night I landed in Pittsburg, PA. My uncle was there to meet me. We drove in silence to the hospital.

I was told my mother was in a semicoma. I walked past my aunt and stopped briefly to say, "You lied. Why did you wait to call me?" My aunt lowered her head and began to cry. I walked past her into my mother's room.

I went to her bedside and took her hand in mine. Her hand was ice-cold. I thought I was too late. "Mom, I'm here." My mother was still, then her hand gently tightened around mine. "Yes, Mom, it's me, Allison. I'm so sorry! They called me this morning. If I had known, I would have been here sooner." I rested my head on her hand and began to cry. "Mom, why? Why didn't you … why couldn't you … it's not your fault. I take all the blame. I never asked because I was afraid I wouldn't get the answer I was hoping for. Whatever moments we did share will have to be enough, because time has run out for us." Silently I thought about the anger I was feeling toward my aunt. Staring at my mother, I confessed, "We never stood a chance, did we? Not with her always there, interfering. Even now she robbed us of our final moments to say goodbye."

My mother's eyes opened, her lips moved, but there were no words.

"Mom."

She closed her eyes for the last time.

My mother was pronounced dead an hour later.

I remained with her another hour then pushed past my family to exit her room. My aunt rushed after me.

"Allison."

"Get away from me! I have nothing to say to you."

"Please, Allison, wait for me."

I turned to face her and screamed, "Why didn't you call me on Monday, when she was first admitted?"

"Sweetheart, she took a turn for the worse during the night. We called as soon—"

"Stop with the sweetheart bullshit! I told you, if anything, *anything* happened, to call me. She didn't suddenly die in her bed. There was time for me to say a decent goodbye. She was my mother, damn you, but you couldn't have that! You controlled her even in death. You bitch, how could you be so selfish?"

My aunt covered her mouth with her hands and cried. My uncle stepped forward to console her. "Allison, you're upset—"

"I'm not upset, I'm pissed! I hate this family. Once my mother is in the ground, I'm through with all of you."

I stormed from the hospital.

* * * * *

I demanded the funeral be held in two days. I kept my distance from everyone. The night before my mother was to be buried, Patrick slipped a note under my bedroom door listing the time of the mass and burial. My aunt and uncle's home would be the gathering place following the funeral. I would not attend.

JoAnne kept a strong hold on my arm as we stood by the grave. I didn't pay much attention to the final prayers being said by the reverend. I took notice of the tombstone in front of me: "Erin Holland, beloved wife and mother," "William James Holland, beloved husband, beloved father," and grandfather; there were two other names, unfamiliar to me, obviously the unborn children of my grandparents.

JoAnne spoke. "Allison, you need to place a rose on your mother's coffin." JoAnne helped me move forward. I placed the white rose, lingering a few seconds, then moved back. Others followed until my mother's coffin was covered with white roses. JoAnne asked, "Do you want a few minutes alone? I'll stay with you if you want."

"No, I'm done. Take me home. I need to pack. I'm leaving tomorrow."

* * * * *

Reaching the foyer of my home, Patrick stepped forward. "We were hoping you'd stay a little while longer."

"No. I need to get back to school and work." Patrick eyes were swollen from crying. I felt sorry for him. His marriage, I suspected, wasn't what he signed up for.

"Patrick, I'm sure my mother discussed her will with you."

"She did."

"I'm not putting you out. You can stay as long as you want."

"If your intentions are to sell the house, please do so. I'll be moving to Pittsburgh in six months."

"Pittsburgh? Why?"

"Work. I'm assuming the CEO position at the bank."

"I thought you wanted out."

"I'm too young not to work. Accepting the offer will give me the security I need to walk away."

Standing in the home I shared with my mother, and with her body only one day lying in a grave not far away, I didn't have the nerve to ask why not New York. Or the question that had haunted me since my teens. My mother's illness had crushed my childhood fantasy where Patrick professed his love for me.

"I wish you luck, Patrick." The cab arrived and beeped the horn.

"You called a cab? I would have driven you and JoAnne to the train."

"Thank you, but I'd rather you didn't."

"Before you go, Allison, can you explain to me why you're angry with your aunt?"

"You have to ask? She should have called me the moment my mother was admitted to the hospital. My aunt robbed me of saying goodbye while my mother was still coherent."

"Your aunt begged for me to call you. You should be upset with me, not her."

"It's over. My mother's gone. I can't listen to another excuse. Whether it was your fault, my aunt's, or my uncle's, one of you should have called."

Lifting my bag, I headed for the door. Turning to Patrick, I said, "Patrick, I'll never forget your kindness. I hope this isn't goodbye." I smiled. "I never thought of you as a stepfather. I want you to know that our relationship meant more to me than you can imagine. If you ever get tired of Pittsburgh, there's always New York."

CHAPTER TWELVE

Sarah

Thinking of Andrew and Julia, I look at my watch and check the time. They should be arriving at camp. I spoke with them earlier this morning, wishing them a safe trip. Both are elated about their time away. I wonder if they are happy to be far away from the unhappiness that has invaded their lives and home.

"What's wrong?" asks George.

"I was thinking about the children. They should be arriving at camp right about now. I was hoping Allison and Pete would spend the day together, but when I spoke with Pete earlier today, he said he was doing some chores around the house while Allison was at the office."

I make a mental note to call Allison this week to ask her to lunch.

"This rough patch they're going through doesn't seem to be easing up. And Patrick's untimely death hasn't helped. I'm sure by this time next year, Pete's business situation will be resolved."

"I've tried not to ask too many questions, but I did ask Pete if he's noticed a change in Allison. Of course the answer was yes. He understands the change in her attitude toward him because of the traveling. He's more concerned about the wedge she has placed between herself and the children."

"I wish I knew what was going through that girl's mind. I think you're doing the right thing by not interfering."

"I know you're right, George, but it's so hard not to be concerned about their marriage. We both know what a sudden death can do to a relationship."

* * * * *

I place a call to Allison at the office and invite her to lunch.

She accepts the invitation. We agree to meet at the Golden Eagle Diner at one. I arrive at twelve forty-five, and Allison arrives ten minutes later. I gasp upon seeing her. She is thinner. As she approaches, I notice the black circles under her eyes.

I greet her with a kiss. "Hi! I'm so happy you could meet me for lunch. You look good. I love your jacket. Is it new?"

"No. I bought it last year, during our summer vacation to Florida."

"I love the boutiques in Florida."

Allison responds with a nod.

"Have you spoken with the children? Uncle George can't wait to talk with Julia. He gets a kick out of her camp stories. I wonder how Ellen and Andrew are getting along."

"I spoke with Julia last night. Haven't heard from Andrew. Ellen is all Andrew thinks about these days. What's the saying? 'A daughter's a daughter for all your life, a son's a son till he takes a wife.'"

"Pete didn't forget his family after he married you, so keep your fingers crossed. Anyway, you'll have him all to yourself in Florida. When do you leave?"

"I'm not going to Florida this year. Too much work. Pete will have to deal with Andrew's bad moods by himself."

I try to suppress my shock. "I'm sure Pete and the children were disappointed when you told them you would not be joining them."

"I haven't told the children yet. Pete wasn't happy, but I don't have a choice. I'm so backed up at work. He has to realize that my work is just as important as his."

"I see. Doesn't sound like Pete to be so inconsiderate about your job. This problem with the Florida office must be weighing on him."

"Maybe Pete's not as perfect as you thought. Since this whole Florida fiasco, I've seen a side of Pete I didn't know existed. You know, he's hired a woman to manage the new office. Her name is Emily Carter. Quite the looker. Have I told you about her? Well, I think he's having an affair."

The look on my face says it all. "Pete's having an affair?"

"I've shocked you, haven't I? Never thought good old Pete had it in him. I didn't mean to upset you. Actually, I'm not sure if he is or he isn't, but it's no surprise. We haven't been seeing eye to eye. That's why I've decided to pass up on vacation. I don't want Mary and Hank to see we're having problems. I'm sure you understand."

"I guess it makes sense not to worry Mary and Hank. You said you weren't sure about this affair. Did you tell Pete you suspected he might—"

"I did. He denied it, but I'm not buying it. I wasn't going to mention it to you because I know how fond you are of Pete, but you are the only other person I can talk to about this. I think Pete and I need this time away from each other. The two weeks apart will give us time to think."

* * * * *

I choose not to share with George Allison's concerns regarding Pete and this Emily Carter woman.

I need time to reflect. Prior to Patrick's death, were there signs that their marriage was strained? I quickly scan over the events leading up to the accident. Nothing jump out at me. Before Patrick's death, I saw nothing but a loving family, happy and content with one another.

Pete is not the kind of man to cheat and jeopardize his family's happiness, but this sort of thing happens all the time. I love Pete like a son, and it pains me to think that there may be some truth to Allison's suspicions. After all, she is a woman, and a woman can sense when something isn't right with a man she has spent half her life with.

Since the beginning of time, it's been said, if a man is unhappy with his current life, he often wonders if the grass is greener on the other side of the fence.

I toss and turn the night away, reflecting on the changes that have occurred after Patrick's passing. Allison is definitely not the Allison before the accident. On the other hand, Pete is facing a business situation that only this Emily Carter can understand. As one who is looking from the outside in, Allison isn't very compassionate toward her husband's plight. Once a doting mother who never complained about the hours spent with the children, she is now missing games and school events. She also is quick-tempered with the children. I can't deny or overlook that her change in attitude can also be related to a woman scorned.

I reach for the book on my nightstand. The photos come loose and fall on my lap. Gathering them together, I wonder what life would have been like if death had taken its natural course. We're born, reach adulthood, age, then die.

My life and the lives of the people I've loved have, in one way or another, been affected by death.

A picture of Lance and me at our college graduation is on the top of the pile. We were in love, looking forward to a future together, marriage, children, grandchildren, maybe great-grandchildren. Staring at the photo, I reflect on my life and the choices I've made.

Resting my head back on my pillow, I think back on my relationships.

* * * * *

Arriving home from Italy, I was embraced by Mrs. Clark and her daughters. I introduced Constance and Christopher to Jimmy and Sally, and these friendships would last the course of our lives on this earth.

I returned to the law firm anxious to see Stephen. Sally informed me that he was still in Europe on business. When he returned late September, our paths never crossed until the office Christmas party.

Jimmy resigned from his position as of December 31 to follow his dream. He was attending school at night; he wanted to design women's clothing. His collection of designs obtained him an interview with a prestigious fashion house. He was offered a junior position.

Celebrating at the company Christmas party, I spotted Stephen immediately when he entered the room. My heart skipped a beat.

He walked to the podium and tapped the microphone. The loud sound caught everyone's attention. "Good evening! I hope everyone is having a good time. Ellen outdid herself this year." The employees cheered. "I know what you're thinking. Good food, expensive liquor don't put food on my table. That's why I'm happy to say that you will receive an additional two weeks' pay next pay period, a Christmas bonus." The room erupted into clapping and cheering Stephen's praise. "We had a good year, thanks to your hard work. Hopefully next year, we can up the ante to a three weeks' bonus! Have fun."

Stephen stepped down, spent several moments conversing with the other partners, then existed the room, shaking hands with the employees as he made his way to the door. I lowered my head, knowing that night meant more to me than it did him.

When Jimmy, Sally, and I said good-night, I ran to the corner in hopes of catching the ten o'clock train back to my apartment. As I reached the corner, I spotted a limo. The back window on the passenger's side slid open. Stephen asked, "Are you on your way home?"

"Yes. I have to hurry. I'm hoping to catch the ten o'clock train."

"Please." Stephen emerged from the car and extended his hand. I took it and enter the car. The car remained at the curb. "Carl will need an address."

"I'm sorry, 5 Beaker Street."

Carl made a right turn heading toward Beaker. feeling uncomfortable, I sat stoic, staring out the window. Stephen asked, "I would have guessed Mrs. Clark had found you a one-bedroom uptown."

"Constance and I have remained close."

"And Mrs. Clark …?"

"And Mrs. Clark and her family as well."

We arrived at my apartment. I didn't wait for Carl to open the door. In minutes, I was on the street and heading toward the steps. Stephen called to me, "Sarah." When I turned, he was right behind me. "Nice building. Is your apartment just as nice?"

"It's one of the smaller apartments."

"Would it be forward of me to invite myself up for coffee?"

"Mr. Collins, maybe another time."

"I'll be on my best behavior. Scout's honor."

I had thought about that night and wanted another just as perfect, but I was wiser now. "I can offer you a cup of tea, and that is all."

When we entered the apartment, Stephen turned around and around. "You weren't kidding. It is small. But it's cozy." He removed his jacket, placing it on the sofa. He sat. I filled the teapot, placed it on the burner, and fixed a platter. I sat across from him, placing a plate of cookies on the coffee table. The teapot whistled. "Excuse me." While I was preparing the tea, Stephen called, "These look interesting." Tasting them, he said, "These are really good."

"It's a family recipe."

"You made these?"

"Yes."

"You're smart, and you can cook."

I smiled. "Yes. Does that surprise you?"

"Not at all. Are you going to put up a Christmas tree?"

Joining him, I placed the hot teapot down. Stephen poured tea into my cup, then his.

"Right in that corner."

"Will you invite me over to see it?"

"Maybe."

Finishing the tea, he said, "Well, this was nice. Your apartment is lovely. Would you mind if I take a few of these for the road?"

"Of course not." I took two napkins, placing several different cookies inside. "This one is for Carl."

Stephen accepted them and walked to the door. Standing outside the door, he said, "Are you free for dinner tomorrow night?"

"Dinner? Are you asking me to dinner?"

"Yes. I would like to thank you for the tea and cookies. Eight o'clock the Plaza. I'll have Carl pick you up at seven thirty."

"The Plaza. I couldn't."

"You can. I'm not taking no for an answer. Tomorrow." Stephen rushed down the stairs before I had a chance to argue.

* * * * *

Before I put on the only black dress I owned, I checked my stocking for runs, then my hair and makeup. Two knocks at seven thirty announced Carl's arrival.

Carl escorted me into the Plaza and left instructions with the Maitre d'. We slowly walked to the dining room. Discreetly I glanced around this magnificent hotel. Entering the dining room, I was informed Mr. Collins was running late. Waiting at the table, I was offered a glass of champagne. I accepted. Twenty minutes later, Stephen entered the dining room.

He kissed me gently on the cheek. "I'm sorry. Have you been waiting long?" Before I could answer, he continued, "I met a friend and his wife for a drink. I could lie and say it was business, but it wasn't. How was your day? Let me guess, school and work?"

"I'm finished with school until January, and work was interesting."

Stephen smiled. "Interesting. What made it so interesting?"

"We went out to lunch to celebrate Jimmy's new job."

"I heard he's leaving the firm. Designing, correct? Constance might have had a hand in helping him land that job."

"She might have gotten him an interview, but his designs got him the job. He's very good."

Raising one brow, Stephen smiled. "I've upset you. I'm happy for your friend." The waiter arrived. Stephen asked, "Do you mind if I order for you? The filet mignon is wonderful. Melts in your mouth."

"You're assuming I like beef?"

"Doesn't everyone like beef?" He smiled. "Please order the beef."

I agreed.

Stephen placed the order. We then talked casually about the office, what my plans were after I finished law school and my plans for the holidays.

Within thirty minutes, I started to relax and enjoy the company of the man who had taken my virginity. After dinner, the conversation turned serious. "You're probably wondering why I haven't been in touch since that night in Italy."

"It was only one night after many bottles of wine."

Stephen smiled. "It was an important night for you."

"It was. I don't think you would have guessed I was a—"

"I can't lie. It did surprise me."

"Can we talk about something else?"

"Of course. Should we have dessert sent to my room? You can't leave without seeing the view of the city. It's magnificent!"

I hesitated.

"I won't lay a hand on you. Scout's honor." Stephen crossed his heart.

We stepped onto the balcony. The view was magnificent. Stephen leaned on the railing. "I love this town. I've seen a lot of cities, but nothing pulls at my heartstrings like this city."

"It is beautiful."

Stephen looked at me. "Your eyes are capturing the city lights. You are a beautiful woman, Sarah Holland."

I blushed. "You're kind. If you think I'm beautiful, you should meet my sister Audrey. She's a beauty."

"You come from good stock."

There was a knock on the door. Stephen said, "Dessert." He had the bellboy set the table on the balcony. "Everything looks delicious, but I can't eat another bite."

Stephen dipped a chocolate-covered strawberry in a bowl of cream. "One bite."

I opened my mouth, and he placed the strawberry gently on my tongue. I bit down, savoring the taste. "It's delicious."

"You have to try the fruit tart."

"I can't. I don't have any more room in this dress."

"I promised you no funny business, but if you need to remove the dress, be my guest."

We laughed. "Let me try the tart. I think I have a little room left."

While we enjoyed another glass of champagne, we resumed our positions at the railing. Without any thought, I asked, "Did you think about me? I mean after?"

Without looking at me, he said, "Many times. I was your first time. I hope I didn't disappoint?"

I smiled. "It was a little uncomfortable at first." I blushed.

Stephen turned toward me. "I'll never force myself on you, but if you decide to have another go at it, well … I'd be happy if you choose me."

Stephen moved away. I reached for his arm. "I'd like to try again, with you, here and now."

* * * * *

I woke up the next morning next to Stephen. He hadn't disappeared as he did in Italy.

"Good morning, Ms. Holland."

"Good morning, Mr. Collins. And how was your night?"

"Exceptional, because I spent it with an exceptional woman."

I smiled and placed my head on his chest, noticing the breakfast set out before us. "Breakfast? When did it arrive? Was someone in the room?"

"No one entered the room. Scout's honor. I met the bellboy in the hall." Stephen stood. He was naked.

"I hope you had a robe on when you answered the door."

"I did, but I removed it just in case—"

"Stop there. I get the picture, but a girl can't live on sex alone."

Sitting across from Stephen, watching him eat and glance over the newspaper, which accompanied the breakfast, I thought him handsome and sexy, but I couldn't help thinking of Lance and wondering if I had betrayed him, or did he betray me by leaving me?

"You're deep in thought. I hope you're thinking about last night."

"I can lie and say I was, but I was thinking about someone else, someone who I thought loved me."

"An old boyfriend?"

"I was involved with someone before I took the job at Clark and Hutch. I thought he was the one, but he wanted to play professional hockey, and hockey was more important than what we shared."

"A jock. Never took you for the jock type."

"He attended NYU, science major, graduated with honors, but his father's dream was to see his son play professionally, so when he was offered a contract, he didn't want to disappoint his father."

"So he really doesn't like the sport, he was intimidated by his father?"

"No, he enjoyed the game. It was his dream as well."

"He followed his dream. I can't fault the guy for putting himself first. There are a few women out there that might have thought we had a future together, but I knew what I wanted and nothing or no one was going to get in my way."

Seeing my expression, Stephen continued, "I know that sounds harsh, but if I didn't follow my dream, I'd be working alongside my father on a milk farm in Upstate New York." Stephen smiled. "Are you sure this man was in love with you?"

"He acted like a man in love, but he left, so I'm guessing he wasn't. Or you and I wouldn't be having this conversation."

"Well, I'm happy he's off spreading his wings, because I love being the man that spread yours."

I flung a piece of toast at Stephen, which ended in our making love for the fourth time. I never told him about the letters, which were tossed in a box, or the phone calls professing eternal love.

Stephen and I met at the Plaza once during the week, twice on the weekends leading up to Christmas.

"Carl will take you to the train after your lunch with Constance and Mrs. Clark."

"Do you think it's a good idea to have Carl take me to the train station? You know Doris will offer her driver."

"I've already told Carl to be discreet. Just turn out your lip, and Mrs. Clark will grant your every wish. If you're going to be a good lawyer, you have to know how to tell a lie that everyone believes."

"Is that what makes a good lawyer? We are all a bunch of liars?"

"Sort of."

I tickled Stephen, and he tickled me where a girl shouldn't be tickled. We spent the next hour making love.

At the door, we kissed. Stephen wished me a merry Christmas. Handing me a present, he said, "This is for you. I hope you like it."

In the box, a white gold bracelet with green emeralds and diamonds. "Stephen, it's beautiful, but I can't—"

"You can, and you will." He reached for the bracelet and placed it on my wrist. "Every time you look at it, you'll think of me and you." Stephen pointed to the bed.

"It's beautiful! Thank you."

We kissed several times before he said, "Go, Carl is waiting, and you wouldn't want to be late for your lunch with the Clarks."

* * * * *

I admired the bracelet and then removed it from my wrist, placing it in my purse. There would be too many questions from where it came.

"Carl, how long have you been Mr. Collins driver?"

"Six years, Ms. Holland."

"Please call me Sarah. Carl, I know Mr. Collins asked that you take me to the train station, and I don't want to cause you trouble, but I'm sure Mrs. Clark will have her driver take me to the train, so can this be our secret?"

"I understand, but you wouldn't mind if I follow the limo, do you? Then it wouldn't be a lie."

"Good thinking." I knew Carl was watching me through the rearview mirror, so I smiled, and he returned the smile.

"Merry Christmas, Sarah."

* * * * *

I entered the foyer of Mrs. Clark's apartment, and Christopher ran to me. I lifted him high in the air. "Hello, little one."

"Where have you been hiding? Do you have a special someone that you're not telling me about?"

"I've only seen him several times. If you're a good friend, you won't push, and don't say a word to anyone."

Constance crossed her heart. "You have to promise that I'll be the first to know. That's the only way I'll keep your secret."

"I promise."

The lunch was fun, but time was slipping away, and I was anxious to get back home to my family. Constance made me promise I'd return for the New Year's Eve bash at Mrs. Clark's, and Mrs. Clark made me promise George would be there.

* * * * *

George and I were relaxing in the living room, eyeing the Christmas tree.

I looked at the tree and said, "Every time I look at a Christmas tree in this living room, I can't help but think about the one that never made it in our home."

"Remember the first year after Mom died? No one had the nerve to ask Dad if we could bring a tree into the house. Then Christmas Eve morning, there it was, just lying in the foyer."

"I remember. I think it would have been easier if she died in January."

George looked over at me. "That bracelet looks expensive."

"I got it at the five-and-dime. Looks like the real thing."

"It *is* the real thing. Do you take me for a fool?"

"I told you I was seeing someone. We are just in the getting-to-know-you stages of our relationship."

"That bracelet alludes that you know each other pretty damn well." George smiled. "I hate to ask, but have you heard from Lance?"

"The letters arrive every other week, but I haven't read one of them."

"You're a piece of work. You're not even curious of what the man has to say?"

"At the beginning, I read two or three. One was no different from the other, and I'm sure the remaining in the box are a repeat of the first three."

"I'm sure they are. Anyway, if there is someone else, then you're better off not reading them. But I'm curious about why you haven't thrown the letters away."

* * * * *

George and I arrived at the Clarks' New Year's Eve party approximately ten minutes late, which was acceptable in high society.

"George, I'm so glad you made it! When are you leaving for Germany?"

"Day after tomorrow, Mrs. Clark."

"Good. Are you available for lunch tomorrow? We always have a New Year's Day lunch, just family." Doris smiled at Sarah.

"Doris, it means so much to me to have you as a dear friend."

Doris reached for my hand. "Friends forever. There isn't anything I wouldn't do for your sister, George. She has a warm and honest heart."

George said, "You'll get no argument from me, but it's not easy being her brother. That warm heart can be a thorn in my side at times."

"My daughters were very protective of their brother, Michael. Now they're very protective of their nephew. Of course, we have Sarah to thank for our good fortune."

Constance greeted us. "Constance, that dress is magnificent!"

"Thank you. A Jimmy original."

I located Jimmy and Sally. They were happy to see George and immediately started teasing him about deserting his country. I sipped my drink and glanced around the room. I spotted Stephen. My heart leaped in my chest. I smiled. He didn't return the smile. *Strange.* A woman with her back to me placed her arm through his. Mrs. Clark notices my stare. Stephen took the woman by the arm, and they walked toward us. The woman was attractive, ebony hair, gray eyes, a slender figure.

"Jasmine, this is Sarah Holland, her brother, George. Sally and Jimmy, you've already had the pleasure of meeting. Sarah, this is Jasmine Collins."

My mind was racing. Stephen never mentioned having a sister who resided in New York. "Sarah, I've been wanting to meet you. Mrs. Clark and Stephen have sung your praises. I personally want to thank you for bringing our dear Constance and her son, Christopher, back home to us." Jasmine leaned in and said, "My husband and Ellen are very impressed with your abilities."

"I knew from the day I met Sarah I might have to watch my back." Ellen leaned in, placing a kiss on my cheek. "Merry belated Christmas, Sarah. Is this handsome man the brother you can't stop talking about?"

I tightened my grip on George's arm as I stared at Stephen. He remained stoic, avoiding my gaze. I felt sick to my stomach, so I asked to be excused. Closing the bathroom door behind me, I looked into the mirror and called myself a fool. I needed to get George and leave. I couldn't sit at the same table with Stephen and his *wife*. A knock came on the door. Hearing my name, I collected myself. "Sarah, it's me, Constance. Are you all right?"

Opening the door, I said, "I'm not feeling well."

Constance placed her hand on my forehead, like she would if she thought Christopher was coming down with fever. "You don't have a fever, but you are sweating. Would you like to rest before dinner?"

"I'd really like to go home. Can you get George? Tell him I'm not feeling well."

"Sarah, can't you at least make it through dinner? I have a big announcement, and I really wanted you to be here. Please stay."

I remained for my friends. They were more important to me than a cheating man who now sat across from me with his wife, who looked adoringly at him whenever he spoke.

Constance announced she had backed Jimmy in his own fashion house. She would remain a silent partner but had first choice on all the new designs. The name of their new adventure: Ji's Designs.

Everyone applauded Jimmy and Constance's partnership. Dessert was severed, the champagne was poured, the clock stuck twelve, and kisses and well-wishes echoed throughout the room. I avoided Stephen and Jasmine. When the party was in full swing, I asked George to get our coats, saying I wasn't feeling well. I said good-night to those closest to me and made my way to the door. Stephen, coming up behind me, whispered, "Sarah, we have to talk."

George handed me my coat. I didn't acknowledge or introduce George to Stephen.

* * * * *

New Year's Day, George sensed something was wrong. "Did you eat something that didn't agree with you?"

I began to cry. "George, I've been such a fool!" I confided in George, including my first encounter with Stephen in Italy.

George consoled me as only a brother could. "It would have been different if you knew he was married, then I'd say you were playing with fire, but you didn't know. And if I remember correctly, you never said you were head over heels in love with this guy, so be happy you got out before you were in too deep."

* * * * *

My time with Stephen was fireworks, and I had to remind myself that it was I who pursued him in the hotel. He said over and over he would never force me. Why was I defending this man? He cheated on his wife. He robbed me of my virginity, never mentioning his beloved wife.

Wednesday of the New Year, I received a call from Stephen's secretary that he requested a meeting.

I retrieved my purse from my desk and walked head held high down the hall toward Stephen's office.

This time wasn't like our first meeting. When his secretary escorted me into Stephen's office, I had his full attention. I didn't sit; I stood directly in front of his desk. Stephen waved his secretary away.

When the door closed, Stephen rose and came toward me.

"Don't come any closer, you selfish son of a bitch!"

"Sarah, I thought you knew."

"Did you just say you thought I knew you were married?"

"Yes, of course. Everyone here knows I'm married. I thought for sure the subject might have come up. Sally is Ellen's secretary, for God's sake. Jimmy bumped into my wife several times at this office. Constance, Mrs. Clark … I was blown away when I realized you had no idea I was married."

"And the thought never crossed your mind to tell me yourself? A decent man would have asked if I wanted to get involved with a married man."

"Assuming you knew, I thought you were all right with it."

I reached in my purse, retrieved the bracelet, and flung it at Stephen. "You're the scum of the earth! When I told you it was my first time, why didn't you stop me? I would have never made love to you if I knew you were married."

"If you remember correctly, the first time, we weren't thinking clearly, but later at the hotel, I told you I wouldn't force you, and—"

"I know what I said. You don't have to repeat it. But I thought I was giving myself to a man who wasn't attached. We even had a conversation about my boyfriend, and you never once mentioned your wife."

Stephen moved closer. I placed a hand before him, and he stopped. "Sarah, it was an honest mistake."

"You call giving myself to you an honest mistake? Did I strike you as the kind of woman who would have an affair with a married man? Did you think I was going to be your mistress, or were you going to leave your wife for me?"

Stephen didn't respond.

"Thank God I didn't fall head over heels in love with you. You were just a good lay." I made my way toward the door.

"Sarah, please, you can't leave until we resolve—"

I turned and smiled. "Resolve, we have nothing to resolve." A light bulb went off in my head. "Oh, I understand, I can't leave until we both agree that no one has to know about our affair, especially Mrs. Clark. If I went running to Mrs. Clark and told her you took advantage of me and never once mentioned you had a wife, you could kiss this job goodbye. I was infatuated with you, and, honey, that's not love, because if I were in love with you, what better revenge than to see you torn down from that pedestal you placed yourself upon." With my hand on the doorknob, speaking directly to the door in front of me but loud enough for Stephen to hear, I said, "I could never hurt your lovely wife, Jasmine. Now, that's a woman who is truly in love. She's too good for you, Stephen, and I hope it isn't long before she realizes it."

* * * * *

I made the decision to leave the firm when February rolled around, and again, I missed my monthly cycle. It was time to visit a doctor.

I scanned the yellow pages and placed a call to several doctors. Most impressed with the receptionist for a Dr. Schultz, OBGYN, I scheduled an appointment.

I walked into the doctor's office and recognized the receptionist by her voice. She was as charming as she was on the phone. "I need you to complete some forms, Mrs. Holland, since this is your first visit."

Embarrassed, I corrected her. "Ms. Holland."

She smiled. "I'm sorry, Ms. Holland."

Sitting on a steel table covered with paper to soften the cold connecting with the warm skin, I waited patiently for Dr. Schultz.

When he entered, I was taken aback by his age. Late sixties, I assumed, but handsome.

"Ms. Holland, it's a pleasure to meet you." We shook hands. "Your hands are cold." With his hands he rubbed mine together.

Releasing my hands, he said, "You've noted you missed two cycles. When was the last time?"

"I believe December. No, I'm sure it was December."

"You're not married, but you are sexually active."

"I *was* sexually active."

"I see. I'm going to check your heart. The nurse will be in to take blood, and I'll do a routine examine. Is that all right with you?"

I nodded.

After the exam, I waited in the doctor's office and glanced at the walls, which were covered with diplomas and certificates.

"Ms. Holland, please sit." Dr. Schultz closed the door behind him.

I looked at Dr. Schultz. "Am I pregnant?"

Dr. Schultz smiled. "It's not conclusive until I get back the blood work, but in my professional opinion, I believe you are."

I placed my hand over my mouth, regained my composure, and said, "I can't have this baby. Can you help me?"

Dr. Schultz, who had been writing in my file, looked up and placed the pen down. "Ms. Holland, I'm not that kind of doctor."

"Can you recommend one?"

"Have you told the father about your current situation?"

"He's married. I didn't know he was married when I was with him. He was my first." I chuckled. "Can you believe I was only with him a month?"

"I've been doing this a long time. It can take years or just one time. The body is a complicated machine." Dr. Schultz looked at my file. "Can I call you Sarah?"

I nodded.

"Sarah, if I were the father, married or single, I'd want to know. He has the right to know. He might surprise you. He might want to know his child or at least help with his care."

"This man doesn't care about anyone but himself. This child will only complicate his life. I was foolish! I should never have gotten involved with him."

"I see. If you were my daughter and we ruled out the father's involvement, then I would advise you to have the baby and place it up for adoption. There are a number of loving couples who would welcome this child into their home."

"You want me to have the baby and place my baby up for adoption?"

"Abortion is illegal in this country, Sarah. The doctors performing this illegal action can do more harm than good. You might not be able to have a child anymore if the procedure is not preformed correctly, in a sterilized facility. Go home, think about your options, and I hope you come back and let me help you through this pregnancy."

* * * * *

I dabbled with contacting Stephen to tell him about the baby, but then I thought of Jasmine and washed the thought from my mind.

Adoption was my only option. I wanted children. What I didn't want was some second-rate doctor destroying my chances of someday having a family of my own. In three months, I would graduate law school. The baby was due in September. With the child being taken immediately from me, I would cram for the boards and sit for them in January. This baby only a mere inconvenience to the goal I had set for myself. I wasn't wise in my decisions regarding men, so it would be some time before I'd allow another to screw with my head.

I called Dr. Schultz and scheduled an appointment.

"You've made a decision?"

"I have. I'm going to place ..."

I couldn't finish the sentence. Dr. Schultz waited patiently for my response. "I've decided to keep my baby. It's going to be hard, but I have the means to provide for the baby and myself."

Dr. Schultz smiled. "You're sure?"

"Yes, I'm sure. I don't have the heart to give up my baby. I lost my mother when I was eleven. I don't want to deprive my baby of their mother. It's too painful. My baby will only have one parent, but I will be a loving parent."

* * * * *

Now, I had to tell the world I was pregnant. The lie I created was one I could live with. I would tell Constance, Doris, Sally, and Jimmy I had spent time with Lance. Doris asked if I had been to a doctor, and I told her I was seeing Dr. Schultz. It came as no surprise that Dr. Schultz and Doris were old friends, since Doris was on the board of the hospital and Dr. Schultz was head of obstetrics.

"You're not going to tell Lance? Are you crazy?" asked Jimmy.

"Lance has a chance to play professionally. If I tell him about the baby, he'll give up his dream and hate this baby and me for the rest of our lives. I'm not taking that chance."

"Sarah, Jimmy's right. You shouldn't go through this alone."

"I'm not alone, Constance. I have all of you, and you know Doris is going to make sure this baby and I are well taken care of. I want you all to stop worrying. You know I'm not hurting for money. My grandparents provided for us, and my father … well, I haven't told him yet, but I'm sure he's not going to desert me, and if he does, I'll have my law degree. I can provide for this baby with or without Lance."

George accepted my decision. Of course, he was the only one that could question my baby's paternity, but I told him the same story I told my friends, that Lance and I had reconnected and I was sure Lance was the father. He didn't press me for the truth.

The time had arrived to call my father. I was five months along before I got the nerve to make the call. "Hello, Dad. It's me, Sarah."

"Sarah." By the sound of my voice, he must have already knew something was wrong.

"Dad, I'm fine. Dad, please don't … Dad, I'm pregnant. Actually, I'm five months pregnant."

"Sarah, are you all right? Are you seeing a doctor? Is the baby all right?"

"Dad, we're doing fine. The baby is moving and kicking. I'm sorry, Dad, it happened, and—"

"You're having a baby, your own child. Are you happy, Sarah? Don't worry, sweetheart, everything will be fine." I could hear a crack in my father's voice when he said, "I'm going to be a grandfather!

Are you sure everything is all right? I wouldn't want to … I love you, Sarah."

During that phone call, the phone call I feared making, for a brief moment, the father I had lost those many years ago emerged. The following day, I answered the door to find my father standing before me. We embraced, I cried, and my father assured me all would be fine.

* * * * *

In June, I finished law school. The rest of the summer, I crammed for the bar and took long walks to the library to lease law books. During one visit, I decided it was time to finish *Gone with the Wind*, in honor of my mother.

After dinner and a hot bath, I retrieved the book and told my unborn child the story of that day so long ago when I watched my mother as she struggled to reach the top of the library steps and how awful it was for Uncle George and me to have her taken from us a few days later. I rubbed my stomach and said, "You and I will finish the book in honor of your grandmother. I know she's watching over us, and she loves you as much as I do."

I started at the beginning even though I could clearly remember the first one hundred and fifty pages. After one week, I placed the book down on the bed and reached for a handkerchief to dry my eyes.

Speaking to my enlarged stomach, I said, "Your grandmother was right, I did enjoy the book. I think Scarlett and I have a lot in common. She was strong, a survivor, determined to follow her own path, and she made bad decisions about her love life. Just like Mommy."

The following day, I asked Constance to join me when I returned the book to the library and accompany me to have a professional picture taken of me in my ninth month. I signed the back of the picture, "Baby and me." I dated it and placed it with the pictures my mother had taken when she was pregnant with her children.

Constance and I walked arm in arm, she supporting me so I didn't take a stumble and hurt myself or the baby. "I could never get through a thousand-page book. It must be the lawyer in you. Why the picture of you and your unborn child?"

I told Constance the story behind the novel *Gone with the Wind* and the tradition of the photo.

"You always speak fondly of your mother. George says she was a beautiful woman inside and out." Constance paused then added, "I couldn't imagine losing my mother at such a young age."

"Like Christopher with his father, my sister, Audrey, has no memory of our mother, but I wouldn't trade the memories I have of her for a stack of gold. Did George also mention he was our mother's favorite?"

"Mothers don't have favorites. I bet if I ask him, he'd say you were her favorite."

I smiled. "My mother and father loved us equally."

Constance stopped walking when I mentioned both my mother and father in the same sentence.

"Why are you stopping?"

"I've only had the pleasure of meeting your father a few times, and I think he's a wonderful man, but when you describe your mother, you describe a woman full of life, your father not so much."

"You know the story. When he lost my mother, the love of his life, he lost the will to live."

"I can understand loving someone so much it hurts. Believe me, I know, but when I look at Christopher, I'm reminded of Michael and I love him even more. Christopher keeps Michael's memory alive. I guess everyone handles grief in their own way."

"It could be worse. My father could have remarried, and I might be standing here complaining about my wicked stepmother."

* * * * *

Two weeks after Labor Day, I had my first contraction, but it was a false alarm. I was one week past my due date. Frustrated, I asked Dr. Schultz if this was normal. He said, "Babies come when the body rejects them. Your body isn't finished with this baby."

On September 23, I woke to a severe pain in my back. When I stood, my water broke.

I called Constance, and fifteen minutes later, a limo was waiting outside my apartment as Constance, Mrs. Clark, and the driver helped me into the limo, promising Mr. and Mrs. Parks updates.

On the drive to the hospital, I tightened my grip on Constance hand. "You told me having a baby was a beautiful experience."

"It is, but I didn't think I had to tell you it was painful."

"I knew there would be pain, but not this much pain. I thought I wanted more children, but this one might be an only child."

Doris laughed. "I said that with my first, and I have four."

Eleven hours later, my son was placed in my arms. I was in love, truly in love. "Hello! You're so tiny and so sweet. I'm your mother. Do you know how much I love you, Eric William James Holland? I love you with all my heart and soul."

Constance and Doris were the first to enter my room. Sally and Jimmy followed. They smiled, watching me gaze adoringly at my little boy. "Come look. He's beautiful! I can't stop looking at him."

"Oh, Sarah, he is beautiful!" Constance asked, "Sarah, did you check to see that he has all ten fingers and toes? That's the first thing I did when I held Christopher."

"He has ten fingers and ten toes, he's twenty-three inches long, seven pounds, eight ounces, and healthy as an ox."

Doris whispered, "I called your father. His first question was about your health, then he asked about the baby, just like a father."

"I can't wait for my family to meet Eric William James Holland."

"Eric William James Holland!" Constance cried. "Sarah, you named him after your mother and father?"

* * * * *

I begged the nurse not to take my son to the nursery. "Please, can he sleep here with me? I promise if he wakes, I'll ring for you."

"Listen, young lady, it's my job to care for this little boy and get you back on your feet. While you're in this hospital, I am in charge. You'll do as I say and get some rest. In four hours, he'll be screaming to be fed. Now, close your eyes."

"Oh, please, promise you won't let him scream too long?"

The nurse wailed, "New mothers!" then removed Eric from the room. I keep my eyes on him until the door closed. I drifted off to sleep after a few minutes.

* * * * *

Someone touched my hand, and I woke. When my vision cleared, my father was patiently watching me.

"Dad, you're here."

My father stood and kissed my forehead then whispered, "I'm so happy you're awake."

I know my father was back in another place and time. He needed assurance. "I'm, fine Dad. I'll be up and walking in no time."

He sat, and his voice trembled. "I'm so happy you and the baby are safe. I saw him, Sarah. He's beautiful, just as beautiful as his mother."

"They didn't tell you his name, did they?"

"No. The nurses said they were given strict orders not to."

"I named him after you and Mom. His name is Eric William James Holland. A little long, but a strong name. Grandmother Holland would be proud."

"I don't know about that. You mixed an Irish name with an English name. She's probably turning in her grave." He paused. "Sarah, I'm sorry your mother isn't here. A girl needs her mother—"

"Dad, I'm happy you're here. Mom is too."

* * * * *

It was one month since Eric William James Holland was born. At the end of the day, he and I would lie together and discuss what we did that day, which I transcribed in a diary of his life, for him to read when he got older. "Today we went to visit Dr. Schultz. He said you're growing like a weed. Tomorrow, Mommy can start you on baby cereal. After lunch, Uncle George and I will take you to the park." From the corner of my eye, I saw George coming toward us with a cup of coffee in each hand. "You want Mommy to tell you your favorite story, about the night you were born?"

"Please spare me. If I hear that story one more time, I'll vomit."

I laughed, knowing George had tired of me describing what it was like to deliver a child.

"Don't mind your uncle. He's jealous because now I have a new man in my life to love and worry about."

"Your mother likes to fib. She doesn't know how not to worry, but I'm happy she has someone else to worry about instead of me."

I placed the baby on the bed when George handed me the cup of coffee.

"I'll never stop worrying about you, George Holland. I just won't worry as much." Gazing upon my baby, I asked, "George, isn't he the most beautiful baby you have ever seen?"

"He's handsome, that's for sure. I have to hand it to you, sis, I knew you were a fighter, but being a single parent in this day and age, with everyone pointing a finger, takes courage."

"I don't care what people think. You know, George, having Eric has changed me. I'm not sure I want to be a lawyer anymore."

"You better get your head out of the clouds. Somebody has to support the boy, and I'm guessing that would be his mother, since she refuses to tell the father."

"The father?"

"Unless this was a miraculous conception, which I strongly doubt, the boy does have a father."

I had completely forgotten about Stephen. The lie I told about Lance was truer to me than the truth. Someday my son might ask about his father. I might tell him the story of how Lance and I met, or not, but I would never tell him about my affair with Stephen. But I could not deny Eric would have questions, but I had a few years to think of another lie.

"So what's your plan?"

"I don't have any plans regarding Eric's father."

"I was asking how you intend on supporting this little one. You can go home. Dad would be glad to help."

"No. There are better possibilities for me in New York. I was talking with Mrs. Parks. She knows a woman, a nanny. I set up an appointment to meet with her on Tuesday. On Thursday, I have an interview with a father-and-son law firm. They handle petty crime, real estate, and fender benders. Great fit for me. I spoke with the son when I called for an interview. I explained my situation, told him I wasn't looking to work around-the-clock, but I'd give it my all. He was impressed when I told him I was sitting for the bar exam in January. I got an interview, so I guess that's a good sign."

"They would be foolish not to give you a job. You're smart and reliable. I'd feel better about boarding a plane if I knew you and Eric were going to be all right."

"What if I told you I needed you and your nephew needs a father figure, would you stay?"

"I don't think Hilda would be too happy with me. I guess this is as good a time as any. I promised to marry her when I got back. Her mother gave me an ultimatum: marry my daughter or take your goods elsewhere."

"She didn't say that?"

"Not in so many words, but she made her point loud and clear. I'm not going to lie, I've been dragging my feet. I'm not sure I got what it takes to be a good husband."

"I was hoping you and Constance might hit it off, but Hilda is a beautiful girl and sweet. If you have to commit, I'm happy with your choice. There is no doubt in my mind that you will be a good husband. Deep down, George Holland, you're a pussycat. I can't say I'm happy that you've chosen Germany as your home."

"Don't give up on us. Hilda's been hinting she might like living in the United States."

Hearing the news, I embraced George. "Oh, George, that would be wonderful! Would you live in New York? Of course you would! And I promise I'll be the best sister-in-law to Hilda, I swear!"

* * * * *

My interview with Hart and Hart went well. Father Hart squawked over the salary, but the young Hart rolled his eyes and quietly informed his father that I was worth every penny. I was offered the job and would begin work at the end of the month, leaving me three weeks before I had to leave my baby.

Laughing to myself as I anxiously rushed home to be with my son, I knew I was going to like working at the Harts' law firm. I got a warm and fuzzy feeling that both father and son were kind and compassionate people.

George was elated for me and boarded the plane back to Germany content that Eric and I would be fine.

Prior to my interviewing with the Harts, I met with Ms. Reiss, who preferred I called her Fanny. I was impressed with her qualification and comfortable to leave Eric in her care. Fanny spent a few hours a day with Eric and me during the three weeks before I was to start work. I thought I was prepared to leave my son, but on my first day of work, I cried like a baby as I went over the instructions I left for Fanny. Eric was fast asleep when I smothered him with kisses and watched as my tears dropped on his precious face. I begged him to forgive me for leaving him, all the while convincing him and myself that I was doing this for us.

It would take two months before I could leave my son without crying. When I returned home from work, I'd spend every waking moment with my son. I never thought I could love another human being as much as I loved my child. I even found a way to forgive Stephen. If it weren't for his cheating ways, I wouldn't have this little treasure to love.

"Mommy's making special cookies that Grandma Erin used to make. She badgered a wonderful woman by the name of Mrs. Peterson to give her the recipe. I had to swear I would not share the recipe with anyone other than Aunt Audrey, but I'm going to break that promise, because I'm going to share the recipe with you. You know boys make the best chefs, or so they say."

Eric was starting to make sounds and responded when I spoke to him. "Eric, you have the cutest laugh. Yes, you do. Yes, you do."

Picking up my baby, I raised him in the air. "Who's going on the train? You are! And when are we going? Next Thursday! And whom are we going to visit? Our family, Grandpa Holland, Aunt Audrey, Uncle George, and Aunt Hilda. That's right, we're going home for Easter. This Sunday, we're going on an Easter egg hunt at Grandma Clark's and Aunt Constance's home. Christopher will be there, and Aunt Sally and Uncle Jimmy, even Fanny. Aren't you a lucky boy having all these people who love you? But not as much as Mommy, because Mommy loves you with all her heart and soul. Yes, she does. Yes, she does."

* * * * *

"Is the baby asleep?" asked George.

"Yes. Hilda rocked him to sleep. I think that wife of yours wants a child of her own. She won't let Eric out of her sight."

"We've been trying. Nothing yet."

"Oh, George, that's wonderful news! You are going to love being a father. It's the best. Makes you forget about all the bad things that happen before your child was born."

"I hope I'm not faced with the Holland curse."

"What curse?"

"Maybe I can't father a child. Remember Mom's miscarriages?"

"Mom had three healthy children, and Eric is four. Getting pregnant isn't easy, unless your name is Sarah Holland."

George smiled. "I've never seen you so happy, Sarah. The only other time was when you and Lance were together. Speaking of Lance, have you heard from him?"

"The letters and calls stopped a while ago. I'm sure he's moved on."

"Too bad. I really liked the guy. Have you considered reaching out to him?"

George didn't know how insane his question was. "No, I told you I haven't heard from him. Why would I want to strap him with a child and wife he never wanted?"

"Sure doesn't sound like the Lance I knew."

"It's over, George. I'm happy with my life just the way it is. Anyway, I don't have time for someone other than Eric."

"Eric isn't going to be a child forever. Might be nice to have someone to share the rest of your life with."

"The only men in my life are here in this house, one's in a crib, one's out here talking with me, and the other is inside, remembering Easters past when our mother was alive and well."

* * * * *

Constance and Christopher met us at the coffee shop that Eric and I frequented each Saturday before a day of shopping and spending an hour or two at the park.

"Did you have a nice holiday with George and Hilda? I really missed you."

"We had a wonderful time. Audrey said she's thinking about spending some time with me next summer. You and I both know she'll change her mind."

"How did Eric and Audrey like Germany?"

"Eric had no idea where he was, as long as he was fed and changed. Audrey seemed to enjoy herself. Lots of history in Germany. We spent most of our time at museums and libraries. Even though my sister and I are nothing alike, I have to admit, we enjoyed each other's company. She likes spending time with Eric."

"I bet George was happy to see you guys."

"He was. I think Hilda is pregnant. While driving through the countryside, we had to stop so she could … well, I don't have to tell you. Looked like morning sickness to me. I kept pressing George, but he wasn't taking any chances that something might go wrong. I got the feeling this might not be Hilda's first pregnancy."

"I'll keep my fingers crossed. So what do you have planned for today?"

"Some shopping. Have to stock the kitchen before I return to work on Monday. Afterwards, a picnic at the part with my little guy. Care to join us?" I love this time of year.

"I'd love to, but Christopher, Doris, and I are going to visit Claire at the country house in Montauk. I wish you were coming along. Claire would love to see you and Eric."

"I wish I could, but the timing is all wrong. Let me know when she's back from the country. We'll plan a Sunday lunch."

"Are you planning something special for this little guy's first birthday?"

"George, Audrey, and I celebrated his first in Germany. I thought I'd keep it simple. Of course, your family, Fanny, Jimmy, Sally. We'll celebrate again at Thanksgiving with the family. He's too young to figure out his grandpa and aunt were not here to celebrate with him. Next year, I promise we'll have a party with lots of balloons and a clown." I smiled at my son, who smiled back, making me wonder if he understood.

"Will you and Eric be joining us for lunch tomorrow at Doris's place?"

"Wouldn't miss it for the world! Eric loves visiting Doris. She's the only grandma he has."

"Well, Christopher and I have to get going. Have a great picnic!"

"Constance, before you go, how did the date go with that good-looking banker? He really likes you."

"It went well. He's really nice. Wants to meet Christopher. I told him I'd rather he get to know the mother better before meeting the son."

"Smart girl. If I ever meet someone, I'll follow your lead."

* * * * *

Mrs. Epstein packed something special for my picnic with Eric at the park. Mr. Epstein showed off Eric to the other customers, who stated that Eric was a handsome baby.

Mrs. Epstein asked, "I guess the old country is back to normal since the war. I lost family in that war. The man was insane!"

"He was mad, that's for sure, killing all those innocent people. I hope we never see the likes of him ever again in my or my child's lifetime."

"I lost two uncles, three aunts, and several cousins. The ones that did survive have nightmares about the time they spent in those camps."

"Selma, enough about the war. It's depressing. Where are you and this little one heading?" said Mr. Epstein.

"We're going to have a picnic at the park. It's such a beautiful day."

"Harold, put some of Sarah's favorite cookies in a bag. And a few of the hard ones for the baby to teeth on."

* * * * *

As we walked, I told Eric how lucky we were to have these good people in our lives. Before we reached the park, Eric was sound asleep.

I laid out a blanket. Sitting, I placed the carriage next to me. I watched the other children jumping, climbing, and running in circles. It wouldn't be long before I'd be chasing Eric.

Feeling lonely with no one to talk to, I decided to eat my lunch before Eric woke. When I opened the bag, Mr. Epstein had packed. I gasped. The bag was filled with cookies and not one but two large sandwiches and a container of potato salad. The entire feast cost me two dollars. Smiling, I decided to purchase three plants on our way home, one for the Epsteins, the Parkses, and of course, Fanny.

Finishing only half of one sandwich, I poured coffee from the thermos and reached for my book. Checking on Eric, I was convinced the minute I finished the first page, he'd be awake.

I was on page 50 when I heard my name. The sun was blocking my vision, so I placed my hand over my eyes to get a better look. The person spoke my name one more time. I immediately recognized the voice.

"Lance."

"Hello, Sarah."

In complete shock, I asked, "What are you doing here?"

"It's a long story. Do you have time to listen?"

I was at a loss for words. Looking around, I noticed a vacant bench. "Would you be more comfortable sitting on the bench?"

"The blanket is perfect. Do you mind if I sit?"

I sat up and made room for Lance to sit beside me. Before he sat, he looked into the carriage to gaze at Eric. When he bent down to sit, I noticed he favored his left leg, leading me to believe his days of playing hockey had come to an end.

"Beautiful little boy."

"Thank you. I guess the blue clothing was a dead giveaway. I think my son looks handsome in blue, so I dress him in it often."

Lance didn't look shocked that I referred to Eric as my own. "He looks like you."

"I think he looks like my mother."

"You always said she was beautiful."

"She was."

Neither of us knowing what to say, we both sat in silence for a few minutes, then Lance said, "You're a single mother?"

I looked at him wondering how he knew. But I didn't ask. "It's a long story."

"I have the time. Do you want to tell your story, or should I tell mine?"

"Why don't you go first?"

Lance started by saying that shortly after he left, he began touring the United States and Canada with the team. He was one week shy of signing a contract that would have paid him $8,000 a year for three years when he was hit hard from behind and fell facedown on the ice. The player that hit him lost his balance, and his skate landed straight across the back of his knee, causing extreme damage. After several surgeries, he went home to recuperate, undergoing excruciating physical therapy before he could even walk on the leg.

I wanted to stop him and ask why he didn't let me know, then I remembered all those phone calls and letters that went unanswered.

"I'm so sorry, Lance."

"You have nothing to be sorry for, Sarah."

Eric stirred. I checked to see if he was awake. "He's still sleeping." Silence again, both of us trying to figure out what to say next. I broke the ice and said, "Why are you here, Lance?"

"I took a job at the university. Been working as a science teacher for eight months. I started in January. I also teach summer classes for extra money."

"You've been in town since January?"

"Yes. You're wondering why I didn't contact you. I guess I was afraid ... You might have noticed the calls and letters were less frequent. Actually, I was happy you never responded. I didn't want to see or talk with anyone after the accident. I felt sorry for myself, but my mother wasn't having it. One day she slapped me hard across the face. It was the first time in her life she ever struck one of her children." Lance smiled. "She said it was time to think about my future. I contacted Professor Powell. He told me there was an opening in the science department. He was instrumental in me getting the job. I owe him."

I got the feeling that Professor Powell had much more in mind when he helped Lance get the job at NYU. I thought Professor Powell enjoyed playing cupid. I wanted to ask Lance why he waited this long to see me, but I let him continue with his story.

"One week after I arrived, I asked Professor Powell about you. He told me about the baby and that you were raising him on your own." Looking directly at me, Lance said, "I didn't want to intrude ..."

Eric began to fuss. "I think he's awake. He must be hungry."

I placed Eric on the blanket, and he began to crawl. Lance stopped him and began to entertain my son while I prepared his lunch. Lance placed the baby on his lap. I fed him. Eric smiled and played with Lance's hair, not at all frightened of the stranger. Lance was enjoying the attention.

"You're a handsome little guy. Maybe after you're finished with lunch, your mommy will allow me to give you a ride on the swing?"

My son attached himself to Lance, and I wondered if he was starving for fatherly affection. When Eric finished his lunch, Lance and I walked over to the swings. Lance pushed Eric and talked the same baby talk that I had grown to love.

"If you're getting tired, I can take him."

"I'm fine."

Sitting Eric in his carriage, I explained, "If I put him on the blanket, he'll just try to crawl away." I placed Eric's favorite toy in front of him, and he entertained himself.

"I think the bench would be more comfortable for you."

"You're probably right. My leg is a little stiff."

Lance folded the blanket and joined me on the bench. I still was waiting for the answer as to why Lance had waited all this time to contact me.

"I see you're still living at the same apartment."

"Professor Powell, I'm guessing?"

"No. I've been passing by your apartment at least three times a week since January. I watch you walk this little one. Once or twice, I've seen you heading home from work. I haven't seen you for a while. Were you on vacation?"

"Audrey and I went to visit George in Germany. He married Hilda. I think she's pregnant, but I don't know for sure."

"That's wonderful news."

"You say you've been keeping track of my comings and goings, so why did you wait so long to approach me?"

"Two reasons. First, I didn't know if there was another man in your life, and second, I was scared shit you'd tell me to get lost."

"Well, you have the answer to number 2, because I haven't sent you away, and in answer to your first question, the only man in my life is my son."

Lance stared at me, hoping for a sign that said, "I forgive you." "I was angry with you when you left, but as you can see, I have a story of my own, so I don't think I have a right to hold a grudge."

"If you want to share your story, I would be happy to listen."

There was a chill in the air. I shivered. "It's getting cool. I should be getting the baby home."

"Can I walk with you?"

Together we walked back to my apartment without another word between us, except Lance cautioning me to watch the oncoming traffic.

When we reached the apartment, I wanted desperately to spend more time with him but shied away from offering a cup of coffee.

"Sarah, do you mind if I stop by once in a while to see you and your son? But if you'd rather I didn't come back, I won't bother you again."

Looking into his eyes, I didn't want our time together to end. "Would you like to come up for a cup of coffee?"

"I would like that very much."

In the apartment, I brewed the coffee while Lance played with Eric on the living room floor. I reflected on another night long ago, when I watched Lance trim our first Christmas tree. While we were together, I often thought of Lance with our children, and many times I envisioned Lance as Eric's father.

"I can't believe it's time for his dinner. Can you sit him in his high chair?" Lance sat in the same seat as he did that night and every night we were together. I smiled, thinking old habits never change. After fastening Eric in the chair and placing a bib around his neck, I asked, "Are you hungry? It's too late for me to prepare dinner, but I can open a can of soup, and there are leftover sandwiches from the diner. You feed Eric, I'll heat the soup."

"I think I can handle feeding a baby."

I smiled. Concentrating on preparing us dinner, I listened as Lance chanted the words that gets a baby to open his mouth. "Open wide, here comes the train, choo, choo, yum, yum."

When I turned to set the table, there was more food on Eric's face than I assumed was in his tummy. "What has this man done to you? Did any of that food get into your mouth?" Taking the spoon from Lance, I ordered, "You heat the soup, I'll feed the baby."

"I thought I did a good job." Lance watched me feed Eric, and my son kept a close eye on Lance.

"Soup's done."

"Can you fill one of those bottles with milk? I can lay him on his blanket while we eat."

Lance spied the bag of cookies. “Hard cookies. I love these cookies.”

“Don’t let Eric see you eating his cookies.”

Lance laughed. I smiled. After dinner, we joined Eric. “It’s almost time for his bath. Do you mind? It will only take a few minutes.”

While I gave Eric his bath, Lance cleaned the kitchen. I placed Eric on his blanket, and he sucked his thumb. He then fell fast asleep.

Lance sat next to me on the sofa. “Is he out for the night?”

“Pretty much. He’ll wake up when I place him in his crib. He’ll cry for a minute or two, then he’ll drift off. If we didn’t have company, I would have read to him while he drank his bottle, but the three little pigs will be there tomorrow.”

“You enjoy being a mother. I knew you would.”

“I wasn’t ready to be a mother when it happened. I … he means the world to me.”

“His father didn’t want him?”

Staring at Lance, I said, “I think it’s time I told you my story. You might not like what I’m about to tell you, because you showing up complicates things.”

There were tears in my eyes when I finished. “I’m sorry I led everyone to believe you were Eric’s father, but in fairness to you, I also told them you had no idea I was pregnant.”

“It doesn’t have to be that complicated. We can set things right.”

“What are you saying?”

“I came back, found out about the baby, I was furious at first that you didn’t tell me, I wanted to wring your neck, but after I got over the initial shock, I was thrilled to know I had a son and begged to be a part of his life and yours, if you will have me.”

I could not believe what I was hearing. I knew why I fell in love with this man. More than anything, I wanted this man to be a part of my son’s life. “Lance, I’ve made mistakes, but my son was not a mistake. I love this child more than life itself. How could I take the chance that you would love him as much as I do?”

Lance reached for me. “I had a lot of time to think, Sarah, and there is nothing I want more than to spend the rest of my life with you and this boy.”

I rested my head on Lance's chest and began to cry. Lance whispered, "Sarah, give me a second chance. I promise to love you and Eric with all my heart and soul."

CHAPTER THIRTEEN

Allison

The camp bus pulls away from the curb, and Pete and I walk home in silence. As we turn the corner within a few feet of our home, and with my being free of any conversation, Pete says, "Lots of new boys this year. I noticed a few trying to get Ellen's attention. I hope Andrew doesn't spend most of the summer fighting off suitors."

"There were a lot of girls checking out our son. I think he'll be fine. If we have to worry about one of our children, it is Julia. The girl has learned the art of flirting quite well."

Pete unlocks the door, and we enter the house. "Thanks for bringing that up. The thought of our daughter being a flirt will definitely keep me up at night."

Closing the door behind us, Pete says, "Beautiful day. Why don't we take our beach chairs and head to the lake and have an early dinner at the lake house?"

The mention of the lake sends my head whirling. "Did you forget it's Saturday? I'm off to work."

"You're off to work. I thought with the kids gone, we could have some time to ourselves. You remember my flight is at two tomorrow?"

"I'm sorry, I have a pile of files sitting on my desk. I need this time to work."

"Allison, I'd rather you didn't go to work today."

"Excuse me, didn't you say you had an early flight tomorrow? And the reason for the early flight, I believe, is because you have an early meeting with the lawyers on Monday."

"Yes, I'm hoping this meeting will resolve a lot of issues and we can get on with our—"

"And did I complain when you said you had to leave early on Sunday? No, because it was work-related. Well, that's why I have to go into the office today. You're going to have to be as understanding as I have been."

"With the kids at camp, you have the whole month to catch up."

Pete's right; with the kids away, it's the perfect time to sit and talk and explain why I've been so distant, but as always, I lose my nerve. "I'm sorry, I have to go." Moving past Pete, I retrieve my car keys. Before I leave, I call to him. "We can go out for dinner. Make a reservation. I should be home around four."

* * * * *

The lake parking lot is packed when I arrive at the place of Patrick's final resting place. There are at least ten children jumping in and out of the water, parents are lounging on beach chairs, and the privacy I was hoping for does not exist. I return to the car and sit for a while. I soon realize my only hope to be alone is at the office.

I turn on my computer at ten and don't turn it off until six that night. I arrive home at seven, and as I pull into the garage, Pete opens the door in the laundry room and waits for me to exit the car. I can tell he's annoyed, so I put on my happy face.

"Hi! Sorry I'm so late. I lost track of time. Happy to say I got through every file. Feels like a weight's been lifted off my shoulders. Did you make a reservation for dinner?"

"I did. It was for seven. We'll never make it."

I look at my watch. "I have an idea. Let's go to Nino's for a quick bite. It's BYOB. You grab a bottle of wine." I head for the car and pull it from the garage, thinking that it's going to be a long night.

On the drive to Nino's, I go on and on about how much work I got done and how the weeks ahead I can concentrate on the families more than the paperwork. Pete's eyes are glued to the road. I'm running out of things to say. Only two more blocks to Nino's.

We manage to get the last table in the restaurant, in the corner, next to the kitchen. "Isn't this better? I'm so sick of fancy restaurants. And you have to admit, the food here is delicious."

It looks like Pete is about to speak, but the waiter interrupts him. "Hi, I'm Jake, and I'll be your waiter tonight. I see you brought your own." Jake points to the wine bottle. "We have several specials tonight. Would you like to hear them?" I nod. Jake reads the specials from a pad. "I'll give you a few minutes to look over the menu. In the meantime, let me grab two wineglasses. Would you like ice water with or without lemon?"

"One with a lot of ice and lemon and one with a little ice, no lemon, for my husband." I look at Pete and smile. "The veal dish sounds good, and so does the chicken." Pete doesn't answer.

Jake returns with our water and two wineglasses. He proceeds to open the bottle. After pouring the wine, Jake asks, "Have you decided?"

"Yes, Jake. I'm going to have the veal special." Pete says he'll have the chicken.

"This is nice, isn't it? Although I miss the kids, I'm not missing Julia's chatting."

"You're doing a good job of idle chat yourself."

I place my glass of wine on the table. "I know you're pissed. I said I'd be home at four. I lost track of time. I'm trying to make it up to you, but you're not having it. All right, get what's bothering you off your chest."

Pete looks wounded. "You know I have to leave by two tomorrow. You couldn't find it in your heart to get home earlier to spend some time with me?"

"I'm with you now, am I not? But that's not good enough for you."

"I don't know how much longer we can go on this way without professional help."

Jake arrives with our salads. I push mine aside, letting Pete know he has ruined our night.

"Here we go, professional help. You mean *I* need professional help, not *we*."

"No, I think we both need to speak with someone. I know my traveling doesn't help. It's only worsened the situation. I hate myself for being away so much, but I have people depending on me, including you and the children."

"I don't need to depend on you. I have a career. I can take care of myself and the children if I have to. My inheritance alone is enough—"

"This isn't about money or inheritances. This is about you, me, and the children. I don't think we're capable of figuring this out without professional help."

Jake arrives. "Still working on the salad?"

Looking upset, I say to Jake, "Something's come up. Can we have our dinners to-go?"

"Sure, no problem."

When Jake is clear from hearing, I say, "I'll be in the car." I storm out of the restaurant and wait for Pete in the car. He exits the restaurant holding the unfinished bottle of wine and a bag. Placing the bottle and food in the back, he enters the passenger's side of the car.

"You can't keep running from the problem, Allison."

"I'm not running from anything." I pull out of the parking lot and slam on the brakes to avoid hitting a car entering the parking lot.

"If you're upset, I can drive."

"I'm fine. I'd appreciate it if you wait till we get home to finish this conversation."

No sooner have we entered the house than Pete says, "We have to talk."

"Then talk."

"I'm going to seek professional help with or without you."

"With all the traveling, how will you find the time?"

"I'm not going to say it again. If you won't come with me, then I'm going on my own. Since you won't tell me what's going on, maybe someone else can. Our marriage is falling apart. We've hit hard times before, but we stuck together—"

"You're just upset that I'm putting my job before yours. Ever since the day we said 'I do,' I've always put your needs before my own, and you can't handle it."

"If that is true, then we definitely need to speak with someone, because I don't think I've ever expressed that my career is more important than yours." Pete's tone softens. "Allison, nothing is the same between us. Our children are being affect. Why are you fighting me? Obviously, you feel I've taken you for granted."

I turn and walk to the den, collapsing in the armchair. Pete follows, standing over me. I say, "I'm tired, the children are away, and I'm going to take this time to relax. You might want to do the same, with Ms. Whatever Her Name Is."

"In all the years we've been together, did I ever give you reason to doubt how devoted I am to you and our family? You know me better than that, and if I did stray, it wouldn't be with someone I work with, especially Emily."

I place my head in my hands. "Pete, I don't know if you're having an affair or not, and personally, I don't care."

I can't see the expression on Pete's face, but I'm sure he isn't happy with my last remark. He doesn't ask for an explanation; he turns and climbs the stairs to find solitude in our bedroom. I decide to sleep on the sofa.

* * * * *

The next morning, I wake late, too late for Sunday services. I picture my aunt turning every time the back door to the church opens. I make a decision; while the children are at camp and then on vacation in Florida, I will not be attending Sunday services. With my arm covering my eyes, I sense Pete's presence.

"I'm leaving for the airport. Think over what we talked about while I'm away. I'll call to let you know what time my flight is on Thursday."

"Have a safe flight."

I hear the front door close, and a strong feeling of freedom washes over me.

* * * * *

That night, my thoughts are consumed with Patrick and his sudden passing. I try closing my eyes, willing sleep and the dream, but the tired feeling is long gone with my family far away.

JoAnne has called earlier. I consider returning her call, but I am not in the mood for a casual conversation. I'm afraid if I hear her voice, the truth will flow from me. JoAnne is the one person I can confide in. She never sugarcoats her opinion, and she speaks the truth whether you want to hear it or not. I believe that is what I fear more than anything. I am not sure what her reaction will be when I tell her I want to end my marriage to Pete and reveal the secret I have hidden from her for years. In the past, I could count on JoAnne to calm the waters when I complained about my family and their imperfections, but this is different. I am about to destroy a man that everyone loves and respects. I will be known as Allison the Selfish Bitch, but only JoAnne will say it to my face.

It's no secret that JoAnne doesn't share my feelings concerning my family. One memory comes to mind.

* * * * *

"Your aunt called again. Are you going to return her call?"

"When I get around to it."

"And when is that? Never? Can I ask you a question? Why do you speak with Patrick when he was just as responsible as your aunt and uncle were for not calling you?"

"I know you've been talking with my aunt. She made you promise to ask me that question, didn't she?"

"No, she didn't. She asked how you were doing, I said you were still a little upset over your mother, and I was hoping a week in Paris would do you good. She was happy for us."

I planned a trip to Paris for JoAnne and me. With the inheritance from my mother's estate lying dormant in the bank and earning a nice return of interest, I didn't think spending a few thousand on one last fling before we started our internships would make a dent in the principal amount. At first, JoAnne objected, but I convinced her I needed to get away.

"Last night I spoke with Patrick to say we were vacationing in Paris, and when we ended our conversation, he made sure to add that he thought it would be nice if I called my aunt and uncle and told them I was going away. But now I don't have to waste the money on a call because you already told them we were going." I smiled, and Joanne grunted.

"I got the feeling Patrick was a little jealous hearing about our trip."

"Why? It's not our first time."

"He's always wanted to travel."

"There's nothing stopping him. Why doesn't he just go?"

"Work is holding him back."

"He gets vacation days. There's nothing holding him back. Also, Gary's not happy I'm going away."

"Gary and Pete can join us if they want."

"Are you getting dementia? They are starting their jobs on Monday."

"I think you can survive not seeing Gary for one week."

* * * * *

Reflecting on Pete's surprise visit to Paris when we were younger, I get an overwhelming need to speak with him. He texted earlier to say his flight was delayed but he was hoping to board shortly. Eyeing the clock, I calculate he should be arriving within the hour. I should call to say I'm happy he's arrived safely. The guilt I am feeling about the remark that I don't care if he is having an affair is eating at me. If Pete ever does cheat on me, it will hurt me deeply. If he's having an affair, what right do I have to judge him when I harbored feelings for Patrick? Aren't my actions a form of cheating? Placing my head in my hands, I have an overwhelming desire to scream. My head is filled with questions, questions I can't answer, questions I don't want to have answered. Pete is right; I need professional help, but if I agree, he will think I'm willing to fight for our marriage.

I reach for my cell phone then place it back on the coffee table. I don't have the strength to call Pete. I lay my head back and think about my life prior to Patrick's dying. I want to turn back time, to the time when JoAnne and I returned from Paris.

* * * * *

The trip did me a world of good. I returned more accepting of my mother's decision in her final coherent moments not to have her only child at her side. If the call were made and I had arrived before my mother slipped into a semicoma, would I have shown compassion, or would I have told her that she had failed as a mother? I was convinced I would have shown compassion.

I didn't allow Patrick to consume my thoughts. First, I stopped calling every Sunday. Patrick, the dutiful stepfather, called once a month. Hearing his voice awakened my feelings for him, but within a few days, I snapped back to reality. I couldn't lie and say I was over Patrick, because in the back of my mind, I was convinced together we could find happiness, but then there was Pete.

I was content with my life. Work and school were going well. My relationship with Pete was evolving. Pete loved to surprise me by planning a special getaway on long-holiday weekends. And the sex was great. During those times I did speak with Patrick and during the depressed days that followed, I considered ending my relationship with Pete. But seeing him, his warm smile, I wondered how I would survive without this man in my life.

Christmastime has a way of softening the hardened heart, so I called my aunt. "I'm coming home for Christmas this year."

"Allison, that's great news! I can't wait to tell your uncle. How long will you be staying?"

"I have to leave on Monday. I'm arriving on Friday, short trip."

"That's fine, sweetheart. It's been a while."

"Patrick wanted to talk with me about the house."

"I guess I can tell you, someone made an offer on your home."

"Why couldn't he tell me that over the phone?"

"I don't know why. It's a good offer, $350,000, but you might not want to sell."

"It's a seller's market, so I should sell. If I wait, the prices might drop."

"I can arrange for you to meet with our attorney."

"I thought I'd speak with Patrick about using the bank's attorney."

"Patrick won't be here for Christmas this year. He said he's spending the holiday in Pittsburgh with friends."

"Funny, I spoke with him last week, told him I was coming home for Christmas, and he never mentioned he wouldn't be there." I hesitated for a moment. "It might be wise to use your attorney."

"I'll call him tomorrow. I hope you're not too disappointed that Patrick won't be here for Christmas."

"It would have been nice if he told me. I might …" I pause, knowing my aunt surmised that I would have changed my plans if I knew Patrick wasn't going to be there. My only salvation was that JoAnne was also going home for Christmas.

* * * * *

Easter was early the following year, and I requested a week off from work so I could attend the closing on my home.

The house was pretty much cleared out except for two boxes in my room. My aunt sold most of the furniture, including my bedroom furniture. The money earned from the sale of the furniture was transferred into my bank account in New York.

Walking into the foyer, I glanced over the empty rooms. The house held only a handful of memories for me, of my father. I thought of the day my mother and father entered this house for the first time. They probably stood in the exact spot where I now stood. They acquired the home shortly after they married. My aunt knew the prior owners, and when she heard they were selling, she called my father, and he and Mother were hooked. They probably envisioned a long and happy life in this home.

Entering my room, I spied two boxes under the window. I didn't hesitate to open the first box. A picture of my mother and father was the first of these small treasures. I wondered if my aunt placed the photo there. The second photo was of my father standing outside the front door with a paintbrush in his hand. A smile flashed across his face. I assumed the photo was taken by my mother. Staring at the picture, I could only envision the happy couple decorating their new home, creating their own memories, which I knew my father would have happily shared with his children.

It had to be twenty minutes before I realized that the childhood and parents I imagined in my mind were gone forever.

Placing the lid on the box, I decided not to look through the second box. I turned and walked toward the closet. I stretched my arm to remove the loosen board. I searched for the wrapped bag that held the red sweater and a picture of Patrick. The picture: a smitten teenager held close to her heart in the middle of the night. As I eyed the picture, my heart skipped a beat. After a few minutes, I placed the picture on top of the sweater and sealed the wrappings. I placed the wrapped package in the first box and picked up the boxes to leave. When I turned, I was startled to see Patrick standing in the doorway.

"Patrick, how long have you been standing there?"

"Minutes. Let me help you with the boxes. They look heavy."

Coming toward me, he stopped when I said, "They are lighter than they look. I don't need any help, but thanks for offering. Why are you here?"

"The realtor called. The new owners will be here shortly for the walk-through." Looking confused, Patrick explains, "They have a right to look over the house before the closing."

I looked around my room. "You might want to tell them about the loose board in the closet. It's a great hiding place for those special things you don't want others to find."

"You could leave the girl that is going to occupy this room a note."

"A girl, is she an only child?"

"No. She has a brother, and her mother is expecting."

I smiled. Looking at the room for the last time, I said, "I hope she's happy here. I should get going. Will you be stopping by Aunt Sarah's later on today?"

"I have to be back in Pittsburgh by seven to celebrate a friend's birthday."

"You always talk about friends in Pittsburgh. I never met any of your friends. Did my mother?"

"Yes, she did. Someone I've been friends with since college."

Patrick and I descended to the lower level. Reaching the bottom, we found the new owners and the realtor entering the house. I avoided eye contact. When the group moved toward the kitchen, I looked back one last time, then gently I closed the screen door, the same screen door I had flung open as a little girl when I saw my father walking down our street.

* * * * *

Patrick did stop by my aunt's later that day to say the closing went well and a check was wired to my account in New York.

"Allison, do you have time for a quick bite before I head back to Pittsburgh? There's a legal matter I'd like to discuss with you."

My aunt looked in my direction. She smiled and motioned for me to accept. I blushed.

Once seated at the diner I ask, "I thought I was through with legal matters once the house was sold?"

"This doesn't pertain to your mother's assets. It's regarding my assets. As you know, my parents are gone, I don't have any siblings, and as far as aunts, uncles, and cousins, from what I was told, there might be an uncle, my father's brother, still living in Europe. For whatever reason, my father never spoke of him. There was no contact that I remember. He wasn't much of a family man. My mother was an only child. She never spoke of aunts, uncles, or cousins."

"And you never bothered to ask?"

"I did question my mother. She'd answer, none that she knew of."

"Didn't you find that strange?"

"I guess, but when my father said enough, I stopped asking. My mother's favorite line was, 'You know how upset you make your father when you ask too many questions, so don't ask so many questions, and life will be easier for you.'"

Patrick was painting a picture of abuse, so I asked, "Was your father abusive?"

"If you are asking if he ever used physical force with my mother or me, he didn't. He was a difficult man. It was his way or not at all. Don't get the wrong idea—my father provided for his family, I was never deprived, and I attended the best schools, music lessons, vacations in the mountains. I never once thought my parents didn't love me. My father always praised my accomplishments. He was proud of me, until the disagreement that tore us apart. When he passed, I didn't beat myself up wondering if we could have put our differences aside."

Since Patrick didn't share what came between his father and him, I didn't pry. "What about your mother? Did you see her after you moved out?"

"Of course. My father mellowed as he got older, but not enough to repair what was broken between us. The relationship I had with my mother was stronger when I got older. She was a part of my life until the end."

"But she wasn't able to change your father's mind regarding you?"

"There wasn't a thing she could do, so she loved us and accepted the separate worlds we created."

"How old were you when you stopped speaking with your father?"

"Twenty-nine."

My bank account was building with inheritance money, but Patrick and I weren't blood, so I asked, "Aren't you curious about your family tree? Why not take some of that hard-earned money and try to locate your family?"

"It's of no interest to me. If my father's brother was anything like my father, I don't need another dominating figure in my life to deal with. I thought long and hard about this, Allison. Your aunt's and uncle's friendship mean the world to me, but as we both know, they don't need the money, so I want you to have it."

There was no arguing Patrick's decision. I didn't want his money; I wanted him to want me as a woman. Changing the subject, I said, "The reason you moved to Pittsburgh was job-related, correct? You signed a one-year contract to stay on with the bank. That year is nearing an end. Are you remaining in Pittsburgh?"

"The bank hasn't found a qualified person to replace me, so I signed on for another year, which could turn into two. I have two years to make a decision."

"You are going to put your life on hold for another two years?"

"Two years isn't that long."

"When are you going to follow your heart?"

Patrick looked confused by the question. "Follow my heart?"

"What about your dream to travel? You're letting this job get in the way of your happiness. What are you afraid of?"

Patrick looked past me. Something had caught his attention. I turned but spotted nothing of interest. I waited for a response.

"You're young. You will soon come to realize loyalty is important in the business world. The company has been good to me. Two years isn't a death sentence."

My questions had caused him to think of me as a child, not as a woman. "I can understand being loyal to the company, but whenever we spoke, I got the impression your job was like a noose around your neck."

"You are so beautiful."

The comment took me by surprise.

"Do I make you uncomfortable when I tell you how beautiful you are? I'm sure Pete tells you all the time. If he doesn't, then he's blind. He's one lucky fellow."

My immediate thought was to discount Pete and our relationship. "We are only friends!"

"Your aunt thinks the relationship has passed the friendship stage."

"My aunt shouldn't be talking to you or anyone about my private life. As I said, Pete and I are friends."

"If you don't mind me asking, does Pete think of you as a friend, or is he hoping to take the relationship to the next level, if it hasn't already happened?"

I froze. Admitting to Patrick that Pete and I had advanced to the next level might hurt my chances of a life with him.

Patrick's voice lowered to a serious tone. Reaching across the table to take my hand, he said, "I've embarrassed you. I'm sorry. I was thinking only of your happiness. In two years, you'll be twenty-six years old. Two years go by quickly."

* * * * *

On the flight home from Cleveland, I was convinced that Patrick's plea was to put my relationship with Pete on hold. His emphasis on *two years* was tormenting me. In two years, I would be a lawyer with a full-time job. Patrick's contract with the bank would have ended, but two years seemed like an eternity. Patrick's feelings for me were still unknown, except for the conclusions I created in my own mind. Why was I afraid to come right out and ask if he had feelings for me? My mother was dead; she wasn't an issue, as far as I was concerned. My aunt and uncle and what they thought of us meant nothing to me. If they exited my life, it was no great loss, although I believed my aunt would come to accept our decision, not wanting to release her hold on me. After I had pondered the question of my inability to confront Patrick, the answer was staring me right in the face: I didn't know how I would react or handle the situation, whether positive or negative. Two years weren't really that long to wait, and during that time, I would grow stronger as a woman, secured with my decision, whether I would value a life with Patrick, Pete, or neither.

* * * * *

My conversation with Patrick, as always, placed a strain on my relationship with Pete.

With the end of my first year of law school approaching, I wasn't any closer to knowing my own heart. I needed to put distance between Pete and myself. The law firm where I presently worked posted a summer position with a satellite office in Port Washington, Long Island. I woke up early, took the Long Island Railroad to my destination, and arrived home by nine each night.

"I miss you. We haven't seen much of each other these last two months."

"I know. I wish things could be different. Taking this job in Port Washington has given me leverage with the firm. They offered me a paid position in September."

"I'm happy for you, Allison. Are you free Saturday for dinner and a movie?"

I did miss Pete. Patrick and I spoke once since our last meeting. For a man that wanted me to wait two years, he was making the wait difficult. I had no one to blame but myself. Asking Patrick bluntly if he had feelings for me would have ended my stress.

I agreed to dinner and a movie with Pete.

Knowing Pete was outside my apartment door, I rushed to open it, rushing into his arms. We couldn't get enough of each other. The lovemaking was fast and furious, and by the third time, it was controlled and just as enjoyable.

Pete jokes, "Absence makes the heart grow founder, and the sex amazing."

"So you forgive me for putting my career before us?"

"Of course." Pete places his mouth on my breast. I shied.

"I think my lady wants me."

* * * * *

I finished law school and graduated with honors. Aunt Sarah and Uncle George attended the ceremony. Patrick was unable to make it. His contract with the bank was nearing an end, and by the month's end, he would clear out his office to begin his new life. He called to say he was coming for a visit.

Hearing of Patrick's visit, I placed my relationship with Pete on hold. I refrained from meeting in the apartment. I limited our time together with long walks and phone conversations.

"Did I tell you Patrick is coming for a visit in July?"

"That's great news. I like Patrick, and I know how important he is to you, but you're not the only one with good news."

"Pete, you got the job?"

"I did. Can you believe it? A six-figure salary to boot! Passing the CPA exam sure did pay off. A few years ago, if someone had told me JoAnne, Gary, and I would be earning a six-figure salary, I would have said, 'From your mouth to God's ears.'"

The comment made me feel like a failure. Pete noticed his statement had struck like a knife. "Sweetheart, I didn't mean—"

"I know there's no money in social work, but it's what I enjoy. My family wasn't impressed with my career choice, especially my aunt. She thinks I should have remained with the firm, but I wanted to give this a try."

"You have to do what makes you happy. Anyway, why don't you let your future husband worry about supporting the family? And if I'm lucky enough to be the one, it would make me happy knowing you're doing what makes you happy."

"You're letting JoAnne and Gary get to you with all their talk about getting married. Of course, someday I'll be ready for marriage and a family, but that day's a long way off."

This visit with Patrick held the key to my future and Pete's as well. Marriage and children might be in my immediate future, but Pete might not be.

* * * * *

My days were consumed with the thought of Patrick's visit. "Do or die. Is this love? If so, what are your intentions?" The question every father asks when his daughter's future is at stake. Since I had no father to ask the question, I was on my own.

* * * * *

Arriving home from work, I found JoAnne sitting on the living room floor, painting her toenails. Without looking up, she said, "Patrick called. He's arriving at ten tomorrow. Pete's picking him up at the airport. You didn't forget about the party at Stew's? You know, the last hurrah before we enter the business world full-time. Goodbye to the lazy days of school and fooling around. Patrick's going to have a blast at Stew's."

I wondered what happened in the last twenty-four hours. When Patrick and I spoke last night, he was taking a cab to the Hilton. Now Pete was meeting him at the airport.

"Pete's picking up Patrick? He told me he would take a cab."

"Pete and Gary were here when Patrick called around four. I told him you weren't home from work. Pete overheard our conversation. Next thing I knew, Pete offered to pick him up. Patrick accepted."

I was furious; I wanted to keep distance between Pete and Patrick. But I couldn't let JoAnne know I was annoyed. "About the party, I have to bail. I'm planning a special night with Patrick."

"You're kidding, right?"

"No. I made a reservation for dinner at the Hilton. Just the two of us."

"The party starts at ten. Won't end till the wee hours of the morning. How long does it take to eat dinner?"

"I don't think Patrick would enjoy Stew's. Alcohol, loud music, it's not his thing."

JoAnne looked annoyed. "You knew about Patrick's visit and the party for over a month. When were you going to tell me you were bailing on the party?"

"I didn't tell you because I knew it would upset you. You think life is nothing but parties and fun, but I'm over that scene."

"Didn't know my lifestyle was upsetting you. Maybe you're exactly like your mother. What was the word you used, oh yes, *Boring.*"

JoAnne was going for the jugular, but I wasn't taking the bait.

She continued, "Pete never mentioned dinner with Patrick."

"I said the reservation is for two, me and Patrick."

"Does Pete know you're not planning on coming to the party?"

"I haven't mentioned it to him. Listen, we're not joined at the hip like you and Gary. I know someday you'll walk down the aisle and spend the rest of your lives together, but that's not in the cards for me."

"Funny, I thought Pete was the one. For the past five years, there hasn't been anyone else. I guess I was wrong."

JoAnne's assumption sent a chill up my spine. I wasn't sure, at least not yet, if I was ready to write Pete off. "I didn't say Pete wasn't the one. I'm just not ready to walk down the aisle. And what is so wrong with me having a private dinner with Patrick?"

"Nothing. As I said, dinner can't last more than two hours. I'm sure Patrick wouldn't mind if you two stopped by to say hi."

I sighed. "I'm not making any promises, and don't give me the silent treatment if we don't make the party. If you need someone to stroke your hurt feelings, I hear your boyfriend's fingers can work magic."

JoAnne laughed. "You got that right."

* * * * *

Pete left a message on my phone to say that Patrick checked in to the Hilton at twelve.

JoAnne asked, "Have you spoken with Patrick?"

"I was just about to call him."

"Pete and Gary invited him to the bar. Patrick never mentioned your dinner plans."

I threw JoAnne a look. "It was a surprise."

I immediately placed a call to the hotel. The hotel manager put my call through to Patrick's room, but the phone went unanswered.

I made several more attempts to reach him. My plans for a quiet dinner with just the two of us were collapsing. Where could he be? Call after call, no answer, and finally at seven, he answered.

"Patrick, where the hell were you? Why didn't you call?"

"Hello, Allison. I was exploring the city. Central Park is beautiful this time of year. Just got back a few minutes ago."

"I made dinner reservation at your hotel. I'll be there in an hour. Our reservation is for eight."

"I'm sorry, I ordered room service. Pete didn't mention dinner. He's picking me up at nine for the party at Stew's."

"You're eating dinner?"

"Allison, I'm so sorry. Dinner with you would have been lovely. What about breakfast tomorrow, just the two of us?"

* * * * *

The party was in full swing when JoAnne and I showed up. Gary greeted us. "I saved a table in the corner, far from the band." Gary pointed to the table. "I'll get a pitcher of beer sent over."

I asked for something stronger. "Order me a Long Island ice tea."

By the time Pete and Patrick arrived, I was on my second drink and fuming.

Pete kissed me on the cheek. "Hi! Sorry we're late. Traffic." Then he leaned in, kissing me square on the lips. I watched Patrick watch Pete and me. Once Pete was seated, Patrick kissed me on the cheek. "You look beautiful, Allison. What are you drinking? Is it good?"

"Long Island ice tea. It's strong."

Patrick smiled. "I'll stick with beer."

The single girls noticed Patrick and invaded the space between us. I was pushed closer to Pete. Pete asked, "Want to dance? I requested the DJ to play our song."

"I didn't know we have a song."

"It's a love song, and every love song is our song."

Pete held me tightly in his arms while I watched Patrick being flirtatious with a few girls I thought were my friends.

The DJ played a fast song, and Pete and I began to move around the floor. Casey dragged Patrick to the dance floor and moved close enough to him that their fronts were touching. Casey made sure Patrick knew her boobs were the real thing, swaying them across his chest gently. I could tell by the look on Casey's face that she had reached her peak. Patrick blushed and moved away.

"I'm getting hot. Can we sit?" Pete agreed. We moved toward the table. Before I sat, I asked the waitress for another ice tea. "Tell Stew to make it a strong one." The waitress got the message loud and clear.

Pete leaned in and whispered, "If Patrick plays his cards right, Casey will show him a good time at the Hilton."

Gary yelled out, "Allison, your stepfather sure does love to dance!" Winking at Pete, Gary gave Pete the thumbs-up sign.

The waitress placed my drink in front of me. JoAnne could smell the alcohol. "Wow, that's number 4, isn't it? Sure does smell strong. Are you sure you can handle it?"

"JoAnne, do I have to remind you my mother is dead and I'm not looking for another?"

Gary chimed in, "Leave her alone. An intoxicated woman is every man's dream, so willing to please."

Keeping my eyes glued to Patrick and Casey, I watched as Connie moved closer to Patrick. Patrick was now the ham between two pieces of bread. Gary looked over at Pete and sang "Oh What a Night." JoAnne laughed out loud.

"Come on, Gary, we can show those three a thing or two about making love while you dance."

Gary and JoAnne put on a show, and to my pleasure, Patrick, Casey, and Connie were forced to the side. Their dancing had come to an end, but not before I noticed Casey whisper in Patrick's ear. Patrick smiled, and Casey placed her hand somewhere off-limits. Patrick turned toward her, and my vision blurred.

I asked Pete to get me another drink. He hesitated, so I threw him a look. "What! I thought we were celebrating?" Pete headed for the bar. I noticed Connie moving on to another guy. Casey's arms were wrapped around Patrick's neck like she was a lioness saying,

"Back off, bitch, he's mine." Patrick kept his hands on her hips and whispered in Casey's ear. She sighed. When he tried to leave, she begged him to stay. He kissed her cheek and made his way to our table.

"Casey's a good dancer."

"It wasn't dancing she was after."

"Allison, I can handle a girl like Casey."

"Patrick, we're still going to meet for breakfast tomorrow?"

Patrick turned to me. "Yes, of course. I made a reservation for two."

"Just the two of us?" Patrick didn't hear the question; he was watching JoAnne and Gary make asses out of themselves on the dance floor.

Patrick laughed. "Those two were carved from the same mold."

"Patrick, what are your plans now that you're retired?"

"Retired? Retirement is for old people. Let's say I'm between jobs."

I repeat the question, "Then, what are you plans?"

Pete sat next to me. Placing the drink in front of me, he said, "The bartender said this is your last drink if you're driving. I told him I'm your ride home."

I wanted to rip Pete's eyes out for interrupting my conversation with Patrick. Lifting the drink to my lips, I swallowed half the drink. My stomach didn't agree with the fifth Long Island ice tea, but I surged forward.

JoAnne and Gary, exhausted from humping on the dance floor, returned to the table. "Patrick, I heard they fired your ass out of the bank."

"You could put it that way. I'm done with the banking industry."

Everyone lifted their drinks and congratulated Patrick. "Fuck the banking industry!"

"So what's next for you?"

"Maybe I'll go back to school here in New York. Seems to have worked for you guys."

Everyone laughed. Gary added, "Not a bad idea. I'm happy I came to New York. If I didn't, I wouldn't have met the love of my life. Right, baby?"

"Oh, Gary, am I really the love of your life?"

I shouted, "Why don't you two get a room? What is wrong with you men? Gary, either shit or get off the pot! Ask the girl to marry you. You know she's dying to be your wife."

"Is that the drink talking? I kind of like the vulgar Allison." Gary turned to JoAnne, "My sweet JoAnne, will you marry me? If you say yes, you'll make me the happiest man alive."

JoAnne gently pushed Gary. "Stop joking about something as serious as marriage."

Gary knelt on one knee and pulled a tiny black velvet box from his jacket. "Baby, I'm not joking." Opening the box, he presented a nice-size diamond ring to JoAnne. "Please, baby, say yes. I knew you were the one the first time I laid eyes on you."

JoAnne jumped from her seat. "Of course I'll marry you! I can't believe the size of this diamond! How could you afford—"

"I know size means everything to you, baby. That's why you and me fit so well."

"Stop bragging, but you do have a nice size."

Everyone screamed, "Too much information."

JoAnne motioned Gary's size with her hands, and the girls cheered. Looking back at Gary, JoAnne said, "Who gives a shit how you paid for it? It's beautiful! But you know we have to wait at least a year before we say 'I do.' If we get married now, my mother will think it was a shotgun wedding."

Gary smiled. "I'm not going anywhere, baby. Just give me the time and date, and I'll get to the church on time."

A loud applaud erupted, and JoAnne jumped into Gary's arms. The DJ took the lead by playing "Shout," and the dance floor was packed with shouting people. I knew this day would come for JoAnne, but not this day. She took my thunder away. This was my night with Patrick.

Patrick was beaming with joy. "I'm happy I was here to celebrate JoAnne's special announcement."

I looked toward Patrick. There were two of him. I spoke to the one closest to me. "You think marriage is in your future, Patrick?" With my question came the nausea. I stood, losing my balance, and Pete braced his arm around me.

"Allison, why don't we go outside? I think the air will do you good." Patrick grabbed my purse and placed his free arm around my waist, helping Pete to get me outside. When I reached the curb, I leaned over and vomited.

Patrick said, "I'll get the car. You parked around this corner, correct?"

Pete handed Patrick the keys. "Yes, about five cars down." Pete kept an arm around my waist and rested his other hand on my neck.

In the car, I placed my head out the open window. Only traveling a few short blocks, I demanded Pete stop the car. Pete pulled to the curb. I opened the door, and for the third time, I vomited.

When we arrived at the apartment, Pete pulled up to the curb and reached into my bag to retrieve the apartment key. "Patrick, you take her up. I'll find a parking space." Before I exited the car, I vomited on the back seat. Over his shoulder, Pete said, "Thank God they're vinyl."

Securing his arms around me, Patrick and I made our way to my apartment. "I'm going to be sick again." Patrick quickly opened the door and found the bathroom, leaving me with my head hung over the toilet. He removed the covers from my bed.

Gently placing me on the bed, Patrick began to remove my shoes. I slumped back onto the pillow, and the light in the room began to fade. Before I passed out, I whispered Patrick's name. As he drew closer, I said, "Patrick, there's something I have to tell you … I've loved you since … and I have to know, do you love me, Patrick?"

Patrick whispered my name, "Allison." I reached for him and pulled him closer. We kissed, and the kissing continued until the room began to spin and darken.

When I woke up, I could feel his presence, so I called to him. "Come closer, please make love to me. I want you so desperately." As he sat beside me, I reached for him. "I love you. Make love to me."

He tried to move away. I reached for him and pulled him closer. "No, I want you, make love to me."

I struggled with the buttons on his shirt. He gently began to unbutton his own shirt as I tried desperately to unbutton my blouse. Seeing my struggle, he helped me unbutton my blouse. I melted when his fingers touched my skin. I lifted my bottom, and he unfastened my skirt. I wiggled out of it. Lying in my panties and bra, I saw a silhouette of a man removing his clothes. He stood before me naked.

I whispered, "You are beautiful."

He dropped on top of me. For a moment I felt dizzy, but I controlled the feeling. Nothing could stop what was about to happen. He removed my bra and placed his lips on each nipple, sucking gently as I climaxed. He removed my panties and repeated the action. I reached for him, but he remained there, finding the spot over and over. My head was spinning. I wanted him to enter me, and I begged for him to enter me. But he refused. I began to plead. When he knew I was reaching my peak, he entered me. The gentle movements subsided. He bent my legs, and when I opened my eyes, a shadow of my knee was the only thing I saw. He thrust into me with such force while tightening his hands around my knees. He groaned. We moved in unison, faster and faster, until we climaxed.

He lay down next to me. The room darkened, and I drifted off.

* * * * *

I woke in the morning. As I forced my eyes open, the first thing I saw was the toilet bowl. I tried to turn, but my head ached. I reached my hand out and found I was alone. I lifted myself up, but the pounding in my head forced me to place my head back on my pillow. I drifted off to sleep.

When I woke, the sun was breaking through the blinds. I covered my eyes to protect them. Sitting up, I tried to stand. After several attempts, I managed to walk. I found JoAnne sitting on the sofa, admiring her engagement ring.

"Good afternoon. You look awful. Does your head hurt? There's aspirin on the table, and the coffee's been sitting all day. It should be strong enough to cure any hangover."

I walked to the coffeepot and poured myself a cup. The smell turned my stomach. I placed the cup on the table and sat. Taking three pills from the bottle, I placed them in my mouth and sipped the coffee to wash them down.

"I thought you were over parties? Didn't seem that way last night. I've never seen you drunk. You're a nasty drunk. I can't believe I'm engaged, and this ring is absolutely beautiful! Did you know about the proposal?"

"What time is it? And no, I didn't have a clue."

"It's five o'clock. I always dreamed when it happened it would be at some romantic restaurant overlooking the Hudson or a bed-and-breakfast in Vermont, never Stew's bar, but I guess Stew's was the perfect place, since Gary and I spend so much time there. I'm so happy you were there to celebrate with me, if only for a little while."

I tried to smile, but my head was pounding, so I asked the only question of interest to me. "Did you see Patrick?"

"Patrick, no. I got home around eleven this morning. I spent the night with Gary. There's a letter on the counter. It's addressed to you."

Rising, I held my head and retrieved the letter. It was from Patrick. I smiled. "I have to lie down. I feel like shit."

"I'm sure you do. Gary was hoping the four of us could go to Picco's for dinner. Do you think you'll be up to it if we make a reservation at eight?"

Holding the letter in my hands and wanting nothing more than to rip it open, I made a plea to my best friend, "JoAnne, you know I love you, you know I'd do anything for you, and you know that I'm as thrilled about your engagement as you are, but Picco's tonight, I think it will be a few days before I can swallow. What about next Saturday?"

JoAnne laughed. "Didn't think you'd be up to Picco's. Next Saturday, mark your calendar." JoAnne waved me away. "Go lie down. You look like shit."

* * * * *

Laying my head gently on my pillow, I opened the letter and gently removed it. I began to read.

Dear Allison,

As I began to write this letter, I knew breakfast was out of the question. I so wanted to share my wonderful news with you.

Tomorrow at six, I board the plane for a one-year trip through Europe, maybe even Africa, if there is time.

I want to thank you for inspiring me to take a chance on life. I intend on enjoying the fruits of my labor before my time is up.

I am sure by the time you read this letter, I would be heading to the airport. I will call, although it might be hard, since I will not be staying in one place longer than a week. But I promised your aunt I would call at least once every two months, and I'm sure she will share with you how I'm doing on this wonderful and long-awaited adventure.

Stay well.

Love,
Patrick

PS: I wanted to add that I'm not sure where life will lead you, but if Pete is part of that journey, you're a lucky woman. He's a wonderful man, and it's no secret the man adores you.

I reached for the phone. The hotel clerk answered on the first ring. Patrick checked out at two. I covered my mouth with my hand and began to sob. A second call to the airport, to have Patrick paged, but what airport? I was sure JFK. I was transferred several times, then the phone went dead. Several more attempts with no success.

Staring at the ceiling, I wondered what went wrong. We made love. The cat was out of the bag. He knew I loved him, and he ran. He ran off to Europe for a year. I loved a man who apparently didn't share my feelings.

Monday, I called in sick to work. I would return on Wednesday, I and my broken heart.

Around JoAnne, Gary, and Pete, I was pleasant, but I only saw Pete when Gary and JoAnne were present. I sat for the bar exam, and surprisingly, I knew after completing the test that I passed.

Three months later, I walked into our local CVS and purchased a pregnancy test. Before I began the process, I prayed to anyone who would listen.

JoAnne had been keeping a close eye on me, knowing something wasn't right. She questioned, "Allison, are you pregnant?"

I didn't answer at first, then the tears gave her the answer. "How did you know?"

"Morning sickness. You haven't been yourself in weeks. What else could it be? Have you told Pete?"

"Pete."

"Yes, Pete, unless you've decided not to keep the baby. I think he has a right to know. Whatever your decision, we'll get through it together. Allison, I know a few girls who made the difficult decision to abort. They are really a mess. Are you strong enough to live with—"

"JoAnne, I'm not as coldhearted as you think. I want to keep the baby, but I can't."

"How far along are you?"

"Almost three months"

"Time is running out."

* * * * *

First, I had to make an appointment at the clinic. Second, I had to end it with Pete.

Sitting on the sofa with the phone and the number of the abortion clinic in my hand, I was startled by a knock on the door. I remained still. I knew the knock and person on the other side of the door.

"Allison, it's me, Pete. JoAnne said you were at home. I was wondering … I was hoping you and I could talk."

I began to shake. Did JoAnne betray me? Had she told Pete I was pregnant?

I opened the door to find Pete standing there with his hands in his pockets and his shoulders slumped.

"Come in." I sat on the sofa, and Pete took his place beside me. "Allison, why are you so upset?"

I stared at those warm green eyes.

"Allison, please talk to me. Tell me what's bothering you. There's nothing you can tell me that's going to change my mind about you. I love you. I think you know that."

"Why do you love me?"

Pete smiled. "I love you because you're beautiful. I love you because you are the smartest woman I know. I love you because you make me laugh. I love spending time with you. I love making love to you. I love your hair, your eyes, the way you walk, the way you talk. I love everything about you!"

"You don't know anything about me."

"I know you love sad movies. I know you prefer a good mystery over a mushy love story. History, pasta, meatballs, kale, which I hate but I eat because I know you love it. You love sunny days, and you're the only woman I know that never complains about her hair when it rains."

"I'm pregnant."

"You're pregnant?" Pete's eyes focused on the floor, and after a few seconds, he looked up and smiled. "You're pregnant, that's wonderful news! Why didn't you tell me sooner? I was worried sick. I thought you wanted to end it between us." Pete wrapped his arms around me and kissed my cheek. "I thought I was going to lose you."

Shocked at Pete's reaction to the news, I decided to end this masquerade once and for all. "Pete, I don't think you understand.

I was just about to schedule an abortion before you showed up." I pushed the paper with the doctor's name and number in his hand.

Pete stared at the paper. "An abortion. You don't want the baby?"

"I'm not ready to be a mother, Pete."

Pete folded the paper in his hand. "I won't ask you to consider having this baby if you already made up your mind not to, but you're right, you wouldn't be a good mother. You'll be a great mother someday."

"I'm my mother's daughter. I don't know how to love a child." As I sobbed, Pete took me into his arms and held me tightly.

"Whatever your decision, I will be there with you. Please forgive me, Allison. I should have been more careful."

I raised my head and looked into Pete's eyes. "It's not your fault."

"I'll never forgive myself for putting you in this position. Making a decision to have an abortion is the hardest decision a woman ever has to make. Please—"

"Pete, it's not your fault, believe me. You had nothing—"

"Don't put the blame on yourself. It takes two to make a baby." Pete paused then whispered, "It's your body and your decision, but if you're not sure you want an abortion, I promise you'll never regret your decision to have the child."

The man before me was hoping I'd change my mind and not abort Patrick's child. If he knew the child wasn't his, would he be willing to love the child and me? I needed to know. "Pete, there's something I have to tell you …"

Pete lifted my chin and turned my face toward him, motioning with his index finger and thumb almost touching. He squinted his eyes. "There's a slight chance you might want to keep the baby?"

"I am having a hard time making this decision. I think of it as a person alive inside me, but …"

Before I could finish, Pete the CPA assumed a lawyer's role fighting a case he wanted desperately to win. "Allison, I have a good job. Money wouldn't be a problem. You can work until the baby is born, and if you want to return to work, fine. We'll find the best nursery or a nanny, whatever makes you feel comfortable. We aren't children, Allison. We can do this."

As Pete continued talking, I realized, with or without Pete, there was a possibility I could care for this child, but was it fair to rob the child of a father? I could make the effort to contact Patrick. Didn't JoAnne say the father had a right to know? Patrick, the father, was a mystery to me. Would he be as elated as Pete was about this unexpected change in his life? Did I need a rock to fall on my head to realize that Patrick running off to Europe proved that the night we spent together meant nothing? Pete loved me. He professed that love openly.

"You really want this baby?"

Pete smiled. "As much as I want this baby's mother to be my wife. I'll make you this promise, if your life is not filled with happiness, I'll set you free. Scout's honor."

* * * * *

My quest was to take the lie to my grave. Pete and I planned to marry in October.

Our families accepted our news without scolding or questioning why we didn't use protection, which I had stopped two months prior due to an infection. I never gave protection a thought when I pleaded with Patrick to make love to me.

Aunt Sarah, JoAnne, Mary, and I shopped for the perfect wedding dress with just enough room to hide the small pouch I was developing.

We were to be married in Pete's parish, and the reception would be held at the country club where Mary and Hank were members.

On a beautiful October day, my uncle George walked me down the aisle. Extending his hand to Pete, he said, "I'm counting on you, son. This girl is precious to my sister and me. All we're asking is that you love her with all your heart and soul."

Pete replied, "I already do, sir."

Standing face-to-face, we vowed to love.

We danced till eleven that night. If not once, then one hundred times, Pete whispered, "I love you. What did your uncle say? I love you with—"

I finished, "With all my heart and soul. My grandmother's mother spoke those words to her, and my grandmother to her children, and so on. It became a family tradition."

Pete placed a hand on my stomach. "I love you, little one, with all my heart and soul."

I smiled and kissed him hard on the lips.

My aunt took a picture of Pete, me, and my eight-month extended stomach, announcing another family tradition. I placed the picture in my child's baby book so it would be the first picture, followed by a picture of the sonogram.

Andrew Henry Cane was born on April 17th, eight pounds, nine ounces, twenty-two inches long. He was healthy, happy, and beautiful. Pete was right; I didn't regret marrying him and keeping my beautiful baby. The lie, at first, frequently entered my thoughts, but as time went on and my new life emerged, I was determined not to allow it to control me.

Pete adored our son. He kept his promise, and he showered us with love. And we loved him. I wrote him a card saying this and ended it with "I love you with all my heart and soul."

* * * * *

It would be nearly two years before Patrick would rejoin our family as a devoted grandfather to Andrew. It was unknown to him that the grandson he loved was his child.

Julia would be born three and half years later. It was with complete joy when I placed Julia in Pete's arms. I felt I had given the gift he so deserved, his own child, a daughter. She belonged to him and him alone. There would be one miscarriage after Julia, but we continued to try without success.

When I saw Patrick for the first time, my heart skipped a beat, but that feeling subsided when I set a place for him in our family as my stepfather and grandfather to our children. We functioned as a family until his death changed our perfect lives.

CHAPTER FOURTEEN

Sarah

George and I are eating lunch. I can't stop thinking of Allison. "I'm concerned, George. I've tried not to interfere. It's been a week since Pete and the children left for Florida. I still haven't heard from her."

"Did you call the house?"

"I did. I left several messages at home and work. She hasn't returned my calls."

The phone rings. I leave George in the kitchen and run to answer the call, thinking it may be Allison.

"Pete, I don't know. I haven't seen her or heard from her. I will. Let us know if we can … all right, I promise."

When I hang up, George is directly behind me. "We have to go. Something's wrong. I'll explain on the way to Allison's."

I ring the bell several times. No answer. I alternate between knocking and ringing the bell. I'm ready to break and enter when Allison finally opens the door. "Aunt Sarah, what are you doing here?" She looks over my shoulder. "Is that Uncle George in the car?"

I walk past her. "We need to talk." Heading for the kitchen, I notice the mess in the den.

Allison asks, "Are you insane, banging on the door that way? I'm surprised my neighbors didn't call the police. And why is Uncle George sitting in the car?"

"I thought it would be best if we talk woman to woman." I wait for her to sit. "Allison, you can tell me to mind my own business, but

I'm not leaving until you tell me what's going on. Pete is beside himself. He hasn't been able to reach you. Why are you avoiding him?"

"I spoke with him last Sunday. He's becoming paranoid. There's nothing wrong. I'll call him tonight. Will that make you happy?"

"Pete called me. He told me you haven't been at work for over a week. What were you thinking? Did you think he wouldn't call the office? The receptionist told him you were on vacation. Do you know how foolish it was to lie to Pete?"

"Stop, stop! Of course I knew Pete would call the office. I guess deep down I was hoping he'd find out I was lying about work."

"Did you find out Pete is having an affair? Is that why you're hiding yourself away?"

Allison laughs. "I hope he is having an affair. He'll need Emily to help him get through this."

"Get through what?"

"I'm leaving Pete, Aunt Sarah. There, I said it. Our marriage is finished. I want a separation. I don't love him. Heck, I'm not sure I ever did!"

"You haven't answered my question. Is Pete having an affair?"

"No, Pete isn't having an affair. The man is head over heels in love with me. Sorry I can't say the same." Allison rises. "I need something stronger than coffee. Do you want a glass of wine?"

"No." I look around the kitchen. There are dishes piled in the sink, and the counters are filled with open boxes and cans. The kitchen looks worse than the den. "If Pete isn't having an affair, then what went wrong?"

Allison pours herself a glass of wine and leans on the kitchen sink. Some of the dishes fall to the side. "I don't know. Shit happens! One day I woke up, took one look at Pete, and realized I never really loved him."

"Did this *awakening* happen after Patrick's death? When someone dies suddenly, at such a young age, it makes you think of your own mortality. You begin to question, 'Is there more to life than being a wife and a mother?' You might even see your spouse as an obstacle. Is this what's going on? Because—"

"Yes, something like that. No, all of it! The dying, the waking up with the same person 365 days a year."

I add, "The needy children?"

By the look on Allison's face, I know she is angry by my mention of the children. She snaps, "I love my children. I'm a good mother. It doesn't make me a bad mother because I didn't want to take a vacation with them. Year after year, the same vacation. Anyway, this is the new norm. Vacations with Dad, vacations with Mom."

Empathetically I say, "I knew something was wrong, but I had no idea it had gone this far. I'm completely at a loss. When are you planning on telling Pete that his life is about to change? From my conversation with him this morning, I assume he doesn't have a clue."

"I should have told him before he and the children left, but I didn't want to ruin their vacation."

I lower my head and say, "There's no right time to break someone's heart."

Allison moves closer to me. We are face-to-face. "I knew it! You're worried about your precious Pete. What about me, your own flesh and blood? You're not worried about my happiness, only Pete's. We shouldn't break poor Pete's heart."

"As I've told you time and again, we're family. Your happiness means everything to me, even more than you can imagine, but your children are also my family, and I'm worried about how this will affect them. Please believe me when I say it's you I'm concerned about." Her face softens. "Please tell me everything. I promise not to judge. It's just that you were happy. You had it all, a loving husband, two beautiful children. What went wrong?"

Allison stares. "Don't go fishing around for answers, Aunt Sarah. You won't like what you hear."

I've seen the expression on Allison's face too many times in the past. She's not ready or willing to share her feelings with anyone. "I can see you've already made up your mind, but I can't help making one last plea. Before you talk with Pete, ask yourself if there is one glimpse of hope that you feel something for this man, and if you find there might be, wait to confront Pete. Try reconnecting with him and the children. If, after a few months, you decide nothing has changed, then you can move forward with my blessing. I don't want you to look back and say, 'I should have handled things differently.' A couple can find love again, but if you break the trust, which a marriage needs to survive, you'll lose him forever."

* * * * *

On the way home, crying, I explain to George what Allison said and what is about to happen to our small precious family.

George sighs. "There's nothing we can do. It's Allison's life. All we can do is be there for them, especially the children and Pete. Poor guy won't know what hit him."

That night, more than ever, I need the pictures of my loved ones. My favorite is a picture of Eric, Lance, and myself. Staring at the photo, I sob. I wonder if my family is cursed. Happiness doesn't seem to be part of our DNA.

I was sure Allison was the lucky one. She was happy and content with her family. She had what most of us long for.

Staring at the photo, I whisper Lance's name.

* * * * *

The first person I called to tell that Lance and I were back together was George. He was overjoyed about the news, and I was overjoyed that Hilda was four months along. I was going to be an aunt. After speaking with George, I called my father and Audrey. They were equally as happy as George.

Lying in bed with Eric between us, I watched Lance watching Eric sleep. "My family is happy for us, and I'm thrilled that George and Hilda are going to be parents. Speaking of parents, when are you going to call yours and tell them the news? In one day you became a father and an uncle. Life really can throw you a curve."

Lance smiled. "I'll call tomorrow. My mother's wish was to be a grandma. She'll be thrilled."

"Will you tell your family the truth?"

"I'll tell her we were together before I got hurt." Staring at Eric, Lance says, "I can't believe I'm lying here with you and this precious boy." I envisioned you walking away, looking back, and saying, '*you had your chance, buddy.*"

"I was a real bitch not taking your calls or answering one of your letters, but I was furious with you. I thought you and I were ... well, that's all behind us. You're here, I'm here, we love each other, and for your punishment, I made you an instant father."

Looking at the clock over Lance's shoulder, I jumped from the bed. "Oh my, it's twelve o'clock! We have to hurry."

"Hurry? Where are we going?"

"We have to be at Doris's at one. I'm going to shower. You watch the baby, then you shower, and I'll dress the baby. No time to give him lunch. Can you heat a bottle of milk?"

"Who's Doris?"

"Oh, I left out that part. Here is the short version. Doris is the reason I got involved with Eric's father. She's really a sweet woman, like Grandma Maggie, but richer than Grandmother Holland. You're going to love her. She'll probably have a few choice words for you, you know, with you knocking me up then running off to play hockey."

"I'm not so sure I'm going to like Doris, especially since she's the one that introduced you to Eric's father. And in my defense, I didn't know about the baby, remember?"

* * * * *

We arrived twenty minutes after one. I introduced Lance to Doris, Constance, Jimmy, Sally, and ran off to the kitchen to heat up Eric's lunch, leaving Lance to face the music. By the time I returned with my happy and content child, Lance had them eating out of his hand.

"This was an interesting lunch. I can't believe he followed you to the park, and I'm assuming you spent the night together. You look like a woman who got laid."

"Jimmy, Lance might overhear you. Go on, Sarah, what happened after he walked you back to the apartment?" asked Constance.

"We argued. He was furious that I didn't tell him about the baby. Then we kissed, ripped each other's clothes off, and made love, and I hate to kiss and tell, but we might have set a record."

"That's the part you didn't bother to share with Doris. Putting aside you didn't bother to tell him he was going to be a father, and I'm happy he didn't knock your lights out, like I would have. The man's a hunk, and you landed him. Perfect ending!" said Jimmy.

"Why don't romantic things like that happen to me?" added Sally.

I touched Sally's arm. "Mr. Hubert seems to be smitten with you."

"I guess, but I'm sure he's not as romantic as Lance, and he's definitely not as good-looking. That man is gorgeous! And that hair as thick as a rug. Thank God Eric inherited his father's good looks and hair."

Watching Lance and Eric playing with Christopher, I couldn't help but notice the strong resemblance between the two. Which eased any doubts Lance wasn't Eric's biological father.

* * * * *

During my weekly phone conversation with my father, he told me, "We're coming to visit. I wouldn't miss my grandson's first birthday."

"Are you sure, Dad? I thought we'd celebrate at Thanksgiving."

"I can't wait until Thanksgiving to see my grandson. Did you invite Lance's parents to the party?"

"That's a great idea."

Hanging up with my dad, I told Lance, "My dad thinks we should have a party for Eric and we should invite your family."

"Great idea."

"My feelings exactly." Holding Eric in my arms, I shared the news with him. "Little one, Mommy and Daddy want your first birthday to be filled with lots of balloons and a whole lot of love."

"I'm going to call my mom. When we last spoke, she said she and my father were making plans to visit. This is as good a time as any."

"I can't believe she wasn't curious. If Eric called to tell me he had a son, I would have asked a million questions until he told me the truth."

Lance picked up Eric, saying, "Buddy, you're going to thank me one day. I'm the buffer you need to stop your mom from asking too many questions. That's what dads do."

* * * * *

Constance and Doris insisted that Eric's first birthday be hosted at Doris's place. Lance and I were happy to hand the reins over to Constance while Lance concentrated on his new role as a father.

Doris managed to convert her place into a circus. She arranged for clowns to entertain the children and a magic show. Eric was afraid of the clowns and had no idea what a magic show was, but he managed to smile and enjoyed all the attention. Christopher was elated with the party and took charge of the other children, which consisted of his friends from the playground.

Lance's mom couldn't stop saying how much Eric looked like Lance when he was a baby, nor could she get enough of my little boy. Lance was right; his mother was too engrossed with being a grandmother and gave no thought to when Eric was conceived.

My dad was polite to Lance's mom but later told me, "I think he looks like your mother."

"I do too, Dad, but she's a proud grandma. Neither you nor I can change her mind."

My dad smiled. "I'm thrilled you and Lance reconnected. I can see how much he loves you and his boy. I never doubted he'd be a good father."

I could hear a sound of regret in my father's voice as he spoke these words to me. "We've been given a second chance, and I couldn't be happier."

Hearing Constance let out a scream of joy, I turned to see George and Hilda standing beside her.

"George, I can't believe you're here!" After hugging and kissing my brother, I reached for Hilda. "Hilda, let me see. Are you showing? Just a little bump. You are so lucky. At that stage in my pregnancy, I was enormous!" I hugged, kissed, and congratulated my sister-in-law. Taking Hilda by the arm, I directed her to the most comfortable chair. "Let me get you something to drink." When I returned, George was holding Eric, sitting on the armchair beside his wife, while Lance, Audrey, and my father looked on. My mother was not far from my thoughts. Thinking of her, I said, "Mom, it took a while, but it seems we finally figured out how to live without you, but oh, how I wish you were here!"

When George and I found a few minutes alone, I asked, "Why didn't you tell me you were coming? Where are you staying?"

"I wanted it to be a surprise. Hilda won't be able to travel during the holidays, so we decided to come for my nephew's first birthday. Dad and Doris knew. Doris made a reservation for us at the Hilton."

I looked toward my dad talking with Lance and Hilda. "I think he's happy with our choices."

"I bet he's happy I settled down."

I looked at George. "You're going to love being a father, George. I don't know how I existed without Eric in my life. I adore that little boy. Although he's probably wondering where his mother ran off to. Lance's mom can't get enough of him."

"Dad looks a little jealous."

"Lance's family is leaving tomorrow. He'll have Eric all to himself."

* * * * *

Hilda gave birth to a boy five months later, Fredrick George Holland, nine pounds, four ounces.

George called to give Lance and me the news. "Nine pounds? He's big, George! How is Hilda feeling? Did you call Dad and Audrey?"

"Hilda is sleeping, and her mother won't leave her side. Yes, I called Dad and Audrey before I called you, and yes, they are thrilled. Dad is planning to come visit with Audrey. I thought you, Lance, and Eric could join them."

"What about the spring? Lance has a week off, and I'm sure I can get some time off to come meet my nephew."

"That's great. Work the details out with Dad then let me know. Sarah, you have to see him. He looks like Mom, dark hair, blue eyes. The nurse said all babies have blue eyes, but I know those eyes. Mom's for sure."

I smile. Seeing our mother in his son's eyes, was George's way of keeping our mother in the present. I didn't have the heart to remind him that both he, and his wife had blue eyes. "I'm so happy for you, George. You're a father with a son of your own to love."

"He's beautiful, Sarah. You know what my first words to him were? 'I love you, buddy, with all my heart and soul.'"

* * * * *

Over the spring break, as promised, we visited with George and Hilda. Hilda was a sweetheart, but her mother wasn't as sweet. She was there to make sure that George's family followed the rules and didn't interfere with the baby's schedule. George was no pushover; he was respectful and firm when he informed his mother-in-law that he would be there during his family's visit so she could attend to her own home during our stay.

While Dad and Audrey were off visiting another museum and Lance, Eric, and Hilda were napping, George and I took the baby for a walk to a nearby park. I started the conversation by saying, "Hilda's mother is worse than Grandmother Holland?"

"She means well. With a husband, two daughters, and a son at home, you'd wonder how she finds the time to help Hilda, but she does." The baby stirred, and George stopped to check on his son.

I told him, "Took me six months before I realized every move doesn't need your attention."

George smiled. "We didn't forget a bottle, did we?"

I smiled. “Right there next to the clean diapers and blanket.”

Sitting on the park bench, I spied George smiling at his son. “And you said you weren’t sure you’d be a good father. From where I’m sitting, I say you’re doing a great job.”

“I remember you being over the top with Eric. I thought you were insane, but when he cries at night for his feeding, I stop Hilda from going. I want to feel him in my arms. Hilda said I’m spoiling her and the baby.”

“Now I know why Mom wanted to fill her house with children. It’s the greatest feeling knowing that you had a part in creating a perfect human being. I never thought I’d say this, but I’d like at least three more.”

George gasped. “Three more? I’d settle for one, maybe two. Babies are a lot of work.”

George and I laughed out loud. I got a warm feeling watching George. He was finally happy. He now had this little boy to love, and yes, he would be a good father.

* * * * *

I still hoped George and Hilda would move back to the States, but once I met Hilda’s mother, I knew she’d convince Hilda to stay close to home.

Life was perfect. With each day that went by, Lance and I became comfortable with our commitment to each other and Eric. By December, Eric was taking steps, using the small coffee table in the apartment as a crutch. He was obsessed with the Christmas tree; the ornaments were placed high and out of his reach. Then he discovered the wires connected to the lights. The lights were moved as high as the ornaments. The tree looked like a woman who spent too much money on a new hat, hoping to disguise her old coat.

By March, Eric was walking without help. Lance and I were exhausted. Work became a relief. We wondered how Fanny managed to keep up with him during the day but were too afraid to ask. The apartment was cramped with Eric’s things.

Then Eric said his first understandable sentence: "Dada moo mook," followed with "Mama, moor ookie." From the joyous reaction Lance and I expressed, you would have thought Eric spoke the first sentence of the Constitution. It wasn't long after that we couldn't get him to stop talking. "Mommy, where's ruck, unny?" "Dada outside, play, read." His wish was our command.

My favorite time with him was when we lay together and read one of his favorite books, then I'd tickle him until he said, "No, Mama, no more funnies."

"No more funnies? Why no more funnies?"

"Funnies make me cry."

I held my son in my arms. "Oh, no, Mommy doesn't want her little boy to cry. Then Mommy will cry."

"Don't cry, Mommy. I don't like Mommy cry."

I smiled. "Mommy won't cry if it makes you sad."

* * * * *

The phone rang, and I crawled over Lance to answer it so the ringing wouldn't wake Eric. "I'll bet it's a wrong number," Lance growled. "If they woke up the baby, tell them I'll hunt them down."

My voice was a whisper. "Hello."

"Sarah."

"George."

I could hear from the sound of his voice that something was wrong. "What's wrong, George?"

Lance sat up. The phone cord was wrapped around his arm.

George began to cry. "My son, Sarah, he's dead. We found him in his crib—"

I began to scream, Eric began to cry, and Lance said, "Sarah." I motioned for him to get Eric. "Oh, no, George, that can't be." When Lance returned with Eric, I reached for my son and held him close to my heart. As I could not control Eric's crying, Lance took him from me and together they went into the kitchen.

George continued, "When Hilda went to wake him this morning, he wouldn't …"

"George, I'm booking the first flight out. Go to Hilda. She needs you."

"She's with her family. She's so upset she won't come home. I understand, it's too painful. I can't believe it. Sarah, hurry. Please hurry."

* * * * *

Constance flew with me to Germany. Lance agreed to stay home with Eric. Constance held my hand during the flight. I cursed George's decision to remain in Germany. He needed me, and I had to fly ten hours to be with him.

When we arrived at George and Hilda's home, I jumped from the cab and rushed inside. George was in Fredrick's room. He was on the floor next to the crib, the phone beside him.

I knelt and took him in my arms. He sobbed. "Sarah, he's gone. My little boy is gone."

It took six hours for Constance and me to convince George he needed to lie down. I had no contact with Hilda that day. I didn't know the phone number to her mother's home. Constance and I waited for George to wake to ask.

Hilda's mother was too upset to talk. Her father sorrowfully asked about George. I said he was concerned about Hilda and was hoping we could stop by. Hilda's father asked if we could wait until tomorrow; his wife wasn't up to a visit.

We did visit the following day, but George and Hilda weren't given time alone to grieve. She was surrounded by her sisters, brother, mother, and father. George was too exhausted to comfort his wife. I worried about them.

My nephew was buried, and three days later, Constance returned home. I stayed another week with George.

When I regained control that night after hearing of my nephew's passing, I called my father. The news of his infant grandson's passing affected him deeply. My father was transported back to another night and time. He insisted on flying to Germany. I didn't know if George could handle seeing my dad, so I insisted my father remain with

Audrey and convinced George I thought it was best for our father to remain home.

During our week together, George and I would be cut off from Hilda. Hilda said she wouldn't return home; she wanted to move. George and I packed away the baby's things and gave it to the local orphanage. I left George alone to disassemble his son's crib.

George was devastated. "Hilda's mother is blaming me. She said I covered the baby during the night and he couldn't breathe, but the blanket was nowhere near him when we found him."

"George, no one is to blame. The doctors are calling it SIDS. The baby just stops breathing. The doctors don't even know the cause. Listen to me, George, you have to go to Hilda. Convince her that you'll find a new place for you to live, far away from here. If you want my advice, far away from her family. We'll start looking tomorrow."

"I think she should remain with her family."

I knew then and there that George's marriage was doomed.

* * * * *

Another Christmas, another tree for Eric to destroy. "The terrible twos are killing me. Eric, listen to Mommy. If you take the ornaments off the tree, Santa won't come visit you. Santa likes when the tree is decorated."

Lance looked over his shoulder and said, "Tried that. He doesn't seem to care much about Santa."

"All right, then, Eric, if you don't stop taking the ornaments off the tree, Mommy won't make those special cookies you like so much."

Lance made Eric believe he was crying. "Son, you're ruining it for me. I love those cookies. Please leave the tree alone?"

"Daddy, don't cry." Eric ran to Lance, and Lance placed him on his lap. "If you don't want Daddy to cry, can you leave the ornaments on the tree?"

"All right, Mommy, cookie."

I handed my son a cookie, and as I did, I informed Lance, "George isn't coming for Christmas."

"I didn't think he would. I guess it's over between him and Hilda."

"She hasn't been to the new place. They see each other for dinner and movies, but listening to George, she doesn't seem interested in getting back together. I'm sure we'll hear they've divorced soon."

Lance placed Eric down and stood. Stepping on a toy, he cried, "Sarah, you can't avoid—"

"I know, I know. We have to move, but I love this place."

"I have an idea. What about we set a date, get married, and then look for a house in Westchester? If you don't accept my proposal this time, I'm not going to ask again."

I smiled. "You don't mean that?"

"It's been over a year since we've been back together. I've proved that I'm not going anywhere. The boy loves me, I think his mother feels the same, so why don't you say yes and set a date?"

"I have no other choice but to marry you. This apartment is definitely too small for four people."

Lance took a moment to digest what he just heard. "You're pregnant?"

"An early Christmas present." Lance lifted me from my chair and spun me around. Eric came running. "Daddy, me!" Lance placed me down and lifted Eric. Spinning him, he said, "We are going to have a baby."

Lance doted on me. He wanted me to give up working, but I told him he was being foolish. "Once we moved to the country, I've decided to be a stay-at-home Mom." Every night Lance cleaned up after dinner, gave Eric his bath, and tucked him in.

"I love all the attention, but you are going to wear yourself out. You better save your strength for this little one."

Lance flopped on the sofa. "Did you come up with a date?"

"You know we didn't plan very well. This baby is due in June, and I'm already beginning to show. We needed to get married yesterday."

"So let's get married tomorrow?"

"And ruin it for Constance, Jimmy, and Sally? They are planning a big wedding with all the frills. I refuse to walk down the aisle as big as a house. I was thinking October, after Eric's third birthday, and when I've lost some of the baby weight."

"October? You want to wait till after the baby is born? Let's go down to the justice of the peace, tie the knot, don't tell anyone, and then we'll spring it on them."

I pouted. "I was looking forward to a church wedding. The white dress, or not, surrounded by family and friends. Look, nothing we've done this far has been conventional, so what's the big deal if our children attend our wedding? October's only eight months away. Please, can I tell Jimmy to start designing my dress?"

Lance frowned. "My mother's not going to be happy when I tell her we're not getting married until October, but I'm happy we've decided on a date. I'll be happier when I know the exact date, church, and time."

* * * * *

Dad, Audrey, and our closest friends, especially Doris, weren't surprised about the baby. But they were thrilled when they heard we were planning an October wedding.

It was April before I told George I was expecting. His news didn't shock me when he said he was getting a divorce. I didn't ask if there was a chance they could work things out.

Jimmy and Constance were in wedding-plan mood. "The baby is due late June, early July. October is the perfect time. I love fall weddings. Will the bride be wearing white?" asked Jimmy.

"I was thinking off-white. White might be pushing it."

"Ivory. I love Ivory! It's in these days. I'll start working on several designs. Have anything in mind?"

"I don't want to look like a princess."

"Then you better control your diet after that baby arrives. No fattening foods. You have to eat healthy. It's better for the baby, and you'll breastfeed. I hear it does wonders for breaking down the fat around the hips and butt."

Constance laughed. "How do you know, Jimmy?"

"I'm a designer, I hear it all. That man of yours must love you to pieces. I can't believe you convinced him to wait until October. Two children born out of wedlock, and you two still haven't tied the knot. You're a vamp, Sarah Holland."

"I'm not taking all the blame. If the man hadn't run off on me to play hockey, we'd be married by now. When he came back, I had to make sure he was going to stick around."

"I hear you, girl. Men are so unpredictable."

* * * * *

June was hot, which didn't help my two already-swollen feet. Lance and Eric were at the park, so I spent this precious time relaxing on the sofa. I was inserting the picture of Lance, Eric, me, and my extended stomach in my baby book.

Lance and I spent two months house-hunting. Every house was smaller than we were hoping for. We decided to place the house-hunting on hold until after the baby was born, which I knew would be extended to after the wedding. I left my job the end of May, promising to return. Like the Parkses, Epsteins, and the Clarks, the Harts were a part of our family as well. I didn't look forward to the day when I had to inform the Harts that Lance and I were moving to Westchester, and my plans of being a stay-at-home mom. But until that time, Fanny was ready and willing to care for two children, so I wasn't ready to close the door on my job.

A knock on the door startled me. "Who is it?"

"Constance and Jimmy."

"Come in, I think the door is open."

"You look relaxed," said Jimmy.

"That was kind of you. Now, tell me what you really think."

"You look like the blimp that flies over the stadium."

"Look at my feet. They're going to burst. Dr. Schultz says he thinks I'm having a girl."

Constance chimed in. "I hope so. I'm so tired of buying boy's clothes."

"Why don't you get that rich guy you've been dating to marry you? Then you can have a little girl of your own."

I was happy Jimmy asked the question, because I was wondering how Constance felt about the guy she was dating, so I added, "Constance, you've been dating Bruce over a year. I know he's met Christopher. Is he the one?"

"You'd know if he was the one. I would have told you. I like him more than any of the other guys I've dated, but I'm not convinced he'll be a good father to Christopher. Deep down, I think he thinks Christopher is a spoiled little boy."

"Christopher? He's as sweet as pie! Dump the bastard," said Jimmy.

"George will be here for the wedding. He's available."

"I love George like a brother. Anyway, we didn't stop by to talk about my love life. Jimmy, show Sarah the designs."

Jimmy placed three sketches before me, one dress more beautiful than the other. "Jimmy, they are stunning! How can I pick one over the other?"

* * * * *

In the fall, Audrey would enter high school. I couldn't attend the middle school graduation ceremony, but afterward, I called, and we talked for an hour, which shocked me. Audrey, of course, graduated top in her class.

"Top of your class? You're a Holland, there's no denying! Dad told me, once the baby is born, you're spending two weeks in New York. Would you like to stay with Lance and me for the summer? You'll get to spend a lot of time with your nephew and the little one."

"Where would I sleep?"

"The baby will be in our room. You can bunk with Eric. We'll make it work."

"Let me think about it. I have a lot to do before I start school."

I knew Audrey wouldn't agree to stay, and she was right—the apartment was too small. She wouldn't be comfortable. "Are you looking forward to the wedding? I want you to be my maid of honor."

"I'm happy for you and Lance, and yes, I am looking forward to the wedding. Dad already arranged for me to be out of school for three days."

"You know, high school goes by quickly. In two years you'll have to start thinking of college. Do you have any idea where you'd like to go? Please say NYU."

"I think I'd like to stay closer to home."

Hearing Audrey's plans to remain close to home brought George to mind. "It will be good to see George."

"He called last night to wish me luck at the graduation. He doesn't live with Hilda anymore. Dad said the divorce will be final at the end of the month."

"He didn't mention it to me. Probably didn't want to upset me in my condition. I hope he meets someone else. I hate thinking of him alone in Germany."

* * * * *

June 19, I woke in pain, sweating profusely. I pushed Lance. "Lance, wake up!" As I lifted myself off the bed, my water broke. "Lance, wake up! It's time!" Another strong pain. I reached behind me and pushed on my back as hard as I could. "Lance, sweetie, did you hear me? Wake up."

"Is Eric crying? Don't get up. I'll check on him."

"No, Lance, my water broke. Call a cab. Call Constance to let her know we're dropping off Eric. His suitcase is behind the door in his room. Mine is in the closet."

Lance jumped from the bed. "Sarah, did you say your water broke? Are you in pain? I'll get you a towel."

I reached and grabbed Lance by the arm. "Listen to me. Forget the towel, the suitcases—"

With the next pain, I shouted, "Forget Constance! Wake Mrs. Parks. She can keep an eye on Eric until Constance arrives. Call the cab company first, tell them to hurry."

* * * * *

As I lay on a gurney, Dr. Schultz held my hand. "Sarah, when did the first contraction start?"

I looked over at the clock behind the nurses' station. "About forty-five minutes ago. Where's Lance?"

"Lance is in the waiting room. Sarah, we're going to take you to the surgical center now. Lance will follow shortly."

The pains were so severe that I didn't have time to argue. "I'm in a lot of pain. I don't think I can—"

Everything went dark. The last word I hear myself say was "Mom."

* * * * *

Someone was holding my hand. I moved my mouth to speak, but my mouth was dry. I whispered, "Dr. Schultz."

"Sweetheart, it's me, Lance." Lance stood and moved closer to me.

"Lance, where's Dr. Schultz?"

"He'll be here soon. I'm so happy you're all right."

I noticed Lance's face glistening in the light. "Lance, you're crying. What's wrong?"

"Dr. Schultz will explain."

"Lance, tell me what's wrong. Is it the baby?"

Lance lowered his head. I tried to move, but the pain was too much for me to bear. I reached for my stomach. "Lance, the baby?"

"I'm so sorry, Sarah, she didn't make it."

I lowered my voice. "She didn't make it? What are you saying?"

"A stillborn. I got to hold her. She … she's so beautiful, our daughter."

"A stillborn? That can't be. Everything was fine when I saw Dr. Schultz only a few days ago. What could have gone wrong?"

Lance placed his head on the bed and sobbed. I placed my free hand on his head. This was Lance's child. He was in pain. His little girl was gone. "Sweetheart, I'm so sorry. I know how much this baby means to you. Don't cry. Please, Lance, don't cry. We will have other children, I promise."

* * * * *

We named our daughter Margaret Catherine Pickett. Lance and I took her home to Cleveland and buried her with the only person I would trust to care for her in heaven, my mother.

Lance tried to hide his grief by focusing on Eric, but I knew deep down he was mourning his little girl. I felt guilty that I had not protected our daughter and hadn't presented a healthy child to this wonderful man who had opened his heart to my son, *our* son. Becoming pregnant became my latest obsession.

Eric turned three in September. We put the wedding plans on hold, as neither of us was up to celebrating. We needed time to heal. Jimmy finished the dress that I would one day wear.

I visited Dr. Schultz's office frequently. "Sarah, you just have to relax. It's only been ten months since your last pregnancy."

"Dr. Shultz, are you sure I'll be able to conceive again? It's important for me to give Lance a child of his own."

"I know, Sarah, but it might be the stress that is complicating your chances. You need something else to focus on. Why don't you move forward with your wedding plans?"

"We haven't even talked about the wedding. Maybe Lance isn't sure he wants to settle down with a woman who cannot—"

"Stop talking that way, young lady. There is nothing wrong with you. You need to relax." Dr. Schultz asked, "Would you consider adopting? A child without a home would be lucky to have loving parents like you and Lance."

* * * * *

Constance and I met for lunch. "How was your visit with Dr. Schultz?"

"He said I'm fine. He thinks I'm stressing too much about—"

Constance finished my sentence. "Getting pregnant? I think he's right. Whenever we are together, it's all you talk about."

"I failed Lance. Dr. Schultz thinks we should go ahead with our plans to get married, but ever since Margaret … well, he hasn't mentioned getting married. I don't think I can go through with a wedding until …" I pause before confessing to Constance that Lance wasn't Eric's biological father.

Constance reached across the table and took my hand in hers. "It will happen. I know it will. Maybe Dr. Schultz is right. Why don't you set a date for the wedding?"

* * * * *

Over the next year, I made several attempts to bring up the wedding with Lance, but each time I lost my nerve. The reason? Lance's neglect to discuss the wedding. I wondered if he changed his mind because I couldn't conceive.

Eric's birthday was approaching. Lance asked, "Someone has a birthday coming up. Do you have any ideas what you'd like for your birthday this year?"

"I want ice skates. Just like the ones you and Mommy bought Christopher for his birthday, and I want you to teach me how to be a better skater. I want to join a hockey team like Christopher. Please, Daddy."

"You're already a good skater for a boy your age."

Eric smiled at his father. "Am I, Daddy? Am I as good as Christopher?"

"Just as good. Remember, Christopher is three years older. I'll show you a few moves I haven't shown Christopher, but you have to promise not to tell Christopher. It's our secret."

"You are the best daddy in the whole wide world! I love you." Eric hugged Lance.

Lance said, "I love you, buddy."

Watching Lance and our son melted my heart. "Hey, what am I, chopped liver? I was going to buy you a new hockey stick and pads. Don't I deserve a kiss and a few words of love?"

"Mommy, you know how much I love you. Are you really going to buy me a new hockey stick and pads for my birthday?"

"Whatever makes you happy makes me happy." Eric gave me a hug, and I placed several kisses on his cheeks. "Mrs. Parks said after breakfast, you could stop by to see the puppies. You know Mr. Parks found homes for them. They will only be around for another week."

"No, Mommy, not all of them?"

"Mr. Parks is waiting for you."

It had become a habit that our door and the Parkses' door remain open while Eric wandered the hall.

With Eric gone, I said, "The realtor thinks she's found the perfect house, and she arranged for us to see it on Sunday. I don't care if it's falling apart. We have to move. The puppy is the last straw. We are running out of room."

Lance smiled. It had been nearly two years since the baby. Last year, right around Christmas, Lance seemed to accept the loss. Because of my inability to conceive, I was finding it hard to move on.

Lance glanced over the newspaper. "I agree, the realtor knows what we like. Let's hope this is the one."

"How hard can it be to find a house with four bedrooms, a guest room, den, living room, at least two fireplaces, a very large kitchen and dining room, two full-size baths, a big backyard, front and back porch, two-car garage … did I forget anything?"

"Nope, that about sums it up."

We laughed. I lowered my voice. "Lance, I was hoping we'd have a few minutes alone. I wanted to ask your opinion …"

Lance placed the newspaper on the kitchen table, giving me his undivided attention.

"What are your feelings on adoption?

Lance questioned, "Adoption? Isn't it hard to adopt?"

"I've been speaking with Dr. Schultz. It's not as hard as you think. There is a Catholic organization and a Jewish organization that help young girls find homes for their babies. Dr. Schultz volunteers at both. He says there is a need for good, loving homes. I like to think we can provide a happy, loving home to a child. Dr. Schultz says if we are interested, he will set up an appointment for us to meet with the directors. We might be able to adopt a child as early as next summer or fall."

Lance pondered the thought. "I think it's a great idea, but I think if we were married, it might give us leverage with the priest and rabbi."

I jumped into Lance's arms. My tears wet his face as I kissed his eyes, cheeks, and mouth. "I am so lucky to have you in my life. I'll call Dr. Schultz on Monday. Do you know how much I love you?"

"With all your heart and soul."

* * * * *

After my call to Dr. Schultz, I called Jimmy. "You need to bring over the wedding dress. I'm sure it will fit."

"You're going through with the wedding? When and where?" shouted Jimmy.

"I'll call Doris to see when the country club is available. In three weeks, Eric starts school, then his birthday. He needs at least a month to get settled in school. We are looking at a house this weekend, not during the holiday. Spring, a spring wedding, the end of March."

"A spring wedding! My favorite time of the year."

"I thought fall was your favorite time of the year?"

* * * * *

The wedding date was set for March 28. Doris confirmed the country club was available. Constance, Doris, Jimmy, and Sally went into wedding mode. Sally, newly married, had a million ideas. I left the four to work out the details.

In late November, with Eric finally adjusting to kindergarten, Lance and I signed a contract on a house in Westchester. The owners needed time to move since their children attended the elementary school. With the wedding in March, we agreed to close the first week in May.

The meeting with the directors went well. Lance and I went through an extensive evaluation, and we passed with flying colors.

In January, we met with several young girls. If we found the right fit, we could have brought our child home in July of that same year. Two girls had agreed to our becoming the adoptive parents to their babies. The babies would be two months apart. Lance and I found it hard to choose and were thrilled when we were approved to adopt both babies.

* * * * *

Three days after we were told about the babies, Lance placed a card on my lap.

"What's this?"

"An early Valentine's present."

I opened the card and found two plane tickets for a two-week vacation in Miami, Florida. I looked at Lance for an explanation. "A honeymoon, and before you try to talk me out of it, I've arranged for Constance to care for Eric while we are gone. I know two weeks is a long time for us to be away from him, but we deserve this. We may never get another opportunity—three kids, a house, a dog. We need this break. Just you, me, the sun and sand. We can make love anytime we want for two weeks."

"I'm in."

CHAPTER FIFTEEN

Allison

Five hours have passed since my aunt left my house, and for four of those hours, I've sat on the sofa in the den staring at a blank screen on the TV.

Pete has stopped trying to reach me. I think about calling him, but I haven't thought of a good excuse as to why I lied about work. The only other person trying to contact me is JoAnne. I wonder if Pete has something to do with her calling so frequently.

I decide to lie down. Closing my eyes, I know the hour of truth is upon me. Pete deserves an explanation of why I lied. An explanation of "I wanted to be alone" won't work. I have played that card too many times. Pete is a good guy, but he isn't a fool. I've told my aunt I'm going to leave Pete, but now I'm questioning my decision. Is she right? Should I hold off and come up with some lame excuse? I'm being selfish. I'm tired of taking the same vacation year after year, or should I pout about being jealous, concerned that Emily's and my paths will cross and I'm not prepared to meet my husband's lover?

My aunt's suggestion is clouding my confession. Should I put off the truth and try to reconnect with Pete and my children? Putting my happiness aside for theirs? But don't I deserve to be happy? And doesn't Pete deserve to know the truth? There is no denying that the thought of Andrew becoming sick and Pete finding out the truth sometime in the future is driving me mad. My mind is running wild with the fear of losing the love of my children. My son will hate me and demand to know the name of his real father. The truth will drive me out of my son's life forever. My daughter, seeing the pain I will cause her father and brother, will take their side and disown me.

The sound of the front door opening doesn't startle me. I know the person entering the house is Pete. He is home. He wants answers. I have seconds to decide what Pete should and shouldn't know. I sit up. From somewhere deep inside, I get the strength to look up at Pete, who is evaluating the condition of our home.

Pete's silence and his just standing over me is infuriating. I'm relieved when he asks, "What's going on?"

I raise my hands in the air in a nonchalant motion.

Pete shakes his head. "Can you tell me why you lied about work?"

"I didn't want to go to Florida this year. I'm sick of Florida, and I'm sick of hearing about Florida."

"Why didn't you just tell me? We could have made other arrangements."

"You had to be in Florida for work. Asking you to go somewhere else would have added additional stress on your life. I was thinking of you." I go for the empathy play card.

Looking around the room, Pete says, "We have known each other half our lives. Why didn't you just tell me this year you would have preferred going somewhere else?" Pete is talking to me, but he continues to look around at the condition of our home. I let him know immediately that I'm not happy with the mess.

"I was going to call Grace in the morning. I thought with her help, together we'd get the house back in order. I don't know what I was thinking letting it go this far."

Pete sits on the chair across from me. "You look tired for someone who has been spending a lot of time alone."

"I haven't been sleeping, and if I do manage to get five hours of sleep, I'm still tired. You might be right. I think it's time. Maybe I do need to speak with someone."

"Allison, it's obvious you're depressed, and you wouldn't be the first person that needed to speak with someone after a shock like you have experienced."

"I've fucked up, Pete. This might look like depression to you, and maybe it is, but there's more to it."

Pete says, "I flew all this way to find out what's going on. If you want to talk, I'll listen. If you want me to help you find someone to talk with, I will. Whatever you want. We can't go on this way."

I look at Pete and wonder how this man can just sit here and be tolerant of my bad behavior, but perfect Pete won't yell or scream. No, he calmly says, "Whatever you want, Allison."

"Do you know what bothers me most, Pete? You are always in control. Nothing bothers you. Aren't you wondering why I choose not to spend time with you?"

Pete ignores the sarcastic remark. "If I got angry with you, would that make you less depressed? No. It's hard watching the person you love most in this world fall apart and there's nothing you can say or do to make them realize they need help. We all know how much Patrick meant to you. His death has affected the person you were. Agreeing to speak to someone is a step in the right direction."

Pete leans over to take my hand. I pull away. "I don't need your pity. You're right, everything changed after Patrick's death, but there's so much more than just his dying that's gotten me upset. You see, Pete, the woman sitting before you is not as perfect as you think she is."

"I'd never asked you to be perfect. Not before or after Patrick's death."

I rise from the sofa. I can't bear to look Pete in the eyes any longer. "You have always placed me on a pedestal. 'Allison, I'm so happy I married you, you're perfect in every way.' But I'm far from perfect. I'm a coward. And a liar! My aunt is right, I never make the right decisions. I'm a failure."

"No one thinks you're a failure except yourself. I think it's time you face your past and deal with what is truly bothering you."

"Believe me, you really don't want me to face my past."

Pete rises. I know he's coming toward me to comfort me. I lift my hand to stop him. "Don't come any closer, please."

"All right, I'll keep my distance. It kills me to see you like this, but I have to think of the children. I can't allow them to see you in the state you're in. I feel for you, but my main concern must be the children."

"What are you saying? If I don't get help, you won't allow me to see my children?"

"That's not what I'm saying. You might not have noticed how the changes in our relationship have affected them."

The fear that Pete will keep the children from me frightens me. "And what would they think if they knew their father was seeing another woman?"

Pete isn't shocked by my accusation, and he doesn't try to defend himself. "This isn't the first time you have accused me of having an affair. You know damn well I don't have to defend myself, because I will never cross that line and jeopardize our family. This is the depression talking, not you. Let's just move forward. You have agreed to seek professional help, which is a start."

Pete turns because he feels comfortable to end our conversation there. I seek help, and all's well with the world. Furious, I say, "Oh, I forgot you're the saintly one. There's not a cheating bone in that body of yours. Sorry I can't say the same."

I want to take back the words, but it's too late. I've spoken them. Now I have no choice but to tell the truth. I can sense the shock and hurt on Pete's face. "What did you just say?"

"There's no easy way to tell you—"

"Is this why you're acting this way? You're seeing someone?"

"Not exactly. It's hard to have an affair with a dead man."

Pete lets out a slow laugh. "Are you insane? Are you telling me you were having an affair with Patrick?"

"I loved him. I've been in love with him since the first time we met. I've always loved him."

Pete moves to the chair closest to him. Bracing himself, he asks, "You were in love with Patrick, your stepfather?" I don't answer. Pete yells, "Damn it, answer me!"

Causing the pain that is invading Pete's world, I need to help him understand. "I swear I never meant to hurt you, but I've been in love with him, and we—"

Pete yells again, "Stop! You're crazy! What's gotten into you? Was this some kind of teenage crush that you manifested after he died?"

"No, it's more than that."

"Are you saying you slept with him?"

"Only once. It was a long time ago, before you and I were married. It happened the night I got drunk. We've talked about that night over the years. You said you'd never forget how drunk I was."

Pete moves closer. I've never seen this look before. I move, afraid that he may reach out and shake me. He says, "Keep talking."

I go on to explain what happened that night. I leave out the part about my becoming pregnant. Pete insists I continue. I explain that the following day, Patrick left a letter. "He never could truly express his feelings for me. He was ashamed of what others might think."

"Is that what he told you in the letter?"

"No. I think he was afraid of my aunt and uncle finding out. He married my mother, but there was this connection between us."

"Those were Patrick's words?"

"No. He never came right out and admitted to me that he loved me, and I was too afraid to ask."

Pete pauses, trying to put the pieces together. "So you married me because you were too afraid to ask Patrick how he felt? Oh, no, that's not the reason. You married me because you were pregnant, and your beloved Patrick ran off after he knocked up his stepdaughter?"

As the tears roll down my face, I can't lighten the blow I'm about to throw Pete. "Andrew is Patrick's son. I'm so sorry. I should have told you. I was going to tell you, but you were so happy about the baby, and I didn't want an abortion."

Pete smirks. "Of course not. If you couldn't have the father, at least you'd have his son. That makes sense!"

"You know that's not true. When I told you I was going to have an abortion, you were the one that told me to give us a chance."

Pete's voice rises. "Us a chance, you, me, and *our* baby." Pete places his hands high on top of his head and spins. "I can't believe this! All these years!" Facing me, he yells, "Sit down! Sit down before I throw you down."

I'm frightened to move, but I manage to get to the sofa and sit.

Pete is fuming. "I find it mind-blowing, after all these years, how easy it is for you to admit you never loved me. What a fool I've been!"

I try to speak.

"Shut up, shut the fuck up!" Pete sits, sliding forward in the chair, moving closer to me. I can feel the heat of his breath when he speaks. "So that's it? You slept with Patrick, got pregnant, passed Andrew off as my son, and now that Patrick is gone, you can't live with the lie? You're afraid that someday you might have to tell me the truth, and it's driving you insane!" I look for permission to explain, but Pete's hand rises to stop me from talking. "All these years, you kept your little secret to yourself. I'm sure you never shared this little secret with Patrick?" Pete waits for an answer then shouts, "Did you?"

"No! We never spoke about that night. Never, I swear."

"I know for a fact why Patrick never put two and two together. Why he never questioned if he could possibly be Andrew's father."

I look confused. Pete smiles. "You know, you aren't the only one who can keep a secret. I have one or two of my own. Would you like me to share them with you?"

I want nothing more than for Pete to lash out at me, but the conversation has taken a new direction with the mention of Pete having secrets of his own. Revenge is what he is after. My heart sinks. I wasn't wrong about Emily Carter. "I know exactly what you are going to say. I was right. You aren't perfect."

"Never said I was. It's too bad you didn't come to me years ago, or better yet … no, it's too soon for that. Let me start from the beginning. That night, the night you thought you fucked Patrick, well, after cleaning up the mess you made in my car, I found Patrick sitting at the kitchen table, writing a letter. I was gone no more than fifteen minutes, maybe enough time to have a quickie, but he didn't look like a man who just got laid." Pete's language to describe that night says it all; he is enraged with hate for me. "Your precious Patrick, before leaving, asked if I'd stay just in case you needed help, and then he said, 'This letter is for Allison. I'm leaving it here on the table. I'll call.' After he left, I rushed in your room and sat beside the bed, watching you sleep, making sure you were still breathing." Pete stares, waiting for me to guess what he was about to say. "You know what happened next? You woke up, and I breathed a sigh of relief. You reached for my hand and asked me to come closer. When I did, you kissed me and told me you loved me. Then you begged me to make love to you. I wanted to resist, but I couldn't. I was head over heels in love with you. I never would have guessed that if the tables were turned and your precious Patrick did grant your wish, I would have been history." Pete pauses. With his eyes glued to my face, he says, "The desire I've felt for you that night and every night since … what a fool I was! All these years, I thought how lucky I was to have you in my life. I'm sorry to blow your world apart, but it was me you slept with that night. It was me you begged to make love to you."

The story causes the bile within me to rise. "It was you?"

Pete sighs. "Sorry to disappoint you, my sweet, but yes, it was me. You made love to me, not Patrick. You can rest your weary head. Andrew is and will always be my son."

I try again to speak. Pete rises and reaches for his duffel bag. I ask, "Where are you going?"

Pete smiles. "Anywhere but here."

"You can't leave now. We have to talk."

"I'm done talking." He turns to leave, then stops. "I said I had two secrets. Do you want to hear the second, or have you heard enough for today?"

"Pete, I'm sorry. I was so drunk and confused, please."

"You're going to need some hard liquor after you hear my second secret. First, I need to know what Patrick said in the letter he wrote you. You owe me that much."

The words rush out of my mouth. "He said he was taking an extended trip to Europe. He thanked me for convincing him to enjoy his life." I lower my head before I say, "And he said I was lucky to have you in my life." I look up. Pete's face lacks expression.

"You were right about one thing. Patrick was afraid about what people might think if they knew."

My eyes question his meaning. "His fear had nothing to do with you. Patrick was afraid of what other people might think of him if they found out he was gay."

I stare at him, trying to comprehend what I've just heard.

"Cat got your tongue? You heard correct. Patrick was gay, and on that extended trip, he wasn't alone. His lover was with him. They met in college. Patrick's one true love. They were still together when he died."

I cover my mouth with my hand. "He wasn't gay! He married my mother. Oh god, did my mother know he was gay when she married him? You said he met this guy in college."

Pete's expression turns to pity. "I don't know what kind of marriage Patrick and your mother shared, maybe one of convenience. You'd have to ask your aunt about their relationship."

"My aunt? She knew Patrick was gay? Did she know about this person? When did you find out? Was it after he died?"

"He told me himself, and he wanted to tell you, but I stopped him. If I only knew then what I know now, but it wouldn't have made a difference. You still would have thought he had a weak moment and slept with you."

"Why didn't you let him tell me? Why didn't you tell me yourself?"

"I wanted to protect you. As I said, I didn't know what kind of marriage your mother had with Patrick. What I did know is you respected and cared for Patrick. I didn't know how his life choice would affected you, so I made the decision to keep things as they were. Patrick was a decent guy. The children adored him. I thought what you didn't know couldn't hurt you. All I cared about was protecting you … Fuck this!"

Pete goes to leave. I jump from the sofa and try to stop him. "Pete, please don't go." Crying, I plead again, "Please, Pete, don't go. We have to figure out a way to—"

"To what? This isn't something we can sweep under the rug, forget it ever happened. It's too late. I'm going back to Florida. I'm going back to my children."

I run after Pete, yelling his name. He slams the door in my face. I fall to my knees, sobbing. I scream, "Pete, please don't leave! Don't leave me. I need you."

* * * * *

After what seems like hours of kneeling, I run for my cell phone and call Pete, knowing he won't answer. I leave message after message, pleading for him to come home so we can talk. I swear and promise first thing in the morning, I will make an appointment and get help. I'm committed to working out my problems for the children and for him. I am relentless, calling every ten minutes, pleading the same message. I beg for a second chance just to talk, nothing more.

Sitting on the floor in our den with my cell phone clenched firmly in my hand, I try to make sense of the story I have been told. *Gay* keeps running through my mind. I never would have guessed in a million years. I think of my mother. What was she thinking? Did she know before she married Patrick or after? And my aunt didn't have the decency to tell me the truth? Why was I born into this family? What did I do to deserve this, or was I just like them?

I wasted more than half my life in love with a man who would never return that love. I threw it all away for what? For a dead gay man. Why didn't I listen to my aunt and just wait? But I had waited, and the waiting was destroying my life and family. Finally, I do what I think is right, and it comes back to bite me. What a joke!

Thinking of Andrew, for the first time since hearing the story, I feel relieved. Pete is Andrew's father. God has answered me. He's lifted this heavy weight from my shoulders. I may have lost Pete, my marriage, even the respect of my children having to deal with a divorce, but Andrew is spared from what I thought would destroy him.

I reach for the phone. I dial Pete's number for the last time. "Pete, it's me. I promise this will be the last time I'll call. Please don't delete this message. My heart is breaking knowing how much I've hurt you. I thought you deserved to know the truth, or what I thought was true. You are not a fool. I'm the fool, but this fool can't help seeing a brighter side of this horrible day. It was finding out that you are Andrew's biological father. The day you asked me to marry you, I knew my son, our son, was blessed to have you in his life. I don't have the answers to why this happened to our family, but I miss the family we were with all my heart and soul."

By two in the morning, the house I neglected is clean. Pete hasn't returned my calls, and why would he? I think of him lying in bed, reliving the words, "I loved Patrick from the first time we met." I lost Pete's trust and love with those words. My aunt is right; there is no turning back.

I need to speak with someone. JoAnne is the first person that comes to mind.

"Hi! Is everything all right? I've been trying to reach you all day. Is Pete with you? What time is it?"

"It is three in the morning! Do you have a few minutes to talk?"

"Of course. What's wrong?"

It's time. I need to tell her the truth. "Remember the night you and Gary got engaged and I got so drunk I couldn't see two feet in front of me?"

"I remember. What's this all about?"

"I couldn't sleep, so I started reminiscing about the happy times in our lives. Your engagement was one."

"I think your news overshadowed my engagement, remember?"

"I was so frightened. Being pregnant was the last thing I wanted, and marrying, you know, I wasn't ready for all of it."

"Is that why you called? Are you having regrets? I believe it's a little too late for regrets."

"No regrets, just feeling down. I needed to hear your voice. Let's do lunch. Are you free next week?"

"I'll make myself available. Talking about that night, you know how I guessed you were pregnant? Well, the morning sickness was a dead giveaway, but I'll never forget Pete's face when I arrived home. He was beaming. I bet you guys talk about it often, the night you conceived that beautiful boy, a night you two will never forget."

My voice cracks. "You're right, JoAnne. We'll never forget that night."

* * * * *

Ten the following morning, the last load of laundry is placed in the drier. I break my promise and dial Pete again. "I said last night was my last call, but you have to know after everything we discussed, we do need to talk. Please call."

Then a light bulb goes off. I'll call the children and ask to speak with Pete. I dial Andrew's cell. He doesn't answer. So I try Julia. "Hi, Mom! What's up?"

"Hi, sweetie. Are you having a good time with Grandma and Grandpa?" I start to cry.

"Mom, what's wrong? Are you crying?"

"No, no sweetie. Well, yes, I am crying. I miss you so much. Can't wait for you to come home."

"Only five more days. How's work? Did you get a lot done?"

"I did, all caught up. Things will be back to normal when you get back."

"Good."

"Where's your brother? I tried calling, but he didn't answer."

"He left his phone at home. Dad, Grandpa, and Andrew went fishing. They should be home at three. I'll tell Andrew and Dad to call you back."

"I'd appreciate that, sweetie. Please tell your father I need to speak with him."

"I will. I have to go. Grandma is waiting for me to go shopping."

"Say hi to Grandma for me."

"Hold on. I'll get her."

"No, Julia, I don't want to hold you up. Just tell her I said hi, and I'll call again during the week."

"All right, Mom. Love you!"

"I love you, sweetie, with all my heart and soul. And I miss you."

My daughter hangs up before I finish my sentence. I sob like a baby, calling Pete's name.

* * * * *

Searching through the phone book, I'm desperate to find a psychiatrist. Turning page after page, I yell out, "Come on, Allison, pick one! You need to do this, just pick one."

I turn the page to the *G*s and locate Dr. David Greenberg. Holding the phone in my hand, I dial his number, but before it rings, I hang up. I repeat this several times before allowing the call to connect.

"Good morning! Dr. David Greenberg's office, how can I help you? Hello? Can you hear me? Are you there?"

Softly I say, "This is Mrs. Cane, I'm a friend of Dr. Greenberg. I was wondering if he had any free time today? Our children go to the same school, and I wanted to speak with him about an upcoming event."

"Just a moment." The line goes dead. For a moment I think we've been disconnected, then I hear a cheerful voice say, "I'm sorry to keep you waiting. Dr. Greenberg said he looks forward to seeing you. He is free from twelve until two o'clock today."

I hold the phone tightly in my hand, trying to convince myself to hang up, but I have already given my name. David will locate my number and call me back. I feel trapped. This is a bad idea.

"Mrs. Cane, are you there?"

"Twelve, of course. I'll be there."

* * * * *

Sitting on the sofa, I eye the clock on the mantel: ten thirty. David's office is thirty minutes away. I leave the house and head for the doughnut shop.

I thank God for the long line ahead of me. I look at the clock: it's was now ten fifty. I order a dozen doughnuts and four large coffees. Five past eleven, I sit in my car, eyeing the coffees. What was

I thinking? Four large coffees! One for the receptionist, one for Dr. Greenberg. I reach for a cup, snap back the lid, and allow the warm coffee to calm me. Eyeing the other, I decide to drink it during my visit.

I hand the sweet girl her coffee and open the box to offer a doughnut.

"Thank you, but I need to watch."

"I've lost some weight myself recently without even trying." Thinking my response inconsiderate, I explain, "I lost a close friend. His death was a shock. I don't think I've eaten a full meal since."

The girl offers her condolences. "What's your name?"

"Nancy."

"Nancy, I've always liked that name. Don't hear it very often anymore. I wonder why."

Nancy thinks me strange and ends our conversation. "You're a little early, but I'll let Dr. Greenberg know you're here. Just have a seat."

I smile and find a seat closest to the door, just in case I lose the courage to stay. Opening the other cup of coffee, I entertain myself watching Nancy do her job, while shaking both legs—a recent habit I developed after hearing of my gay stepfather's death.

Nancy gets up and motions to me. "You can go in."

As I enter the office, David comes from behind his desk to greet me. "Allison, I'm so glad you stopped by. What's this? You didn't have to bring your own coffee. We have coffee, but I'm glad you brought the doughnuts. I haven't had breakfast. I was supposed to have lunch with a friend, but he had to cancel."

I present David the box of doughnuts. "Help yourself." David motions for me to sit.

"Is this coffee for me?"

"Yes, but it's a little cold."

Nancy immediately takes the cup and begins to walk from the room. "Thank you, Nancy. I owe you one."

Nancy smiles. "No problem, Dr. Greenberg."

As she closes the door behind her, David says, "Nancy said you wanted to see me regarding an upcoming school event?"

After noticing me wring my hands together, David figures out that may not be the reason for my visit. He gently says, "Allison, how can I help you?"

Nancy knocks and enters with his coffee. "Thank you, Nancy," says David. Nancy smiles. I also thank Nancy before she closes the door behind her.

I stare at David for several minutes before saying, "I have this friend, and she's been going through a rough time. I think she needs to speak with someone, and soon."

"How long has your friend been going through this rough time?"

"Almost two years. I've noticed a complete change in her personality. It's affecting her family. Her husband shared with me that he thought she needed professional help. I spoke with her, told her about her husband's concerns, and she finally realizes he might be right. She asked if I could recommend someone. I thought of you, but I wanted to speak with you first."

David offers me a doughnut. I refuse. "I see."

"She would have been here herself, but she was embarrassed. I told her I would talk with you, explain how uneasy she felt."

"I know you're trying to be a good friend to this person, but by sending you, it sounds like she's not ready or willing to accept there's a problem."

"No. Believe me, she knows she has to talk with someone. I guess we went about this all wrong. I'll give her your number, tell her if she wants to speak with you, she has to set up her own appointment. Thank you. I'm sorry I took up your time. There's still time to get lunch." Getting up, I point to the doughnuts. "A gift. Enjoy."

"Allison, please don't rush off."

After several minutes of silence, with my back to David, I say, "You know I'm lying. I'm the person in need of your help." David doesn't respond, so I turn to him and say, "If you'd rather I see someone else because … well, we are sort of friends and all, I understand."

I reach into my purse, searching for a tissue to dry my eyes. David stands before me with a box of tissues. "Thank you."

David smiles. "You're welcome. Please sit."

Now it's my turn to smile. "I'm a mess. Pete thinks I'm depressed. I think he's right. This all happened after my stepfather, Patrick, died in a car accident. I just haven't been able—"

"How long after he died did Pete notice your depression?"

"Immediately."

"Are you sure the depression was immediate?"

"Absolutely. I heard he died, and I couldn't function."

David takes a moment before speaking. "You mentioned that our being friends might affect my not wanting to take you on as a patient, but that is the question you should be asking yourself. Will you feel comfortable sharing personal issues with me? If not, there are a number of excellent doctors I can recommend."

"I was going to close my eyes, direct my finger to a name, and call the number, then it dawned on me how comfortable I felt whenever we spoke."

"Even though you feel comfortable with me, the only way I can help you is if you are completely honest and open with me. Can you do that?"

"I can promise I'll try. I'm not proud of something I've done. It hurt the people I love most in the world. It might take me a couple of sessions to open up."

David smiles. "Why don't I block out an hour. How do Wednesdays work for you? Mornings or afternoons? Your office isn't far from here, correct?"

"The children will soon be back at school. Lunchtime works best for me."

"You might be a little upset after a session. Is that going to be a problem?"

"I can alter my work schedule."

"All right, then, next Wednesday at twelve. A session lasts one hour. If you need more time, I leave thirty minutes open after each session. Are you sleeping?"

"Not soundly. Some nights I get two hours, sometimes three, but not more than four."

"I'm going to prescribe a mild sedative to take the edge off. I don't believe in medicating when it isn't necessary. I'm convinced once we begin our sessions, sleep will not be an issue. Also, I want you to start exercising at least four times a week, or thirty minutes a day, if possible. Walk, bike, run, swim, workout classes—your choice. But no less than four times a week. During this time, I want you to think of Allison and only Allison. What makes her tick, what makes her happy, what makes her sad? You see where I'm going with these questions?"

CHAPTER SIXTEEN

Sarah

I call the children in Florida. Julia tells me that Pete is flying back home, something to do with work, but I know better. I want to call Allison to say Pete is on his way, but I'm sure she won't take the call.

I know Pete isn't a fool. He knows Allison is hitting rock bottom. Seeing her, and the shape of their home, may help. I pray that Allison takes the advice I offered, to think twice before telling her husband she never loved him.

Seeing Allison in that state awakens memories of love, hope, and loss in me.

* * * * *

Lance's gift of a honeymoon was a surprise, but January offered another surprise. I wasn't expecting. I didn't get my period that month. I didn't give it a lot of thought to skipping a month. Things were moving quickly, two babies, the wedding. I didn't feel stressed, but I did have a lot going on in my life, so skipping a month wasn't uncommon.

The house needed to be painted from the inside and out, but other than paint, the house was perfect. Mr. and Mrs. Parks said we could stay two extra months rent-free as a wedding gift to us. What they didn't know, although a generous offer: one of our children was due in July, and we wanted our baby to rest their little head in their own home, not cramped in an apartment.

The pup, whom we named Spotty, needed to be walked. Spotty stared up at me, his little eyes begging. I smiled, reached down, and patted his head. I lifted him and cuddled him close. Feeling the warmth of his small body made me think how comfortable I was with my life.

"I spoke with a painter. Donald said they will be out of the house May 1. Anyway, the painter said it will take him three weeks to paint the inside of the house. Sarah, you still haven't picked the colors for the bedrooms. On my way home from work, I'll stop by the paint store and get a swatch of every color. I don't think I'm going to have the outside of the house painted. Blake was telling me he and his wife aluminum-sided their home, and it looks great. I thought we should do something in gray, with black shutters, but if you want white, that's fine too." Lance looked over his shoulder. "The pup looks comfortable. Eric will be home soon. Constance said the movie was two hours long, then ice cream. When they get here, I'll take Christopher, Eric, and the pup for a walk. Want to join us?"

"It's too cold. Anyway, Constance and I need a little time to finalize the wedding flowers. Lance, how are we going to manage two babies, the pup, getting Eric settled in another school? I'm really worried Eric is going to be jealous of baby number 1. And what happens when two months later, we show up with number 2?" Then I thought, *What if I am pregnant? Baby number 3 … four kids.* I laughed out loud.

"What's so funny?"

"Nothing. You didn't answer my question. With you off at work, how am I going to do it?" I smiled. "Also, me, you, sex—it's not happening after we settle down in our new home."

Lance chuckled. "We'll manage. I got it all figured out. After all the kids are asleep, we'll cuddle up in front of the fire. I'll pour two glasses of wine, we'll toast having a few moments to ourselves, fall asleep, and dream about having sex."

"I have needs."

Lance raised an eyebrow. "All kidding aside, I spoke with Fanny. She's considering our offer, but she wants weekends off. I think she has a boyfriend. Wait till she sees the guest room. I told her it's large enough to be a bedroom / living room."

"Lance, that's wonderful! Do you think she'll accept our offer?"

"The pay is good, and she loves Eric. Of course she'll accept the offer."

Eric crashed through the door. "Mommy, Daddy, can we take Spotty for a walk?"

"I'll get my coat. Mommy and Aunt Constance need sometime alone."

With the boys and pup gone, Constance asked, "I thought you and I were friends, Sarah. Ever since you got Eric that puppy, Christopher thinks I'm the worse mother in the entire world."

"Why? There are several dogs at the vineyard."

"They don't live with us. I guess I can get a puppy. Other people in the building have dogs. The doorman walks their dogs for a fee. Maybe I'll consider it. Why are you moving to Westchester? I'm going to miss just dropping by. Why couldn't you just move uptown? You and Lance can afford it."

"I want a house. I want my children to experience my life before … well, before my mother died."

"I was raised in a house, and if you tell anyone what I'm about to admit, I'll hate you forever. I like being rich. Does that make me a snob?"

I burst out laughing. "You owe me. If it weren't for me, you'd be living in that hut you called a house in Italy."

* * * * *

Sitting in Dr. Schultz's office, I waited patiently for him to arrive. When the door opened, I smiled. "Boy or girl? How's the mother doing?"

"Little girl, mother and daughter are fine. This is baby number 5. I'm just there to hold her hand and tell her when to push. She says she's done, but she said that after baby number 3." Dr. Schultz chuckled. "I saw Doris earlier. She said she was having lunch with you this afternoon."

"I'm meeting her at one. I just wanted to stop by and ask about the girls."

"They are fine. You know, there is a window of thirty-six hours. They have a right to change their minds."

"Lance and I have prepared ourselves. I'm sure this isn't an easy decision, so it must be the right decision for them. Dr. Schultz, there's another reason I stopped by. I missed my January cycle, and I'm three days late this month."

Dr. Schultz stopped updating the chart in his hands. "Sarah, it's too early for an internal. I'd like to wait another month, but this changes everything. Three little ones."

"Fanny has agreed to live with us, and Lance will be there to help."

Dr. Schultz sighed. "I know you wanted a large family. That's why I worked hard at getting the board to agree on you and Lance adopting two children. But if you are pregnant, you might want to consider one at this time."

"No, Dr. Schultz, we want both babies. I have it all figured out. Anyway, babies don't stay babies forever. It was only a short time ago I thought Eric was a handful. Now he gives himself a bath, cares for the puppy, and holds the light bulbs for Mr. Parks so he can climb the ladder.

* * * * *

Doris was like a mother to me. I shared my news with her, and she promised to keep my secret. If I missed again in March, I'd confirm my pregnancy with Dr. Schultz and break the news to Lance on our honeymoon. I made a mental note to pack smelling salts.

* * * * *

The beginning of March was warmer than normal. Enjoying the weather, I took the long way home, swinging my purse back and forth as I walked. Three weeks to go, and I'd be Mrs. Lance

Pickett, mother of three children, maybe four, and a homeowner. Life couldn't be better.

I tried not to dwell on the girls changing their minds, but if they did, I would understand. If God was in my corner and there was a child developing inside me, there would be another baby for Lance and me to love, but only if God was in my corner.

Smiling, I entered the building. "What's with the big smile, Sarah?"

"Just life, Mrs. Parks, just life."

"Life is good. I couldn't be happier for you. I'm going to miss you, especially that little boy. You're the best tenants I ever had." Mrs. Parks choked up.

"We're not going that far. We will visit, I promise. I'll never forget everything you and Mr. Parks did for me. I couldn't have done it without you. Do you think I'd forget family? Mrs. Clark's driver would be happy to pick you and the Epsteins up when she comes to visit."

"Mrs. Clark is a fine woman, but Mr. Parks would never agree to be driven. We will find our way to and from. Nothing can keep me away."

I leaned over and placed a kiss on Mrs. Parks's cheek and noticed a tear or two building in her eyes. "Mrs. Parks, please don't cry. You will make me cry and ruin this perfect day."

"Oh, go on now. Eric's been out several times, looking for his mommy."

Opening the door to my apartment, I blew Mrs. Parks a kiss. She smiled.

"Mommy, Mommy, where have you been? It's getting dark outside. You never come home when it's dark."

"I'm not that late, my sweet boy. Mommy was just taking her time walking home. It's warm for March." Spotty rushed to get my attention.

"Mommy, you have to give Spotty a kiss. He missed you." After taking my son's direction, I placed Spotty down, and the two ran off to Eric's room to play.

"Where's Daddy?" I called as they disappeared.

"I'm in here, running Eric's bath." Hearing Lance, Eric and Spotty ran past me, almost knocking me off balance.

Eric yelled, "After my bath, will you read me a story from one of the new books Aunt Audrey gave me for Christmas? Mommy, my teacher sent home a note. Daddy already knows. It's on the table."

I read the letter and covered my mouth with my hand. There was an outbreak of chicken pox at Eric's school. My first thought was to call Dr. Schultz and ask if I should be concerned. Lance entered the room and interrupted my thoughts.

"Chicken pox with the wedding three weeks away. We are doomed. If this wedding doesn't get off the ground, we're getting married by the minister and the celebration can follow after the honeymoon."

Three nights later, I woke. Call it mother's instinct. I went to check on my son. It didn't take long for me to notice the beading sweat on his brow. When I placed my hand on his forehead, he was burning with fever.

"Lance, Eric is sick. I have to call Dr. Schultz." Lance went to Eric, who began to moan. Forty-five minutes later, there was a knock on our door.

"Dr. Schultz, thank you so much for coming. I'm sorry, but Eric is burning up. We took his temperature. It's 103."

I rushed Dr. Schultz into Eric's room. Lance was sitting vigil over our son.

"Let me look." Lance moved out of the way. Dr. Schultz removed Eric's PJs, and he moaned. "I know it's cold, little fellow, but Dr. Schultz is looking for … and there it is." Inside Eric's thigh was a small sore. "Chicken pox. I heard there was an outbreak at the local schools."

"Yes. We got a letter the other day. Lance, can you get the letter?" I knew the letter had little meaning for Dr. Schultz, but I needed a few minutes alone with him. "Dr. Schultz, I haven't told Lance yet. If I'm pregnant, what harm …?"

Lance rushed back, letter in hand. "Here's the letter." Dr. Schultz read it quickly. "Standard letter. Have you both had the chicken pox?" We nodded. "Good. Sarah, with the wedding weeks away, I want you to stay far away from Eric." Dr. Schultz raised an eyebrow at me. I nodded in agreement. "Lance, can you keep this woman away from Eric?" Lance agreed.

I interjected, "Dr. Schultz, my son needs me. It's impossible for me to keep my distance."

Dr. Schultz stood very close to me and said, "Sarah, within three days, all the sores should be visible. Incubation occurs two weeks prior. Give the sores time to dry."

Nodding, I knew it was too late. The harm, if any, had been done. Dr. Schultz left a list of items we could purchase at the local drugstore to make the next two weeks comfortable for our little boy. At the door, I thanked Dr. Schultz for his time. Dr. Schultz said, "It won't do you any good to worry, young lady. Come see me in three days. In the meantime, I'll confer with several other physicians."

I placed a call to my dad to ask if I had contracted chicken pox when I was younger. I knew the answer was yes; George and I were out of school for two weeks. "Is that so? Thanks, Dad."

Hanging up, I informed Lance, "My father isn't sure if I had the chicken pox. I thought I did, but he thinks it was the mumps," I lied.

Lance sighed. "I can't believe it! What bride wants to have pockmarks all over her face? Our wedding pictures are going to be something we won't soon forget. Let's hope your father is wrong. Chicken pox, mumps, they are all the same to a father."

My lie worked. That first day, Lance sent me off to work while he nursed Eric. On the second day, the sores were visible, and Lance prepared oatmeal baths. On the third day, Eric slowly returned to a normal child. I made an appointment with Dr. Schultz. Lance returned to work on the fourth day, and Fanny took over Eric's care.

During the examination, Dr. Schultz took blood work and preformed a routine exam. "The blood work will confirm if you are pregnant. I want to hold off on an internal exam, but if I were a gambling man, I'd say you are pregnant."

I sat up and threw my arms around Dr. Schultz. "I knew it! I'm so happy. I couldn't be happier. Oh, I'm not kidding myself, it's going to be hard, but Lance and I, we will get through it. Years from now, we'll laugh, telling the children how quickly our family grew."

When I got home, from the doorway of my son's room he pleaded, "Mommy, can you read me a story? When I'm sick, you always sit with me and read."

I walked into his room and lay down next to him. While he rested his head close to my heart, I asked, "Which book?"

"The bunny book. It's our favorite, right, Mommy?"

"Yes, sweetheart, it's our favorite."

I placed a kiss on the top of my son's head. "Eric, don't be mad at Mommy for not cuddling you while you were sick. There is a good reason Dr. Schultz wanted me to keep my distance."

"Daddy said you didn't have the pox when you were little. Daddy said you could get really sick since you are a big girl. I don't want you to be sick and miss the party, but I don't like being away from you."

Tightly I hugged my son. A tear rushed down my cheek. "I'm here now, and I promise never to leave you."

I started to read, knowing my little boy was sound asleep before I finished page 1. I remained with him, drifting off. I woke with Eric securely wrapped in my arms. Spotty was nestled between us. I remained still, watching my son and the puppy's chest rise and fall. Eric stirred and woke, the pup did the same, and the two rushed off for another day at play.

I was happy it was Friday. I asked if I could leave early. The Harts, who were still confused as to why I didn't take the week off to nurse my sick son, were happy to see me off. When I got home, Eric was running through the living room like a wild animal.

"I think he's better," said Fanny.

"Why don't you call it a day, Fanny? You earned it. We will be fine."

Saturday morning, Lance and I woke at eight. Confused as to why Eric and Spotty didn't wake us, I went to check on them. Spotty raised his head and wagged his tail, but did not leave Eric's side. Smiling, I left them and prepared breakfast.

Eric emerged from his room as soon as breakfast was ready. He took his seat at the table. "You must have been exhausted from all that running around you did yesterday."

My son didn't respond. Lance questioned, "Mommy asked if you were tired, buddy. You slept late today."

With Lance and I looking on, Eric's head fell back. I could see the whites of his eyes roll upward. I dropped the frying pan. Lance reached for his head. I screamed, "Something's wrong!" I held my son in my arms while Lance got Mr. Parks, who drove us to the emergency room. When we arrived, a nurse took Eric from my arms and ran to the first open room she could find. An older nurse pushed a buzzer and announced immediate assistance. Lance and I remained with our son. We each held one of Eric's little hands in ours. It was then I noticed that Eric's palms were red and had rashes.

The doctor arrived and looked at Lance to step aside. Knowing I wasn't moving from my position, Lance joined me. He checked Eric's vitals and opened and checked his eyes. When he lifted Eric's pajama top, I noticed a rash on his stomach. The doctor lowered his shirt and checked the bottom of his feet, which were also red and had a rash, then his hands. The doctor questioned us, noting our answers in Eric's chart. He asked the nurse to see if a private room was available in pediatrics.

Dr. Schultz arrived an hour later. He examined Eric, read the chart, checked out the rashes that were noted by the previous doctor, lowered his head, and then removed his glasses. Speaking to Lance, he said, "I called Dr. Kemp. He's a good friend of mine. He'll be here shortly."

"Dr. Schultz, there are rashes on Eric's stomach, feet, and hands that weren't there yesterday." Lance spied Eric's feet and hands then asked, "Is that from the virus?"

I was numb. My little boy lay silent. I was sure what I saw earlier was a seizure, so my next question was obvious. "Dr. Schultz, did Eric have a seizure?"

Dr. Schultz took my hands in his. "Sarah, I'd rather wait for Dr. Kemp. This is not my field. Dr. Kemp will answer all your questions. I know you and Lance are anxious for answers, and you will have them, but I'd rather Dr. Kemp—"

Before Dr. Schultz could finish his sentence, the door swung open, and a man younger than Lance walked in. He greeted Dr.

Schultz, glanced in our direction, and went directly to Eric. His examination of Eric went on for twenty minutes. He spoke to the attending nurse, she left the room, and within minutes, machines were rolled in. Dr. Kemp proceeded to attach wires to Eric's chest and head. The machines immediately came to life when Dr. Kemp hit several switches. I watched as my son's heart and brain rate were printed on a piece of paper coming from the machine. Dr. Kemp read these small pieces of paper intently. The sound of the machines made me dizzy. I leaned into Lance. Dr. Schultz located two chairs, and we sat.

Dr. Kemp stood before us but talked directly to Dr. Schultz. When he turned to Lance and me, he spoke in layman's terms and referred to my son by name. "Eric is in a coma."

I gasped, tightening my grip on Lance's arm. An inaudible word swept from deep within me. "No, please, God, no!"

Lance questioned Dr. Kemp, "A coma? Why? How is this possible? He was fine yesterday. He didn't mention banging his head. I'm sure if he did, his nanny would have mentioned …"

Dr. Kemp knelt so he was facing Lance and me. "The coma was caused by the chicken pox, not trauma to the head."

I shouted, "I noticed the rashes, they weren't there yesterday!"

"I'm afraid it might be Reye's syndrome."

I covered my mouth, knowing nothing about the disease. "Is it fatal?"

"I like to tell you we know how to treat this disease, but it is as foreign to us as SIDS. The next forty-eight hours are crucial. There have been cases where a child comes out of the coma perfectly fine, but the longer he remains in the coma, could cause damage to the brain."

I buried my head in Lance's chest. "This can't be happening. He has to wake up!"

Lance held me tight and whispered, "Sarah, we are not going to lose another child."

Dr. Kemp gestured for Dr. Schultz to step outside, leaving Lance and me alone. When Dr. Schultz returned, he found Lance and me sitting across from each other, holding Eric's tiny hands, pleading for him to wake up.

Dr. Schultz placed a hand on my shoulder. "Dr. Kemp said Eric's vitals are good. His brain and heart are functioning at a normal rate. Sarah, I'm not leaving the hospital until Eric is up and out of danger.

After the closing of the door by Dr. Shultz, the only sound in the room was of the machines monitoring our son. I looked over at Lance and pleaded with him to go to the library and find out all he could about this disease."

Lance kissed Eric. Before leaving, he placed a kiss on the top of my head. "I promise I won't be long."

The door opened, and Doris leaned over me, placing her face close to mine. I began to sob and whispered, "Doris, my baby, my baby is very sick. He's so tiny." Doris stayed with me until Lance returned. When I saw the expression on Lance's face, I knew my little boy was in jeopardy of being taken from us.

Twenty-four hours later, Eric's condition had not changed. Lance and I pleaded for him to wake up. We read his favorite stories, and Lance told him funny stories about Spotty. When our voices were hoarse from talking, I laid my head on the bed. I watched Lance with his head back on the chair, and the hand that once held our son's was at his side. I wondered how he could sleep with our boy's life hanging on the edge.

Dr. Schultz kept his promise; he remained at the hospital, and every four hours, he stopped by to see if there was a change. By the tenth visit, he didn't bother to check Eric's chart.

Thirty-six hours later, with my head close to my son's side, I drifted off to sleep.

I dreamt about the night Eric was born, him lying next to me, swaddled in a blanket, only a few hours old. The room was white, and sunlight was all around. It was a warm and happy feeling. Then the room went dark, and I was sitting next to my mother, reliving the day we sat together and watched Dad and George playing on the front lawn. My mother turned to me. I smiled. She didn't. She was crying.

I felt a hand on my shoulder. I awoke and looked up to find my father standing beside me. "Dad." I melted into his arms and sobbed.

Forty-eight hours, and still no change. I asked Lance to ask everyone to leave the room, including him. "I need time alone with my son."

Lance was the last to leave, but before he did, our eyes locked. He whispered, "I love you."

Lying next to my son, taking him in my arms, I placed him close to my heart. I rested my head on his, kissing the soft hair that adorned his head. I whispered, "Eric William James Holland, Mommy needs you to wake up. Please, baby, wake up. You can't leave me. Do you know you are the only person that belongs only to me? You are my heart and soul. If you leave me, I don't know what I'll do. Please come back to me, baby, please."

The doctors didn't sugarcoat what Eric's chances were of making a full recovery. If he did wake, there most likely would be brain damage, but brain damage seemed easier to face than never seeing him again.

That night, while Lance slept, I watched Eric's breathing labor. I sat on the bed, held him close, and listened as he took his last breath. When the machines went flat, Lance woke and found me sobbing while I held my baby boy close and whispered, "I love you, baby, with all my heart and soul."

Lance and I sat with our child, who was white and still for three hours. It was morning when the door opened and Dr. Schultz stood behind us. He placed a hand on Eric's head. Speaking to me, he said, "Sarah, it's time to leave."

"I can't … I can't leave him here. I don't want anyone to touch him. I want Lance to go home and get his clothes. I want to dress my son. I'm taking him home to Cleveland. Lance, please make the arrangements."

"Do as she says, Lance. Doris and Constance are waiting to help. I'll stay with them until you get back."

When Lance returned, he placed the clothes that Eric would have worn to our wedding. A navy-blue suit, white shirt, red bow tie, and undergarments. A nurse brought me a pan filled with warm water for me to wash my son. I dressed him, kissing him many times as I completed the task, never noticing that Lance was only a few feet away. When he stepped forward, I asked, "Can we leave tomorrow?"

Lance, filled with grief, cried silently and said, "We can."

There was nothing left for me to say to my tiny son, but Lance needed to say goodbye, so I stepped aside and gave him a few minutes alone with Eric. Supporting each other, both physical and emotionally, we left the hospital.

Doris gave up her bedroom to Lance and me. As Lance sat in an armchair, staring out the window, I was reminded of another man so filled with grief that all he could do was stare out of a window. Lying in bed, I stared out the same window and watched the stars twinkle in the sky.

When I woke the following morning, there was a pain so heavy in my heart that I thought I would never be able to move from the bed. Doris sat in a chair beside me, holding my hand. I acknowledged her. "What time does the train leave?"

"Eleven."

I looked at the clock. It was eight thirty. I get out of bed with my back toward Doris, and she called my name. She was staring at the back of my nightgown, and tears were building. I pulled the nightgown around and spotted the blood. I comforted Doris by saying, "Don't be upset, Doris. God wasn't in my corner. Actually, he never was, and never will be."

* * * * *

On the train ride back home, I placed my shaking hand on my son's small coffin. Lance sat on the other side. His hands braced his head. Neither he nor I spoke except for an occasional thank-you when he handed me a cup of tea I couldn't drink. There were no words that could ease the pain he and I were feeling.

On a cold and blustery March day, I buried my son beside his grandmother and sister. With George, who held on tightly to our father, and Audrey, whose head was bowed so all that was visible was her dark-brown wool hat. Pearl stood close to Audrey, and beside her was her son and his wife. Our friends remained a short distance in the front of the tiny white coffin—Doris, Constance, Christopher, Jimmy, Sally and her husband, Mr. and Mrs. Parks, Mr. and Mrs. Epstein, Professor and Mrs. Powell, Dr. and Mrs. Schultz, and of course, Fanny.

Several times during the service, my legs weakened. Lance held on to me while I prayed that I'd wake up from this awful nightmare. As the preacher spoke, I stared into the open grave, my boy's final resting place, hoping to spot my mother's casket. I swore I could see a tip of another tiny white casket. I went limp. I heard someone call Lance's name, then another calling for a chair. I sat with Doris and Constance standing beside me. The preacher ended the prayer service seconds later.

I was asked to place the first white rose, Lance the second, then each person in attendance followed our lead. When the service was over, Lance and I were left alone. We said our goodbyes quietly, then together we walked from the cemetery as I repeated over and over in a soft whisper, "I will always love you, my precious little boy, with all my heart and soul."

CHAPTER SEVENTEEN

Allison

Today marks my fourth session with David. The pills he's prescribed have taken the edge off, and since stopping the pills, I've been able to function.

Pete doesn't confide in me when he tells our children he is renting an apartment in town. It's the children who inform me of Pete's plans upon their return home from Florida. "Dad said you and he need a little time apart. He also said that is why you didn't take vacation with us. Mom, what is going on?" asks Andrew.

Julia, who can't control her tears, doesn't hold back when she accuses me of lying. "Mom, you promised everything was fine. Why did you lie to us?"

I want to hate Pete, but I can't. I need to step up to the plate and face the music, so during the next two weeks before school, I speak the truth, and it feels good.

"I'm not going to sugarcoat what is going on. You both know I haven't been myself after Pop died. Medically, I'm depressed. I don't want you to blame your dad. He did everything he could to get me to join a grieving group, and when I was getting worse, he begged me to see a therapist. In a nutshell, I wouldn't take your father's advice. I'm seeing a therapist, once a week, and it's helped, but I have a long road ahead of me, and I need to do this on my own. Your father has been kind enough to give me the time and space I need to work this out."

Andrew says, "I don't get it. Isn't that what married people do? Stay together through the rough times?"

"Yes, normally that is what couples do, but there are times when a little time apart can also help in tough situations."

Julia is crying uncontrollably. I draw her nearer to me. "I know I've disappointed you, and I know you're thinking your dad and I are the adults, we should be able to figure this out." I sigh, trying to find a way to explain to my children without telling them that their mother is a total fuck-up. "You know the fear that overcomes you when you can't find your way out of a maze? That's how I'm feeling. I need someone other than your father to make me whole again, help me find my way back."

"What about Dad? Is he getting help?" asks Andrew.

"Your father isn't the problem. I am."

Julia speaks her opinion. "It's all the traveling Dad's been doing. He's become a part-time husband, and so soon after Grandpa died. I met that lady Emily. She stopped by the house to drop off some legal papers. I bet she has something to do with Dad spending so much time in Florida."

"No, Julia, Emily is working her butt off to get the Florida office open and operating. We should be grateful she's there to help. Never doubt the love your father has for his family. He's a loyal and righteous man."

* * * * *

With the second week of school in full swing, football and soccer begin. Every other weekend, Pete arrives at five on Friday and beeps the horn to announce his arrival. On Sundays, he deposits the children at the curb by six, avoiding all contact with me.

I return to work after Labor Day. I welcome being away from my home because working doesn't allow me the luxury to sit and reflect on how badly I have messed up my life. Saturdays and Sundays are difficult, when the children are with Pete.

By my fifth visit with David, we still have not scratched the surface in finding the root of my problem.

"Saturday is the first football game of the season. Do you think Pete will be there? And if so, how will you handle seeing him for the first time since you separated?"

"I'm anxious to see him, but I'm sure he will keep his distance."

"Have either of you told anyone other than the children that you're not together?"

"I haven't. I have spoken with our best friends, JoAnne and Gary, and they are clueless, so Pete hasn't either. If he had, JoAnne would be standing at my front door, reading me the riot act."

"Have you given any thought to why Pete has been so secretive about your living arrangements?"

"Yes, I have thought about it."

"And your conclusion?"

"He's embarrassed. Everyone envied what we had. We were the perfect couple. How do you explain we weren't?"

* * * * *

Saturday, I drop off Julia at soccer practice and Andrew at the football field. I tell Andrew I'm going to get coffee.

I decide to purchase two coffees and four doughnuts, as a peace offering. Walking toward the stands, I spot Pete sitting alone. My heart leaped in my chest. My reaction to seeing my husband doesn't surprise me. Since the day I told him I never loved him, I wanted nothing more than to spend the rest of my life with him. Seeing me heading toward him, Pete becomes uncomfortable, but I don't give him a chance to move. I smile, assuring everyone around us that we are still a happy and loving couple.

Sitting next to him, loudly I say, "I stopped for coffee."

Pete accepts the coffee but doesn't offer any thanks. I whisper, "I haven't eaten breakfast. Have you?" I place the open bag of doughnuts before him.

"No thanks. I've already had breakfast."

At halftime, without a word, Pete stands and makes his way toward the field. My peace offering of fresh doughnuts hasn't worked, so I eat another and save the last two for the kids. David and his wife approach Pete. They talk for a few seconds, then Pete disappears, returning by the fourth quarter with Julia. Pete points to where I'm sitting, and Julia makes her way over. I offer her a doughnut.

"Did you text your dad to say practice was over?"

"No. He texted me and said he was on his way. Mom, do you mind if I have lunch with Dad? I know it's your weekend and all."

"Of course not, sweetie. Is Andrew tagging along?"

"No. He's going out with the team."

Walking off the field, I see Pete and walk toward him. "Julia said you are taking her to lunch?"

"I'll have her home by four."

Julia spots a friend. "Dad, I'll be right back."

To soften the tension between us, I ask, "Did Andrew tell you he was having lunch with a few friends?"

"It's your weekend. He doesn't have to check in with me."

His tone is upsetting, so calmly I say, "You didn't seem to care about my weekend when you asked Julia to lunch."

"I didn't invite Julia to lunch. She asked me to lunch. I told her if it was all right with you, then yes, I'd have lunch with her."

"I'm sorry. I shouldn't have assumed you asked her. But if we were able to communicate, it would be helpful."

The lids of Pete's eyes narrow. He manages to control himself because the couples we socialize with are nearby. I look in their direction. "I've been avoiding them like the plague. It won't be long before they figure out we're not together. That is why I think it's important for us to be able to sit down and talk this out." I wait for an answer from Pete. Julia arrives before I get an answer to my question.

"Are you ready to go? Say goodbye to your mother." Pete walks away, and Julia runs to catch up.

I don't know how I'm able to drive, because the tears are clouding my vision. I need to find a way to get through to Pete. The weather, over a course of three hours, has turned to rain. I grab my raincoat and an umbrella and plant myself at the curb. When the car pulls up, Pete spots me. He stops short in front of our house. I run to open the car door. When Julia exits, I hand her the umbrella and tell her I need a few minutes to talk with her dad. Soaking wet,

I sit in the passenger's seat and close the door behind me. I watch our daughter enter the house and turn to Pete. "You can't avoid me forever. We share two children. We owe it to them to find a common ground of communication."

Pete stares ahead. "I'd rather we keep things as they are. The less I see you, the better I feel." Pete manages to turn my way. "I wasn't going to Andrew's game today. I was going to go next weekend, but when I told Andrew my plan, he said he didn't care what was going on between us. He wanted his parents at his games. That's why I showed up."

I take this opportunity to make my point. "That's why it's important for us to communicate. If you had made your feelings known to me, I could have supported your decision. I'm not saying he would have understood, but together we might have convinced him it would be best."

Pete scolds me, "Finding a way to communicate is not going to make their lives any easier! They have to accept the truth. We can't be in each other's company."

"If they have to accept the truth, then why haven't you told anyone we've separated?"

Pete stares ahead in silence. I give an opinion. "Maybe deep down, just like me, you are looking for an answer to why I've chosen to fuck up our perfect life. And if the answer is an acceptable one, one we can deal with, then maybe you're thinking we might have a chance to salvage what we had."

Not speaking directly to me, Pete says, "I try not to think about you at all."

"And how is that working for you? Because I think of you every minute of the day. I fucked up, I made a mess of our lives, and I wish I knew why."

"Isn't that a question for your therapist?"

I begin to cry. "After five visits, I've talked about nothing but finding a way for you and me to be civil with each other, for the children's sake. If I can manage to wrap my head around that, I might be able to tackle serious issues, like what makes Allison fuck up so much."

"Don't waste your money or time on me."

I soften. "Pete, I know you hate me, I can accept that, but if you have one small feeling left toward me, please talk to me, if only about the children."

* * * * *

Office visit number 6. "I saw you and Pete at the game on Saturday. I spoke with him. He thinks within a few months, the Florida office will be up and operating."

"I wouldn't know. He doesn't talk to me. He'd prefer to keep it that way."

David makes a clicking sound with his lips.

"What? What was that sound you made?"

"It's a reaction to what split you guys up, because after six sessions, I don't have a clue. Here's a recap of our five sessions: Your stepfather's death drove Pete and you apart. Your father died when you were a little girl, leaving you with a cold and uncaring mother. You hate your aunt, your uncle. You want Pete to forgive you. For what, I have no idea. JoAnne is the only other person other than your children you love. Did I miss anything?"

I stare, unable to come up with an answer to David's analogy of my pitiful life.

So he continues, "If you were sitting in my place, wouldn't you think it strange that a man who fathered two children with you apparently cannot manage to have a simple conversation with you because you wedged a wall between you when you were overcome with grief?"

Stoic, I wait for him to continue.

"Allison, it is a waste of your money and time, not including my time, which could be spent helping someone else. I think it best—"

"Are you ending our sessions?"

"Yes. Here are several names of doctors I think you'd be more comfortable seeing. When you are ready, I strongly advise you give one of them a call, but the decision is entirely yours."

"I don't want to meet with another doctor."

David, sympathetic to my situation, says, "This is against my better judgment. I won't remove your next appointment from my appointment book. I'll give you a week to decide if therapy is right for you."

* * * * *

The next week is impossible for me. Pete has managed to avoid me at the game on Saturday. My last plea has done nothing to soften his disgust toward me. David has my number. I think I'm doing a good job of opening up without truly being open. Am I using David in hopes that Pete will see I'm making an effort and give me the second chance I feel I deserve?

Wednesday, I confess everything to David. I make a mental note to purchase several boxes of tissues and bring them to the next session.

David says, "Now we can start the mending process."

The following week, I prepare myself for my hour with David. I'm convinced we will focus on Patrick and my teenage crush. Instead, David starts the session by asking, "You were five when your father died, or were you turning five?"

"I was three weeks shy of turning five."

"How did you celebrate your birthday?"

"My aunt, uncle, and grandfather Holland were fixtures in our home after my father passed. Aunt Sarah cooked dinner, then after dinner, there was a cake and lots of presents. I remember my uncle bought me a doll whose hair grew when you pulled her ponytail. I vaguely remember me mentioning it to my father. The doll had to have dark hair just like mine."

"Were you happy that your uncle remembered you wanted the doll?"

"No. I hated him and the doll. I threw her in the toy chest, and that's where she remained until I turned twelve and threw her in the garbage."

"You clearly remember hating the doll." David never jots down anything I say during our sessions, but today he does. I assume he's written, "Allison hates dolls."

"Do you remember any of the other gifts?"

"My mother bought me books. She loved to read, but strangely, she never read to me. That was my aunt's job."

"What were some of the other presents you received?"

"My grandfather bought me a red bike with training wheels. My aunt bought me clothes. I remember this one dress I pointed out to her when we were shopping before my father died. It had ruffles around the collar, sleeves, and one big ruffle at the bottom. It was pink-and-white. She also got me a gold heart locket, which I was sure she purchased after my father died, because it held a picture of my mother and father on their wedding day."

"Did you treasure the locket?"

"No. I flushed it down the toilet when no one was looking."

David doesn't note the flushing of the locket.

Three weeks later, with thirty more of David's simple questions regarding my father's death, I come to realize I didn't hate my father for dying; I hated him because he risked his life to save a boy he didn't know and left his little girl waiting at home for him.

It takes two more weeks for me to speak of my father without hatred in the tone of my voice.

* * * * *

Thanksgiving is closing in on me. When my aunt inquires of my plans, I easily respond, "We are spending the holiday with you and Uncle George."

She is elated with my answer. I'm sure she thinks my response will be I'm not celebrating this year because it's the one-year anniversary of Patrick's death, but she thought wrong.

"I'd be happy to host. Will Pete's family be joining us?"

"I'll let you know."

* * * * *

The following Saturday, I wonder if I'm losing my mind. Pete is heading toward me. "Do you have a few minutes to talk?"

I could have thought of a million jokes in response to his question, but my answer is simple and to the point. "Sure."

"What are your plans for Thanksgiving this year? Because I was thinking, I can take the kids Wednesday night, plan a nice breakfast, and drop them off at twelve on Thanksgiving. Christmas Day, we could do the same."

I confess, "I haven't told my aunt you moved out. Just the other day, she asked if your family would be joining us for the holidays. I said I would ask you. I haven't even told JoAnne about our situation."

Pete stares. "My mother was disappointed when I told her with all the traveling, I thought it best that we spend Thanksgiving as a family. She asked if we were planning on spending Christmas week in Florida. The children don't have to this year."

"Whatever they want to do is fine with me. If they want to spend Christmas week in Florida, I'll call your mother to explain I just can't afford the time away from work."

Pete is a little taken aback by my response. "I'll talk with them. If they want to go, I'll make the arrangements."

I feel sick to my stomach knowing it's only right that I convince my children to spend Christmas week with their grandparents. I don't want our casual conversation to end, so I ask, "Any progress with the Florida office?"

"Some." Pete realizes this question does not involve our children. It's off-limits. Pete, anxious to make a quick getaway, says, "Maybe next year, we can work on a schedule. One year I'll have Thanksgiving, one year Christmas. I've got to go. Have a nice day."

As Pete steps away, I say, "You too."

* * * * *

David doesn't waste any time. "Describe your mother in four words."

"Later. Something strange happened this weekend. I wanted to get your opinion—"

"I have eyes. I saw Pete talking with you on Saturday."

"I guess our friendship ended when I became a patient. You avoid me like the plague at the games."

"There's a reason I keep my distance, and the reason is Pete. All right, I'll bite. What did he say? Then I want those four words."

I tell David about our discussion regarding the holidays. I'm over-the-top happy. "I think we are making progress. We had a conversation like two civilized people, or should I say parents, and we managed to put our children's needs before our own. What's your professional opinion?"

"The holidays needed to be discussed. Each parent has a right to spend time with their children. Now, in four words, describe your mother?"

"Bookworm, cold, uncaring, and strange."

* * * * *

Thanksgiving, I arrive at my aunt's home. Before I can close the door, Pete's car pulls up behind mine. I gasp.

My aunt rushes past me. "Pete, you were able to get a flight?" Turning toward me, she says, "Allison, did you know?"

The children and I remain frozen in place.

* * * * *

I can't wait to tell David the news regarding Thanksgiving. "He drops the kids off at twelve, at the curb, not even a wave. Seconds after we arrive at my aunt's, his car pulls up behind mine."

"Why do you think he decided to come?"

"I have no idea. My aunt said they spoke earlier in the week. Pete told her he was unable to make it back for Thanksgiving. When she questioned how I felt about him not being there, it seemed I was very understanding, according to my aunt's version. Stranger yet, the day moved along as it did Thanksgivings past. The men watched football, and Julia, my aunt, and I played board games. The conversation during dinner and desert was light and airy. It was a great holiday."

"Must have been hard for the two of you to keep up this masquerade."

"We were every pleasant with each other, joking with the children. I think we did a good job of fooling my aunt and uncle."

"Allison, don't get your hopes up. Holidays make people do strange things. This was the first holiday Pete had to spend alone, away from his children. Don't read too much into his actions. He's probably hating himself for having a weak moment."

"I'm not going to lie and tell you I didn't see this as a ray of hope. Pete could have said he couldn't get back, and I would have kept the lie going. All right, maybe he was miserable without the children. Maybe he sucked it up to be with his children. Whatever. He was there, and it was a beautiful day."

The session moves on, and we elaborate on my word descriptions relating to my mother.

"It took you less time to describe your eighteen-year relationship with your mother than it did for you to reflect on the five years you spent with your father."

"Five years, and I still can remember how much I was loved by my father. Eighteen years, and maybe there was a moment or two with my mother. Remember, *strange* was one of the words I used in my description."

David renders his own description of my mother. "From what I'm hearing, your mother wasn't warm and fuzzy. She wasn't physically abusive. She wasn't a drunk or an addict. In your opinion, her life was dull and boring, and she died sooner than she should have. Sad."

I throw up my hands. "That sums up her life."

"She married your father, then married a second time. She obviously loved your stepfather. She kept his secret."

I answer, "Go figure."

"That discounts the uncaring and cold theory. How does that make you feel?"

The question leaves me stunned. "Like shit. If there is something worse than shit, that's how I feel.

* * * * *

The revelation that my mother was not uncaring or cold hurts so much that I fake being sick and pass up on Saturday's football game. I text Pete, say I'm not feeling well, and ask if he can help out with the kids. I remain in bed.

Tuesday at work, I open an email from Pete. "Here is a list of what the kids want for Christmas. Why don't we divide the gifts equally between you, me, and our families?"

I loudly curse at my computer. "Fuck you, Pete!" Seeing Kathy standing in the doorway, I say, "Not my husband, someone else. I'm fine, just close the door. I need a few minutes to calm down."

* * * * *

David stares when I rush into his office and announce, "This isn't working for me. I spend one hour with you, then you send me out there to deal with my emotions. I buried my feelings for my mother the day I buried her. Did I tell you she didn't even want me around to hold her fucking hand when she was dying? Oh, she was really compassionate. Fuck her! Fuck Pete! I fucked up, I get it, I could have aborted … but is he happy his son, our son, is alive and well? No. All he can think about is how we can divide presents for the kids. Fuck the holidays."

David and I play the staring game, then he says, "Bad weekend?"

I burst out laughing. "No, bad fucking life."

"Allison, I would like to continue talking about your mother, but seeing how upset you are—"

"What would cause a mother to hate her own child? Did she blame me for my father's death? Do you think my father forced her to have a child? There were times, David, when she was sick, she opened up to me. She spoke of a life with my father, children, travel. She spoke as if my father and she were in agreement on the path their lives would take. I was my father's child. I was a part of him. Why couldn't she love me? All the times I could have asked her why, I never did."

"From what you have told me, there were also many opportunities before marrying Pete that you could have asked Patrick if he had feelings for you."

"And I never did."

"Allison, I would like to stop here and take a few weeks off. During this time, I would like you to consider speaking with your aunt. I think she holds the key to the questions you're asking now. Pete said your aunt knew the truth about Patrick. Find out what she knew. There is one other thing I'd like you to consider. I know you're close with JoAnne, and I'm assuming she would be the first person you told about the separation, but I'd like you to consider your aunt as your first choice. I'll end by saying I'm only suggesting. Ultimately, it's your decision."

CHAPTER EIGHTEEN

Sarah

It was June, three and half months since my precious son was laid in the ground. Lance was getting anxious to return to New York and life as we knew it.

Every day around noon, together we would visit our children's grave.

Most days, we stood at the grave in silence, but today I could sense Lance wanted to talk. "Lance, why don't you just say what's on your mind?"

Lance lowered his head. "Dr. Schultz called. He said the baby arrived earlier than expected. It's a girl, six pounds, five ounces, nineteen inches long."

"Are the mother and baby doing well?"

"Yes. The mother hasn't changed her mind about the adoption. Sarah, I think it's time to go home."

"This is my home, Lance."

"No, Sarah. It's our children's final resting place, it's not our home, and it wasn't theirs. Our home and our lives are back in New York."

"Lance, you're not thinking I can go back to New York and possibly be a mother to this little girl? I can't believe so soon after Eric's death, you are ready to be a father to this child."

Lance came toward me. I stepped away, and he softly said, "Nothing is going to make the pain go away, but living every day visiting their grave doesn't bring them back. I have a job in New

York. School starts the third week in August." Lance whispered, "I already told Dr. Schultz I didn't think we were ready to be parents to this child. The second baby is due in August. There's the house, I was hoping … if not, I'll put it back on the market. We can rent an apartment uptown, closer to Constance and Doris. Once we are settled, you might want to reconsider adopting the second child. If not, we'll wait until the time is right."

I didn't want Lance's logic. I wasn't sure I wanted to be a mother, not now, or ever. I yelled, "A baby doesn't heal a broken heart! Trust me, I know firsthand. My father never noticed Audrey existed after my mom died, and I am my father's child. These children deserve better. Anyway, we committed ourselves under different circumstances. Being a parent is the last thing I want."

Lance stepped forward again. I moved farther away. "Sarah, the love we have for each other will get us through this. Don't give up on us. Not again."

I sensed Lance was coming closer. This time, I remained still. When he placed his arms around me, I cried. "You have it all figured out. We go back, find somewhere to live far from the place we shared with our son, bring this innocent child into this sad situation, and everything is going to be all right?"

Lance placed his head close to mine. "Sarah, you are my heart and soul, but remaining here, dwelling on our loss, is not what our children want for us."

It was then I knew Lance and I had to go our separate ways, for now. I tightened my hold on him. My action convinced him going home was the right thing to do.

* * * * *

George came to visit the end of June. I knew his visit was to check up on me and to find out why Lance and I hadn't returned to New York.

"Lance told me he's taking the train back to New York on Saturday. I hope you're going back with him. It's time."

"He has to go back. School is starting, and he must find a place to live. Doris said the Parkses rented the apartment." Facing George, I said, "I can see right through you. You don't have to walk on eggshells with me. You're wondering why Lance and I haven't already gone back to New York. Am I right?"

George looked off in the distance. "Watching you throw your life away is depressing. Dad lives his life knowing that one day we will place him in the ground next to Mom. I hate to see you go down that same road."

"Your analogy doesn't change the fact that less than four months ago, I buried my son, and with him went my hopes of happiness."

George leaned closer. "I know exactly how you're feeling. I've been there, and there isn't a day that goes by that I don't think of my son. I didn't want Hilda to leave me. I was willing to try, save our marriage. I spoke of having other children, but I couldn't reach her. She turned away from me, just like you're turning from Lance. He loves you, Sarah, and maybe you and Lance can't have children of your own, but there can be children in your lives. Don't be a fool. Saturday, get on that train, go home."

* * * * *

Friday morning, I hid a small suitcase in the trunk of my dad's car. When everyone was asleep, I slipped away and drove to Pittsburgh, where I rented a motel room and hid for several days. I called my dad on Sunday, and he said Lance had left as planned. George was leaving on Monday. When George grabbed the phone from my father's hand, I hung up. George left on Monday. I returned home on Wednesday.

* * * * *

While I was at the motel, I called Constance to tell her Lance was returning home. I asked that she give him the number to where I was staying. I also asked her to help him find a place to live. I told her all I wanted was Eric's baby book, the empty baby book that would have told the story of my daughter's life, and the book *Gone with the Wind.*

When Lance called, I cried my apology to him. "Lance, I am so sorry. I wasn't ready to go back. I know you are right, we need our friends to help us heal, but right now all I want is to be alone. I beg you to understand."

Lance whispered, "I'd do anything for you, Sarah. I love you. That hasn't changed. If you need more time, I understand. I won't put pressure on you, but I'm frightened. The longer you wait to begin life without Eric, the harder it is going to be to leave there."

I cried. "Don't be frightened. I still love you. I'm not forgetting how much you loved Eric, and he loved you so much. You were his daddy. Thank you, thank you for giving our precious boy the father he deserved." I hung up and sobbed alone in a motel room far away from home, something I hadn't done since my dying child lay in my arms.

* * * * *

Lance and I found a common ground. He called once a week and gave me an update on our friends. He took a one-year lease on a two-bedroom apartment, much larger than the one we shared. He said during the year, he would look for a larger place. His comment that he was tired of small apartments made me sad. My small apartment held nothing but happy memories for me. He finished our conversation by asking if I had plans on returning home.

When I gave no time frame, Lance stopped asking. August came and went. The baby, I assumed, was born and placed with another family. Lance never brought up the child, and I never asked.

At Christmas, Lance came to visit. We went to the grave together and prayed. Lance boarded the train one day later. When I kissed him goodbye, he said, "Please come home. I miss living with you. I miss us."

Constance and Doris wrote and called often. During my phone conversations with Constance, I asked that she, Jimmy, and Sally keep a close watch over Lance. "Include him in all your plans, Constance. He needs a life."

"Sarah, are you ever going to come back? I miss you. We miss you."

"I wish I could, but every time I think, 'Okay, you can do this,' I think about my children lying in a grave and my being so far away."

Doris and Constance came to visit when Christopher turned nine. Christopher brought Spotty along, and I couldn't believe how excited the dog was to see me. We brought Spotty to visit Eric's grave. When Constance, Christopher, and Doris left, I spent most of the following day at the grave, crying for the life my son didn't share with his two best friends, Christopher and Spotty.

* * * * *

January, I was walking through town when I eyed the perfect spring dress for Audrey. Since returning home, I devoted most of my time doting on her. It didn't take me long to realize she hated the attention. I passed the law office of Stark, and I thought I'd stop in and say hi to Mr. Stark, who defended George all those years earlier.

Walking in, I found Mr. Stark filing. "Don't you have a secretary to do that?"

He turned. "Sarah Holland, how are you?"

"You remember me?"

"Of course I remember you! Your brother stops by whenever he's in town. In answer to your question, I did have a secretary, until she ran off and married a boy from North Carolina."

I smiled. "Are you looking to replace her? If so, I might be able to help you out. I need to keep busy. Maybe I can work part-time or full-time, if you're interested?"

"Sarah, I heard about your boy. I'm so sorry."

I sighed. "That's one of the reasons I need to keep busy."

"Aren't you an attorney? Heard you graduated law school top in your class. You may be a bigger help to me than you think. What about paralegal work?"

"I'm your girl."

* * * * *

I didn't tell Lance I had taken a job. It wasn't until he visited on the one-year anniversary of Eric's death that Audrey accidentally mentioned my job. Lance saved his questions until we left our children's grave. Walking behind Audrey and Dad, Lance asked, "Why didn't you mention you were working?"

"I only took the job to keep busy."

Lance stopped in his tracks. "I knew something like this would happen. Taking a job means you have no intentions of returning to New York. That's why you didn't tell me."

"You have no idea how I feel. You think I can just hop on a train and leave them here alone?"

Lance reached for my hand. "Do you hear yourself? You're not deserting your children. The children are gone." Lance pointed to the grave. "That place holds the remains of what was."

Audrey and Dad stopped when I cried and screamed, "They're alive in my mind! In my imagination, they are growing taller every day! Our little girl is three. I bought her a pretty new dress. Eric is six. He's jealous of his little sister's new dress. To distract him, I send him off to play with Spotty. That's life for me. I don't expect you to understand. I never asked you to leave, you left on your own. You chose to go back there, to New York, where life once was beautiful and good!"

I ran past my father and Audrey. I ran from the cemetery. When I was exhausted from running, I walked at a fast pace, not knowing where I would wind up. A car slowed, then stopped. Lance exited my father's car.

"Sarah, stop. Stop running away."

"I'm not running away, Lance. I'm walking."

He reached out and pulled me back. He took notice of the park across from where we were standing. He crossed the street, dragging me along. I went willingly. Sitting on a bench, he asked, "Sarah, just tell me the truth. Have you decided to remain here in Cleveland?"

I lowered my head and shook it left then right. "I have no idea what I want."

"Obviously, you don't want to live with me in New York."

"I miss you, I miss our friends, but I don't have the strength to leave them here all alone without someone who cares they existed."

"That's where you're wrong. I care they existed. There isn't a day that goes by that I don't think of them. I don't need a grave to remind me they were a part of my life, our lives."

"I hate myself for putting you through this. I hate myself more for not having the strength to get on that train and leave with you. I can't ask you to wait forever, but if and when I am ready, I hope it won't be too late."

* * * * *

Lance called every Sunday and wrote, but his words of love were more of friendship as time passed.

On a beautiful Saturday morning in November, I rose and thought I'd give myself a break. No visits to the cemetery. But as the day was moving along, I found myself wondering if my children were waiting. When I walked up to the grave, I just stood there, looking up at the sky. A rainbow streaked across the sky on a perfectly clear day. I smiled. A strong wind took the scarf from my neck. I heard a strange sound. The sound was from me. I laughed. For the first time in nearly two years, I laughed. I envisioned my mother. Beside her were my children. They were smiling. My mother's expression spoke to me, saying, "I'm here, and it's time."

I smiled, knowing I was ready to leave this place and return to New York. To the place where there were so many good memories. The time I spent with my grandmothers, where I met and fell in love with Lance, sweet memories of Eric, the happiness I felt when I touched my swollen stomach that held my baby girl. I knew it was going to be rough, but I was ready and willing to try.

When I turned, I gasped, not expecting to see the person standing behind me.

"Hello, Sarah."

"How did you find this place?"

"I've been here before. This isn't the first time."

I questioned, "Stephen, why are you here?"

"I've visited several times, hoping to bump into you. I guess today's my lucky day."

"You didn't answer my question. Why are you here?"

"I already know the truth, but I need to hear it from you. Eric was my son, wasn't he?"

Stephen hadn't changed. He was still a handsome man, but his eyes told a different story. I sighed. "He was your son and the greatest gift a man could give a woman. He meant the world to me. He was my heart and soul. During his short life, he was the light in my world. I loved him more than you can imagine. He was so easy to love, and I showered him with love. He was a happy child."

"I know. I've watched you and him many times from a distance. I even know the name of the man he called Daddy, Lance."

"He was a wonderful father."

Stephen began to cry. I reached for his hand. "Oh, Stephen, I wish I could offer some words of compassion. Was I wrong not to tell you? Maybe. But there was Jasmine. And truth be told, I didn't want to share Eric. He was mine and mine alone, until Lance."

Stephen nodded. He understood. "I won't bother you again."

Wrapping my arms around myself, I said, "There's a diner down the road. I'll treat you to a cup of coffee, and you can ask me about Eric. It makes me happy to talk about him."

As we turned to leave, I stopped. "Stephen, I can't stop you from visiting the grave, but Eric is gone, and with him went the secret you fathered a child. Don't torture yourself anymore asking, 'What if?' Today I saw a rainbow. I know we can never forget, but I think the rainbow is a sign there is life after death. Don't you agree?"

* * * * *

The following day, I sat at the desk in my room, wondering if I should call or write Lance. I decided a letter over a phone call since letters had been a part of Lance and my relationship.

It took me two days to come up with the words and two days to get the nerve to mail the letter.

Dear Lance,

I wrote letter after letter, but this letter says it all.

I love you, I miss you, and I'm ready to come home, if you'll have me.

I'm happy you moved in to a larger apartment. I hope you haven't had time to decorate, because I think you should leave the decorating to me.

And I have every intention of filling those bedrooms with children. Adopted or biological, whatever way God sees fit. Yes, I said God. I made my peace with him as well.

I hope it's not too late.

Love you with all my heart and soul,
Sarah

* * * * *

I ran down the stairs, ready to mail my letter, when my father asked, "Sarah, what's your rush?"

Kissing my father on the cheek, I said, "I have to mail this letter before the post office closes."

"Speaking of letters, the postman just dropped two of them off for you today. They're on the table by the steps."

I looked at my watch, grabbed the letters, and headed for my car. When I placed the letters on the passenger's seat, the handwriting on the envelope got my attention. I opened the letter written by Lance first.

> *Dear Sarah,*
>
> *I hope you're well. Please accept my apology for writing instead of calling, but what I have to tell you can't be said over the phone, and forgive me for not being strong enough to tell you in person.*
>
> *This is the hardest letter I've ever had to write. Sarah, I'm getting married.*

Laying my head back, I returned Lance's letter to the envelope and reached for the second letter. My hands shook as I tore open the envelope and began to read.

> *Dear Sarah,*
>
> *Please forgive me. You know how much your friendship means to me. That is why it is so hard to tell you I've fallen in love with Lance. Sarah, I know my action is a betrayal of our friendship, and I'm hoping you'll find it in your heart to forgive me. Lance and I want to start a life together and want to share our happiness with everyone, but not before we told you of our intentions.*
>
> *Sarah …*

I folded the second letter and placed it in the envelope with Lance's letter. I didn't finish reading either. I wasn't surprised that Lance and Constance had fallen in love; their calls had lessened over the last six months. I should have put two and two together.

Was I hurt? Of course. But I only had myself to blame. Or was death to blame? Lance wanted to go on with his life, and I wasn't ready to return to that life knowing Eric wouldn't be a part of our future.

In my room, I placed the letters, including the one I wrote to Lance, in the book *Gone with the Wind*, which held all my special photos. Then I sat and wrote another letter addressed to the two people who meant the world to me.

Dear Lance and Constance,

When I received your letter, I danced with joy that my two favorite people in this entire world found love, and even happier to know it was with each other.

Please don't wait to say 'I do,' and of course, Jimmy has to design the perfect wedding dress!

I have some news of my own. I've accepted a job in Pittsburgh. It's not New York, but it is a big city, and you know this girl is a city girl at heart.

George is coming home for Christmas, and then I'm flying back with him for a little R & R before I start my new job.

I hope by the time I return, you two would have tied the knot, but I promise I'll be there for the birth of your first child.

I'm sure Christopher is thrilled, as he should be, to have Lance in his life, and I'm sure he wants Spotty to be the ring bearer.

Love each other forever.

Sarah

Doris called to confirm if I was truly happy for Lance and Constance. She divulged that she noticed they were becoming close and was concerned their union would affect our relationship.

"Sarah, you know how I feel about you and Constance. I love you as if you were my own daughters. I'm sure you understand how concerned I am that this union will affect the bond you have with Constance, Lance, and myself."

"Doris, believe me, I'm happy for them, and nothing will sever our relationship. I'll never forget your support in good times and bad. Nothing can break the bond we share. Now, tell me, when is the wedding?"

"New Year's Day, then they're off to Italy for their honeymoon."

"I'm happy for them. They deserve to be happy. You don't know how relieved I was to hear that Lance was moving on. I fell out of love with him after Eric died. I didn't mean for it to happen, but I don't have to explain to you how losing a child can affect life as you knew it."

* * * * *

After visiting with George in Germany, I landed a great job in Pittsburgh. I was finally ready to practice corporate law. I worked my butt off proving my worth. After three years, I made partner, winning a trial in favor of a wealthy client's daughter who was knee-deep in an ugly divorce after marrying a loser who was spending her trust fund money on women and booze.

One year after moving to Pittsburgh, I bumped into my high school flame, Michael Pratt. Michael had married his college sweetheart, and they divorced one year later. Michael described a woman who wanted more than he could give. He ended the story by saying, "Thank God no children."

After I made partner, Michael and I moved in together. Was it love? No. A relationship of convenience? Yes. It was easier to have someone to share my life with than living alone with my memories. Lance was and will always remain my one true love.

Children and marriage were never discussed since we were married to our careers. Another reason our relationship worked so well. We saw little of each other because of our demanding schedules. When we found the time to be together, the sex was good. The money we earned gave us the privilege to play hard, sparing no expense on trips, cars, clothes, five-star hotels, the opera, and so much more.

A client gave me sound advice when he said I shouldn't invest in the stock market hoping to get rich. Invest in art, then you can retire and live like a queen. I purchased eight pieces that would triple in value.

I didn't have the fairy-tale ending, but life was good.

As I guessed, Constance presented Lance with his first child one year after they were married, a girl named Emily. I was asked to be godmother, and I accepted. Over the course of five years, two more daughters would complete the Pickett family, Caroline and Amanda. Christopher turned fourteen and was entering high school in the fall. His dream was to earn a hockey scholarship to Boston University.

My friendship with Doris, her children, Jimmy, Sally, the Parkses, the Epsteins, the Harts, the Powell's, Dr. Schultz, Fanny, and of course, Constance, Lance, and their children was never severed.

I took sour grapes and made wine of my life. There wasn't a day that went by that I didn't think of my daughter, Margaret, but mostly I grieved Eric, my adorable son. I often wondered what his dreams and accomplishments would have been at each age if Reye's syndrome hadn't cut his life so short.

CHAPTER NINETEEN

Allison

After my visit with David, I do as he asks. I consider telling my aunt the truth about Pete and me. Two seconds later, I convince myself it's a terrible idea. Two days later, I think it's a good idea, then knock it down again and opt for telling JoAnne the truth and nothing but the truth.

Time is running out. Christmas Eve is tomorrow, and I still haven't decided.

Taking a break from work, I decide to call JoAnne. I dial her number then chicken out telling her, so we talk about the children and work.

The plan for Christmas Eve and Christmas Day will remain as it did Christmas past. Christmas Eve dinner at my aunt's, then attend Christmas Eve service as a family. Christmas Day, Pete will arrive forty-five minutes before my aunt and uncle, and we will celebrate as a family. The following day, Pete and the children will fly off to visit with Pete's parents for the Christmas week break. I will remain home.

While my aunt and I clear the dishes Christmas Eve, I inform my aunt that the children and Pete are leaving for Florida the day after Christmas. I immediately announce, "I'm not going. I was wondering, after they leave on Monday, if I could stop by and spend the day with you."

The decision is made; my aunt will be the first person I'll tell about our separation.

I'm not fooling my aunt. Her look proves she knows Monday is going to be an interesting day. "I hate thinking of you all alone in that house. Why don't you pack a few things just in case you decide to spend the night?"

* * * * *

Monday, I kiss my children goodbye. While sipping coffee alone in my kitchen, I wipe my tears, wishing I were boarding the plane with my family.

I do as my aunt suggested: I pack a duffel bag with clothes and toiletries, which I leave in the car when I arrive at her home.

My aunt is waiting at the front door. "Your uncle and I waited to have lunch. I hope you didn't eat?"

"I didn't, but I did have way too much coffee, so just water for me."

After lunch, my aunt and I clear the table. My uncle wishes us a good day and goes off to play cards with his buddies.

My aunt prepares tea and a plate of Christmas cookies. Eating little of my lunch in anticipation of my talk with her, I reach for a cookie. "These are my favorite. Your mother's recipe, correct?"

"Not exactly. She strong-armed her best friend, Claire, into giving her the recipe."

"I'm glad Grandma won out. I can't get enough of them."

My aunt smiles and then refreshes my tea. "You know, I'm curious as to why you aren't on that plane."

I place my teacup back on the saucer. "I wish I had taken your advice, but as usual, I didn't." I tell my aunt that Pete and I have been living apart since August. "The day you stopped by to tell me Pete knew I lied about working, well, we got into it, and I said things I shouldn't have said."

"I'm not surprised. I knew Pete's arrival on Thanksgiving Day was as much a shock to you and the children as it was to your uncle and me. Although Christmas went off without a hitch, when we left your house, I mentioned to your uncle something wasn't right."

Minutes after my aunt finishes her sentence, I'm crying. "Do you know how hard it was for me not to run after the car and beg Pete to take me with him?"

My aunt reaches for me. I fall into her arms. "I'm sure it was very hard, sweetie."

"I messed up really bad. I threw it all away, my marriage, my children's happiness. Why didn't I listen to you when you said, 'Once the trust is broken, there's no turning back'? Pete hates me, he hates me."

"*Hate* is a strong word. I don't know what you said to each other, but I don't think Pete could ever hate you."

"Once you hear the truth, you'll understand."

Aunt Sarah gently squeezes my shoulders. "I learned a long time ago, life doesn't come with a map. You can't avoid the bad times and only travel the good."

Seconds later, my aunt rises and says, "I'll be right back." When she returns, she hands me a book, *Gone with the Wind.* My expression questions the meaning.

"Did you ever read it?"

"No. Isn't it, like, a thousand pages? I don't have the patience."

Sitting next to me, my aunt opens the book to the middle and removes several photos. She places one to her heart then hands it to me. The boy in the photo looks familiar. I think Andrew, but the clothes he's wearing are dated. I look to my aunt for an answer.

"That's my son, Eric William James Holland. Looks a little like Andrew when he was that age."

"You had a son?"

My aunt hands me a second picture of her son, a very handsome man, and her around eight months pregnant. I gasp. "You were married, with children?" I immediately think tragic accident. "Why didn't you tell me?"

"It's the Holland way. What we can't change, we bury deep inside, but today I decided it was time to share a part of my life with you. See, your aunt also messed up a few times in her life, so you're not alone."

After hearing the story of my aunt's life, I stare at the picture of her with her family. "You were a handsome family. Did Eric and Margaret's passing destroy your relationship with Lance?"

"No. Death had a way of complicating my life, but I had only myself to blame." My aunt hands me another picture of a baby boy. This one had blond hair and blue eyes. "Uncle George's son. His name was Fredrick George Holland."

"I surmised Uncle George was married through your conversations with my mother, but I didn't know he had a child."

"Yes, Uncle George was married to a sweet girl named Hilda. Fredrick died of SIDS. His passing destroyed their marriage."

"How sad."

All these years, I was cruel and disrespectful to my aunt and uncle, especially my uncle. Now I saw them in a different light. Once they were happy, with families of their own.

Aunt Sarah takes the photo from my hand and smiles, seeing her nephew's sweet face. "Death has always been knocking on our door and messing up our lives. I thought he gave up on us until Patrick died. Your mother had her share as well."

When Aunt Sarah mentions my mother, I immediately say, "David, the doctor I'm seeing, thinks you have the answers to the questions I have about my mother. After hearing your story and Uncle George's, I'd like to know more about your families."

"Why don't we spend today talking about your mother? I'll tell you all I know, and hopefully, I'll have the answers to most of your questions."

"I guess the most important question: Why didn't my mother love me? And please don't try to sugarcoat your answer. I never felt loved by the woman."

My aunt looks bewildered. "I never forgave myself for not calling the day your mother was admitted in the hospital. I wish I could turn back the clock, but there's no going back. I'm so sorry."

"I can't lie, I resented you for not keeping your promise, but I'd be in denial if I said my mother would have wanted me there. You haven't answered my question. Why didn't she love me?"

My aunt sighs. "When our mother died, so did our father, and your mother paid the price. This beautiful baby girl came home to a house filled with grief. If it weren't for Pearl, her caregiver, she could have faded away and no one would have cared." Her voice cracks. "There were times I blamed myself. I should have been there for her. I was her big sister. But deep down I resented her. She was the reason my mother and father were taken from me. When I was older and realized she herself was a victim, I tried to be there for her, but it was too late. She was a loner who rarely showed emotion. Reading was her refuge from the dysfunctional family we created. Then I was off to New York, and Uncle George joined the Marines. I often wondered what life was like for your mother after George and I left. Please don't misunderstand—we were never abused physically, but emotionally we were. Our father was a good man, a hard worker, but after my mother's death, I don't think he was capable of loving."

I interrupt, "My father loved her?"

"He did love her, and she loved him. It was the first time I saw her happy, but it was your father's outward personality that she loved most. In their case, opposites were attracted to each other. Your father saw what we all did. She was beautiful, kind, and caring, a good person."

I lower my head into my hands. Of course, my aunt will defend my mother. She's her sister, and she doesn't want to hurt me more than I'm already hurting.

My aunt lifts my head with her fingertips. "Allison, I'm not trying to find the right words to make you feel better. Your mother was as much a mystery to me as she was to you. I saw your father as her only hope to find what love was all about, and then he was gone."

"But I was here, I was a part of him. If she could love him, why couldn't she love his child?"

My aunt continues, "I've asked myself that question many times after my mother died. Why couldn't my father be the father he was before my mother's passing? Your mother never knew that man, but your uncle and I did, so the loss was just as great as with losing our mother. We came to terms with the cards we were dealt. We accepted the good and overlooked the bad. Your mother loved you. Your wants and needs came before hers. She wanted you to reach your goal and never be a burden. I know there were a few precious moments with her. Hold on to them. Think of that little baby never being held by her family, ignored to create her own world. Think of her as one of the children you work with daily, the neglected ones, who find it so hard to be hugged because they were never hugged."

I want to accept that my mother's life wasn't a piece of cake, but what she did for Patrick proved that the woman could love. "You say she didn't know how to love, but she must have loved Patrick. She kept his secret. Pete told me he was gay, said you knew, my mother knew, everyone knew but me."

My aunt takes a moment before answering. "I think you're confusing love with friendship. During one of your mother's chemo treatments, I was angry with Patrick traveling so often. I said the same to your mother." Taking my hand, she said, "Sarah, there is something you need to know. One year after Patrick and I married, he confessed he was gay. She told me he was going to quit his job, and leave town. She convinced him to stay."

I question, "Why didn't she leave him?"

"When they met, she thought he was handsome, interesting, but I don't know if she was considering marriage. I might have had a hand in pushing her down the aisle. My aunt pauses. "I don't have to tell you how shocked I was, finding out Patrick was leading a double life. As you know, he had a partner in Pittsburg. On and off since college, but during your mother's marriage, this man was a constant. Times were different then. A gay person didn't feel comfortable coming out. They had their careers to think about. I do know that Patrick loved your mother for accepting him."

"How did you manage to remain friends with him once you knew the truth?"

My aunt smiles. "Of course, when I discovered the truth, I confronted your uncle. He calmed me, saying it was your mother's life, not ours, and did I really want to upset the applecart when she was so sick? So as time went on, I saw the devotion. He washed her, held her head when she was sick, carried her when she could no longer walk. How can you hate such a man?" My aunt asks, "If you knew the truth and your mother's decision to remain in her marriage, would you have accepted her decision?"

"No, I would have told her to pack his bags and place them and his sorry ass on the curb, and if she hadn't listened, I would have lost any respect I had for her."

"That's why your mother didn't tell you. Nor did Pete or I. Patrick's life choice didn't change the person he was. When he told his family the truth, they sent him away. He wanted to tell you the truth, but Pete wanted to leave well enough alone. I think Patrick was relieved when Pete's decision was to keep things as they were. He was afraid of your reaction. It meant the world to Patrick to remain a part of your family."

I think of my friends who are gay. Never have I been judgmental of their life choices, but I'm conflicted about my mother's acceptance of Patrick's life choice. More than conflicted, I'm finding it hard to believe that my mother could show compassion to this man who lied to her. Then I'm reminded of the night of my graduation, when she presented me with the bracelet I now wear every day since receiving it. Was I so blind that I didn't see compassion other times in my life, such as her not wanting my life interrupted by her illness?

"You look tired. Did you pack an overnight?"

"I left it in the car."

"You've decided to stay the night?"

"Yes. I have so many questions."

"Tomorrow's another day."

* * * * *

Lying in bed, thinking about my children, I question how this separation, and ultimately divorce, will affect them. Pete is making an effort to keep life as normal as he can. Thanksgiving and Christmas have proved he loves our children more than life itself. He is an exceptional man whom I've managed to destroy.

My cell phone buzzes. I reach for my bag. The book *Gone with the Wind* is lying on top of it. I place the book on the bed and hurry to answer the call.

"Hello."

"I'm calling to let you know we arrived an hour ago." Pete has waited a whole hour before letting me know they arrived safely. Another change I'll have to accept. Normally, he would have called as soon as he was allowed to use his cell phone. I hear excitement in the background. Dolores is saying how tall Andrew is getting, and Gale is teasing Julia.

"Do you want to speak with the kids?"

"I'll speak with them tomorrow. It sounds like they're having a good time with Dolores and Gale."

"Okay, then, I'll have them call you tomorrow."

Pete hangs up, and I cry. Hearing the happiness in my children's voices upsets me. Are they happy to be away from their mother and all her issues? Don't they care I'm a broken woman with a broken heart?

The buzzing of my phone startles me. "Hello."

"Hello, Mom. Why did you hang up without speaking with Julia and me?"

The tears begin to fall. "I'm sorry Andrew, but it sounded like you were having a good time with you aunts."

Julia yells into the phone, "Mom, Aunt Gale says my jeans are really cool."

"Julia, give me five minutes. Mom, how are you? Did you spend the day with Aunt Sarah?"

"I did. It was great. I'm spending the night. I might decide to stay a few days."

Andrew whispers, "I'm glad. I don't want you to be alone. Dad said we'll be home for New Year's Eve. We want to spend it with you."

"You'll be home for New Year's Eve? I'm so happy! I miss you guys, and never forget, I love you with all my heart and soul."

"Same to you. Julia wants to talk. I'll call you tomorrow night."

"Good night."

"Mom, did you hear? Aunt Gale is jealous of my jeans! We are going shopping tomorrow to buy her a pair. Thanks, Mom, you're the best!"

"I bet they won't look as good on Aunt Gale, but don't tell her I said that."

Julia laughs. "Mom, Andrew told you we're coming home on New Year's Eve? Andrew and I insisted Dad take us home. We didn't want you to be alone, not on New Year's."

"Thank you. I was wondering how I was going to ring in the New Year without my two most favorite people in the entire world."

* * * * *

After wishing my daughter a good night and telling her how much I love and miss her, I lay my head on the pillow and drift off to sleep. Waking at two in the morning, unable to sleep, I reach for the book, "*Gone With the Wind*", which slipped onto the floor. After glancing at the photos and letters, place so carefully in the middle of the book, I begin to read the story of *Scarlett O'Hara's* life.

CHAPTER TWENTY

Sarah

At four thirty that afternoon, I check on Allison. She is sound asleep, a sleep she badly needs. I linger in the doorway, watching her sleep, thinking what a beautiful woman she is, as beautiful as her mother. I wish I had found the words that would have convinced the child her mother truly loved her. There were times I questioned the love my sister felt for the child. I never saw the delight in Audrey's face, as the one I experienced the first time I saw my son. I sigh, closing the door. I hope someday she'll find peace and be able to forgive her mother, as I did my father, for a persona developed through no fault of their own.

George arrives home at five with dinner. "I brought fried chicken with all the fixings. I was tired of bland meat and vegetables."

"I'll allow it this time, but keep in mind, fried chicken is a heart attack waiting to happen."

George smiles. "I'll keep that in mind. Where's Allison?"

"She's upstairs, asleep. She's had a hard day. Wouldn't be surprised if she sleeps through the night. I'll prepare a plate for her."

"So what's going on between her and Pete?"

"They've separated for now."

"She told you they separated, and you're not freaking out?"

"I'm not happy their marriage is in trouble, and I'm not sure exactly what happened, but I think before the week is over, I'll have a better idea."

I tell George what I told Allison about our past lives. "She was shocked to hear we had families of our own."

"I bet she was. She always thought me boring, and I have to agree, I am boring."

"She should have known you in high school."

George and I reminiscence about our high school days over dessert and coffee. At nine o'clock, we retire for the night. I check on Allison one last time.

I notice the book on the floor. I'm reminded of the photos that I'm sure she'll look at over and over and the letters Lance and I wrote each other before he married Constance. I'll need a good night's sleep to answer all her questions. Even though I feel exhausted and am sure I will drift off as soon as my head hit the pillows, I lie awake thinking of Lance.

* * * * *

I loved the hustle and bustle of my life in Pittsburgh. Michael was traveling overseas quite often. Three years earlier, the parent company moved their headquarters to China.

Audrey's engagement to marry Albert Marks was making me homesick for my family, but I wasn't sure I was ready to move back into my father's home. I went home for Audrey's wedding in October. Michael was in China, unable to make it back. George met our friends in New York, and together they traveled to Cleveland.

I cleared my calendar for three weeks, two before the wedding and one after to spend time with George. Arriving home, I was shocked to find my father had aged since Christmas. I questioned Audrey regarding his health. She said our dad contracted the flu in August, which lingered on for a month. I immediately made an appointment with Dad's doctor, who gave him a clean bill of health.

I told my father I wanted him to do nothing but rest now that I was home to help Audrey with the final wedding plans. When the weather permitted, my dad and I took long walks to the park. We'd find a bench and talk.

"Are you feeling better?"

"I'm fine, Sarah, just a little tired is all. Did you stop by the boardinghouse to make sure they are ready for Doris and her family? She always made sure our stay at the Hilton was top-notch. I want her to feel just as comfortable here in our hometown."

"Dad, it's not called a boardinghouse, it's now known as a bed-and-breakfast."

"You can't teach old dogs new tricks. To me it will always be the boardinghouse."

I smiled, moving my hand over his. "I'm sure Doris hired outside help to see that everyone is comfortable but courteous not to offend Craig." Craig and his wife Camille bought the boardinghouse, now known as the bed-and-breakfast, ten years earlier.

My father questioned, "Over the years, you remained close with the Clark family and your friends, especially Lance and Constance. Is it hard, Sarah, to be a part of their lives?"

"Dad, are you worried about me seeing Lance and Constance? For heaven's sakes, I'm godmother to their daughters. Our paths have crossed quite a few times over the years."

"I know, but what you and Lance had was something special, just like your mom and I."

I never lied to my father, but today I had. I was anxious to see Lance and, of course, Constance. I had wondered over the years what life would have been like for Lance and me if I had returned to New York. There were no guarantees that he and I would have been happy. I might have stepped off the train and jumped back on, knowing I couldn't face the past. I was certain that life for us had taken the right turn. He and Constance found love, they were happy, and they adored their children.

Audrey Holland married Albert Marks on October 24. As maid of honor, I proudly walked down the aisle, making eye contact with George. We smiled, thankful our baby sister had found this wonderful man who truly loved her.

When Audrey entered the church, everyone gasped. She was radiant. The next time I would see an equally beautiful bride would be when Allison married Pete. After my father kissed his daughter and presented her to her future husband, my brother-in-law, the salt of the earth, whispered, "Forever I will love you, Audrey, this day and forever, my beautiful bride."

Lance found me staring at my sister and her husband while they greeted their guests. "I know how long you have waited to see your sister happy."

I turned and faced Lance, thinking how handsome he looked in his tux. "Lance, where's Constance?"

"She's dancing with Christopher. I left the two little ones to dance with each other. Doris has the baby. I slipped away when no one was looking."

I laughed. "They are beautiful, those goddaughters of mine. Emily is growing tall. Before you know it, she'll be dating."

"Dating, not on my watch."

"Spoken like a true father."

"Sarah, I'm happy to find you alone. We are going to visit the grave tomorrow. We were wondering if you'd like to come along."

I smiled. "Thanks for asking. George and I were planning on going next week. We want to clear the grounds before the winter."

Lance accepted my response. He then asked, "How is Michael?"

"He's doing well, traveling more than he wants to," I said. "Audrey needs me. I believe it's time to cut the cake. Let's go find that family of yours."

* * * * *

As I was sitting on the sofa, looking through a catalog for the perfect gift for Audrey and Al's one-year anniversary, the phone rang. Michael whispered, "Sarah, Constance is on the phone." Michael covered the phone. "She's upset."

I took the phone from Michael. "Constance?"

"Sarah." Michael was right; Constance was upset, and crying.

"Constance, what's wrong? Is it Lance?"

"No, Sarah. Doris had a massive stroke."

Twelve hours later, I entered Doris's hospital room. I greeted the family, asked about Doris's condition, and then waited in the hall with Sally, Herb, and Jimmy.

Jimmy hugged me and said the doctors didn't think Doris would make it through the night. I asked Constance if I could spend a few precious moments with Doris. Constance had everyone move to the back of the room, allowing me privacy. I took Doris's hand in mine. "Doris, you're more than a friend. I want you to know I thank God every day for bringing us together." I placed a kiss on her hand and continued, "If tonight is the night you will be with our loved ones in heaven, I have one request, my dearest friend. Kiss my son and daughter. Let my family know that I still and will always love them with all my heart and soul, as I do you."

My father, Audrey, and Al attended Doris's funeral, flying back from New York. Audrey announced she was expecting. "One leaves this world, one enters."

Allison was born on May 5, 1971, at seven pounds, six ounces, twenty-one inches long. I fell in love all over again.

Four years later, Michael was offered a position in China. He wanted to take the job, so I saved him a lot of anxiety when I announced I was giving up corporate law and returning home. I rented an apartment not far from the local college. I became certified to teach law. I was offered a job and taught three classes, leaving enough time for me to take complete charge of our father's care, allowing Audrey time to care for her family. Shortly after my returning home, Al died. The newspapers would call his actions heroic.

George retired from military life when Allison turned thirteen. He chose to move in with our father. Two years later, I would also move back home.

One year after moving back home, I received the shock of all shocks. Constance called, saying she was diagnosed with stage III breast cancer and needed me. I flew back and forth from Cleveland to New York, supporting my friend and her family. Two years later, the cancer would take Constance's life. On the day Dad, Audrey, and I were to return home, I received a call from Christopher. "Aunt Sarah, we are worried about Dad. He won't leave his room."

I gently knocked on the bedroom door. "Lance, can I come in?"

Lance opened the door. I had been in this bedroom many times over the past two years, comforting Constance, but today it felt awkward being alone with Lance in this room.

Lance walked to the window and stared out. I went to him. I wondered again why one found solace looking toward the heavens for answers.

"You think she's out there somewhere? Each time someone in our lives is taken from us, we look to the heavens for a sign that all is well. She's fine, Lance. She's no longer in pain."

Lance began to cry, walking away from the window and me. He sat on the bed, and I stood over him, avoiding to sit on the bed he shared with Constance. Taking his hand in mine, I said, "Lance, there are children who are worried sick about you. So am I."

Lance removed his hand from mine and placed his head in his hands. "I can't live with myself. She knows."

I asked, "Who knows?"

"Constance." Lance faced me. "Sarah, do you believe after we're gone, we know what's in the hearts and minds of the ones we left behind?"

I softened my voice. "I want to believe we can."

Lance stood, taking my hands in his. "I was a good husband to Constance. I was devoted to making her happy. She's was the mother of my three beautiful girls, and I loved her, but I didn't love her the way I loved and will always love you."

I pulled back my hands, placing them over my mouth. After a few minutes, I found the strength to say, "Lance, it was clear from your letters that you and Constance were in love. You wrote me to say you wanted to marry her."

Lance's voice slightly elevated as he explained, "When I came back, I was a broken man. I knew when you didn't get on that train with me that there was a good chance you never would. At first, there was nothing between Constance and me but a strong friendship. As time passed, we kissed, held hands, and there was Christopher. Sharing in his life helped me go on without Eric. Then your letter arrived. You gave your blessing for us to marry. I knew then you were never coming back. Constance was confident that together we could find happiness."

"Your letter said you were marrying Constance. How did you expect me to respond?"

Lance stared into my eyes. "In my letter, I begged if there was a chance for you and me ..." By the expression on my face, Lance questioned, "You never read the entire letter, did you?"

Remembering I hadn't, I said, "No. Reading that you were marrying was enough. Constance wrote that she had fallen in love with you. I thought ..."

Lance sighed. "How ironic. You never read the entire letter. If only you would have read the letter___?"

"I still have the letter, and all the letters you ever wrote me."

"When you get home, finish reading it. Then you will understand why I'm finding it hard to face my children."

That same night, I finished the letter.

> *Sarah, Constance believes we can have a life together. She has been a kind and considerate friend, but my feelings for you haven't changed. I was foolish to ask you to come back to New York and put aside the precious memories we shared with Eric. Say we belong together, and I will live with you anywhere in this crazy world.*
>
> *I can't beg you to love me, but if there is hope, please tell me.*
>
> *In time, Constance will understand that a love as strong as ours can survive even the hardest of times.*
>
> *Sarah, I love you with all my heart and soul. Don't give up on us.*

I placed the letter back in the book. Lance picked up the phone on the third ring. I read the letter I had written to him all those years ago. I told him about the rainbow in the cemetery, how I saw it as a sign from our children that it was time for me to begin my life, except that life wasn't to be with him.

Lance and I spoke often after that night, never asking why. Ironically, death had gotten in the way of Lance and me finding that pot of gold at the end of our rainbow.

One year after Constance's death, Lance and I arranged to meet in California, far away from our families. For two weeks, we took long walks, held hands, leaving the past behind. We talked about the present. We held each other close after making love, searching for the answers to the rest of our lives. We knew marriage was out of the question. Christopher and the girls thought of us as best friends, and above all, we felt we had to honor their mother's memory. My dad, George, Audrey, and precious little Allison were my life, and because of all the pain and sorrow Lance and I had shared, I chose not to bring it back into my immediate family.

We shared a wonderful and filling life over a span of eighteen years without our families' blessing. If Lance's children suspected that our relationship was more than friendship, they never questioned.

I'd visit Lance and the children from time to time as an aunt and friend. The girls married. Emily resided in California, Caroline in Texas, and Amanda in Colorado. Christopher's first marriage ended in divorce, and six years later, he married again. Two years later, his wife gave birth to their only child, a son, Michael Eric Clark Pickett. Christopher moved his family out to the vineyard several years later after retiring. Several years later, Lance joined Christopher and his family. He resided in a small cottage not far from the main house.

Lance and I would sneak away to exciting and exotic places. We never regretted putting the feelings of others before our own. We were happy and in love. Lance was right when he said a love and bond such as ours could only end when we cease to exist.

On a cold and windy day in October, Christopher called to say that morning, he found Lance's body cold and still in his bed.

Another light in my world had grown dark.

CHAPTER TWENTY-ONE

Allison

On Thursday, I return home from my aunts. New Year's Eve is Saturday, so I give myself a few days to digest what my aunt told me about my family and their lives.

Aunt Sarah had loved and lost, and yet she remains strong. I can't imagine myself able to move past all the sorrow and pain and still find the strength to be a caring and loving person. I develop a respect for this woman, my aunt, whom I resented and hated without cause. She learned to love with all her heart and soul. She describes herself as the character Scarlet from *Gone with the Wind*, a survivor, which she was, but Scarlet was selfish and conniving, my aunt neither.

I have several questions the following morning after finding out about my family's secret lives.

I wake that morning finding her in the kitchen. Sunlight filters through the window onto her face. She is beautiful, but most of all, she is happy and content. I know my presence is the cause.

"Good morning."

"Morning. In ten minutes, it will be noon. Are you hungry? I thought we could go out for lunch."

"I need to shower. Where's Uncle George?"

"He's helping his friend Gus repair the roof on his house. He'll be gone most of the day."

"You two are so generous."

"What else do we have to do in our old age? 'Give and you shall receive'—isn't that what the Good Book says?"

I smile. "I guess." Feeling hungry, I say, "I'll be down in twenty minutes. I know a great place to have lunch. They won't rush us."

I take my aunt to an Italian restaurant. After placing our order, I share with my aunt what life was like before Pete and I separated.

"You know all those Saturdays when I said I was working? I wasn't always at the office. I spent a lot of time at the lake where we spread Patrick's ashes."

My aunt adds, "I visited my children's grave every day for two years."

"I don't know how you had the strength to go on after they died, especially Eric."

"A rainbow changed my life, made me realize I didn't want to end up like your grandfather, a shell of a man. No, sir, not me. Lance once said our children wouldn't want that for us."

"What happened to Lance?"

The food arrives. While we eat, my aunt tells the love story that she and Lance finally got to share.

"How did you manage to keep Lance from me? He died when I was in my teens, and I don't believe I've ever met Christopher, his family, or his sisters. Why?"

"When Lance and I made the decision to have a small part in each other's lives, I made the decision to keep that part of my life separate. Neither he nor I ever talked about marrying. His children were happy knowing he had a dear friend to see him through the hard times, and their happiness was all that mattered to us. I believe I did what was best for everyone."

I'm sick inside after hearing my aunt's explanation of how she and Lance set aside their feelings for each other to avoid hurting his children. I didn't think twice about destroying the lives of Pete and my children.

"I read one hundred and fifteen pages of *Gone with the Wind.* Scarlet's strength and determination reminds me of you, but her selfish and conniving ways, that pretty much describes me."

Aunt Sarah reaches across the table. Taking my hand in hers, she asks, "Why are you so hard on yourself?"

"After all I put Pete through, I want nothing more than for him to forgive me, no matter how much I've hurt him. I'd say that's pretty selfish. I've always thought of myself as a good person, yet I can't forgive my own father for running into a burning building to save a boy he didn't know. I can't forgive my mother for not being the mother I needed after my father died."

My aunt sighs. "I couldn't forgive my mother for getting pregnant or my father for getting her pregnant. I hated my sister, your mother, for living, and our mother for dying. I hated my father for turning into a zombie after my mother died. I hated God for taking my children from me. I don't think that's selfish. I'd call it normal. You're the strongest woman I know. It might have taken some time, but you're getting the help you need. Far be it from me to discount your feelings toward your mother, because your feelings are your feelings. She might not have been the mother we picture ourselves having, but she did love you the only way she knew how."

"I can remember a few special moments with my mom before she died. David thinks I should focus on them, try to focus on the positive. My mother didn't beat me, she didn't drink or take drugs, and she could keep a secret."

* * * * *

Before leaving my aunt's house on Thursday, I tell her the whole truth why Pete and I are living apart.

Hearing my story through tears and my cracking voice, she listens without being judgmental or condescending.

When I'm done, my aunt wraps her arms around me, saying, "Allison, you were young, and young people do foolish things. I got pregnant with a married man. Everyone knew he was married but me. Talk about feeling foolish! The end result of my foolishness was Eric. You and Pete have Andrew, and finding out Pete is his father has to be an enormous relief. I can't promise that you and Pete can salvage your marriage, but I do know that you are strong enough to go on with or without him.

* * * * *

Pete calls the following day to say they will be arriving at twelve on New Year's Eve. I thank him.

"Is everything all right? You sound different."

"Everything is fine. How was your vacation?"

"Fine. I'm flying back to Florida on Monday. I won't be back for two weeks."

"All right. See you on Saturday."

Pete drops the kids off at the curb far away from the front door of our home.

New Year's Eve, Aunt Sarah convinces the children and me to attend the church party. The children and I dance until two. New Year's Day, we sleep until eleven. Afterward, we go out to dinner with my aunt and uncle. Pete doesn't stop by to wish us a Happy New Year. He calls the children and doesn't ask to speak with me. Pete's actions are upsetting, but not gut-wrenching painful.

* * * * *

I arrive ten minutes late for my scheduled appointment with David.

"Happy New Year, Allison."

I smile. "Happy New Year."

Sitting across from David, I wait for him to begin our session.

David stares at me for several moments before saying, "Something is different about you."

"Funny you say that. Last time I spoke with Pete, he felt I sounded different too."

"One difference is you're ten minutes late. Traffic?"

"No. I just left the office a little later than usual."

"If there was something pressing at work, you could have called and canceled. I have a one-time no-charge cancellation policy."

"Wow, business must be good if you can afford to write off an hour's fee."

David smiles. "Did Pete spend Christmas with you and the kids?"

"Christmas Day and Christmas Eve."

"Good. Did you plan something special for yourself while the children were in Florida?"

Now it's my turn to smile. "Why don't you come right out and ask if I took your advice?"

David remains silent, waiting for me to continue. "Since Pete didn't offer for me to tag along, I decided to spend several days at my aunt's house. Funny, for a little over a year, I wanted nothing more than to be left alone, but when Pete pulled away from the curb with our children, I wanted nothing more than to be in that car."

"You have to start getting out more. When it's Pete's weekend with the kids, call a friend. Do you have friends who are single?"

"I do, but then I'd have to tell them about my present situation, and I'm hoping in time, Pete and I … well, you get the picture."

"I have to applaud your positive thinking, but keep in mind, Pete can't speak ten words to you. Do you really think you'll get back together before everyone figures out you've separated?"

"Good point." I question David, "You never asked whom I chose to air my dirty laundry to."

"I'm guessing Aunt Sarah?"

I laugh. "What gave it away?"

"I can say, 'Blood is thicker than water,' but JoAnne would never have understood. After all these years, she would have questioned why you chose to tell Pete the truth. And there was the fear that she might have chosen Pete's friendship over yours. Your aunt was the safer choice."

"Far be it from me to disagree, but eventually, I'm going to tell JoAnne the truth, and there is a good possibility I might lose her friendship. My aunt was the safer choice, and the right choice. Aren't you curious to know how she responded?"

"She loves you, Allison. Nothing you do or say is going to change her love for you. We've run out of time. My curiosity will have to wait until our next session."

* * * * *

The children speak with Pete often during the two weeks he is away. JoAnne is asking too many questions. I want to give Pete a heads-up that I'm going to tell JoAnne the truth, but I have put off talking with him because I'm not sure I'm ready.

Andrew hands me the phone. "Dad."

"Pete."

"Hello. I'll be back on Thursday. It's your weekend with the kids, but since I've been away, I was hoping we could work something out. Do you have plans this weekend?"

"Nothing special. Did you ask if they had plans? Mostly, I just drive them to and from a friend's house."

"I told them if it was all right with you, I would like to spend the entire weekend with them, no friends. I've missed them."

I add, "It's hard to accept that we're no longer the center of their universes. Wow, no contact with friends. Are you sure you can handle the mood swings?" Dead silence. "Pete, I wanted to discuss JoAnne and Gary. JoAnne's been asking for a long-overdue couple's weekend, and I've been using your travels as an excuse, but I think it might be time to tell them about our present living situation."

"Gary's been pushing for information. Says JoAnne thinks something might be wrong. He called several times last week. I haven't returned his calls. I really wanted this weekend with the kids. Would your aunt be willing to stay at the house on Friday so we can talk?"

"I can ask. We can talk here. Or I can come to your place?"

"No. Make a reservation for dinner. Text me the restaurant and time."

* * * * *

I call my aunt after speaking with Pete. "Are you free on Friday? If you aren't, is Uncle George available?"

"Your uncle is helping out at the senior center, but I'm free."

"I spoke with Pete. He invited me to dinner."

"He called to invite you out? Like on a date? That's great news!"

"No. When he asked, it wasn't in a pleasant way. It was more like a command."

"Maybe he was nervous?"

"He might want out of this marriage permanently."

* * * * *

I search online for a restaurant. Scrolling down, I spot a restaurant on the lake. Romantic, yes, but not let's-have-drinks-and-then-a-quick-stop-at-the-corner-motel romantic. On second thought, the lake is Patrick's final resting place. I decide on Enzo's, not too romantic, but the tables are far enough apart to have a civil, at times heated conversation.

I text Pete, "Enzo's, 41 Baltic Place. Seven."

I arrive ten minutes early for my appointment with David. He's with a patient, so I spend the time talking with Nancy until the green light appears.

When I say hello, David stares. I ask, "What's wrong?"

"Every week a different change. Last week calm and demure. This week, I sense a slight edge to your demeanor."

I rest my coat and purse on the chair. "Pete invited me to dinner on Friday night."

"Dinner Friday night."

"I mentioned telling JoAnne and Gary about our living situation. He suggested we talk. Maybe he's having second thoughts."

David stares.

"I know what you're thinking. I'm getting my hopes up. Well, maybe just a little, but his voice wasn't all that pleasant when he asked. For all I know, he might have contacted an attorney and wanted to save me the shock when the divorce papers arrive."

David agrees. "That explains the edge."

David listens for forty-five minutes while I tell him my aunt's life before and after her mother's death and what life was like for my mother growing up in the Holland household.

"I've seen your aunt at the field, but I haven't had the pleasure of speaking with her. She sounds like an amazing woman."

"She's one strong lady. She says she owes it all to her mother and Scarlet."

"Scarlet?"

"Three days before my grandmother Erin died, she suggested my aunt read *Gone with the Wind.*" David tilts his head. "Margaret Mitchel's classic novel? Anyway, Scarlett O'Hara, the main character in the book, she was a girly girl but possessed a strong will to survive life's atrocities. My aunt believes, coincidentally, her mother left Scarlet as a role model to get her through the hard times."

"Interesting." David writes in his notepad.

I ask, "Thinking of recommending the book to your patients? Believe me, it works. I'm almost finished with the book."

"How has it helped?"

"Scarlet is conniving, selfish, and ruthless in a loving way. Her decisions, good or bad, she believes, will benefit everyone, but first and utmost, herself. From the first to last page you want to be her."

"I saw the movie, if I'm correct, and the book mirrors the movie. Her self-indulgence cost her Rhett, correct?"

I narrow my stare. "Yes. She lost the man who truly loved her."

"I guess Scarlet is to women what John Wayne is to men."

"She didn't let losing the love of her life stop her from having a life."

"If you are telling me you're ready to begin a new phase in your life, then I guess Scarlet did help." David smiles before continuing, "Last session, you said you confided in your aunt. Did you speak about your mother?"

"Yes. We did speak about my mother and my father. I expressed to her what I've told you. I want to be forgiven more than I want to forgive. She understood how I found it hard to think of my father as a hero rather than the person that deserted me, feeling deserted by her own parents. See, it wasn't easy being a child in the Holland home after my grandmother died. My aunt wished her sister, my mother, had died instead of her mother. My grandfather became a zombie. Uncle George ... well, I really don't know how he felt about my mother. Yesterday, I wondered if my mother blamed herself for her mother's death. Of course, I'll never know." I smile. "All these questions went unanswered because my mother and I never communicated."

"After you had spoken with your aunt, if I asked you to describe your mother in four words again, would your answer be the same?"

My answer is quick. "No. I'd describe her as a victim, survivor, beautiful, very beautiful, but I believe you already knew my answer would change, because my feelings toward my mother have changed."

"Accepting the things we can't understand is a form of forgiveness."

* * * * *

It's seven fifteen. I'm starting to worry Pete isn't going to show. I search my purse for my compact mirror to check my hair and makeup. I apply a hint of lip gloss to my lips. I brush my hands over my dress then touch the back of my hair. I wonder if Pete will notice I'm wearing my hair down, allowing a few curls to frame my face.

Pete enters the restaurant. I wave to get his attention. I control my excitement at the sight of him.

"Sorry I'm late. I got stuck at the office." It's hard to accept the new Pete; the old Pete would have called to explain. The new Pete didn't even text.

"No problem."

The waiter rushes over to get Pete's drink order. He spies the glass of red wine in my hands. "I'll have a martini, dry, three olives. Thanks."

"Would you like tap or bottled water?"

"Tap is fine."

Another change. Pete is curt with the waiter. Long gone was cheerful Pete.

"Rough day at the office?"

Pete doesn't respond. A sword can't cut through the tension Pete is feeling sitting across from me. I feel uncomfortable as well. I don't know this man.

"I spoke with Andrew. Your aunt is at the house."

"Yes, I was lucky she wasn't busy. She and uncle—"

Pete cuts me off. "I know Andrew can be trusted, but I'd rather Julia with an adult."

"Julia? Did something happen at your place?"

"No."

"Then why this sudden concern that Julia can't be trusted?'

"Did I say she couldn't be trusted?"

"If you're holding back telling me something I should know about Julia's behavior—"

Pete cuts me off again. "I told you nothing happened."

The waiter places Pete's drink in front of him. New Pete finishes half the drink in less than a minute.

"Pete, I see how concerned you are about the children. Do you think we need family counseling? I could ask David to recommend someone."

"David who?"

"David Greenberg. He's been a great help to m—"

For the third time, Pete cuts me off. "David Greenberg, Ellen's father? How has he helped you?"

"David Greenberg is my therapist."

"You're fucking kidding me!"

Thank God for the space between the tables. I look around to see if anyone has heard the outburst.

"Do you have a problem with me seeing David?"

Pete lowers his voice. "Of course I have a problem with you seeing David. I know the man, for Christ's sake. Did you tell him everything?"

I can see how my selection of doctors isn't the best choice for Pete. "I'm sorry, I didn't think how this would affect—"

For the fourth time, Pete cuts me off.

"You never think. You do exactly what you want without considering anyone else's feelings."

"You're right, I didn't think, but there's nothing I can do about it now. I went to see David because I felt comfortable talking with—"

Fifth time, I'm cut off. "You feel comfortable telling someone we know how you fucked me over?"

"You wanted to talk. Maybe we should change the subject."

The waiter arrives to take our order. I order dinner; Pete another drink, no food. I'm concerned he's drinking on an empty stomach. I can't allow him to drive home, which I'm sure will cause a scene.

"That's you're second drink. You should order something to eat. I can't allow you to drive home unless you eat something and drink a lot of water."

Pete stares. I stare back. He motions the waiter over. "Cancel the drink. I'll have what she's having and a bottle of sparkling water."

"Thank you."

We sit in silence, waiting for our dinner. Pete pushes the food around his plate, taking one or two bites. It is then I notice. He has lost weight.

After finishing half my dinner, I say, "We were going to discuss JoAnne and Gary. What are your thoughts?"

Pete glares at me. "My parents are getting suspicious. My mother knows something's wrong. I've decided to tell my parents next week."

"My aunt and uncle already know."

"I bet your aunt freaked out."

"Actually, she was very compassionate. I'm sure your mother will be as well."

This time, Pete's glare is frightening. "Did you tell your aunt the truth, or did you make up some lie to appease her?"

"She knows the truth."

Pete squeezes his lips. He's pissed. "You told her you tricked me into marrying you? Did you tell her you were in love with her sister's husband?"

"It was hard, but yes, I told her everything."

Pete looks past me. "Are you going to tell JoAnne the truth?"

"If you'd rather I didn't, but she's never going to accept we fell out of love with each other."

"I'm not telling Gary the truth, or my parents. You can tell JoAnne whatever the fuck you want."

"Pete, I'm sorry. If you'd rather JoAnne didn't know, I understand, but you know as well as I do that she will never accept we just stopped loving each other." I take a moment to apologize. "Pete, I know you're hurting. I treated you badly, and I am truly sorry."

The waiter asks if we've saved room for dessert. Pete responds, "No. Just the check."

"Pete, please, can we talk? If not here, let's go outside."

We head outside. I point to my car, which is parked far away from the restaurant.

I start the car and raise the heat. I'm elated Pete has agreed to speak with me. "I don't know where to start except to say, again, that I hurt you and it's killing me. I've learned a lot about myself since I've been seeing David."

"And what have you learned, that you are a conniving, deceitful bitch?"

"I accept the insult graciously. There is no easy way to explain. I was young, foolish. I had issues with my mother. I created this fantasy life with Patrick, but after you and I married, I never fantasized about him again, I swear on our children. I was committed to you and our family. After hearing of Patrick's death, I panicked. I truly believed you needed to know the truth, that I thought Andrew was Patrick's son."

"Bullshit! You could have kept your dirty little secret hidden in that cold heart of yours."

"I was going to tell you after the funeral. Two weeks turned into a month, then a month into six. I thought about keeping the secret, but I was frightened. If something happened to Andrew and you discovered I lied, what then? I lose you and the children. I couldn't take that chance. I knew if I told you the truth, you wouldn't turn your back on Andrew. How could you, after all these years? Can't you see I was stuck between a rock and hard place? I believe I procrastinated telling you the truth because I didn't want what we had to end. But waiting for the ball to drop … you saw what was happening to me. I was losing it. I needed to tell you. There was no other way."

"You should have told me ages ago. You never loved me. Now all I feel for you is disgust."

"And you have every right." A few seconds of silence before I ask, "Pete, did I ever once, in our marriage, give you a reason to doubt that I loved you? I know I destroyed the trust in our marriage, but if there is a chance for us, would you consider couples therapy? Maybe if you hear from a third party that I'm—"

Pete cuts me off for the sixth time. "Couples therapy? I'm not ready for any kind of therapy with or without you. As far as I am concerned, you can—"

"I can drop dead tomorrow and you'll piss on my grave."

Pete's eyes fill. Without saying a word, he exits the car, slamming the door in my face. I watch his car pull out of the parking lot.

* * * * *

Another session. Nancy motions for me to go in. When I enter the office without removing my coat, I place my hands on my hips and ask, "Let me guess, I look like a woman who hasn't slept in days. Well, I haven't, not more than four hours a night." I raise my fingers, making the quotation sign, saying, "Since my dinner date with Pete."

"Tylenol PM works well."

I remove my coat and slump into the chair. "I'll make a mental note to stop at the drugstore on my way home."

Waiting a few minutes for me to settle down, David begins the session. "At our last session, you had a breakthrough. Am I correct in saying you found a way to forgive your parents?"

"Oh god, David, can't we move on? Yes, I forgave my father for dying. I forgave my mother, my aunt, and my uncle is the only man in my life that cares what happens to me. I've moved on, left the past far behind. Now let's deal with the rest of the shit in my life."

"All right, why do you think you were attracted to Patrick?"

"I was a teenager, he was handsome, and the obvious reason, I hated my mother."

"If your feelings for Patrick evolved from your hatred for your mother, explain to me why you waited so long to tell the man how you felt about him."

"I have no idea why I waited. Am I correct in saying that will be today's topic of discussion?"

David stares, which is a sign he wants me to continue. "All right, I knew sooner or later, I'd have to answer this question: 'Allison, why do you procrastinate?' Because deep down, I loved my mother, and I couldn't find it in me to hurt her. You know what they say, 'We always love the ones that do not return our love.'

"It's obvious to me you loved your mother, and hurting her was the last thing you wanted to do, but what isn't clear is why you didn't break it off with Pete, knowing you were going to confront Patrick."

"I was a conniving bitch—Pete's words. I didn't want to let Pete go."

"But you would have if Patrick had shared your feelings?"

"I guess."

"You guess. You weren't considering keeping both men in your life, were you?"

"Of course not. If Patrick felt the same as I did, I would have broken it off with Pete."

"Patrick's leaving saved your relationship with Pete, correct?"

"After Patrick deserted me, I tried to keep my distance from Pete. I only saw him if JoAnne and Gary were present."

"But you still didn't break it off, but you were going to when you discovered you were pregnant, or would you have had the abortion and continued your relationship with Pete?"

"I wasn't thinking about Pete. My only thoughts were of the baby and aborting it. I had no intentions of tricking Pete into marrying me. I'm not as conniving as Pete thinks. If Pete had not showed up that night, I would have made the appointment, taken care of the problem, and mourned the loss."

"Pete showing up threw a wrench in your plan, but why tell him you were pregnant?"

"He kept asking what was wrong. I don't know why I told him."

"Did you want to keep the baby, Patrick's child?"

"Yes and no. I didn't want to have an abortion. I didn't want to kill my baby, but not because it was Patrick's child. I just didn't want to …"

"So you allowed Pete to change your mind?"

"Yes. I trusted him. I knew if anyone would love my baby, it was Pete. He would never desert me. He loved me unconditionally." I realize at that moment the reason I never broke it off with Pete. "Patrick leaving only proved that he never loved me. It was all a figment of my imagination. So I was free to begin a life with Pete. The baby was all that connected Patrick to me. When he reconnected with the family, I allowed him to be a part of my life because I believed he was Andrew's father. Over time, he was a good friend and grandfather to my children. That is why I'm telling the truth when I say I never fantasized about him once I married Pete."

David leans across the table and offers me a tissue. "Why do you think Patrick's death resurrected the feelings you had as a teenager?"

"I thought he was Andrew's father. If Pete found out the truth other than my confession, my children would have lost all respect for me. I had one choice and one choice only: tell Pete, let him digest that he wasn't Andrew's biological father, and together we would protect Andrew from finding out the truth."

"What if Pete turned away from Andrew?"

"This is Pete we're talking about. He loves that boy. I trusted him with my life, so how could I not trust him with my son's life?"

"I guess you're right. Pete is a protector. He kept the truth from you regarding Patrick's life choice."

"You understand, he wanted to protect his family. He worried that by opening up a can of worms, I would have a million and one questions, why he married my mother, what effect this would have on my children …"

"So Pete made the right decision to keep things as they were. I wonder, if Pete gave his permission, how would you have handle Patrick's sexuality, assuming you slept with the man?"

I know the answer to this question because I've asked myself the same question many times. "I would have dissolved my friendship with him, keeping him far from my family. I would have hated him for endangering my life and my family's."

"Even though you believed he was Andrew's father?"

"If you think I was a basket case after he died, I would have been insane with worry that I had contracted the HIV virus and passed it on to my family. Thank God he wasn't Andrew's father."

"You might have found out sooner that you never slept with Patrick if he had confided in you."

"Patrick could have been bi. He married my mother and consummated their marriage. Considering it's not in my DNA to ask the difficult questions, don't you think I would have worried myself sick knowing my secret was compounding itself?"

David moves on. "It can't be easy knowing that your marriage was destroyed for nothing."

"It's sad. I love my husband, always have, always will, but there is no way I'll ever convince him he was always the one."

David leans forward, tissue box in hand. I pull several tissues from the box. David smiles."Better to have loved and lost, then to have never loved at all."

"You're trying to get me to accept my marriage is over, treasure the good years I had with Pete, and move on? I don't have a chance in hell convincing Pete, do I?"

"Pete has an image of you and Patrick together and a confession of true love. He's human, Allison, deceived by the woman he loved and adored. You want him to set aside his feelings and forgive you for the sake of your family? The only way your marriage is going to be saved is if both you and Pete agree it's worth saving, and we both know Pete is not ready and may never be ready. My advice is to take it slow with Pete. Don't push. You will only drive him farther away. I'd suggest that you think of yourself and a life without Pete."

"David, I know the right thing to do is let Pete go, but I can't. For the first time in my life, I'm not haunted by the past. Why is it wrong for me to want to right the wrong?"

David consoles, "Pete may not be acceptable to you trying to right the wrong, but who am I to say what's right or wrong? I just don't want you sitting around waiting for Pete to come home. When the children are with Pete, make plans with friends. Maybe in time you'll consider dating. Only a suggestion."

I smile. "Know any single guys?"

"One or two come to mind." David smiles. "All kidding aside, I believe you love your husband, Allison. You've convinced me. Maybe if all the planets align correctly, you'll be able to convince Pete. One more question before you go. Did you ever consider that it wasn't your mother you were trying to hurt by your teenage crush?"

The words flow like water down a cliff. "I have. My aunt."

"She was instrumental in Patrick's marriage with your mother. You stated she was the obstacle between your mother and yourself. Do you still feel that way?"

I laugh. "I wanted so much to hurt her. Can you imagine how she would have felt knowing Patrick and I had run off together? And she was the one that wanted him to be a part of our family. It would have killed her. When I was young, that was all I dreamed about, hurting her. Now hurting her would kill me."

"Why?"

"Right or wrong, good or bad, she loves me, always has. But you already knew that."

David nods, acknowledging my statement.

"I'll make you a promise, David. I won't push Pete, but I can't promise that I won't remind him every chance I get about how much in love we were before I messed up. My aunt says, 'True love never dies.' I hope she's right. I do have one thing in my corner: I never slept with Patrick before or after marrying Pete. Thank God."

David smiles. "Scarlett O'Hara, *Gone with the Wind* determination, correct?"

I smile. "You bet."

"Well, as your friend, and Pete's as well, I hope you two work things out."

"Remember, David, I'm half a Holland. We don't give up that easily."

* * * * *

David cuts my sessions to every other week. He says it's time to go out into the world and begin life free of the baggage. Soccer season begins in April, and contact with Pete is next to none. The next stop on this train of truth is JoAnne, but before I jump into the icy water, I ask my aunt if she wants to take a little trip.

President's Weekend, I buy the cheapest shuttle flights I can find to Cleveland. I'm taking my children to visit my hometown, and the grave. Not a glorious trip, but we will fit in a little sightseeing before returning home.

When we arrive at the cemetery, the temperature is comfortable for February. My aunt has purchased a few disposable yard tools, and while Julia, Andrew, and Aunt Sarah clean around the grave, Uncle George goes looking for water pails to hold the flowers we've purchased.

I'm sitting on a blanket, watching my aunt instruct Julia and Andrew what weeds to pull and what are true buds that will blossom in the spring. When Uncle George returns, he takes over for Aunt Sarah, and she comes to sit next to me on the blanket.

"The cemetery is the only part of this old town that hasn't been hurt by the economy," says Aunt Sarah.

"It's a ghost town. The only decent place around is where we are staying."

"The bed-and-breakfast changed hands several times, but it manages to stay afloat."

I look over at the names on the tombstones and spy my mother's, Audrey Holland Marks Pickett. "My mother sure did have a long name."

My aunt laughs. "Did you know your grandmother wanted to name her Rose? I fought like hell with Grandmother Holland. She was appalled by the name." Aunt Sarah sticks her nose in the air. "She wouldn't even agree to call her Audrey Rose. Said the name only fit if you lived in the southern part of the country. She was a tough old broad, my Grandmother Holland."

"Did you like her?"

"Not at first, but in the end, she did find her way into my heart. Grandma Maggie was our favorite." Aunt Sarah looks up at the sky.

"Grandmother Holland knew Grandma Maggie held a special place in our hearts, and in hers as well. Later in life, they were the best of friends."

I smile. "Andrew and Julia love hearing your stories about the family."

Watching as Andrew clears dirt from the name Eric James Holland Pickett, I ask, "Aunt Sarah, did you ever see Eric's father again?"

"I did, right in this very spot. He came to visit his son's grave, and I just happened to be here."

"He didn't want Eric?"

"I never told him I was pregnant. Remember, he was married. Once I met his wife, I knew telling him wasn't an option. I didn't find out he knew about Eric until he showed up here. Seems he kept a close watch on us. Knew I was involved with Lance. He claimed he had no intentions of working his way into Eric's life, but who knows? People mellow as they grow older. Maybe Stephen would have contacted Eric and told him the truth."

"Weren't you afraid that might happen?"

"I wasn't given a hell of a lot of time to worry. Anyway, I took the Scarlet O'Hara approach. If I think about this, I'll go crazy. I'll think about it tomorrow. Tomorrow is another day."

I hug my aunt. We chuckle. Uncle George asks, "What's so funny?"

CHAPTER TWENTY-TWO

Allison

Since Christmas, JoAnne and I have met for lunch several times. Pete has sent an email asking that I wait telling her the news because he hasn't talked with his parents but he will let me know once he has. JoAnne is off to Korea on business and will be gone for three weeks. I have until the end of March before I have to drop the bomb.

One night, as I arrive home from work, the phone rings. I rush to answer it. The caller ID says Cane.

"Hello."

"Hello, sweetheart. It's Mary."

"Mary, how are you?" I know by the sound of her voice that Pete has spoken with his parents. Since the separation, whenever Mary and I speak, I know she's dying to ask if everything is all right. I do my best to keep our conversations light and safe.

"I'm not good, and neither is Hank. Allison, I'm sick over this. Please, sweetheart, tell me everything is going to work out." Mary begins to cry.

"Mary, what did Pete tell you?"

"He told me he moved out of the house. Said you and he haven't been getting along. I blamed him, all this traveling, leaving you alone to care for the children and the house. He was upset with me. Said I didn't know what I was talking about. He stormed out of the house. Hank went after him, but he drove off. He frightened me, Allison. I never saw my son act this way. Allison, is there something you're keeping from me? Dolores says I need to question Pete about his relationship with Emily Carter. Sweetheart, is this woman the problem?"

"Mary, believe me, Emily Carter is not the problem. It's true, the Florida office has put a strain on our marriage. The children were being affected by our arguing. That was why we decided to separate. Did you try Pete's cell phone? Is he all right?"

"I did. He's not picking up."

"We are both taking this separation pretty hard, especially Pete. Mary, your son needs all your understanding. Don't be hard on him. It's more my fault than his. Patrick's sudden death … Pete's issues with the Florida office."

"I love my son, Allison, that is never going to change, but I love you and the children as well. You're my family. I've often bragged to my friends how my daughter-in-law and I are not just family, we are friends."

"Mary, you're so kind, and yes, we are friends and will always be friends, but you have to stop worrying about me. I'm fine. My aunt and uncle have been very supportive of me, and you have to do the same for Pete. The children, although they're not happy their parents aren't together, are coping. Together we'll get through this no matter what the outcome."

"My son needs to know that you and the children are his family, and he will curse the day he let it slip through his fingers."

"I don't have to tell you marriage isn't always fun and games. Sometimes there are bumps in the road. We are finding it a little hard to get over the bumps, but we are trying, I promise."

"Oh, sweetheart, after talking with you, I feel better. My son loves you, you're his rock, and I know you love him. Keep that in mind, and everything will turn out fine."

"And you promise to take care of Pete for us, Mary. I'm counting on you."

After hanging up with Mary, my children find me crying at the kitchen table. They comfort me with hugs and kisses.

* * * * *

The following day, I email Pete. "Spoke with your mother last night. She was calm after we spoke. I hope all is well. I wanted to get your opinion about having the children speak with someone."

Three hours later, I receive an answer. "Speak with David. I'm sure he can recommend someone."

The following week, I enter David's office, and on my seat is a Congratulations balloon.

I smile. "What's with the balloon?"

"Please sit."

When I sit, I notice a cupcake with a candle. "It's not my birthday."

"No, but it is graduation day."

"Graduation day?"

"I'm releasing you, Allison Cane. Go, be free, live your life to the fullest, smell the coffee, hear the birds singing, the wind blowing softly through the trees …"

"Enough. Is this your way of saying you're kicking my ass out the door?"

"That's right. Now, turn around, bend over. I've never kicked a patient before."

An overwhelming feeling of helplessness invades me. "David, I don't think I'm ready."

"You are ready. You've been ready. In the last three visits, we talked about Ellen and Andrew, Julia's new outfits. I told Nancy not to charge you for the last two visits."

"But we haven't discussed how I'm going to resolve this issue with Pete. What about the children? I was going to ask if you knew a child physiologist."

David searches his black book and hands me a business card. "Dr. Jewel. I'll give her a call on your behalf. She'll probably want to meet with you first. You'll like her."

"David, you didn't answer my question. What about my problems with Pete?"

"Allison, you'll be wasting your money. We can sit here and discuss Pete until we are blue in the face, but it will not resolve the issue between you. Both of you have to be willing to try. We've discussed this many times."

"David …"

"Allison, if you were acting like a lovesick woman, there would be no balloon or cupcake. I know from our conversations, you haven't picked up the phone and begged Pete to come back. You made the decision to put your children's needs before Pete's and your own. You are in a different place than Pete. Once things settle down with the Florida office, I hope he is smart enough to find a therapist of his own."

* * * * *

I place a call to Dr. Jewel's office and arrange to meet with her. David is right; I'm impressed with Dr. Ruth Jewel. Julia and Andrew will meet with her separately. If and when she needs Pete or me to attend, she will contact us. I verify with Pete if I can share his cell phone number and email address with Dr. Jewel. When I receive his reply, I forward the information.

Soccer practice is in full swing. I anticipate seeing Pete at the field on Saturday. On Thursday, arriving home from work, I find Pete waiting for me at the front door.

"Why didn't you go in? The kids should be home."

"They're out to dinner with your aunt and uncle."

"My aunt never called—"

"I called your aunt. I need a few minutes of your time."

"Of course, come in."

Walking to the kitchen, I announce, "I picked up fried chicken for dinner. There's plenty. Are you hungry?" Before Pete could answer, I grab two plates, drinking glasses, and utensils. I place the chicken and sides between us. "What can I get you to drink? I'm having a glass of white wine."

"White wine is fine."

From the corner of my eye, I watch as Pete looks around the house. I know he misses living here. When I sit, I say, "Are you going to eat with your coat on?"

Slightly Pete's lips move up. A smile. I can't help myself. I smile back. Pete removes his coat.

"Dig in. Where are the kids having dinner? No, let me guess, the Pancake House? Aunt Sarah loves that place."

Another smile.

"Your smile gave it away. The woman loves her pancakes."

"Your aunt and you are getting along finally."

"I have one better. I really, really like my uncle. He tries to be all macho, but he's a big old pussycat."

Pete fills his plate, and slowly he begins to relax. It feels right having my husband here with me. My eyes fill. I lower my head and pat my napkin to my cheeks. Sipping my wine, I ask, "So what brings you to our neck of the woods?"

"I wanted to ask about the kids' therapy. How's that going?"

"At first, Andrew was against it. I told him if he just gave it five visits, I wouldn't nag him about his schoolwork for two weeks. He hasn't complained about going. Julia, on the other hand, thought it was a great idea. Give Julia a chance to run her mouth, and she's as happy as a pig in shit. Sorry." I smile.

Pete nods in agreement. I continue, "I can't ask them how it's going. Dr. Jewel said that's a no-no. If they want to share, they will. She said if something was terribly wrong, she'd contact us."

"I'm available whenever she needs me," says Pete.

"I told her you travel. She'll work with you."

"I will be traveling less now that the Florida office is open and operating."

"Oh, Pete, that's great news."

"You know it's the busy season until the end of April, so there'll be a trip or two, but nothing major."

"We did a pretty good job on this chicken. Coffee? I have cookies."

"Coffee, please. Allison, I also stopped by to talk with you regarding …" Pete reaches into his coat pocket and pulls out a white envelope. My stomach cramps. He places several pages before me. I look closely. A statement, not divorce papers.

"What's this?"

"The kids' college fund."

I look it over. Staring at Pete, I say, "Do I need to sign something?"

"Did you notice the balance?"

Looking at the balance, I notice the account has depleted by $250,000. "I thought we decided on a conservative approach?"

"We did. I borrowed money to get the Florida office off the ground. Next month I will deposit $100,000 back into the account."

I try to find the words to make this right. "I understand. With what happened between us, you weren't able to look me in the face, much less ask if you could borrow against the children's college account."

"Pete avoids discussing the past." I smile.

"I'm not worried. The kids have enough money. Did you forget I inherited Patrick's estate? I sure didn't need the money, so I created a trust for the kids."

Pete's mood hardens. Realizing I mentioned Patrick, I freeze but quickly regain my composure. I shouldn't be afraid to speak Patrick's name in front of Pete. Patrick existed; he was a part of our lives, and his name will come up now and then.

"I don't need your inheritance to pay for my kids' college."

"I know. I was just saying, if we ran into a problem, we could always use the money Patrick left me. I'm still wondering why he didn't leave it to his partner." I wait for a reaction from Pete. He's wondering how much I know about Patrick's life. "You did know about his partner? He lives in Pittsburgh. When Patrick was married to my mother, he was leading a double life. Of course, my mother knew. She was fine with it. Long story. Did he ever mention Bruce to you?"

Pete doesn't respond.

"Technology. I found him on Facebook. Seems like a nice guy, not as good-looking as Patrick, but I guess opposites attract." Dropping the subject, I say, "I have no doubt you will come up with your share of our children's college education. And so will I."

Pete nods, saying, "I don't think either of us is going to have to dig too deep into our own pockets. As I said, the company will pay back more than half before Andrew sets foot in college."

* * * * *

I sit in Dr. Jewel's office, waiting. She has called several days earlier to say she needs to meet with me. I'm nervous. This nervous feeling I relate to when JoAnne and I were called to the principal's office for drawing ugly faces on Sheila Frost's locker.

To calm myself, I go over the list in my mind of things I have to do today. Julia has soccer practice at five, I will drop Andrew off at Sean's, and the science project they are working on is due on Monday. My cell phone buzzes. The assistant gives me a look, so I whisper, "Hello."

"I'm back."

"JoAnne, can I call you back?"

"I'm going into a meeting in five minutes. I want to come out this weekend, girls' weekend. I'm leaving early on Friday. Only been home one day, and Gary and the boys can't wait to get rid of me."

"I can't do it this weekend. I'm hosting a bridal shower on Sunday for Kathy."

"Is that this weekend? Well, I could crash the party, but I really wanted you and me to spend the weekend together, just us girls. I was hoping you could send Pete and the kids off somewhere."

The following weekend is Pete's weekend with the kids. "What about next weekend?"

This Saturday, I have arranged to have drinks with a few single friends, claiming with Pete traveling so often, I need a night away from the kids. This will be the third time I've joined one or two of my friends for a drink.

"All right, next weekend. I'm taking the train at four. Can you pick me up at the station?"

"Of course. I've got to go. Love you."

"Love you too."

When I hang up, I smile at the assistant, who is annoyed I answered my phone. "Sorry, it was important."

I'm glad when the office door opened, as it takes the attention from me, placing it upon the new arrival. I'm surprised to see it's Pete.

"Pete, I didn't know you were going to be here."

"Dr. Jewel called earlier in the week."

"Same here. I thought she would see us separately, but I guessed wrong."

The assistant motions for us to go in.

"Hello, Mr. Cane. Allison, nice to see you again."

We sit next to each other, but far enough apart to avoid any part of our bodies touching. Dr. Jewel notices.

"I wanted to see you today to talk about the children. I've met with Andrew and Julia separately and two sessions together.

I interject, "Julia mentioned she held back talking too much so Andrew wouldn't tease her when the session was over."

Ruth smiles. "She is a chatty one, but chatty in this case is good." She turns to Pete. "Mr. Cane, we've never met. Would you mind if I begin with you? Any problems with the children when they spend the weekend with you?"

"Are you asking because they said there was?"

"It's no surprise the children aren't comfortable being displaced."

"I think I did a good job making my place feel like home. Fifty-four-inch TV, Xbox—what more do teenagers need these days?"

Pete's nonchalant response doesn't go unnoticed with me or Dr. Jewel.

"You realize the children don't think of your apartment as their home? Their home is the home you shared as a family."

Pete doesn't take his scolding with a grain of salt. "They seem happy when they're with me. Isn't that what we all want, for them to be happy? It's not like I pick them up from school on Friday and lock them in the apartment for the weekend. I plan day trips, things they like to do, no different from when we lived together."

"And the children enjoy their time with you, no complaints there. Feeling displaced is a normal reaction from children of divorced parents."

I speak out. "We're not divorced, we're separated."

Dr. Jewel corrects herself. "Separated parents."

Pete speaks directly to Dr. Jewel. "I'm not discounting my children's feelings, but I'm not giving up my time with my kids. So what do you suggest I do to make them feel comfortable?"

Dr. Jewel smiles. "If I suggested you spend less time with your children, I would have to rip up the pigskins hanging on the wall. No, my suggestion would be to change the pickup and delivery process. Instead of picking the children up at school, give them time to go home. Pete, may I call you Pete?" Pete nods. "Pete, on Sunday, when they return home, walk them to the door. Allison, if Pete needs to stop in, for whatever reason, do you have a problem with him coming into the home?"

"Absolutely not. It's still Pete's home."

I can feel the heat radiating off Pete's body.

"Pete, I would like to quote Andrew during one of our sessions. 'Dad drops us at the curb like Monday's trash.'"

Dr. Jewel waits for a response. I need to defend Pete's actions. "Dr. Jewel, Pete feels uncomfortable seeing me. What can we do to make this right? I could find things to do on Friday and be out on Sunday when they return?"

"They will see right through your actions, Allison. No, you will have to come up with a better solution. Pete, it is obvious to the children and me that your seeing Allison makes you uncomfortable. Do you have any suggestions on how we can make your being together easier on the children?"

Pete reaches his boiling point. "This is the first time I'm hearing that my children feel I'm treating them like 'Monday's trash.' I'll need a few days to think about a better solution. I'll email you." Pete stands, grabs his coat, and heads for the door.

I whisper, "I'm sorry." I run after Pete.

In the parking lot, I call, "Pete, I can't run in these heels! Damn it, stop acting like a baby, for Christ's sakes!" Pete turns. I catch up.

"Thanks. There's a coffee shop across the street. Do you have time to talk?"

"I don't want coffee. If you want to talk, talk."

I sigh and roll my eyes. "If it makes you feel any better, I didn't know Andrew felt like trash. I'm just as upset as you are. I don't think you should be driving when you're so upset."

Pete looks up. "Dr. Jewel made it sound like it was my fault." Pete defends himself, "I'm treating my children like Monday's trash? What a joke! They should only know how hard it is for me to look at you after what I know. My own mother is blaming me, says I put work before you and my children. Dolores thinks I'm having an affair. She put my father up to asking me. He said he knew how easy it was for a man to become infatuated with an attractive woman. He hoped I hadn't stepped over the line."

I reach for Pete's arm. He pulls away, saying, "You come out smelling like a fucking rose when you … Why the fuck didn't you get help before you destroyed us?"

I begin to cry. "I swear, if I could go back, I would, but I can't. Pete, seeing you like this is eating me up inside!"

Pete stares. His eyes grow soft. "Why, Allison? Why wasn't my love enough?"

"Are you going to believe me if I tell you it was and still is enough? I love you. I miss us and what we had. I'm begging for a second chance. I'm willing to work on our marriage. Won't you consider couples therapy?"

"I can't talk about this." Pete turns and begins to walk toward his car. I run after him and grab his arm. He turns.

"Pete, I have to make this right. You can move back home. I should have been the one who left, not you. It's not right that I get to see the children every day, and you only every other weekend. It's not right."

Pete's response is quick. "Haven't we fucked up the kids enough? Now you want me to agree to take their mother from them?"

"You're their father. They need you as much, if not more, than they need me. You have always been our rock."

"I'll call Dr. Jewel in a few days. I've gotten to a point where I can talk to you without being sick to my stomach. I'm sure I can handle seeing you inside and outside the house. I've got to go."

"Pete, won't you give me a chance to explain why I was so screwed up? Please?"

"I know your childhood, your adult life sucked. Your mother was as cold as ice, and you were in love with your stepfather, the father of your son. When you lost him, you lost everything."

Pete walks away. I run after him. "Pete, please listen to me. The love of my life is alive and well. I want to spend the rest of my life with him. I'm not fragile. I made a mistake. I've changed … please."

Pete doesn't stop. He reaches his car and gets in. I move to the side, allowing him to drive off. Walking toward my car, I notice people have stopped to watch. I get into my car. Hitting the steering wheel, I ask, "God, please help me. Please help me."

* * * * *

Friday, Pete tells the kids to take the bus home after school and he'll pick them up at six. He rings the bell. Andrew answers the door. I'm carrying a laundry basket when I pass him. I say, "Hi." Julia passes me on the steps. When she reaches the bottom, I tell my kids to have a good weekend.

Ascending two more steps, I hear Pete say, "I'll be right out. I need to talk to your mother."

I stop in my tracks.

"I'm going to bring the kids back at four on Sunday. I think we can trust them to stay alone for a few hours. I was thinking we'd go to the diner to talk."

I smile. "I'm hosting a bridal shower for Kathy on Sunday. Four might be a little early."

"Kathy's getting married?"

"She is, June 6."

"Does six work?"

"If everyone isn't gone by six, I'll kick them out."

*****

Pete drops the kids off at six. I kiss them hello and goodbye and tell them I'll be home in several hours. Pete opens the car door for me. I get a warm feeling in my stomach, a sign that old Pete has emerged. I begin the conversation. "Before I forget, I mentioned to the kids, if they wanted to spend a day or two with you during the week, it was fine with me. Also, I could pick them up on Sunday, and maybe I could come up and see your place?"

Pete doesn't respond.

The diner is a short distance from our house, and we drive in silence the rest of the way.

Ordering two cups of coffee and a Danish, I suddenly feel uncomfortable sitting across from my husband.

Stirring his coffee, Pete says, "The kids did tell me that you said it was all right if they wanted to spend a day or two at my place during the week. I told them they shouldn't feel obligated or change their schedules for me." Pete places the spoon on the table. "It would be kind of nice to spend more time with them now that I'm not traveling as much. Whatever makes them comfortable." Pete adds, "It was a little awkward the last time I was at your home, our home. I guess as time goes by … but having you come by my place doesn't work for me."

I make light of the situation. "You don't want me to see how messy your apartment is?"

"Allison, I know you're trying, but I'm not ready for any of this."

"I understand. I've asked myself several times, if the shoe were on the other foot, how would I feel? Exactly the way you're feeling. I deeply hurt you, and I have to let you go."

My saying I have to let him go hits a nerve. "I know you were hoping I'd give you a chance to explain. This might sound harsh, but fool me once, all right, fool me twice, not happening. I'm not ready to hear your bullshit about you having this amazing revelation that it was always me. I'm getting used to the way things are. I told my family I'm not having an affair, and if they don't stop the nagging, they can forget they have a son or a brother. They got the message loud and clear." Pete is gaining strength from our separation. I'm losing hope of a reconciliation. "What I would like to know is why you never broke up with me, knowing how you felt about Patrick."

"If you think whatever I'm going to say is bullshit, why ask?"

"I'm curious."

"I thought about breaking up with you several times."

"What stopped you?"

"I didn't want to let you go. It's as simple as that. And don't ask what I would have done if Patrick weren't gay and returned my love. I probably would have made the biggest mistake of my life. I was a teenager when I fell in love with Patrick. Heck, he was the only one that ever showed an interest in me. I was out to hurt the people I thought had hurt me. Patrick was that weapon. Thinking I slept with him and assuming I was carrying his child was a fucking nightmare after he walked away. How could I, the levelheaded Allison, even consider falling for her stepfather?"

"When I left the house that day, I had to stop the car several times to vomit. The thought of you and Patrick together was turning my stomach. I hated myself for loving you."

"You're forgetting one thing: I never slept with Patrick."

"You're forgetting I was there that night. You desperately wanted him to make love to you, not me."

Crying, I say, "Stop, I can't hate myself more than I already do. Pete, I swear I was faithful to you after we married. Patrick had a place in our family as the children's grandfather."

"Fifteen years, Patrick was a part of our family. Are you telling me you never looked at him or our son and wondered, 'What if?'"

"I swear I never gave it a second thought. When Patrick left, rejecting me for reasons unbeknownst to me, you were there. You loved me and the baby inside of me. Fate stepped in and chose you, and I never regretted one day of my married life with you. Believe me or not, I love you, and will love you till the day I die."

Pete doesn't look at me. Staring off in the distance, he says, "It's too late for us. The children should not suffer. I'm going to put my feelings aside for their sake."

* * * * *

Upon entering the house, I shout, "I'm back!" adding, "I'm tired. I'm calling it a night." Lying awake, alone in the room I shared with Pete, I softly cry into my pillow. The marriage is over. There is no going back. Pete will have to deal with seeing me until our children are off and on their own. How will I survive without him?

When Pete picks up the kids the following weekend, I tell him JoAnne needs to know the truth. I can't put her off any longer.

That same week, we get our first report from Dr. Jewel. It's no surprise that our children are affected by the separation, but in her professional opinion, they are dealing with the situation. She isn't surprised by their hoping for a reconciliation. If we are thinking divorce, we should start a dialogue with the children. In this case, honesty is highly recommended. She suggests counseling for Pete and me so we aren't blindsided by the change in our children's personalities hearing the news.

I laugh at her last suggestion. If only she knew Pete's feelings toward therapy.

The train pulls into the station at five thirty. JoAnne waves. Opening her arms, she pulls me in for a hug. "I've missed you! Where are we eating? I'm starving."

"I made a reservation at Pierre's, six thirty."

At Pierre's, JoAnne removes her coat, and the men at the bar stare. As we pass the bar, she sways, walking toward our table. Two extremely distinguished men ask if they can buy us a drink.

"No, thank you. It's ladies' night. Men are excluded."

At the table, I ask, "Are you ever going to grow up?"

"No. Why should I? I'm not dead. Anyway, those guys don't stand a chance, not with the hunk I have waiting for me at home."

"Well, you sure dress to please. Did you think they wouldn't notice you?"

"You don't look too shabby in the number you're wearing. Doesn't it make you feel good to know we still have it?"

I lift the menu. "Oh, put that down. I'm not ready to eat. I want a martini." JoAnne smiles at the waiter. He rushes over.

"My friend and I would like a dry martini, three olives for her, four for me." JoAnne winks at the waiter. He smiles back. I interrupt the flirtation.

"Can you make mine an apple martini, no olives? Thank you."

"I haven't seen you since February. It's almost May. How was your Easter?"

"Easter was good. Spent it with my aunt and uncle. I took the week off, and Aunt Sarah and I spent a lot of time shopping with Julia. She never seems to have enough clothes."

"She's a chip off the old block—that's my block, not yours. Therapy has done wonders for you. You're finally able to mention your aunt without smoke coming out of your ears."

The waiter arrives with our drinks. JoAnne smiles, and the waiter smiles back. "He likes me. Maybe we can take him back to your place. You did get rid of Pete and the kids?"

"Did you forget he doesn't have a chance in hell? Not with Gary waiting in the wings? To answer your question, they're spending the weekend at the Cape."

"Music to my ears! How's life with Pete back home? Gary said he's not traveling as much. Heard Emily Carter is doing a great job. Have you met her?"

"No."

"She was in town last weekend."

I don't respond. JoAnne finishes her drink and motions for another. "Gary said there was a company dinner. Didn't you go?"

My head is spinning, knowing that Emily was in Connecticut last weekend. Now I have an image of Emily and Pete together. "JoAnne, Pete and I are separated."

JoAnne stares. "What did you say?"

"We're separated, as in we are not living under the same roof."

The waiter places another drink in front of JoAnne. Before he clears our table, JoAnne asks, "He's fucking that Emily Carter! When

I get my hands on Gary, I'm going to strangle him! I told him not to recommend her for the job. I would never allow that woman anywhere near my husband. I hope you called the bitch."

I wonder why so many people assume Pete is having an affair after hearing we've separated. "Maybe I'm the one having an affair."

"Pete's a man, he's weak. She's a cougar. Women like her take what they want and don't care who gets hurt."

"Did she strike you as a cougar?"

"No. She was sweet, but I've met a lot of sweet women who are sluts. How did you find out? You followed him to Florida and caught them in the act? I knew something was wrong." JoAnne eyes my expression. "He came right out and told you? That doesn't sound like Pete." Before I can explain, JoAnne tries to defend Pete. "Sweetie, he isn't the first man that strayed, and I can understand you leaving him, but that just makes it easier for her to make her move. Is he sorry? Has he asked you to forgive him? Allison, you have to think of the children.

JoAnne finishes her drink, and she orders another. The waiter looks at me. His expression asks, "How is she getting home?"

"Cancel the martini. We'll have a bottle of your best red wine. You choose. I'm the designated driver."

"I hope he hurries with that wine. I can't believe Pete is having an affair. Men! So many of my friends' husbands have had affairs. I blame it on the forty-year itch. They look at that bucket list and think, 'Oh, I haven't had an affair. Let me fit that in before I die.' Heck, for all I know, Gary could have had a one-night stand, with all the traveling we do, but if I ever found out, he'd be down a body part."

"Pete is like a brother to you. Do you really think the reason we aren't together is his having an affair?"

"If my sister-in-law told me she and my brother were separated, you bet your ass I know he was having an affair. My brother's a jerk."

"Look over the menu. You need to eat something."

"You just blurted out you and Pete aren't living together. Do you think the first thing I want to do is have a full-course meal?"

"Pete is not having an affair. Two hours ago, you were starving. Let's order dinner, and I promise once we finish, I'll tell you everything."

"If he's not having an affair, then what the fuck happened? Does Gary know? Because he hasn't said a word."

"Gary doesn't know. Pete hasn't told him, but he'll know soon enough. I'm not saying another word until we've ordered."

JoAnne waves the waiter over. "We'll have today's cut, medium rare, a side of potato au gratin, asparagus, Béarnaise sauce on the side. A fresh garden salad to start and another bottle of this fabulous wine, thank you."

"I was going to have the sea bass."

"You can have fish tomorrow. What happened?"

"How was your trip to Korea?"

"Great. Now talk."

"Can we enjoy dinner before I tell you the whole truth and nothing but the truth, please?"

After finishing our salads, JoAnne grows impatient. "Allison, I can't wait another minute. Tell me what happened, or I'll make a scene."

"JoAnne, I'm going to tell you everything. I would rather I ate before spilling my guts."

During dinner, we discussed JoAnne's trip. The wine seemed to calm her. I drank two glasses of wine in anticipation of my confession.

After dinner, I confess falling in love with Patrick as a teenager and how I destroyed my marriage in less than an hour. I finish with "Pete can't forgive me, and I don't expect him to. I'm sure we will be divorced before the New Year."

JoAnne is stoic; I've never seen her this way.

"You understand, I never planned to fall in love with Patrick. You know what my childhood was like …"

JoAnne lowers her head. "How could you? How could you be so cruel? What the fuck were you thinking? You felt Pete deserved to know the truth? Are you a fucking idiot?"

JoAnne's reaction shocks me. "I didn't—"

"Didn't what? Didn't mean to rip the guy's heart from his chest? He's a fool if he forgives you. You don't deserve his forgiveness. I can't believe he has to deal with you for the rest of his life for Julia and Andrew's sake. If I were him, I'd sue for custody."

I gasp. "JoAnne, please. I was counting on you to under—"

"Counting on me to what? Take your side? Fifteen years, you didn't say one word, not even to me." JoAnne has a revelation. "You were going to tell me the day of the funeral, weren't you? That's why you freaked out."

"I was embarrassed to admit I was in love with Patrick, even to you, the one person in this entire world I told everything to."

"Not everything. Were you planning on running off with your mother's husband and sending me a postcard from paradise? Why didn't you tell me, so I could have smacked some sense into that screwed-up head of yours? What I'd really like to know is, why didn't you talk to me before telling Pete the truth? Are you insane?"

"I know you don't agree with me telling him the truth, but I had to think of my son. What if something happened to him and some doctor told him his blood type didn't match his father's? What would have happened? I'll tell you, I would have lost not only Pete but my children as well. I put my children before Pete. Any mother would have. JoAnne, I fucked up. Once I knew the truth, I realized I've always loved Pete. I've begged for a second chance. Pete hates me, and I've come to accept that I can't change the past. I got help, and it feels good to be normal again. My only regret is Pete got hurt and I lost him forever, and if I have to lose your friendship, it will hurt, but I understand. I don't know why this happened, but it did, and I have to live with the pain I've caused."

JoAnne stares. I reach for the wine bottle and pour myself a full glass. The waiter walks over to take the bottle from my hands. "Don't worry, I'm not driving." I reach for my phone and text my aunt. "JoAnne and I out to dinner. Not going well. Need a ride. I'll text when we are ready to leave. Bring Uncle George. He'll need to drive my car." I include the name of the restaurant and the address. She responds, "Will pick you up. Good luck."

"Whom are you texting?"

"Aunt Sarah. She'll pick us up. Uncle George will drive my car back." I show the waiter the text and ask him to open the other bottle of wine.

"Does your aunt know the truth?"

"Yes. She knew what my life was like. She didn't judge me. I guess blood is thicker than water."

"You want me to believe your aunt, who corrected your placing the fork on the wrong side of the plate, isn't freaked out that you wanted to screw her sister's husband? Please!"

"Shit happens, JoAnne. Life isn't always peaches and cream. With my father dying before I was five, my mother, through no fault of her own, couldn't comfort her only child. As strong as you thought I was, maybe, just maybe, I was a little screwed in the head. Seems like my aunt and uncle thought I deserved a little pity. Sorry I can't say the same for my best friend. My aunt showed compassion. She didn't judge me. I didn't think you would be happy when you heard the truth, but I thought we could forgive each other anything."

JoAnne's expression softens. "Where are you living?"

"What?"

"Where are you living? I'm sure Pete asked you to leave?"

"No, I'm living in the house with the kids. He rented an apartment in town."

I drink most of the wine in my glass. JoAnne reaches for the wine bottle and pours herself a full glass.

Placing the bottle back in the holder, JoAnne asks, "Is Pete planning on telling Gary the truth?"

"No. He doesn't want him to know. Would you?"

"No, I don't want him to know. If Gary ever found out the truth, he'd insist I drop you as a friend." JoAnne notices the expression on my face. "Don't worry, as much as I'd like to wring your neck, I'm not going anywhere. If you shot the pope, I'd defend you. Actually, life would have been easier if you shot the pope." JoAnne smiles. "All right, I might have acted a little crazy. Maybe your life wasn't all peaches and cream, but I'm having a hard time trying to understand why telling Pete was the right thing to do."

I breathe a sigh of relief when JoAnne softens. The thought of losing her friendship is more than I can bear.

"Your therapist must be top in his field. When you referred to your mother, you said it wasn't her fault the way she acted toward you. And you managed to mend the fences with your aunt. I'm not surprised she didn't judge you. She loves you, Allison. I'm sure you figured that out by now."

I fill our glasses and tell JoAnne what I've learned about my family. When I was done, there wasn't a drop of wine left in the bottle.

JoAnne runs out of tissues. "Do you have any tissues? I can't believe Aunt Sarah had children and two lovers. It's even harder to believe that someone actually married your uncle and he had a son. I think his wife used the baby's death to get out of the marriage. She was probably bored out of her mind."

We burst out laughing. JoAnne crosses her legs. "I think I wet my pants. Your aunt and uncle were getting more ass than us."

"I don't think Uncle George is as boring as we thought. He goes out a lot. For all I know, he might have a woman on the side. I have to remember to ask my aunt."

The restaurant is packed, and JoAnne's and my behavior becomes the subject of conversation. The waiter rushes over. "Can I get you ladies anything else? Alcohol isn't an option." Laughing, JoAnne and I ask for the check.

Sitting in the hall of the restaurant, I beg JoAnne. "Please don't let on that I told you about my aunt and uncle's past. I don't want to break her trust."

"I won't. I feel so bad for her and your uncle. Losing their families … how sad."

My aunt walks in, and JoAnne leaps into her arms. "Aunt Sarah!"

In the car, JoAnne sits forward, wrapping her arms around my aunt. "Aunt Sarah, thank you for everything. You're the best. If it weren't for you, I'd be stuck in Cleveland. Who knows what I'd be doing today? It is because of you, and of course my parents, that I have this wonderful life. I owe you, Aunt Sarah. I love you so much! Did I tell you you're the best?"

My aunt turns to me and says, “You told her everything, didn’t you?”

I pout and answer, “I’m sorry.”

* * * * *

The following afternoon, JoAnne and I share the sofa, holding ice packs to our foreheads. “I really could use another cup of coffee, but I can’t stand up. Why didn’t you bring the coffee-pot in here?”

“I was afraid I’d drop it.”

“Good point.”

I sit up. I’ve had a full weekend planned for us, museum, theater, dinner.

“I would have crossed the museum off the list.”

“You have no class.”

“Hey, I’m not the one who was in love with my stepfather.”

We laugh. “True. I’m the one without any class.”

“I can’t deny that I didn’t have the hots for Patrick when I first met him. There was something about him that wasn’t doing it for me. I would have never guessed he was gay. He must have been good in bed for your mother to keep him around.”

“He had a partner in Pittsburg. I don’t think my mother and he had sex after he confessed he was gay.”

“Of course, they were having sex. I bet Patrick was bisexual.”

“I don’t think we should be talking about my mother’s sex life. She loved my father, that’s all I know. I think it was easier for her to keep Patrick around than to deal with my aunt. You know my aunt’s goal in life was to see her brother and sister happy. She overcompensated because her mother died so young.”

“Starting with your grandmother’s death, it just went downhill for your family from that day forward. How sad.”

“My aunt thought I beat the Holland curse, but no such luck. Death controls the outcome of our existence.”

JoAnne’s knowing the truth is another weight lifted off my shoulders. JoAnne tells Gary that Pete and I have been having problems long before Patrick died. Gary calls Pete to confirm, and Pete has stuck to the story. Our best friends are hoping for a reconciliation.

* * * * *

It's the third week of June, and the following week, school will end and the children will be off to camp after the fourth.

Aunt Sarah treats Julia to a pedicure and manicure after school. In the rearview mirror, I notice my son staring out the window. "Hey, buddy, can I buy you dinner?"

"I'll have something when we get home. I've got a lot of homework."

"Homework with one week left to the school year?"

"Extra credit homework."

Mother's intuition. "Andrew, did something happen at school?"

My son doesn't answer my question. He asks, "Mom, you met Dad in college. How many guys did you date before Dad?"

Bingo! Either Ellen or Andrew is moving on. "Let me guess."

I start to count on my hand and keep going before my son says, "Get real, Mom."

I laugh. "Three, but my relationships didn't last more than six months, tops."

"I wish I were more like Julia. She has a different boyfriend every three weeks."

I make a mental note to have a long discussion with my daughter about sex.

"Ellen thinks we should see other people. Last year at camp, we were kind of stuck with each other. It was fun, but we didn't meet a whole lot of other kids."

My son needs some motherly advice. I pull to the curb, shut off the engine, and turn to face him. "Sorry, buddy, but I have to agree with Ellen on this one. Sounds like camp was a bust last year."

"We had fun, and I really like Ellen, but this is my last year as camp counselor and my last year of high school."

"Sounds like you agree with Ellen. Your aunt JoAnne didn't believe in having a steady fellow."

Andrew smiles. "I bet Aunt JoAnne was a piece of work in high school."

"Hey, now, don't get the wrong idea. Your aunt and I saved ourselves for college. That's an accomplishment these days."

"Too much information, Mom, but I get the point. I'm really not sure how I'm going to feel when I see Ellen with another guy."

"The same as she is going to feel when she sees you with another girl."

"Mom, are you dating? I ask because I really don't know how I'm going to feel if you or Dad start dating."

"No, I don't think I'm ready, but maybe someday. Andrew, I know it is hard to accept, but you father and I might not be able to work things out." I can see Andrew becoming uncomfortable, so I ask, "Have you talked to Dr. Jewel about your situation with Ellen?"

"I did. She said first loves are hard to get over. You always remember your first love."

"See? It's working out already. As you grow old, you'll have fond memories of Ellen."

Andrew smiles. "Thanks, Mom. I've missed talking with you."

As I pull away from the curb, I can sympathize with my son's current situation. His first broken heart, but soon his heart will heal, whereas Pete's and mine will never mend.

* * * * *

I'm running around like a chicken without a head when my phone buzzes.

"Hi! What's up, Aunt Sarah?"

"What's up? Funny, you sound like Julia. I need a favor. Marge just called. Carl and her are fighting summer colds. Can you and the kids come by the parish to help set up for the picnic on Saturday?"

I have several more stops to make, gathering last-minute items for camp. "What time?"

"Five. Don't bother with dinner. We're ordering sandwiches."

"I think I can swing five if I don't have to cook dinner. See you at five!"

"Allison, did I tell you I invited Pete on Saturday? I'm just following your lead trying to include him so the children won't think we've deserted him. He always got a kick out of the July 4 picnic."

"I also invited him. He said he'll try. No promises."

"He said the same to me. I hope he comes. I haven't seen him since the baseball season ended."

* * * * *

Julia and Andrew are helping Uncle George, while Aunt Sarah and I wipe down the tables.

When my back is turned, Aunt Sarah calls out, "Jason, over here." I turn to look and spot a good-looking, salt-and-pepper-haired man walking in our direction.

"Jason, I don't believe you ever met my niece, Allison."

"No. Hello, Allison. Jason Paul. Nice to meet you."

We shake hands, and my aunt explains that Jason is the accountant for the parish. "Jason, I'm going to need a little more money for the entertainment, and I hope that isn't going to be a problem."

"Sarah Holland, every year you go over budget and leave me the task of explaining the shortfall to the reverend."

"Don't mind the reverend. I'm no fool. We have more than enough money in the budget. The reverend always lowballs what we can spend. You think by this time he's figured out I'm wise to him."

Jason and my aunt share a laugh. "Your aunt is one smart cookie."

"You'll get no argument from me."

Jason goes to talk with the reverend. I help gather the folding chairs. Spotting coffee and dessert, I sneak away, finding a table far from the other workers.

"Do you mind if I sit?" I turn to find Jason behind me with a cup of coffee and a large slice of chocolate cake.

I smile. "That chocolate cake looks good. Can I steal a bite?"

"You're in a holy place. I don't think the word *steal* is acceptable."

I move over, making room for Jason. He offers a piece of cake. I refuse. "Did you get Aunt Sarah her money?"

"Of course. Your aunt is right. The reverend is a little tight."

I laugh. "My aunt lives for these events. She especially likes being with the children."

"She's a sweet lady, your aunt, and your uncle George does whatever she asks."

An image of my aunt and uncle as children emerges in my mind. "They're a team."

The silence becomes uncomfortable, so I ask, "Is your family attending the BBQ?"

"My family lives in California. I'm not married, no children, just me, and yes, I intend on making an appearance. You're married. Pete, correct? We met Christmas Eve."

"Soon-to-be ex-husband, not sure. Please don't mention this to anyone. We're separated. I don't know why I told you. I guess I wanted to test saying it to someone outside of the family."

"I'm sorry to hear. I was married, but only for a year."

"One year. What happened?"

"I met her on the rebound. We married, six months later, her ex shows up. They are happily married with three kids."

"There are so many stories about failed relationships."

"If you don't mind my asking, what's yours?"

"Work, Pete was traveling, we fought, separated. I haven't given up on us, but I think he might have."

"Are we talking about the same guy, Pete Cane?"

"That's him."

"Pete's a smart man. I don't think he'd let a beautiful woman such as yourself slip away."

"Thanks. I hope you're right."

* * * * *

I wake early on July 4. I wake Andrew and tell him I'm going to the drugstore. I want to buy one more bottle of shampoo for Julia, wanting to avoid the frantic call when she runs out.

Returning home, I take a shower, grab a bathing suit, cover-up, towels, sun lotion, and pack a duffel bag. I put on my favorite shorts and tank top. Checking myself in the mirror, I decide to wear my hair loose and grab several hair ties for later in the day. Sunglasses, makeup, brush, money. *Am I forgetting anything?* Yes, a sweater. I open the closet, and there, staring me in the face, is the red sweater. *Sorry,* I think, *not today.*

I park the car, the kids gather their stuff, and they run off. Closing the car trunk, I walk toward the lake. The picnic area is far from where we released Patrick's ashes. Today my thoughts are of another day and this lake.

* * * * *

After Pete and I had walked through our home with the realtor, we asked if there were any other offers and how long we had to make our decision. She said time was of the essence; the owners had already found a new home and wanted to move before the school year began. She suggested we take a tour of the area and said there was a lake nearby. The grounds consisted of a children's playground, picnic area, and beach area. She gave us directions and said she thought visiting the area would help us decide.

Cruising the neighborhood, we were amazed at how well the homes and lawns were maintained. Following the realtor's directions, we found the lake. With Julia in my arms and Andrew, a toddler, holding Pete's hand, together as a family we walked to the shoreline of the lake. Pete removed Andrews little sneakers and socks, then he removed his own. Pete held Andrew's hands as they splashed each other's feet. I remember calling to remind Pete not to let him wet his shorts. I danced with Julia, feeling the excitement my husband and son were experiencing. When Andrew tired, father and son came to stand beside me. "What a magnificent view!"

"It is. So what do you think, Mrs. Cane, do we make an offer on the house?"

"Oh, yes! Pete, do you think they will accept our offer? Should we increase the offer? The master's bath is fine, but we will have to update the guest bath and make a few changes to the downstairs powder room. The outside of the house is lovely, and the gardens are so pretty."

"What about the kitchen? Can you live with it until we have enough money to remodel?"

"I can live with it. I'll paint the cabinets. I have so many ideas. Pete, I love the house! Do you think we stand a chance of getting it? I can see us growing old in that house. I'm going to put a swing on the front porch, where we can rock our grandchildren to sleep."

Pete put on his comic voice and said, "Baby, I'll make them an offer they can't refuse."

This lake held many memories for Pete and me. It was the place I took my young children to play and the place Pete and I came to relax and meet up with the friends we made over the years.

* * * * *

Before I make my way toward the tables, I glance in the direction where we spread Patrick's ashes, thinking, *Therapy has taught me not to dwell on the past.* So I whisper, "Rest in peace, Patrick."

* * * * *

"You look great in those shorts. JoAnne's going to envy how good you look!"

"Aunt Sarah, how long have you known JoAnne? The woman grows more beautiful with age."

"You're much prettier."

"We're family. You have to say I'm prettier."

Aunt Sarah places her arm around my waist and leans in to kiss my cheek. "I have a surprise for you. I'm so excited I'm ready to burst! I invited Christopher and his family."

"Christopher, Constance's son?"

"Yes. It is time you two met. Christopher was thrilled I called."

"That is pretty exciting news. I can't wait to meet him."

Uncle George and Andrew are tossing a baseball, warming up for the annual baseball game. I spot Julia talking with a boy. After

Andrew dropped the bomb that Julia had a different boyfriend every three weeks, I've spent an hour with my girl talking about boys. Seems my girl is smarter than I think.

"Mom, I'm not a flirt, I'm friendly. I don't lead the boys on. I'm up front with them. I make them know from the start we are just friends, nothing more. I find them interesting. I want to know what makes them tick. I'll be more careful, Mom, I promise."

I know the boy Julia is talking with. They have known each other since first grade, so I put my worries to rest and feel confident my girl can handle herself.

"Hey, you look great in those shorts. I'm jealous." JoAnne spins me around and bear-hugs me. "How are you doing, girlfriend? Has that husband come to his senses?"

"Aunt Sarah and I invited him today, but I'm not sure he'll show."

"Gary asked if he was coming. He said he'll try to make it. Things aren't any better, are they?"

"When he comes by to pick up the kids, I keep my distance. We've spoken several times about camp, his vacation with the kids in Florida, but nothing major. You already know that Gale arranged her wedding around the kids' visit. Andrew only wants to stay the week of the wedding. We told him he was old enough to make his own decision."

"That was really nice of Gale. Do you think you will be invited?"

"Mary said I will, but I don't think I'm going to go, unless—"

"Unless Pete asks?"

"Exactly."

Gary yells out, "Hi, Allison! Isn't it a beautiful day?" Kissing me on both cheeks, he asks, "How's my girl? Where are the kids?"

"I'm fine." I point in the direction to where my uncle and children are standing. JoAnne's sons, Carson and John, greet me with a kiss.

"JoAnne what are you feeding these boys? I think they grew at least two-inchs taller."

"Those are your exact words every time you see us, Aunt Allison," says John.

"Would you rather I ask about the girls in your lives?"

"Not in front of Mom."

"What do you mean not in front of Mom? If either of you has girlfriends, I'd like to meet them, so—"

Before JoAnne can finish her sentence, the boys run off and meet up with Andrew.

My aunt calls my name, and when I turn, she is waving me toward her. Her arm is locked through the arm of a handsome man from the pictures I've seen of his mother. I know it's Christopher.

"Who is that gorgeous man with Aunt Sarah? Don't tell me she's trying to hook you up?"

"No. The pretty woman next to him is Terri, his wife, and next to her is their son, Michael Eric Clark Pickett." JoAnne connects the dots. "Constance's son Christopher."

Everyone is introduced to the Pickett family.

The festivities are underway. Balloons for the younger children are being passed around. The older kids grab a few, untie them, and fill them with water. Julie and her friend Grace are assigned to the face-painting booth. They are surrounded by at least thirty little ones. Uncle George is navigating the trucks that hold the rides. The older boys are practicing in anticipation of the baseball game that is to begin in fifteen minutes. The adults, minus the kid's, are enjoying a cold lemonade. Still no Pete.

JoAnne leans in. "I don't think he's coming."

I sigh. "Would you?" I excuse myself and walk to the lake. Several minutes later, Christopher is standing beside me.

"Isn't it strange, only a highway between us, and we never met?"

"Six months ago, I didn't know you existed."

"She never failed to talk about you to me. All good things. She's very proud of you."

"How often do you see her?"

"At least twice a year."

"You're a lawyer, correct?"

"Retired lawyer. I sit on the board of my grandfather's law firm, but the vineyard is my first love. My father's as well. Not Lance, my biological father. I never met him, but my grandmother kept him alive by sharing his life with me, especially his dream of running a successful vineyard."

"I'm a lawyer, social work, not corporate. My aunt was instrumental in my wanting to be a lawyer."

"I guess you know by now that your aunt came to rescue me. I have her to thank for my childhood. I got to grow up surrounded with love from both my mother's and father's families."

"My aunt told me, your grandmother was like a second mom, and grandmother to Eric."

"Eric was my best friend as a child. Did you know he had a puppy named Spotty? When Eric died, I told my mother your aunt couldn't give Spotty away. Of course, Aunt Sarah knew I would take good care of him. I can't think of one without thinking of the other. My father Lance was sick when we had to put the dog down. Only my mother and I understood why."

"I still find it hard to believe my aunt lost two children. I would have liked having cousins. I wish we had met sooner."

Christopher smiles. "I don't know how your aunt managed to remain friends with my family after Lance and my mother married."

I don't think it my place to respond to Christopher's question. If I have to guess, I'll say she thinks of his family as her extended family, and her family's happiness is what she lives for. "She's a strong lady, that aunt of ours."

"You know, it was Lance that taught Eric and me how to play hockey. As a child, I envied Eric for being blessed with a father like Lance. You can imagine how guilty I felt when I heard my mother and he were getting married. He was a great father to me and my sisters."

"Parents' decisions have a way of changing the lives of their children. You're lucky you were blessed with great parents."

"I was blessed, a great mom and dad and three nagging sisters."

I smile. "I wouldn't know. I'm an only child."

“Thank God my father and Sarah got to have their happy ending.”

I shoot a look in Christopher’s direction. “You knew about your father and my aunt?”

“Yes. One of the last things my mother said to me before she died was, ‘Christopher, I’m going home to your father. Lance and Sarah were cheated of a life together. I hope they find each other when I’m gone.’ When my father died, I found a book in his dresser, *Gone with the Wind*. When I removed the book, one picture fell to the floor. A picture of him, Aunt Sarah, and Eric. Your aunt was eight months pregnant. I never questioned either about their relationship while my father was alive or after he was gone.”

As Christopher finishes his story, I hear Pete’s voice call, “Allison.”

Lowering my head to brush the tears from my cheeks, I’m elated, saying, “Just in time for the baseball game.”

Pete extends a hand to Christopher. “Hi, I’m Pete.”

“Pete, I’ve waited a long time to meet you. I’m Christopher Clark Pickett. I’m an old friend of Aunt Sarah and Uncle George.”

“Aunt Sarah mentioned you might be here.” Although Pete finds it hard to be in my presence, he never refuses a call from my aunt.

Christopher escorts Pete to his family. “I’d like you to meet my wife and son.” I follow.

Uncle George’s team includes Andrew, Pete, Gary and his sons, Christopher and his son, and several fathers and sons from the parish. We cheer the team on, but not as loudly as Aunt Sarah. I sense she’s happy to have the people she loves most in this world finally together. She smiles at me, and I return the smile, privileged to be related to this loving and compassionate woman.

As we enjoy our picnic feast together as a family, Uncle George talks about high school days. Aunt Sarah proudly tells the stories that it was Uncle George that had won state three years in baseball and two in football. Only JoAnne asks, “I bet you had a lot of girlfriends in high school, being the star athlete. I fell in love with Gary the first time I saw him in his football uniform.”

Uncle George, being a wise man, says, "A guy never kisses and tells. Right, boys?" The boys laugh. It's at that moment I notice Pete is laughing right along with the boys.

I am sitting between Aunt Sarah and JoAnne. Aunt Sarah says, "He looks happy being here with you and the kids."

"He's happy to be with the kids, not me."

JoAnne chimes in, "I agree with you, Aunt Sarah. I saw him checking out her ass at least five times."

It's time for the three-legged race. The kids run to get the feed bags, while JoAnne reminds everyone, "Allison and I won this race five years in a row. Remember, Allison? You swore after the fifth year, you'd never run this race again until you had children."

The teams consisted of; Andrew and Pete, Julia and me, JoAnne and Carson, Gary and John, Christopher and Michael. I watch as Pete places his leg in the bag with Andrew's assistance. He is smiling at Andrew as he points out the strategy they will use to win.

"Mom, Andrew is determined to win. Aunt JoAnne, and you hold the record with five wins, and Uncle Gary had too many beers to see straight. So what do you think Aunt JoAnne has up her sleeve?"

"Whatever she's planning, keep in mind, she devoured five hot dogs and a ton of potato salad. Your father can't run without the use of both legs. You're right about Uncle Gary, he's had too many beers. And Christopher and Michael are city boys. I say we have a pretty good chance of winning." After the race, the only voice you can hear is Julia's as she shouts, "Eat our dust!" When she is presented with a three-inch trophy, I remain on the ground, trying to catch my breath. Thin or not, I'm out of shape.

A hand reaches down to lift me from the ground. I know the hand. "She's something else, that girl of ours."

"She sure is competitive. I don't know whom she takes after." Pete points to JoAnne. "She might not be blood, but I'd say we have her to blame."

JoAnne is hugging Julia and trying to wrench the trophy from her hands.

Later in the day, JoAnne is giving Terri the third degree. Aunt Sarah is at the dessert table, Uncle George is overseeing the rides, and

I'm watching Pete as he, Gary, Christopher, and the boys chat. He looks happy. Several times, he wraps an arm around Andrew's shoulder. I ask myself, "All those years, how did I not see the resemblance between the two?"

Dusk is falling. Soon the fireworks show will begin, ending this beautiful day. I search for my daughter, who is splashing around in the lake with several of her friends. I walk to the lake to watch. Ten minutes later, I'm crying, watching her. Not wanting anyone to see, I find a private place under a tree and have myself a good cry.

"Need a few minutes alone?"

"Pete." He can see I'm crying, "I lost it watching our daughter. Can you believe Andrew has one year before he's off to college, and Julia three? I'm not ready. You know he's applying to Stanford? You have to talk him Pete, Boston U or NYU, nothing farther."

Pete smiles and leans on the tree. "I think his first choice is Boston. Did you know Julia's thinking Northwestern?"

"Over my dead body! If Boston is good enough for her brother, it's good enough for her."

"The decision is theirs, not ours."

"You're not fooling me. You're just as upset they grew up so fast."

"We always knew this day would come. If it makes it any easier, we still have three years before Julia is off."

"Seems like a death sentence. Three years, and then bingo, another change in my life. Back to being single." Pete doesn't respond. I look up at him. "Dating anyone?"

Pete is puzzled by the question. "No. The thought hasn't crossed my mind. You?"

"No. Since you're available, maybe we could ..."

Pete smiles, pauses, then says, "I've been seeing a therapist."

"You have? Who?"

"You're not going to believe. David."

"Isn't that against some doctor's oath? If you've treated the wife, it would be against protocol to treat the husband."

"I don't think so. If anything, it might help."

I take that as a positive sign. "I might have to call David and set up a few sessions to help me accept my little birds are ready to book the nest."

Pete sits next to me. "The circle of life."

"You always know exactly what to say. I miss that."

The first of many fireworks erupts in the sky.

CHAPTER TWENTY-THREE

Allison

I rush the kids out the door. The Fourth of July weekend has been perfect, and so is this beautiful Tuesday morning.

Spying Andrew's duffel bag, which is half-empty, I ask, "Are you sure you've packed everything?"

"Everything you left for me to pack." Andrew opens the trunk of the car and drops in his bag. Plopping himself in the passenger's seat, he calls, "If you don't want us to be late, you better run up and drag your daughter out of her room."

Taking Andrew's advice, I run up the stairs to find Julia ripping her room apart. I freak out, knowing the mess will be cleaned up by me. "What are you doing?"

"I've checked my duffel bag, the carry bag, my closet, and the dresser. I can't find my yellow sweater!"

"You don't have time to waste looking for it. You can borrow one of my sweaters."

When I open my closet, I quickly realize I don't have a yellow sweater. Black and beige—boring. I pull a light-blue sweater from the hanger. Underneath is the red sweater. I take both to Julia.

"Which one?"

Julia stares at the sweaters in my hands. "Mom, you'd let me borrow the red one? It's perfect!"

I smile. "It's yours. I'm not fond of red."

"Thanks, Mom. I love this sweater."

Pushing Julia from her room, I say, "When you get back, I'll tell you who gifted me the sweater."

When I turn the corner, the bus is already there and waiting. Andrew spots Pete grabbing his bag. He's off to greet him.

Crying, I hold on to my children for as long as I can. Andrew is the first to break away. Julia follows his lead. I notice David and Alice off in the distance. I wave.

Pete and I wait for the bus to pull away from the curb. Mothers wipe their tears, frantically waving as the bus drives out of sight. The few fathers that are able to make the send-off are welcoming six weeks of freedom, except Pete and me, because the children are all that we have left in our world.

I say goodbye to Pete. We linger. I hope he will say something other than goodbye. He touches my arm, and the warmth of his hand makes me shiver. Our eyes meet. I can't find the old Pete in those eyes, but they are softer, kinder. I'm sad by the realization that he has found a way to survive in this world without me. He wishes me a good summer and says he hopes I plan to do something special. Then he's gone.

* * * * *

Two days later, as I arrive home from work, Marie, my neighbor, calls my name. With a bottle of wine in her hand, she makes her way toward me.

"Allison, I rang the bell earlier. Late night at work?"

"I was at the salon. Root touch up."

"Looks nice. This is for you. Maybe one night you might want to have a few of your old friends over." Marie pauses. "I rehearsed what I was going to say a hundred times. Allison, please don't take this as interfering, but the gals couldn't help but notice that you and Pete are going through a difficult time. We miss you at the tennis club. As you know, Grace moved. We were wondering if you would like to take her place. Grace was also our foursome for golf. Do you play golf? I wasn't sure if you did. Anyway, the club offers lessons. We play at four on Tuesday. Would you be interested?"

I have no response, so Marie continues, "I promise we aren't prying. No questions. I just think, with the kids away, you might want to get out more."

Without a second thought, I say, "I'm in. Thanks for thinking of me. I'll call the club and inquire about the golf lessons. Tennis at eight on Fridays, correct?"

"Is that going to work for you? I mean, can you get the time off work?"

"I've arranged to have Fridays off during the summer months. Count me in."

* * * * *

After my first golf lesson, my aunt and I meet for dinner.

"How was the golf lesson?"

"Great! The instructor thinks I have a natural talent for the sport. I also invited a few of the ladies to the house next Wednesday, drinks and pizza. I'm playing tennis with them on Friday. I'm sure I'll be hurting on Saturday. I was going to spend the day at the lake. Care to join me?"

"I wish I could. I'm having lunch with the ladies. After, we are going to the movies for the live Met performance of *Romeo and Juliet*. If you haven't been, you should give it a go. It is fabulous and much cheaper. Although I love the Met and spending time in the city."

I imagine my aunt strolling through the park where she spent so much time with Eric, passing by the old apartment.

"Have you heard from Pete?"

"Only one email saying he heard from the kids. Did I mention he's seeing a therapist? Guess who?"

"Dr. David Greenberg?"

"You got it. I thought it was against some ethical code, but apparently not."

"It might be to your benefit that Pete is seeing someone so close to the problem." My aunt pauses. "Before I forget, are you busy next weekend?"

"Nothing much. Why?"

"Christopher invited us out to the vineyard. We can leave after your tennis game. Bring a bathing suit and racket. This isn't your typical vineyard. It's more like a country club with vines."

* * * * *

That Saturday, as I've predicted, my legs are sore. I find a sunny spot near the lake that will shade as the sun moves west. Sitting on my beach chair, I whisper to myself, "What a beautiful day." I watch the younger children play in the freshwater while their parents keep watch. I'm reminded of Pete and me planting our chairs as close to the water as possible. I sigh, allowing my eyes to wander. I compliment Patrick on his choice to spend eternity on this lake. I pour myself a cool drink and begin to catch up on the years' worth of *People* magazines, old but still enjoyable to read. Bored with the rich and famous, I reach for the current book I've chosen to read. I drift off and am awakened by the sound of my name.

"Hello, Allison."

I cover my eyes from the sun. "Jason? Long time no see."

Realizing I'm covered with nothing but a bathing suit and suntan lotion, I reach for my cover-up when I stand to greet him. "Missed you at the picnic. My aunt said you were helping a friend."

"I heard it was a great success. To answer your question, I was with a friend. It was my friend Jean's last chemo treatment. It was scheduled for Friday, then postponed to Saturday. She didn't do well this time around, so I remained with her until Monday."

Jason's hazel eyes mist when he speaks about his friend. "I hope the prognosis is good?"

"The doctors are hopeful. It's stage III, but curable."

"Doesn't sound like you're as confident as the doctors."

"She's a close friend. She and I were divorced around the same time. We were there for each other."

"She sounds like a special lady. Please give her my best." I notice the running attire. "Great day for a run. I got back into running when I started therapy. I try to get out at least four times a week. The other days, I catch up on my beauty sleep."

"It's working, the running and the beauty sleep."

"Thanks."

Jason and I spend an hour talking about our jobs and my children. Jason looks at his watch. "I should be heading back. Are you busy this evening? I've been wanting to try the new steak house on Main Street. Would you like to join me for dinner?"

Dinner with a man is tempting, but accepting Jason's invitation is acceptance that my marriage is officially over.

"Jason, I would love to have dinner with you, but—"

"Allison, if I say this isn't a date, just two friends checking out the new streak house, would that make it easier for you to say yes to dinner?"

"You read my mind. Accepting a date would mean I was giving up on Pete and me ever getting back together." The thought of another Saturday alone at home makes me think twice. "Nothing more than a dinner with a friend, correct?" Jason agrees. "Then I would love to go to dinner with you. What time should I meet you at the restaurant?"

I pull into the parking lot at the same time as Jason. He is a gentleman, greeting me by saying I look lovely, nothing more—no kiss on the cheek, no taking my arm as we walk toward the restaurant. Just two friends sharing dinner.

I'm home by ten.

* * * * *

I juggle three pizza boxes, unlocking my front door. I set the boxes on the kitchen counter, set the warming tray in the oven, and place one box inside. I gather chips, dips, napkins, plates, and wineglasses on a tray and carry them into the living room. Taking two steps at a time to reach the bedroom, I change from my work clothes into jeans, a tee, and flip-flops. I run a brush though my hair, blush on my cheeks, and lipstick. As I'm heading down, the phone rings. I'm going to let the call go to voice mail when the children come to mind, so I take the call.

"Hello."

"Hello, Allison."

I feel dizzy at the sound of his voice. "Pete." I pause. "How are you?"

"I'm doing well. And yourself?" The doorbell rings.

"Pete, I need to answer the door. Can you hold?"

"Of course."

Every friend I have invited is standing on my front porch. I tell them to help themselves, pointing to the phone. As ladies do, they begin to chat and laugh, filling the house with noise.

"Pete, I'm back."

"Are you having a party?"

"Just a few friends over for drinks and pizza."

Pete doesn't respond. I ask, "Most of our friends know about the separation. I thought it was time for me to get back part of my life."

"I see. I'm calling about the wedding." I jump the gun, thinking Pete is going to ask if I'm attending Gale's wedding. I wait. "Gale doesn't want a formal wedding, so no tux. I was wondering if Andrew had a suit that fits, or should I purchase another?"

Disappointed, I answer, "He has a blue suit he wore to the junior prom. I believe it's suitable for the wedding."

"Great. Have you heard from the kids?"

I want to cut the conversation short after I'm not asked if I'm planning on attending the wedding. "Pete, I've got to go."

"Yes, of course. Have fun."

When I join the ladies, I pour myself a glass of wine and gulp. Marie is the first to ask, "Pete?"

"Yes. His sister is getting married in August. He was calling to ask if Andrew had a suit. I received my invitation three weeks ago. I thought he might be calling to ask if I was going."

Denise asks the question that the others are too afraid to ask. "Is Pete bringing someone else to the wedding?"

"No. Pete is not having an affair. The problems in our marriage are business-related. The fights over his traveling … well, we said things we shouldn't have said, and it put a crack in our relationship."

Lori inhales. "Thank God. I thought it was another woman. I don't want to interfere, but have you considered couples therapy?

When Joel hired a knockout assistant, oh, she wasn't the problem. It was Joel. He talked about how wonderful she was 24-7. It affected our marriage. We went to couples therapy, and Joel realized quickly that his obsession with this girl was hurting me."

Denise asks, "What happened in therapy that made Joel realize he was being an ass?"

Lori smiles. "I'll never know. His assistant found a new job. Joel could have counteroffered, but he chose life over death."

The room erupts in laughter. I hear myself laughing louder than everyone.

"Allison, I think Lori is right. You have to set a fire under Pete. Tell him couples therapy or it's over," says Marie.

Denise questions, "Are you going to the wedding?"

I've already decided, if Pete doesn't ask, I'm not going. Sunday, I will call Gale to let her know.

* * * * *

I speak to the kids before calling Gale on Sunday.

Sitting at the kitchen counter, I speak with Julia after calling Andrew, because she and I have more to discuss. My conversation with Andrew is short and to the point.

"Hi, Mom."

"Hi, sweetheart, how are you?"

"Fine."

"How's camp?"

"Good."

"Have you met a lot of new people?"

"Yes."

"How many kids are in your group?"

"Ten."

Etc., etc.

"Remember, I love you with all my heart and soul, and I miss you."

End of conversation.

Counting to ten, I call Gale's cell.

"What? You're not coming? If you don't come, I'm postponing the wedding."

I laugh. "You are not going to postpone the wedding. Your mother will have me killed. Gale, your brother and I … well, it's difficult to explain. I don't want him to feel uncomfortable. Please understand."

Gale's voice cracks, but she controls herself when she says, "It won't be the same without you. Allison, the family is frightened. The longer you guys remain apart … We know my brother loves you. He's miserable without you. I know he hates living it that apartment alone. What are you guys doing to fix this?"

I'm over lying, so truthfully, I say, "Nothing."

"Nothing? What about marriage counseling?"

I don't think it's my place to discuss Pete's private life, so I answer for myself, "I was seeing a therapist."

"Was? Are you still seeing someone?"

"No. I was told to go off and figure out what I wanted to do with my life, and that is what I'm doing. I'm sure Pete is doing the same."

"This is insane! Are you telling me you're considering divorcing?"

"Neither one of us has discussed divorce. First, let me put your mind at ease. There isn't another woman or man. I know this separation was a blow to your family. We were fighting a lot, a first in our marriage. Things were said, and for the children's sake, we decided to take a break from each other."

"This doesn't make any sense. Do you know why I agreed to marry Michael? Because I wanted what you and my brother had, a beautiful life filled with love and happiness. Nothing lasts forever."

"Gale, walk down that aisle. I know you and Michael will grow old together."

Gale and Michael are off to Italy for their honeymoon, flying out of JFK. We make plans to meet in the city for dinner so I can congratulate them in person.

* * * * *

On the drive to the vineyard, I drift off when we hit the Long Island Expressway. Aunt Sarah is right; the house Constance and Michael had built is breathtaking.

Christopher's son, Michael, is off to camp, so the adults enjoy the peace and quiet of having no children to cater to.

"I haven't told your aunt. My sisters and their families are in town and will be joining us tomorrow. I wanted to surprise her."

My aunt and uncle are thrilled to see the girls and their families and embrace them.

After dinner, I find my aunt lounging by the pool. Her expression says it all: she is lost in the past.

"Hi, sweetie. Is it time for dessert and coffee?"

"No. Christopher is catching up with his sisters, so I thought I'd come find you. Uncle George is napping in the den."

"Come pull up a chair. The girls really like you, and Christopher is so happy having you in his life. I should have my head examined for keeping you apart. With the girls living so far away, it would have been good for him to have you in his life. I'm sorry."

"We have a lot of time to get to know each other."

"I'm happy. Do you know Michael's, Constance's, and Lance's ashes were spread around that oak tree? Well, not all of Lance's ashes. He requested to have a little place on our children's grave. I toyed with the idea of cremation then decided my children and I have been separated for far too long."

"You believe in life after death?"

"My grandma Maggie's last words were my grandfather's and my mother's name. My father's my mother's. I believe we are reunited with our loved ones when we pass from this world."

My aunt is feeling sad thinking about Lance. "Aunt Sarah, Christopher told me something, something that binds you and Lance together forever. He told me after his father died, he found a copy of *Gone with the Wind*, and in the center of the book was a picture of you pregnant, Eric, and himself. The identical picture that is in your copy. He truly did love you with all his heart and soul."

"As I did him."

*****

I meet Gale and Michael for dinner in New York. When we part, I whisper in Gale's ear, "A good marriage is built on love and trust."

On the train ride home, the anger I feel toward Pete is building. He had to know how much I wanted to attend the wedding.

Another school year, another football game. I sit on the far end of the bleachers to avoid Pete.

When he walks onto the field, he goes to David and Alice to chat and remains with them the entire game. Seeing how comfortable they are with one another makes my blood boil. When the game is over, I rush off the field and to my car. It's Pete's weekend. As I place my hand on the door handle, David calls my name. "Fuck."

"Allison, I just wanted to say hello. I won't keep you."

"Hello, David." In the distance, I spot Pete walking to his car with the children. He waves. I don't return the wave.

"How are you?"

I'm curt. "Fine. How are you?"

"Fine. Did I do something to upset you?"

"Why didn't you tell me you were seeing Pete as a patient? Isn't that against some medical oath?"

"To answer your question, no, but there is a thing called patient's rights, and Pete is a patient."

"I'm sure you already know your patient's sister got married in August, and it's clear to me he didn't want me at the wedding."

"And you're blaming me?"

"He must have mentioned in one of your session that I was invited. Do you know how hurt I was he didn't ask?"

"You didn't answer my question. Are blaming me because Pete didn't ask you to the wedding?"

"Yes. You're his doctor. You had to know I'd be upset. Why didn't you—"

"I suggest, if you are upset with Pete, tell him. It was nice seeing you, Allison. Have a nice day."

David walks away, and Pete is walking toward me. "Hi! Is it all right if I bring the kids back at seven on Sunday, football …?"

"Of course, no problem. I have to go. I'm late for a nail appointment."

* * * * *

The following weekend, my weekend, Andrew is off to a sweet sixteen party, and Julia is invited to a sleepover. After dropping Julia off, I go home, take a hot shower, make dinner, and channel-surf until I notice that *Fried Green Tomatoes* is starting in ten minutes. On the coffee table is my dinner, a hot cup of tea, cookies for dessert, a bag of chips for later, and the tissue box. The movie ends at eight. I finish the last chip in the bag and dry the last tear. I need a glass of wine, so I go into the kitchen, pour myself a tall glass, and am about to insert the DVD *Gone with the Wind* when the doorbell rings.

I go to the door and ask who is on the other side. My mouth drops open when I hear Pete's voice.

"It's Pete, Allison."

I repeat, "Pete?"

"Yes. Do you have a few minutes to talk?"

I run to the mirror in our foyer to check my appearance. I rush around, looking for my purse to apply lipstick. Realizing my purse is in my bedroom, I run up the stairs. Emptying my purse onto the bed, I can't find lipstick. Cursing out loud, I go to the bathroom and find one in the makeup drawer. I brush my hair and quickly apply a little blush to my cheeks. I almost fall, running down the stairs. When I open the door, no Pete.

Disappointed, I'm ready to close the door when I notice his car. Stepping outside, I lower my head to look inside. No Pete.

"Hi."

I jump out of my skin and look to my left to see Pete sitting on the porch swing. "You scared me! Sorry I took so long. I had to … I wasn't expecting anyone. If you were hoping to spend time with the kids, you're out of luck. They're out."

"I wanted to speak with you. I should have called."

"You should have. It's Saturday. I could have been out."

Pete stares. "I wanted to ask if I did something to upset you. You weren't very friendly the last time we saw each other."

Leaning on the porch railing, I say, "I guess I was a little upset."

"With me? I thought for the kid's sake, we were going to make this work. If I did something to upset you, tell me."

I try to suppress my anger. I know there is no easy way to tell Pete I'm hurt over the wedding. I lie, "I'm trying to move on. Isn't that what you want?"

Pete doesn't respond, so I turn to him, "I'm doing the best I can trying to understand why you … Never mind, it doesn't matter."

"Does this have anything to do with Gale's wedding?"

The blood in my body rushes to my head. "I'm not a part of your world anymore. What I did was unforgivable, I get it. Just because I am your children's mother doesn't give me the right to be at your sister's wedding."

"You received an invite. Wasn't it your decision not to attend?"

Pete doesn't have a smug look on his face when he asks the question.

I sigh. "I thought it might be uncomfortable for you if I showed up."

"That explains the cold shoulder. You would have attended if I gave you the okay?" Pete sighs. "When Gale said you didn't want to come, I respected your decision. I was wrong, I apologize. Aunt Sarah must be upset with me. She goes out of her way to make me feel comfortable. My mother would be furious if she knew that if I had asked, you would have been at the wedding."

I fantasized about Pete and me being at the wedding together. Watching Gale and Michael profess their love might have ignited a feeling within him. "My feelings were hurt. It's over."

Pete stands. "I'm glad we talked. I'm sorry it didn't work out. I know how close you are with my sisters. I'll try to be more considerate in the future."

Pete makes his way toward the steps. I don't want him to leave. "Andrew said you're off to Florida on Monday. Say hi to your parents, and tell your mother I'll call. I promise I won't mention anything we've talked about."

Pete smiles, and I can't remember a time he looked more handsome. "Thanks."

He steps down. I move toward the steps. "Why the trip?"

"What?"

"I thought everything was going well with the Florida office. Why the trip?"

"I need to meet with Emily to go over some of the older clients' files. It's difficult over of the phone."

The mention of Emily's name makes my stomach ache. "Can't Hal handle it?"

"I bought out Hal's half of the company. Emily's made an offer to buy his share, but I've decided to be the sole owner. It turns out the Florida operation is paying off. I have Hal to thank."

Pete makes a move. I ask, "That's great. I guess you've paid back all the money you borrowed from the kids?"

Pete stops in his tracks. I can sense he is offended by the question. He smiles. "You should receive a statement shortly. You'll see every dime was paid back and much more."

"I never doubted you. I'm sorry if my question was offensive."

"I'm not offended. Well, maybe just a little, but I'm a big boy. I'll get over it."

I can't allow Pete to walk away. I want him to stay. "Can I offer you a glass of wine or a cup of coffee?"

Pete pauses. Looking back, he says. "I'll take a rain check. I have to be somewhere at nine thirty. If I leave now, I'll just make it."

My heart leaps from my chest. "A date? Can't be business. Saturday night, nine thirty, a little late for an appointment? I'm sorry. What you do with your time is none of my business. Have a good night."

I turn my back on Pete as the tears begin to form and drop slowly down my cheek.

Hearing Pete's voice, I stop at the front door. "Allison, I was invited for drinks at a client's house. He's expecting me."

I face Pete. He can see the tears. I quickly ask, "Don't you miss us?"

Pete lowers his head. "What would it matter if I did?"

I move closer to Pete. "It does matter if you miss us. There is a chance we can work this out. You know I miss us. I miss the dreams we shared. The day of the picnic, I was thinking about the day we found this house, the lake, where we enjoyed time with our children. The hope that someday we'd be sitting on this very porch, loving and enjoying our grandchildren." I stare at Pete, hoping for a sign.

"I didn't come here to upset you. That wasn't my intention."

"You came because it bothered you that I was avoiding you."

Pete doesn't answer immediately. "I'll confess, it did bother me."

A ray of hope rushes through me. "Maybe you miss how easy it was for you and me to just talk about anything or nothing. There is only one way to find out. We should be spending time together. I know you have a commitment to your client, but afterward, you can stop by. We can talk." Pete is silent. I'm at the end of my rope, exhausted. I stare into Pete's eyes, hoping for a sign of hope, but all I see is pity, pity for the woman he once loved.

I breathe out, frustrated. I say, "I've begged, I've pleaded for a second chance. I can't keep hoping and praying if you won't meet me halfway. If it's over, why don't you file for divorce and put me out of my misery?" Pete doesn't respond. "You loved me once. Do you just wake up and, *poof*, that love is gone forever?" I lift my chin high in the air. "I love you. Won't you give me a chance to prove I do? You might be surprised to learn I'm telling the truth." Pete continues to stare. "Say something, damn it!"

"I have to go." Pete moves away.

I call to him. "You know this would be easier if we didn't have children. Maybe then, after not seeing me at all, you might realize that life sucks without me. Have you asked yourself that question, Pete? Is your life better without me? Are you happy?"

Pete turns toward me, he pauses, and I patiently wait for an answer. He slowly walks to his car. He looks back before getting in. I whisper, "Pete."

* * * * *

I sit on the sofa until twelve in hopes that Pete will return. Andrew returns home at one. Giving up, I secure the house and go to bed.

Sunday, I wake at seven, go for a run, dress for Sunday services, and leave the house with Andrew in toe. After services, Andrew pleads, "Mom, would you mind if I passed on lunch? Sean's cousin Carolyn is spending the day with him. He invited me to tag along."

"Andrew, I was so looking forward to having lunch, just you and me. You know your sister won't be home until five."

"I know, Mom, it's your weekend. Forget I asked."

My son is feeling guilty. I have to be the adult. "I'll make you a deal. You're off school on Wednesday. Teacher conference, correct?" Andrew agrees. "I'm cutting out of work at twelve. You and Julia owe me a movie and dinner. Deal?"

"Deal."

I return to an empty house. I make a decision; once Julia is off to college, I will sell the house and move in to a condo. Maybe I'll move back to the city, closer to JoAnne and Gary, and find a better job at a big law firm. I'll convince Aunt Sarah and my uncle to do the same.

The phone rings. I reach for it, hoping it's Pete.

"Hey, girlfriend! I'm glad you're home. How are things going?"

"Shitty as usual, JoAnne."

"Still mad at Pete?"

"He stopped by last night. I got to tell him how I felt. He apologized but basically said I was a big girl, got my very own invite, and if I wanted to attend, I should have."

"You should have listened to Gary and me and went. It's not like Pete's family disowned you. They want what we all want, for Pete and you to get back together."

"I don't want to involve you or Gary in this mess, but has Pete mentioned where he sees himself, say, in a year?"

"Pete made it clear from the start that he doesn't want to discuss his personal life, so their conversations are about the kids, work, sports, and golf."

"Next Saturday is Pete's weekend with the kids. I might call Jason and ask him to dinner. I can't take another Saturday home alone."

"I think it's a great idea, and if Pete finds out his little bird is stepping out, it might ruffle his feathers."

"You might be right. Maybe it's time this little bird gave flying a try."

"I'm so jealous! The dating scene is so romantic and lustful. You can't keep your hands off each other. Hey, is there any chance you might jump this guy's bones? It's been a while, and a girl has needs."

"I'm hanging up. When you get like this, there's no stopping you. I'll call you tomorrow."

* * * * *

Later that day, my aunt and uncle stop by the house. Aunt Sarah and I sit in the backyard, watching Uncle George rake the leaves in the garden.

"Pete stopped by last night."

"Why?"

"He wanted to know why I was giving him the cold shoulder."

"Interesting."

"Why?"

"He missed talking with you."

"I asked him the same question. You know what the answer was? He didn't have one. I wish I had listened to you."

"Allison, if you learned anything these past months, you learned not to dwell on the past. He's gotten control over his anger. That's an accomplishment. He's working on expressing his feelings. Give him time. It took me two years before I had the answers to all those questions after Eric died."

"That was different, Aunt Sarah. You lost your son. Pete and I are alive. We can share our feelings with each other."

"A loss is a loss. I don't have to explain that to you. Ask yourself this question, If Pete did say there was a chance, are you ready and strong enough to handle the times he will doubt your sincerity? It's not going to be easy. You're going to have to deal with his ups and downs, and that can be stressful."

"I love him, Aunt Sarah. I want him back, and not for the children's sake. Three years, Julia will be off to college. Why would I fight for our marriage if I weren't sincere? If I wanted him out of my life, I would have gotten a divorce. He has to know I'm hoping we can work this out."

My aunt smiles. "There's a bright side to all this. Pete hasn't asked for a divorce."

* * * * *

At ten Monday morning, I reach for the phone. After six rings, Nancy answers.

"Dr. Greenberg's office. How can I help you?"

"Hello, Nancy. It's Allison Cane. Is Dr. Greenberg available?"

"I'm sorry, Mrs. Cane, he's with a patient."

"Can you give him a message? Tell him I'm free for lunch today or any day this week."

"I'll give him the message, Mrs. Cane."

Forty-five minutes later, Nancy returns my call. David is free at one on Tuesday. He will meet me at Rick's Café.

* * * * *

I arrive ten minutes late. David is already seated.

"I'm sorry I'm late. Custody hearing."

"I only arrived five minutes ago." David isn't his chatty self. I smile.

Waiting for our lunch to arrive, I ask about David's family. "Is Ellen seeing anyone?"

"Yes. She met him at camp. He attends the same school, Cliff O'Neal."

"Cliff. Good kid. I know the family."

"How is Andrew?"

"If you're asking if he's seeing anyone, he hasn't mentioned anyone in particular."

"How are the children doing?"

"Much better than I thought. We underestimate our children. I'm sure they would love to have Pete and me back together. What child wouldn't? I had a meeting with Dr. Jewel two weeks ago. She says they're doing well. She's going to leave it up to them if they wish to continue." I pause. "David, I want to apologize for my behavior at the field. I had no right to ask you to intercede on my behalf. It was wrong of me, and I'm truly sorry."

"Apology accepted."

I smile. "You've been a good friend, David. I hope that hasn't changed?"

"You were hurt. I understand."

"As my friend, you'll be happy to know I've been on two dates with a man from my parish. His name is Jason."

"Two dates?"

"Yes, but just as friends, nothing more. I've been playing golf and tennis with old friends, but *Saturday night is the loneliest night of the week*. It's nice spending time with the opposite sex."

"Nothing wrong with that."

Lunch arrives, and David and I talk about the children. One more year, and his and my baby will be off to college.

"What colleges is Ellen applying to?"

"Stanford, Northwestern, NYU, Boston."

"Are you hoping for NYU or Boston?"

"I'm neutral. Alice is beside herself. She's hoping NYU. I heard Andrew is applying to the same schools."

"Pete assures me Boston is his first choice. I light a candle every week at church. I hope God is listening."

"How is your relationship with Pete?"

David's question causes me to joke. "I invited you to lunch, so lunch is on me, but if you're going to charge me for a session, lunch is on you."

"I'm asking as a friend and nothing more."

"I want him back, David. Nothing's changed. As I said, I'm not sitting around, waiting for him to come home. We are able to have civil conversations. He did stop by to ask why I was giving him the cold shoulder. After we spoke, I asked him if he missed us and if he was happy. He had no response. It seems the only conversation we can have is about the children."

"You've come a long way."

"I guess. I just wish I knew what he … I mean, good or bad, I'd like to know. Don't think I'm fishing for answers. Believe me, I'm not. I just want to know."

* * * * *

I receive an email from Pete on Thursday. He's flying to Florida that weekend. He's already told the children he has to go. I don't ask. I don't want to burst Pete's bubble, but the children are tiring of the every-other-weekend thing. Hearing the news, Andrew immediately makes plans with Sean. Julia makes plans to go shopping with Aunt Sarah, dinner, and a sleepover.

I call Jason and invite him for a burger and movie, as friends. He accepts. I wonder if this is considered a third date.

Saturday night, when I arrive home, my son is sound asleep. I go to my room, take a hot shower to relax, and get into bed. The cell phone buzzes. *Pete.*

"Hi, Pete."

"Hi, Allison. I'm sorry I didn't call sooner. The past several weeks, the auditors ran an audit. I meet with them on Monday. I thought it best I give myself a few days to review the report."

"Nothing serious, I hope. Are we still in the black? Because I was hoping to retire. I think I can get used to making salon appointments during the day, shopping, tennis, and golf at my leisure."

I can sense that Pete is smiling. “Sounds like a plan. Cross my heart, your investment is secure.”

“That’s a relief. Are Gale and Michael back from their honeymoon?”

“Their flight arrives on Thursday. I hope to be back on Wednesday. I told them I’d meet their flight. They want to spend the weekend catching up with the kids. It’s your weekend. Is that going to be a problem?”

“No. They are usually off with their friends when it’s my weekend, anyway.”

Pete speaks softly. “I think they are getting bored with …”

I know the feeling, so I drop the subject. “Andrew got his learner’s permit. Did he tell you?”

“He told me.”

“Chauffeuring the kids around has been a big part of my life. I’m not ready to give up that job.”

“I got a knot in my stomach when I heard he got his permit.”

“I’m not looking forward to that call when he calls to say he’s had his first fender bender.” We chuckle. “Did you want to leave a message for the kids?”

“No. I spoke with them earlier. I actually called to talk with you.”

“With me?”

“Yes. I wanted to explain, the other night, I couldn’t get out of my commitment.”

“If I remember correctly, I invited you back.”

“You did. I did consider coming back, but I know you have questions. Questions, I don’t have answers to.”

“Which question?”

“You asked if I am happier without you.”

“You don’t have to answer the question Pete. I already know the answer. Telling you I was in love with another man, well, I hurt you deeply. I broke the trust in our marriage. I have no right to ask for your forgiveness. If there is one thing I’ve learned, you can’t change the past. I made my bed, and I have to deal with the consequences.

Knowing your Andrew's biological dad, is the happiest I've been in a very long time."

Dead Silence.

"Pete I know this conversation is making you uncomfortable, so let's just end it there, we'll talk soon."

"Allison, don't hang up."

My heart skips a beat. "I won't if you don't want me to."

Silence.

"Pete, is there something you want to say?"

"You're so sure we can put this mess behind us. And I'm convinced the truth will always come between us."

"I'm not a fool. I know what I'm asking is selfish. I want you back. I want you, me, and our children under one roof."

"I can answer one question, I do miss living with my children. I miss watching them grow, going out with their friends. The time I spend with them is precious, because they are all I have left. I will say therapy is helping. I'm in a better place. I can accept that your childhood wasn't the best. I've accepted that I lost my wife, and my best friend as well."

"Oh Pete. I know you're not going to believe me, but I love you, and I also miss my best friend. I've tried not to pressure you, but if you would only give us a chance. If not as husband and wife, as friends, best friends. You say therapy is helping, then why couldn't couples therapy work as well?"

"I'm not ready for couples therapy."

"All right, not couples therapy. But seeing each other as friends, is that asking too much. We can discuss the past, not discuss the past. It might help you decide if you can tolerate me, or not. Pete, you don't have to answer, but if you think about me, and you've gotten past wanting me dead, then we owe it to ourselves to at least try."

Silence.

"Are you ready to throw away eighteen-years of marriage? I don't care if you believe me or not, I love you Pete Cane. For a year, I tried to convince myself that I didn't love you. It was my way of dealing with losing you, once you knew the truth?"

"I need time to think."

"Pete, you said you considered coming back that night. Why didn't you? Was it because you feared you wouldn't be able to leave?"

Pete sighs. "I have to go, Allison."

The phone disconnects. I stare at the phone and whisper, "You love me, Pete, and I know you do."

* * * * *

That night, while I sleep, the dream appears. I'm running through the field, the clipped daisies in hand. I reach the chairs draped in white and notice the chairs are filled with people. I slowly walk down the aisle.

My aunt and uncle are sitting in the second row. In the first are my mother and father. Reaching them, I take their hands in mine, saying, "I love you with all my heart and soul."

I step forward and smile at the reverend. The man in white suit is beside me. I can see him vividly. We make eye contact. Smiling, I say, "I'll love you, Pete, till the day I die."

I wake from the dream knowing what I must do. I jump from bed, pack a duffel bag, shower, and place my first phone call. "Hi, JoAnne."

"Hey, girlfriend."

"Pete called last night. He loves me, JoAnne, I know he does."

"Pete called to say he loves you?"

"He didn't say he loves me. He wanted to talk. I'm going to Florida, and I'm not leaving until I've convinced my husband we belong together."

"Are you sure?"

"I'm sure."

"Did you pack sexy underwear, boots, stockings, all black, nothing but black?"

I laugh. "I'm not a call girl. I'm a wife on a mission."

"Listen to me. No man can resist a woman in black. If you want him back, you have to control the penis. The penis will convince the brain he can't live without you. Trust me."

"You might be right. Sex first, talk later."

"Allison, all kidding aside, good luck. I want you guys back together more than I want Gary to buy me that diamond necklace I've been eyeing."

"I don't know. I saw the diamond necklace. You might want to reconsider."

Second call: I book a flight to Florida.

Third call. "Aunt Sarah, I need you to come stay with the kids for a few days."

"Where are you going?"

"I had a dream and decided I'm flying to Florida to confront Pete."

I wake my children from a sound sleep. "Andrew, I'm going to be gone for a few days. Aunt Sarah is staying at the house. She's going to drive me to the airport. She'll be back in a few hours."

"Mom, where are you going?"

I don't want to get my son's hopes up. "Please trust me."

"Are you going to Florida?"

The cat is out of the bag. I confess, "Andrew, I don't want you to get your hopes up, but I think your father is ready to talk, and I can't wait for him to come back on Wednesday."

My son smiles. "Good luck, Mom." Placing his head back on the pillow, he says, "I told Dr. Jewel everything would be back to normal before I left for college."

Julia isn't as easy to say goodbye to. "Mom, did Dad call and ask you to meet him in Florida? How romantic! Did you pack something sexy?"

I'm convinced JoAnne is my daughter's biological mother.

"Black or red—those two colors work best."

"And how would you know?"

"Mom, fashion magazines. How else would I know? And I rummage through your nightie drawers every so often. Just to make sure you're keeping up with the women your age."

Before I can reprimand my daughter for invading my private space, my aunt rushes in. "I'm so excited! This is a great idea, the best idea you've had in a long time! On the phone, you said you had a dream. Must have been some dream? Did you pack something sexy?"

I'm convinced the women in my life are perverted. I kiss and hug my daughter. Before I get the words out, she says, "I know you love me with all your heart and soul. Good luck, Mom."

My aunt is mumbling as we leave the house, "Are you going to tell me about the dream?"

"I'll tell you in the car."

The only part of the story I left out, when I confessed all to my aunt, was the dream.

* * * * *

"We have to say goodbye here. New regulations." I bear-hug my aunt. When I look over her shoulder, I see my uncle entering the airport. "Uncle George!"

My aunt turns. "George, what are you doing here?"

"A note, you leave me a note saying Allison has to leave for Florida. Why didn't you wake me?" My uncle turns to me. "Allison, why are you going to Florida? Did something happen to Pete?"

"He's fine, Uncle George. I'm going to Florida to beg my husband to take me back, and I won't take no for an answer. Wish me luck?"

My uncle hugs me. "Of course I'll wish you luck. If Pete doesn't take you back, he's a fool."

"Thanks, Uncle George."

I kiss my aunt once again then eye my aunt and uncle standing side by side. I wish I could turn back the clock and get back all the years I wasted hating the two people in the world who love me and want nothing more than for me to be happy and safe.

I feel a strong desire to let them know how much they mean to me. "I know it's taken me a long time … you know you're the closest I have to a mother and father. Please forgive me for being such a jerk. And thank you for loving and never giving up on me. What's the saying, 'Better late than never'?" I smile. "One last hug and kiss, then I have to go." I whisper the words that mean so much to my family, "I love you both with all my heart and soul."

My aunt smiles and says, "Go get your Rhett, Scarlett."

* * * * *

Sitting on the plane, I have a change of heart. My first thought is to exit the plane and call my aunt and uncle and tell them I got cold feet. Instead, I firmly grip the armrest and remain in place.

Once in flight, I rehearse what I'm going to say when I see Pete. The attendant offers me a drink. "White wine, please."

Repeating over and over in my head what I'm going to say to Pete, after a stream of begging and pleading, I speak out loud, "Hell, I'm just going to wrap my arms around his neck and kiss him over and over until he says, 'I'm not promising anything, but I'll give it a try.'"

"Did you say something, deary?" asks the mature woman sitting in the seat next to me.

"I'm sorry, just thinking out loud."

"Well, I hope your plan works."

I smile. "Thanks. Me too."

I reach for the headphones, dial the number for the Love Song Channel, and finish the wine. Within minutes, I feel myself drifting off to sleep, happy knowing love conquers all.

* * * * *

In the cockpit, the copilot watches the newly blinking red light. He turns to the pilot. "Joe, the warning light for the left engine just went on. How does it look on your side?"

The pilot adjusts the mirror to check out the left engine. "Oh my god, I think I see smoke coming out the engine." The pilot calls back to the control tower. "Control tower, this is Flight 763. There is smoke coming from the left engine of the plane. Please advise the nearest airport we need to make an emergency landing."

When the pilot glances at the engine, there are flames. "Control tower, please advise the nearest airport. I will need to make an emergency landing. Flight 763, flames emerging from left engine." The pilot advises the copilot, "Andy, notify the attendants. Tell them to do a quick run through the cabin. Make sure the passengers have their seat belts in place. I'm going to turn on the seat belt sign."

The passenger in row 4, seat A, is dreaming. Smiling at Pete in the dream, she says, "I love you with all my heart and soul."

ABOUT THE AUTHOR

Antoinette Zam, nee Pellegrino, was born in Williamsburg, New York in March of 1948. She now resides in West Windsor, New Jersey, and has been married to her greatest supporter, her husband Arnold, for thirty two years. They have 4 adult children between them from previous marriages. She is a grandmother of seven, ranging in age from twenty-six to one year. She worked for thirty-two years in the banking industry.

Her grandparents were Italian immigrants and when she was young, she spent her Sundays visiting her grandparents, where the entire family would gather. The day was filled with plenty of food and conversation. The eldest would talk of their arrivals to Ellis Island and share their worries and concerns about the new world and the families they left behind in the old country. Her parents would share stories of the Great Depression and World War II. Over the years, she would share these stories with friends and family who would always tell her that she had enough interesting stories to write a book.

Antoinette's mother, Sylvia, was diagnosed with colon cancer in 2005, ultimately succumbing to the disease in the summer of 2006. In her mother's waning days, Antoinette would sit with her in the sun reminiscing about the past and she would share with her mother updates about family and friends. Antoinette would add a little spice to the stories, which always brought a smile to her dear mother's face.

Three days before her passing, her mom suggested to Antoinette that she give writing a chance. Antoinette informed her mother that she was not a writer, but her mom told her to just give it a shot and that she might be surprised with the outcome.

Shortly after her mother's passing, Antoinette position with the bank was downsized. Inspired by her mother's suggestion to write, she created her first novel and her oldest granddaughter helped in the editing process. It took her ten-years to complete the book and another five to have it published.

She hopes you enjoy the story she has crafted as much as she enjoyed creating it. She would like to thank the readers in advance for taking the time to read her novel.

CPSIA information can be obtained
at www.ICGtesting.com
Printed in the USA
LVHW040906301018
595214LV00009B/828/P

9 781643 503943